Lecture Notes of the Institute for Computer Sciences, Social Informatics and Telecommunications Engineering   280

T0211700

More information about this series at http://www.springer.com/series/8197

Min Jia · Qing Guo · Weixiao Meng (Eds.)

Wireless and Satellite Systems

10th EAI International Conference, WiSATS 2019
Harbin, China, January 12–13, 2019
Proceedings, Part I

 Springer

Editors
Min Jia 🄳
Harbin Institute of Technology
Harbin, China

Qing Guo
Harbin Institute of Technology
Harbin, China

Weixiao Meng
Harbin Institute of Technology
Harbin, China

ISSN 1867-8211   ISSN 1867-822X (electronic)
Lecture Notes of the Institute for Computer Sciences, Social Informatics
and Telecommunications Engineering
ISBN 978-3-030-19152-8   ISBN 978-3-030-19153-5 (eBook)
https://doi.org/10.1007/978-3-030-19153-5

This Springer imprint is published by the registered company Springer Nature Switzerland AG
The registered company address is: Gewerbestrasse 11, 6330 Cham, Switzerland

Preface

We are delighted to introduce the proceedings of the 10th edition of the European Alliance for Innovation (EAI) International Conference on Wireless and Satellite Systems (WiSATS 2019). This conference has brought researchers, developers, and practitioners together from around the world who are leveraging and developing wireless and satellite systems. The theme of WiSATS 2019 was "Wireless and Satellite Systems."

The technical program of WiSATS 2019 consisted of 137 full papers. The conference tracks were: Main Track; Workshop 1 - Machine Learning for Satellite-Terrestrial Networks; Workshop 2 - Human–Machine Interactive Sensing, Monitoring, and Communications; Workshop 3 - Integrated Space and Onboard Networks; Workshop 4 - International Workshop Intelligent Signal Processing, Wireless Communications and Networks; Workshop 5 - Vehicular Communications and Networks; Workshop 6 - Intelligent 5G Communication and Digital Image Processing Technology; Workshop 7 - Security, Reliability, and Resilience in Internet of Things; Workshop 8 - Advances in Communications and Computing for Internet of Things.

Aside from the high-quality technical paper presentations, the technical program also featured three keynote speeches. The three keynote speeches were given by Dr. Wei Zhang from the University of New South Wales, Dr. Yi Qian from the University of Nebraska-Lincoln, and Pengren Ding from National Instruments.

Coordination with the steering chairs, Imrich Chlamtac, Kandeepan Sithamparanathan, and Mario Marchese, was essential for the success of the conference. We sincerely appreciate their constant support and guidance. It was also a great pleasure to work with such an excellent Organizing Committee and we than them for their hard work in organizing and supporting the conference. In particular, we also thank the Technical Program Committee, led by our TPC co-chair, Hsiao-Hwa Chen, who completed the peer-review process of technical papers and compiled a high-quality technical program. We are also grateful to the conference manager, Radka Pincakova, for her support and all the authors who submitted their papers to the WISATS 2019 conference and workshops.

We strongly believe that the WISATS 2019 conference provided a good forum for all researchers, developers, and practitioners to discuss all the scientific and technological aspects that are relevant to wireless and satellite systems. We expect that future WISATS conference will be as successful and stimulating as indicated by the contributions presented in this volume.

April 2019

Qing Guo
Weixiao Meng
Min Jia
Hsiao-Hwa Chen

Organization

Steering Committee

Imrich Chlamtac	Bruno Kessler Professor, University of Trento, Italy
Kandeepan Sithamparanathan	RMIT, Australia
Mario Marchese	University of Genoa, Italy

Organizing Committee

General Co-chairs

Qing Guo	Harbin Institute of Technology, China
Weixiao Meng	Harbin Institute of Technology, China
Min Jia	Harbin Institute of Technology, China

TPC Chair

Hsiao-Hwa Chen	National Cheng Kung University, Taiwan

Advisory TPC Chairs

Gengxin Zhang	Nanjing University of Posts and Telecommunications, China
Lidong Zhu	University of Electronic Science and Technology of China, China
Qihui Wu	Nanjing University of Posts and Telecommunications, China
Mugen Peng	Beijing University of Posts and Telecommunications, China
Wei Chen	Tsinghua University, China
Zan Li	Xidian University, China
Shi Jin	Southeast University, China
Feifei Gao	Tsinghua University, China
Xiaoming Tao	Tsinghua University, China
Sheng Zhou	Tsinghua University, China
Caijun Zhong	Zhejiang University, China
Junhui Zhao	East China Jiaotong University, China

Panels Co-chairs

Qinyu Zhang	Harbin Institute of Technology (Shen Zhen), China
Haibo Zhou	Nanjing University, China

Workshops Co-chairs

Xuejun Sha   Harbin Institute of Technology, China
Hongbin Chen   Guilin University of Electronic Technology, China

Publicity and Social Media Chair

Shaochuan Wu   Harbin Institute of Technology, China

Publications Chair

Xin Liu   Dalian University of Technology, China

Sponsorship and Exhibits Co-chairs

Zhutian Yang   Harbin Institute of Technology, China
Wei Wu   Harbin Institute of Technology, China

Local Co-chairs

Xuanli Wu   Harbin Institute of Technology, China
Shuai Han   Harbin Institute of Technology, China

Web Chair

Yanfeng Gu   Harbin Institute of Technology, China

International Advisory Chair

Imrich Chlamtac   University of Trento, Italy

Contents – Part I

**International Workshop on Integrated Space and Onboard
Networks (ISON)**

Intelligent Signal Processing, Wireless Communications and Networks

Contents – Part II

International Workshop on Advances in Communications and Computing for Internet-of-Things

Late Main Track

Main Track

Alternative Extended Block Sparse Bayesian Learning for Cluster Structured Sparse Signal Recovery

Lu Wang[1], Lifan Zhao[1], Guoan Bi[1(✉)], and Xin Liu[2]

[1] School Electrical and Electronic Engineering,
Nanyang Technological University, Singapore, Singapore
{wanglu,zhao0145,egbi}@ntu.edu.sg
[2] School of information and communication,
Dalian University of Technology, Dalian, China
liuxinstar1984@dlut.edu.cn

Abstract. Clustered sparse signals recovery with unknown cluster sizes and locations is considered in this paper. An improved alternative extended block sparse Bayesian learning algorithm (AEBSBL) is proposed. The new algorithm is motivated by the graphic models of the extended block sparse Bayesian learning algorithm (EBSBL). By deriving the graphic model of EBSBL, an equivalent cluster structured prior for sparse coefficients is obtained, which encourages dependencies among neighboring coefficients. With the sparse prior, other necessary probabilistic modelings are constructed and Expectation and Maximization (EM) is applied to infer all the unknowns. The alternative algorithm reduces the unknowns of EBSBL. Numerical simulations are conducted to demonstrate the effectiveness of the proposed method.

Keywords: Clustered structure · Bayesian sparse learning · Expectation · Maximization method

1 Introduction

Traditional sparse representation attempts to find a parsimonious coefficient vector $\mathbf{x} \in \mathbb{R}^{N \times 1}$ from noisy observation $\mathbf{y} \in \mathbb{R}^{M \times 1}$

$$\mathbf{y} = \mathbf{A}\mathbf{x} + \mathbf{n}, \tag{1}$$

where $\mathbf{A} \in \mathbb{R}^{M \times N}$ is an representative dictionary and n is the noise. To further include the inherent structure onto the signal, structured sparse recovery is proposed with improved recovery performance. Among which, block structure is one of the mostly observed structures in practice [1,2,4,5]. In block structure, elements of sparse coefficient $\mathbf{x}$ are likely to be nonzero or zeros in blocks. Particularly, when the block sizes or the localizations are unknown, the structure is referred to cluster structure.

M. Jia et al. (Eds.): WiSATS 2019, LNICST 280, pp. 3–12, 2019.
https://doi.org/10.1007/978-3-030-19153-5_1

Algorithms dealing with the simple block sparse signal with known block partition have been widely studied and can be generally divided into three categories. The greedy pursuit algorithms are one of the categories including Model-CoSaMp [6], Block-OMP [7], and their variations. The second category is the convex optimization, such as GLasso algorithm [8], GBasis Pursuit [9], l_2/l_1 Programming [10], etc. The third one is the sparse Bayesian learning method known as block-sparse Bayesian learning (BSBL) [11]. They performs competitively with each other in ideal situation with known block partition and size. Obvious performance degradation is observed when such algorithms are applied to the cluster structure where knowledge on the block partition is unavailable. Signal with cluster structure is generally much harder to recover. However, under such a circumstance, it is observed that neighboring elements of the sparse coefficients are statistical dependent on each other, which may be potentially used to capture the underlying structure of the signal. This fact has been studied by recently proposed methods, such as extended block-sparse Bayesian learning (EBSBL) in [11] as well as pattern-coupled sparse Bayesian learning in PC-SPL [12].

In EBSBL, an augmented vector is artificially constructed and linearly combined to represent the sparse coefficient to introduce interactions among its neighboring elements. Due to the augmented vector, an extended problem with higher dimensionality has to be solved in EBSBL. This paper tries to derive an explicit interaction expression of the neighboring coefficients and reduce the problem size of EBSBL. By studying the underlying relationship of the hidden variables in the graphic model of EBSBL, a clustered-sparsity imposed prior can be derived by integrating out the hidden augmented vector artificially constructed. The newly derived prior of one certain sparse coefficient introduces interactions of its own hyperparameter and those of its neighbors, thus imposing dependencies among neighbors. By constructing structured prior and other proper probabilistic models for all hidden variables, the original sparse representation problem is easily treated by Bayesian method. The expectation-maximization is used to estimate all the unknowns. The relationship between the alternative EBSBL with the original EBSBL is also revealed. Simulations are conducted to demonstrate its effectiveness.

2   The Review of the Idea of EBSBL

Since the proposed alternative method is motivated by the EBSBL, we first briefly review the basic idea of EBSBL.

2.1   EBSBL

The basic idea of EBSBL to recover clustered sparse signal is to try to reformulate the signal with unknown location and size by expanding its sparse coefficients into known blocks. The processing can be illustrated by Fig. 1. The constructed augmented vector is denoted by $\mathbf{z} = [\cdots \mathbf{z}_{i-1} \mathbf{z}_i \mathbf{z}_{i+1} \cdots]^T$, where block

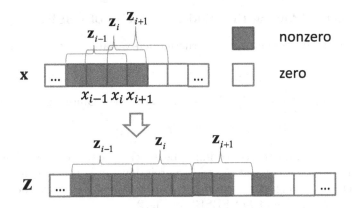

Fig. 1. The illustration of the expanding procedure.

$\mathbf{z}_i = [x_{i-1}x_ix_{i+1}]^T$. Since merely neighboring information is used, the block size in Fig. 1 can be reasonably set to 3. For clustered signal, due to the fact that neighboring coefficients are likely to behave in the same way, it is highly probably that the augmented vector is of block sparse with equally partitioned blocks of size 3. Therefore, $\mathbf{z}$ can be effectively recovered by the BSBL method. With the augment vector $\mathbf{z}$, the original problem can be approximately transformed into a block sparse recovery problem with known block partition:

$$\mathbf{y} = \sum_{i=1}^{g} \mathbf{AE}_i\mathbf{z}_i + \mathbf{n} = \mathbf{\Phi}\mathbf{z} + \mathbf{n} \qquad (2)$$

where $\mathbf{\Phi} = [\mathbf{\Phi}_1, \cdots, \mathbf{\Phi}_g]$ with sub-dictionary $\mathbf{\Phi}_i = \mathbf{AE}_i$. $\mathbf{E}_i \in \mathcal{R}^{N \times 3}$ is a zero matrix with its rows from i-th row to $i + h - 1$-th row being an identity matrix. The original coefficient $\mathbf{x}$ is then a linear transformation of $\mathbf{z}$:

$$\mathbf{x} = \sum_{i=1}^{g} \mathbf{E}_i\mathbf{z}_i. \qquad (3)$$

2.2 Discussion of EBSBL

It should be emphasized that the problem of cluster sparse signal recovery in (2) can only be approximately solved by the BSBL, since the block sparsity of each block $\mathbf{z}_i$ does not exactly hold. This is the fact with great probability. However, for those block $\mathbf{z}_i$ containing the edge of the clusters of $\mathbf{x}$, the block sparsity cannot be applied. This approximation will result in inaccuracies in the edge recovery of the clusters of $\mathbf{x}$.

3 Graphic Model of EBSBL

In this section, the graphic model of EBSBL is constructed to explicitly show the relationship of each hidden variable. And a new structured prior of $\mathbf{x}$ is constructed based on the graphic model.

3.1   Interaction Among the Hidden Variables of EBSBL

To apply the BSBL method to infer the hidden variable $\mathbf{z}$, $\mathbf{z}$ has to be hierarchically modeled:

$$p\left(\mathbf{z}; \{\gamma_i\}_i, \mathbf{B}\right) = \mathcal{N}\left(0, \mathbf{\Sigma}_0\right) \tag{4}$$

with $\mathbf{\Sigma}_0 = \mathrm{diag}\left(\gamma_1 \mathbf{B}, \cdots, \gamma_g \mathbf{B}\right)$. Each block $\mathbf{z}_i$ follows Gaussian distribution as below:

$$p\left(\mathbf{z}_i; \gamma_i, \mathbf{B}\right) = \mathcal{N}\left(0, \gamma_i, \mathbf{B}\right), \tag{5}$$

where γ_i is the parameter controlling the block sparsity degree. With those probabilistic model in (4) and (5) and the relationship between $\mathbf{x}$ and $\mathbf{z}$ in (3), The interactions among all the hidden variables of x, z and γ can be explicitly shown in the Graphic model of EBSBL in Fig. 2.

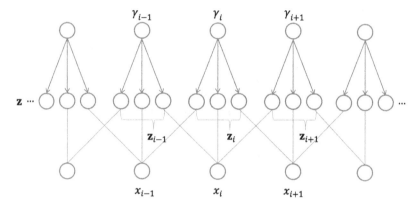

Fig. 2. The graphic model of EBSBL.

In Fig. 2, the ith element of x_i directly is connected to $\mathbf{z}_{i-1}\{3\}$, $\mathbf{z}_i\{2\}$ and $\mathbf{z}_{i+1}\{1\}$ according to the linear transformation in (3). Since $\mathbf{z}_{i-1}\{3\}$, $\mathbf{z}_i\{2\}$ and $\mathbf{z}_{i+1}\{1\}$ depends on γ_{i-1}, γ_i and γ_{i+1}, then x_i is implicitly connected to γ_{i-1}, γ_i and γ_{i+1}. Similarly, it is concluded that x_{i-1} depends on γ_{i-1}, γ_i and γ_{i+1}, and x_{i+1} depends on γ_{i-1}, γ_i and γ_{i+1}. Therefore, x_i implicitly interacts with its neighbors x_{i-1} and x_{i+1}. By this hierarchical probabilistic modeling, EBSBL easily exert the dependency on neighboring sparse coefficients in a probabilistic way. That statistical dependency will be used in EBSBL to enhance the performance of sparse recovery for signals with cluster structure.

It is noted that EBSBL requires to infer an extended vector $\mathbf{z}$ of size 3 times that of $\mathbf{x}$. To maintain the problem size to that of $\mathbf{x}$, we try to derive an explicit structured prior for the sparse coefficients, which is motivated by the graphic model of EBSBL.

3.2 Structured Prior for Clustering Sparse Signal

It should be emphasized that the graphic model in Fig. 2 only tells us that x_i is implicitly and jointly depending on γ_{i-1}, γ_i and γ_{i+1} through the intermediate hidden variables of $\mathbf{z}_{i-1}\{3\}$, $\mathbf{z}_i\{2\}$ and $\mathbf{z}_{i+1}\{1\}$. Actually, the explicit relationship of x_i on γ_{i-1}, γ_i and γ_{i+1} can possibly given by integrating out the intermediate variables $\mathbf{z}_{i-1}\{3\}$, $\mathbf{z}_i\{2\}$ and $\mathbf{z}_{i+1}\{1\}$. Since we previously assume that blocks of $\mathbf{z}_{i-1}$ for different i are independent as shown in the probabilistic model in (4), $\mathbf{z}_{i-1}\{3\}$, $\mathbf{z}_i\{2\}$ and $\mathbf{z}_{i+1}\{1\}$ are independent Gaussian random variables with variances γ_{i-1}, γ_i and γ_{i+1}. Therefore, $x_i = \mathbf{z}_{i-1}(3) + \mathbf{z}_i(2) + \mathbf{z}_{i+1}(1)$ according to (3) follows normal distribution with a variance of $\gamma_i + \gamma_{i+1} + \gamma_{i-1}$, i.e.,

$$p\left(x_i; \gamma_i, \gamma_{i-1}, \gamma_{i+1}\right) = \mathcal{N}\left(0, \left(\gamma_i + \gamma_{i-1} + \gamma_{i+1}\right)\right). \tag{6}$$

The overall prior of $\mathbf{x}$ also depends on the expression of $\mathbf{B}$ in (5). If $\mathbf{B}$ is an identity matrix, elements inside each $\mathbf{z}_i$ are independent. Therefore, x_i will be independent for all i and an explicit prior of $\mathbf{x}$ over $\boldsymbol{\gamma}$ can be given as below

$$p\left(\mathbf{x}; \boldsymbol{\gamma}\right) = \prod_i p\left(x_i; \gamma_i + \gamma_{i-1} + \gamma_{i+1}\right). \tag{7}$$

The probabilistic graphic model of prior in (7) can be given by Fig. 3. As illustrated in Fig. 3, prior for coefficient x_i directly involves its own hyperparameter γ_i and those of its neighbors x_{i-1} and x_{i+1}. The hyperparameters are coupled together to introduce the dependency.

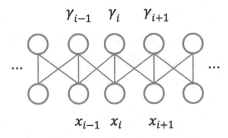

Fig. 3. The graphic model of the proposed structured prior.

It should be noted that if $\mathbf{B}$ in (5) has nonzeros on its off-diagonal, elements inside each $\mathbf{z}_i$ will not be independent. Under this case, neighboring x_i will be correlated with each other and the distribution of $\mathbf{x}$ over $\boldsymbol{\gamma}$ can not be written explicitly. For simplicity, we always assume an identity matrix for $\mathbf{B}$. In contrast, EBSBL theoretically allows arbitrary form of $\mathbf{B}$.

3.3 Discussions on the Constructed Prior

The hyperparamter coupled prior in (7) coincidently shows a similar form of the pattern-coupled prior proposed in [12]. However, it should be noted that coupling of the hyperparameter is modeled as the precision of x_i in [12], while coupling of the hyperparameter in our case is the variance of sparse coefficient x_i and statistically implies x_i of a linear combination of three independent normal variables.

The assumption of an identity matrix for $\mathbf{B}$, though exerts more restriction, is reasonable. The independence of elements in $\mathbf{z}_i$ somehow decreases the aforementioned inaccuracy of edges in the non-zero cluster, since it allow totally different elements in $\mathbf{z}_i$. To see this, first let us assume each element of $\mathbf{B}$ is 1. Consider $x_i = \mathbf{z}_{i-1}(3) + \mathbf{z}_i(2) + \mathbf{z}_{i+1}(1) \neq 0$ is on the edge of the nonzero cluster and $x_{i-1} = \mathbf{z}_{i-2}(3) + \mathbf{z}_{i-1}(2) + \mathbf{z}_i(1) \neq 0$ and $x_{i+1} = \mathbf{z}_i(3) + \mathbf{z}_{i+1}(2) + \mathbf{z}_{i+2}(1) = 0$. In this situation, block $\mathbf{z}_i$ should be nonzero and $\mathbf{z}_i(3) \approx \mathbf{z}_i(2) \approx \mathbf{z}_i(1) \gg 0$ with the most probability according EBSBL, thus leading to a large inaccuracy in estimation of x_{i+1}. On the other hand, if elements in $\mathbf{z}_i$ are independent, $\mathbf{z}_i(3)$ is allowed to be close to 0, which makes it easy to estimate x_{i+1}.

4   Alternative to EBSBL for Cluster Sparse Signal Recovery

In order to formulate our problem under Bayesian framework, in addition to the cluster-structured prior of $\mathbf{x}$ in (7), necessary proper probabilistic models are need to be constructed for other hidden variables in Bayesian treatment. After that, Expectation and Maximization algorithm can be applied to infer all the hidden variables and unknown parameters.

4.1   Updating Rules for Unknowns

The noise $\mathbf{n}$ is assumed to be Gaussian distributed with variance α_0, so that the likelihood function of $\mathbf{y}$ in (1) is as follows:

$$\mathbf{y} \,|\mathbf{x}; \alpha_0 \sim \mathcal{N}\left(\mathbf{Ax}, \alpha_0 \mathbf{I}_M\right), \tag{8}$$

where $\mathbf{I}_M$ is an identity matrix with size M.

We can then easily calculate the posterior of $\mathbf{x}$ given likelihood in (8) and its prior of (7), which is of a Gaussian distribution with mean and covariance

$$\tilde{\mathbf{x}} = \boldsymbol{\mu} = \alpha_0^{-1} \boldsymbol{\Sigma} \mathbf{A}^T \mathbf{y} \tag{9}$$
$$= \mathbf{D}\mathbf{A}^T \left(\alpha_0 \mathbf{I} + \mathbf{A}\mathbf{D}\mathbf{A}^T\right)^{-1} \mathbf{y},$$

and

$$\boldsymbol{\Sigma} = \left(\alpha_0^{-1} \mathbf{A}^H \mathbf{A} + \mathbf{D}\right)^{-1}. \tag{10}$$

In (10), $\mathbf{D}$ is a diagonal matrix and the i-th element on its diagonal is $(\alpha_{i-1} + \alpha_i + \alpha_{i+1})^{-1}$.

For the unknown parameters estimation in Bayesian treatment, the algorithm of Expectation-Maximization is mostly used. In EM, $\boldsymbol{\gamma}$ and α_0 can be found by maximizing

$$E_{\mathbf{x}|\mathbf{y}, \boldsymbol{\gamma}, \alpha_0} \left\{ p\left(\mathbf{y}|\mathbf{x}; \alpha_0\right) p\left(\mathbf{x}; \boldsymbol{\gamma}\right) \right\}, \tag{11}$$

where $E_{\mathbf{x}|\mathbf{y};\gamma,\alpha_0}\{\cdot\}$ denotes an expectation with respect to the posterior of $\mathbf{x}$. According to (11), γ can be given by maximizing

$$E_{\mathbf{x}|\mathbf{y};\alpha}\{\log p(\mathbf{x};\alpha)\} = \tag{12}$$

$$-\sum_{i=1}^{N}\log(\alpha_{i-1}+\alpha_i+\alpha_{i+1}) - \sum_{i=1}^{N}\frac{E_{\mathbf{x}|\mathbf{y};\alpha}\{x_i^H x_i\}}{\alpha_{i-1}+\alpha_i+\alpha_{i+1}},$$

with $E_{\mathbf{x}|\mathbf{y};\alpha}\{x_i^H x_i\} = \mu_i^2 + \Sigma_{i,i}$ and $\Sigma_{i,i}$ being the i-th diagonal component of Σ. Let $v_i = \alpha_{i-1}+\alpha_i+\alpha_{i+1}$ and $w_i = \mu_i^2 + \Sigma_{i,i}$. γ can be found by letting the gradient of (12) with respect to γ_i to zero:

$$\frac{\partial E_{\mathbf{x}|\mathbf{y};\alpha}\{\log p(\mathbf{x};\alpha)\}}{\partial \alpha_i} \tag{13}$$

$$= \frac{w_i}{v_i^2} + \frac{w_{i-1}}{v_{i-1}^2} + \frac{w_{i+1}}{v_{i+1}^2} - \frac{1}{v_i} - \frac{1}{v_{i-1}} - \frac{1}{v_{i+1}} = 0.$$

The root of (13) can not be given in a close-form, since γ_i is entangled with other unknowns of γ_{i-1} and γ_{i+1}. There are three possible ways to find the estimation of γ_i. One simple way is to iteratively find the root γ_i of (13) by using the previously estimated γ_{i-1} and γ_{i+1}. This will be time-consuming. The other possible method is to find the lower and upper bound of (13) following [12] to analyze the approximation of the root.

Let us define

$$\bar{\gamma}_{\max} = \max\{\bar{\gamma}_{i-2}, \bar{\gamma}_{i-1}, \bar{\gamma}_i, \bar{\gamma}_{i+1}, \bar{\gamma}_{i+2}\}$$

and

$$\bar{\gamma}_{\min} = \min\{\bar{\gamma}_{i-2}, \bar{\gamma}_{i-1}, \bar{\gamma}_i, \bar{\gamma}_{i+1}, \bar{\gamma}_{i+2}\},$$

where $\bar{\gamma}_{i-2}, \bar{\gamma}_{i-1}, \bar{\gamma}_i, \bar{\gamma}_{i+1}, \bar{\gamma}_{i+2}$ are the optimal solution to (13). Therefore, we have the following equation:

$$\frac{w_i}{\bar{v}_i^2} + \frac{w_{i-1}}{\bar{v}_{i-1}^2} + \frac{w_{i+1}}{\bar{v}_{i+1}^2} = \frac{1}{\bar{v}_i} + \frac{1}{\bar{v}_{i-1}} + \frac{1}{\bar{v}_{i+1}}. \tag{14}$$

Since $\bar{v}_i^2 = (\bar{\gamma}_{i-1}+\bar{\gamma}_i+\bar{\gamma}_{i+1})^2 \leq 9\bar{\gamma}_{\max}^2$, $\bar{v}_{i-1}^2 = (\bar{\gamma}_{i-2}+\bar{\gamma}_{i-1}+\bar{\gamma}_i)^2 \leq 9\bar{\gamma}_{\max}^2$, and $\bar{v}_{i+1}^2 = (\bar{\gamma}_{i+2}+\bar{\gamma}_{i+1}+\bar{\gamma}_i)^2 \leq 9\bar{\gamma}_{\max}^2$, we have the left hand side of (14) satisfy

$$\frac{w_i}{\bar{v}_i^2} + \frac{w_{i-1}}{\bar{v}_{i-1}^2} + \frac{w_{i+1}}{\bar{v}_{i+1}^2} \geq \frac{w_i + w_{i-1} + w_{i+1}}{9\bar{\gamma}_{\max}^2}. \tag{15}$$

And because $\bar{v}_i = \bar{\gamma}_{i-1}+\bar{\gamma}_i+\bar{\gamma}_{i+1} \geq 3\bar{\gamma}_{\min}$, $\bar{v}_{i+1} = \bar{\gamma}_{i+2}+\bar{\gamma}_{i+1}+\bar{\gamma}_i \geq 3\bar{\gamma}_{\min}$ and $\bar{v}_{i-1} = \bar{\gamma}_{i-2}+\bar{\gamma}_{i-1}+\bar{\gamma}_i \geq 3\bar{\gamma}$, the right hand side of (14) should satisfy

$$\frac{1}{\bar{v}_i} + \frac{1}{\bar{v}_{i-1}} + \frac{1}{\bar{v}_{i+1}} \leq \frac{1}{\bar{\gamma}_{\min}}. \tag{16}$$

Therefore, it is easy to show

$$\frac{w_i + w_{i-1} + w_{i+1}}{9\bar{\gamma}_{\max}^2} \leq \frac{1}{\bar{\gamma}_{\min}}. \tag{17}$$

Since $\bar{\gamma}_{\min} \leq \bar{\gamma}_i \leq \bar{\gamma}_{\max}$, if we make additional constraint that $\bar{\gamma}_{\max} \to \bar{\gamma}_{\min}$, then we have an approximation to the optimal root of (13) from (17) as follows:

$$\bar{\gamma}_i = \frac{w_i + w_{i-1} + w_{i+1}}{9}. \tag{18}$$

Similarly, α_0 is calculated according to (11) by maximizing

$$E_{\mathbf{x}|\mathbf{y};\alpha} \left\{ \log p\left(\mathbf{y}\,|\mathbf{x};\alpha_0\right) \right\}$$

$$\propto -\frac{M}{2}\log\alpha_0 - \frac{E_{\mathbf{x}|\mathbf{y};\alpha}\left\{\|\mathbf{y}-\mathbf{Ax}\|_2^2\right\}}{2\alpha_0}$$

$$= -\frac{M}{2}\log\alpha_0 - \frac{\|\mathbf{y}-\mathbf{A\mu}\|_2^2 + \mathrm{Tr}\left(\Sigma\mathbf{A}^T\mathbf{A}\right)}{2\alpha_0}. \tag{19}$$

Setting the derivative of (19) with respect to α_0 to be 0, α_0 is estimated by the root:

$$\tilde{\alpha}_0 = \frac{\|\mathbf{y}-\mathbf{A\mu}\|_2^2 + \mathrm{Tr}\left(\Sigma\mathbf{A}^T\mathbf{A}\right)}{M}. \tag{20}$$

The algorithm iteratively estimates $\mathbf{x}$, α_0, and γ_i by μ in (9), $\tilde{\alpha}_0$ in (20) and $\bar{\gamma}_i$ in (18) till convergence.

4.2   Discussion

To find the close-form sub-optimal solution to (12), a constraint that $\bar{\gamma}_{\max} \to \bar{\gamma}_{\min}$ is assumed. This is somehow similar to the assumption that x_{i-1}, x_i and x_{i+1} share variance $\gamma_{i-2} = \gamma_{i-1} = \gamma_{i+1} = \gamma_{i+2} = \gamma_i$ as used in [3]. Same updating rule for γ_i is obtained as that in [3].

5   Simulations

The performance of the alternative to the EBSBL algorithm has been evaluated and comprehensively compared in [3]. For completeness, we quote the main performance evaluation results here. Two measures of support recovery rate and normalized root mean squared error (NRMSE) [3] are used for performance evaluation under the signal to noise ratio of 25 dB. The achieved support recovery and NRMSE are shown in Figs. 4 and 5, respectively, using 100 independent trials.

Figure 4 gives the support recovery rates against the sampling ratio while Fig. 5 gives the achieved NRMSE against the sparsity. As shown in sub-figures (b) of both figures, the NRMSEs of all algorithms decrease as the under-sampling

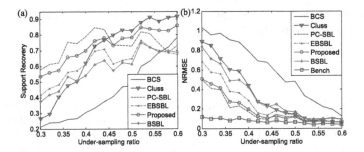

Fig. 4. Support recovery and NRMSE against sampling ratio when the signal is of a sparse degree of 25. (a) the support recovery; (b) the NRMSE.

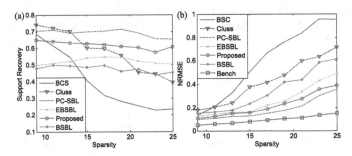

Fig. 5. Support recovery and NRMSE against sparsity level using 35 measurements. (a) the support recovery; (b) the NRMSE.

ratio increases and the sparsity level decreases. When the under-sampling ratio or the sparsity increases as shown in sub-figures (a) of both figures, the achieved support recovery rates of different algorithms all decrease.

It is easy to note that the structured sparse recovery algorithms generally achieve better NRMSE than that of BCS as shown in Fig. 4(a). The inaccuracy aforementioned in Sect. 2.2 can be noticed by the result that as the observations increase, the support recovery rates of all structure considered sparse representations hardly increase. This inaccuracy can also be noted in Fig. 5(a). We see that as the sparsity decreases, the support recovery rate achieved by either BSBL or EBSBL is lower than that achieved by conventional BCS [14]. It is noted that Cluss in [13] achieves a better support recovery rate as there are enough observations since prevention of structure over fitting is considered in [13].

6   Conclusion

This paper serves mainly as a supplementary for our prior work in [3]. The alternative extended block sparse Bayesian learning algorithm is re-investigated. More discussions on the relationship among the original problem, EBSBL and the alternative EBSBL are made for better understanding. A new interpretation of the derivation of close-form updating rules for the disentangling of the unknowns is provided. Problems of the edge inaccuracy in both the EBSBL and its alternative will be further investigated.

References

1. Mishali, M., Eldar, Y.C.: Blind multi-band signal reconstruction: compressed sensing for analog signals. IEEE Trans. Signal Process. **57**(3), 993–1009 (2009)
2. Wang, L., Zhao, L., Bi, G., Wan, C., Zhang, L., Zhang, H.: Novel wideband DOA estimation based on sparse bayesian learning with dirichlet process priors. IEEE Trans. Signal Process. **64**(2), 275–289 (2016)
3. Wang, L., Zhao, L., Rahardja, S., Bi, G.: Alternative to extended block sparse Bayesian learning and its relation to pattern-coupled sparse Bayesian learning. IEEE Trans. Signal Process. **66**(10), 275–289 (2018)
4. Wang, L., Zhao, L., Bi, G., Wan, C., Yang, L.: Enhanced ISAR imaging by exploiting the continuity of the target scene. IEEE Trans. Geosci. Remote Sens. **52**(9), 5736–5750 (2014)
5. Wang, L., Zhao, L., Bi, G., Wan, C.: Sparse representation based ISAR imaging using Markov random fields. IEEE J. Sel. Top. Appl. Earth Observ. **8**(8), 3941–3953 (2015)
6. Baraniuk, R.G., Cevher, V., Duarte, M.F., Hegde, C.: Model-based compressive sensing. IEEE Trans. Inf. Theory **56**(4), 1982–2001 (2010)
7. Eldar, Y.C., Kuppinger, P., Bolcskei, H.: Block-sparse signals: uncertainty relations and efficient recovery. IEEE Trans. Signal Process. **58**(6), 3042–3054 (2010)
8. Yuan, M., Lin, Y.: Model selection and estimation in regression with grouped variables. J. R. Statist. Soc. B **68**(8), 49–67 (2006)
9. Van Den Berg, E., Friedlander, M.: Probing the pareto frontier for basis pursuit solutions. SIAM J. Sci. Comput. **31**(2), 890–912 (2008)
10. Eldar, Y.C., Mishali, M.: Robust recovery of signals from a structured union of subspaces. IEEE Trans. Inf. Theoy **55**(11), 5302–5316 (2009)
11. Zhang, Z., Rao, B.D.: Extension of SBL algorithms for the recovery of block sparse signals with intra-block correlation. IEEE Trans. Signal Process. **61**(8), 2009–2015 (2013)
12. Fang, J., Shen, Y., Li, H., Wang, P.: Pattern-coupled sparse Bayesian learning for recovery of block-sparse signals. IEEE Trans. Signal Process. **63**(2), 360–372 (2015)
13. Yu, L., Sun, H., Barbot, J.P., Zheng, G.: Bayesian compressive sensing for cluster structured sparse signals. Signal Process. **92**(7), 259–269 (2012)
14. Ji, S., Xue, Y., Carin, L.: Bayesian compressive sensing. IEEE Trans. Signal Process. **55**(6), 2346–2356 (2008)

Design of GEO/LEO Double-Layered Satellite Network Based on Rateless Code for Global Information Distribution

Chuang Wang[1] , Dongming Bian[1]([⊠]) , Xingchen Xu[1], Jian Cheng[1], and Feilong Li[2]

[1] Army Engineering University of PLA, Nanjing 210007, China
biandm_satlab@163.com
[2] Troops 31006 PLA, Beijing 100030, China

Abstract. This paper proposes a double-layered satellite network based on the rateless code, which can globally distribute the information with a few satellites. The satellite network is composed of Geostationary Earth Orbit (GEO) and Low Earth Orbit (LEO) satellites. The GEO satellites which cover the low and middle latitudes serve as the backbone network, whereas the LEO satellites are considered the enhanced network to make up for the shortage of the backbone network. Due to the interruption tolerance of the rateless code, only a few satellites are employed to achieve worldwide information distribution in the design of the satellite network. The coverage performance and the average elevation angle of the user are simulated, and results demonstrate that the network can achieve globally information distribution.

Keywords: Satellite communication · Rateless code · Double-layered network · Information distribution

1 Introduction

Compared with other communications, the satellite communication has the inherent characteristics, especially the broad coverage which can support global services. With the continuously increasing requirement of information business, the satellite communication can contribute to alleviating the pressure, such as distributing information globally. It is necessary to design a network that can achieve worldwide information distribution.

Satellites can be divided into Geostationary Earth Orbit (GEO), Medium Earth Orbit (MEO) and Low Earth Orbit (LEO) satellites according to the orbital altitude. They show different characteristics in the communication

Supported by National Natural Science Foundation of China (No. 91338201, 91738201 and 91438109).

system, as listed in Table 1. It reveals that there are respective advantages and disadvantages, and the restrictions are difficult to overcome in the single-layered satellite network.

Table 1. Advantages and disadvantages of different satellites.

Satellites	Advantages	Disadvantages
GEO	The broad coverage	Unable to cover the high latitudes
	The mature manufacturing technology	Large propagation loss and delay
	Easy to keep aligned with the satellite	Large manufacturing and launch risk
	Communicate without frequent switch	Vulnerable to jam and physical destruction
	The negligible doppler shift	The scarce orbital position resource
MEO/LEO	The small launch risk	The limited single satellite capacity
	Small propagation loss and delay	The complex network control
	Cover the Earth globally	More satellites required
	Backup and anti-interference ability	The severe doppler shift
	The small user terminal	Large total investment and operating cost

Consequently, the double-layered satellite network was proposed, which combines with the pros and cons of different satellites [1–4]. Compared with the single-layered network, the double-layered network has more advantages, e.g., the coverage of multiple satellites, the high elevation angle of the user and the flexibility in choosing satellites. Furthermore, some researchers proposed the multi-layered satellite network [5,6]. However, many satellites are required to achieve worldwide information distribution, and the networking between satellites is very complicated.

This paper proposes a double-layered satellite network based on the rateless code to address the challenge, which can achieve worldwide information distribution with fewer satellites. The network is composed of the GEO constellation which acts as the backbone network and the LEO constellation which serves as the enhanced network. The backbone network distributes information in the low and middle latitudes, whereas the enhanced network provides enhanced support through the multiple coverage in low and middle latitudes and the supplemental coverage in the high latitudes and the polar regions. Along with the characteristics of reliable, fast and interruption tolerant of the rateless code, the double-layered satellite network can achieve an efficient and reliable information distribution.

The rest of the paper is as follows. Besides briefly introducing the characteristics of the rateless code, Sect. 2 depicts the double-layered satellite network. Next, Sect. 3 designs the backbone network and the enhanced network. Section 4 analyzes the coverage performance and the average elevation angle of the user. Finally, Sect. 5 concludes the paper.

2 Satellite Network Architecture Based on the Rateless Code

The satellite communication is a useful platform for distributing information around the globe. However, the channel condition may be deteriorated by the bad weather, the interference or the invisibility between the source and the receiver, which will cause a sharp rise in the bit error rate. The packet error rate will arise as well during the data distribution. Therefore, it is necessary to take measures to guarantee the reliability of the information distribution. Lots of techniques are put forward to solve the problem, such as network code [7], block code [8], FUN code [9] and rateless code [10]. Among them, the rateless code possesses some excellent characteristics, which is an effective encoding method for both unicast and multicast system, and plays an essential role in the satellite communication, especially for those without feedback from the receiver.

In 1998, Byers and Luby firstly proposed the concept of rateless code in binary erasure channel [10]. The definition of the code length does not exist for the rateless code, which means that the code length tends to be infinity. Correspondingly, the definition of the code rate does not exist, so it is called rateless code. The basic idea of the rateless code is that the source node continuously generates encoded packets, and as long as the receiver receives sufficient encoded packets whose quantity is slightly larger than the original packets, it is possible to recover the original information, regardless of what the specific packets it receives. Specifically, the source node transmits sufficient packets encoded from k original packets, and when the receiver receives arbitrary $k(1+\varepsilon)$ encoded packets, the decoder can recover all original packets at a high probability, where ε is the decoding overhead. It should be noted that the decoding overhead of the elaborately designed rateless code can be very small, and the encoding and decoding algorithm can be simple as well. In addition, the rateless code can also improve the channel capacity and the network robustness.

In satellite broadcast, when users can not continuously receive the information from one satellite, the information can be transmitted from different satellites with the help of the rateless code, which can significantly improve the efficiency of the broadcast. We propose the GEO/LEO double-layered satellite network to achieve reliable, efficient and interruptible information distribution based on the rateless code. The rateless code shows the following characteristics when adopted in satellite broadcast:

- Reliability: If the Automatic Repeat Request (ARQ) mechanism is adopted to distribute data to users in heterogeneous channel conditions, it may result in ACKnowledgement (ACK) storm because each user has been reporting the ACK. If the Forward Error Correction (FEC) is chosen, it cannot ensure the reliability because of the deteriorated channel condition. If the rateless code is adopted, there is only one ACK when the entire data are completely received. Therefore, the information can be reliably distributed to all users.
- Fastness: Since the user only confirm once after the entire data have been received, the number of ACK or retransmission is reduced compared with the

ARQ mechanism. Therefore, the transmission delay is effectively shortened. The information transmission is fast.

- High efficiency: As long as the receiver receives arbitrary $k(1+\varepsilon)$ encoded packets, original packets can be recovered at a high probability. Recently, some elaborately designed rateless code whose decoding overhead approaches zero has been proposed [11,12]. The number that the receiver needed is almost the same as the original. Thus the efficiency is high.
- Interruption tolerance: During the transmission, the user can access the network and download the data at any time. In addition, the downloading can be interrupted, and the user can access the network later to continue the downloading. When the quantity of the received packet is enough, the original information can be obtained as well.
- Large chunks of data: The encoding and decoding complexity of ordinary code increases exponentially with the data size, while the relationship between the encoding and decoding complexity and the data size reaches linear in Raptor [13]. So the rateless code is very suitable for the transmission of large chunks of data.

The study presents a double-layered satellite network based on the rateless code. The GEO satellites cover the low and middle latitudes, and the LEO satellites cover the high latitudes and the polar regions as a supplement. The rateless code is used for broadcasting information between the backbone network and the enhanced network and between the network and the user. The asynchronous and intermittent reception can be realized With the help of the interruption tolerance. In other words, the user can access, quit and rejoin the network at any time. Therefore, the information can be distributed efficiently and reliably. Furthermore, the total number of satellites can be effectively reduced by using the rateless code. Because even if the entire network cannot achieve seamless global coverage, the region that is not covered temporarily can be broadcasted by the next satellite because of the interruption tolerance. Therefore, as long as the network can achieve periodical coverage globally, it can achieve worldwide information distribution.

The architecture of the double-layered satellite network is shown in Fig. 1. It consists of three parts, i.e., the space segment, the control segment and the user segment. The space segment is made up of the GEO constellation and the LEO constellation. The GEO constellation is comprised of three evenly distributed GEO satellites, and the Inter Satellite Link (ISL) is established between each GEO satellite. The LEO constellation is comprised of LEO satellites which are distributed in polar orbit. The GEO constellation serves users in the low and middle latitudes whereas the LEO constellation is responsible for users globally, especially in the high latitudes. The control segment is made up of the Network Control Center (NOC) and gateways, and it is responsible for the monitoring and control of the space segment, the network operation management and the user management. The user segment includes different types of user terminals and the information source.

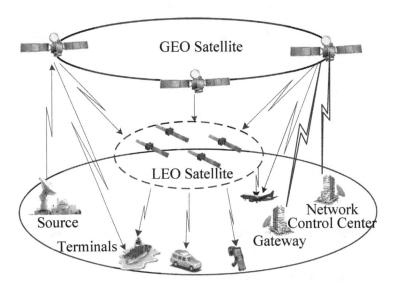

Fig. 1. The architecture of the double-layered satellite network.

3   Design of the Double-Layered Network

The double-layered satellite network consists of a GEO constellation which works as the backbone network and an LEO constellation which works as the enhanced network. In extreme cases, only a GEO satellite and an LEO satellite can realize worldwide information distribution based on the rateless code. However, if then, most of the regions in the world are covered shortly, and the network capacity is notably limited. Therefore, the design of GEO and LEO constellations is required. We should balance between the number of satellites and the coverage performance to achieve better performance with fewer satellites.

3.1   Design of the Backbone Network

According to the features of the GEO satellite, the backbone network is set to use three GEO satellites. The three satellites evenly distribute in orbit, and the longitude of each differs 120°. The fixed ISLs are built between GEO satellites for the information exchange. Figure 2 shows the coverage performance of the backbone network when the user's elevation angle is 10°, where the green denotes that the zone is covered by single satellite with 100% time; the yellow represents two satellites, and the white denotes it cannot be covered with 100% time. Figure 2 shows that the backbone network can cover areas within 50° north and south latitudes, which are about 468 million km^2, as large as 91.75% of the global surface.

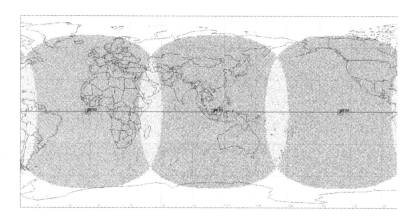

Fig. 2. The coverage performance of the backbone network.

3.2   Design of the Enhanced Network

The backbone network can cover most of the global surface, but the regions near the north and south poles are not covered. We decide to use polar LEO satellites to compose the enhanced network. Firstly the orbit altitude is optimized, and the selection of orbit altitude should take the following two factors into account:

(1) avoid the Van Allen radiation belts and the atmospheric drag [14]

The Van Allen radiation belts are two high-energy particle radiation belts around the earth, in the range of 1500–5000 km and 13000–20000 km. They will cause damage to the electronic circuit, so the two ranges should be excluded. Furthermore, when the orbit altitude is less than 700 km, the atmospheric drag will slow the velocity of the satellite and shorten the lifetime of the satellite. Therefore, the orbit altitude of the LEO satellite should be in the range of 700–1500 km.

(2) facilitate the operation of the satellite control

We choose the quasi-regression orbit to facilitate the satellite control, which means that the satellite passes the same place on the ground every day or every several days. The orbit period T_s follows the formula:

$$\frac{T_s}{T_e} = \frac{k}{n} \tag{1}$$

where k and n is the integer. T_e is a sidereal day, and the value is $T_e = 86164$ s. According to Kepler's Third Law, the relationship between the orbit altitude and the period confirms:

$$h = \frac{T_s^{\frac{2}{3}} \mu^{\frac{1}{3}}}{(2\pi)^{\frac{2}{3}}} - R \tag{2}$$

where μ is Kepler Constant, and $\mu = 3.986 \times 10^{14}$ m^3/s^2. R is the radius of the Earth, and $R = 6371$ km. After simulation, we choose $k/n = 2/25$, which means that the sub-satellite point will return to the same position after 25 laps around

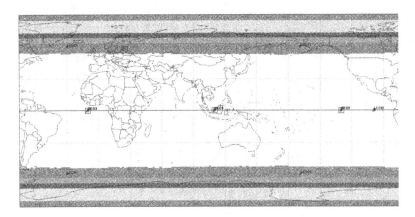

Fig. 3. The coverage performance of the enhanced network (6 satellites). (Color figure online)

the Earth in 2 days. $T_s = 6893\,\mathrm{s}$ according to (1), and then substitute into (2). We get $h = 1457\,\mathrm{km}$, and the value meets the requirement 700–1500 km.

The diameter of the LEO satellite coverage area is $D = 5943.5\,\mathrm{km}$ when the elevation angle is 10°. If fewer satellites are used to cover the polar regions, the overlapping region between satellites should be minimized. The minimal number of satellites needed can be calculated by:

$$S = \left\lfloor \frac{2\pi R}{D} \right\rfloor \tag{3}$$

After calculation, we get $S = 6$. The six LEO satellites are distributed in different orbit planes to cover the polar regions evenly. It is known that when the quantity of the polar orbit planes is more than 2, satellites may collide over the polar regions. Therefore, the inclination angle from 80° to 100° (except 90°) is usually used, and the inclination angle is set 84.5°.

After the design, we use the LEO satellite with 1457 km orbit altitude, 84.5° inclination angle to compose the enhanced network, and the quantity of the orbit plane is 6. It should be pointed out that the total number of LEO satellites is flexible. If the excellent coverage performance is required, the quantity can be large. If the cost is low, the quantity had better be small.

Figure 3 shows the coverage performance of the enhanced network when the enhanced network is composed of 6 LEO satellites, where the red denotes that the zone is covered above 90% time, the yellow zone above 80% time, the blue zone above 70% time, the gray zone above 60% time, the purple zone above 40% time, and the white zone below 40% time. Figure 3 shows that 6 LEO satellites can provide periodic coverage for regions above 50° north and south latitudes. When the enhanced network is composed of 24 LEO satellites, the satellites follow the Walker constellation with the parameter of 24/6/3. The coverage performance is shown in Fig. 4, where the green denotes that the zone is covered by with 100% time, the red zone above 90% time, the yellow zone above 80% time, the blue

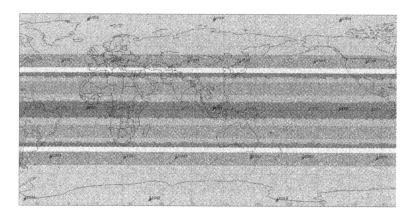

Fig. 4. The coverage performance of the enhanced network (24 satellites). (Color figure online)

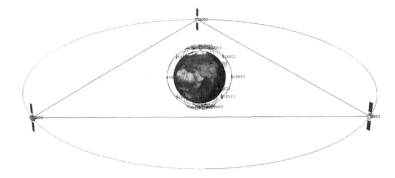

Fig. 5. The configuration of the double-layered satellite network (24 LEO satellites).

zone above 70% time, the gray zone above 60% time, and the purple zone above 40% time. Figure 4 shows that 24 LEO satellites can achieve seamless coverage for regions above 50° north and south latitude.

In practice, the configuration of the double-layered satellite network is quite flexible. A primary network that consists of 3 GEO and 6 LEO satellites can be first established in the initial stage. It can achieve worldwide information distribution with the help of the rateless code. Then LEO satellites can be added at any time to shorten the interruption time. If the seamless coverage is required, the quantity of LEO satellites can be increased to 24 or higher. Figure 5 shows the configuration of the double-layered satellite network when 24 LEO satellites are used.

4   Simulation Analysis

The longitudes of the ascending node of the three GEO satellites are 110° E, 10° W and 130° W, and the fixed ISLs are built between the GEO satellites. Then

Table 2. The ephemeris data of the GEO and LEO satellites.

Satellite	Perigee altitude	Apogee altitude	Inclination angle	Argument of perigee	RAAN	True anomaly
GEO1	35786 km	35786 km	0°	0°	110°	0°
GEO2	35786 km	35786 km	0°	0°	230°	0°
GEO3	35786 km	35786 km	0°	0°	350°	0°
LEO1	1457 km	1457 km	84.5°	0°	0°	0°

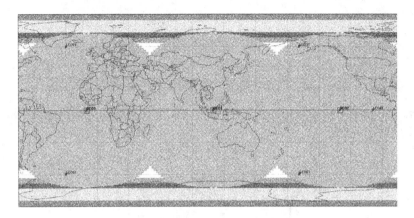

Fig. 6. The coverage performance of the double-layered network (6 LEO satellites). (Color figure online)

generate three GEO and one LEO satellites by the software Satellite Tool Kit (STK) according to the ephemeris data of the GEO and LEO satellites listed in Table 2. The other satellites are created based on 6/6/1 constellation parameter When the enhanced network is composed of 6 LEO satellites. The user's elevation angle is set to be 10° in the simulation. The coverage performance of the double-layered satellite network is shown in Fig. 6, where the green denotes that the zone is covered by with 100% time, the red zone above 90% time, the yellow zone above 80% time, the blue zone above 70% time, the gray zone above 60% time, and the purple zone above 40% time.

Figure 6 demonstrates that the double-layered network can cover the low latitudes with 100% time, and the area occupies 91.75% of the global surface when the enhanced network consists of 6 satellites. Besides, it can cover 96.29% of the global surface above 80% time. Thus we know that although it cannot achieve seamless coverage globally, the polar regions that are not completely covered can be covered periodically, and the interruption time is short. The information distribution can continue through the next satellite based on the interruption tolerance of the rateless code after the interruption.

When the enhanced network is composed of 24 LEO satellites, the enhanced network is a Walker constellation with the constellation parameter of 24/6/3. The other simulation conditions are the same. Figure 7 shows the coverage performance of the double-layered satellite network, where the green denotes that

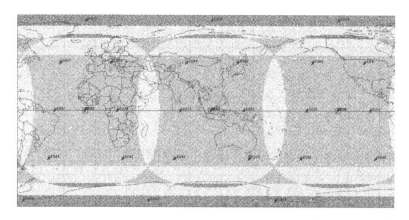

Fig. 7. The coverage performance of the double-layered network (24 LEO satellites). (Color figure online)

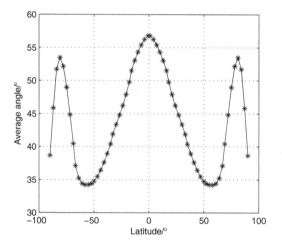

Fig. 8. The average elevation angle versus the latitude.

the zone is covered by single satellite with 100% time; the yellow represents two satellites, and the red represents three satellites. Figure 8 shows the average elevation angle of global users versus the latitude.

Figure 7 demonstrates that the double-layered satellite network achieves seamless coverage globally when the enhanced network consists of 24 satellites. Besides, it achieves multiple coverage in the high latitudes. In addition, the double-layered satellite network provides good communication elevation angle for users, especially in the low and high latitudes according to Fig. 8. Therefore, the designed network can improve the system availability, and alleviate the problem of information distribution in valleys, mountains, high latitudes and polar regions.

5 Conclusion

The multi-layered satellite network can combine characteristics of different typological orbits and utilize varieties of spatial resources to the uttermost, which indicates a significant development direction in the future. This paper proposes a double-layered satellite information distribution network combined of the GEO satellites and LEO satellites, which is based on the disruption tolerance of the rateless code. The designed network can use fewer satellites to achieve global information distribution. This paper simulates the coverage performance and the average elevation angle of the designed network, and the results prove that the network performs well, and the system availability is high.

References

1. Kimura, K., Inagaki, K., Karasawa, Y.: Global satellite communication network using double-layered inclined-orbit constellation with optical intersatellite links. In: Free-Space Laser Communication Technologies VIII, pp. 12–24. International Society for Optics and Photonics (1996)
2. Yang, L., Sun, J.: Multi-service routing algorithm based on GEO/LEO satellite networks. In: 2016 International Conference on Network and Information Systems for Computers (ICNISC), pp. 80–84 (2016)
3. Liu, R., Sheng, M., Lui, K.S., Wang, X., Zhou, D., Wang, Y.: Capacity analysis of two-layered LEO/MEO satellite networks. In: 2015 IEEE 81st Vehicular Technology Conference (VTC Spring), pp. 1–5 (2015)
4. Jiang, M., Liu, Y., Xu, W., Tang, F., Yang, Y., Kuang, L.: An optimized layered routing algorithm for GEO/LEO hybrid satellite networks. In: 2016 IEEE Trustcom/BigDataSE/ISPA, pp. 1153–1158 (2016)
5. Qi, J., Li, Z., Liu, G.: Research on coverage and link of multi-layer Satellite Network based on STK. In: 2015 10th International Conference on Communications and Networking in China (ChinaCom), pp. 410–415 (2015)
6. Kawamoto, Y., Nishiyama, H., Kato, N., Yoshimura, N., Kadowaki, N.: A delay-based traffic distribution technique for Multi-Layered Satellite Networks. In: 2012 IEEE Wireless Communications and Networking Conference (WCNC), pp. 2401–2405 (2012)
7. Borkotoky, S.S., Pursley, M.B.: Broadcast file distribution in a four-node packet radio network with network coding and code-modulation adaptation. In: Proceedings - IEEE Military Communications Conference, MILCOM 2015, pp. 1144–1149 (2015)
8. Ryoo, S., Kim, S., Ahn, D.S.: Layered coding with block turbo code for broadcasting and multicasting services. In: IEEE Vehicular Technology Conference, pp. 1–4 (2006)
9. Zhang, H., Sun, K., Huang, Q., Wen, Y., Wu, D.: FUN Coding: Design and Analysis (2016)
10. Byers, J.W., Luby, M., Mitzenmacher, M., Rege, A.: A digital fountain approach to reliable distribution of bulk data. ACM SIGCOMM Comput. Commun. Rev. **28**, 56–67 (1998)
11. Zhang, Q., Zhang, S., Zhou, W.: Enhanced LT decoding scheme in satellite communication. In: 2014 6th International Conference on Wireless Communications and Signal Processing, WCSP 2014, pp. 1–6 (2014)

12. Suo, L., Zhang, G., Lv, J., Tian, X.: Performance analysis for finite length LT codes via classical probability evaluation. IEEE Commun. Lett. **21**, 1957–1960 (2017)

13. Mladenov, T., Nooshabadi, S., Kim, K.: Efficient GF (256) raptor code decoding for multimedia broadcast/multicast services and consumer terminals. IEEE Trans. Consum. Electron. **58**, 356–363 (2012)

14. Cordeau, J.F., Laporte, G.: Maximizing the value of an earth observation satellite orbit. J. Oper. Res. Soc. **56**, 962–968 (2005)

A Modified Model-Based Resistance Estimation of Lithium-Ion Batteries Using Unscented Kalman Filter

Jing-Long Chen and Ri-Xin Wang

Deep Space Exploration Research Center, Harbin Institute of Technology,
Harbin, China
wangrxhit@163.com

Abstract. Lithium-ion batteries are critical components for satellite, and it is necessary to monitor their state of health (SOH). At present, the most common Ah-count method in satellite has errors in long-term health monitoring. Therefore, in this work, resistance is adopted to describe SOH and a resistance estimation method is developed based on unscented Kalman filtering (UKF). To reduce the impact of unstable work condition and battery aging, a simplified electrochemistry model of lithium-ion batteries is built to replace equivalent circuit model (ECM) in UKF. In consideration of battery aging, a linear lithium ions loss model is used in this model. Then, the linear relationship between resistance and capacity is analyzed to demonstrate the ability for SOH description by resistance. Experimental data suggests that this model can effectively track the resistance in discharge process and yield satisfactory results with battery aging. Besides, this method is applicable to estimating battery SOH, as suggested by the linear relationship between estimation of resistance and actual measurements of capacity.

Keywords: Lithium-ion battery · Resistance estimation · Unscented Kalman filter · State of health

1 Introduction

Satellite is critical for communication, navigation, and military in modern society. As the core of energy source and storage component in satellite, battery would determine the life span of satellite. Lithium-ion batteries are becoming the broadest choice in satellite power system due to high-energy density and long lifetime. At present, lithium-ion batteries have been applied in new satellites by United States and European Space Agency (ESA) [1, 2]. Besides, lithium-ion batteries are also selected as Chinese third-generation satellite power storage batteries to replace NiMH and NiCd batteries. Compared to NiMH battery, lithium-ion battery requires more accurate battery manager system (BMS) to ensure the normal operation of satellite system and extend the service life [3]. The core of achieving BMS function is to monitor SOH accurately. The commonly used battery health index (HI) includes capacity, resistance, and an indirect HI. Capacity reflects SOH directly, but changes with work-condition-like temperature and varying discharge rate in practical. Otherwise, discharge capacity measurement

© ICST Institute for Computer Sciences, Social Informatics and Telecommunications Engineering 2019
Published by Springer Nature Switzerland AG 2019. All Rights Reserved
M. Jia et al. (Eds.): WiSATS 2019, LNICST 280, pp. 25–40, 2019.
https://doi.org/10.1007/978-3-030-19153-5_3

requires battery to discharge from fully charged state to cut-off voltage. Indirect HI is estimated capacity through data future point, including constant-voltage current charging time [4], interval capacity [5], feature points of differential voltage analysis (DVA) and incremental capacity analysis (ICA) [6–8]. These indirect HI can estimate SOH accuracy, but require voltage data under time-invariant currents. Above-mentioned HI is hard to apply in satellite because their special requirements cannot be satisfied in orbital satellite generally. Resistance is inherent character of battery and can be measured directly or estimated through measured battery signals (voltage, current and temperature). It is insensitive to discharge rate and has steady relationship with capacity. The relationship between resistance and SOH has been studied extensively. Maheshwari et al. [9] study the degradation characteristic of lithium-ion battery impedance with cycle aging based on test date. Chen et al. [10] analyze the relationship between internal resistance increases and capacity decreases, and define SOH directly according to internal resistance. Resistance in these researches is measured by dedicated devices which are hard to install on satellite. Cui et al. [11] investigate the real-time relationship between impedance and battery cycle and propose a method in which rapid identification of the impedance is built on charge and discharge curves. In this method, the calculation of transfer impedance is very complex, and the calculation of internal impedance ignore the error derived from varied SOC.

Generally, current-pulse technique and electrochemical impedance (EIS) are major approaches to measure battery internal resistance. Current-pulse technique offers a current pulse (ΔI) for battery and measures the voltage drop (ΔV). Then the resistance, also known as direct current resistance (DCR) in this case, can be calculated by R = $\Delta V/\Delta I$. This technique is superior for simple online implementation, yet is hard to apply in satellite directly for requiring high-quality pulse to ensure measurement accuracy. Whereas, EIS analyze resistance on the basis of impedance spectrum. It is highly precise, but only suitable in laboratory due to the necessity for special equipment.

Given the weakness of current-pulse technique and EIS, Kalman filter-based parameter estimation methods have aroused abundant research attention recently. Those approaches attain optimal state estimation from measured parameters including voltage, current, and temperature. Plett et al. [12–14] firstly estimate battery parameter using Extended Kalman filter and acquire accurate estimation results. Tian et al. [15] estimate battery SOC and capacity through UKF. Than Lim et al. [16] estimate electric vehicles battery parameters by Fading Kalman filter. In those Kalman filter methods, the system state equation has three types of lithium-ion battery model in general, i.e. electrochemical model, mathematical model, and electrical model [17]. Mathematical model has fastest operation, and yet lower accuracy and applicability. Electrical model is much simpler compared with electrochemical model. It can be applied into comprehensive system-level dynamic models and track how battery responds to transient loads with high accuracy. Unfortunately, this model requires the correlation between OCV and SOC which is hard to obtain in practice. To address this problem, Wei et al. [18] use a function to describe OCV in capacity estimation, yet it may not be suitable for aging battery. To suit for aging battery, Lavigne et al. [19] propose an OCV curve adjustment algorithm with aging, but this method is difficult to apply in on-orbit satellite because it needs at least two OCV measurements in normal operation or in specific operation (for instance, charge phase).

Electrochemical model has no need for OCV-SOC curve, and encompasses transport phenomena and electrochemical kinetics. This model is very accurate due to the development of electrochemical theory, whereas it needs sophisticated battery parameters for estimation. Accordingly, to avoid that constant OCV-SOC curve is employed to estimate battery parameters under different SOHs, a resistance estimation method using simplified electrochemical model is proposed herein. Through this model, resistance as health index is estimated accurately during battery aging process.

2 Relationships Between Resistance and Capacity

Establishing relationships between SOH and internal resistance lays the foundation for estimating SOH by internal resistance. The primary ageing mechanisms of battery lies on the loss of active lithium [20]. Lithium is primarily consumed with the growth of solid electrolyte interphase (SEI) which consequently increases resistance [21]. The SEI layer is assumed to be homogeneous, and the ionic conductivity κ_{SEI} is constant. Thus, the resistance at the SEI film can be noticed as [22]:

$$R_{SEI} = \frac{\delta_{film}}{\kappa_{SEI}} \qquad (1)$$

Where δ_{SEI} is the thickness of SEI film and can be calculated through equation below:

$$\frac{d\delta_{film}}{dt} = -\frac{i_s}{2F} \frac{M_{SEI}}{\rho_{SEI}} \qquad (2)$$

Where F is Faraday's constant, M_{SEI} is molecular weight of SEI, while ρ_{SEI} represents for SEI density, and i_s is the side-reaction current density referred to as interfacial surface area of anode. The time integral of i_s is the mount of loss of active lithium q_{loss}. Then the R_{SEI} can be noted that:

$$R_{SEI} = \int_0^t \delta_{film}/\kappa_{SEI} dt = R_0 - K_1 q_{loss} \qquad (3)$$

Then $K_1 = M_{SEI}/2F\rho_{SEI}\kappa_{SEI}$

Following Daigle's model [23], the capacity of battery decreases linearly with the q_{loss}.

$$Q_t = Q_0 - K_2 q_{loss} \qquad (4)$$

Where, Q_t is capacity in current time, Q_0 is initial capacity, K_2 is the coefficient.

This relationship is also verified by simulating the degradation of battery performance. The simulation is implemented in Comsol Multiphysics 5.2a and the results are presented in Fig. 1:

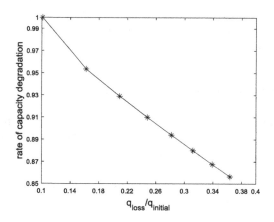

Fig. 1. Correlation of capacity and q_loss/q_initial

Accordingly, the relationship between resistance R and capacity loss Q_{loss} can be expressed as:

$$Q_{loss} = \alpha R - \beta \tag{5}$$

Where α, β denoted as the coefficient.
The traditional battery SOH is defined by battery capacity [10]

$$SOH = \frac{Q_t - Q_{end}}{Q_0 - Q_{end}} \tag{6}$$

Taking Eqs. (5) to (6)

$$SOH = \frac{R_{end} - R_t}{R_{end} - R_0} \tag{7}$$

Where R_t is current resistance, R_0 is resistance at start of the lifetime and R_{end} is resistance at end of the lifetime.

3   Resistance Estimate Method

3.1   Li-Ion Battery Discharge Model

Pseudo-two-dimensional (P2D) model, a frequently employed electrochemical model, describes the internal behavior of lithium-ion following concentrated solution theory. The sandwich structure of lithium-ion encompasses positive and negative porous electrodes, a separator and a current collector [24]. Then, lithium ions (Li+) can diffuse between positive and negative electrodes, and intercalate and deintercalate from active materials in different electrodes during charge or discharge processes. Under P2D model, battery model originates from a simplified set of electrochemical equations about charge flow and voltage drops at the cathode, anode, and separator layers of a Li-ion battery. This model is elucidated by Daigle [23] and summarized by Bole [25]. Herein, Daigle's model is adopted and modified to estimate the state of age-dependent resistance according to current-voltage dynamics of batteries in operation.

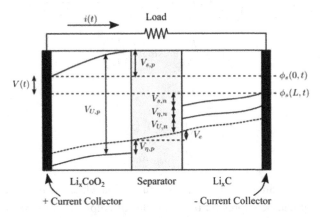

Fig. 2. Battery voltage [23]

As shown in Fig. 2, pressure drop $V(t)$ of overall battery voltage is potential difference between positive current collector $\phi_s(0,t)$ and negative current collector $\phi_s(L,t)$ minus pressure drop caused by internal resistance at the current collectors, which is not diagramed. $V(t)$ is superposed by voltage drops though further analysis and research about all parts of the battery. The equilibrium potential is $V_{U,p}$ at the positive current collector (subscript p). This voltage is then reduced by the solid-phase ohmic overpotential $V_{s,p}$ and the surface overpotential $V_{\eta,p}$. The electrolyte ohmic resistance then causes another drop V_e. There are additionally voltage drops caused separately by surface overpotential $V_{\eta,n}$ and solid-phase ohmic overpotential $V_{s,n}$ at the negative electrode (subscript n). Eventually, the voltage drops again, which is attributed to the equilibrium potential $V_{U,n}$ at the negative current collector. The resistance at current collector also causes voltage drop $V_{cc,p}$ and $V_{cc,n}$. All the voltage drops derived from resistance ($V_{cc,p}, V_{s,p}, V_e, V_{s,n}, V_{cc,n}$) can be lumped together:

$$
\begin{aligned}
V_0 &= V_{cc,p} + V_{s,p} + V_e + V_{s,n} + V_{cc,n} \\
&= i_{app}\left(R_{cc,p} + R_{s,p} + R_e + R_{s,n} + R_{cc,n}\right) \\
&= i_{app}R_0
\end{aligned}
\tag{8}
$$

Each electrode, either positive or negative, is split into two volumes, i.e. a surface layer (subscript s) and a bulk layer (subscript b), respectively. These voltage terms of battery are expressed as functions of the amount of charge in the electrodes and the equations are described by the set of equations below:

$$V = V_{U,p} - V_{U,n} - V_0 - V'_{\eta,p} - V'_{\eta,n} \tag{9}$$

$$V_{U,i} = U_0 + \frac{RT}{nF}\ln\left(\frac{1 - x_{s,i}}{x_{s,i}}\right) + V_{INT,i} \tag{10}$$

$$V_{INT,i} = \frac{1}{nF}\left(\sum_{k=0}^{N_i} A_{i,k}\left((2x_i - 1)^{k+1} - \frac{2x_i k(1 - x_i)}{(2x_i - 1)^{1-k}}\right)\right) \tag{11}$$

$$V_{\eta,i} = \frac{RT}{F\alpha}\arcsin h\left(\frac{J_i}{2J_{i0}}\right) \tag{12}$$

$$J_i = i_{app}/S_i \tag{13}$$

$$J_{i0} = k_i\left(1 - x_{s,i}\right)^a \left(x_{s,i}\right)^{1-\alpha} \tag{14}$$

$$V'_0 = i_{app}R_0 \tag{15}$$

$V'_{\eta,p}, V'_{\eta,n}$ is observed value, and $V_{\eta,p}, V_{\eta,n}$ is actual value which change instantaneously. Their relationship can be expressed by parameter of empirical time constants $\tau_{\eta,i}$.

$$\dot{V}'_{\eta,p} = \left(V_{\eta,p} - V'_{\eta,p}\right)/\tau_{\eta,p} \tag{16}$$

$$\dot{V}'_{\eta,n} = \left(V_{\eta,n} - V'_{\eta,n}\right)/\tau_{\eta,n} \tag{17}$$

Where the subscript i is electrode, where $i = n$ or $i = p$. U_0 is a reference potential, R is the universal gas constant, while T is the electrode temperature (in K), and n is the number of electrons transferred in the reaction ($n = 1$ for Li-ion), F is Faraday's constant, and $V_{INT,i}$ is denoted as the activity correction term (0 in the ideal condition). The Redlich-Kister expansion is employed with $N_p=12$ and $N_n=0$ [23]. i_{app} is the applied electric current. J_i represents for the current density, and J_{i0} is the exchange current density, k_i is a lumped parameter of several constants, including rate coefficient, electrolyte concentration, and maximum ion concentration.

Each electrode, either positive or negative, is split into two individual control volumes (CVs), i.e. a surface layer (subscript s) and a bulk layer (subscript b), respectively. The mole fractions ($x_i, x_{s,i}, x_{b,i}$) can be expressed by equations below:

$$x_i = q_i/q^{\max}; \quad x_{s,i} = q_{s,i}/q_{s,i}^{\max}; \quad x_{b,i} = q_{b,i}/q_{b,i}^{\max} \tag{18}$$

Where q_i is the amount of charge in electrode i, $q_{s,i}$ is the amount of charge in surface of electrode i, $q_{b,i}$ is the amount of charge in bulk of electrode i. Abiding by the principle of charge move in these volumes, the charge (q) variables are expressed as following differential equations:

$$\dot{q}_{s,p} = i_{app} + \dot{q}_{bs,p} \tag{19}$$

$$\dot{q}_{b,p} = -\dot{q}_{bs,p} + i_{app} - i_{app} \tag{20}$$

$$\dot{q}_{s,n} = -i_{app} + \dot{q}_{bs,n} \tag{21}$$

$$\dot{q}_{b,n} = -\dot{q}_{bs,n} + i_{app} - i_{app} \tag{22}$$

The term $\dot{q}_{bs,i}$ expresses diffusion from the bulk to surface layer for electrode i and the express as follows:

$$\dot{q}_{bs,i} = \left(c_{b,i} - c_{s,i}\right)/D \tag{23}$$

Where D is the diffusion constant. The c terms are lithium ion concentrations:

$$c_{b,i} = q_{b,i}/v_{b,i}; \quad c_{s,i} = q_{s,i}/v_{s,i} \tag{24}$$

Where, for CV v in electrode i, $c_{v,i}$ is the concentration of charge in electrode i, and $v_{v,i}$ is the volume of CV. Note $v_i = v_{b,i} + v_{s,i}$ and the following relations:

$$q_p = q_{s,p} + q_{b,p} \tag{25}$$

$$q_n = q_{s,n} + q_{b,n} \tag{26}$$

$$q^{max} = q_{s,p} + q_{b,p} + q_{s,n} + q_{b,n} \tag{27}$$

$$q_{s,i}^{max} = q^{max} \frac{v_{s,i}}{v_i} \tag{28}$$

Considering that this model is used to estimate resistance with aging, the variation of parameter with aging cannot be neglected. At present, there are three commonly reported degradation modes [26]: (1) loss of lithium inventory, (2) loss of active material in positive electrode, (3) loss of active material in negative electrode. Those degradation modes in this work appear as the decrease of maximum charge amount. The decay trajectory of the maximum amount of charge can be estimated by a linear model [27]:

$$q^{max} = q_0^{max} - a \cdot N_{cyc} \tag{29}$$

Where a is lithium ions loss coefficient, N_{cyc} is number of cycle.

In summary, this model involves as states $q_{s,p}, q_{b,p}, q_{b,n}, q_{s,n}, R_0, V'_{\eta,p}, V'_{\eta,n}$. The model output is denoted by V. Parameter values for a typical 18650 Li-ion cells are given in Daigle's literature [23]. In this model, the R_0 is variable to be estimated, differing from Bole's literature [25].

3.2   UKF Framework

Kalman filter is mathematical technique which offers an efficient recursive means to estimate the states of a process and ultimately minimize the mean of the squared error [28]. For the highly nonlinear electrochemical battery model, UKF is more accurate than KF or EKF [29, 30]. This chapter summarize the filter basics to be mentioned, and more details may be found in Haykin's book [31].

The battery model is sophisticated and on-board measurement may not be very accurate. Therefore, noise items should be involved for both the process model and measurement model. The covariance of the process noise is assumed as R_p, associated with the system noise and current measurement error, while the covariance of the measurement noise is R_m, associated with the terminal voltage measurement error. The steps of applying the UKF to estimate resistance are summarized as follows.

Step1. Initialize the state and covariance for every discharge test date.
Step2. Calculate the weighted sigma points:

$$S = \{w_i, X_i; i = 0, 1, \cdots, 2L\} \tag{30}$$

where the sigma points are:

$$X_0 = \hat{x}_{k-1} \tag{31}$$

$$X_i = x + \left(\sqrt{(L+\lambda)P^x_{k-1}}\right)_i, i = 1, 2, \cdots, L \tag{32}$$

$$X_i = x - \left(\sqrt{(L+\lambda)P^x_{k-1}}\right)_i, i = L+1, L+2, \cdots, 2L \tag{33}$$

where the parameter $\lambda = \alpha^2(L+\kappa) - L$ and the weights w_i can be calculated by the equations below:

$$w^m_0 = \lambda/(L+\lambda) \tag{34}$$

$$w^c_0 = \lambda/(L+\lambda) + (1 - \alpha^2 + \beta) \tag{35}$$

$$w^m_i = w^c_i = 1/(2(L+\lambda)), i = 1, \cdots, 2L \tag{36}$$

where the α, β is parameter for unscented transform. In this paper, the common parameters $\alpha = 1, \beta = 0, \kappa = 0$ are adopted.

Step3. Update each sigma point via the time-update equation to predict the system state and calculate the covariance of the estimated state

$$X_{k|k-1} = h(X_{k-1}, u_k) + R_p \tag{37}$$

$$x_k^- = \sum_{i=0}^{2L} w_i^m X_{i,k|k-1} \tag{38}$$

$$P_k^{x-} = \sum_{i=0}^{2L} w_i^c \left(X_{i,k|k-1} - x_k^- \right) \left(X_{i,k|k-1} - x_k^- \right)^{\mathrm{T}} \tag{39}$$

Step4. Update the measurement as followed:

$$Y_{k|k-1} = g\left(X_{k|k-1}, u_k \right) + R_m \tag{40}$$

$$y_k^- = \sum_{i=0}^{2L} w_i^m Y_{i,k|k-1} \tag{41}$$

$$P_k^{y-} = \sum_{i=0}^{2L} w_i^c \left(Y_{i,k|k-1} - y_k^- \right) \left(Y_{i,k|k-1} - y_k^- \right) \tag{42}$$

$$P_k^{xy-} = \sum_{i=0}^{2L} w_i^c \left(X_{i,k|k-1} - x_k^- \right) \left(Y_{i,k|k-1} - y_k^- \right) \tag{43}$$

$$K_k = P_k^{xy} \left(P_k^{xy} \right)^{-1} \tag{44}$$

Step5. Update the state and covariance as followed:

$$\hat{x}_k = x_k^- + K_k \left(y_k - y_k^- \right) \tag{45}$$

$$P_k^x = P_k^{x-} - K_k P_k^{y-} K_k^T \tag{46}$$

For the resistance estimation in this paper, observe various is V and state variable of UKF include $V_0, V'_{\eta,p}, V'_{\eta,n}, q_{b,n}, q_{s,n}, q_{b,p}, q_{s,p}$. The state equation consists of Eqs. (6) and (10–26) and observe equation consist of Eqs. (7–9). The parameters of battery vary slightly in one discharge cycle, inclusive of $q^{\max}, D$ [32]. Accordingly, the parameters are assumed being constant for each discharge cycle except for resistance in single discharge. Besides, $q^{\max}$ change with cycle and the value can be obtain from Eq. (27).

4   Resistance Estimation Algorithm Verification

4.1   Experimental Data Source

This work employs public battery life test data originating from Prognostics CoE at the U.S. National Aeronautics and Space Administration (NASA) Ames to verify the resistance estimation algorithm for different SOHs. As Fig. 3 shows, experimental setup primarily consists of a set of Li-ion cells which may reside either inside or outside an environmental chamber, chargers, loads, EIS equipment for battery health monitoring(BHM), a suite of sensors (i.e. voltage, current and temperature), some custom switching circuitry, data acquisition system and a computer for control and analysis. The experiments are operated through 3 different operational profiles (i.e. charge, discharge and EIS) at ambient temperature, 23 °C. Charging is performed in CC-CV mode at 1.5 A. Discharging is performed at a constant current level of 2 A until cut-off voltage. The charge and discharge continue to loop until the capacity degraded to 30% of rated capacity. Data set B0006 is adopted here.

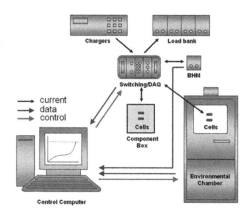

Fig. 3. The experimental setup schematic diagram.

4.2   Verification Through Battery Degradation Data

Without loss of generality, complete life test data of B0006 battery is employed. B0006 data set involves 616 operational profiles (168 discharge profiles and 141 EIS after charging completes). Measurement encompasses battery current, terminal voltage, surface temperature and stationary resistance. For each discharge profile, current and temperature serve as controlled quantity, and terminal voltage serves as observed quantity for UKF algorithm. Battery parameters are critical for resistance estimation. In this paper, lithium ions loss coefficient a is 30, and other battery parameters are given by Daigle [23], as summarized in Tables 1 and 2.

Internal resistance varies with SOC [33, 34], and the correlation between ohmic internal resistance and SOC is presented in Fig. 4, originating from battery test data of UR 18650ZY. As suggested in the test data, the resistance decreased at initial discharge and rose rapidly at the end of discharge. For each discharge profile, this law is consistent with estimated results of the resistance, and one estimated result is illustrated in Fig. 5. To compare with the internal resistance from EIS, the mean of estimated values from UKF during overall process of single charge is denoted as the estimated value of battery resistance. Then, the mean of EIS measurements at full charge discharge states is employed as the actual value of battery resistance.

Table 1. Battery parameters

Parameter	Value
q_0^{max}	1.32×10^4 C
R	8.314 J/mol/K
T	292 K
F	96487 C/mol
n	1
D	7×10^6 mol s/C/m^3
τ_0	10 s
α	0.5
R_0	0.085 Ω
S_p	2×10^{-4} m^4
k_p	2×10^4 A/m^3
$v_{s,p}$	2×10^{-6} m^3
$v_{b,p}$	2×10^{-5} m^3
$\tau_{\eta,p}$	90 s
S_n	2×10^{-4} m^4
k_n	2×10^4 A/m^3
$v_{s,n}$	2×10^{-6} m^3
$v_{b,n}$	2×10^{-5} m^3
$\tau_{\eta,n}$	90 s

Table 2. Battery activity correction term coefficient

Parameter	Value
$U_{0,p}$	4.03 V
$A_{p,0}$	−33642.23 J/mol
$A_{p,1}$	0.11 J/mol
$A_{p,2}$	23506.89 J/mol
$A_{p,3}$	−75679.26 J/mol
$A_{p,4}$	14359.34 J/mol
$A_{p,5}$	307849.79 J/mol
$A_{p,6}$	85053.13 J/mol
$A_{p,7}$	−1075148.06 J/mol
$A_{p,8}$	2173.62 J/mol
$A_{p,9}$	991586.68 J/mol
$A_{p,10}$	283423.47 J/mol
$A_{p,11}$	−163020.34 J/mol
$A_{p,12}$	−470297.35 J/mol
$U_{0,n}$	0.01 V
$A_{n,0}$	−86.19 J/mol

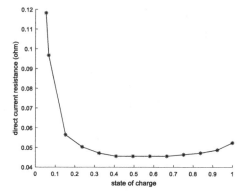

Fig. 4. The correlation of ohmic internal resistance and SOC at 1C

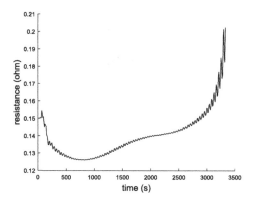

Fig. 5. Resistance estimate result for one of discharge profiles.

The ohmic internal resistance is estimated, and the actual ohmic internal resistance is equal to the sum of *Rct* and *Re* according to the battery model in Sect. 3.1 [7]. Comparison results of actual and estimated resistance in all degradation processes are plotted in Fig. 6, and the estimation errors are plotted in Fig. 7 to verify the estimated results. The estimated results are found very close to actual resistance, and maximum estimate error is under 10%. In first 80 discharges, the estimated resistance estimation does not vary apparently as new lithium battery needs some charge-discharge cycles to complete activation. Then, the resistance increases progressively with the degeneration of battery. By analyzing overall degradation process, estimated internal resistance is approximate 5% greater than measured value from EIS. This phenomenon is associated with the simplification of the models. For instance, a constant is adopted to replace *D*. In normal conditions, *D* changes with SOC and SOH. And the actual *D* change rule and the impact on estimation result is to be majorly studied in the future.

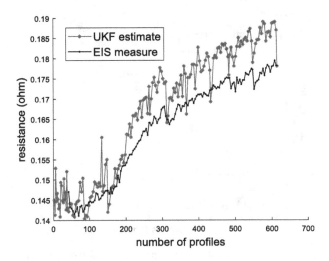

Fig. 6. Resistance estimation results at different degradation

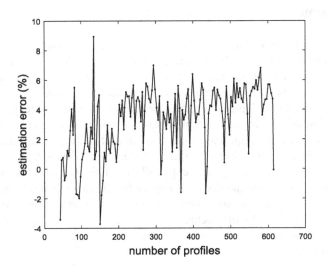

Fig. 7. Resistance estimation error at different degradation

The linear relationship between resistance and capacity is proved by these estimation results as well. As Fig. 8 presents, the relationship between resistance estimation results and capacity loss satisfies the linear rule well except in first 80 discharges. Data of Fig. 8 are fitted through Eq. 44. Thus, the battery state of health can be expressed by resistance very well R-square: 0.9992.

$$Q_{loss} = 15.151 * R - 2.0347 \qquad (47)$$

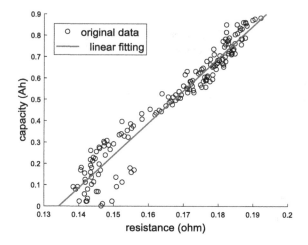

Fig. 8. Capacity loss of B0006 battery with different resistance

5   Conclusion

In this paper, UKF-based battery resistance estimation technique is developed and validated experimentally using B0006 battery from NASA. Then, the linear relationship between resistance and capacity loss is deduced and validated. Accordingly, this technique can be applied to estimate SOH. To estimate the resistance, a simplified electrochemical model is adopted to express the changes of battery voltage. This model could express the battery dynamics approximately, and OCV-SOC curve varied with battery degeneration is not required. Besides, the impact of temperature and parameter changes with aging has also been considered in this model. Thus, this algorithm can estimate battery resistance under different SOH and different conditions more accurately. Moreover, this technique does not require full discharge data. Hence, the proposed method is appropriate for satellite battery health monitoring with unfixed operating current and depth of discharge. For further work, the change of charge amount and diffusion coefficient with battery degeneration will be considered for more accurate estimation.

References

1. Wang, D., Li, G.X., Pan, Y.L.: The technology of lithium ion batteries for spaccraft application. Aerosp. Shanghai **17**, 54–59 (2000)
2. Ping, L., Ling-Sheng, T., Jie, W., Ya-Lin, L., Zhen-Hai, C.: Application of li-ion battery in GEO satellite. Chin. J. Power Sources 1–2 (2018)
3. Berecibar, M., et al.: Online state of health estimation on NMC cells based on predictive analytics. J. Power Sources **320**, 239–250 (2016)
4. Yang, J., Xia, B., Huang, W., Fu, Y., Mi, C.: Online state-of-health estimation for lithium-ion batteries using constant-voltage charging current analysis. Appl. Energ **212**, 1589–1600 (2018)

5. Yang, Q., Xu, J., Cao, B., Xu, D., Li, X., Wang, B.: State-of-health estimation of lithium-ion battery based on interval capacity. Energy Procedia **105**, 2342–2347 (2017)
6. Zheng, L., Zhu, J., Lu, D.D., Wang, G., He, T.: Incremental capacity analysis and differential voltage analysis based state of charge and capacity estimation for lithium-ion batteries. Energy **150**, 759–769 (2018)
7. Li, Y., et al.: A quick on-line state of health estimation method for Li-ion battery with incremental capacity curves processed by Gaussian filter. J. Power Sources **373**, 40–53 (2018)
8. Wang, L., Pan, C., Liu, L., Cheng, Y., Zhao, X.: On-board state of health estimation of LiFePO4 battery pack through differential voltage analysis. Appl. Energ **168**, 465–472 (2016)
9. Maheshwari, A., Heck, M., Santarelli, M.: Cycle aging studies of lithium nickel manganese cobalt oxide-based batteries using electrochemical impedance spectroscopy. Electrochim. Acta **273**, 335–348 (2018)
10. Chen, L., Lü, Z., Lin, W., Li, J., Pan, H.: A new state-of-health estimation method for lithium-ion batteries through the intrinsic relationship between ohmic internal resistance and capacity. Measurement **116**, 586–595 (2018)
11. Cui, Y., et al.: State of health diagnosis model for lithium ion batteries based on real-time impedance and open circuit voltage parameters identification method. Energy **144**, 647–656 (2018)
12. Plett, G.L.: Extended Kalman filtering for battery management systems of LiPB-based HEV battery packs - Part 1. Background. J. Power Sources **134**, 252–261 (2004)
13. Plett, G.L.: Extended Kalman filtering for battery management systems of LiPB-based HEV battery packs - Part 2. Modeling and identification. J. Power Sources **134**, 262–276 (2004)
14. Plett, G.L.: Extended Kalman filtering for battery management systems of LiPB-based HEV battery packs - Part 3. State and parameter estimation. J. Power Sources **134**, 277–292 (2004)
15. Tian, Y., Xia, B., Sun, W., Xu, Z., Zheng, W.: A modified model based state of charge estimation of power lithium-ion batteries using unscented Kalman filter. J. Power Sources **270**, 619–626 (2014)
16. Lim, K., Bastawrous, H.A., Duong, V., See, K.W., Zhang, P., Dou, S.X.: Fading Kalman filter-based real-time state of charge estimation in LiFePO4 battery-powered electric vehicles. Appl. Energ **169**, 40–48 (2016)
17. Cao, Y., Kroeze, R.C., Krein, P.T.: Multi-timescale parametric electrical battery model for use in dynamic electric vehicle simulations. IEEE Trans. Transp. Electrification **2**, 432–442 (2016)
18. Wei, Z., Zhao, J., Ji, D., Tseng, K.J.: A multi-timescale estimator for battery state of charge and capacity dual estimation based on an online identified model. Appl. Energ **204**, 1264–1274 (2017)
19. Lavigne, L., Sabatier, J., Francisco, J.M., Guillemard, F., Noury, A.: Lithium-ion Open Circuit Voltage (OCV) curve modelling and its ageing adjustment. J. Power Sources **324**, 694–703 (2016)
20. Cao, W., Li, J., Wu, Z.: Cycle-life and degradation mechanism of LiFePO4-based lithium-ion batteries at room and elevated temperatures. Ionics **22**, 1791–1799 (2016)
21. Spotnitz, R.: Simulation of capacity fade in lithium-ion batteries. J. Power Sources **113**, 72–80 (2003)
22. Safari, M., Morcrette, M., Teyssot, A., Delacourt, C.: Multimodal physics-based aging model for life prediction of li-ion batteries. J. Electrochem. Soc. **156**(3), A145–A153 (2009)
23. Daigle, M., Kulkarni, C.S.: Electrochemistry-based battery modeling for prognostics. In: Conference of the Prognostics and Health Management Society (2013)

24. Ramadesigan, V., Northrop, P.W.C., De, S., Santhanagopalan, S., Braatz, R.D., Subrama-
    nian, V.R.: Modeling and simulation of lithium-ion batteries from a systems engineering
    perspective. J. Electrochem. Soc. **159**, R31–R45 (2012)
25. Bole, B., Kulkarni, C.S., Daigle, M., Kulkarni, C.S.: Adaptation of an electrochemistry-
    based li-ion battery model to account for deterioration observed under randomized use. In:
    Conference of the Prognostics and Health Management Society (2014)
26. Birkl, C.R., Roberts, M.R., McTurk, E., Bruce, P.G., Howey, D.A.: Degradation diagnostics
    for lithium ion cells. J. Power Sources **341**, 373–386 (2017)
27. Xiong, R., Li, L., Li, Z., Yu, Q., Mu, H.: An electrochemical model based degradation state
    identification method of Lithium-ion battery for all-climate electric vehicles application.
    Appl. Energ **219**, 264–275 (2018)
28. He, H., Xiong, R., Guo, H.: Online estimation of model parameters and state-of-charge of
    LiFePO4 batteries in electric vehicles. Appl. Energ **89**, 413–420 (2012)
29. Li, J., Klee Barillas, J., Guenther, C., Danzer, M.A.A.: A comparative study of state of
    charge estimation algorithms for LiFePO4 batteries used in electric vehicles. J. Power
    Sources **230**, 244–250 (2013)
30. He, Y., Liu, X., Zhang, C., Chen, Z.: A new model for State-of-Charge (SOC) estimation for
    high-power Li-ion batteries. Appl. Energ **101**, 808–814 (2013)
31. Haykin, S.: Kalman Filtering and Neural Networks. Adaptive & Learning Systems for Signal
    Processing Communications & Control, pp. 170–174 (2001)
32. Daigle, M., Kulkarni, C.S.: End-of-discharge and end-of-life prediction in lithium-ion
    batteries with electrochemistry-based aging models. In: AIAA Infotech@Aerospace
    Conference (2015)
33. Chen, M., Rincon-Mora, G.A.: Accurate electrical battery model capable of predicting,
    runtime and I-V performance. IEEE Trans. Energy Convers. **21**, 504–511 (2006)
34. Ning, G., Haran, B., Popov, B.N.: Capacity fade study of lithium-ion batteries cycled at high
    discharge rates. J. Power Sources **117**, 160–169 (2003)

A Joint Technology of UAV SAR Based on OFDM Waveform

Yun Zhang[(✉)], Xin Qi, Lupeng Guo, and Nan Qiao

Institute of Electronic Engineering Technology, Harbin Institute of Technology,
Harbin 150001, China
zhangyunhit@hit.edu.cn

Abstract. This paper presented a method based on compressed sensing that can be used for a joint technology of unpiloted aerial vehicles (UAV) radar detection and with the orthogonal frequency division multiplexing (OFDM) signal. OFDM is promising waveform in the next-generation future radar, it also brings the possibility of radar detection and wireless communication time-sharing processing under compatibility mode. An imaging method was performed by synthetic aperture radar imaging (SAR) with OFDM signals on the UAVs platform in this paper. Due to burden on data storage and transmission, an effective imaging algorithm is proposed to achieve high resolution with less collection data by UAV SAR based on compressive sensing focusing method. At the same time. The experimental data and simulation testified the proposed method.

Keywords: OFDM · UAV SAR · Radar-communication integration ·
Radar imaging

1 Introduction

In recent years, UAVs plays an important role in typical environment monitoring, target acquisition and information transmission [1]. Some researchers have studied the joint-design methodology of multicarrier detection technique and orthogonal frequency division multiplexing (OFDM) communication technique [2]. Kenneth Vines and his team also provide a C-Band UAV SAR based on integrated radar and communication design [3]. Several experiments have been taken to verify the usage of UAV SAR in typical working mode and GMTI based on radar- communication integration [4].

According to the characteristics and requirements of the UAVs, it can reduce the volume, power consumption and cost of the system through the joint design of radar detection and communication based on OFDM signal. The orthogonal frequency division multiplexing (OFDM) has become a crucial technique for the new generation at home and abroad [5]. OFDM radar signal processing was first proposed by Janki-raman in 1998, and recently researched in radar applications, such as target detection [6], high-resolution and wide-swath imaging [7]. Furthermore, UWB OFDM radar and GPS combination system is designed by Garmatyuk D, his team also used it as SAR imaging signal and proposed imaging algorithm which an improvement can be effected by use of the least squares estimate part [8, 9].

© ICST Institute for Computer Sciences, Social Informatics and Telecommunications Engineering 2019
Published by Springer Nature Switzerland AG 2019. All Rights Reserved
M. Jia et al. (Eds.): WiSATS 2019, LNICST 280, pp. 41–50, 2019.
https://doi.org/10.1007/978-3-030-19153-5_4

Meanwhile, limited by shannon Nyquist sampling theorem, high resolution and large scene ground observation bring rigorous challenges to A/D sampling, data storage and transmission systems. However, the development of compressed sensing technology has brought great possibilities for solving this problem. A compressed sensing imaging method is presented based on wavelet sparse representation of scatter coefficients for strip map mode SAR [10]. As long as the signal satisfies the precondition of sparse in a specific transformation domain, the signal can be reconstructed without distortion with a high probability using a small amount of observed data. Some researchers have explored the problem of SAR [11, 12]. However, few studies have been on OFDM SAR with compressed sensing.

The primary focus of this paper is on radar imaging technology based on UAV OFDM SAR. The radar detection performance of OFDM signal is obtained by analyzing the ambiguity function. The imaging results of target can be obtained by two-dimensional matching filter. Meanwhile, high resolution large scene SAR imaging imposes a heavy burden on data storage and transmission systems. To alleviate this problem, a compressive sensing imaging method is proposed based on OFDM SAR.

2 Theory Basis

2.1 The Construction of Scenario Model

UAVs could implement orthogonal frequency multiplexing (OFDM) communications and radar detection joint modules simultaneously. It means target detection is performed by the means of radar signal processing. The UAV platform continuously emits OFDM signals to main objects in the surrounding environment, such as vehicles and buildings during movement. When the OFDM signal is scattered by the target, the time delay and doppler frequency of the echo signal will change. Reconstruction of original image can be achieved by the use of echo information, as shown in Fig. 1.

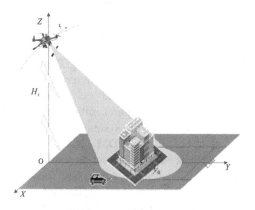

Fig. 1. OFDM UAV SAR model

2.2 The Ambiguity Function

As a means of radar waveform design and analysis, ambiguity function can describe the characteristics of the waveform and corresponding matched filter. When the optimal matching filter is adopted, it can be used to measure the resolution, measuring accuracy and ambiguity of the radar system. There are many ways to define the ambiguity function. This article adopts the definition as shown in Eq. 1.

$$\chi(\tau_d, f_d) = \int_{-\infty}^{+\infty} u(t)u^*(t + \tau_d)e^{j2\pi f_d t} dt \tag{1}$$

2.3 SAR Echo Model Based on OFDM Waveform

In the principle of orthogonal frequency division multiplexing (OFDM), an available signal bandwidth is divided into multiple sub band. It is assumed that the OFDM signal which the number of subcarriers is N can be represented by

$$u(t) = \frac{1}{N} \sum_{n=}^{N-1} d_n(t) \exp(j2\pi f_n t) \tag{2}$$

$$d_n(t) = C_n(t)\exp(j\, \varphi_n(t)) \tag{3}$$

The diversity of communication waveform design is mainly reflected in the carrier modulation envelope $d_n(t)$. $C_n(t)$ represents the term of envelope amplitude, and $exp(j\varphi_n(t))$ is the envelope phase term.

The imaging of SAR based on OFDM is considered into account of the establishment of the scene model. Assuming that the shared signal transmitting platform moves along the x-axis at a constant velocity v, the stationary point target P, the distance from the radar to the target is $R(t)$. Radar will transmit OFDM signal of N sub carrier in the state of motion, then the echo can be clearly expressed as

$$ss\left(t_f - \frac{2R(t_s)}{c}, t_s\right) = \sigma w_r\left(t_f - \frac{2R(t_s)}{c}\right)w_a(t_s)\frac{1}{\sqrt{N}}$$
$$\sum_{n=0}^{N-1} d_n\left(t_f - \frac{2R(t_s)}{c}\right) \exp\left(j2\pi f_n\left(t_f - \frac{2R(t_s)}{c}\right)\right) \tag{4}$$

Where σ is scattering coefficient, w_r presents time domain distance window function, time domain azimuth window function can be expressed as w_a, t_f is fast time series, t_s is defined as slow time sequence, R is regarded as the distance from radar to target, and c is the speed of light.

Assuming that the signal envelope, $d_n(f_r)$ is phase encoded, the reference signal of the corresponding matched filter can be represented as

$$u(t_f) = ss^*(-t_f) = \frac{1}{\sqrt{N}} \sum_{n=0}^{N-1} \exp(-j\phi_m) \exp(-j2\pi f_n t_f) \qquad (5)$$

After range matching filtering, the echo signal can be expressed as

$$
\begin{aligned}
s(t, t_m) &= F^{-1}\left\{ F\left\{ ss\left(t_f - \frac{2R(t_s)}{c}, t_s\right) \right\} * F\{u(t_f)\} \right\} \\
&= \sum_{n=1}^{N_0} B\sigma_n \sin c\left[\Delta f_r\left(t - \frac{2(R0 + x_n \sin\theta_0)}{c}\right)\right] \\
&\quad \cdot \exp\left(-j\frac{4\pi}{\lambda} R_0\right) \cdot w_a(t_m - x_n/v) \cdot \exp\left(j\pi\gamma_m(R_0)(t_m - x_n/v)^2\right)
\end{aligned}
\qquad (6)
$$

Assuming that $\rho_n = B\sigma_n \sin c\left[\Delta f_r\left(t - \frac{2(R_0 + x_n \sin\theta)}{c}\right)\right] \cdot \exp\left(-j\frac{4\pi}{\lambda} R_0\right)$, the Eq. (6) can be regarded by

$$s(t, t_m) = \sum_{n=1}^{N_0} \rho_n w_a(t_m - x_n/v) \cdot \exp\left(j\pi\gamma_m(R_0)(t_m - x_n/v)^2\right) \qquad (7)$$

2.4 The UAVs SAR Imaging Under-Sampled Measurement

High resolution and large scene ground observation bring a heavy burden on A/D sampling, data storage and transmission systems. This paper is designed to realize the recovery of under-sampled measurement echo data for UAVs OFDM SAR by the use of compressed sensing.

Compressed sensing is a method of recovering signals from linear observations by solving a highly nonlinear optimization problem. An N-dimensional real signal is consisted of a set of orthogonal bases $\{\varphi_i\}_{i=1}^{N}$

$$\rho = \Psi\theta \qquad (8)$$

$\psi = [\varphi_1, \varphi_2, \cdots \varphi_N] \in R^{N \times N}$ is the dictionary matrix. This paper chooses the Fourier orthogonal basis, $\psi\psi^T = \psi^T\psi = I$, $\theta = [\theta_1, \theta_2, \cdots \theta_N]^T$. The compression of $\rho_{M \times 1}$ can be accomplished by an observation matrix Φ which is not related to an orthogonal basis dictionary matrix. And the radar echo signal is the following expression:

$$s_{M \times 1} = \Phi_{M \times N} \rho_{N \times 1} \qquad (9)$$

Therefore, the observation matrix can be expressed as

$$\Phi = [s(t_m - (\frac{N}{2} - 1) \cdot \Delta\tau), \cdots s(t_m + \Delta\tau), \cdots s(t_m + (\frac{N}{2} - 1)\Delta\tau)]$$

$$s(t_m - i\Delta\tau) = \exp\left\{j\pi\gamma_m(R_0)(t_m - i\Delta\tau)^2\right\}$$

The data $s_{M \times 1}$ after range matching filtering is the under-sampled measurement echo data and $\rho_{N \times 1}$ is the data to be restored.

The purpose of compression sensing is to recover x from y. Convex optimization can be very simple to describe the situation, and the original signal will be solved as solving such a convex optimization problem.

$$\min\|y - T\theta\|_2 + \lambda\|\theta\|_1 \tag{10}$$

The recovery matrix. $T = \Phi\Psi^H$, $\rho_{N \times 1} = \Psi\theta$, is the reconstructed complex image of the range cell scene.

3 Simulation and Results

In this section, simulation results are used to validate the analysis previously. The OFDM signal is obtained by a series of random sequence with QPSK modulation, serial and conversion, IFFT transform. The carrier frequency of the signal is 38 GHz. The number of sub carriers is set as 512, the symbol cycle length is 16.67 us, the signal bandwidth is 100 MHz, and the number of symbols per carrier is set as 12. As the method shown above, the ambiguity function is shown in Fig. 2, which shows resolution performance intuitively.

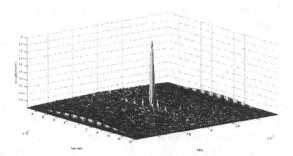

Fig. 2. The ambiguity function of OFDM signal

Theoretically, the range resolution only depends on the signal bandwidth $\Delta R = \frac{c}{2B} = 1.5$ m, the velocity resolution, which is related to the signal carrier frequency and the accumulated time length, is $\Delta v = \frac{1}{2}\lambda\Delta f = \frac{1}{2}\frac{c}{f_c}\frac{1}{T_{all}} = 23.68$ m/s. As is shown in Figs. 3 and 4, the equivalent bandwidth at the 4 dB point which corresponds to range resolution is $0.763 \times 2 = 1.526$ m and the velocity resolution is $11.85 \times 2 = 23.7$ m/s The result of the simulation is consistent with the theoretical value.

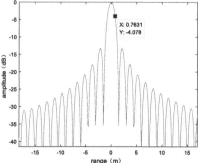
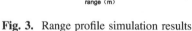
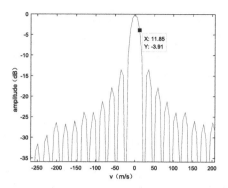

Fig. 3. Range profile simulation results   **Fig. 4.** Doppler frequency simulation results

The signal for radar detection and communication is transmitted simultaneously by UAVs. Considering the storage and transmission burden of large amount of data, the reconstruction of image is carried out by using down-sampling data. The processing of signal is shown in Fig. 5. The echo signal is convoluted with the reference signal in the fast time domain. The observation matrix is constructed in the slow time domain, which transforms the azimuth compression into solving the convex optimization problem. There are 5 point targets near the center of the scene at (Xc, 0), (Xc + 10 m, 0), (Xc − 10 m, 0), (Xc, 20 m), (Xc, −20 m) in the simulation. Assuming that echo data is down sampling at random, the echo received by radar is 0.8 times that of the original data. Figure 6 shows the echo data of the descending sampling. The results of range matching filtering with the loss of signal are presented in Fig. 7.

Results are shown in Fig. 8, where it could be seen that the target distance position can be obtained after correlation processing. As shown in Fig. 9, there are five targets in the scene which could be obtained by the means of compressed sensing. Compressive sensing parameters are set as discussed in Sect. 2.5 where η is equal to 2.

Compressed sensing is of great significance for the recovery of missing data in radar imaging. The influence of compressive sensing on SAR imaging performance is mainly reflected in the result of azimuth data compression. The use of compressed sensing has certain limitation on the amount of missing data. In the absence of random 0.3 times the original data of the information, it could still get accurate the position information. If the sampling rate continues to be lowered, the signal cannot be recovered well and the azimuth will appear blurred. The position of the target cannot be obtained accurately because of the elevation of side lobe in Table 1. It can be described that the trend of peak side lobe rate (FSLR) with the percentage of echo data is shown in Fig. 11 (Fig. 10).

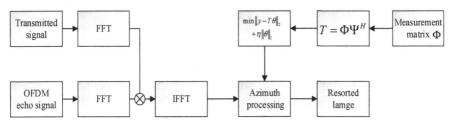

Fig. 5. The flow chart for signal processing

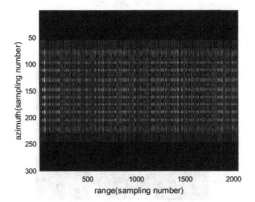

Fig. 6. The echo data of the descending sampling results

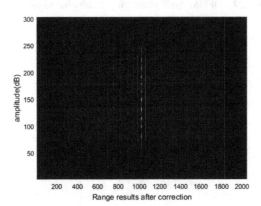

Fig. 7. Range compression simulation results

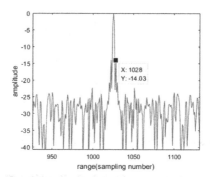

Fig. 8. Range profile results

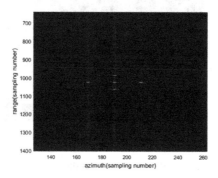

Fig. 9. OFDM SAR simulation results based on CS

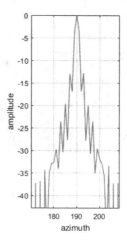

Fig. 10. 80% down sampling results.

Table 1. The relationship between echo data percentage and FSLR

Echo data percentage	FSLR
100%	−34.9 dB
90%	−34.7 dB
70%	−27.3 dB
40%	−22.83 dB
20%	−19.34 dB
1%	−8.17 dB

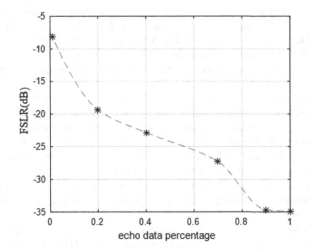

Fig. 11. The FSLR with echo data percentage

4 Conclusion

A joint technology of unpiloted aerial vehicles (UAV) radar imaging system based on OFDM signal is established to get the high-resolution imaging of the target, and it is applied to the actual situation. By using sparse reconstruction algorithms and the imaging processing the imaging of target was successfully focused by less raw data, which is suit for UAV radar with the waveform of the orthogonal frequency multiplexing (OFDM). The experimental data and simulation testified the proposed method. This research will enhance the understanding of radar-communication integration with small unpiloted aerial vehicles.

Acknowledgement. This work was supported by the National Natural Science Foundation of China 61201304 and 61201308, it also thanks for the Aerospace Innovation Foundation. The author wants to express their gratitude to the Key Laboratory of Marine Environmental Monitoring and Information Processing, Ministry of Industry and Information Technology.

References

1. Wang, W.-Q.: Space–time coding MIMO-OFDM SAR for high-resolution imaging. IEEE Trans. Geosci. Remote Sens. **49**(8), 3094–3104 (2017)
2. Riché, V., Méric, S., Baudais, J.Y., Pottier, É.: Investigations on OFDM signal for range ambiguity suppression in SAR configuration. IEEE Trans. Geosci. Remote Sens. **52**(7), 4194–4197 (2017)
3. Yan, X., Chen, J.: A light-weight SAR system for multi-rotor UAV platform using LFM QUASI-CW waveform. In: IGARSS, pp. 7346–7349 (2016)
4. Zhang, T., Xia, X.G., Kong, L.: IRCI free range reconstruction for SAR imaging with arbitrary length OFDM pulse. IEEE Trans. Signal Process. **62**(18), 4748–4759 (2017)
5. Garmatyuk, D., Morton, Y., Mao, X.L.: Radar and GPS system inter-operability with UWB-OFDM signals. IEEE Trans. Aerosp. Electron. Syst. **42**(4), 265–274 (2011)
6. Garmatyuk, D., Brenneman, M.: Slow-time SAR signal processing for UWB OFDM radar system. In: 2010 IEEE Radar Conference, USA, pp. 853–858 (2010)
7. Liu, X., Shen, D., Liu, Y.: Research on the micro small UAV system carrying SAR. Aero Weaponry (3), 33–47 (2017)
8. Xiao, Z., Gu, C., Gao, F.: Research on detection and communication for unmanned aircraft based on multicarrier techniques. Aerosp. Shanghai (1), 69–74 (2016)
9. Wu, Q., Zhao, F.: Compressive-sensing-based simultaneous polarimetric HRRP reconstruction with random OFDM pair radar signal. IEEE Access **6**, 37837–37849 (2018)
10. Wang, W., Liao, G., Wu, S.: A compressive sensing imaging approach based on wavelet sparse representation. J. Electron. Inf. Technol. **33**(6), 1140–1146 (2011)
11. Jung, S.H., Cho, Y.S., Park, R.S., Kim, J.M., Jung, H.K., Chung, Y.S.: High-resolution millimeter-wave ground-based SAR imaging via compressed sensing. IEEE Trans. Magn. **54**(3), 1–4 (2018)
12. Yang, X., Zheng, Y.R., Ghasr, M.T., Donnell, K.M.: Microwave imaging from sparse measurements for near-field synthetic aperture radar. IEEE Trans. Instrum. Meas. **66**(10), 2680–2692 (2017)

Multi-satellite Non-cooperative Communication Based on Transform Domain Communication System

Cheng Chang$^{(\boxtimes)}$, Zhe Li, Guowei Yao, Yun Xia, and Shuo Shi

Research and Development Department,
China Academy of Launch Vehicle Technology, Beijing 100076, China
loeibx@163.com

Abstract. Cognitive communication based on the unoccupied channels of transparent transponders in commercial satellites is a promising method to solve the shortage of satellite spectrum resource. However, most opportunity spectrum access systems cannot obtain real-time channel information from a commercial satellite. Although some systems can achieve non-cooperative communication, they usually utilize single satellite, which limits their overall performance. In this paper, to take full use of unoccupied satellite spectrum without disturbing primary users, a non-cooperative communication method by using satellites of different types is proposed based on transform domain communication system. Compared with existing methods, it is compatible with different transparent transponder parameters, such as frequency, bandwidth, primary user type, and delay. Besides, it also can achieve transmitting rate adaptation without signaling overhead.

Keywords: Non-cooperative communication · Transparent transponder · Transform Domain Communication System (TDCS) · Multi-satellite

1 Introduction

The increasingly rapid growth in wireless communications has made the frequency spectrum an extremely precious resource. Spectrum crowding in commercial satellites is more visible with limited transponder resource [1]. However, recent studies suggest that spectrum congestion is mainly due to inefficient spectrum usage rather than spectrum scarcity [2]. Considering payloads weight and reliability, most commercial satellites carry transparent transponders [3]. Channels of different transparent transponders are allocated to certain primary users or services, which implies that some spectrum would be idle when the corresponding primary users or services are absent. Hence, fully utilizing transparent transponder resource of commercial satellites without disturbing primary users has been the focus of some recent research efforts.

For most opportunity spectrum access systems, the real-time channel information obtaining of commercial satellites is the prerequisite to utilizing unoccupied spectrum. Shi [4] designed a non-cooperative communication system via satellite transparent transponders based on direct sequence spread spectrum (DSSS) technique. It roughly

M. Jia et al. (Eds.): WiSATS 2019, LNICST 280, pp. 51–58, 2019.
https://doi.org/10.1007/978-3-030-19153-5_5

lays the DSSS signal on channels whether or not the primary users exist. However, the lack of real-time channel information increases the risk of disturbing primary users. Xie [5] proposed utilizing satellite transparent transponders to achieve covert communication based on transform domain communication system (TDCS). TDCS is an overlay cognitive radio system [6, 7], where spectrum sensing is used to obtain real-time channel condition. Nevertheless, systems above only consider single satellite and the transmitting rate could not change with the real-time channel condition of the transparent transponders, which limits the spectrum efficiency improvement.

In this paper, a multi-satellite non-cooperative communication system is proposed to achieve reliable communication. Transparent transponders from different commercial satellites are analyzed to design a multi-satellite channel model. Based on this model, the system is designed detailedly. Then adaptive transmitting structure is proposed to improve the spectrum efficiency. Finally, delays of different satellites are estimated and compensated to accurately recover the modulated data. Compared with existing methods, the proposed system is compatible with different satellites. Besides, it also can achieve transmitting rate adaptation without signaling overhead.

The next section of this paper will briefly introduce TDCS. The new system is proposed detailedly in Sect. 3, where multi-satellite channel model, adaptive transmitting rate structure, delays estimation and compensation are designed. Simulations and analysis are presented in Sect. 4. The paper is then concluded in Sect. 5.

2 Preliminary

The TDCS model is depicted in Fig. 1. The transmitter and the receiver independently sense the spectrum, to create the spectrum mask $A(k)$, with a value 1 or 0 if the k th frequency bin is unoccupied or interfered, respectively. Pseudo-random phases θ_k are created by a pseudo-random sequence generator and applied element by element to the spectrum mask. The resulting vector is passed through an inverse fast Fourier transform (IFFT) and normalized to obtain the basis waveform. Basis waveform is used to generate cyclic code shift keying (CCSK) symbols. Then data is modulated with the symbols in Gray code. The i th transmitting symbol can be expressed on complex baseband notation as

$$s_{TDCS,i}(n) = \frac{1}{\sqrt{NN_1}} \sum\nolimits_{k=0}^{N-1} A(k) e^{\theta_k} e^{-j2\pi m_i k/M} e^{j2\pi nk/N}, \tag{1}$$

where N and N_1 are the numbers of the total and the unoccupied frequency bins, respectively. $m_i \in [1, M]$ is the i th transmitting data with M-ary CCSK modulation.

In the receiver, data is restored by maximum peak detection based on the correlations between the received signal and local generated CCSK symbols.

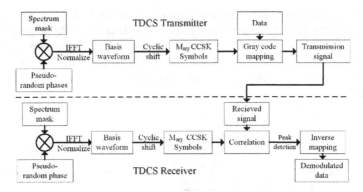

Fig. 1. Diagram of the TDCS.

3 System Structure

As the communication scenario shown in Fig. 2, ground terminal A transmits data to ground terminal B via two maritime satellites and one broadcasting TV satellite, simultaneously. The communication links are composed of uplinks from A and downlinks to B. In the following parts, the key points of the terminals and links are designed detailedly.

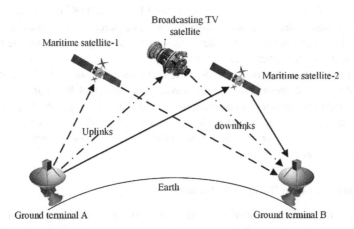

Fig. 2. Communication scenario.

3.1 Non-cooperative Channels Design

In Fig. 3, the non-cooperative channels are designed. Data is divided into three parts depending on the transmitting rates of the three channels. Assume maritime satellites are Inmarsat-4, which use L band (1634–1675/1518–1559 MHz up/downlink) with total relay bandwidth 36 MHz of total 41 MHz. However, due to the transmission rate requirement of primary users and frequency division multiplexing access structure, the beam bandwidth covering certain area is limited within 3.5 MHz. The bandwidths of transparent transponders and guard intervals are 200 kHz and 20 kHz, respectively. For broadcasting TV satellites, their relay bandwidths are much wider, such as 36 MHz, 54 MHz, and 72 MHz in C and Ku band. Considering broadcasting TV signal usually needs 8 MHz bandwidth, the beams are much wider to cover the whole relay bandwidths.

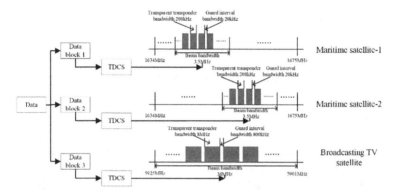

Fig. 3. Non-cooperative channels design.

The communication waveforms are generated based on TDCS. Terminal A and B independently sense the channel conditions of three satellites to generate spectrum masks. The idle transparent transponders are selected as the channels for the proposed communication system. Every satellite owns a unique pseudo-random phase sequence, based on which terminals generate basis waveforms for each satellite. Then data blocks are modulated with corresponding basis waveforms. Terminal B separates composite signal with different down-conversions to demodulate. For signals from the same frequency range, when one signal is demodulating, other signals can be regarded as noise according to the quasi-orthogonal of pseudo-random phase sequences and noise-like waveform characteristics [8].

3.2   Adaptive Transmitting Rate Structure

To achieve data blocks allocation as well as transmitting rate changing with channel conditions, an adaptive transmitting rate structure is proposed in this section. As shown in Fig. 4, synchronizations are used as an index to represent different modulation types. In the receiver, every frame is synchronized in P channels to locate the start point and determine the modulation type. Based on the index information above, signals are modulated in the corresponding way. Obviously, no signaling overhead is need in this structure.

According to [9, 10], the symbol error rate (SER) and bit error rate (BER) of TDCS modulated with CCSK are approximated as

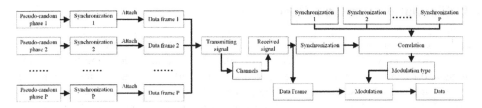

Fig. 4. Adaptive transmitting rate structure.

$$P_s = 1 - \int_0^\infty e^{-(x+\gamma)} \cdot I_0\left(\sqrt{4\gamma x}\right) \cdot (1 - e^{-x})^{M-1} dx, \tag{2}$$

$$P_b = \left(2^{b-1}/(2^b - 1)\right) P_s, \tag{3}$$

where $\gamma = E_s/\sigma_n^2$ is the ratio of symbol energy to noise power (SNR). $I_0(.)$ is the modified Bessel function of the first kind and zero order. M is the order of CCSK, and b is the bits carried by each symbol. The correlating of the synchronization for each satellite is actually the same as data, therefore, the SER of the synchronization P_{syn} and the total BER of one satellite P_e are given as

$$P_{syn} = 1 - \int_0^\infty e^{-(x+\gamma_{syn})} \cdot I_0\left(\sqrt{4\gamma_{syn}x}\right) \cdot (1 - e^{-x})^{P-1} dx, \tag{4}$$

$$P_e = 1 - \sum \xi_1(1 - P_{b1})(1 - P_{syn}) + \ldots + \xi_P(1 - P_{bP})(1 - P_{syn}), \tag{5}$$

where $\gamma_{syn} = E_{syn}/\sigma_n^2$ is the ratio of synchronization energy to noise power ratio. P is the variety of the modulation types in one satellite. P_{b1}, P_{b2}, ..., and P_{bP} are the BERs of different modulation types. ξ_1, ξ_2, ..., and ξ_P are the scales of different modulations in on satellite.

3.3 Delay Estimation and Compensation

The signal space transmission characteristic as well as delays are different with different frequency bands. For maritime and broadcasting TV satellites are Geosynchronous, once the terminals are fixed, the delays would not change much. Therefore, delay estimation can be regarded as a stable multi-path estimation. Terminal A transmits specific preset signals which are known to terminal B via satellites. In terminal B, delays are estimated with the preset signals (as pilots) by correlations. In the demodulation, corresponding delays are composited to recover data from different satellites. The total BER P_{eall} is then obtained,

$$P_{eall} = \zeta_1(1 - P_{e1}) + \zeta_2(1 - P_{e2}) + \zeta_3(1 - P_{e3}), \tag{6}$$

where P_{e1}, P_{e2}, and P_{e3} are the BERs of three satellites as in (5). ζ_1, ζ_2, and ζ_3 are the scales of data allocated to corresponding satellites.

4 Simulations and Analysis

In this section, some numerical examples are simulated to verify the proposed system.

Figure 5 shows the delay estimation of different satellites. According to the communication scenario above, the preset signals of three different satellites reach terminal B with different delays. To simplify the process, N is set as 128, the communication bandwidths are 3.5 MHz and 36 MHz for maritime and broadcasting TV satellites, respectively. Taking the time of the first reached preset signal as standard, the delays are estimated. In Fig. 5, the delay of maritime satellite-1 is regarded as standard with $\tau_{m1} = 0$, whereafter, the delays of maritime satellite-2 and broadcasting TV satellite are estimated as τ_{m1} and τ_b. Then delays are compensated for each satellites to restore the separated data.

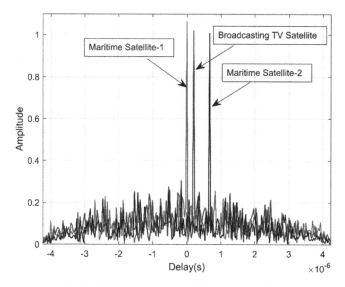

Fig. 5. Delay estimation of different satellites.

Figure 6 illustrates the BER performance of the adaptive transmitting rate structure. To overcome Doppler shift, synchronization is usually much longer than symbols. Simulation parameters are set as $N_{syn} = 1023, N = 128, N_1 = 50,\ 80, P = 2, \xi_1 = 1/3$ and $\xi_2 = 2/3$. According to dimensionality theory [10], without adaptive modulation, satellites use 32CCSK to fit $N_1 = 50$ spectrum condition. Modulation cannot adaptively turns to 64CCSK when spectrum condition is $N_1 = 80$. Based on the proposed method, modulation changes with spectrum condition, as the result, system can carry extra 0.6 bit per symbol on average. Besides, the BER performance is better than 32CCSK based on $N_1 = 50$.

The synthetical transmitting rate can be regarded as the sum of every satellite. According to the scenario above, assume three satellites share the same adaptive modulations, the transmitting rates can be calculated

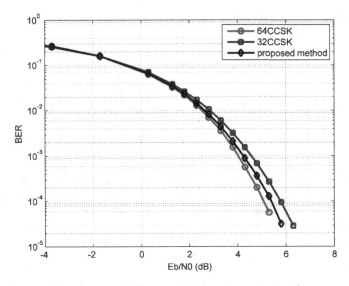

Fig. 6. Bit error rate (BER) performance of the adaptive transmitting rate structure.

$$R_b = \frac{b}{T_s} = \frac{b.B}{N}, \tag{7}$$

where b is the bits carried by each symbol on average in the proposed method. T_s and B are the duration and bandwidth of each symbol. The transmitting rates of two maritime satellites are $R_{b,m1} = R_{b,m2} = 0.155$ Mbps, the transmitting rate of the broadcasting TV satellite is $R_{b,bt} = 1.6$ Mbps, and the total transmitting rate is $R_{b,all} = 1.91$ Mbps. Obviously, the transmitting rate of multi-satellite method is much fast than that with single satellite.

5   Conclusions

This paper shows that cognitive communication system can be designed utilizing multiple satellites in a non-cooperative way. Compared with existing methods, the proposed system utilizes discrete and unoccupied spectrum of transparent transponders to fully use the satellite resource. Besides, the distributed data structure is safer to achieve a low detection and interception characteristic. The transmitting rate is also improved to meet applications requirement on high-speed and large-bandwidth.

References

1. Knab, J.: Optimization of commercial satellite transponders and terminals. IEEE Trans. Aerosp. Electron. Syst. **49**(1), 617–622 (2013)
2. Chakravarthy, V., Li, X., Wu, Z., Temple, A., Garber, F., Kannan, R.: Novel overlay/underlay cognitive radio waveforms using SD-SMSE framework to enhance spectrum efficiency- part i: theoretical framework and analysis in AWGN channel. IEEE Trans. Commun. **58**(6), 1868–1876 (2009)
3. Liang, W., Ng, X., Hanzo, L.: Cooperative overlay spectrum access in cognitive radio networks. IEEE Commun. Surv. Tutor. **19**(3), 1924–1944 (2017)
4. Shi, R., Hu, S., Xu, J.: Concealed adaptive spectrum spread transmission for satellite communication by transparent repeater. Ship Electron. Eng. **37**(1), 54–57 (2017)
5. Xie, T., Xinyu, A., Chu, Z., Gao, W.: Satellite covert communication system based on the transform domain communication system. Inf. Control **43**(5), 524–528 (2014)
6. Chakravarthy, V., Nunez, S., Stephens, P., Shaw, K.: TDCS, OFDM, and MC-CDMA: a brief tutorial. IEEE Commun. Mag. **43**(9), S11–S16 (2005)
7. Zhao, Q., Sadler, M.: A survey of dynamic spectrum access. IEEE Signal Process. Mag. **24**(3), 79–89 (2007)
8. Sun, H., Cao, F., Qin, H.: Multiple access applications of transform domain communication system based on phase coding. In: Proceedings of Fifth International Conference on Big Data and Cloud Computing, Dalian, China, pp. 217–222 (2015)
9. Dillard, M., Reuter, M., Zeiddler, J., Zeidler, B.: Cyclic code shift keying: a low probability of intercept communication technique. IEEE Trans. Aerosp. Electron. Syst. **39**(3), 786–798 (2003)
10. Proakis, G.: Digital Communications, 5th edn. McGraw-Hill Higher Education (2011)

Intelligent Dynamic Timeout for Efficient Flow Table Management in Software Defined Satellite Network

Shahid Jan[1(✉)], Qing Guo[1], Min Jia[1], and Muhammad Kamran Khan[2]

[1] School of Electronics and Information Engineering,
Harbin Institute of Technology, Harbin, China
sjanwardag@yahoo.com,
{qguo,jiamin}@hit.edu.cn
[2] Department of Electronics, University of Peshawar, Peshawar, Pakistan
kamranmu@uop.edu.pk

Abstract. Software Defined Network (SDN) modify the architecture of traditional satellite network into Software Defined Satellite Network (SDSN) by decoupling its control and data planes. However, SDSN encounter several issues, such as satellite link handover and limited space of Ternary Content Addressable Memory (TCAM), which results into increasing the number of flow rule entries and flow drop. To solve these issues this paper presents a novel three-layer architecture of SDSN and propose Intelligent Dynamic Timeout (IDT) algorithm. The algorithm predicts dynamic timeout for the eviction of unused flow entries in order to reduce the size of flow table, drop flow rate and number of table miss packets. Simulation results show that the average size of flow table, drop flow rate and number of table miss packets are reduced by 39.55%, 11.2% and 10.18% respectively when comparing the performance of IDT with different static idle timeout values.

Keywords: Software Defined Satellite Network ·
Flow table management · Dynamic timeout · IDT

1 Introduction

Satellite communication play a vital role in information transmission and it has been widely used for military purposes, live television, weather broadcast and internet of things [1]. However, traditional satellite network led the resources underutilization and it does not guarantee the requirements of future [2]. Software Defined Network (SDN) is an emerging network paradigm, which modify the architecture of distributed network by decoupling its control and data planes [3]. Traditional satellite network has adopted the architecture of SDN and results into Software Defined Satellite Network (SDSN). SDSN is explained by many recent researches e.g. OpenSAN [4] divide the architecture of SDSN into three planes. Similarly, [5] also present the architecture of SDSN.

M. Jia et al. (Eds.): WiSATS 2019, LNICST 280, pp. 59–68, 2019.
https://doi.org/10.1007/978-3-030-19153-5_6

SDN switches install flow rules given by controller in Ternary Content Addressable Memory (TCAM) and a single SDN switch can accommodate 1500 flow rules, because TCAM are power hungry and more costly [6]. In SDSN frequent satellite link handovers occur in network topology, which create more flow table entries and results into flow drop [7]. Different timeouts, ranging from 5 s to 60 s, have been used to evict the unused flow entries from switch [8]. However, all these timeouts are fixed and do not consider the occupied space of the switch.

This paper uses dynamic timeout to evict the unused flow entries from switch and thus reduces the size of flow table, drop flow rate and number of table miss packets. The technical contributions of this paper are given below.

- It presents a novel three-layer architecture of SDSN and propose an algorithm of Intelligent Dynamic Timeout (IDT) for efficient flow table management.
- The proposed algorithm considers the key points of limited TCAM space at forwarding satellites and priority based classified traffic of satellite network to predict a dynamic idle timeout.
- Simulation results show that the average size of flow table, drop flow rate and number of table miss packets are reduced by 39.55%, 11.2% and 10.18% respectively when comparing the performance of IDT with the static idle timeout of different values.

The rest of this paper is organized as follows. Section 2 explains related work. Section 3 explains the proposed architecture of SDSN and algorithm. Section 4 explains prototype implementation. Section 5 explains the experimental results and performance analysis. Finally, Sect. 6 conclude this paper.

2   Related Work

Flow Table management in ground network is explained by many researches and we have divided it into three directions. The first direction explains the designing of local policies inside SDN switches to reduce the number of requests sent to the controller. This concept has been used by DevoFlow [6] to reduce the number of flow entries in TCAM of the switch and minimize the communication between switch and controller. Similarly, DIFANE [8] uses middle switches in data plane and install flow rules in these switches to keep the traffic flow in data plane.

Second direction is the use of wildcard rules to reduce the size of flow table in switches. Leng et al. [9] proposed the scheme of flow table reduction by splitting the large groups of addresses into smaller groups and rewrite smaller groups in flow table. H-SOFT [10] proposed optimization algorithms to reduce the high-dimensional and complex fields of flow table into low-dimensional and multiple flow tables.

Third direction is to assign an appropriate static or dynamic idle timeout values to flush out the unused flow entries. Zarek et al. [11] explains the assigning of proper static idle timeout to evict flow entries from the flow table. Zhu et al. [12] proposed a scheme to assign different timeout to the newly arrived flows according to their characteristics. Vishnoi et al. [13] present Smart Time which combines adaptive timeout with proactive eviction of flow rules to calculate well-organized idle timeout and result in effective utilization of TCAM space. However, all these approaches are not appropriate for flow table management in SDSN, because it does not consider the satellite link handover, limited resources of satellite network and its priority based classified traffic.

3   SDSN Architecture and Algorithm

3.1   SDSN Architecture

The proposed SDSN architecture is based on the basic paradigm of SDN and comprises of three planes: Control Plane (GEO Satellites), Data Plane (LEO Satellites) and Management Plane (Ground Stations) as illustrated in Fig. 1.

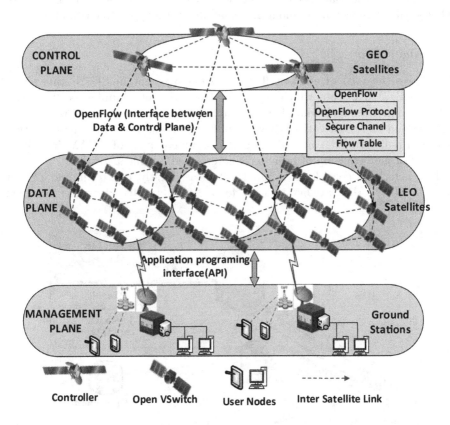

Fig. 1. Software Defined Satellite Network architecture

Control Plane: In this plane Geostationary Earth Orbit (GEO) satellites reside due to its wide coverage and stationary to the ground characteristics. This framework contains three GEO satellites for monitoring and control of data plane. GEO satellites monitor the LEO satellites flow status, link status and share it with the management plane for satellite network view. It also receives the routing rules from data plane and translate it to OpenFlow rules.

Data Plane: This architecture consider Low Earth Orbit (LEO) satellites in data plane due to less distance from the ground. A constellation of 40 LEO satellites is enough for global seamless coverage. Each satellite has four intersatellite links: two bidirectional links with the satellites of same orbit and two links with the corresponding satellites of different orbits. Each LEO Satellite contains Open Vswitch to run flow table and perform the packets forwarding function.

Management Plane: The ability of satellite to process network routing algorithms, perform the task of network security and manage all other resources are limited, therefore management plane will process all these responsibilities. The view of whole network collected from GEO satellites by Ground Stations will make able the management plane to run network policies. These network policies will be distributed among LEO satellites through GEO satellites.

3.2   Algorithm

To achieve the goal of efficient flow table management in SDSN, this paper proposes IDT algorithm which consist of two different Modules as illustrated in Fig. 2. The Feedback Module sends tableStatus request to each switch after every second and records the last value of flow entries. The Timeout Prediction Module Predict timeout according to the occupied space of TCAM in switch. Table 1 list the definition of basic parameters used by this algorithm.

IDT algorithm consider two important ideas. Firstly, due to limited TCAM space in SDSN, IDT predict timeout for a flow entry based on the occupied

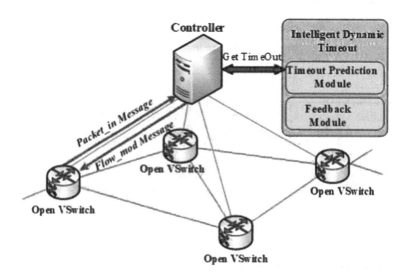

Fig. 2. Intelligent dynamic timeout modules description

Table 1. Definitions of basic parameters.

Parameters	Definitions
TCAM(peak)	Total TCAM space boundary limit
TCAM(max)	90% of the Total TCAM space boundary limit
TCAM(start)	80% of the Total TCAM space boundary limit
TCAM_Occup	Current TCAM occupied space by flow rule entries
T(idle)initial	Initial idle timeout
T(idle)ct	Initial idle timeout used for classified traffic
df1, df2, df3	Decreasing factor for traffic of group1, group 2 and group 3
T(idle)flow(x)	Idle timeout install for flow(x)
T(idle)IDT	The idle timeout of flow(x) by IDT

space of the switch and decreases the value of timeout according to increase in number of flow entries. Secondly, due to limited resources of SDSN it is difficult to allocate each user enough resources. Thus, we have classified users into three different groups based on their MAC/IP addresses. The timeout of these groups reduces in different proportion according to the decreasing factors.

Algorithm 1. Intelligent Dynamic Timeout Algorithm

Input: TCAM(peak), TCAM(max), TCAM(start), T(idle)ct, T(idle)initial, df1, df2, df3

Output: T(idle)IDT

   For every Switch: Monitor the number of Flow entries and Record the last n value

1: **for** Packet_in message **do**
2:     Check TCAM_Occup:
3:     **if** TCAM_Occup <TCAM(start) **then**
4:         K = (TCAM_Occup – TCAM(start)) / TCAM(max)
            T(idle)flow(x) = T(idle)initial – ($K \times$ T(idle)initial)
5:     **else if** TCAM(start) <= TCAM Occup <TCAM(max) **then**
6:         K = (TCAM Occup – TCAM(start)) / (TCAM(start)– TCAM(max))
            T(idle)flow = T(idle)initial – ($K \times$(T(idle)initial - 6))
7:     **else if** TCAM_Occup >= TCAM(max) **then**
8:         **if** *user* $\in$ group 1 **then**
9:             T(idle)flow(x) = $T(idle)ct \times$ df1
10:        **else if** *user* $\in$ group 2 **then**
11:            T(idle)flow(x) = $T(idle)ct \times$ df2
12:        **else if** *user* $\in$ group 3 **then**
13:            T(idle)flow(x) = $T(idle)ct \times$ df3
14:        **end if**
15:    **end if**
16:    T(idle)IDT = T(idle)flow(x)
17: **end for**
18: **return** $T(idle)IDT$

The execution process of IDT is divided into five Phases. Phase 1 accepts the input data. We consider T(idle)initial as 12 s, T(idle)ct as 10 s. df1, df2 and df3 are 0.7, 0.6 and 0.5 respectively. Phase 2 check flow table statistics every second and record the last value of flow table entries in a csv file. In Phase 3, the controller check TCAM occupied status of each switch. As T(idle)initial is 12 s, if there is no flow table entry T(idle)IDT will be 24 s. As the number of flow entries increases, it decreases the timeout linearly and when the TCAM Occupied space reaches to TCAM(start), timeout decreases to 12 s. In phase 4, the idle timeout value decreases fast to avoid reaching the TCAM(peak). In Phase 5, timeout value decreases suddenly in correspondence with the decreasing factors, to ensure the traffic flow from high priority users and avoid flow drop. The time complexity of IDT algorithm is O(n).

4   Implementation

To implement IDT algorithm, we used Mininet, Pox Controller and Open Vswitches to create a realistic virtual network. In addition, we developed 2-layer satellite constellation in Satellite Tool Kit (STK) with the parameters of its orbit as listed in Table 2 [14]. Figure 3 illustrate 3D view of the whole constellation.

Table 2. Parameters of GEO and LEO satellite orbits.

Orbit planes	Altitude in km	No of satellites	Inclination	True anomaly
GEO	36000	3	0°	0
LEO 1	887	8	86°	0
LEO 2	887	8	86°	333
LEO 3	887	8	86°	353
LEO 4	887	8	86°	328
LEO 5	887	8	94°	351

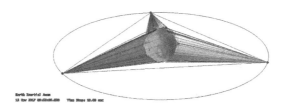

Fig. 3. 3D view of satellite constellation

The designed constellation has two ground stations at Sydney and Beijing. The purpose of satellite constellation is to measure satellite access to the ground

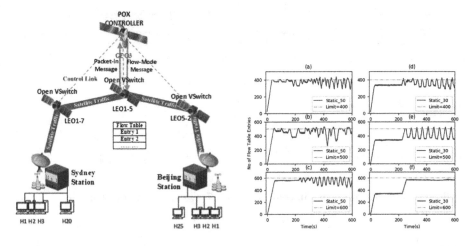

Fig. 4. Network topology

Fig. 5. Flow entries of static timeout 50 s and 30 s

stations which leads us to define a static network topology as illustrated in Fig. 4. This topology is fixed and use only three satellites of LEO1-7, LEO1-5 and LEO5-2 to transmit data from 20 hosts connected to Sydney station to the 25 hosts connected to Beijing station as illustrated in Fig. 4.

5 Experimental Results and Performance Analysis

5.1 Experimental Results

Four sets of experiments are created to estimate the performance of our proposed algorithm. Time of each experiment is 10 min (600 s). In each experiment random traffic flows from 20 hosts connected to Sydney station to the 25 hosts connected to Beijing station as illustrated in Fig. 4.

First experiment considers static idle timeout of 50 s. The results of this timeout strategy under TCAM space limit 400, 500 and 600 are shown in Fig. 5. (a), (b) and (c) respectively. In each case, the number of flow table entries cross the final limits, because the timeout value is larger and the unused flow entries reside in switch for more time due to which packets drop will occur. Second experiment considers static idle timeout of 30s. Simulation results of this timeout strategy is explained in Fig. 5. (d), (e) and (f) under the TCAM limit 400, 500 and 600 respectively. Figure 5(d) and (e) show that the number of flow table entries cross the final limit of TCAM due to maximum timeout which result into packets drop. But in Fig. 5(f) the maximum number of flow table entries do not cross the TCAM limit, because the TCAM space is enough to accommodate more flow entries. There will be no packets drop in this case.

Third experiment considers static idle timeout of 15 s. Results of this timeout strategy under the TCAM space limit of 400, 500 and 600 are shown in Fig. 6. (a),

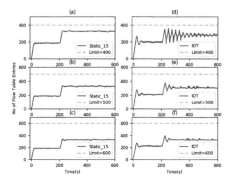

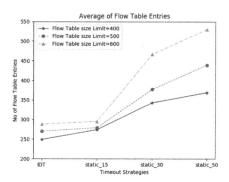

Fig. 6. Flow entries of static timeout 15 s and IDT

Fig. 7. Comparison of flow entries.

(b) and (c) respectively. In each case, number of flow table entries do not cross TCAM limit because the idle timeout is less and it evict the flow entries more quickly. In this case there will be no packets drop, but the number of table miss packets will increase. Fourth experiment considers dynamic idle timeout of IDT to evict the flow table entries from switch. The results of IDT under the TCAM space limit 400, 500 and 600 are shown in Fig. 6. (d), (e) and (f) respectively. In each case, flow table entries do not reach the final limit of TCAM space and there are no packets drop in IDT.

5.2   Performance Analysis

(a) Comparison of Flow Table Entries: The Comparison of average flow table entries of different timeout under the TCAM limit 400, 500 and 600 are shown in Fig. 7. The analysis shows that, Static_30 reduced the average number of flow table entries as compared to Static_50 by 7.04%, 14.12% and 12.07% under the TCAM limit 400,500 and 600 respectively. Similarly, Static_15 reduced the average number of flow table entries as compared to Static_30 by 20.11%, 25.99% and 36.69% under the TCAM limit of 400, 500 and 500 respectively. IDT reduced the average number of flow table entries as compared to Static_15 by 9.12%, 3.22% and 2.37% under the TCAM limit of 400, 500 and 600 respectively. Thus, using dynamic timeout of IDT instead of static idle timeout for evicting flow entries, can shrink the size of flow table dramatically.

(b) Drop Flow Rate: Figure 8 illustrates the drop flow rate of Static_50, Static_30, Static_15 and IDT. Here the drop flow is only due to the limited space of TCAM. Figure 8 shows that, the drop flow rate of static_50 is reduced 10.12%, 10.28% and 4.54% by static_30 under the TCAM limit of 400, 500 and 600 respectively. Similarly, drop flow rate of Static_30 is reduced 5.76%, 2.47% and 0.06% by Static_15 and IDT under the TCAM limit of 400, 500 and 600 respectively. The drop flow rate decreases when TCAM space limit increases and

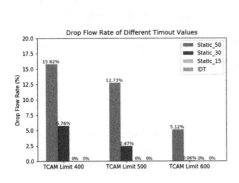

Fig. 8. Drop flow rate of different timeout.

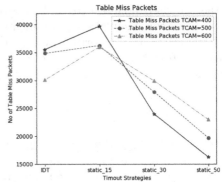

Fig. 9. Table miss packets of different timeout.

the value of timeout decreases. In our case as the idle timeout approaches to 15s drop flow rate turns to 0%. But using static timeout of less value triggers more table miss packets, which create additional overheads on controller. Thus, using dynamic timeout like IDT is more suitable in SDSN than static timeout of less value.

(c) Table Miss Packets: Figure 9 illustrates the total number of table miss packets, flows from three switches at LEO satellite nodes to one controller at GEO satellite node. When TCAM limit is 400, in Static_50 table miss packets are 32.1% less than Static_30. In Static_30 table miss packets are 39.58% less than Static_15. Similarly, in IDT table miss packets are10.51% less than Static_15. When the TCAM limit is 500, in Static_50 table miss packets are 29.43% less than Static_30. In Static_30 table miss packets are 22.90% less than Static_15. In IDT table miss packets are 3.74% less than Static_15. When TCAM limit is 600, in Static_50 table miss packets are 23.32% less than Static_30. In Static_30 table miss packets are16.71% less than Static_15 and table miss packets of IDT are 16.29% less than Static_15. Thus, using static timeout of more values reduces the number of table miss packets but increases packets drop while timeout of less value avoid packets drop but increases the number of table miss packets which is unacceptable in case of SDSN.

6   Conclusion

This paper has addressed issues of flow table management faced by SDSN. A scalable novel three-layer architecture of SDSN and IDT algorithm is proposed to solve these issues. The algorithm considers limited resources of satellite network and its priority based classified traffic to predict a dynamic idle timeout. In addition, a satellite constellation has been developed to evaluate the scalability of the proposed architecture and achieve the real parameters of satellite network. Extensive Simulation experiments have been performed to compare the performance of IDT algorithm with static timeout. The performance analysis demonstrated that IDT algorithm can efficiently reduce the size of flow table, drop flow rate and number of table Miss packets.

References

1. Dexin, D., Zengwei, Z., Meimei, H.: A survey: the progress of routing technology in satellite communication networks. In: 2011 International Conference on Mechatronic Science, Electric Engineering and Computer (MEC), Jilin, pp. 286–291 (2011)
2. Li, T., Zhou, H., Luo, H., Yu, S.: SERvICE: a software defined framework for integrated space-terrestrial satellite communication. IEEE Trans. Mob. Comput. **17**(3), 703–716 (2018)
3. Kreutz, D., Ramos, F.M.V., Veríssimo, P.E., Rothenberg, C.E., Azodolmolky, S., Uhlig, S.: Software-defined networking: a comprehensive survey. Proc. IEEE **103**(1), 14–76 (2015)
4. Bao, J., Zhao, B., Yu, W., Feng, Z., Wu, C., Gong, Z.: OpenSAN: a software-defined satellite network architecture. In: ACM SIGCOMM Computer Communication Review, vol. 44, no. 4, pp. 347–348. ACM (2014)
5. Bertaux, L., et al.: Software defined networking and virtualization for broadband satellite networks. IEEE Commun. Mag. **53**(3), 54–60 (2015)
6. Curtis, A.R., Mogul, J.C., Tourrilhes, J., Yalagandula, P., Sharma, P., Banerjee, S.: DevoFlow: scaling flow management for high-performance networks. ACM SIGCOMM Comput. Commun. Rev. **41**(4), 254–265 (2011)
7. Li, T., Zhou, H., Luo, H., You, I., Xu, Q.: SAT-FLOW: multi-strategy flow table management for software defined satellite networks. IEEE Access **5**, 14952–14965 (2017)
8. Yu, M., Rexford, J., Freedman, M.J., Wang, J.: Scalable flow-based networking with DIFANE. ACM SIGCOMM Comput. Commun. Rev. **40**(4), 351–362 (2010)
9. Leng, B., Huang, L., Wang, X., Xu, H., Zhang, Y.: A mechanism for reducing flow tables in software defined network. In: 2015 IEEE International Conference on Communications (ICC), London, pp. 5302–5307 (2015)
10. Jingguo, G., Zhi, C., Yulei, W., Yuepeng, E.: H-SOFT: a heuristic storage space optimization algorithm for flow table of OpenFlow. In: 2014 14th January Concurrency and Computation, pp. 3497–3509. Wiley Online Library (2014)
11. Zarek, A., Ganjali, Y., Lie, D.: OpenFlow Timeouts Demystified. University of Toronto, Toronto, Ontario, Canada (2012)
12. Zhu, H., Fan, H., Luo, X., Jin, Y.: Intelligent timeout master: dynamic timeout for SDN-based data centers. In: 2015 IFIP/IEEE International Symposium on Integrated Network Management (IM), pp. 734–737. IEEE (2015)
13. Vishnoi, A., Poddar, R., Mann, V., Bhattacharya, S.: Effective switch memory management in OpenFlow networks. In: Proceedings of the 8th ACM International Conference on Distributed Event-Based Systems, pp. 177–188. ACM (2014)
14. Qu, Z., Zhang, G., Cao, H., Xie, J.: LEO satellite constellation for internet of things. IEEE Access, **5**, 18391–18401 (2017)

A Spectrum Prediction Technique Based on Convolutional Neural Networks

Jintian Sun[✉], Xiaofeng Liu, Guanghui Ren, Min Jia, and Qing Guo

School of Electronics and Information Engineering,
Harbin Institute of Technology, Harbin 150001, China
18s105097@stu.hit.edu.cn, jiamin@hit.edu.cn

Abstract. Secondary users in cognitive radio system use spectrum sensing technology to detect the primary users in the frequency band and use spectrum holes to communicate. Spectrum prediction technology is based on the existing spectrum sensing results to predict the future channel occupancy, so as to reduce the blocking rate, avoid malicious dynamic interference and other purposes. In this paper, a spectrum prediction method based on convolution neural network is proposed and some applications of this method in practical communication systems are given. This method can be trained in real time and has a certain adaptability to the dynamic environment. Using this method, the predicted results can be used to allocate resources reasonably, and the spectrum resource utilization rate is high. In addition, the time-consuming of broadband spectrum sensing can be shortened by combining the spectrum prediction method based on convolution neural network. At the end of this paper, the simulation results of spectrum prediction method based on convolution neural network are given and the efficiency of the algorithm is discussed.

Keywords: Cognitive radio · Spectrum prediction ·
Convolution neural network

1 Introduction

In recent years, the number of mobile wireless communication devices continues to grow, and the types of services are complex and diversified, which has led to a surge in demand for spectrum resources. On the other hand, there is a lot of waste in the existing spectrum resource allocation schemes. Cognitive radio (CR) is an important technology to solve the contradiction between the shortage of spectrum resources and the low utilization of spectrum resources. Using this technology, unauthorized secondary user (SU) can sense the spectrum environment and access the idle frequency band that the authorized primary user (PU) does not use temporarily, effectively improve the utilization of spectrum resources, to a certain extent, solve the problem of spectrum resource shortage.

However, in current CR technology, it is common for SU to sense the idle channel in the frequency band and occupy it for data transmission, and continuously sense the current channel while communicating, stop the transmission immediately when the PU reactivate signal is received, and then re-select other idle channels. However, when the

M. Jia et al. (Eds.): WiSATS 2019, LNICST 280, pp. 69–77, 2019.
https://doi.org/10.1007/978-3-030-19153-5_7

number of PUs is large and they frequently access/leave the channel or have dynamic malicious interference in the available frequency band, SU needs to frequently re-sensing the spectrum environment, re-select the channel and retransmit the data. This will result in the waste of SU resources, the increase of communication delay, the increase of packet loss rate and the decrease of throughput. Moreover, this problem is particularly serious when the frequency band of the system is wide and the spectrum sensing time is long.

Spectrum prediction technology is an effective way to solve the above problems. Its basic principle is to predict whether the channel will remain idle in the future by some method, so as to select a good channel to access. At present, there are some related researches, such as spectrum prediction based on hidden Markov model [1–3] de, spectrum prediction based on BP neural network [4] and many improved methods based on it [5, 6], spectrum prediction based on Q-learning [7], etc. The spectrum prediction based on Markov model needs to know some prior information about the spectrum environment in advance, which is often difficult to obtain. BP neural network needs to train a fully connected neural network. Generally, the weight of this network is very large and needs a large number of training samples. In addition, most of the above spectrum prediction methods are not easy to change after the model is determined, cannot adapt to the dynamic environment, and can only output an optimal channel. Q-learning and spectrum waterfall model are used to deal with dynamic interference [8], but the relationship between the algorithm and spectrum prediction is not discussed.

To solve above problems, this paper presents a spectrum prediction technique based on convolution neural network (CNN) classification model, and gives its application in practical communication system. The main features are as follows:

1. After completing the model training, we can continue to train in real time and have better dynamic environment adaptability.
2. It can output more than one good channel with long idle time in the future, so as to allocate resources reasonably to SU in the future.
3. By sharing spectrum prediction and spectrum sensing information, spectrum sensing aided spectrum prediction is realized, and spectrum prediction guides spectrum sensing, thus saving overall time consumption.
4. Using relay cooperative spectrum sensing and data fusion center, SU resources are allocated reasonably to improve resource utilization efficiency.

2   System Model and Problem Description

It is assumed that there are multiple PU using frequency bands $F = [f_1, f_2]$ to communicate in one area. At the same time, some SU want to use the same frequency band F for communication. These SUs do not have spectrum sensing capabilities, and all spectrum sensing tasks are handed over to a cognitive data fusion center (DFC) in the region [9]. DFC continuously senses frequency band F by periodic T, and divides F into N channels according to the communication bandwidth requirement of SU, which are $c_1, c_2, \cdots c_N$. At time t, the DFC senses the spectrum of the current environment, and then decides whether there is a PU in the channel $c_n(n = 1, 2, \cdots, N)$ according to energy detection [10]. The binary detection model for the detection of PUs in the AWGN channel can be written as:

$$
\begin{cases}
c_n = 0 & : \quad r(t) = n(t) \\
c_n = 1 & : \quad r(t) = x(t) + n(t)
\end{cases}
\tag{1}
$$

Where $x(t)$ is the PU signal in the current detection channel, and $n(t)$ is the Gaussian white noise with the double-band power spectral density N_0. Take the test statistic as:

$$
V(t) = \frac{1}{N_0} \int_{t-T}^{t} r^2(t) dt
\tag{2}
$$

After setting the threshold with a certain false alarm probability, it is possible to detect whether there is a PU in the c_n with a certain detection probability. If there is no PU in c_n at t time, that is, channel c_n can be called as $c_n = 0$, otherwise it is called $c_n = 1$. And all channel occupancy conditions at time t are defined as the channel environment state vector s_t at time t. The element in this $1 \times N$ vector is only 0 or 1. All the environment state vectors from time $t - (m-1)T$ to time t are defined as the channel environment state matrix $S_t = \{s_{t,1}, s_{t,2}, \cdots s_{t,N}\}$ in chronological order. Obviously, S_t is a matrix of $m \times N$, of which elements are only 0 or 1. In addition, $C_{t,1}$, is defined as the longest idle channel number after t. Define $C_{t,2}$, whose value is equal to the channel number of second long idle time after t time. And so on.

If the current time is recorded as t_c. Our problem is how to predict $C_{t_c,1}, C_{t_c,2}, C_{t_c,3} \cdots$ in the case of known $S_{t_c}, S_{t_c-T}, S_{t_c-2T} \cdots$. These predicted results are used to allocate resources reasonably, so as to reduce the collision between SU and PU as much as possible, avoid waste of resources, and ultimately improve the overall performance of the system. Using CNN based spectrum prediction technology can accomplish this task.

3   CNN-Based Spectrum Prediction Technology

Enlightened by the good performance of CNN in image classification and recognition, this idea can be applied to spectrum prediction. When using CNN to classify and recognize images, a certain number of pictures and labels which can correspondingly represent the content of each picture are needed to make a data set, and then the data set is used to train a well-designed CNN structure. After getting a trained CNN, the new picture can be input into the CNN to determine the category of the picture with high accuracy [11]. Based on the similarity between picture and channel environment state matrix, label and channel number, a spectrum prediction technique based on CNN is proposed.

As shown in Fig. 1, for simplicity, the principle of spectrum prediction based on CNN is illustrated by predicting the optimal channel $C_{t_c,1}$ at the current time, (similarly $C_{t_c,2}, C_{t_c,3} \cdots$).

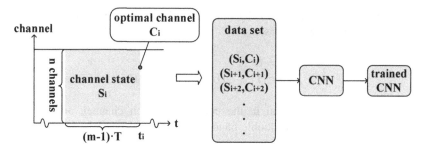

Fig. 1. Schematic diagram of spectrum prediction technology based on CNN.

The first is the training session. At the time t_i, DFC can obtain channel environment state matrix S_{t_i} and optimal channel $C_{t_i,1}$, abbreviated as S_i and C_i by spectrum sensing. The channel environment state matrix S_{t_i+T} and the optimal channel $C_{t_i+T,1}$, which are abbreviated as S_{i+1} and C_{i+1} respectively, can be obtained from the DFC at the time of $t_i + T$ by spectrum sensing. Many pairs of spectrum state, optimal channel pairs $(S_i, C_i), (S_{i+1}, C_{i+1}), (S_{i+2}, C_{i+2}), \cdots$ can be obtained by many times of spectrum sensing. Use them as data and labels to input CNN as a training set and train CNN accordingly.

Then the prediction session. At time t_n, the channel environment state matrix S_{t_n} can be obtained by DFC through spectrum sensing, and the optimal channel $C_{t_n,1}$ can be obtained by inputting S_{t_n} into the trained CNN.

The CNN-based spectrum prediction technique has the following two features worthy of explanation.

Training a CNN requires data and data corresponding labels. Generally speaking, when a trained CNN is in use, only data is input into the network, and it is impossible to determine whether the network output is correct or not. This has led to the inability to adjust network parameters after the training is over. For the spectrum prediction technology based on CNN, the label is the future idle channel number. Therefore, in actual applications, not only data can be obtained, but also a label corresponding to the data can be obtained after a short delay. That is to say, new training data sets can be obtained during use. These new data sets can be used to fine-tune existing network parameters in real time if necessary. Thereby further improving the prediction accuracy and enabling the system to obtain a certain dynamic environment adaptability.

Generally speaking, a CNN contains many parameters, and forward propagation takes a long time. However, spectrum prediction technology based on CNN can solve this problem by using the characteristics of channel environment state matrix. The value and arrangement of most data in the channel environment state matrix at the adjacent time are exactly the same. For example, at time t, $S_t = \{s_{t,1}, s_{t,2}, \cdots s_{t,N}\}$, at the adjacent time $t + T$, $S_{t+T} = \{s_{t+T,1}, s_{t+T,2}, \cdots s_{t+T,N}\}$, there is

$$s_{t,k} = s_{t+T,k-1}, (k = 2, 3, \cdots, N) \tag{3}$$

$$S_{t+T} = \left\{ s_{t+T,1}, s_{t+T,2}, \cdots, s_{t+T,N-1}, s_{t+T,N} \right\} = \left\{ s_{t,2}, s_{t,2}, \cdots, s_{t,N}, s_{t+T,N} \right\} \qquad (4)$$

S_{t+T} can be viewed as a result of translation and additions and deletions of S_t. Because of the principle of data forward propagation in CNN [11], when the adjacent data is highly repeatable, most of the data in the convolution layer and pool layer of CNN need not be recalculated in the two forward propagation calculations at adjacent times. Although the fully connected layer does not have this property, in most cases the computational complexity of the fully connected layer is much less than that of other hidden layers. In practical application, the corresponding intermediate results of the previous time operation can be saved, and then the changed data are calculated and combined with the saved data in the next calculation. This can greatly reduce the time of forward propagation.

Based on the same principle, training multiple different CNN can predict $C_{t_c,2}, C_{t_c,3} \cdots$ respectively. When several SUs have service requirements, DFC can reasonably allocate channel resources according to the demand of SU for channel idle time. Avoid waste of resources and improve resource utilization.

In addition, when there is malicious dynamic interference in the environment, the interference signal will be directly regarded by the SU as a PU. Therefore, based on the same principle, this method can also be applied to avoid malicious dynamic interference.

4   Combination of Spectrum Prediction and Spectrum Sensing

In addition to the channel selection for SU based on the spectrum prediction results mentioned above, spectrum prediction can also be used to speed up spectrum sensing.

When the available frequency band is wider, the longer spectrum sensing time will reduce the overall performance of the system. The traditional idea is to use compressed sensing algorithm or other solutions to solve this problem [12]. The application of spectrum prediction technology can solve this problem from another angle.

As shown in Fig. 2, suppose the system works in a relatively wide bandwidth environment. Firstly, data fusion center A performs full-band spectrum sensing for a period of time, and trains CNN with the sensing results. The trained CNN is used to predict several channels $\{C_1, C_2, C_3 \cdots\}$, which will remain idle for some time in the future, through the current channel environment state matrix S. At this point, the full-band spectrum sensing is no longer carried out, but narrow-band spectrum sensing is carried out for several bands where $\{C_1, C_2, C_3 \cdots\}$ are located. After a period of time, the full band spectrum sensing is resumed to cope with environmental changes. After that, repeat the above process. In summary, spectrum sensing results are used to complete the spectrum prediction, and then the spectrum prediction results are used to guide the next period of spectrum sensing. With this method, SU can be accessed more quickly when the service requirement of SU occurs in the partial spectrum sensing stage. This method reduces the overall system delay from reducing the average time of spectrum sensing.

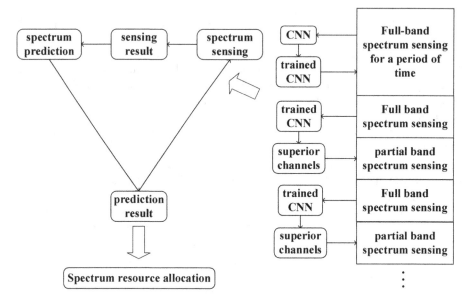

Fig. 2. The process of combining spectrum sensing with spectrum prediction.

5 Numerical Results and Discussion

In this paper, a simple CNN is designed, which contains two convolution layers and a full connection layer. The activation functions use tanh function, and the output data of convolution layer is pooled by 2×2 average. The output layer function uses the softmax function.

First, the idle channel prediction capability of CNN-based spectrum prediction technology is simulated. The simulation parameters are set such that the PU number obeys the Poisson distribution with the parameter λ at each perception. The size of the channel state matrix S_t is set to 200×9. In order to assess the performance of the proposed algorithm, the blocking rate of the proposed spectrum prediction algorithm is compared with the blocking rate based on BP neural network spectrum prediction. The parameter for assessment is the reduction rate of blocking rate relative to accessing by a random selection of all idle channels.

$$\Delta R = \frac{r_0 - r}{r_0} \tag{5}$$

Where ΔR means the reduction rate of blocking rate, r means the blocking rate of using spectrum prediction algorithms, r_0 means the blocking rate of accessing by a random selection of idle channels. Obviously, higher ΔR means better performance of the algorithm. The ΔR of various spectrum prediction algorithms change with training times under different λ settings are shown in Fig. 3. In Fig. 3, the red solid line represents using CNN-based spectrum prediction, the black dotted line represents using

BP neural network spectrum prediction, and the blue dotted line represents a random selection of idle channels.

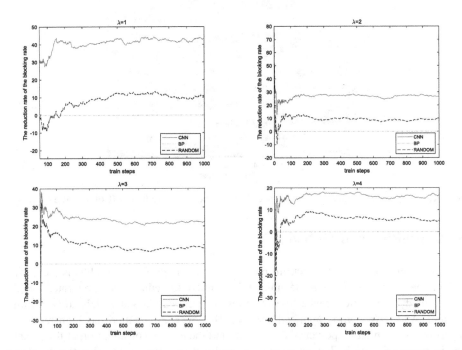

Fig. 3. Relationship among ΔR, train steps, idle channel selection strategies and λ (Color figure online)

After the training results have stabilized. It can be seen that when $\lambda = 1, 2, 3, 4$ the ΔR of CNN-based spectrum prediction is approximately equal to 40%, 25%, 20% and 15%. But the ΔR of BP neural network spectrum prediction is always lower than 10%. The performance of CNN-based spectrum prediction is always better than BP neural network spectrum prediction under various user densities.

After that, the CNN-based spectrum prediction technology was simulated to avoid malicious interference. The interference type is set to sweep interference with an unknown frequency hopping interval. The interference power is set to be much higher than the user's signal power. The user can hop frequency once every 10 spectrum sensing periods at the fastest.

In Fig. 4, the yellow strip indicates the channel on which the frequency sweep interferes at each moment. The green block is the channel that the user selects through spectrum prediction. It can be seen that the user avoids malicious interference under the support of spectrum prediction technology. From the results, when the interference mode is relatively fixed, it only takes dozens of rounds of training to complete the task of avoiding interference.

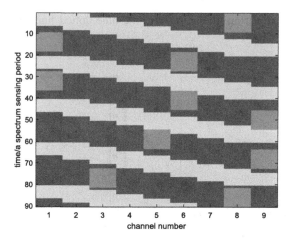

Fig. 4. Users avoid malicious interference through spectrum prediction (Color figure online)

6   Conclusion and Outlook

This paper proposes a new spectrum prediction technology for the problems faced by SU in the existing CR. This technique is applied to reduce blocking rate, avoid malicious dynamic interference, spectrum resource allocation and wideband spectrum sensing. And have a good application effect. However, the method has high requirements on the computing power of the device, and the energy consumption in the actual application is also high. This is a common problem of artificial neural networks. The focus of future research should be on how to reduce the amount of system computation as much as possible while continuing to maintain a high probability of accurate prediction. Thereby reducing system hardware requirements.

Acknowledgement. This work was supported by the National Natural Science Foundation of China (No. 61671183, 61771163 and 91438205) and the State Key Laboratory of Space-Ground Integrated Information Technology (2015_SGIIT_KFJJ_TX_02).

References

1. Eltom, H., Kandeepan, S., Liang, Y.C., Evans, R.J.: Cooperative soft fusion for HMM based spectrum occupancy prediction. IEEE Commun. Lett. **22**(10), 2144–2147 (2018)
2. Saad, A., Staehle, B., Knorr, R.: Spectrum prediction using hidden Markov models for industrial cognitive radio. In: IEEE International Conference on Wireless and Mobile Computing (2016)
3. Eltom, H., Kandeepan, S., Liang, Y.C., Moran, B., Evans, R.J.: HMM based cooperative spectrum occupancy prediction using hard fusion. In: IEEE International Conference on Communications Workshops (2016)
4. Bai, S., Zhou, X., Xu, F.: "Soft decision" spectrum prediction based on back-propagation neural networks. In: International Conference on Computing. IEEE (2014)

5. Supraja, P., Pitchai, R.: Spectrum prediction in cognitive radio with hybrid optimized neural network. Mob. Netw. Appl. 1–8 (2017)
6. Bai, S., Zhou, X., Xu, F.: Spectrum prediction based on improved-back-propagation neural networks. In: International Conference on Natural Computation. IEEE (2016)
7. Han, G., Xiao, L., Poor, H.V.: Two-dimensional anti-jamming communication based on deep reinforcement learning. In: Proceedings of the 42nd IEEE International Conference on Acoustics, Speech and Signal Processing, March 2017
8. Liu, X., Xu, Y., Jia, L., Wu, Q., Anpalagan, A.: Anti-jamming communications using spectrum waterfall: a deep reinforcement learning approach. IEEE Commun. Lett. **22**(5), 998–1001 (2017)
9. Wu, K., Tang, M., Tellambura, C., Ma, D.: Cooperative spectrum sensing as image segmentation: a new data fusion scheme. IEEE Commun. Mag. **56**, 143 (2018)
10. Ali, A., Hamouda, W.: Advances on spectrum sensing for cognitive radio networks: Theory and applications. IEEE Commun. Surv. Tutor. **19**(2), 1277–1304 (2017)
11. Krizhevsky, A., Sutskever, I., Hinton, G.E.: Imagenet classification with deep convolutional neural networks. In: Advances in Neural Information Processing Systems, pp. 1097–1105 (2012)
12. Qin, Z., Gao, Y., Plumbley, M.D., Parini, C.G.: Wideband spectrum sensing on real-time signals at sub-Nyquist sampling rates in single and cooperative multiple nodes. IEEE Trans. Signal Process. **64**(12), 3106–3117 (2016)

TOA Estimation of Unknown Chirp Signal Based on Short Time FRFT and Hough Transform

MengZhu Liu, YiCheng Jiang$^{(\boxtimes)}$, Yun Zhang, and Min Jia

Harbin Institute of Technology, Harbin, China
jiangyc@hit.edu.cn

Abstract. This paper studies the time-of-arrival (TOA) estimation problem for unknown chirp signals. The signal envelope is assumed to be trapezoidal, and TOA is defined as the arrival time for envelope to rise to the half-platform value. The current state-of-the-art technique is based on short time fractional Fourier transform (STFRFT). It utilizes STFRFT to obtain the time-profile of time-frequency spectrum, and proves that the profile can be used to estimate TOA. However, this method uses only the peak of profile, which induces information losses and thus degrades the estimation accuracy. To alleviate this, in this paper, Hough Transform is combined with STFRFT to make better use of the time-frequency spectrum. On the other hand, the chirp rate of signal is conventionally assumed to be accurately detected by a previous FRFT step. But the accuracy is actually limited by the computational complexity of FRFT. Hence, a dechirp technique is also involved to make improvements on this aspect. Numerical results show that the dechirp technique brings advantages in detecting chirp rate; and combining Hough Transform with STFRFT is beneficial for TOA estimation.

Keywords: TOA estimation · Chirp signal · FRFT ·
Hough Transform

1 Introduction

Time-of-arrival (TOA) estimation is an important topic in the area of radar signal processing for its usage in source localization, source identification and signal sorting [1]. In this paper, the TOA estimation of pulse linear frequency modulated (LFM) signal is studied. The signal comes from a noncooperative source so that the parameter is unknown; and the source and sensors are asynchronous. Notably, the estimated TOA can still be used to sort signals or generate the TDOA between different sensors [2].

Two classical TOA estimators are the thresholding estimator (TE) [3] and the auto convolution estimator (ACE) [4]. TE works by comparing signal energy

Supported by National Natural Science Foundation of China 61671490.

with a predetermined threshold, and ACE works by taking the auto-convolutions of signals. Some priori information of signal is explored in ACE, which results in its better performance than TE. However, for a chirp signal fractional Fourier transform (FRFT)-type methods can make further improvements since chirp signal is more concentrated in fractional Fourier domain (FRFD)-spectrum than Fourier domain (FD)-spectrum [5,6].

The current state-of-the-art FRFT-type method is short time FRFT estimator (STFRFTE) which is proposed in [7]. For convenience, short time FRFT will be abbreviated as STFRFT. STFRFTE segments the signal by a series of sliding short windows and uses FRFT to obtain the time-profile of STFRFT-spectrum [8]. It is then found that the profile owns a similar shape with signal envelope [7]. On these foundations, the half-peak value of time-profile can be used to estimate TOA.

However, STFRFTE impractically assumes that the signal chirp rate is accurately estimated by a previous FRFT step [7]. The assumption is obviously not reasonable because the accuracy of chirp rate is limited by the searching step of FRFT, which cannot be infinitely small due to complexity limitations. On the other hand, only the peak information of STFRFT-spectrum time-profile is used to determine TOA, which leads to performance losses. Thus, this paper will make improvements on both aspects.

Firstly, by making partial derivatives, it is observed that the precision of an estimated chirp rate is generally inversely proportional to the chirp rate, when the search step is constant. This is because the FRFT-order of signal and the chirp rate thereof are not uniformly one-to-one mapped. Therefore, this paper proposes to iteratively dechirp the signal to reduce its chirp rate, which brings benefits in chirp rate estimation and the subsequent STFRFTE process.

More importantly, Hough Transform (HT) is combined with STFRFTE to generate HT-STFRFTE, where HT is a classic image shape detection technology in automated digital image analysis [9–11]. Since HT makes the information of STFRFT-spectrum more fully used, better results are promised.

The main contributions of this paper are twofold. On one hand, we propose a modified chirp rate estimation technique based on dechirping, which generates DFRFT. Compared with FRFT, it can improve the accuracy of result with the same computational complexity. On the other hand, we propose a novel TOA estimation method based on HT. A HT-based TOA estimation method has been proposed in [12], but its focus is on mapping the signal amplitude into a high-dimension parameter space, which means it is very computationally expensive. Alternatively, we apply HT in FRFT spectrum analysis and the computational cost is very small. We are also aware of some modified HT algorithms, e.g., generalized Hough Transform [13] and randomized Hough Transform [14]. When the signal envelope is not an ideal trapezium, it is an interesting topic for future research to construct modified TOA estimators with them.

Outline of this paper is described as follows. In Sect. 2, the basic signal model is formulated and the STFRFTE method is briefly introduced. Section 3 derives the DFRFT and HTSTFRFT method. Numerical results are given in Sect. 4 and conclusions are drawn in Sect. 5.

2   Basic Fundamentals

2.1   Signal Model

To start with, the model of pulse LFM signal $x(t)$ is formulated as

$$x(t) = w(t)e^{j\frac{u_0}{2}t^2 + j\Omega_0 t + j\phi_0} \tag{1}$$

where u_0 denotes the chirp rate of $x(t)$, Ω_0 the carrier frequency, ϕ_0 the initial phase and $w(t)$ the signal envelope.

The unknown received signal is

$$s(t) = x(t - \bar{t}_a) + n(t) \tag{2}$$

where $\bar{t}_a$ denotes the time delay between source and receiver and $n(t)$ is the Gaussian white noise.

When source and receiver are synchronous, TOA is $\bar{t}_a$. However, when they are asynchronous, TOA is aliased by a constant C_a, i.e., $t_a = \bar{t}_a + C_a$. Although t_a is an aliased estimate of TOA, it can be estimated by the envelope of received signal $(w(t - t_a))$. Following [7], $w(t - t_a)$ is formulated as

$$w(t - t_a) = \begin{cases} k_r(t - t_a) + \frac{A_0}{2}, & t_1 \leq t \leq t_2 \\ A_0, & t_2 \leq t \leq t_3 \\ k_f(t - t_a - t_{PW}) + \frac{A_0}{2}, & t_3 \leq t \leq t_4 \\ 0, & otherwise \end{cases} \tag{3}$$

where $t_1 = t_a - \frac{t_r}{2}$, $t_2 = t_a + \frac{t_r}{2}$, $t_3 = t_a + t_{PW} - \frac{t_f}{2}$, $t_4 = t_a + t_{PW} + \frac{t_f}{2}$, A_0 is the platform-value of trapezium, t_{PW} the pulse width (PW), k_r the slope of the rising edge, k_f the slope of the falling edge, t_r the duration of the rising edge and t_f the duration of the falling edge. $w(t - t_a)$ is also shown in Fig. 1. As depicted in Fig. 1, the shape of envelope is assumed to be trapezoidal and t_a is defined by the arrival time for $w(t - t_a)$ to rise to $\frac{A_0}{2}$. The purpose of this paper is to estimate t_a through $s(t)$.

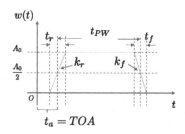

Fig. 1. The ideal envelope of the chirp pulse.

2.2 STFRFT Fundamentals

Since STFRFT is developed based on FRFT, FRFT is firstly described as follows. The pth order FRFT of $x(t)$ is defined as a linear integral transform with kernel $K_p(u,t)$:

$$X_p(t) = F^p[x(t)] = \int_{-\infty}^{\infty} K_p(u,t)x(t)dt \qquad (4)$$

where $F^p[\bullet]$ denotes the FRFT operator, $K_p(u,t) = e^{j\pi(t^2\cot\alpha - 2tu\csc\alpha + tu^2\cot\alpha)}$, $\sqrt{1-j\cot\alpha}$, $\alpha = \frac{p\pi}{2}$ (when $p \neq 2n$), $K_{p=4n}(u,t) = \delta(t-u)$ and $K_{p=4n\pm2}(u,t) = \delta(t+u)$. Hence the interval of definition for α is $\alpha \in [-\pi, \pi)$ with period 2π.

According to the principle of FRFT, $|X_p(t)|$ achieves its maximum value when $\alpha = \alpha_0 = \alpha_m + \frac{\pi}{2}$, where $\alpha_m = \arctan(\mu_0)$. Then signal is in the time-frequency line $(\mu_m = \mu_0)$ and α_0 is the rotation angle between the time-frequency line and the time domain $(\mu_m = 0)$. The geometric relation between $\mu_m = \mu_0$ and α_0 is shown in Fig. 2. For convenience, α_0 is called the matched rotation angle and $p_0 = \frac{2\alpha_0}{\pi}$ is called the matched order, leading to $u_0 = -\cot(\alpha_0)$ and $p_0 = \frac{2}{\pi}\text{arccot}(-u_0)$.

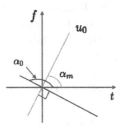

Fig. 2. Geometric relation between the chirp rate u_0 and the matched angel α_0.

STFRFT of $x(t)$ is obtained by multiplying $x(t)$ with a window $g(t)$ before taking the FRFT, that is

$$\underset{x,p}{\text{STFRFT}}(t,u) = \int_{-\infty}^{\infty} x(\tau)g(\tau - t)K_p(\tau, u)d\tau. \qquad (5)$$

The performance of STFRFT is affected by the shape and length of the window. Commonly used windows are rectangular window, Gaussian window, etc. As discussed in [15,16], Gaussian window generally leads to the best performance. Thus in this paper, the Gaussian window to be used is expressed as

$$g(t) = (\pi\sigma^2)^{-1/4}e^{-t/2\sigma^2}. \qquad (6)$$

where σ is the mean square deviation that determines the length of Gaussian window. According to (5), STFRFT can analyze how the FRFT-spectrum changes by time, which means it is possible to estimate when the signal starts and ends. So an STFRFT-based TOA estimation method (i.e., STFRFTE) was proposed in [7].

2.3 STFRFT-Based TOA Estimation

To perform STFRFT-based TOA estimation, chirp rate μ_0 should be known in prior.

By moving the window, the STFRFT-spectrum at different moments can be obtained. When the window is within the duration of chirp pulse, the peak of STFRFT-spectrum is located at (t, u_0) where t is the window center [6]. Thus along the line $u_0 = -\cot(\alpha_0)$, the time-profile of STFRFT-spectrum $\tilde{w}(t)$ is obtained by

$$\tilde{w}(t) = |\underset{x,p_0}{\mathrm{STFRFT}}(t, u_0)|. \tag{7}$$

In [7], it is proved that TOA is obtainable via

$$\hat{t}_\alpha = \arg\{\tilde{w}(t) = 0.5 \max \tilde{w}(t),\ t < \arg \max_t \tilde{w}(t)\} \tag{8}$$

which means, when signal envelope rises to the half of platform-value ($\frac{A_0}{2}$), the STFRFT-spectrum also rises to the half of platform-value in the time-frequency domain in the noise-free situation. This builds the fundamental basis for this paper.

However, STFRFTE has two limitations: (1) Chirp rate is needed in STFRFTE, hence the result is affected by the accuracy of chirp rate estimation; (2) Due to the influences of noise, there is a large fluctuation in the signal amplitude during the pulse duration [16]. To make improvements on these aspects, next section will describe a chirp rate estimation method based on dechirping and a TOA estimation method based on Hough Transform.

3 Proposed Theory and Method

3.1 An Improved Chirp Rate Estimation Method

The chirp rate estimated by FRFT is always erroneous due to the existence of noise and the limitation in computational complexity. Define $\hat{\alpha}_0$ as the estimated matched angle and $\hat{u}_0$ the estimated chirp rate, then $\hat{u}_0 = -\cot(\hat{\alpha}_0)$. It is obvious that the accuracy of $\hat{\alpha}_0$ is determined by the search step length when SNR is high enough. Notably, traditionally the search values of α_0 are uniformly spaced between $\frac{1}{\pi}$ and $\frac{3}{\pi}$, which means the search step is constant.

Hence $\Delta\hat{\alpha}_0$ is almost inevitable and we propose DFRFT to reduce the effect of $\Delta\hat{\alpha}_0$ by exploring the relationship that $\partial\hat{u}_0/\partial\hat{\alpha}_0 = \sin^{-2}\hat{\alpha}_0$, where ∂ denotes the partial derivative notation. Then the derivative is positively correlated with $|\hat{\alpha}_0 - 90°|$, and it reaches the minimum value when $\hat{\alpha}_0 = 90°$. In other words, the smaller $|\hat{\alpha}_0 - 90°|$ is, the more accurate $\hat{u}_0$ is.

On these foundations, we iteratively multiply $s_i(t)$ by $e^{j\hat{u}_i t^2/2}$, where $i = 1, 2, \cdots$, $s_1(t) = s(t)$ and $\hat{u}_i$ is the estimated chirp rate in the ith iteration. In this way, both the chirp rate u_i of $s_i(t)$ and $|\hat{\alpha}_i - 90°|$ can be iteratively reduced which gradually improves the accuracy of $\hat{u}_i$. When the iteration stops, $\hat{u}_0$ is calculated by $\hat{u}_0 = \sum_i \hat{u}_i$.

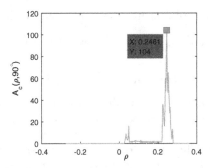

Fig. 3. A typical result of HT.

3.2 STFRFTE Based on Hough Transform

As mentioned before, in STFRFTE, TOA is estimated by finding where the STFRFT-spectrum time-profile $\tilde{w}(t)$ grows to be $\max_t \frac{1}{2}\tilde{w}(t)$. This means TOA should be more accurate with $\max_t \frac{1}{2}\tilde{w}(t)$ approaching the half platform value of $\tilde{w}(t)$. However, $\tilde{w}(t)$ is typically fluctuant with t, leaving $\max_t \frac{1}{2}\tilde{w}(t)$ greatly affected by the local changes of $\tilde{w}(t)$. The value of $\frac{1}{2}\tilde{w}(t)$ is therefore a bad estimator of the half platform-value and a better method is required.

To describe the global feature of the platform-part in $\tilde{w}(t)$, a classical graphics detection theory (i.e., Hough Transform) will be used to identify the graphics components in $\tilde{w}(t)$. It is noteworthy that to combine the graphics detection method with STFRFT is an idea that has not been addressed elsewhere to our best knowledge. The basic theory of Hough Transform is briefly given as follows.

A 2-D straight line (L_1) can be described by the polar coordinate (ρ, θ), where ρ denotes the length of the vertical-line (L_2) from the origin to L_1, θ is the rotation angle of L_2 with the x axis. Then a point (x, y) on L_1 satisfies

$$\rho = x\cos\theta + y\sin\theta. \tag{9}$$

Equation (9) implies that each point on L_1 corresponds to a subset of polar parameter space (e.g., (x, y) corresponds to $(\rho_1, \theta_1), (\rho_2, \theta_2), \cdots$). Then the subsets of different points comprise different curves, which intersect at (ρ, θ). Hence, we define $\boldsymbol{\Theta}_\rho = \{\rho_1, \cdots, \rho_N\}$ as well as $\boldsymbol{\Theta}_\theta = \{\theta_1, \cdots, \theta_N\}$, calculate $\hat{\rho}(\theta_j) = x\cos\theta_j + y\sin\theta_j$ for each θ_j and create a two-dimensional accumulative matrix $\boldsymbol{A}_c$, where the (j_1, j_2)th element of $\boldsymbol{A}_c \in \mathbb{R}^{M \times M}$ is $(\rho_{j_1}, \theta_{j_2})$. Following these, for each θ_j we find ρ_i which belongs to $\boldsymbol{\Theta}_\rho$ while minimizing $||\hat{\rho}(\theta_j) - \rho_i||_2$ and add the (i, j)th element in $\boldsymbol{A}_c$ with 1. Once the points in $\tilde{w}(t)$ are enumerated, the maximum peak of accumulator $\boldsymbol{A}_c$ should generate the required result. Recall that the top line of trapezoid has the value $\theta = 90°$, then the maximum peak $\boldsymbol{A}_c(\rho, 90°)$ is used instead.

Readers are referred to [17] for more implementation details of Hough transform. A typical result of $\boldsymbol{A}_c(\rho, 90°)$ is shown in Fig. 3.

With ρ_e the estimated platform-value (trapezoid height), we have

$$\tilde{w}(t)|_{t=t_a} = 0.5\rho_e, \; t < \arg \max_t \tilde{w}(t). \tag{10}$$

3.3 Implementation Details of DFRFT and STFRFTE

TOA estimation system flow chart is shown in Fig. 4. It should be emphasized that to dechirp signal, TOA is an essential estimate.

Firstly, using FRFT and STFRFTE one can roughly estimate the chirp rate and the TOA of signal. Then the Hough Transform step is used to update the TOA. The estimated chirp rate and TOA can be further used in DFRFT. After iterating several times, one can finally get a high-precision TOA.

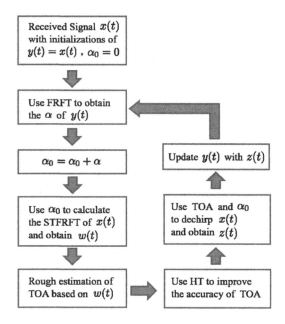

Fig. 4. Flow chart of TOA estimation system.

4 Numerical Results

To illustrate the superiorities of DFRFT and HT-STFRFTE, both FRFT and STFRFTE will be involved for comparison. The parameters of the pulse LFM signal in (1) are $\Omega_0 = 0$, $\phi_0 = 0$, $A_0 = 1$, $t_{PW} = 10\mu s$, $t_r = t_f = t_{PW}/25$ and $k_r = k_f = A_0/t_r$. Sampling frequency is $f_s = 100\,\text{MHz}$ and the chirp rate u_0 is a random variable uniformly distributed between $[\frac{f_s}{2t_{PW}}, \frac{3f_s}{4t_{PW}}]$.

In the simulation for DFRFT, $t_a = 0\mu s$ and there are three times of iteration, with the search steps being $\Delta\alpha_1 = 0.01\pi\,\text{rad}$, $\Delta\alpha_2 = 0.005\pi\,\text{rad}$ and $\Delta\alpha_3 = 0.0025\pi\,\text{rad}$, respectively. In the simulation for HT-STFRFTE, $t_a = 500\,\text{ns}$.

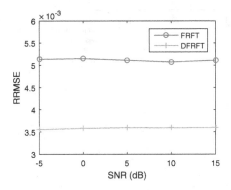

Fig. 5. RRMSEs of the chirp rate estimation in terms of the DFRFT and FRFT.

4.1   Test for DFRFT

In Fig. 5, relative root mean square error (RRMSE) of the estimated chirp rate $\hat{u}_0$ is defined by RRMSE $= 1/V \cdot \sqrt{\sum_{v=1}^{V} ||\frac{\hat{u}_0 - u_0}{u_0}||_2^2}$, where $V = 200$. RRMSE is used here because it is barely influenced by the value of u_0.

Figure 5 demonstrates the RRMSE curves in terms of DFRFT and FRFT. Since search step can not be infinitely small, the accuracies of DFRFT and FRFT converge to approximately 3.5×10^{-3} and 5×10^{-3}, respectively. We can also observe that DFRFT produces better results than FRFT in the interested SNR range. Thus the novelty of DFRFT is validated.

4.2   Test for HT-STFRFTE

In this subsection, root mean square error (RMSE) of estimated TOA $(\hat{t}_\alpha)$ is RMSE $= 1/V \cdot \sqrt{\sum_{v=1}^{V} ||\hat{t}_\alpha - t_\alpha||_2^2}$, where $V = 200$.

Figure 6 demonstrates the relation between the time-profile of STFRFT-spectrum and its noise-free version. It can be observed that the time-profile of STFRFT-spectrum is fluctuant compared with the noise-free one. The other three curves stand for the estimated half trapezoid height (also the half-platform value). We can see the value estimated by HT-STFRFTE is much closer to the ideal value than that by STFRFTE.

Additionally, Fig. 7 depicts the RMSE curves in terms of HT-STFRFTE and STFRFTE. Clearly, HT-STFRFTE provides better results under both low and high SNR conditions. For example, when SNR $= 10$ dB, RMSE$_{\text{STFRFTE}} = 24.2$ ns and RMSE$_{\text{HT-STFRFTE}} = 16.9$ ns. Hence, the benefits from the additional HT step have been certified.

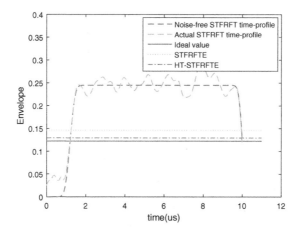

Fig. 6. STFRFT-spectrum time-profile as well as its noise-free version and the estimated half trapezoid heights by HT-STFRFTE and STFRFTE.

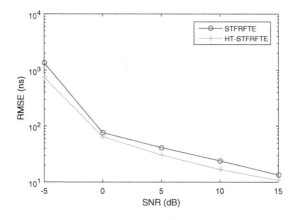

Fig. 7. RMSEs of TOA in terms of HT-STFRFTE and STFRFTE.

5   Conclusion

To estimate TOA of unknown chirp signals, FRFT-type method is studied in this paper. Two contributions are made, i.e., the propositions of dechirp FRFT (DFRFT) and Hough Transform FRFT estimator (HT-STFRFTE), with DFRFT providing the chirp rate required by HT-STFRFTE. DFRFT works by adding an extra step between two iterative FRFT steps, which reduces the signal chirp rate and thus makes the estimated result less sensitive to errors from the search step of matched-order. Compared with FRFT, DFRFT requires approximately the same computational complexity while providing better performances. In STFRFT based TOA estimation, the time-profile of STFRFT-spectrum is observed to fluctuate with the time-frequency domain, which makes the result sensitive to local changes. Compared with it, HT-STFRFTE can subtract the platform-value more accurately. Numerical results show that, the proposed methods provide better results in terms of chirp rate and TOA.

References

1. Hara, S., Anzai, D., Yabu, T., Lee, K., Derham, T., Zemek, R.: A perturbation analysis on the performance of TOA and TDOA localization in mixed LOS/NLOS environments. IEEE Trans. Commun. **2**(5), 99–110 (2013)
2. Wang, Z.L., Zhang, D.F., Bi, D.Y., Wang, S.Q.: Multiple-parameter radar signal sorting using support vector clustering and similitude entropy index. Circ. Syst. Sig. Process. **33**(6), 1985–1996 (2014)
3. Guvenc, I., Sahinoglu, Z.: Threshold selection for UWB TOA estimation based on kurtosis analysis. IEEE Commun. Lett. **9**(12), 1025–1027 (2005)
4. Chan, Y.T., Lee, B., Inkol, H.R., Chan, F.: Estimation of pulse parameters by convolution. In: Canadian Conference on Electrical and Computer Engineering, CCECE 2006, vol. 2, no. 5, pp. 99–110. IEEE (2016)
5. Almeida, L.B.: The fractional Fourier transform and time-frequency representations. IEEE Trans. Signal Process. **42**(11), 3084–3091 (1994)
6. Ozaktas, H.M., Aytr, O.: Fractional Fourier domains. Sig. Process. **46**(1), 119–124 (1995)
7. Tao, R., Li, Y.-L., Wang, Y.: Short-time fractional Fourier transform and its applications. IEEE Trans. Signal Process. **58**(5), 2568–2580 (2009)
8. Awal, M.A., Ouelha, S., Dong, S.Y., Boashash, B.: A robust high-resolution time-frequency representation based on the local optimization of the short-time fractional Fourier transform. Digit. Sig. Process. **70**, 125–144 (2017)
9. Duda, R.O., Hart, P.E.: Use of the Hough transformation to detect lines and curves in pictures. Commun. ACM **15**, 11–15 (1972)
10. Jiankui, Z., Zishu, H., Sellathurai, M., Hongming, L.: Modified Hough transform for searching radar detection. IEEE Geosci. Remote Sens. Lett. **5**(4), 683–686 (2008)
11. Illingworth, J., Kittler, J.: The adaptive Hough transform. IEEE Trans. Pattern Anal. Mach. Intell. PAMI **9**(5), 690–698 (1987)
12. Sobhani, B.: Target TOA association with the Hough transform in UWB radars. IEEE Trans. Aerosp. Electron. Syst. **52**(2), 743–754 (2016)
13. Ballard, D.: Generalizing the Hough transform to detect arbitrary shapes. Pattern Recognit. **13**, 111–122 (1981)
14. Xu, L., Oja, E., Kultanen, P.: A new curve detection method: randomized Hough transform (RHT). Pattern Recognit. Lett. **11**(5), 331–338 (1990)
15. Durak, L., Arikan, O.: Short-time Fourier transform: two fundamental properties and an optimal implementation. IEEE Trans. Signal Process. **2**(5), 99–110 (2016)
16. Awal, A., Ouelha, S., Dong, S., Boashash, B.: A robust high-resolution time-frequency representation based on the local optimization of the short-time fractional Fourier transform. Digit. Sig. Process. **70**, 125–144 (2017)
17. Mukhopadhyay, P., Chaudhuri, B.: A survey of Hough transform. Priyanka. Pattern Recognit. **48**, 993–1010 (2015)

International Workshop on Machine Learning for Satellite-Terrestrial Networks

A Deep Learning Method Based on Convolution Neural Network for Blind Demodulation of Mixed Signals with Different Modulation Types

Hongtao Zhu[1], Zhenyong Wang[1,2(✉)], Dezhi Li[1], Qing Guo[1], and Zhenbang Wang[1]

[1] School of Electronics and Information Engineering,
Harbin Institute of Technology, Harbin, Heilongjiang, China
zhuhongtao@stu.hit.edu.cn,
{ZYWang, lidezhi, QGuo}@hit.edu.cn, zhenbangw@163.com
[2] Shenzhen Academy of Aerospace Technology, Shenzhen, Guangdong, China

Abstract. In recent years, deep learning is becoming more and more popular. It has been widely used in image recognition, automatic speech recognition and natural language processing. In the field of communication, the signal is considered as time data, which can identify the intrinsic characteristics and information of the signal by the way of deep learning. In the aspect of cognitive radio, if the signal adopts different modulation methods in different time slots for adaptive modulation, it is difficult for the existing signal demodulation system to demodulate it effectively. Usually, it is necessary to identify the modulation mode of the signal first. In this context, the deep learning is introduced into signal demodulation. On the basis of analyzing the structure of convolutional neural network (CNN), an improved CNN structure is proposed, which does not need to recognize modulation methods and realizes blind demodulation of mixed signals with different signal-to-noise ratio (SNR). Through transfer learning and denoising auto-encoder, the network is further optimized to further reduce the bit error rate (BER).

Keywords: Signal demodulation · Convolution neural network · Transfer learning · Denoising auto-encoder

1 Introduction

With the development of cognitive radio, it becomes more and more important to identify the modulation mode and demodulate the signal. For general signal demodulation process, first of all, it is necessary to identify the modulation mode of the signal, so a series of algorithms are needed to estimate the parameters, and then the signal is demodulated when the modulation mode and other synchronization parameters are known. In order to adapt to different hardware and communication environments, different modulation modes, such as PSK, QAM, FSK, are usually needed when transmitting signals. Considering such a situation, if the transmitter modulates the

M. Jia et al. (Eds.): WiSATS 2019, LNICST 280, pp. 91–103, 2019.
https://doi.org/10.1007/978-3-030-19153-5_9

signal randomly in different time slots by different modulation methods, it can greatly increase the degree of confidentiality of the information, and also can choose the modulation mode independently according to the actual requirements in transmitting the information. Thus, if the modulation classification and other technical communications are not the same. The modulation of the signal is recognized, and the existing system is unable to demodulate the signal effectively.

Based on the above problems, how to realize the unified demodulation of mixed signals with multiple modulation modes without changing the hardware circuit is a challenging research problem. In recent years, with the development of computer hardware and the application of distributed computing, it is possible to train large-scale neural networks. More and more people are devoting themselves to the study of deep learning. Deep learning is a nonlinear model that captures and learns the abstract representation of data. It can be used in one layer with neural networks. A large number of neurons adapt to [1]. Abstract learning in depth learning can be understood as a demodulation process, which means extracting useful information from the original data [2]. In signal demodulation, Milad and Azizm adopt ANN demodulation quadrature amplitude modulation (QAM) [3]. Compared with general QAM demodulator, this method is helpful to reduce the bit error rate. In reference [4], a deep neural network (DNN) and a long-term and short-term memory (LSTM) for FM demodulation are proposed. It uses a learning-based method to use the priori information of the voice message sent in the demodulation process. Their reconstruction depends on the use of memory, so their demodulation schemes may fail without strong memory. Mira proposed an adaptive radial basis function (RBF) neural network in reference [5] for multiuser communication demodulation in direct sequence spread spectrum multiple access (DSSSMA). The results show that it has fast convergence and near optimal performance. Akan and Dogan proposed a NN-based software radio receiver in the literature [6] considering the unknown channel model of training sequence. The receiver has the same performance as the correlation receiver. It is suitable for additive white Gaussian noise (AWGN) channel and has the advantages of processing interference and phase offset channels. In addition, the receiver can also be used for fading channels with improved performance.

The main idea of this paper is to propose a neural network model based on CNN, which can demodulate a variety of mixed modulation signals in a unified way. The rest of this paper is arranged as follows: Sect. 2 studies the basic principle of CNN and analyzes the characteristics of CNN for signal demodulation. Section 3 presents a signal demodulation model suitable for various mixed modulation signals. Based on this model, the model is improved by using transfer learning and denoising autoencoder. Section 4 compares the demodulation performance of the improved model with that of the original model through experiments, and verifies that the network model can demodulate the mixed signals with different SNR. Section 5 conclude the paper.

2   The Principle of Convolutional Neural Network

CNN is different from general neural network in that it is formed by stacking convolution layer and pool layer. The convolution layer of convolution neural network usually contains three levels. In the first stage, the convolution layer uses multiple convolution kernels in parallel to generate a set of linear activation functions. In the second stage, nonlinear activation functions such as rectifier linear element functions act on each linear output at the first stage. In the third level, the pooling function is used to further adjust the output of the volume layer.

The convolution nucleus can be seen as a layer of neuronal structure, which can also weigh inputs and produce output signals. The characteristic graph is the output of a convolution kernel. A given filter is dragged across the entire previous feature map or input, and each move of a step produces activation of neurons at each location and outputs to a feature map. From the point of view of communication, each convolution kernel is equivalent to a filter, which can extract the corresponding data features.

2.1   Basic Convolution Function

Convolution operations used in neural networks are usually not the standard discrete convolution operations used in mathematical literature, and they are slightly different from them. Former usually refers to a specific operation, which involves the parallel use of multiple convolutions. Convolution with a single kernel can only extract one type of feature, although it acts on multiple spatial locations. But we often hope that one layer of neural network can extract many types of features in multiple locations.

Suppose that there is a four-dimensional kernel tensor K, each of which is $K_{i,j,k,l}$, indicating the connection strength between an output unit in channel i and an input unit in channel j, and there is a k-row l-column offset between the output unit and the input unit. Suppose the input is composed of observation data V, each element being $V_{i,j,k}$, representing the value in column k and row j in channel i. Assuming that the output Z and the output V have the same form, if the output Z is obtained by convoluting K and V, and it is given by:

$$Z_{i,j,k} = \sum_{l,m,n} V_{l,j+m-1,k+n-1} K_{i,l,m,n} \tag{1}$$

Sometimes it is desirable to reduce the overhead of network computing by downsampling. If you want to sample only s pixels in each direction of the output, then you can define a downsampling convolution function C as shown in Eq. (2).

$$Z_{i,j,k} = c(K, V, s)_{i,j,k} = \sum_{l,m,n} [V_{l,(j-1)\times s+m,(k-1)\times s+n} K_{i,l,m,n}] \tag{2}$$

Where s is called the step size of downsampling. Figure 1 is a convolution with step size.

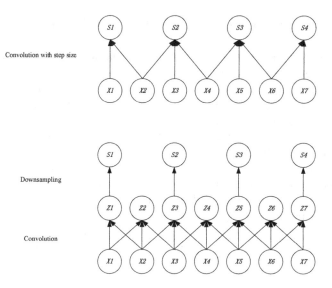

Fig. 1. Convolution with step size

2.2   Characteristics of CNN

Convolution operation helps to improve the model through two important ideas: sparse interactions and parameter sharing [7].

Sparse Interactions. Each output unit of traditional neural network interacts with each input unit. However, CNN has the characteristics of sparse interaction. By using kernel function, the parameters of model storage are greatly reduced. For example, when detecting and recognizing signals, the input signal sample points may contain millions of sample points, but small meaningful features such as frequency hopping can be detected by occupying only a few to hundreds of core signal sample points. This means that fewer parameters need to be stored, which not only reduces the storage requirements of the model, but also improves its statistical efficiency. Graphical explanations of sparse connections are shown in Fig. 2.

Parameter Sharing. Parameter sharing is to use the same parameters in multiple functions of a model. In traditional feedforward neural networks, each element of the weight matrix is used only once when calculating the output of a layer. In convolution neural network, the convolution kernel will do convolution operation with each position of input, and optimize the network by learning a set of parameters, thus greatly reducing the network parameters. Figure 3 shows how the parameter sharing is implemented.

2.3   Optimization Method and Selection of Activation Function

Optimization plays a crucial role in deep learning algorithms. Optimization refers to minimizing or maximizing a task function $f(x)$ by changing x, which is called a cost

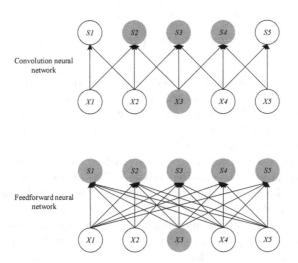

Fig. 2. Comparison of connections (above is a convolution network, the following is a traditional feedforward neural network).

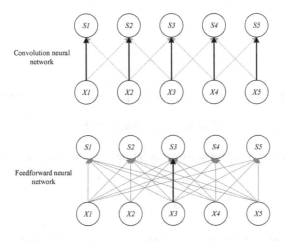

Fig. 3. Parameter sharing (above is a convolution network, the following is a traditional feedforward neural network).

function. How to choose the cost function is an important link in the design of neural network. The choice of error function will affect the convergence of the model, optimization speed and other aspects. In this paper, the mean square error function is chosen as the cost function to train.

Considering a set of data sets $X = \{x^{(1)}, \ldots, x^{(m)}\}$ with m samples and corresponding data sets labeled $Y = \{y^{(1)}, \ldots, y^{(m)}\}$, the error function can be expressed as follows:

$$\theta_{MSE} = \arg \min_{\theta} \prod_{i=1}^{m} E(\bar{y}_i - y_i)^2 \tag{3}$$

If $\bar{y}$ is an unbiased estimate of y, then the estimator evaluated by mean square error is consistent with the estimator evaluated by variance, so the unbiased estimator can be examined by variance. When $\bar{y}$ is not an unbiased estimate of y, the two are no longer equivalent, then the mean square error is reasonable, that is, through the variance and deviation of two parts of the judgment.

Suppose there is a function $y = f(x)$ in which x and y are real numbers. The derivative of this function is $f'(x)$. The derivative $f'(x)$ represents the slope of $f(x)$ at point x. The size of the slope shows how to input the size of the change to the desired output $f(x + \varepsilon) \approx f(x) + \varepsilon f'(x)$.

The derivative is useful for minimizing a function because it specifies how to change x to improve y slightly. So x can move $f(x)$ to a smaller step in the opposite direction of the derivative to reduce the amount of it. Stochastic Gradient Descent (SGD) is a common algorithm used to train neural networks. The loss function in the deep learning algorithm is usually the sum of the loss functions of each sample. For example, the negative conditional logarithmic likelihood of training data can be written as Eq. (4).

$$J(\theta) = \frac{1}{m} \sum_{i=1}^{m} L(x^{(i)}, y^{(i)}, \theta) \tag{4}$$

Where L is the loss function for each sample, and it can be expressed as Eq. (5).

$$L(x, y, \theta) = -\log p(y|x; \theta) \tag{5}$$

For these additive loss functions, gradient descent requires the following formula.

$$\nabla_{\theta} J(\theta) = \frac{1}{m} \sum_{i=1}^{m} \nabla_{\theta} L(x^{(i)}, y^{(i)}, \theta) \tag{6}$$

Considering the computational complexity and the computational efficiency, a general approach is to randomly and evenly extract a small number of samples from the training set called minibatch $B = \{x^{(1)}, \ldots, x^{(m')}\}$. Here m' is the number of samples per batch, and the selection criterion is to select as few samples as possible under the premise of meeting the task requirements. The estimation of gradient can be expressed as follows.

$$g = \frac{1}{m'} \nabla_{\theta} \sum_{i=1}^{m'} L(x^{(i)}, y^{(i)}, \theta) \tag{7}$$

By using samples from B, the stochastic gradient descent algorithm uses the following gradient estimation:

$$\theta \leftarrow \theta - \varepsilon g \tag{8}$$

Where ε is the learning rate.

In this paper, the Sigmoid function is used as the final output layer function. Sigmoid has exponential function form and is a nonlinear action function. It is the closest biological neuron in physical sense, and it is also the most widely used activation function type. Neural network learning is based on a set of samples, including the input and output of the samples, which are one-to-one corresponding to the input and output neurons. The weights and thresholds of the neural network are initially arbitrarily initialized. The learning process is to adjust the weights and thresholds again and again by iteration to minimize the mean square error of the actual output and the expected output of the network. Given the input, a continuous output can be obtained based on Sigmoid function, and the output of Sigmoid function can also be expressed as probability, because the model finally decodes bit outputs 0 and 1. With this activation function, the output can be limited to the range of (0, 1) for subsequent threshold decoding. The form of the Sigmoid function is as follows:

$$Sigmoid(x) = \frac{1}{1 + e^{-x}} \tag{9}$$

3 Demodulator Based on Convolutional Neural Network

3.1 Building a Signal Demodulation Model

Through the experimental analysis, it is found that reducing the total connection layer can greatly reduce the number of model parameters, and will not have a great impact on the accuracy. Based on the above analysis, the final network structure is shown in Fig. 4.

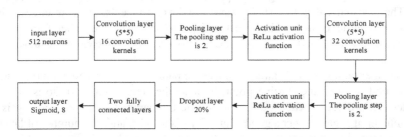

Fig. 4. Structure model of signal demodulation model based on convolution neural network.

In this paper, 8-bit information is used as a group, modulated to the carrier, each bit information is collected 64 points through the AWGN channel, so a group of 8-bit information is used for 512 sampling points as a sample input to the model. The number of input neurons is set to 512, which corresponds to 8 bit data of each sample and 512 sampling points. In this paper, there are two convolution layers in the neural network architecture, each layer is followed by a maximum pooling layer. The intermediate convolution layers are all modified linear elements. The output structure of the network is the Sigmoid unit of 8 neurons, which is used to output 8 bit demodulated bit data. The convolution kernel length is set to 5 * 5 size, and the convolution kernel number is 16 and 32 respectively. In addition, the maximum pooling step size is 2, and the width is set to 3. Because the network parameters are less, and random deactivation layer is added in the middle, the over-fitting phenomenon of the network can be effectively prevented.

In this paper, the mean square error between training data and model prediction is used as a cost function. For many tasks, even if small random noise is added to the input, the task should still be able to solve. However, the neural network proved to be not very robust to noise [8]. One of the ways to improve the robustness of neural networks is to simply apply random noise to its input and then train it. Therefore, in this experiment, when testing the accuracy of the algorithm under different SNR conditions, the signal data of different modulation modes under the SNR is collected first, 75% of the data is used as training set, and the rest as test set. The stochastic gradient descent algorithm is used as an optimization algorithm and the learning rate is set to 0.0001. Because the optimization algorithm is iterative, it needs to specify the initial value, here the Gaussian distribution initializer is used to randomly initialize the parameters.

3.2   Improved Demodulation Model

Transfer Learning. On Transfer learning refers to the use of what has been learned in one setting (Distribution P_1) to improve generalization in another setting (Distribution P_2). In transfer learning, the learner must perform two or more different tasks, but assume that many of the factors that explain the P_1 change are related to the changes that learning P_2 needs to grasp. In these cases, the goal is to take advantage of the data advantages of the first setting to extract information that may be useful in learning in the second setting or in making direct predictions. For example, identify a picture of a dog. These visual categories share some low-level concepts, such as edges, visual shapes, geometric changes, the effects of photo changes, etc. Therefore, transfer learning can be achieved by simply sharing low-level parameters to achieve better performance.

When the training model starts to update the parameters iteratively with the random initialization point as the starting point, because the signal-to-noise ratio is high, the samples can provide a better gradient to update the parameters, so the training is not very difficult, it is easy to get a good result. This is also because the number of layers is not very deep, the solution space is not very complex, resulting in any initial iteration can reach the global optimal point or close to it. However, as the SNR decreases, minibatch can only provide gradient estimation with severe noise disturbance, resulting in unstable training. In this case, only very small learning rates and carefully tuned hyper parameters can be used to train. But this greatly increased the workload of the experiment. Using transfer learning method and using the model parameters obtained under high signal-to-noise ratio to initialize low signal-to-noise ratio can greatly speed up the training speed and accuracy of the network.

Denoising Auto-Encoder. Denoising auto-encoder (DAE) is a kind of encoder which takes corrupted data as input and is trained to predict the original undamaged data. The DAE training process is shown in Fig. 5. First, a damage process $C(\tilde{x}|x)$ is introduced. This conditional distribution represents the probability of a given data sample x to produce a damaged sample $\tilde{x}$. The automatic encoder learns the reconfiguration distribution $p_{reconstruct}(x|\tilde{x})$ from the training data pair $(x, \tilde{x})$ according to the following procedure:

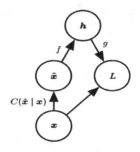

Fig. 5. Structure of denoising auto-encoder.

(1) Sampling a training sample from training data.
(2) Pick up a damaged sample $\tilde{x}$ from $C(\tilde{x}|x = x)$.
(3) $(x, \tilde{x})$ is used as a training sample to estimate the reconstruction distribution $p_{reconstruct}(x|\tilde{x}) = p_{decoder}(x|h)$ of the automatic encoder, where h is the output of the encoder $f(\tilde{x})$, and $p_{decoder}$ is defined according to the decoding function $g(h)$.

It is usually easy to minimize the gradient descent of the negative log likelihood $-\log p_{decoder}(x|h)$. As long as the encoder is deterministic, the denoising auto-encoder is a feedforward network and can be trained in the same way as other feedforward networks.

CNN is a suitable choice for the application of deep learning in signal demodulation. Convolution operation is a kind of operation that transforms time domain to frequency. Although the convolution form of convolution neural network is somewhat different, it is essentially similar. For signals, the characteristics are mainly reflected in the frequency domain. In addition, unlike most of the tasks performed by CNN, neural networks used in signals do not require a strong ability to extract features, which is attributed to the ease of feature extraction in signal demodulation. The use of high capacity deep networks can easily lead to overfitting. However, due to the poor robustness of the neural network to noise, the error performance of demodulation still needs to be improved. Experiments show that the difficulty of signal demodulation lies in how to resist noise rather than enhance the ability to extract features. Based on this analysis, this paper adopts the improved scheme of denoising auto-encoder pre-training and signal demodulation, and uses two-layer convolution neural network to build the encoding and decoder to de-noise the data. The final model training flow chart is shown in Fig. 6.

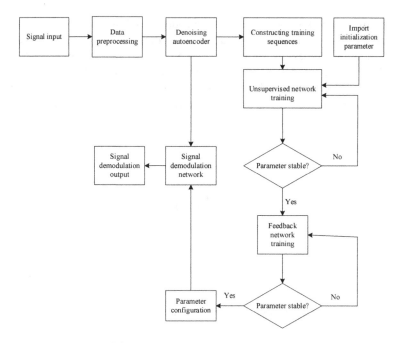

Fig. 6. Flow chart of training mode.

4   Experiments and Results Analysis

In Fig. 7, the CNN model is used to demodulate a single modulated signal (FSK). Although there are some differences in BER performance compared with the coherent demodulation theory, the preconditions are different. The BER curve of the coherent demodulation theory is the precondition that the frequency interval equals the symbol transmission rate. The convolution neural network model is obtained under the premise that the frequency interval is equal to half of the symbol transmission rate. Therefore, the spectrum efficiency of this design is higher. At the same time, for incoherent demodulation, the frequency interval becomes smaller, which will greatly reduce the bit error performance. Under the same conditions, the demodulation performance of CNN model is 3.5 dB higher than that of incoherent demodulation. Compared with the best incoherent receiver, the performance of our model is better than that of the best incoherent detection when the signal-to-noise ratio is lower than 11 dB, and slightly lower than that of the best incoherent detection when the signal-to-noise ratio is higher than 11 dB. The reason for this analysis is that the test set data is not big enough. If we want to get the BER below 10–6 accurately, we must test at least one million data. Because of the limitation of hardware, we can't detect such huge data at one time.

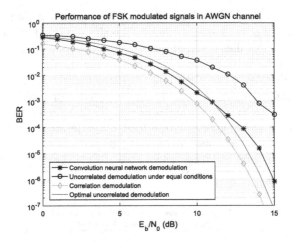

Fig. 7. Performance of FSK modulated signals in AWGN channel.

The demodulation performance curve of 4-PAM signal is shown in Fig. 8, and the improvement of the model by transfer learning and denoising auto-encoder is compared. The experimental results show that both transfer learning and denoising auto-encoder can improve the performance of the model by 0.5–1 dB, which indicates the demodulation performance of the network model is very close to correlated demodulation.

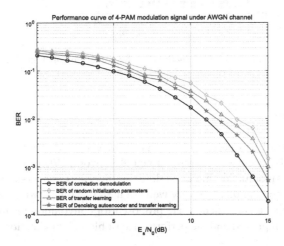

Fig. 8. Performance curve of 4-PAM modulation signal under AWGN channel.

Figure 9 shows the performance curve of the model for blind demodulation of mixed modulation signals. The experimental results show that the CNN model can blind demodulate the mixed modulation signals without knowing the modulation mode, and the improved model can improve the performance of blind demodulation about 2 dB. Through the comparative analysis of the experiments, we can see that the capacity and potential of the model are not fully realized when demodulating a single signal. The reason is that the characteristics of the signal needed for demodulation are not very large, so the performance advantages of the training methods of transfer learning and denoising auto-encoder are not obvious, but in a variety of ways. Under the condition of unified signal demodulation, the feature extracted by the model will increase linearly. At this time, the model is easy to converge to the local optimum, and the influence of noise will be greater. At this time, the performance of the model will be greatly improved. At the same time, after training the parameters, the network has good generalization performance, and it can achieve the expected goal of blind demodulation of multiple mixed modulation signals.

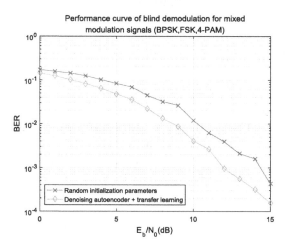

Fig. 9. Performance curve of blind demodulation for mixed modulation signals (BPSK, FSK, 4-PAM).

5   Conclusions

The main purpose of this paper is to design a blind demodulation method of mixed modulation signals based on convolution neural network. When transmitter transmits signals of different modulation modes at different time slots, the model can perform the corresponding demodulation tasks very well. At the same time, two methods of transfer learning and denoising auto-encoder are proposed for convolution neural network. The network model is improved and the performance of blind demodulation is improved by about 2 dB.

Acknowledgments. This work was supported by National Natural Science Foundation of China (Grant Nos. 61601147, 61571316) and Fundamental Research Funds of Shenzhen Innovation of Science and Technology Committee (Grant No. JCYJ20160331141634788).

References

1. Nielsen, M.A.: Neural Networks and Deep Learning. Determination Press (2015)
2. Simpson, A.J.R.: Abstract Learning via Demodulation in a Deep Neural Network. Computer Science (2015)
3. Milad, A.N., Aziz, M.M., Rahmadwati, A.: Neural network demodulator for quadrature amplitude modulation (QAM). Int. J. Adv. Stud. Comput. Sci. Eng. **5**(7), 10–13 (2016)
4. Elbaz, D., Zibulevsky, M.: End to End Deep Neural Network Frequency Demodulation of Speech Signals. arXiv preprint, pp. 1–6 (2017)
5. Mitra, U., Poor, H.V.: Neural network techniques for multi-user demodulation. In: IEEE International Conference on Neural Networks-Conference Proceedings, pp. 1538–1543. Institute of Electrical and Electronics Engineers Inc., San Francisco (1993)
6. Önder, M., Akan, A., Doğan, H., et al.: Advanced neural network receiver design to combat multiple channel impairments. Turkish J. Electr. Eng. Comput. Sci. **24**(4), 3066–3077 (2016)
7. Müller, J., Müller, J., Tetzlaff, R.: Hierarchical description and analysis of CNN algorithms. In: International Workshop on Cellular Nanoscale Networks and Their Applications, pp. 1–2. IEEE Computer Society, Notre Dame (2014)
8. Nam, H., Han, B.: Learning multi-domain convolutional neural networks for visual tracking. In: 29th IEEE Conference on Computer Vision and Pattern Recognition, CVPR 2016, pp. 4293–4302. IEEE Computer Society, Las Vegas (2016)

Robust UAV Communications with Jamming

Haichao Wang[1][(✉)] ⓘ, Junnan Yao[1], Jin Chen[1], Guoru Ding[1,2] ⓘ, and Ling Yu[1]

[1] Army Engineering University, Nanjing 210007, China
whcwl0919@sina.com, tms3216@163.com, chenjin99@263.net,
dr.guoru.ding@ieee.org, yl28112844340126.com
[2] Southeast University, Nanjing 210096, China

Abstract. Unmanned aerial vehicle (UAV) communication has attracted increasing attention recently, benefiting from its high mobility. However, most existing studies concentrate on a perfect scenario, without considering the unintentional interference/intentional jamming and uncertain channel/location information. In addition, the UAV-to-UAV (U2U) communication scenario has not been widely investigated as the UAV-to-Ground case. To fill this gap, this paper investigates the robust U2U communications in the presence of jamming, where the U2U communication channel and jammer location are considered to be uncertain, i.e., only having partial information. For the non-convex optimization with the aim of minimizing the flight time, we propose a successive convex approximation method by introducing S-procedure and slack variables. The inner optimization is transformed into a semidefinite programming problem, which can be optimally solved by standard convex techniques. Simulation results validate the proposed path planning method in the presence of jamming.

Keywords: Unmanned aerial vehicle · Jamming · Path planning · Robust optimization

1 Introduction

The high-data rate and low-delay requirements for wireless communications pose a critical threat to the existing terrestrial communication system with limited network resource. To this end, many aerial/space communication platforms, such as unmanned aerial vehicles (UAVs) and satellites, have been leveraged to provide better service for terrestrial users, which forms a widely known Space-Air-Ground Integrated Network (SAGIN).

UAV, as one of critical elements in SAGIN, has been attracted increasing attentions in wireless communications due to its wide applications [1–3], such as aerial base station [4–6], relay [7–10], energy source [11,12], etc. Specifically, authors in [1] proposes a surveillance system for amateur UAVs based on cognitive internet of things. UAV' potentials in wireless communications versus

M. Jia et al. (Eds.): WiSATS 2019, LNICST 280, pp. 104–116, 2019.
https://doi.org/10.1007/978-3-030-19153-5_10

traditional fixed infrastructure based communications have been studied in [2]. Furthermore, authors in [3] show its advantages in communications, caching, and energy transfer. As aerial base stations [4–6], they embody a three-dimensional (3D) characteristic, where the UAV altitude has an important impact on the system performance. The reason is that, in general, increasing the UAV altitude results in a higher path-loss, but it also improves the probability of having line-of-sight (LoS) link. The optimal altitude for both static and mobile UAVs as relays has been investigated in [7]. In [8], a joint 3D location and transmit power optimization problem in a UAV relaying network with multiple mobile users is studied. On the other hand, authors in [8–10] utilized the UAV horizontal mobility to improve the terrestrial network performance. In addition, UAV-enabled wireless power transfer has been investigated in [11,12] for mobile case and static case, respectively.

The aforementioned studies focus on a perfect scenario, i.e., no interference and jamming signals. In practice, UAV communications may experience jamming, however, with few researches. In this paper, we study the robust UAV-to-UAV (U2U) communications in the presence of jamming. Specifically, the contributions of this paper are summarized as follows:

– We formulate a path planning problem for U2U communications in the presence of jamming, which considers the air-to-air channel uncertainty, jammer location uncertainty, UAV maximum flight speed, and the signal-to-interference-plus-noise-ratio (SINR) requirement. The aim is to minimize the flight time via designing the UAV path.
– We develop a path planning algorithm with the aid of S-procedure, successive convex approximation (SCA), and semidefinite programming (SDP). In particular, the probability constraint is firstly transformed into a tractable equivalence by introducing the slack variables and S-procedure. Then, the SCA is leveraged to tackle the determined optimization problem, where SDP is embedded.

The rest of this paper is organized as follows. In Sect. 2, we illustrate the investigated scenario and formulate the optimization problem. Then, we design a path planning method in Sect. 3 by leveraging the SCA and SDP. Simulation results are presented to verify the effectiveness of the proposed approach in Sect. 4. Finally, we conclude this paper in Sect. 5.

2   System Model and Problem Formulation

2.1   System Model

Consider two UAVs cooperatively perform a series of tasks and exchange information while flying in the air. As an example, two mobile UAVs aim to share the transport and surveillance information collected by the ground sensors in vehicle networks. Meanwhile, a set of terrestrial jammers, denoted as the set $\mathcal{M}$, attacks the UAV communications, as shown in Fig. 1. To enable efficient communications, UAVs maintain a small distance during the flight. Since the distance between UAVs is much smaller than the space of interest and the distances between UAVs and jammers, their positions ($\mathbf{w}_1$ and $\mathbf{w}_2$) are approximated by the coordinate $\mathbf{w} = \{x, y, H\}$, measured in meters. The term $\{x, y\}$ represents the UAV horizontal position, whereas H indicates the UAV altitude. The UAV positions for performing current and next tasks are denoted as the start and end locations, respectively, represented by $\mathbf{w}^{\text{start}}$ and $\mathbf{w}^{\text{end}}$. Let T denote the time length which UAVs speed flying away to the end location from the start location. At any time instant $t \in [0, T]$, the UAV location is given as $\mathbf{w}(t) = \{x(t), y(t), H\}$. The total time length is discretized into N time slot, with each of $T[n]$ length [13]. The UAV location is $\mathbf{w}[n] = \{x[n], y[n], H\}$ at the n-th time slot. Thus, the UAV path $\{\mathbf{w}[n]\}_{n=0}^{n=N}$ is discretized into N line segment, and $\mathbf{w}[0] = \mathbf{w}^{\text{start}}, \mathbf{w}[N] = \mathbf{w}^{\text{end}}$. To ensure an almost continuous path, the length of each line segment is limited by $\Delta_{\max}$:

$$\|\mathbf{w}[n] - \mathbf{w}[n-1]\| \le \Delta_{\max}, \forall n, \tag{1}$$

where $\Delta_{\max}$ is the maximum length of line segment.

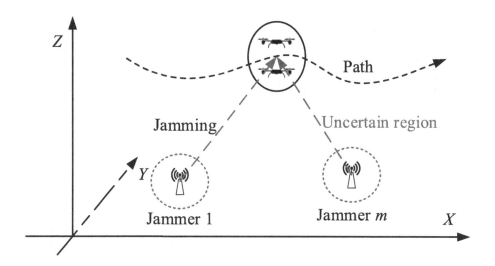

Fig. 1. Considered UAV-to-UAV communication scenario in the presence of jammers.

Based on the network state information, a ground node is responsible of planning UAVs behaviors, including altitude, velocity, etc. However, only partial information can be mastered by the ground node. Specifically, the UAVs parameters have been acquired. Due to the lack of cooperation between ground node and jammers, jammers locations cannot be acquired accurately. The errors between the exact location $\mathbf{w}_m^J = \{x_m^J, y_m^J, 0\}$ and estimated location $\bar{\mathbf{w}}_m^J = \{\bar{x}_m^J, \bar{y}_m^J, 0\}$

of m-th jammer is $\Delta \mathbf{w}_m^J = \mathbf{w}_m^J - \bar{\mathbf{w}}_m^J = \{\Delta x_m^J, \Delta y_m^J, 0\}$, and $\Delta \mathbf{w}_m^J$ is given by

$$\Delta \mathbf{w}_m^J \in \mathcal{U}_m = \left\{ \left(\Delta x_m^J\right)^2 + \left(\Delta y_m^J\right)^2 \leq (L_m)^2 \right\}. \tag{2}$$

Therefore, for a terrestrial jammer, it locates in a circular region with the estimated location $\bar{\mathbf{w}}_m^J$ as center and L_m as radius. Notably, the uncertain region may be irregular, but there is always a circle containing the irregular region. Thus, the studied uncertain region actually provides a conservative estimation for other irregular form.

The U2U (air-to-air) channel power gain g_u is modeled by average channel power gain along with a random variable accounting for the fading component, i.e.,

$$g_u = \beta_0 d_u^{-\alpha} \xi, \tag{3}$$

where β_0 is the channel power gain at the reference distance d_0, d_u is the distance between UAVs of interest, α is the path loss exponent, and ξ represents the fading and small scale effect. Since the air-to-air channel consists of dominant LoS link and non-dominant NLoS link, respectively, the Rice distribution is used to account for the small scale effect ξ and is given as [14, 15]

$$f\left(\xi|\rho, \mu\right) = \frac{\xi}{\rho^2} \exp\left(-\frac{\xi^2 + \mu^2}{2\rho^2}\right) I_0\left(\frac{\xi\mu}{\rho^2}\right), \tag{4}$$

with $\xi \geq 0$, where $I_0(x)$ is the modified Bessel function of the first kind with order zero, and ρ and μ reflecting the strength of the scattered (non-dominant) and dominant paths. It can be observed that Rice channel model reduces to a Rayleigh model when there is no dominant signal $\mu = 0$, i.e., $f\left(\xi|\rho\right) = \frac{\xi}{\rho^2} \exp\left(-\frac{\xi^2}{2\rho^2}\right)$.

The channel of the interference link from the m-th jammer to the UAV is dominated by LoS transmission [9],

$$g_m^J[n] = \beta_0 \left\| \mathbf{w}[n] - \mathbf{w}_m^J \right\|^{-\alpha} = \beta_0 \left\| \mathbf{w}[n] - \bar{\mathbf{w}}_m^J - \Delta \mathbf{w}_m^J \right\|^{-\alpha}, \forall m \in \mathcal{M}, \tag{5}$$

at the n-th line segment, where $\|\mathbf{a}\|$ provides the Euclidean norm for vector $\mathbf{a}$. Notably, $g_m^J[n]$ is not perfectly known since we only have partial information on $\Delta \mathbf{w}_m^J$. It can be observed that the location uncertainty is finally mapped to the channel state. Thus, the studied location uncertainty can be understood from different perspectives. On one hand, it initially characterizes the location uncertainty. Besides, it can be also regarded as the CSI uncertainty, which results from the random small scale fading or estimation errors.

2.2   Problem Formulation

The received SINR at the n-th line segment is given by

$$SINR[n] = \frac{P_u g_u}{\sum_{m=1}^M P_m^J[n] g_m^J[n] + \sigma^2}, \tag{6}$$

where P_u is the transmit power of UAV-Tx, P_m^J is the jammer power of m-th jammer, σ^2 is the noise power, and unit bandwidth is considered. Since future jammer power $P_m^J[n]$ cannot be acquired accurately, average jammer power is used in this paper and considered to be known. Then, the received SINR in the worst case is

$$\min_{\{\Delta\mathbf{w}_m^J\}} SINR[n] = \frac{P_u g_u}{\max\limits_{\{\Delta\mathbf{w}_m^J\}} \sum_{m=1}^{M} P_m^J[n] g_m^J[n] + \sigma^2}. \tag{7}$$

To ensure the U2U communication, the outage probability in the worst case is limited as follows:

$$\Pr\left[\min_{\{\Delta\mathbf{w}_m^J\}} SINR[n] \leq \gamma_{th}\right] \leq \varepsilon, \forall n, \tag{8}$$

where $\Pr[A]$ represents the occurrence probability of an event A, γ_{th} is the required SINR, ε is maximum allowable outage probability, and "min" makes it still work in the worst case since the jammers locations are uncertain.

In addition to the communication constraint, there is maximum flight speed on UAV. UAV path is limited by UAV maximum flight speed, i.e.,

$$\|\mathbf{w}[n] - \mathbf{w}[n-1]\| \leq V_{\max}T[n], \forall n, \tag{9}$$

where $V_{\max}$ is the maximum speed.

The aim of this paper is to minimize the completion time T, i.e., flying toward the end location as soon as possible, by designing UAV path. The problem can be formulated as follows:

$$(P1): \min_{\{\mathbf{w}[n],T[n]\}} \sum_{n=1}^{N} T[n]$$

$$s.t.\ C1: \Pr\left[\min_{\{\Delta\mathbf{w}_m^J\}} SINR[n] \leq \gamma_{th}\right] \leq \varepsilon, \forall n,$$

$$C2: \|\mathbf{w}[n] - \mathbf{w}[n-1]\| \leq \Delta_{\max}, \forall n,$$

$$C3: \|\mathbf{w}[n] - \mathbf{w}[n-1]\| \leq V_{\max}T[n], \forall n, \tag{10}$$

where $C1$ is outage probability constraint, $C2$ and $C3$ are the path constraints.

3   Time Minimization Algorithm for Robust UAV Communications

In $(P1)$, the probability constraints $C1$ is non-convex although there is a linear objective, and thus $(P1)$ cannot be efficiently solved by existing standard convex optimization methods.

Denote

$$I[n] = \max_{\{\Delta\mathbf{w}_m^J\}} \sum_{m=1}^{M} P_m^J[n] g_m^J[n] + \sigma^2. \tag{11}$$

Algorithm 1. One-dimensional search for obtaining parameter b

---
1: Initialize the parameters b^s, Δb, and set $s = 0$
2: **Repeat**
3:    Update $b^s \leftarrow b^s + \Delta b$
4:    Update $s \leftarrow s + 1$
5: **Until** $Q_1(a, b^s) < \varepsilon$
6: Output b^s

Then, the constraint in $C1$ can be rewritten as follows:

$$\Pr\left[\xi \leq \frac{I[n]\, d_u^\alpha \gamma_{th}}{P_u \beta_0}\right] \leq \varepsilon, \forall n. \tag{12}$$

Since random variable ξ follows Rice distribution, its cumulative distribution function (CDF) is given as standard Marcum Q-function $Q_1(a, b)$

$$Q_1(a, b) = \int_b^\infty x \exp\left(-\frac{x^2 + a^2}{2}\right) I_0(ax) dx. \tag{13}$$

Then, there is

$$\Pr\left[\xi \leq \frac{I[n]\, d_u^\alpha \gamma_{th}}{P_u \beta_0}\right] = 1 - Q_1\left(\frac{\mu}{\rho}, \frac{1}{\rho} \bullet \frac{I[n]\, d_u^\alpha \gamma_{th}}{P_u \beta_0}\right) \leq \varepsilon. \tag{14}$$

The standard Marcum Q-function $Q_1(a, b)$ is nondecreasing with respect to a and non-increasing with respect to b. Thus, given parameter a and probability ε, the parameter b can be obtained via one-dimensional search, denoted as $b = Q_1^{-1}(a, \varepsilon)$ [16]. Algorithm 1 provides the procedure for obtaining b with a given a and probability ε.

Now, the constraint in (14) can be rewritten as

$$\frac{I[n]\, d_u^\alpha \gamma_{th}}{P_u \beta_0} \leq \rho Q_1^{-1}\left(\frac{\mu}{\rho}, 1 - \varepsilon\right), \forall n, \tag{15}$$

or the following intractable form:

$$I[n]\, d_u^\alpha \gamma_{th} \leq \rho \beta_0 Q_1^{-1}(\mu/\rho, 1 - \varepsilon)\, P_u, \forall n. \tag{16}$$

Since the interference from each jammer is independent, there is

$$I[n] = \max_{\{\Delta \mathbf{w}_m^J\}} \sum_{m=1}^M P_m^J[n]\, \beta_0 \left\| \mathbf{w}[n] - \bar{\mathbf{w}}_m^J - \Delta \mathbf{w}_m^J \right\|^{-\alpha} + \sigma^2$$

$$= \sum_{m=1}^M \frac{P_m^J[n]\, \beta_0}{\min_{\Delta \mathbf{w}_m^J} \left\| \mathbf{w}[n] - \bar{\mathbf{w}}_m^J - \Delta \mathbf{w}_m^J \right\|^\alpha} + \sigma^2, \forall n. \tag{17}$$

Introducing additional variable $\{U_m[n]\}$, the constraint in (16) can be replaced with

$$\left(\sum_{m=1}^{M} P_m^J[n]\beta_0 U_m^{-\alpha/2}[n]+\sigma^2\right) d_u^\alpha \gamma_{th} \le \rho\beta_0 Q_1^{-1}(\mu/\rho, 1-\varepsilon)P_u, \forall n, \quad (18)$$

$$U_m[n] \le \min_{\Delta \mathbf{w}_m^J} \left\| \mathbf{w}[n] - \bar{\mathbf{w}}_m^J - \Delta\mathbf{w}_m^J \right\|^2, \forall m, n \quad (19)$$

The Eq. (19) can be rewritten as

$$\left(\Delta x_m^J\right)^2 + \left(\Delta y_m^J\right)^2 \le L_m^2, \forall m \in \mathcal{M}, \quad (20)$$

$$U_m[n] \le \left(x[n] - \bar{x}_m^J - \Delta x_m^J\right)^2 + \left(y[n] - \bar{y}_m^J - \Delta y_m^J\right)^2 + H^2, \forall m \in \mathcal{M}, n, \quad (21)$$

The constraints in (20) and (21) are intractable to be addressed since there is infinite number of parameters $\left\{\Delta x_m^J, \Delta y_m^J\right\}$. To this end, we resort to the S-Procedure defined as follows [17]:

S-Procedure: Denote $\mathbf{F}_i$, $\mathbf{g}_i$, and h_i as the $n \times n$ symmetric matrix, n dimensional column vector, and real number, respectively. Then, the implication

$$\mathbf{x}^T\mathbf{F}_1\mathbf{x} + 2\mathbf{g}_1^T\mathbf{x} + h_1 \le 0 \Rightarrow \mathbf{x}^T\mathbf{F}_2\mathbf{x} + 2\mathbf{g}_2^T\mathbf{x} + h_2 \le 0, \quad (22)$$

holds if and only if there is a $\lambda \ge 0$ such that

$$\begin{bmatrix} \mathbf{F}_2 & \mathbf{g}_2 \\ \mathbf{g}_2^T & h_2 \end{bmatrix} \preceq \lambda \begin{bmatrix} \mathbf{F}_1 & \mathbf{g}_1 \\ \mathbf{g}_1^T & h_1 \end{bmatrix} \quad (23)$$

provided there exists a point $\bar{\mathbf{x}}$ with $\bar{\mathbf{x}}^T\mathbf{F}_1\bar{\mathbf{x}} + 2\mathbf{g}_1^T\bar{\mathbf{x}} + h_1 < 0$.

In the sequel, we address the constraints (20) and (21). It can be observed that $\left(\Delta x_m^J\right)^2 + \left(\Delta y_m^J\right)^2 - L_m^2 < 0$ with $\left(\Delta x_m^J, \Delta y_m^J\right) = (0,0)$. Based on the S-Procedure, (20) implies (21) if and only if

$$\Gamma\left(x[n], y[n], U_m[n], \lambda_m[n]\right) \succeq 0, \forall m \in \mathcal{M}, n, \quad (24)$$

where

$$\Gamma\left(x[n], y[n], U_m[n], \lambda_m[n]\right) = \begin{bmatrix} \lambda_m[n]+1 & 0 & \bar{x}_m^J - x[n] \\ 0 & \lambda_m[n]+1 & \bar{y}_m^J - y[n] \\ \bar{x}_m^J - x[n] & \bar{y}_m^J - y[n] & \varphi_m[n] \end{bmatrix} \quad (25)$$

with

$$\varphi_m[n] = -\lambda_m[n]L_m^2 + \left(x[n] - \bar{x}_m^J\right)^2 + \left(y[n] - \bar{y}_m^J\right)^2 - U_m[n] + H^2. \quad (26)$$

However, it is intractable to be addressed with the form in Eq. (24) since it results in a non-convex feasible region. Considering the fact that x^2 is convex, there is

$$x^2[n] \ge -(x^s[n])^2 + 2x^s[n]x[n],$$
$$y^2[n] \ge -(y^s[n])^2 + 2y^s[n]y[n]. \quad (27)$$

Algorithm 2. Path planning for U2U communications with jamming

---
1: Initialize the parameters $P^s = \{\mathbf{w}\,[n]\,, T\,[n]\,, U_m\,[n]\,, \lambda_m\,[n]\}$, and set $s = 0$
2: **Repeat**
3:    Solve the SDP problem in (P2) with a feasible point P^s and find optimal solution P^*
4:    Update $P^s \Leftarrow P^*$
5:    Update $s \leftarrow s + 1$
6: **Until** the terminal condition is met
7: Output the path $P^* = \{\mathbf{w}\,[n]\,, T\,[n]\}$

Therefore, Eq. (24) is lower bounded by the following linear matrix inequality (LMI):

$$\tilde{\Gamma}\left(x\,[n]\,, y\,[n]\,, U_m\,[n]\,, \lambda_m\,[n]\right) = \begin{bmatrix} \lambda_m\,[n] + 1 & 0 & \bar{x}_m^J - x\,[n] \\ 0 & \lambda_m\,[n] + 1 & \bar{y}_m^J - y\,[n] \\ \bar{x}_m^J - x\,[n] & \bar{y}_m^J - y\,[n] & \tilde{\varphi}_m\,[n] \end{bmatrix} \quad (28)$$

with

$$\tilde{\varphi}_m\,[n] = -\lambda_m\,[n]\,L_m^2 - \left(x^s\,[n]\right)^2 + 2x^s\,[n]\,x\,[n] - \left(y^s\,[n]\right)^2$$
$$+ 2y^s\,[n]\,y\,[n] - 2\bar{x}_m^J x\,[n] - 2\bar{y}_m^J y\,[n] + \left(\bar{x}_m^J\right)^2 + \left(\bar{y}_m^J\right)^2 - U_m\,[n] + H^2. \quad (29)$$

We should iteratively solve the following problems:

$$(P2): \min_{\{\mathbf{w}[n],T[n],U_m[n],\lambda_m[n]\}} \sum_{n=1}^{N} T\,[n]$$

$$s.t.\ C1: \begin{cases} \sum_{m=1}^{M} P_m^J\,[n]\,\beta_0 U_m^{-\alpha/2}\,[n] \leq A, \forall n, \\ \tilde{\Gamma}\left(x\,[n]\,, y\,[n]\,, U_m\,[n]\,, \lambda_m\,[n]\right) \succeq \mathbf{0}, \forall m, n, \\ \lambda_m\,[n] \geq 0, \forall m, n, \end{cases}$$

$$C2: \|\mathbf{w}\,[n] - \mathbf{w}\,[n-1]\| \leq \Delta_{\max}, \forall n,$$

$$C3: \|\mathbf{w}\,[n] - \mathbf{w}\,[n-1]\| \leq V_{\max}T\,[n]\,, \forall n, \quad (30)$$

where $A = \frac{\rho\beta_0 Q_1^{-1}(\mu/\rho,1-\varepsilon)P_u}{d_u^\alpha \gamma_{th}} - \sigma^2$. The $P2$ is a semidefinite programming (SDP) and can be solved by convex optimization techniques.

Finally, the algorithm to solve (P1) is summarized in Algorithm 2.

4   Simulations and Discussions

In this section, we illustrate the UAV behavior in the presence of jamming, and demonstrate the effectiveness of the proposed algorithm by conducting in-depth simulations. Consider a horizontal 1000×1000 m^2 scenario with two terrestrial jammers located at $(300, 300)$ and $(700, 700)$, respectively. Unless otherwise specified, the main simulation parameters are set as that listed in Table 1.

Table 1. Key parameters used in simulations.

Parameter	Value	Comments
P_m^J	0.5 W	Jammer power
β_0	−60 dB	Channel power gain at the reference distance d_0
ρ, μ	1.347, 6.469	The strength of the scattered and dominant paths
ε	0.1	Outage probability
P_u	0.1 W	UAV transmit power
d_u	20 m	Distance between UAVs
α	−3	The path loss exponent
γ_{th}	1	The required SINR
σ^2	−110 dBm	Noise power
$\Delta_{\max}$	100 m	The maximum length of line segment
$V_{\max}$	20 m/s	The UAV maximum flight speed
H	100 m	The UAV altitude
L_m	40 m	The uncertain radius

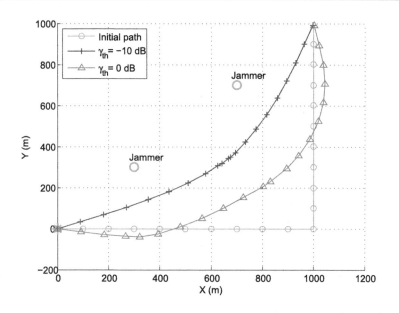

Fig. 2. UAV path in the presence of jammers with different considerations.

Figure 2 illustrates the UAV path in different considerations, where "∗" and "∘" represent the UAV start (end) location, jammer location, respectively. The initial path for start our algorithm has also been given in Fig. 2. It can be first observed that, in the presence of jamming, the UAV is intentionally far away

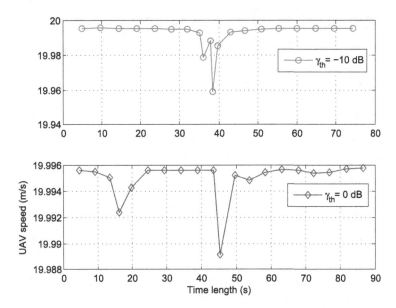

Fig. 3. UAV flight speed versus the time length.

from the jammer during the flight. Moreover, with higher SINR requirement, longer distance is required to avoid jamming.

To make the UAV path more intuitive, Fig. 3 presents the UAV speed versus the flight time, where the maximum flight speed is set to be 20 m/s. It can be found from Fig. 3 that the UAV passes through the jammer region at a maximum speed in all cases. This is expected since higher speed can save the flight time, without other considerations, such as the energy consumption.

The convergence behavior of the proposed path planning algorithm is plotted in Fig. 4. The time length consumed goes to a stable value after some iterations. Furthermore, it can be known from Fig. 2 that the initial path in the case of $\gamma = 0$ dB is not a feasible point. However, the proposed path planning algorithm can also achieve a feasible and high-performance solution, which is expected and proves the robustness of the algorithm.

Figure 5 plots the time length comparison versus the uncertain region with different SINR requirements. As expected, high uncertainty results in greater flight costs for the UAV. This is because the UAV must fly a longer distance to be away from jammers.

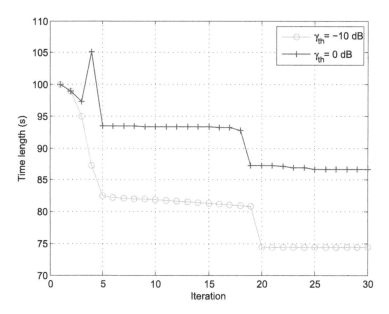

Fig. 4. The convergence behavior of the proposed path planning algorithm.

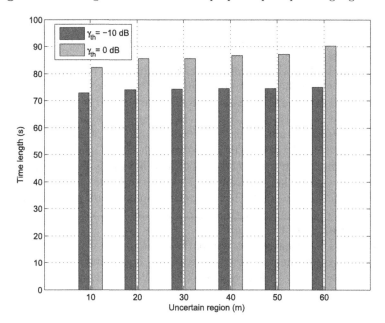

Fig. 5. Time length comparison versus the uncertain region with different SINR requirements.

5   Conclusions

UAVs have been attracted increasing attentions in wireless communications. In this paper, we studied the robust UAV communications in the presence of jamming. First, we formulated a path planning problem for U2U communications in the presence of jamming, which considered the air-to-air channel uncertainty, jammer location uncertainty, UAV maximum flight speed, and the SINR requirement. Then, we developed a path planning algorithm with the aid of S-procedure, successive convex approximation (SCA), and semidefinite programming (SDP). Simulation results validate the effectiveness of the proposed algorithm.

Acknowledgement. This work was supported in part by the National Natural Science Foundation of China under Grant 61871398 and Grant 61501510, and in part by the China Postdoctoral Science Foundation Funded Project under Grant 2018T110426.

References

1. Ding, G., Wu, Q., Zhang, L., Lin, Y., Tsiftsis, T.A., Yao, Y.D.: An amateur drone surveillance system based on the cognitive internet of things. IEEE Commun. Mag. **56**(1), 29–35 (2018)
2. Zeng, Y., Zhang, R., Teng, J.L.: Wireless communications with unmanned aerial vehicles: opportunities and challenges. IEEE Commun. Mag. **54**(5), 36–42 (2016)
3. Wang, H., Ding, G., Gao, F., Chen, J., Wang, J., Wang, L.: Power control in UAV-supported ultra dense networks: communications, caching, and energy transfer. IEEE Commun. Mag. **56**(6), 28–34 (2018)
4. Al-Hourani, A., Kandeepan, S., Lardner, S.: Optimal lap altitude for maximum coverage. IEEE Wirel. Commun. Lett. **3**(6), 569–572 (2014)
5. Alzenad, M., El-Keyi, A., Lagum, F., Yanikomeroglu, H.: 3-D placement of an unmanned aerial vehicle base station (UAV-BS) for energy-efficient maximal coverage. IEEE Wirel. Commun. Lett. **6**(4), 434–437 (2017)
6. Mozaffari, M., Saad, W., Bennis, M., Debbah, M.: Unmanned aerial vehicle with underlaid device-to-device communications: performance and tradeoffs. IEEE Trans. Wirel. Commun. **15**(6), 3949–3963 (2016)
7. Chen, Y., Feng, W., Zheng, G.: Optimum placement of UAV as relays. IEEE Commun. Lett. **22**(2), 248–251 (2018)
8. Xue, Z., Wang, J., Ding, G., Wu, Q.: Joint 3D location and power optimization for UAV-enabled relaying systems. IEEE Access **6**, 43113–43124 (2018)
9. Zeng, Y., Zhang, R., Teng, J.L.: Throughput maximization for UAV-enabled mobile relaying systems. IEEE Trans. Commun. **64**(12), 4983–4996 (2016)
10. Wang, H., Wang, J., Ding, G., Chen, J., Li, Y., Han, Z.: Spectrum sharing planning for full-duplex UAV relaying systems with underlaid D2D communications. IEEE J. Sel. Areas Commun. **36**(9), 1986–1999 (2018)
11. Xu, J., Zeng, Y., Zhang, R.: UAV-enabled wireless power transfer: trajectory design and energy optimization. IEEE Trans. Wirel. Commun. **17**(8), 5092–5106 (2018)
12. Wang, H., Wang, J., Ding, G., Wang, L., Tsiftsis, T.A., Sharma, P.K.: Resource allocation for energy harvesting-powered D2D communication underlaying UAV-assisted networks. IEEE Trans. Green Commun. Netw. **2**(1), 14–24 (2018)
13. Zeng, Y., Xu, J., Zhang, R.: Energy minimization for wireless communication with rotary-wing UAV (2018). http://cn.arxiv.org/pdf/1804.02238

14. Goddemeier, N., Wietfeld, C.: Investigation of air-to-air channel characteristics and a UAV specific extension to the Rice model. In: IEEE GLOBECOM Workshops, pp. 1–5. IEEE (2015)
15. Kim, M., Lee, J.: Outage probability of UAV communications in the presence of interference (2018). http://cn.arxiv.org/pdf/1806.09843.pdf
16. Zheng, G., Ma, S., Wong, K.K., Ng, T.S.: Robust beamforming in cognitive radio. IEEE Trans. Wirel. Commun. 9(2), 570–576 (2010)
17. Boyd, S., Vandenberghe, L.: Convex Optimization. Cambridge University Press, Cambridge (2004)

DQN Aided Edge Computing
in Satellite-Terrestrial Network

Fangmin Xu[✉], Fan Yang, Chao Qiu, Chenglin Zhao, and Bin Li

Beijing University of Posts and Telecommunications, Beijing, China
xufm@bupt.edu.cn

Abstract. In order to support a mass of current satellite applications, it becomes a trend to integrate satellite networks with terrestrial networks, called satellite-terrestrial networks. However, traditional network protocols cannot adapt to the dynamic and complex satellite-terrestrial network. Moreover, the computing and communication capabilities of some satellites cannot meet the requirements of supporting various applications. As a result, the paper proposes an edge computing based software-defined satellite-terrestrial network architecture, which can manage network flexibly by logically centralizing network intelligence and control. Furthermore, a networking and edge computing scheme is proposed by formulating a jointly optimization problem, which is solved by using novel deep Q-learning approach. Simulation results show the effectiveness of the proposed scheme.

Keywords: Satellite-terrestrial networks ·
Software defined networking (SDN) · Networking · Edge computing ·
Deep-Q-learning

1 Introduction

Satellite network is developing fast recently and has been widely used in many fields, such as emergency assistance, navigation, remote sensing and so on [1]. Thus, variety of satellite applications are developed. However, the capability of satellites is not high enough to support the explosion of current satellite applications. So there is an emerging trend to integrate satellite networks with terrestrial networks, called satellite-terrestrial networks [2].

Traditional satellite network protocols have poor mobility, high costs and complexity, and it cannot adapt to the dynamic changing satellite-terrestrial network. Satellite-terrestrial needs a flexible and intelligent network architecture and protocols. Thus, there is a growing trend to use software-defined network (SDN) to reconstruct the satellite-terrestrial networks. SDN decoupled control and data plane, logically centralized network intelligence and state, and

Supported by the Key Program of the National Natural Science Foundation of China (61431008).

M. Jia et al. (Eds.): WiSATS 2019, LNICST 280, pp. 117–127, 2019.
https://doi.org/10.1007/978-3-030-19153-5_11

abstracted the underlying network infrastructure [3]. Feng *et al.* in [4] proposed an architecture for heterogeneous satellite-terrestrial networks, they use SDN and network virtualization to improve the flexibility of networks. Li *et al.* in [5] proposed a multi-strategy flow table management scheme, called *SAT-FLOW*. Boero in [6] constructed a SDN-based terrestrial-satellite network architecture to minimize the mean time to deliver the data of a new traffic flow from source to destination including the time required to transfer SDN control actions. Liu in [7] proposed an optimal controller and gateway placement algorithm in SDN enabled 5G-satellite integrated network which increased the network reliability and decreased the latency. It is obvious that, by abstracting and allocating networking resources dynamically, satellite-terrestrial networks can get better performance such as reliability, latency, flexibility and so on.

Moreover, traditional satellite-terrestrial network apply cloud computing to assist the satellite in computing complex tasks. For example, Huang in [8] proposed a novel layered architecture for the space-based cloud infrastructure to aid space network. However, due to the long distance and huge amount of data to be delivered, it is not economical and feasible to offload computation tasks to the cloud center. So there is an increasing trend to use edge computing to aid satellite-terrestrial network. Edge computing is a new paradigm of shifting computation resources to the network edge to improve network service performance. This brings higher network resource utilization and computation performance. Specially, our contributions are:

- Proposed an edge computing based software-defined satellite-terrestrial network architecture and formulate a jointly resource allocation problem based on it.
- Utilize deep Q-learning approach to solve the jointly resource allocation problem.

The rests of the paper is organized as follow. In Sect. 2, system description and model are presented. The joint optimization problem of networking and edge computing is formulated as a Q-learning process and solved in Sect. 3. In Sect. 4, we present the simulation results. Finally, conclusions presented in Sect. 5.

2   System Model

In this section, we first present the proposed architecture of edge computing based software-defined satellite-terrestrial network. Then system model is given, including network model, communication model and computing model.

2.1   Proposed Framework of Software-Defined Satellite-Terrestrial Network

This paper take a joint consideration of both networking and computing in software-defined satellite-terrestrial network architecture. The architecture includes data plane, control plane and application plane, as shown in Fig. 1

In the data plane, there are two types of infrastructures to provide network resources and edge computing resources. Networking resource infrastructure includes LEOs and MEOs. And computing resource infrastructure consists of MEC servers which provide computation resources for the network users. In the control plane, the control intelligence is abstracted in GEO satellites and land-based controllers. They are responsible for centralized management of the LEO/MEO satellites and MEC servers. Controllers receive the requests from devices in data plane and consider both the networking resources and MEC server status to make a decision, i.e. which LEO/MEO should server the user, and which MEC server should assist the LEO/MEO on processing raw data. In the application plane, a number of applications are provided, including remote sensing, navigation, communicating and monitoring.

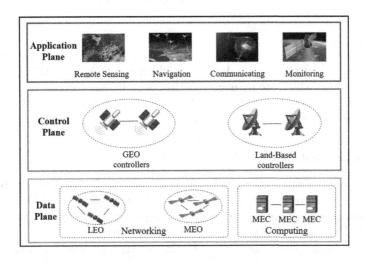

Fig. 1. The framework of Software-Defined Satellite-Terrestrial network.

The workflow of the architecture includes several steps. First, a user sends a request to the GEO/land-based controller, i.e. requests to identify an objects (such as vehicles or vessels) in a video/image of a certain area. Controller runs the algorithm and returns decision to the user, the decision includes which LEO satellite could the user connect to get satellite networking resource and which MEC server should aided the LEO satellite with processing raw data by complex image/video identification algorithms. Then, user connects to the selected LEO according to controller decision. LEO retrieves for the content and pass the raw data to the selected MEC server. If the MEC server is busy, then the tasks need to queue up. Till the MEC server finishes the previous tasks. MEC server begin to execute the tasks and return the result to the LEO, and then the content will be returned to the user. To visualize the description, we give the workflow diagram in Fig. 2.

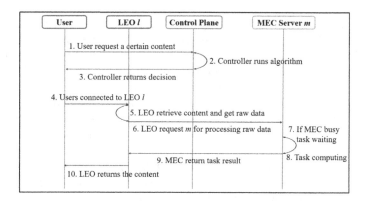

Fig. 2. Workflow in the proposed architecture.

2.2 Network Model

There are two resource pools in data layer which includes LEO/MEO satellites, and MEC servers, which are managed by the controllers in the control plane. Let $\mathcal{L} = \{1, ..., L\}$, $\mathcal{M} = \{1, ..., M\}$, $\mathcal{U} = \{1, ..., U\}$ denote the set of LEOs/MEOs, MEC servers, and users.

2.3 Communication Model

We assume that the wireless channels between users and LEO/MEOs are realistic time-varying, it can be modeled as finite-state Markov channels (FSMCs). In this model, channel quality can be expressed by the received SNR h_u^l of a user u from LEO/MEO l. We split the range of h_u^l into L' discrete intervals, each interval is a state of Markov chain, i.e., $\mathcal{H} = \{\mathcal{H}_0, \mathcal{H}_1, ..., \mathcal{H}_{L'-1}\}$. The received SNR h_u^l at time t can be represented by $\mathbf{h}_u^l(t)$, where $t \in \{0, 1, 2, ..., T-1\}$. Based on a certain transition probability, the received SNR $\mathbf{h}_u^l(t)$ changes from a state to another, and the transition probability from one state $\vartheta_{\bar{s}}$ to another state $\varphi_{\bar{s}}$ at time slot t could be denoted as $\gamma_{\vartheta_{\bar{s}}\varphi_{\bar{s}}}(t)$. Then, the transition probability matrix $\Upsilon_u^l(t)$ could be represented as:

$$\Upsilon_u^l(t) = [\gamma_{\vartheta_{\bar{s}}\varphi_{\bar{s}}}(t)]_{L' \times L'}, \qquad (1)$$

where $\gamma_{\vartheta_{\bar{s}}\varphi_{\bar{s}}}(t) = Pr(\mathbf{h}_u^l(t+1) = \varphi_{\bar{s}}|\mathbf{h}_u^l(t) = \vartheta_{\bar{s}})$, and $\varphi_{\bar{s}}, \vartheta_{\bar{s}} \in \mathcal{H}$.

We assume that the available spectrum bandwidth of LEO/MEO l is B^l Hz, among which B_u^l Hz is allocated to user u. The available backhaul capacity of LEO/MEO l is Z^l bps. The spectrum efficiency of user u is $\nu_u^l(t)$ at time t. The communication rate of user u associated with LEO/MEO l is:

$$ComR_u^l(t) = a_u^l(t)B_u^l(t)\nu_u^l(t), \forall u \in \mathcal{U}, \tag{2}$$

$$s.t. \sum_{u \in \mathcal{U}} ComR_u^l(t) \le Z^l, \forall l \in \mathcal{L}, \tag{3}$$

where $a_u^l(t)$ means whether user u connects LEO/MEO l. Let $a_u^l(t) = 1$ represent user u connects certain LEO/MEO l. Otherwise, $a_u^l(t) = 0$.

2.4 Computing Model

We assume $T_l = \{o_l, n_l\}$ is the computation task of LEO/MEO l, with the data size of o_l, and required CPU cycle of n_l.

Since we have no idea on exactly know how many computation capabilities are allocated to LEO/MEO l. Thus, we model the computation capabilities of MEC server m allocated to LEO/MEO l as a random variable $\mathcal{Q}_l^m$. The value of $\mathcal{Q}_l^m$ can be splited into M' discrete intervals, i.e., $\Pi = \{\Pi_0, \Pi_1, ..., \Pi_{M'-1}\}$. The computation capability $\mathcal{Q}_l^m$ at time instant t can be represented by $\mathcal{Q}_l^m(t), t \in \{0, 1, 2, ..., T-1\}$. Computation capability $\mathcal{Q}_l^m(t)$ changes from one state to another based on transition possibility. Here $\varepsilon_{\alpha_{\bar{s}} \varpi_{\bar{s}}}(t)$ represent the transition probability of $\mathcal{Q}_l^m(t)$ from one state $\alpha_{\bar{s}}$ to another state $\varpi_{\bar{s}}$ at time instant t. The transition probability matrix $E_l^m(t)$ could be denoted as:

$$E_l^m(t) = [\varepsilon_{\alpha_{\bar{s}} \varpi_{\bar{s}}}(t)]_{M' \times M'}, \tag{4}$$

where $\varepsilon_{\alpha_{\bar{s}} \varpi_{\bar{s}}}(t) = Pr(\mathcal{Q}_l^m(t+1) = \varpi_{\bar{s}} | \mathcal{Q}_l^m(t) = \alpha_{\bar{s}})$, and $\varpi_{\bar{s}}, \alpha_{\bar{s}} \in \Pi$.

The task execution time T_l at MEC server m can be denoted as

$$t_l^m = \frac{n_l}{\mathcal{Q}_l^m(t)}. \tag{5}$$

So the computation rate is:

$$CompR_l^m(t) = a_l^m(t)\frac{o_l}{t_l^m} = a_l^m(t)\frac{\mathcal{Q}_l^m(t)o_l}{n_l}, \tag{6}$$

$$s.t. \sum_{l \in \mathcal{L}} a_l^m(t)o_l \le O_m, \tag{7}$$

where $a_l^m(t)$ means whether LEO/MEO l offloads computation tasks to certain MEC server m. Let $a_l^m(t) = 1$ denote LEO/MEO l offloads tasks to MEC server m. Otherwise, $a_l^m(t) = 0$. O_m is the maximum size of tasks that can execute simultaneously on MEC server m.

Thus, jointly optimize the networking and computation offloading strategy is a complex and high-dimensional system. Tradition approach is difficult to work out. So it is necessary to use machine learning algorithms, such as deep Q-learning, to learn the law of the system. In this way, a viable solution could be given. Thus, in this paper, we propose a deep Q-learning approach to solve computation offloading problem in satellite-terrestrial networks.

3   Problem Formulation

In this section, we formulate a joint optimization problem of networking and edge computation capability in satellite-terrestrial network. Then we propose a deep Q-learning approach to solve it.

3.1   State Space

The state space is consists of networking state, computing state. Then, state space $S(t)$ at time slot t is represented as:

$$S(t) = \begin{bmatrix} \mathbf{h}_u^1(t) & \mathbf{h}_u^2(t) & ... & \mathbf{h}_u^l(t) & ... & \mathbf{h}_u^L(t) \\ \mathcal{Q}_l^1(t) & \mathcal{Q}_l^2(t) & ... & \mathcal{Q}_l^m(t) & ... & \mathcal{Q}_l^M(t) \end{bmatrix}, \tag{8}$$

3.2   Action Space

In this system, controller needs to decide which LEO/MEO l should provide networking resource to u, and which MEC server m should execute the computation task for LEO/MEO l. Thus, action space $a_u(t)$ at time instant t is represented as:

$$a_u(t) = \{ComA_u(t), CompA_l(t)\}, \tag{9}$$

where $ComA_u(t)$, and $CompA_l(t)$ mean:

(1) $ComA_u(t) = [ComA_u^1(t), ..., ComA_u^L(t)]$, where $ComA_u^l(t), \forall l \in \mathcal{L}$ means whether or not LEO l provide networking resource to user u. $ComA_u^l(t) \in \{0, 1\}$, where $ComA_u^l(t) = 0$ means LEO l is not assigned to user u at time instant t, otherwise $ComA_u^l(t) = 1$. Note that, in one time slot, only one LEO to provide user u with networking resources.
(2) $CompA_l(t) = [CompA_l^1(t), ..., CompA_l^M(t)]$, where $CompA_l^m, \forall m \in \mathcal{M}$ means whether or not the LEO/MEO l offload tasks to MEC server m. And $CompA_l^m(t) \in \{0, 1\}$, where $CompA_l^m(t) = 0$ means LEO/MEO do not offload to MEC server m, otherwise $CompA_l^m(t) = 1$. Note that there is only one MEC server to do the computation task for LEO/MEO l at one time slot.

3.3   Reward Function

According to the work in [9], the controllers need to pay the usage of wireless spectrums in LEO/MEO l, and the computation fee in MEC server m, which are denoted as δ_l per Hz and η_m per Joule.

In addition, the controllers charge user u for the fees of accessing the networks, and using the computation resources, which are represented by τ_u per bps, and ϕ_u per bps.

$$R_u(t) = \sum_{l \in \mathcal{L}} R_{u,l}^{comm}(t) + \sum_{m \in \mathcal{M}} R_{l,m}^{comp}(t)$$

$$= \sum_{l \in \mathcal{L}} ComA_u^l(t)(\tau_u ComR_u^l(t)/\delta_l B_u^l(t))$$

$$+ \sum_{m \in \mathcal{M}} CompA_l^m(t)(\phi_u CompR_l^m(t)/\eta_m n_l e_m) \tag{10}$$

$$= \sum_{l \in \mathcal{L}} ComA_u^l(t)(\tau_u B_u^l(t)\nu_u^l(t)/\delta_l B_u^l(t))$$

$$+ \sum_{m \in \mathcal{M}} CompA_l^m(t)(\phi_l \frac{\mathcal{Q}_l^m(t)o_l}{n_l}/\eta_m n_l e_m)$$

$(utility/resource).$

We define reward function $R_u(t)$ at time instant t as the expected utility per resource. It is the ratio between the charging fee of using the resource and the paid fee of having the resource. The larger expected utility per resource means the higher efficiency of unit resource. Thus, $R_u(t)$ can be expressed as (10), where e_m denotes the energy consumption for performing one CPU cycle.

3.4 Deep Q-Learning Algorithm

DQN use the interaction of agent-environment to optimize the action choosing. At one decision episode, the learning agent senses state $S(t)$ from the environment. According to a given policy, the agent chooses action $a_u(t)$ to execute. Then the environment turns to a new state $S(t+1)$, and the agent gains the corresponding reward $R_u(t)$.

In tradition Q-learning algorithm, the given policy is defined by Q-table. However. when the state space and the action space are high-dimensional. It is difficult to have all $Q(s,a)$ and put them into Q-table. Therefore, we use deep networks to evaluate $Q(s,a)$, i.e., $Q(s,a,w) \approx Q(s,a)$, where w is the set of weights and biases in deep networks [10]. In each learning iteration, deep networks are trained to minimize loss function $L(w)$, so as to evaluate real $Q(s,a)$.

There are two innovations to make DQL more efficient and more robust, includes experience replay and fixed target deep networks [10]. Deep Q-learning is shown in Algorithm 1, where ϵ-greedy policy is used to balance exploitation and exploration.

4 Simulation Results and Discussions

In this section, we evaluate the performance of the proposed algorithm in satellite-terrestrial networks. First, we present simulation settings, followed by some discussions about simulation results.

Algorithm 1. Deep Q-learning

1: Initialization:
   Initialize evaluated deep networks with the set of weights and biases w.
   Initialize target deep networks with the set of weights and biases w'.
2: **for** $k = 1 : K$ **do**
3:    Reset the environment with an arbitrary observation S_{ini}, and $S(t) = S_{ini}$.
4:    **while** $S(t)! = S_{terminal}$ **do**
5:       Select action $a_u(t)$ based on ϵ-greedy policy.
6:       Obtain immediate reward $R_u(t)$ and next observation $S(t+1)$.
7:       Store the experience $(S(t), a_u(t), R_u(t), S(t+1))$ into the experience replay memory.
8:       Randomly sample some batches of them from the experience replay memory.
9:       Calculate target Q-value $Q_{target}(t)$ in target deep networks:
         if s' is $s_{terminal}$
            $Q_{target}(t) = R_u(t)$,
         else
            $Q_{target}(t) = R_u(t) + \gamma_q \max_{a'} Q(s', a', w')$.
10:      Train evaluated deep networks to minimize loss function $L(w)$.
11:      Every some steps, update target deep networks.
12:      $S(t) \leftarrow S(t+1)$
13:   **end while**
14: **end for**

4.1   Simulation Settings

In this simulation, hardware environment is a GPU-based server, and this server has 8 GB 1867 MHz LPDDR3, 2 GHz Intel Core i5, and 256G memory. Software environment is Python 2.7.10 with Tensorflow 1.4.0. Note that, we use a seven-layer deep networks in the simulation.

We assume that the state of wireless channels between user u and LEO/MEO l can be strong (spectrum efficiency $\nu_u^l = 10$), commom (spectrum efficiency $\nu_u^l = 2$), and poor (spectrum efficiency $\nu_u^l = 0.2$), whose transition probability matrix is

$$\Upsilon = \begin{bmatrix} 0.5\ 0.4\ 0.1 \\ 0.1\ 0.5\ 0.4 \\ 0.4\ 0.1\ 0.5 \end{bmatrix}. \tag{11}$$

We also assume the computation capability states of MEC servers are strong (computation rate $\mathcal{Q}_u^m(t) = 50$), common (computation rate $\mathcal{Q}_u^m(t) = 10$), and poor (computation rate $\mathcal{Q}_u^m(t) = 1$), whose transition probability matrix is

$$E = \begin{bmatrix} 0.5\ 0.3\ 0.2 \\ 0.2\ 0.5\ 0.3 \\ 0.3\ 0.2\ 0.5 \end{bmatrix}. \tag{12}$$

The values of the rest parameters in the simulation are listed in Table 1.

Table 1. Parameters setting in the simulation.

Parameters	Values	Descriptions
B_u^l	5 MHz	The bandwidth of LEO l allocated to user u
δ_l	2 units/MHz	The unit paid-price of using wireless spectrums
η_m	2 unit/J	The unit paid-price of using MEC servers
τ_u	10 unit/Mbps	The unit charging-price of using networking resources
ϕ_u	10 unit/Mbps	The unit charging-price of using computing resources
n_u	5 Mcycles	The required number of CPU cycles to finish each computation task
e_m	1 J	The energy consumption for performing one CPU cycle
o_u	2 Mbits	The computation task size

4.2 Simulation Results

Figure 3 shows the relationship between training episodes and the expected utility per resource, including networking and computing. The learning agent runs in AdamOptimizer [11] with the learning rate of 0.001, and ϵ-greedy linearly decreasing from 1 to 0.1 in 500 training episodes. As shown in (10), with the increase of training episodes, the expected utility per resource increases until convergence. Finally, the expected utility reach a stable value. And with the joint consideration of networking and edge computing resources, the proposed DRL-based scheme has the better performance than only consider single aspect.

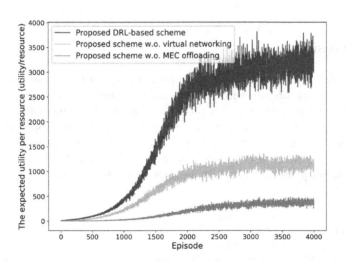

Fig. 3. Training curves tracking the expected utility per resource under different schemes.

Figure 4 shows the relationship between the learning loss and training steps, when the learning agent runs in AdamOptimizer with the learning rate of 0.001. At the beginning, target deep networks and evaluated deep networks have the similar weights and biases, thus the loss values are low. Along with the training process, evaluated deep networks learn the environment and store experiences into the experience replay memory, this increase the differences between target deep networks and evaluated deep networks. Evaluated deep networks are trained by these differences to decrease the learning loss. The decrease of learning loss represents the effectiveness of the deep networks.

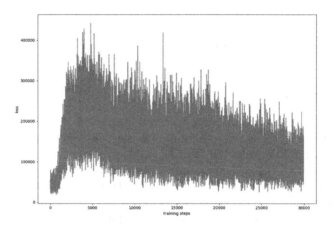

Fig. 4. Training curves tracking the learning loss under the proposed DRL-based scheme.

5 Conclusions

In this paper, we proposed an edge computing based software-defined satellite-terrestrial network architecture. Additionally, based on the architecture, we formulated the joint optimization problem of networking and edge computing resources in the network. Then we utilized a deep Q-learning approach to solve it. Simulation results showed the effectiveness and the convergence performance of our proposed scheme with different scenarios. Some future works should consider the mobility scenarios, which is used to better generalize the proposed approach.

References

1. Kaneko, K., Nishiyama, H., Kato, N., Miura, A., Toyoshima, M.: Construction of a flexibility analysis model for flexible high-throughput satellite communication systems with a digital channelizer. IEEE Trans. Veh. Technol. **67**(3), 2097–2107 (2018)
2. Yao, H., Wang, L., Wang, X., Lu, Z., Liu, Y.: The space-terrestrial integrated network (STIN): an overview. IEEE Commun. Mag. **16**(99), 2–9 (2018)
3. Yang, B., Yue, W., Chu, X., Song, G.: Seamless handover in software-defined satellite networking. IEEE Commun. Lett. **20**(9), 1768–1771 (2016)

4. Feng, B., et al.: HetNet: a flexible architecture for heterogeneous satellite-terrestrial networks. IEEE Netw. **31**(6), 86–92 (2017)

5. Li, T., Zhou, H., Luo, H., You, I., Xu, Q.: SAT-FLOW: multi-strategy flow table management for software defined satellite networks. IEEE Access **5**, 14952–14965 (2017)

6. Boero, L., Marchese, M., Patrone, F.: The impact of delay in software-defined integrated terrestrial-satellite networks. China Commun. **15**(8), 11–21 (2018)

7. Liu, J., Shi, Y., Zhao, L., Cao, Y., Sun, W., Kato, N.: Joint placement of controllers and gateways in SDN-enabled 5G-satellite integrated network. IEEE J. Sel. Areas Commun. **36**(2), 221–232 (2018)

8. Huang, H., Guo, S., Wang, K.: Envisioned wireless big data storage for low-earth-orbit satellite-based cloud. IEEE Wirel. Commun. **25**(1), 26–31 (2018)

9. He, T.Y., Zhao, N., Yin, H.: Integrated networking, caching and computing for connected vehicles: a deep reinforcement learning approach. IEEE Trans. Veh. Technol. (2017)

10. Mnih, V., et al.: Human-level control through deep reinforcement learning. Nature **518**(7540), 529 (2015)

11. Chilimbi, T.M., Suzue, Y., Apacible, J., Kalyanaraman, K.: Project adam: building an efficient and scalable deep learning training system. In: OSDI, vol. 14, pp. 571–582 (2014)

Adaptive Compressed Wideband Spectrum Sensing Based on Radio Environment Map Dedicated for Space Information Networks

Xiaoluan Zhang[1,2], Youping Zhao[1(✉)], and Hongbin Chen[3]

[1] School of Electronic and Information Engineering,
Beijing Jiaotong University, Beijing 100044, China
{xiaoluan_zh,yozhao}@bjtu.edu.cn
[2] Central Radio & TV Tower, National Radio and TV Administration,
Beijing 100142, China
[3] School of Information and Communication,
Guilin University of Electronic Technology, Guilin 541004, China
chbscut@guet.edu.cn

Abstract. Spectrum sensing is the basis of dynamic spectrum access and sharing for space information networks consisting of various satellite and terrestrial networks. The traditional spectrum sensing method, guided by the Nyquist-Shannon sampling theorem, might not be suitable for the emerging communication systems such as the fifth-generation mobile communications (5G) and space information networks utilizing spectrum from sub-6 GHz up to 100 GHz to offer ubiquitous broadband applications. In contrast, compressed spectrum sensing can not only relax the requirements on hardware and software, but also reduce the energy consumption and processing latency. As for the compressed measurement (low-speed sampling) process of the existing compressed spectrum sensing algorithms, the compression ratio is usually set to a fixed value, which limits their adaptability to the dynamically changing radio environment with different sparseness. In this paper, an adaptive compressed spectrum sensing algorithm based on radio environment map (REM) dedicated for space information networks is proposed to address this problem. Simulations show that the proposed algorithm has better adaptability to the varying environment than the existing compressed spectrum sensing algorithms.

Keywords: 5G · Dynamic spectrum access · Compressed spectrum sensing · Radio environment map (REM) · Space information network

1 Introduction

1.1 Background

Terrestrial wireless networks have evolved into the Internet of Things (IoTs) paradigm, in which different terrestrial wireless networks will be integrated and millions of objects will be connected. In addition, satellite networks support more connections from the space, which cannot be solely supported by terrestrial wireless networks. Terrestrial wireless networks and satellite networks will be integrated into space

M. Jia et al. (Eds.): WiSATS 2019, LNICST 280, pp. 128–138, 2019.
https://doi.org/10.1007/978-3-030-19153-5_12

information networks to provide ubiquitous coverage, massive connectivity, and enhanced capacity. Though satellite-terrestrial networks offer many advantages over terrestrial wireless networks, the topology and radio environment are much more complicated with high dynamics, making the efficient resource allocation extremely difficult. Furthermore, dynamic resource scheduling and efficient cooperative transmission are critical problems for space information networks, particularly, the sparse representation and fusion processing of massive data obtained by multiple platforms with heterogeneous sensors [1]. In the past decades, cognitive radio has been introduced as a new paradigm for enabling much higher spectrum utilization efficiency, providing more reliable and personal radio services, reducing harmful interference, and facilitating the interoperability or convergence of different wireless communication networks such as various satellite and terrestrial communication networks. Cognitive radios are goal-oriented, autonomously learn from experience and adapt to changing operating conditions [17, 18]. Cognitive radios have the potential to drive the next generation of radio devices and wireless communication system design and to enable a variety of niche applications in demanding environments such as dynamic spectrum access and sharing for unmanned aircraft systems [16] and integrated space and terrestrial networks.

Along with the rapid increase of wireless communication applications, available radio spectrum becomes a limiting factor mainly due to fairly low utilization and out-of-date regulations. By sensing spectrum holes, secondary users (SUs) can make use of them to realize the communication without generating harmful interference to primary users (PUs). Cognitive radio technology has changed the traditional fixed allocation mode of spectrum resources, thus improving the spectrum utilization efficiency. Spectrum sensing, as the key step of cognitive radio, is the basis of dynamic spectrum access and sharing for the integrated space and terrestrial networks. In the context of evolution towards the fifth-generation mobile communications (5G) which cover spectrum from sub-6 GHz up to 100 GHz, wireless communication employs even broader channel bandwidth at even higher frequency band than ever before, which also results in higher requirements on both hardware and software. The wider frequency band SUs can sense at a time with less scanning time, the more chance to find and use the spectrum holes to realize the communication tasks. As showed in Fig. 1, to achieve the above aim, SUs need a wideband antenna, a wideband radio frequency (RF) front-end, and a high speed analog-to-digital converter (ADC), and a powerful signal processor as well.

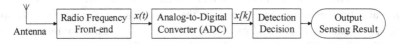

Fig. 1. Traditional spectrum sensing

The wideband antenna and the wideband filter were well developed [2]. By contrast, the most challenge module is the high-speed ADC. According to the Nyquist-Shannon sampling theorem, the sampling frequency must be at least twice the highest frequency of the signal. In the context of evolution towards high-speed and broadband, wireless communication works at a frequency from several hundred MHz to dozens of GHz, that means a high demand for the sampling rate of ADC, usually more than several GHz. So far the achievable sampling rate of the state-of-the-art ADC is only 6.4 GSPS [3]. And usually the higher sampling rate of ADC, the greater power it will consume. For spectrum sensing conducted by SUs, the most important thing which we care most is simply to find the available spectrum holes. For SUs, it is not necessary to take care of the detail of the spectrum resources which are utilized but the spectrum holes. Data we acquired through the Nyquist-Shannon sampling usually contains massive redundancies we do not need or do not care about. "Why go to so much effort to acquire all the data when most of what we get will be thrown away? Can not we just directly measure the part that will not end up being thrown away?" Donoho asked this question in his paper [4].

1.2   Related Work

Donoho, Candès and Tao proved that sparse signal may be reconstructed with even fewer samples than the Nyquist-Shannon sampling theorem requires which is the basis of compressed sensing (CS) [4, 5]. CS offers a joint compression- and sensing-processes, based on the existence of a sparse representation of the treated signal and a set of projected measurements [6]. Tian and Giannakis introduced CS into spectrum sensing field firstly [7]. And Polo and others proposed a hardware structure called analog-to-information converter (AIC) to replace the ADC in spectrum sensing [8]. Compressed spectrum sensing has become matured gradually. However, in the compressed measurement (low-speed sampling) process of the existing general compressed spectrum sensing algorithms, the compression ratio is set to a fixed value, which limits their adaptability to the radio environment with different sparseness.

Radio Environment Map (REM) has been introduced as a vehicle of network support to cognitive radios, which is basically an integrated database that provides multi-domain environmental information and prior knowledge for cognitive radios, such as the geographical features, available services and networks, spectral regulations, locations and activities of neighboring radios, policies of the users and/or service providers, and past experience [10, 13]. The REM can be exploited by the cognitive engine for most cognitive functionalities, such as situation awareness, reasoning, learning, planning, and decision support. In recent years, REM has been viewed as "enabler for practical cognitive radio networks" [19]. As an example, REM has been developed for the cognitive wireless regional area networks (IEEE 802.22), especially from the perspective of interference management and radio resource management [14]. REM has also been exploited to compensate the dynamically changing Doppler spread for high-speed railway broadband mobile communications [15]. Coordinated resource allocation based on REM was proposed to support satellite-terrestrial coexistence [12].

1.3   Contribution

In this paper, an adaptive compressed spectrum sensing algorithm based on REM for space information networks (REM-SIN) is proposed, which has better adaptability to the dynamically changing radio environment with different sparseness. Simulation results demonstrate that the proposed algorithm has a better adaptability to the channel environment with different sparseness than the existing general compressed spectrum sensing algorithms.

1.4 Organization

The remainder of this paper is organized as follows: In Sect. 2, we introduce compressed sensing and general compressed spectrum sensing algorithm at first. Then an adaptive compressed spectrum sensing algorithm is proposed based on REM-SIN. In Sect. 3, the adaptive algorithm is simulated with MATLAB. At last, the conclusion is drawn in Sect. 4.

2 System Model

2.1 Compressed Sensing

For a signal x, if it can be expressed as $x = \Psi s$ and many elements of N-dimensional vector s is zero or close to zero, we call x is sparse or compressible. And we call Ψ sparse projection matrix.

Using an $M \times N$ matrix called measurement matrix Φ, we can measure the sparse signal x as shown by Eq. 1. And we can use the M-dimensional vector y to reconstruct the signal x via some reconstruction algorithm. That is the core of compressed sensing.

$$y = \Phi x = \Phi \Psi s \qquad (1)$$

Suppose that the maximum frequency of x is f_M and the time window for sensing is $t \in [0, NT_0]$, where T_0 is the Nyquist-Shannon sampling interval, $T_0 = \frac{1}{2f_M}$. The process of converting an analog signal to a digital signal can be expressed in the discrete-time domain as shown by Eq. 2:

$$x_t = S r_t \qquad (2)$$

where S is an $K \times N$ projection matrix and r_t is a N-dimensional vector and acquired by Nyquist-Shannon sampling, $r_t[n] = x(t)|t = nT_0, n = 1, \ldots, N$. Rows $\{S_k\}_{k=1}^{K}$ of S can be viewed as a set of basis signals or matched filters [7], while the measurements $\{x_t[k]\}_{k=1}^{K}$ are in essence the projection of $x(t)$ onto the basis. If S is the identity matrix of size-N, Eq. 2 represents Nyquist-Shannon sampling. And if $K < N$, Eq. 2 represents compressed sampling.

Compressed sensing supposes that x is sparse or compressible. So we can use the measurements $x_t[k]$ and the projection matrix S to reconstruct the signal r_t and $x(t)$ via solving the Eq. 3:

$$\hat{r}_t = \arg \min_{r_t \in \Re^N} ||r_t||_0, \text{ subject to } x_t = S r_t \qquad (3)$$

Equation 3 is a non-deterministic polynomial-time hard (NP-hard) problem. So we usually use an approximate Eq. 4 to replace Eq. 3 and convert the NP-hard problem to a convex optimization problem. In some sense, Eq. 4 is the 'closest' convex optimization problem to Eq. 3 [9]. More explicitly, when the projection matrix S satisfies the $(2k, \delta_{2k})$-Restricted Isometry Property (RIP) and $0 < \delta_{2k} < \sqrt{2} - 1$, the solution to Eq. 4 is the same as the solution to Eq. 3 [20]. And the (k, δ_k)-RIP property is defined by (5) below.

$$\hat{r}_t = \arg \min_{r_t \in \mathfrak{R}^N} ||r_t||_1, \text{ subject to } x_t = S r_t \tag{4}$$

$$(1 - \delta_k)||x||_2^2 \leq ||S_T x||_2^2 \leq (1 + \delta_k)||x||_2^2 \tag{5}$$

Note that in (5), $x \in \mathfrak{R}^{|T|}$, $||x||_2^2 = \sum_i x_i^2$, $\delta_k \in (0, 1)$, and k is a constant; $T \subset \{1, 2, \ldots, N\}, |T| \leq k$; S_T is a submatrix of S, and S_T is composed of columns of S as indicated by index T; and $|.|$ represents the number of elements in a set. Equation 4 is a convex optimization problem. There are many solutions, such as the basis pursuit (a kind of linear programming algorithms) [21] and orthogonal matching pursuit (a kind of greedy algorithms) [22].

2.2 General Compressed Spectrum Sensing

Since Tian and Giannakis introduced compressed sensing for wideband cognitive radios [7], scholars have made a lot of further investigations. The framework of general compressed spectrum sensing algorithms is shown in Fig. 2.

Fig. 2. General compressed spectrum sensing

For spectrum sensing, SUs use antenna and radio frequency front-end to receive a wideband analog signal $x(t)$ whose maximum frequency is f_M Hz. Under the guidance of the measurement matrix, we use AIC to compress the analog signal $x(t)$ into the digital signal $y[k]$. Even the AIC's sampling rate is lower than $2f_M$ (Nyquist-Shannon sampling rate), we still can use $y[k]$ to reconstruct $x(t)$' digital form $x[k]$ by related algorithms. Using the digital signal $x[k]$, SUs can make detection decision and finish the spectrum sensing. That is the main process of general compressed spectrum sensing algorithms.

In compressed measurement (low-speed sampling) process of compressed spectrum sensing algorithms, AIC samples and transforms the analog signal $x(t)$ into the digital signal $y[k]$ with sampling rate which is lower than Nyquist-Shannon sampling rate and makes the signal can be reconstructed. Generally speaking, the more measurements, the more accuracy reconstructed signal has which makes the sensing result more accurate. However, more measurements needs higher sampling rate which means more data is produced.

We define the compression ratio as a parameter which controls the number of measurements. Specifically, the compression ratio is defined by

$$\rho = k/2f_M \tag{6}$$

where k is the length of $y[k]$ and equals to the number of rows of measurement matrix, and $2f_M$ is the Nyquist-Shannon sampling rate of $x(t)$.

The sparser the signal is, the less measurements it needs when reconstructing the signal. For the existing compressed spectrum sensing algorithms, the compression ratio is usually set to a fixed value. Therefore, their adaptability to the channel environment with different sparseness is fairly limited.

2.3 Adaptive Compressed Spectrum Sensing

To solve the problem that the adaptability to the channel environment with different sparseness of general compressed spectrum sensing algorithms is not strong, we propose a new adaptive compressed spectrum sensing algorithm, which is based on radio environment map dedicated for space information networks (REM-SIN). Its framework is shown in Fig. 3.

Under the guidance of the measurement matrix and the check matrix, we use AIC to compressed measure (sample) the analog signal $x(t)$ to get the digital signal $y[k]$ and $y'_1[k]$. In the subsequent steps, $y[k]$ is used to reconstruct the digital signal $x[k]$. Corresponds to the progress of getting $y'_1[k]$, we use the check matrix to compressed measure (sample) $x[k]$ to get the digital signal $y'_2[k]$. We call $y'_1[k]$ and $y'_2[k]$ the check sequence.

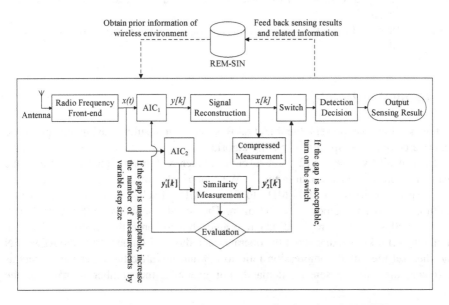

Fig. 3. Adaptive compressed spectrum sensing based on REM-SIN

Because $x(t)$ is unknown to us, we do not know how similar the reconstructed signal $x[k]$ to $x'[k]$ is ($x'[k]$ is a digital signal sampled at Nyquist-Shannon sampling rate from $x(t)$). That is to say, we cannot evaluate or ensure the sensing result's accuracy.

Inspired by cross validation, we can use the similarity between $y'_1[k]$ and $y'_2[k]$ to evaluate the similarity between $x[k]$ and $x'[k]$, and evaluate the sensing result's accuracy in the end. As we have known how accurate the sensing result is, we can adjust the compression ratio and repeat the sensing again when the sensing result's error is unacceptable.

If we have known the prior knowledge of radio environment, we can set an initial compression ratio and other parameters to accelerate the adaptive process of compressed sensing.

The adaptive compressed spectrum sensing algorithm based on REM-SIN is detailed as follows:

Step 1: PUs obtain the prior knowledge of radio environment from the REM-SIN and combine with the sensing demand, then set the initial compression ratio and other parameters, and then create the measurement matrix and the check matrix.

Step 2: PUs receive $x(t)$ and use AIC to compressed measure (sample) $x(t)$ to get $y[k]$ and $y'_1[k]$ under the guidance of the measurement matrix and the check matrix.

Step 3: PUs use $y[k]$ to reconstruct $x[k]$ and use the check matrix to compressed measure (sample) $x[k]$ to get $y'_2[k]$.

Step 4: PUs measure the similarity between $y'_1[k]$ and $y'_2[k]$ to evaluate the reconstruction and sensing result's accuracy. If the gap between $y'_1[k]$ and $y'_2[k]$ is unacceptable, increase the number of measurements by variable step size and return step 2. Else, use the reconstruction result $x[k]$ to spectrum sensing.

Step 5: PUs feed back the sensing result and other related information to the REM-SIN.

3   Simulation Results

In this section, we present the MATLAB simulation resulting using the proposed adaptive compressed spectrum sensing algorithm.

First of all, we use a 512-point discrete-frequency-domain signal to simulate the channel environment as shown in Fig. 4. We suppose that there are 4 wideband signals in the spectrum between 4900 MHz to 5102.4 MHz. Each wideband signal's bandwidth is 6 MHz and its power is −83 dBm. The signal-to-noise ratio (SNR) is 20 dB.

Then, SUs use the proposed adaptive algorithm to sense the spectrum. SUs can obtain the prior knowledge about the operational radio environment from the REM-SIN and then set the initial compression ratio to 0.3 and initialize the other parameters as well according to the sensing demand. For example, the number of rows of the measurement matrix and check matrix are initially set to 150 and 40, respectively; the step size for both long step and small step are set to 40 and 10, respectively; the threshold Euclidean distance between $y'_1[k]$ and $y'_2[k]$ is preset as 4×10^{-12}. The reconstruction algorithm employed in our simulation is the sparsity adaptive matching pursuit (SAMP) [11].

We can choose many statistics to measure the similarity between $y'_1[k]$ and $y'_2[k]$ like Euclidean distance, Minkowski distance, vector cosine angle, and so on. In this simulation, we choose Euclidean distance to measure the similarity between $y'_1[k]$ and $y'_2[k]$. The true value of error we defined is the Euclidean distance between $x[k]$ and $x'[k]$. And we call the Euclidean distance between $y'_1[k]$ and $y'_2[k]$ the alternative value of error. Figure 5 show that two kind values of error have the same variation trend with the row number of measurement matrix with a high probability.

When the Euclidean distance between $y'_1[k]$ and $y'_2[k]$ is greater than 1×10^{-11}, we deem that there is a great disparity between $x[k]$ and $x'[k]$, and increase the number of rows of measurement matrix with a large step, then repeat the compressed sensing. When the Euclidean distance between $y'_1[k]$ and $y'_2[k]$ is greater than 4×10^{-12}, it indicates there is a small disparity between $x[k]$ and $x'[k]$, and increase the row number of measurement matrix with a small step, then repeat the compressed sensing. When the Euclidean distance between $y'_1[k]$ and $y'_2[k]$ is less than 4×10^{-12}, the disparity between $x[k]$ and $x'[k]$ can be ignored, and then the reconstruction result $x[k]$ is used for spectrum sensing.

The spectrum sensing results are shown in Figs. 6 and 7. Note that it is assumed that when the received signal power is lower than −90 dBm, the channel is idle.

The simulation results show that by using the proposed adaptive algorithm, the compression ratio can be adjusted according to the channel environment so as to get accurate sensing results efficiently.

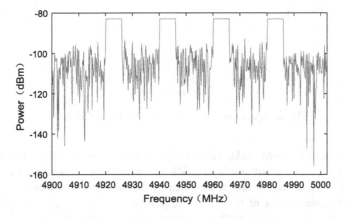

Fig. 4. Simulated channel environment

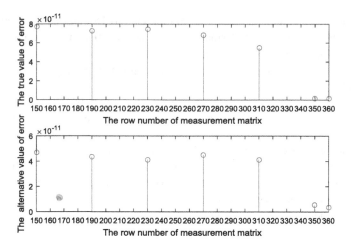

Fig. 5. Error's variation with the row number of measurement matrix

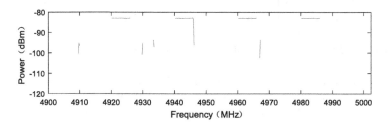

Fig. 6. Spectrum sensing results

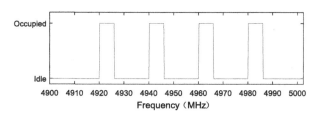

Fig. 7. Spectrum sensing results after binary decision

Figure 8 show the area under curve (AUC) value of the receiver operating characteristic (ROC) curve when employing different number of rows of the measurement matrix. As for the detection and false alarm performance, our proposed algorithm is basically the same as that of the SAMP algorithm. The advantage of our proposed algorithm is that it can evaluate the spectrum sensing results automatically and then make adjustment adaptively. In this way, there is no need to accurately estimate the spectrum sparsity of radio environment, which is essential yet challenging for the traditional compressed spectrum sensing algorithms.

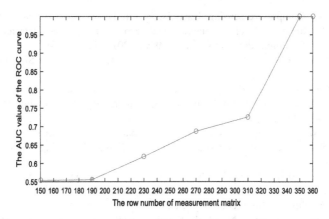

Fig. 8. Area under curve (AUC) value of the receiver operating characteristic (ROC) curve vs. the number of rows of the measurement matrix

4 Concluding Remarks

With the development of integrated satellite-terrestrial networks utilizing spectrum from sub-6 GHz up to 100 GHz to offer ubiquitous broadband applications, the topology and radio scenarios will become much more complicated with extremely wide radio spectrum to be shared. Accordingly, it is important to make compressed spectrum sensing more efficiently and adaptively to the dynamically changing radio environment. In this paper, an adaptive compressed spectrum sensing algorithm is proposed, which is based on REM dedicated for space information networks (REM-SIN) to improve the adaptability of compressed spectrum sensing algorithms to the channel environment with different sparseness. The simulation results show that by using the proposed algorithm, the compression ratio can be adjusted adaptively according to the channel environment and get accurate sensing results efficiently. For future work, it is worthwhile to analyze the impact of many practical factors (such as mobility of satellites and weather condition) on the spectrum sensing results and construct the REM-SIN for various applications.

Acknowledgments. This work is supported in part by the Beijing Natural Science Foundation (4172046) and the Key Laboratory of Cognitive Radio and Information Processing, Ministry of Education (Guilin University of Electronic Technology, CRKL150203).

References

1. Yu, Q., Wang, J., Bai, L.: Architecture and critical technologies of space information networks. J. Commun. Inf. Netw. **1**(3), 1–9 (2016)
2. Sun, H., Chiu, W.Y., et al.: Adaptive compressed spectrum sensing for wideband cognitive radios. IEEE Commun. Lett. **16**(11), 1812–1815 (2013)
3. ADC12DJ3200 12-Bit, Dual 3.2-GSPS or Single 6.4-GSPS, RF-sampling analog-to-digital converter (ADC). http://www.ti.com/product/ADC12DJ3200. Accessed 07 Oct 2018

138   X. Zhang et al.

4. Donoho, D.L.: Compressed sensing. IEEE Trans. Inf. Theory **52**(4), 1289–1306 (2006)
5. Candès, E.J., Romberg, J., et al.: Stable signal recovery from incomplete and inaccurate measurements. Commun. Pure Appl. Math. **59**(8), 1207–1223 (2006)
6. Elad, M.: Optimized projections for compressed sensing. IEEE Trans. Signal Process. **55** (12), 5695–5702 (2006)
7. Tian, Z., Giannakis, G.B.: Compressed sensing for wideband cognitive radios. In: 2007 IEEE International Conference on Acoustics, Speech and Signal Processing, Honolulu, HI, pp. IV-1357–IV-1360 (2007)
8. Polo, Y.L., Wang, Y., et al.: Compressive wide-band spectrum sensing. In: 2009 IEEE International Conference on Acoustics, Speech and Signal Processing, Taipei, pp. 2337–2340 (2009)
9. Donoho, D.L., Elad, M.: Optimally sparse representation in general (nonorthogonal) dictionaries via $\ell1$ minimization. Proc. Natl. Acad. Sci. U.S.A. **100**(5), 2197–2202 (2003)
10. Fette, B.: Cognitive Radio Technology. Elsevier (2006)
11. Do, T.T., Gan, L., Nguyen, N., et al.: Sparsity adaptive matching pursuit algorithm for practical compressed sensing. In: 42nd Asilomar Conference on Signals, Systems and Computers, Pacific Grove, CA, pp. 581–587 (2009)
12. Wang, Y., Lu, Z.: Coordinated resource allocation for satellite-terrestrial coexistence based on radio maps. China Commun. **15**(3), 149–156 (2018)
13. Zhao, Y., Le, B., Reed, J.H.: Network support – the radio environment map. In: Fette, B. (ed.) Cognitive Radio Technology, chap. 11, pp. 337–363. Elsevier (2006)
14. Zhao, Y., Morales, L., Gaeddert, J., Bae, K.K., Um, J., Reed, J.H.: Applying radio environment map to cognitive wireless regional area networks. In: Proceedings of the Second IEEE International Symposium on Dynamic Spectrum Access Networks (DySPAN 2007), Dublin, Ireland, pp. 115–118 (2007)
15. Li, J., Zhao, Y.: Radio environment map-based cognitive Doppler spread compensation algorithms for high-speed rail broadband mobile communications. EURASIP J. Wirel. Commun. Netw. **1**, 1–18 (2012). https://doi.org/10.1186/1687-1499-2012-263
16. McHenry, M., Zhao, Y., Haddadin, O.: Dynamic spectrum access radio performance for UAS ISR missions. In: Proceedings of IEEE MILCOM 2010, San Jose, California, pp. 2446–2451 (2010)
17. Mitola III, J., Maguire Jr., G.Q.: Cognitive radio: making software radios more personal. IEEE Pers. Commun. **6**(4), 13–18 (1999)
18. Haykin, S.: Cognitive radio: brain-empowered wireless communications. IEEE J. Sel. Areas Commun. **23**(2), 201–220 (2005)
19. Yilmaz, H.B., Tugcu, T., Alagöz, F., Bayhan, S.: Radio environment map as enabler for practical cognitive radio networks. IEEE Commun. Mag. **51**(12), 162–169 (2013)
20. Candès, E.J.: The restricted isometry property and its implications for compressed sensing. C.R. Math. **346**(9–10), 589–592 (2008)
21. Chen, S.S., Donoho, D.L., Saunders, M.A.: Atomic decomposition by basis pursuit. SIAM Rev. **43**(1), 129–159 (2001)
22. Cai, T.T., Wang, L.: Orthogonal matching pursuit for sparse signal recovery with noise. IEEE Trans. Inf. Theory **57**(7), 4680–4688 (2011)

International Workshop
on Human-Machine Interactive Sensing,
Monitoring, and Communications
(HiSMC)

An Adaptive Fingerprint Database Updating Scheme for Indoor Bluetooth Positioning

Haifeng Cong$^{(\boxtimes)}$, Liangbo Xie, and Mu Zhou

School of Communications and Information Engineering,
Chongqing University of Posts and Telecommunications, Chongqing, China
1034188564@qq.com

Abstract. The accuracy of fingerprint based Bluetooth positioning technology depends on the fingerprint database established in offline phase. However, the change of environment and Access Point (AP) locations has significant impact on wireless signal distribution, resulting a decline in indoor Bluetooth positioning accuracy. In order to solve this problem, this paper presents a fingerprint database updating algorithm. Firstly, RSSI sequence, head, and speed information are extracted from crowdsourcing date. Secondly, the extracted information is used in Pedestrian Dead Reckoning Modification (PDRM) algorithm to get candidate fingerprint. Finally, we propose concepts of standard fingerprint, negative exponential time model, and similarity filtering to update original fingerprint database. The experimental results show that after the proposed fingerprint database updating, fingerprint database positioning accuracy is improved by 0.5 m.

Keywords: Indoor positioning · PDRM · Crowdsourcing ·
Fingerprint database updating · Bluetooth

1 Introduction

With rapid development of mobile computing, communication network brings a strong impetus for personal Position information service. Therefore, the Location-Based Service (LBS) receives extensive attention. At present, the Global Navigation Satellite System (GNSS) can basically meet the demand of outdoor positioning accuracy. However, satellite signals are easily shielded and have serious multipath effects inside a building, which make GNSS positioning accuracy descend. In response to this phenomenon, many research institutes have proposed a variety of indoor localization systems, including BLE [1], Wireless Local Area Network (WLAN) [2], Radio Frequency Identification (RFID) [3], MEMS sensors [4], Ultra Wideband (UWB) [5].

Some factors such as universality and robustness limit the development of traditional positioning technologies. BLE fingerprint positioning technology has

© ICST Institute for Computer Sciences, Social Informatics and Telecommunications Engineering 2019
Published by Springer Nature Switzerland AG 2019. All Rights Reserved
M. Jia et al. (Eds.): WiSATS 2019, LNICST 280, pp. 141–150, 2019.
https://doi.org/10.1007/978-3-030-19153-5_13

the advantages of low power consumption, low cost and long-term high accuracy. In indoor environment, wireless signal propagation environment is constantly changing, so fingerprint database needs regular updating. Traditional fingerprint database update means require professionals to periodically re-collect fingerprint data to update fingerprint database, which is inefficient [6].

The remainder of paper is organized as follows. Section 2 reviews several methods of fingerprint database updating. Section 3 describes the proposed fingerprint database updating framework. Section 4 shows experimental results. Finally, conclusion is provided in Sect. 5.

2 Related Work

In recent years, in order to maintain the stability of fingerprint positioning accuracy, fingerprint database adaptive updating technology has received widespread attention. The authors [7] proposed a completely user-independent fingerprint database updating method, providing an interactive interface for users to actively participate in fingerprint database updating, almost no Professionals are involved in updating fingerprint database, but for larger indoor environments, users are frequently bothered when they first start using the system, which increases the user's burden. The authors [8] proposed a method that does not require prior mapping. Users sensor information can be used to complete the fingerprint database updating process, with the help of inertial sensor in mobile phone and PDR algorithm. However, it is difficult to obtain pedestrian steps and heading information accurately. And current position calculation depends on historical location information of target, which leads to positioning cumulative errors and poor long-time positioning accuracy. Therefore, choosing PDR algorithm as an updating means will inevitably lead an error to updating, and even reduces positioning accuracy. The authors [9] explored indoor plan thoroughly by digging out path information, so as to judge the position of user's moving track in a specific shape on indoor map to realize the fingerprint database updating. However, due to the complexity of indoor environment, there is a certain probability of identifying wrong the location where the user trajectory appears, and this will have a negative impact on fingerprint database updating.

In view of these problems, this paper proposes a fingerprint database adaptive updating method based on crowdsourcing [10]. In positioning phase, users will gradually accumulate a large number of positioning data, and the fingerprint database may be adaptively updated by the data to avoid the high investment caused by the participate of professionals, which improves the universality of fingerprint localization technology, with good engineering application prospects.

3 Algorithm Description

3.1 Algorithm Overview

The overall system framework is shown in Fig. 1, including data preprocessing module and fingerprint database updating module. Firstly, the data of users

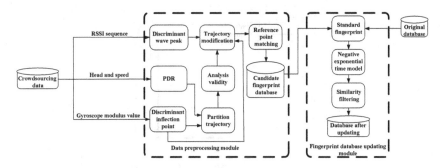

Fig. 1. Framework of fingerprint database updating.

is uploaded to server, which mainly includes Micro Electro Mechanical System (MEMS) and Bluetooth Low Energy (BLE) information. Then, RSSI sequence is extracted to identify AP position beacon by RSSI peak. At the same time, we use corner determination with map information to identify corner position beacon. Then, the AP and corner beacons geographical coordinate information are used to correct PDR trajectory in process of positioning, so as to eliminate accumulated error in positioning information, and generate candidate fingerprint data according to corrected position coordinates of PDR track with corresponding RSSI. Finally, fingerprint database updating is completed based on standard fingerprint, negative exponential time model and similarity filtering.

3.2 Data Preprocessing

Pedestrian Dead Reckoning. PDR algorithm is a kind of algorithm that uses MEMS information to estimate user's speed and head, and deduces user's position. However, most existing smartphones use inexpensive builtin sensors, speed and head obtained from sensor information contains error. Errors will accumulate over time with iteration of PDR algorithm, eventually track will gradually deviate from real track. Figure 2 shows PDR experimental trajectory, red trajectory is result of PDR algorithm and black solid line is real walking trajectory. As we can see from Fig. 2, it is unreliable to use PDR directly to deduce coordinates of each point in moving process as coordinates of fingerprint, so a correction method is proposed to correct PDR trajectory later in this paper.

Trajectories Modification. The signal propagation model is shown in (1), the farther the smart phone is from AP, the weaker the RSSI is. The RSSI is the highest when smartphone is just below AP.

$$RSSI = -(10n \log d + A) \tag{1}$$

where A is RSSI at a distance of 1 m from AP, d is distance from AP, and n is value trained on the measured data.

Therefore, based on time when AP's RSSI peak appears, it is possible to recognize that user has passed AP at that moment. Figure 3 shows RSSI trend

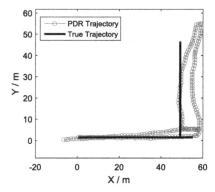

Fig. 2. PDR and true trajectories. (Color figure online)

in a certain test track. When a user passes an AP, peak must be greater than the threshold $RSSI_{min}$ and since it is impossible for user to continuously pass through same AP in a relatively short period of time, peak occurrence interval must be greater than threshold T_{min}. In summary, the time of pedestrian passing AP can be identified by peak discrimination, AP coordinates at this time can be regarded as current position of user, and it is called RSSI peak beacon in this paper.

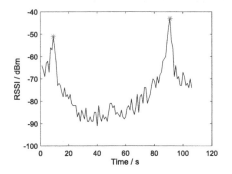

Fig. 3. The RSSI trend of AP.

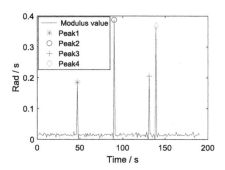

Fig. 4. Gyroscope modulus value.

The other type of beacon proposed in this paper is called corner beacon. Firstly, calculate total modulus of 3-axis gyroscope. Secondly, turning behavior of users can be discriminated according to change of modulus of gyroscope. Figure 4 shows change of gyroscope modulus value of a certain trajectory. When user moves forward gently, modulus value of gyroscope fluctuates slightly from a small value to a small value, and once the pedestrian makes a turning behavior, gyroscope modulus value will change suddenly, the bigger the angle of gyration is, the bigger the variation of modulus of gyroscope is. Finally, RSSI information, which at specific time of user's turning, are matched with RSSI information collected from different corner to determine the corner that pedestrian is passing through. The coordinates of that corner can be used as current position of pedestrian, which is called corner beacon.

After completing beacon recognition, we can segment PDR trajectory according to time of turning beacons, segmenting large segments into small straight lines, which is convenient for subsequent effectiveness identification and trajectory correction. Trajectory shows in Fig. 5 are segmented into five segments, different colors and symbols represent different trajectory after segmentation.

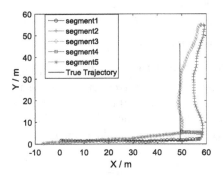 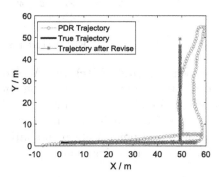

Fig. 5. Trajectories after segmentation. (Color figure online)   **Fig. 6.** Trajectory modification.

In this paper, RSSI peak beacon and corner beacon are used to correct PDR trajectory and reduce the cumulative error, so as to improve the accuracy of coordinate estimation of each candidate fingerprint data. The i-th point coordinates correction manner is shown in (2).

$$
\begin{cases}
x_i = x_0 + \sum_{n=1}^{i} v_n * \sin(\theta_n) + \sum_{n=1}^{i} \varepsilon_{xn} \\
y_i = y_0 + \sum_{n=1}^{i} v_n * \cos(\theta_n) + \sum_{n=1}^{i} \varepsilon_{yn} \\
\varepsilon_{xi} = \frac{v_i \sin(\theta_i)}{\sum v_i \sin(\theta_i)} (L \sin(\psi_1) - L_{PDR} \sin(\psi_2)) \\
\varepsilon_{yi} = \frac{v_i \cos(\theta_i)}{\sum v_i \cos(\theta_i)} (L \cos(\psi_1) - L_{PDR} \cos(\psi_2))
\end{cases}
\tag{2}
$$

where v_n and θ_n denote velocity and angle information at time n respectively; ε_{xi} and ε_{yi} are error compensation in X and Y directions respectively. L is real trajectory length and $L_{PDR} = \sum_{i=1}^{N} v_i$ is trajectory length deduced by PDR algorithm. ψ_1 is the angle between latter beacon coordinate (x_{end}, y_{end}) and previous beacon coordinate (x_0, y_0); ψ_2 is the angle between PDR estimated end coordinate (x_{PDR}, y_{PDR}) and starting coordinate (x_0, y_0). Figure 6 shows comparison between original PDR trajectory, modified trajectory and real trajectory. Modified trajectory in Fig. 6 is more suitable for real trajectory.

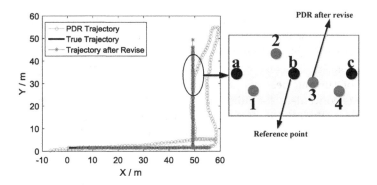

Fig. 7. Reference point matching.

Reference Point Matching. According to modified PDR results, geographic coordinates are extracted and combined with RSSI at corresponding time to generate candidate fingerprint data. The approach of matching reference points is shown in Fig. 7, point a, point b and point c are reference points. Point 1, point 2, point 3 and point 4 are points after PDR result revised by beacon. Formula (3) is specific matching manner.

$$(x_{RF}, y_{RF}) = \arg\min(\sqrt{(x - x_{RF})^2 + (y - y_{RF})^2}) \tag{3}$$

where x_{RF} and y_{RF} are reference point coordinates, x and y are coordinates of revised PDR result. By matching RSSI sequence to corresponding reference point, we can get candidate fingerprint data.

3.3   Fingerprint Database Updating

Standard Fingerprint. After obtaining candidate fingerprint data, the original fingerprint database can be updated by negative exponential time model, standard fingerprint, and similarity filtering updating rules.

First of all, according to candidate fingerprint data and original fingerprint database, we calculate the standard fingerprint. Suppose a reference point which from original fingerprint database already have contained M fingerprint sequences, and the mth fingerprint sequence is

$$S_{\text{original}}^{\text{m}} = \{RSS_{\text{m1}}, RSS_{\text{m2}}, ..., RSS_{\text{mn}}\} \tag{4}$$

At the sametime the same reference point has K candidate fingerprint sequences and the kth fingerprint sequence is

$$S_{\text{candidate}}^{k} = \{RSS_{k1}, RSS_{k2}, ..., RSS_{\text{kn}}\} \tag{5}$$

Then standard fingerprint of the reference point can be defined as (6). Standard fingerprint can be used for similarity calculation with the original fingerprint database and candidate fingerprint to regulate fingerprint data of reference point. Accuracy and stability of fingerprint database can be dynamically maintained by filtering low similarity fingerprint and retaining high similarity fingerprint.

$$S_{\text{standard}} = \frac{\Sigma_{i=1}^{M} S_{\text{original}}^{i} + \Sigma_{i=1}^{K} S_{\text{candidate}}^{i}}{M + K} \tag{6}$$

Negative Exponential Time Model. Then, when the amount of updated data $S_{candidate}$ is small, candidate data has a smaller impact on standard fingerprints in (6). As a result, standard fingerprint is still similar to original fingerprint database and it is difficult to accurately reflect changes in fingerprint database. Therefore, negative exponential time model is introduced to standard fingerprint. Original fingerprint information will gradually reduce its weight and reduce its impact on standard fingerprint. The standard fingerprint is then redefined as (7), where $R(t)$ is negative exponential time model and defined as (8).

$$S_{\text{standard}} = \frac{\Sigma_{i=1}^{M} S_{\text{original}}^{i} \times R(t_i) + \Sigma_{i=1}^{K} S_{\text{candidate}}^{i} \times R(t_i)}{\Sigma_{i=1}^{M} R(t_i) + \Sigma_{i=1}^{K} R(t_i)} \tag{7}$$

$$R(t) = \begin{cases} \exp(-3.725 \times 10^{-6}(t - t_0)) & t - t_0 < days \\ 0 & t - t_0 \geq days \end{cases} \tag{8}$$

Where t is the time when fingerprint data to be updated are collected, t_0 is the time when original fingerprint data are collected.

Similarity Filtering. Finally, fingerprint of same reference point are filtered according to similarity with standard fingerprint, and some fingerprints with low similarities will be filtered. Similarity is related to Euclidean distance of signal strength between fingerprints, defined as (9).

$$Sim_i = (|S_i - S_{\text{standard}}|)^{-1} \tag{9}$$

where $|S_i - S_{\text{standard}}|$ is Euclidean distance of signal strength between candidate fingerprint and standard fingerprint. The larger $|S_i - S_{\text{standard}}|$ is, the smaller similarity is.

4   Performance Evaluation

One floor of a building is selected as experimental environment, plane structure is shown in Fig. 8. This environment is a typical office environment consists of hall, corridor and several office rooms. Experimental environment has a total area of about $65 \times 17 \, \text{m}^2$, of which hall area is about $140 \, \text{m}^2$, corridor area is about $116 \, \text{m}^2$. Small red tower in Fig. 8 is positions of AP. Red linear trajectory distributed area is test area.

Bluetooth AP in experiment is made by TI's CC2540 chip. Millet 4 phone are selected as terminal device, which integrate BLE module, magnetometer, gyroscope, accelerometer, and other sensor modules. Through Bluetooth RSSI and MEMS data acquisition APP under Android 6.0 operating system and Java positioning server, experimental platform can simultaneously detect RSSI and MEMS sensor data from each Bluetooth AP and locate users. APP can upload data to positioning server to complete the fingerprint database updating process.

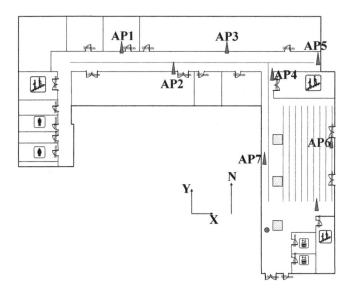

Fig. 8. Physical layout of target environment. (Color figure online)

Project personnel holds smart phones walking in test area at a uniform speed. Updating data is collected for three days and time of collection is 30 min a day. Test data is collected in third day at same place. Figure 9 shows Bluetooth positioning result, black solid line is real test trajectory, green trajectory is result of fingerprint positioning before updating, and red line is result of fingerprint positioning after three times updating. As shown in Fig. 9, after updating fingerprint database, result of positioning is more close to the real trajectory than result of positioning by original fingerprint database.

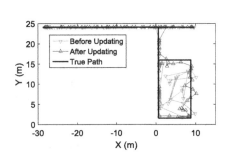
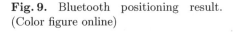
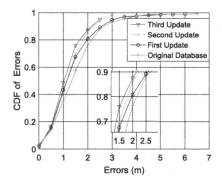

Fig. 9. Bluetooth positioning result. (Color figure online)

Fig. 10. CDFs of positioning errors.

Table 1 shows different percentile localization errors which use original and updated fingerprint database. In addition, Fig. 10 shows localization Cumulative Distribution Function (CDF) of original fingerprint database and after three updating. After three times updating, average positioning accuracy is increased from 1.4 m to 1.1 m, while tailing error is reduced from 6.8 m to 2.5 m.

Table 1. Positioning error under different percentile values

Percentile value	Original database	First update	Second update	Third update
50%	<1.4 m	<1.2 m	<1.2 m	<1.1 m
70%	<1.8 m	<1.6 m	<1.5 m	<1.4 m
90%	<2.7 m	<2.6 m	<2.3 m	<2.2 m

5 Conclusion

Aiming at the problem that fingerprint database needs to be updated due to change of environment in BLE indoor positioning technology, this paper presents an algorithm that uses crowdsourced data to realize adaptive fingerprint database updating. Experimental results show that the proposed algorithm can updating fingerprint database and improve positioning accuracy. At the same time, the proposed algorithm only uses users positioning data to update fingerprint database. Comparing with traditional fingerprint database updating methods which need participation of professionals this methods can reduce labor cost.

Acknowledgment. This work was supported partly by the Scientific and Technological Research Foundation of Chongqing Municipal Education Commission under grant KJ1704083, the National Natural Science Foundation of China under 61704015, the Fundamental and Frontier Research Project of Chongqing under grant cstc2017jcyjAX0380.

References

1. Faragher, R., Harle, R.: Location fingerprinting with bluetooth low energy beacons. IEEE J. Sel. Areas Commun. **33**(11), 2418–2428 (2015)
2. Zhuang, Y., Syed, Z., Li, Y., et al.: Evaluation of two WiFi positioning systems based on autonomous crowd sourcing on handheld devices for indoor navigation. IEEE Trans. Mob. Comput. **15**(8), 1982–1995 (2016)
3. Lu, S., Xu, C., Zhong, R.Y., et al.: A RFID-enabled positioning system in automated guided vehicle for smart factories. J. Manuf. Syst. **44**(1), 179–190 (2017)
4. Abd, R.M., El-Rabbany, A.: Integration of GPS precise point positioning and MEMS-based INS using unscented particle filter. Sensors **15**(4), 7228–7245 (2015)

5. Song, L., Zhang, T., Yu, X., et al.: Scheduling in cooperative UWB localization networks using round trip measurements. IEEE Commun. Lett. **20**(7), 1409–1412 (2016)
6. He, S., Lin, W., Chan, S.H.G.: Indoor localization and automatic fingerprint update with altered AP signals. IEEE Trans. Mob. Comput. **16**(7), 1897–1910 (2017)
7. Park, J.G., Charrow, B., Curtis, D., et al.: Growing an organic indoor location system. In: International Conference on Mobile Systems, Applications, and Services, pp. 271–284. ACM, San Francisco (2010)
8. Huang, J., Millman, D., Quigley, M., et al.: Efficient, generalized indoor WiFi GraphSLAM. In: IEEE International Conference on Robotics and Automation, pp. 1038–1043. IEEE, Shanghai (2011)
9. Kim, D.H., Hightower, J., Govindan, R., et al.: Discovering semantically meaningful places from pervasive RF-beacons. In: UbiComp, pp. 21–30. ACM, Orlando (2009)
10. Luo, H., Zhao, F., Jiang, M., et al.: Constructing an indoor floor plan using crowdsourcing based on magnetic fingerprinting. Sensors **17**(11), 2678–2692 (2017)

Backscatter Signal Blind Detection and Processing for UHF RFID Localization System

Liangbo Xie[✉], Xin Xiong, Qingfei Kang, and Zengshan Tian

School of Communications and Information Engineering,
Chongqing University of Posts and Telecommunications, Chongqing, China
xielb@cqupt.edu.cn

Abstract. Radio frequency identification (RFID) is widely used in many fields and more recently, there has been a continuously growing interest in RFID-based indoor localization. Compared to RSS and AOA based RFID localization algorithms, the carrier phase-based ultra-wideband localization algorithm has better performance. To implement 3D indoor localization with this method, carrier phase of multiple receivers must be obtained in different frequencies. However, existing RFID systems do not meet the requirement. Therefore, this paper proposes a system consisting of a software-defined radio with custom-made RF front-end (SRCF) and ImpinjR420 COTS reader (R420), which can realize data communication between R420 and tags, and achieve the channel coefficient estimation. Moreover, an algorithm is proposed to detect the EPC data backscatter by the tag without any prior information. Experiment results show that the proposed algorithm can correctly decode the EPC data and obtain the channel coefficient information.

Keywords: RFID · SDR · Indoor localization · Signal detection · Carrier phase

1 Introduction

In recent years, RFID-based localization technology is getting more and more attention, especially in the field of virtual reality and factory automation [1], such as warehouse cargo location management, posture detection [2] and other fields. Received signal strength (RSS) [3], angle of arrival (AOA) [4] and carrier phase-based ultra-wideband localization [5], are the most popular RFID localization methods, and carrier phase-based ultra-wideband localization method has better performance than RSS and AOA. The key to carrier phase-based algorithm is how to obtain carrier phase of multiple receivers. Therefore, multiple receivers are needed to receive the data backscattered by tag, as shown in Fig. 1.

M. Jia et al. (Eds.): WiSATS 2019, LNICST 280, pp. 151–159, 2019.
https://doi.org/10.1007/978-3-030-19153-5_14

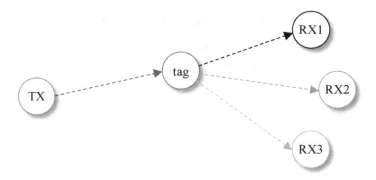

Fig. 1. System structure which is suitable for carrier phase-based ultra-wideband localization algorithm.

At present, we can easily to communicate with tags use a Commercial-Off-The-Shelf (COTS) RFID reader (R420), but the original data cannot be directly obtained and cannot work in ultra-wideband. On the other hand, although physical layer communication between software-defined radio (SDR) and tag at different frequency is implemented [6], but the SDR transmission power is low, and cannot implement a transmitter, multiple receivers, which is not suitable for carrier phase-based localization algorithm.

To solve this problem, this paper proposes a system that uses a R420 to communicate with tag while an SDR with custom-made RF front-end (SRCF) is used to send carrier and receive data backscattered by the tag. When transmitting a high-power signal in ISM and a low-power signal outside ISM the tag is powered up and reflects data both frequencies simultaneously [7]. Thus, if the number of SRCF receivers is enough, the carrier phase of multiple links can be obtained.

The rest of this paper is organized as follows. Section 2 presents the system model when the tag uses FM0 encoding. Section 3 offers signal detection and carrier phase estimation. Section 4 is the experimental results.

2   System Model

When a tag is powered up by R420 at frequency f_1, an SRCF is used to transmit the carrier wave (CW) at frequency f_2. The tag modulates its information on both f_1 and f_2, then reflects, as shown in Fig. 2. In this way, the SRCF receiving antenna will receive four types of signals, directly by SRCF and R420. Due to in different frequencies, we can filter out the signal from the R420 with the frequency f_1, and only the signal with the frequency f_2 is left, but this will leave a small number of harmonic components. The complex baseband equivalent of the received signal at the SDR is [8]:

$$y(t) = [m_{dc} + m_{mod}x(t)]e^{+j2\pi\Delta ft} + z(t) + n(t) \tag{1}$$

Where the DC component m_{dc} is caused by CW and an unmodulated component scattered back by the tag; the modulated m_{mod} component depends on the channel coefficients of the SRCF transmitting antenna-to-tag and tag-to-SRCF receiving antenna links, the tag antenna reflection coefficients, the tag scattering efficiency and the carrier transmitting power, which the channel coefficients are mainly composed of two parts: amplitude and phase. $x(t)$ is a binary real-valued tag scattered waveform; $z(t)$ is the residual harmonic component of the signal with frequency f_1. Δf is the carrier frequency offset (CFO) between CW transmission and SRCF reception chain. $n(t)$ is the complex thermal (receiver) Gaussian noise. The system of this work is based on a local oscillator for both transmission and reception, so $\Delta f = 0$; Because the difference between f_1 and f_2 is much larger than the frequency of returning data from the tag, thus $z(t) = 0$.

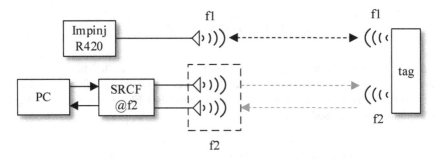

Fig. 2. System structure

3 Signal Detection and Carrier Phase Estimation

3.1 SDR Receive Signal Representation

According to Gen2 [9], in FM0 encoding, level transitions always occur on the bit boundaries. In addition, a level transitions will occur in the middle of the symbol 0, and the symbol 1 will not. Thus, there are 4 waveforms that can be generated per symbol data, as shown in Fig. 3.

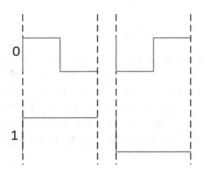

Fig. 3. FM0 symbols

If the starting position of the bit in the received waveform is found and the starting position is shifted back by $T/2$, where T is the bit (symbol) period, only two possible pulse shapes can be generated (instead of four) [10], shown in Fig. 4.

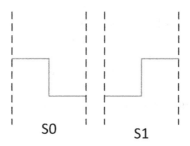

Fig. 4. Tow possible pulse shapes

Finally, differential decoding can be used to detect a transmitted bit.

Assume that the SRCF receiver accurately detects the bit signal reflected by the tag and removes m_{dc} from the received waveform (zero-offset FM0). The received digital signal should be expressed:

$$y[k] = y(kTs) + n(kTs) = hx[k] + n[k], x[k] = \sum_{n=0}^{N} S_{d(n)}[k - nL - \tau] \qquad (2)$$

where $n[k]$ is the sampling of Gaussian white noise; Ts represents the sampling interval, T represents the symbol period, τ represents the delay before tag starts transmitting its information, $L = \frac{T}{Ts}$ represents the number of sampling points of each symbol. $S_{d(n)}$ represents two forms of received waveform:

$$S_0[k] = \begin{cases} 1, if\ 0 \le k < \dfrac{L}{2} \\ 0, if\ \dfrac{L}{2} \le k < L \end{cases}, S_1[k] = \begin{cases} 0, if\ 0 \le k < \dfrac{L}{2} \\ 1, if\ \dfrac{L}{2} \le k < L \end{cases} \qquad (3)$$

3.2   Signal Detection and DC Offset

Since the SDR is always transmitting the carrier wave, it does not know when the received data contains the bit sent by the tag. Therefore, the SRCF needs to detect in real time whether the received data contains bit sequence reflected by the tag. Due to the characteristics of FM0 coding, the amplitude spectrum distribution is similar to the pulse signal with a period T of $T/2$. By analyzing the amplitude spectrum of the received waveform, it can be determined whether the tag modulation information is included [11].

The double-sided band amplitude spectrum of a pulse signal with a period T of $T/2$ can be expressed as:

$$|F_n| = \frac{A}{2}\left|Sa(\frac{nw_0 T}{2})\right| \qquad (4)$$

where $w_0 = \frac{2\pi}{T}$, $F_{\pm 1}$ represents the amplitude of the fundamental component when $n = \pm 1$.

Supposing the SDR receives a sequence $y(n)$ of length M, by performing an N-point FFT transformation on $y(n)$, transformed sequence $Y(k)$ can be expressed as:

$$Y(k) = FFT[y(n)]_N \qquad (5)$$

Because the characteristics of FFT, if the complex sampling rate of the signal is B Hz, the frequency bandwidth represented by $Y(k)$ after the FFT of the N point is B Hz.

By calculating the ratio of the fundamental frequency w_0 and B, the position of the pulse signal in $Y(k)$ can be determined.

$$k_1 = N/2 + k_w, k_2 = N/2 - k_w, k_w = \left\lfloor \frac{w_0 N}{B} \right\rfloor \qquad (6)$$

In the double-sided band amplitude spectrum, k_1, k_2 are symmetric about the midpoint $N/2$. By accumulate the $Y(k)$ near these two positions and the entire $Y(k)$, we can obtain:

$$P_1 = \sum_{n=k_1-a}^{k_1+a} Y(k) + \sum_{n=k_2-a}^{k_2+a} Y(k), P_2 = \sum_{n=0}^{N} Y(k) \qquad (7)$$

where a is the summation width. When the received signal contains tag-modulated information, the ratio of P_1 and P_2 should be significantly larger than not included.

Once the tag-modulated bit sequence in the received signal is detected, the bit starting point can be roughly determined with the above method, and the average value of the data point of a certain length before the starting point is regarded as m_{mod}, and then m_{mod} will be removed from the entire piece of data by subtracting this value.

3.3   Synchronization and Phase Estimation

After the previous work is completed, we need to synchronize the receiving bit with a known preamble. The offset of the bit start point and the received data start point can be found by the following equation.

$$\tau = \arg\max_{\tau \in \{0,...,L\}} \left| \sum_{n=0}^{N_p} s_p[n]y[\tau+n] \right| \qquad (8)$$

where the s_p is a known 6 symbol lengths preamble, N_p is the number of samples in the preamble.

The channel coefficient h can be estimated by solving a least squares problem:

$$\hat{h} = \arg\min \sum_{k=\tau}^{\tau+N_p-1} \left| y[k] - h s_p[k-\tau] \right|^2 \tag{9}$$

$$= \frac{\sum_{k=\tau}^{\tau+N_p-1} y[k] s_p[k-\tau]}{\|s_p\|^2} \left(\frac{\pi}{2} - \theta \right) \tag{10}$$

where $\| \bullet \|$ denotes the Euclidean norm.

After the channel coefficient h is known, the phase difference caused by the propagation of the CW in the channel can be calculated as [8].

$$\varphi = angle(h) \tag{10}$$

where φ is a complex value.

When correlation synchronization is completed, a bit sequence with known starting point can be obtained. Through moving the bit start point back by $T/2$, the data can be decoded by differential decoding.

$$b(n) = d(n-1) \otimes d(n), n = 1, \ldots, N \tag{11}$$

when the received signal waveform is S_0, $d(n) = 0$, when it is S_1, $d(n) = 1$. $b(n)$ is the decoded bit. operation $\oplus \leftarrow$ denotes modulo-2 addition (xor).

4 Experimental Results

The experimental platform is shown in Fig. 5, which contains three antennas, a commercial tag, a SRCF and a R420. The backscatter parameters of the tag are set to FM0 encoding with a reverse link rate of 400K by R420. At the SRCF receiver, 4M complex sampling rate is set. Therefore, the sampling point of each symbol is 10. According to Gen2 protocol, the data modulated by the tag including RN16 and EPC,

Fig. 5. Experimental setup.

wherein the sequence length of RN16 is 22, and the sequence length of EPC is 135. We extract phase information from the EPC at the SRCF receiver because EPC is longer than RN16 and has CRC-16 check.

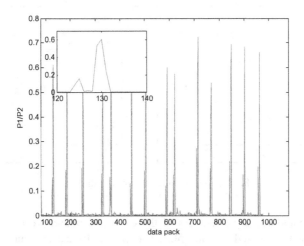

Fig. 6. The P1/P2 of different data pack.

Figure 6 shows the value of P1/P2 under the following experimental conditions, (1) treat 512 samples as a data packet, (2) the SRCF signal transmission power was 17.2 dBm and the R420 signal transmission power was 25 dBm, (3) the distance between tag and SRCF receiver, about 2 meters away. In Fig. 6 a larger peak and a smaller peak can be found in the round frame, which correspond to EPC and RN16, respectively. Because the EPC corresponds to a wider peak width and a larger amplitude, we can easily distinguish between EPC and RN16.

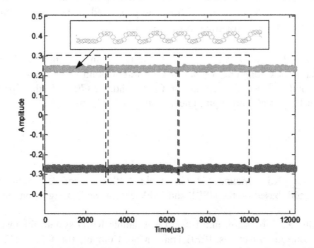

Fig. 7. The dotted box is the EPC sequence detected by the gate block.

Figure 7 shows the data detected by SRCF, which contains EPC. Useful information can be obtained by processing these data.

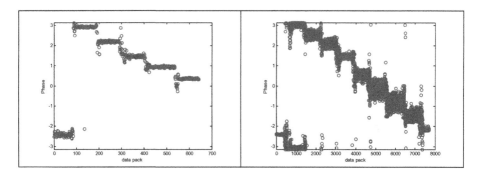

Fig. 8. The *phase* value changes with distance.

In order to validate the correctness of the estimated phase, we move the tag two centimeters at each time, and get multiple carrier phases for each distance. As shown in Fig. 8, the carrier phase changes by about 0.75 for each change of distance, which is in line with the theory. Thus, the proposed channel coefficient algorithm can extract the phase correctly.

5   Conclusion

Existing RFID systems do not meet the requirements of the carrier phase-based ultra-wideband localization algorithm. This paper presents a system consisting of a SRCF and R420, which can be easily extended to one transmitter multiple receivers structures. A channel coefficient estimation algorithm is proposed, which can extract the phase and decode the EPC correctly. Thus, the proposed system is suitable for carrier phase-based ultra-wideband localization algorithm.

Acknowledgement. This work was supported partly by the Scientific and Technological Research Foundation of Chongqing Municipal Education Commission under grant KJ1704083, the National Natural Science Foundation of China under 61704015, the Fundamental and Frontier Research Project of Chongqing under grant cstc2017jcyjAX0380.

References

1. Wang, Y., Man, K.L., Maunder, R.G., et al.: A flexible software defined radio-based UHF RFID reader based on the USRP and LabView. In: SoC Design Conference, pp. 217–218 (2016)
2. Wang, L., Gu, T., Tao, X., et al.: Toward a wearable RFID system for real-time activity recognition using radio patterns. IEEE Trans. Mob. Comput. **16**(1), 228–242 (2017)

3. Ni, L.M., Liu, Y., Lau, Y.C., et al.: LANDMARC indoor location sensing using active RFID. Wirel. Netw. **10**(6), 701–710 (2004)
4. Azzouzi, S., Cremer, M., Dettmar, U., et al.: New measurement results for the localization of UHF RFID transponders using an Angle of Arrival (AoA) approach. In: IEEE International Conference on RFID, pp. 91–97. IEEE (2011)
5. Ma, Y., Selby, N., Adib, F.: Minding the billions: ultra-wideband localization for deployed RFID tags. In: Proceedings of the 23rd Annual International Conference on Mobile Computing and Networking, pp. 248–260. ACM (2017)
6. Buettner, M., Wetherall, D.: A software radio-based UHF RFID reader for PHY/MAC experimentation. In: IEEE International Conference on RFID, pp. 134–141. IEEE (2011)
7. Kargas, N., Mavromatis, F., Bletsas, A.: Fully-coherent reader with commodity SDR for Gen2 FM0 and computational RFID. Wirel. Commun. Lett. **4**(6), 617–620 (2015)
8. Kimionis, J., Bletsas, A., Sahalos, J.N.: Increased range bistatic scatter radio. IEEE Trans. Commun. **62**(3), 1091–1104 (2014)
9. EPC Radio-Frequency Identity Protocols, Class-1 Generation-2 UHF RFID Protocol for Communications at 860 MHZ–960 MHZ, version 2.0.1, EPC Global, Wynantskill, NY, USA (2015)
10. Bletsas, A., Kimionis, J., Dimitriou, A.G., et al.: Single-antenna coherent detection of collided FM0 RFID signals. IEEE Trans. Commun. **60**(3), 756–766 (2012)
11. Joo, T.H., Oppenheim, A.V.: Effects of FFT coefficient quantization on sinusoidal signal detection. In: International Conference on Acoustics, Speech, and Signal Processing, vol. 3, pp. 1818–1821. IEEE (2002)

Centimeter-Level Localization Algorithm with RFID Passive Tags

Liangbo Xie, Die Jiang$^{(\boxtimes)}$, Xiaohui Fu, and Qing Jiang

School of Communications and Information Engineering, Chongqing University
of Posts and Telecommunications, Chongqing, China
1046646101@qq.com

Abstract. Indoor localization technology of radio frequency identification
(RFID) had gained much attention in recent years, but previous works usually
need relative motion between a reader and a tag, or reference tags. Such operation brought about more complexities and difficulties for system deployment.
This paper proposes an algorithm that enables centimeter accuracy on ranging
and localization in line-of-sight (LOS) and non-line-of-sight (NLOS) environments without relative motion and reference tags. By exploiting physical
properties to emulate a large virtual bandwidth on off-the-shelf passive RFID
tags and combining with frequency hopping continuous wave (FHCW) algorithm, we can achieve centimeter-level ranging accuracy and perform
centimeter-level 3D localization at x/y/z dimensions. In case of missing some
channel information, we put a Non-uniform Discrete Fourier Transform (NDFT)
to identify LOS path and obtain 1D ranging result with centimeter accuracy. For
indoor multi-path environments, we propose an optimized multipath suppression
algorithm to ensure centimeter-level accuracy on ranging and localization.
Emulation results demonstrate that the algorithm can achieve 2 cm ranging
accuracy within the distance of 7 m, and the accuracy probability is above 97%.

Keywords: LOS path identification · Optimized multipath suppression ·
3D localization

1 Introduction

With the increase of large and complex indoor environments such as large shopping
malls, large parking lots, airports and so on, there is an urgent need for powerful indoor
localization technology to satisfy self-localization and target localization in unfamiliar
environments. However, due to indoor multipath effect, the Global Navigation Satellite
System (GNSS) signal is rapidly attenuated and even cannot be detected [1–3], leading
to a sharp drop in indoor localization accuracy. A variety of indoor localization
technology came into being under such circumstance. Owing to low cost and simple
deployment, the topic of radio frequency identification (RFID) localization has gained
much attention from the academic community over the past decade [4, 5]. More
generally, RFID localization can enable many applications in libraries, retail stores,
warehouses and smart environments.

© ICST Institute for Computer Sciences, Social Informatics and Telecommunications Engineering 2019
Published by Springer Nature Switzerland AG 2019. All Rights Reserved
M. Jia et al. (Eds.): WiSATS 2019, LNICST 280, pp. 160–170, 2019.
https://doi.org/10.1007/978-3-030-19153-5_15

Many researches have been conducted on RFID localization. In [6, 7], they use the received signal strength (RSS) to achieve localization, however, these methods suffer from poor accuracy and reliability due to indoor multi-path environment since RSS is not sensitive to distance. The localization accuracy can be greatly improved by utilizing reference tags or anchor nodes, but the number of required reference tags or anchors is so large, resulting in extra costs. Besides, reference tags or anchors also need initial deployment with accuracy positions, which increases additional complexity to system deployment. Several arts have also shown tens of centimeter to centimeter accuracy about RFID localization, such as Holographic localization [8], Tagoram [9], PinIt [10] and so on. Unfortunately, they all require relative motion between readers and tags. When motion is required, the system latency is usually high.

Carrier phase-based methods are preferred for their ultra-high sensitivity as a function of distance. TOF obtained by carrier phase is the time that signal travels between a reader and a tag. Emulating a large virtual bandwidth on off-the-shelf passive RFID to obtain carrier phase and compute accurate TOF measurements, we can localize target tag without reference tags and any restrictive assumptions on motion of readers and tags [11]. Based on [11], in this paper, we propose an algorithm that we can leverage Non-uniform Discrete Fourier Transform (NDFT) to identify LOS path under the condition of missing some channel information. In addition, we propose an optimized multipath suppression algorithm to ensure centimeter-level accuracy on ranging and localization.

The rest of this paper is organized as follows. The discussion of virtual bandwidth emulation is presented in Sect. 2. The whole frequency hopping continuous wave (FHCW) algorithm is discussed in Sect. 3, including NDFT and optimized multipath suppression algorithm. The related evaluation results is presented in Sect. 4. And Sect. 5 concludes this paper.

2 A Large Virtual Bandwidth Emulation on Narrowband RFID Passive Tags

In the proposed algorithm, we need to acquire the absolute TOF, so we have to face the challenge – i.e., centimeter-level ranging and localization rely on accurate TOF, and accurate TOF depends on the ability to measure time at a very fine granularity. To achieve the above purpose, a specific hardware would be required to support very high sampling rate or very large bandwidth. However, billions of RFID tags already deployed in today's world have narrow bandwidth so they can't meet the requirement. If we design new RFID tags, not only would such a way make non-compliant with today's FCC regulations and RFID communication protocols, but it would also waste a number of off-the-shelf narrowband RFID tags. Under such background, we present an approach that directly takes advantage of off-the-shelf passive RFID tags to enable centimeter-level ranging and localization.

When a passive tag receives a reader inquiry signal, it responds to the reader by switching its internal impedance between two states, i.e., reflective and non-reflective called the backscatter technology. Since the downlink (reader-to-tag) signal and the uplink (tag-to-reader) signal are on the same carrier frequency, the backscatter is linear.

We hence can utilize the physical property to emulate a large virtual bandwidth by frequency hopping pattern. Two reader transmit continuous waves at a frequency f_1 inside the (Industrial Scientific Medical) ISM band and another frequency f_2 outside the ISM band respectively and simultaneously. It uses high power f_1 to power up and communicate with the passive tag, and uses lower power f_2 to hop over time and collect the channel state information at each of these carriers. The space between adjacent carriers is denoted as Δf. Then we stitch the channels at the various frequencies to realize a large virtual bandwidth in the time domain as shown in Fig. 1. Such an approach still remains compliant with FCC regulations.

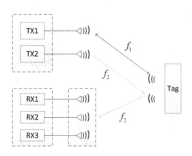

Fig. 1. In the linear backscatter, a tag responds to the readers. The two readers transmit f_1 and f_2 respectively and simultaneously, the tag reflects all the frequency. But after reaching the receiver, f_1 has already been filtered.

3 FHCW Algorithm Description

The proposal algorithm can enable centimeter localization of UHF (ultra-high frequency) RFID passive narrowband tags in LOS and NLOS environments, so it can operate in multipath-rich indoor environment. The whole algorithm consists of three components: (1) LOS path identification; (2) Optimized multipath suppression and phase cycle ambiguity resolving; (3) 3D localization. The flow diagram of 1D ranging estimate is shown in Fig. 2.

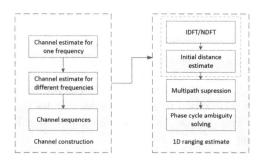

Fig. 2. The flow diagram of 1D ranging estimate.

3.1 LOS Path Identification

In indoor environment, RF signals bounce off different obstacles (such as ceilings, walls, and furniture). As a result, the receiver obtains several copies of the signal and every copy has experienced a different TOF. In Sect. 2, to obtain accurate TOF, we have already realized a large virtual bandwidth. Multipath resolution is inversely proportional to the bandwidth, given by [12]:

$$Multipath\,Resolution = 1/B \tag{1}$$

note that the larger bandwidth is, the higher resolution is. Thus it is not difficult to identify LOS path in the multi-path environments and obtain a rough TOF estimate of that path. Next, we discuss how the TOF of direct path from all the remaining paths teases apart.

To identify the LOS path, we leverage the fact that the LOS path has the shortest distance without experiencing reflectors in contrast to indirect paths, so it arrives the earliest in time under indoor conditions. The visual representation is the first peak in the channel impulse response (CIR) profile, and we can use the TOF corresponding to the first peak as an initial estimate for the LOS distance. If we, however, directly use off-the-shelf narrowband RFID tags with 26 MHz of bandwidth, there are many different paths merge into each other including direct path and indirect paths, since such a small bandwidth results in too low multipath resolution to disentangle the TOF of LOS path according to Eq. (1).

To illustrate, let us consider a transmitter sending a signal to its receiver without multipath effect. Then we can write the wireless channel h as [13]:

$$h = \alpha e^{-j2\pi ft} \tag{2}$$

where α is the signal magnitude, f is the frequency and t is the round trip TOF. When the signal propagates in complex indoor environment, we can write the wireless channel h as:

$$h_i = \sum_{k=1}^{m} a_k e^{-j2\pi f_i t_k} = a_0 e^{-j\frac{2\pi}{c}f_i d_0} + \sum_{l=1}^{L} a_l e^{-j\frac{2\pi}{c}f_i d_l} \tag{3}$$

note that the equation stands for the sum of several Eq. (2). Where k is the number of path to the receiver, i is the number of frequency, l is the number of multipath, a_0 is the LOS signal magnitude, a_l is the each multipath signal magnitude, d_0 is the distance of the LOS path, d_l is the distance of each multipath.

From the above equation, we obtain the channel estimates in the frequency domain. To identify the LOS path, we need to transform the channels from the frequency domain to time domain and find the first peak. Namely we need to perform an Inverse Discrete Fourier Transform (IDFT) following the operation:

$$h(n) = IDFT[H(k)] = \frac{1}{N} \sum_{k=0}^{N-1} H(k) e^{j\frac{2\pi}{N}nk} \tag{4}$$

where $H(k)$ denotes the wireless channel in frequency domain obtained by Eq. (3). We can directly realize time domain representation and CIR profile through inverse fourier transform function in Matlab as shown in Fig. 3. Due to a large bandwidth leading to high time resolution, we can observe that the peak in the profile is sharp.

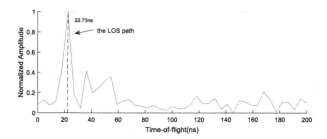

Fig. 3. CIR profile at 220 MHz bandwidth. Due to a large bandwidth leading to high time resolution, we can directly leverage IDFT to identify LOS path and obtain the TOF (i.e. to compute initial distance estimate.)

There is a premise for such a method, which leverages IDFT to identify LOS path that the reader transmits continuous carrier wave f_2 over time by a way of hopping and the receiver obtains the channel measurements at many uniformly-spaced frequencies. If these measurements are not equally spaced frequencies, due to losing packets at some frequencies, IDFT cannot be simply used to separate individual paths and identify LOS path. In order to solve this problem, Inverse Non-uniform Discrete Fourier Transform (INDFT) is proposed. Here, we still use the principle of NDFT [14] instead of INDFT which gives:

$$H(k) = \sum_{n=0}^{N-1} h(n)e^{-j\frac{2\pi}{T}kt_n} \tag{5}$$

where T represents total sampling time, t_n denotes different time per sampling. The equation transforms the channels from the time domain to frequency domain. Now we replace total sampling time with hopping frequency band and use each of hopping frequencies instead of time per sampling to achieve time domain profile, and Eq. (5) can be modified as:

$$h(n) = \sum_{n=0}^{N-1} real[H(k)]e^{-j\frac{2\pi}{F}kf_n} \tag{6}$$

It should be noted that we only choose real part of the channel measurements. Where F is hopping frequency band, f_n is each of the hopping frequencies, hopping interval Δf is non-uniform because of packet missing at some frequencies. Figure 4 shows the time domain profile lacking four frequencies with the same distance of LOS path as Fig. 3.

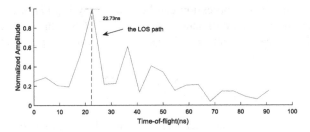

Fig. 4. CIR profile at 220 MHz bandwidth lacking four frequencies. Such means can realize CIR profile that is symmetrical distribution with half of time as the axis of symmetry. It does not affect initial distance estimate that we only take a part of symmetrical distribution for analysis since actual localization distance is within 10 m in indoor environment.

Compared with Fig. 3, Fig. 4 demonstrates that although the receiver lacks some packet corresponding to several frequencies, we can also identify the LOS path and obtain a TOF estimate of that path to compute initial distance estimate. Even if there are some missed packets, IDFT and NDFT have the same effect on identifying LOS path.

3.2 Optimized Multipath Suppression and Phase Cycle Ambiguity

After identifying the LOS path and obtaining initial distance estimate $\tilde{d}_0^c$ corresponding to the estimated TOF, we can strengthen the LOS path and suppress the multipath in frequency domain through the following operation [11]:

$$\theta_k = \angle \sum_{i=1}^{K} h_i e^{j\frac{2\pi}{c}(f_i - f_k)\tilde{d}_0^c} \tag{7}$$

where c is the speed of signal propagation, $\angle$ denotes phase solving. And we can observe that LOS phase can reinforce about K times but NLOS phase strengthen far less than K times by expanding the equation. By this way, suppressing the multipath is achieved. Figure 5 demonstrates we can obtain better phase through multipath suppression to achieve centimeter ranging and localization.

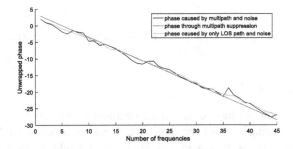

Fig. 5. Unwrapped phase with hopping frequencies. The black line is phase collected in multipath indoor environment. The blue line denotes phase obtained by multipath suppression. The red line represents phase of only LOS path. Noise effects in all three cases. (Color figure online)

Even though multipath suppression can be realized by Eq. (7), the effect of multipath on phase still exists and influences the phase of LOS path. As a result, we can exploit some phase measurements to achieve better multipath suppression, given by:

$$\theta_l = \angle \sum_{i=1}^{K} h_i e^{j\frac{2\pi}{c}(f_i - f_l)\tilde{d_0^c}} \tag{8}$$

where $l = (K + 1)/2$. K is odd number. For example, when we take i from 1 to 39, thus $l = 20$ and θ_{20} is just what we want. What our improvement is that we perform five or more times such operation and combine the obtained multiple phases to solve phase cycle ambiguity. The suppression approach is always applicable regardless of whether the packets corresponding to some frequencies are missed.

After the filtered phases are obtained, the phase ambiguity can be resolved by the Chinese Remainder Theorem (CRT) [15]. Since the collected phase is always within $[0, 2\pi)$, cycle ambiguity exists when the distance is longer than one wavelength. When the collected phase is θ, the actual phase can be $\theta + 2n\pi$, where n is the cycle integer. The standard modular arithmetic algorithm can be reflected in distance as following equation:

$$d_l = \frac{\theta_l c}{2\pi f_l} \mod \lambda_l \tag{9}$$

where θ_l is the filtered phases at different frequencies, λ_l is the wavelength at different frequencies. By computing multiple such d_l at different frequencies and picking the solution satisfying the most number of equations (i.e., the d with most number of aligned lines in Fig. 6), we can obtain the unique and centimeter-level ranging result d.

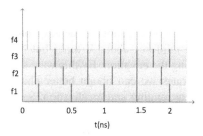

Fig. 6. Resolving phase cycle ambiguity by CRT. We pick the d with most number of aligned lines.

3.3   3D Localization

In the previous section, we have obtained the centimeter-level 1D ranging. Since each ranging result is a distance from the target tag to an Rx antenna, in 3D space, one ranging gives a sphere as shown in Fig. 7(a). To uniquely localize the target tag through trilateration [16] given by Eqs. (10) and (11). Three spheres are required to compute the intersection point as depicted in Fig. 7(b).

$$(x_1 - x_0)^2 + (y_1 - y_0)^2 + (z_1 - z_0)^2 = d_1^2$$
$$(x_2 - x_0)^2 + (y_2 - y_0)^2 + (z_2 - z_0)^2 = d_2^2 \qquad (10)$$
$$(x_3 - x_0)^2 + (y_3 - y_0)^2 + (z_3 - z_0)^2 = d_3^2$$

$$\begin{bmatrix} x_0 \\ y_0 \\ z_0 \end{bmatrix} = \left(A^T A\right)^{-1} A^T b \qquad (11)$$

where $A = \begin{bmatrix} 2(x_1 - x_3) & 2(y_1 - y_3) & 2(z_1 - z_3) \\ 2(x_2 - x_3) & 2(y_2 - y_3) & 2(z_2 - z_3) \end{bmatrix}$, $b = \begin{bmatrix} x_1^2 - x_3^2 + y_1^2 - y_3^2 + z_1^2 - z_3^2 - d_1^2 + d_3^2 \\ x_2^2 - x_3^2 + y_2^2 - y_3^2 + z_2^2 - z_3^2 - d_2^2 + d_3^2 \end{bmatrix}$

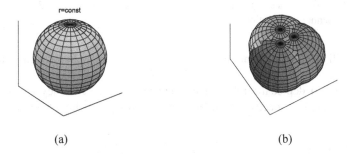

(a)   (b)

Fig. 7. 3D localization by three spheres intersection. (a) A sphere obtained by a ranging. (b) Intersection sphere obtained by three ranging.

4   Evaluation Results

We perform intensive emulation experiments and prove that the presented approach can realize centimeter accuracy on ranging and localization. In our emulation, the bandwidth is 220 MHz and hopping space is 5 MHz, so the multipath resolution is about 4.5 ns and the corresponding distance resolution is around 1.35 m. We assume the receiver obtained four copies of the transmitted signal in indoor environment, including one LOS path and three NLOS paths. We take the first ten energy columns in CIR histogram to analyze the performance of proposed method and obtain the initial distance estimate since RFID localization distance is generally within 10 m.

Figure 8(a) (b) show the 1D ranging accuracy under different distances. Figure 8(a) and (b) correspond to two cases of whether packets are missed, respectively. We can observe that the algorithm can achieve 2 cm accuracy on ranging within 7 m in both cases. The 2 cm accuracy probability is above 97%.

Figure 8(b) demonstrates that the 1D ranging accuracy is worse than Fig. 8(a) since the missed packets have influence on subsequent multipath suppression algorithm. However, as long as the number of missed packets is not very much, the 1D ranging

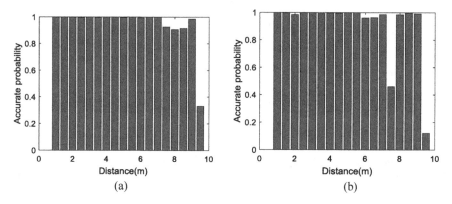

Fig. 8. 1D ranging accuracy with distance variety. (a) shows that the 1D ranging accuracy gradually decreases with distance without missed packets. (b) shows that the 1D ranging accuracy gradually decreases with distance and is worse than (a) for missed four frequencies corresponding channel information.

accuracy is still able to satisfy our centimeter-level requirement in most cases as shown in Fig. 8(b).

Figure 9(a) (b) depict the relationship between ranging accuracy and bandwidth and hopping space respectively under the condition of without missed channel information.

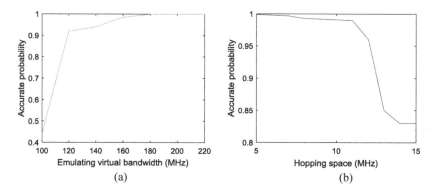

Fig. 9. 1D ranging accuracy vs. different factors. (a) shows that 1D ranging accuracy gradually increases with bandwidth. (b) shows that 1D ranging accuracy gradually decreases with hopping space.

Figure 9(a) demonstrates that the 1D ranging accuracy gradually improves with increased bandwidth when the hopping space is 5 MHz. Besides, bandwidth is only close to 200 MHz, which can achieve centimeter-level ranging and localization when the energy of LOS path is enough high. Figure 9(b) demonstrates that the 1D ranging accuracy gradually decreases when the bandwidth is 220 MHz and the hopping space slowly increases from 5 MHz to 15 MHz. Therefore we generally take the hopping space to be equal to 5 MHz or 10 MHz, by doing so, we can make the performance of ranging and localization better and take integer number of frequencies when emulating a bandwidth of 220 MHz via frequency hopping.

After obtaining the 1D centimeter-level ranging, we can leverage two receiver antennas to achieve centimeter accuracy on 2D localization through Least squares [17] or weighting method. To perform 3D localization, we can exploit three receiver antennas and trilateration [16] to compute the optimal solution in intersection area of three sphere.

5 Conclusion

This paper presents an algorithm that enables centimeter accuracy on ranging and localization without relative motion or any reference tags. For this purpose, we first exploit off-the-shelf passive RFID tags to emulate a large virtual bandwidth, and then perform FHCW algorithm including LOS path identification, multipath suppression optimization, phase cycle ambiguity solving and 3D localization. We believe the proposed approach can provide a new idea for RFID indoor localization technology.

Acknowledgement. This work was supported partly by the Scientific and Technological Research Foundation of Chongqing Municipal Education Commission under grant KJ1704083, the National Natural Science Foundation of China under 61704015, the Fundamental and Frontier Research Project of Chongqing under grant cstc2017jcyjAX0380.

References

1. Jia, M., Gu, X., Guo, Q., Xiang, W., Zhang, N.: Broadband hybrid satellite-terrestrial communication systems based on cognitive radio toward 5G. IEEE Wirel. Commun. **23**(6), 96–106 (2016)
2. Jia, M., Liu, X., Gu, X., Guo, Q.: Joint cooperative spectrum sensing and channel selection optimization for satellite communication systems based on cognitive radio. Int. J. Satellite Commun. Netw. **35**(2), 139–150 (2017)
3. Jia, M., Liu, X., Yin, Z., Guo, Q., Gu, X.: Joint cooperative spectrum sensing and spectrum opportunity for satellite cluster communication networks. Ad Hoc Netw. **58**(C), 231–238 (2017)
4. Ni, L.M., Liu, Y., Lau, Y.C., Patil, A.P.: LANDMARC: indoor location sensing using active RFID. Wireless Netw. **10**(6), 701–710 (2004)
5. Yang, L., Chen, Y., Li, X.-Y., Xiao, C., Li, M., Liu, Y.: Tagoram: real-time tracking of mobile RFID tags to high precision using COTS devices. In: Proceedings of the 20th Annual International Conference on Mobile Computing and Networking, pp. 237–248. ACM (2014)
6. Nikitin, P.V., Rao, K.V.S.: Theory and measurement of backscattering from RFID tags. IEEE Trans. Antennas Propag. Mag. **48**(6), 212–218 (2007)
7. Chawla, K., McFarland, C., Robins, G., Shope, C.: Real-time RFID localization using RSS. In: 2013 International Conference on Localization and GNSS (ICL-GNSS), pp. 1–6. IEEE (2013)

8. Miesen, R., Kirsch, F., Vossiek, M.: Holographic localization of passive UHF RFID transponders. In: IEEE International Conference on RFID, pp. 32–37. IEEE (2011)
9. Yang, L., Chen, Y., Li, X.Y., et al.: Tagoram: real-time tracking of mobile RFID tags to high precision using COTS devices. In: International Conference on Mobile Computing and NETWORKING, pp. 237–248. ACM (2014)
10. Wang, J., Katabi, D.: Dude, where's my card? RFID positioning that works with multipath and non-line of sight. ACM SIGCOMM Comput. Commun. Rev. 43(4), 51–62 (2013)
11. Ma, Y., Selby, N., Adib, F.: Minding the billions: ultra-wideband localization for deployed RFID tags. In: Proceedings of the 23rd Annual International Conference on Mobile Computing and Networking, pp. 248–260. ACM (2017)
12. Adib, F., Kabelac, Z., Katabi, D., et al.: 3D Tracking via Body Radio Reflections, pp. 317–329 (2014)
13. Tse, D., Vishwanath, P.: Fundamentals of Wireless Communications. Cambridge University Press, Cambridge (2005)
14. Bagchi, S., Mitra, S.K.: The Nonuniform Discrete Fourier Transform and Its Applications in Signal Processing. Kluwer Academic Publishers, Boston (1999)
15. Weisstein, E.: Chinese Remainder Theorem. http://mathworld.wolfram.com/ChineseRemainderTheorem.html
16. Manolakis, D.E.: Efficient solution and performance analysis of 3-D position estimation by trilateration. IEEE Trans. Aerosp. Electron. Syst. 32, 1239–1248 (1996)
17. Sheynin, O.: On the history of the principle of least squares. Arch. Hist. Exact Sci. 46(1), 39–54 (1993)

Precise Direction Detector: Indoor Localization System Based on Commodity Wi-Fi

Xiaolong Yang[(✉)], Xin Yu, Jiacheng Wang, Qing Jiang, and Mu Zhou

Chongqing Key Lab of Mobile Communications Technology,
Chongqing University of Posts and Telecommunications, Chongqing 400065, China
yangxiaolong@cqupt.edu.cn

Abstract. This paper aims to present a novel algorithm for indoor localization by employing the channel state information (CSI) which is collected by Wi-Fi chips that are on common Wi-Fi device to estimate the angle of arrival (AoA) of multipath components accurately. In a complex indoor environment, the proposed direct path identification algorithm can be used to identify the line of sight (LOS) and non-line of sight (NLOS) scenario with the averaged detection rates of 0.814 and 0.920, respectively. Finally, by using the widely-known least squares localization algorithm to locate the target. Extensive experimental results have demonstrated that our system can achieve the median localization error of 0.7 m and be robust to the environment variations.

Keywords: Wi-Fi · Indoor localization ·
Channel state information (CSI) · Angle of arrival (AoA)

1 Introduction

With the rapid growth of Wi-Fi infrastructure and devices, a booming increase of applications based on indoor localization has been witnessed [1], such as shopping navigation [2] and augmented reality [3]. The mainstream of Wi-Fi localization systems is based on the received signal strength (RSS), location fingerprinting, time of flight (ToF), and angle of arrival (AoA). The RSS-based system measures RSS from multiple APs to build the propagation models, and then uses the triangulation approach [4] to locate the target. Another popular system is based on location fingerprinting, which collects the fingerprints, such as the RSS, to build a relationship between the fingerprints and physical locations [5]. Benefitting from the multiple input multiple output (MIMO), the AoA-based system has been carefully studied. The basic idea is to use the antenna array to calculate the AoA of multipath signal at the wireless access point (AP). Besides, there

Supported by the Science and Technology Research Program of Chongqing Municipal Education Commission (Grant No. KJQN201800625).

M. Jia et al. (Eds.): WiSATS 2019, LNICST 280, pp. 171–178, 2019.
https://doi.org/10.1007/978-3-030-19153-5_16

are some other existing indoor localization systems based on radio frequency identification (RFID) [6] and ultra-wideband (UWB) [7]. Summary Cognitive radio has attracted considerable attention because of its ability to make full use of the available spectrum resources for wireless terrestrial communication networks [8–10].

The most accurate systems, like the ArrayTrack [1] and Ubicarse [11], can reach an accuracy of 30–50 cm in indoor environment. However, these systems cannot meet the requirements of cost efficiency and universality, which make them hard to apply. The ArrayTrack and LTEye [12] work on AoA estimation which are accurate and universal, but they both need to modify the hardware. The ArrayTrack requires the AP to be equipped with 6 to 8 antennas, which contradict the common AP with three or less antennas. SpotFi [12] overcomes the constraints on number of antennas, but still cannot solve the problem of coherent signal and need the help of received signal strength indicator (RSSI) to complete localization. The LTEye uses the motorized rotating antenna which is more difficult to be applied. Other localization systems, such as the Ubicarse and Wi-Fi/MEMS system [13], can also be cost-efficient and accurate by combining the data from different sensors, but they require the target to be equipped with accelerometer and gyroscope, which are hardly found in many types of terminals.

2   System Description

2.1   Super-Precision Estimation Model

It is known that the signals experience the attenuation and time delay during the propagation, and there are generally 6–8 significant propagation paths in dense indoor multipath environment [1]. So we describe the channel frequency response (CFR) as

$$h(f) = \sum_{l=0}^{k} \gamma_l e^{-j2\pi f \tau_l}, \tag{1}$$

where γ_l is the attenuation, τ_l is the time delay and f denotes the frequency of the transmitted signal. The CSI can be recognized as a sample edition of the CFR.

For the kth propagation path, τ_k is the distance from the AP to receiver, d is the antenna spacing, and θ_k is the signal incident angle. Thus, the received signals at the mth antenna travels an additional distance $d(m-1)\sin\theta$, which results in a phase shift $-2\pi \times (m-1) \times d \times \sin(\theta_k) \times f_0/c$. Then the phase shift related to AoA on the kth propagation path, at the mth antenna can be described as

$$\Phi(\theta_k, \tau_k) = e^{-j2\pi f \times d \times (m-1) \times \sin(\theta_k)/c}, \tag{2}$$

where c is the speed of light. The vector of received signals on the kth path can be written as

$$\mathbf{a}(\theta_k, \tau_k) = \begin{bmatrix} 1 & \Phi(\theta_k, \tau_k) \cdots \Phi(\theta_k, \tau_k)^{m-1} \end{bmatrix}^{\mathsf{T}}. \tag{3}$$

By assuming that there are L propagation paths, we define the steering matrix as

$$\mathbf{A} = [\mathbf{a}(\theta_1, \tau_1), \cdots, \mathbf{a}(\theta_L, \tau_L)]. \tag{4}$$

Thereby, the received signal is constructed with the superposition of multipath signal, which can be expressed as

$$\mathbf{x} = \sum_{i=1}^{L}(\mathbf{a}(\theta_i, \tau_i)\gamma_i + n_i) = \mathbf{A\Gamma} + N, \tag{5}$$

where $\mathbf{\Gamma}$ denotes the vector of attenuations on the L paths and $\mathbf{N}$ is the noise. Then, we build the measurement $\mathbf{X}$ through received signal vectors for N subcarriers

$$\mathbf{X} = [\mathbf{x_1} \cdots \mathbf{x_N}] = \mathbf{A}[\mathbf{\Gamma_1} \cdots \mathbf{\Gamma_N}], \tag{6}$$

where $[\mathbf{x_1} \cdots \mathbf{x_N}]$ denotes the vectors obtained from all subcarriers and $[\mathbf{\Gamma_1} \cdots \mathbf{\Gamma_N}]$ are the corresponding complex attenuation. The impact of channel on signals is entirely recorded in CSI which is presented by Wi-Fi card. So, for a system equipped with Intel 5300 and 3 antennas, the CSI matrix can be expressed as

$$\mathbf{CSI} = \begin{bmatrix} \overbrace{c_{1,1}...c_{1,30}}^{antenna1}, \overbrace{c_{2,1}...c_{2,30}}^{antenna2}, \overbrace{c_{3,1}...c_{3,30}}^{antenna3} \end{bmatrix} = \begin{bmatrix} c_{1,1} & c_{1,2} & \cdots & c_{1,30} \\ c_{2,1}...c_{2,3} & & \cdots & c_{2,30} \\ c_{3,1}......c_{3,4} & & \cdots & c_{3,30} \end{bmatrix}. \tag{7}$$

The goal of our system is to use $\mathbf{X}$ to estimate $\mathbf{A}$. The AoA can be easily estimated when $\mathbf{A}$ has been obtained. The multiple signal classification (MUSIC) algorithm works well for the relations between $\mathbf{A}$ and $\mathbf{X}$, because the eigenvectors of $\mathbf{XX}^H$ corresponding to the eigenvalue 0 are orthogonal to the steering vectors in $\mathbf{A}$. $\mathbf{X}^H$ is the conjugate transpose of $\mathbf{X}$. Thus, we calculate the eigenvectors of $\mathbf{XX}^H$ corresponding to the eigenvalue 0, construct the steering vectors which are orthogonal to the eigenvectors, and extract the AoA from the steering vectors. The covariance matrix $\mathbf{R}_x$ with respect to the received signal is expressed as

$$\begin{aligned} \mathbf{R}_x &= E[\mathbf{XX}^H] \\ &= \mathbf{A}E[\mathbf{SS}^H]\mathbf{A}^H + E[\mathbf{NN}^H], \\ &= \mathbf{AR}_s\mathbf{A}^H + \sigma^2\mathbf{I} \end{aligned} \tag{8}$$

where $\mathbf{R}_s$ is the covariance matrix of signal vectors. As we know, the smallest $90 - L$ eigenvalues are corresponding to the noise subspace, while the other L eigenvalues are corresponding to the signal subspace. Based on this, we employ the spatial spectrum function in (9) to estimate the steering vectors $\mathbf{a}(\theta, \tau)$ when the denominator is close to 0. Then, the angle corresponding to sharp peak is selected as the incident angle of the AoA.

$$P(\theta, \tau)_{MUSIC} = \frac{1}{\mathbf{a}(\theta, \tau)^H \mathbf{E}_N \mathbf{E}_N{}^H \mathbf{a}(\theta, \tau)}. \tag{9}$$

2.2 CSI Matrix Smoothing and Direct Path Identification

In indoor environment, the received signals are likely to be coherent, which is not beneficial for the angle estimation. To address this issue, our system performs spatial smoothing on $\mathbf{R}_x$. The covariance matrices are constructed by increasing the serial number of subcarriers from 1 to $E_2 = 30 - N_2 + 1$ and the serial number of antennas from 1 to $E_1 = 3 - N_1 + 1$. In our system, $N_2 = 15$ and $N_1 = 2$. Then, the total number of sub-arrays and the elements in each sub-array equals to $E_1 \times E_2$ and $N_1 \times N_2$. In this case, the covariance matrix of CSI can be modified into

$$\mathbf{R}_{smoothed} = \frac{1}{E_1 \times E_2} \sum_{i=1}^{E_1} \sum_{j=1}^{E_2} \mathbf{R}_{i,j}. \tag{10}$$

The $\mathbf{R}_{i,j}$ is the sub-covariance matrix of $\mathbf{R}_x$, which can be written as

$$\mathbf{R}_{i,j} = \begin{bmatrix} x_{i,j} \times x_{i,j} & \cdots\cdots & x_{i,j} \times x_{i+1,j+15-1} \\ \vdots & \vdots \; \vdots & \vdots \\ x_{i,j+15-1} \times x_{i,j} & \cdots\cdots & x_{i,j+15-1} \times x_{i+1,j+15-1} \\ x_{i+1,j} \times x_{i,j} & \cdots\cdots & x_{i+1,j} \times x_{i+1,j+15-1} \\ \vdots & \vdots \; \vdots & \vdots \\ x_{i+1,j+15-1} \times x_{i,j} & \cdots\cdots & x_{i+1,j+15-1} \times x_{i+1,j+15-1} \end{bmatrix}, \tag{11}$$

where $x_{i,j} \times x_{i,j}$ is the first element of the sub-covariance matrix.

In the direct path identification section, we use least squares method to get better fitting effect. First, we perform the affinity propagation clustering on the peak points from the result of MUSIC. Second, to detect the outliers, we calculate the density of each point by

$$\rho(\mathbf{x}, k) = \left(\frac{\sum_{y \in N(\mathbf{x}, k)} d(\mathbf{x}, \mathbf{y})}{|N(\mathbf{x}, k)|} \right)^{-1}, \tag{12}$$

where $N(\mathbf{x}, k)$ is the set of k nearest neighbors of $\mathbf{x}$, $|N(\mathbf{x}, k)|$ denotes the size of set $N(\mathbf{x}, k)$, and $\mathbf{y}$ refers to the nearest point. We divide (12) by the averaged density of its k nearest neighbors to obtain the average relative density.

$$\bar{\rho}(\mathbf{x}, k) = \frac{\rho(\mathbf{x}, k)}{\left(\sum_{y \in N(\mathbf{x}, k)} d(\mathbf{y}, k)/|N(\mathbf{x}, k)| \right)}. \tag{13}$$

Third, an outlier score is distributed to each point and the points with significantly high scores need to be deleted. The algorithm used for outlier deletion is described in Algorithm 1.

Finally, we select the path with the highest score as the direct one to locate the target by

$$score_i = exp(\alpha_n N_i - \alpha_\theta \sigma_{\theta i} - \alpha_\tau \sigma_{\tau i} - \alpha_{m\tau} \bar{\tau}_i). \tag{14}$$

In the ith cluster, where $\sigma_{\theta i}$ and $\sigma_{\tau i}$ stand for the variance of AoA and ToA of the points, N_i denotes the number of points, and $\bar{\tau}_i$ is the average ToF of the points. Besides, $\alpha_n, \alpha_\theta, \alpha_\tau$, and $\alpha_{m\tau}$ express the weights.

Algorithm 1. Outlier Deletion

   Input: Raw data from one cluster
   Output: Modified data without outliers
1 if *the number of point in cluster* > 5 **then**
2   **for** *all x* **do**
3 | determine $N(x, k)$; calculate $\rho(x, k)$;
4   **end**
5   **for** *all x* **do**
6 | distribute an outlier score to each point, outlier score=average relative $\rho(x, k)$;
7   **end**
8   **if** *the number of point in cluster* < 10 **then**
9   delete the point with the highest outlier score from x;
10   **else**
11 | delete (the number of point*0.1) outliers
12   **end**
13   **end**
14 **end**

---

3 Experiments and Evaluation

As shown in Fig. 1, 27 test points are uniformly calibrated with every two adjacent points spacing 0.6 m in each column and the distance interval between the neighboring columns of test points is about 3 m.

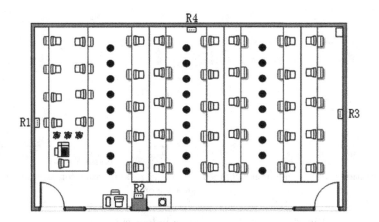

Fig. 1. Testbed of indoor environment

So as to verify the ability of system to identify LOS and NLOS, we place 4 APs in which two of them are blocked with the metal plates to create NLOS scenario during the tests and analyze its detection rate. In LOS and NLOS

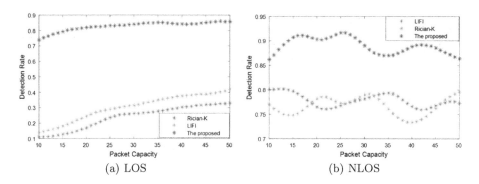

Fig. 2. Detection rate in LOS and NLOS scenarios

scenarios, compared with other two typical systems, namely the LIFI [14] and Rician-K, we can see from Fig. 2(a) and (b) that the proposed system can at least achieves the detection rates above 0.7 and 0.85, respectively. While the two typical systems only can at most achieve the detection rates of 0.42 and 0.8. Besides, the proposed system achieves the higher averaged detection rates of 0.814 and 0.920 in this two scenarios, respectively.

For comparison, the schemes proposed in SpotFi and CUPID [15] are also used to process the same data. From Fig. 3(a) we can see that the proposed system achieves higher positioning accuracy with the median error of 0.502 m, while the SpotFi and CUPID are only with the median errors of 0.652 m and 2.12 m, respectively.

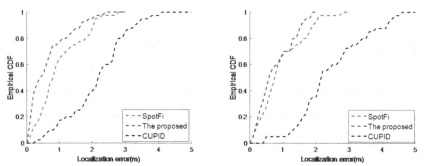

(a) Localization errors in indoor environment (b) Localization errors for the off-the-shelf smartphone

Fig. 3. Localization errors in indoor environment

To verify the practicability of our system, we select the off-the-shelf Samsung i9500 smartphone as the target for the testing. The tester holding the smartphone walks around with random directions in detected area. Each receiver collects 100 packets per second and 20 of them are used to locate the target. As we can see in

Fig. 3(b), when the experimental condition become complex, the performance of CUPID degrade significantly which can only reach a median accuracy of 2.57 m. Obviously, the proposed plan is more robust than CUPID and SpotFi which can achieve an impressive median accuracy of 0.7 m, while SpotFi can only reach 0.743 m.

4   Conclusions

In this paper, the proposed system is proved to be able to estimate the AoA and ToF of the signal accurately based on the existing Wi-Fi device without any extra hardware. At the same time, the smoothing algorithm can resist the coherent signal effectively. Furthermore, our system is capable of picking out the APs operating in LOS scenario with high detection rate and extracting the information of direct path to locate the target. The extensive experiments conducted in the indoor environments demonstrate its robustness and practicability. In the future, we will continue to investigate the approach of self-adaptive threshold setting to improve the detection rate of direct path in NLOS scenario.

References

1. Xiong, J., Jamieson, K.: ArrayTrack: a fine-grained indoor location system. In: USENIX Conference on Networked Systems Design and Implementation, Lombard, IL, USA, pp. 71–84 (2013)
2. Shu, Y., et al.: Last-mile navigation using smartphones. In: International Conference on Mobile Computing and Networking ACM, Paris, France, pp. 512–524 (2015)
3. Wang, H., Bao, X., Roy Choudhury, R., Nelakuditi, S.: Visually fingerprinting humans without face recognition. In: Proceedings of the ACM MobiSys, Paris, France, pp. 345–358 (2015)
4. Tian, Z., et al.: Fingerprint indoor positioning algorithm based on affinity propagation clustering. EURASIP J. Wirel. Commun. Netw. 1–8 (2013)
5. Youssef, M.: The Horus WLAN location determination system. In: International Conference on Mobile Systems, Applications, and Services, Seattle, Washington, USA, pp. 205–218 (2005)
6. Wang, J., Katabi, D.: Dude, where's my card? RFID positioning that works with multipath and non-line of sight. In: Proceedings of the ACM SIGCOMM 2013 Conference on SIGCOMM, Hong Kong, China, pp. 51–62 (2013)
7. Wang, J., Vasisht, D., Katabi, D.: RF-IDraw: virtual touch screen in the air using RF signals. In: ACM SIGCOMM Computer Communication Review, Maui, Hawaii, pp. 1–4 (2014)
8. Jia, M., Gu, X., Guo, Q., Xiang, W., Zhang, N.: Broadband hybrid satellite-terrestrial communication systems based on cognitive radio toward 5G. IEEE Wirel. Commun. **23**, 96–106 (2016)
9. Jia, M., Liu, X., Gu, X., Guo, Q.: Joint cooperative spectrum sensing and channel selection optimization for satellite communication systems based on cognitive radio. Int. J. Satell. Commun. Netw. **35**, 139–150 (2017)

10. Jia, M., Liu, X., Yin, Z., Guo, Q., Gu, X.: Joint cooperative spectrum sensing and spectrum opportunity for satellite cluster communication networks. Ad Hoc Netw. **58**, 231–238 (2016)
11. Kumar, S., Gil, S., Katabi, D., Rus, D.: Accurate indoor localization with zero start-up cost. In: International Conference on Mobile Computing and Networking, Maui, Hawaii, USA, pp. 483–494 (2014)
12. Kotaru, M., Joshi, K., Bharadia, D., et al.: SpotFi: decimeter level localization using WiFi. In: ACM Conference on Special Interest Group on Data Communication, London, United Kingdom, pp. 269–282 (2015)
13. Tian, Z., et al.: Smartphone-based indoor integrated WiFi/MEMS positioning algorithm in a multi-floor environment. Micromachines **6**(3), 347–363 (2015)
14. Zhou, Z., et al.: LiFi: line-of-sight identification with WiFi. In: INFOCOM IEEE, Toronto Canada (2014)
15. Sen, S., et al.: Avoiding multipath to revive inbuilding WiFi localization. In: Proceeding of the, International Conference on Mobile Systems, Applications, and Services ACM, pp. 249–262 (2013)

A Novel AoA Estimation Algorithm Based on Phase Compensation of Linear Array

Xiaolong Yang$^{(\boxtimes)}$, Yuan She, Jiacheng Wang, Mu Zhou, and Zengshan Tian

Chongqing Key Lab of Mobile Communications Technology,
Chongqing University of Posts and Telecommunications, Chongqing 400065, China
yangxiaolong@cqupt.edu.cn

Abstract. This paper presents a novel algorithm for angle of arrive (AoA) estimation by employing the phase of received signal. First, the phase of the received signal is compensated in all directions. Then, the AoA is estimated by evaluating the fluctuation of the compensated phases from sensors of the array. Meanwhile, since matrix decomposition is not required, the complexity is greatly reduced compared to the conventional methods. Our implementation and evaluation on commodity WiFi devices demonstrate that the proposed algorithm achieves better or comparable performance to SpotFi. In terms of estimation accuracy, the proposed algorithm can estimate the incident angle of the multipath and the coherent signals effectively. In terms of complexity, since matrix decomposition is not required, the complexity is greatly reduced compared to the conventional methods.

Keywords: Wi-Fi · Indoor localization · Channel state information · Angle of arrival · Coherent signal

1 Introduction

Recent years, the ever-fast development of indoor localization [1–6] has attracted people's attention. Mainstream indoor positioning techniques are based on ultra wide band (UWB), fingerprinting, radio frequency identification (RFID), MEMS and Wi-Fi. Those positioning techniques based applications are required to be accurate, universal and efficient for meeting user needs and Summary Cognitive radio has attracted considerable attention because of its ability to make full use of the available spectrum resources for wireless terrestrial communication networks [7–9].

The accuracy of ArrayTrack [10], SpotFi [11] and UWB [12] based system is sufficient in most cases. But ArrayTrack needs 16 antennas to overcome the multipath effect which is not universal for modifying the hardware. UWB based system is more real-time and accurate than ArrayTrack and SpotFi while the related

Supported by the Science and Technology Research Program of Chongqing Municipal Education Commission (Grant No. KJQN201800625).

M. Jia et al. (Eds.): WiSATS 2019, LNICST 280, pp. 179–186, 2019.
https://doi.org/10.1007/978-3-030-19153-5_17

expensive equipment makes it unattractive. SpotFi uses ToF based approachs and AoA based approachs for joint estimation, which needs matrix decomposition and smoothing to remove the influence of coherent signals and results in SpotFi inefficient and time complex. In sample environment, SpotFi can achieve better estimation accuracy than other methods. However, for complex indoor environment, due to the effect of coherent signal and noise, the estimation accuracy decreased.

In order to reduce the influence of coherent signal on angle of arrival estimation and solving the problem of high algorithm complexity caused by a large number of operations in SpotFi. We present a novel AoA estimation algorithm, which uses phase compensation to solve the coherent signal and algorithm complexity problems of SpotFi effectively.

The three key contributions of this paper are listed as follow:

(1) The proposed algorithm solves the problem of AoA estimation with respect to the coherent signal and multipath signal effectively.
(2) The AoA estimation efficiency is improved without any loss of accuracy.
(3) The time complexity of the algorithm is greatly reduced.

The rest of this paper is organized as follows. The related work about localization technologies is introduced in Sect. 1. The proposed one-dimensional and 2D AoA estimation is described in Sect. 2. Section 3 conducts the experiments and analyzes the results. And Sect. 4 draws the conclusion and provides some future works.

2   System Description

In the indoor environment, the signal could arrive at the receiver after multiple reflections, and the arriving directions of the signals can be estimated by considering the phase shift. Our system makes full use of the phase difference to estimate incident angle.

2.1   AoA Estimation Based on Linear Array

Let $H(f)$ be the channel frequency response (CFR) as the signal is influenced in transmission channel with both amplitude and phase, and the amplitude attenuation is attributed to the energy loss during signal propagation while the phase change is caused by ToF of signal. Thus, can be denoted as:

$$H(f) = |H(f)| \, exp(-j \times 2\pi \times sin(\angle H(f))) \qquad (1)$$

where $|H(f)|$ and $\angle H(f)$ is amplitude and phase of the channel frequency response $H(f)$ respectively.

More generally, we suppose there are M antennas placed in a uniform equidistant linear array with equal spacing d as shown in Fig. 1. For each propagation path, the ToF contains the time proportional to the distance between the transmitter and receiver, and the time is related to incident angle of signal. Let Θ be

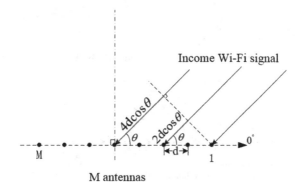

Fig. 1. Uniform linear array diagram

the incident angle of signal corresponding to the normal direction of the linear array and γ be the signal attenuation during path traveling.

Combining with Eq. (1), the signal arriving at first antenna of the array can be expressed as:

$$S_{r_1}(f) = \gamma S(f)_s e^{-j2\pi \times \tau_d \times f} \tag{2}$$

where τ_d is the time from the transmitter to the first antenna; f is the frequency of transmitted signal. Due to the AoA and array spacing, the signal arriving at the second antenna needs to fly another distance about $d \times cos\theta$ which results in a phase shift about $\Phi(\theta) = e^{-j2\pi \times (d \times cos\theta/c) \times f}$. Thus the signal received by the second antenna is shown below:

$$S_{r\,2}(f) = S_{r\,1}(f) e^{-j2\pi \times (d \times cos\theta/c) \times f} \tag{3}$$

In a uniform line array, the signal phase received from each antenna can be recorded as:

$$P(\theta) = \begin{bmatrix} 1 & \Phi(\theta) & ... & \Phi(\theta)^{M-1} \end{bmatrix}^T \tag{4}$$

where $\Phi(\theta) = e^{-j2\pi \times d \times sin(\theta) \times f/c}$, and c is the speed of light and f is the frequency of the transmitted signal. Considering the first antenna as a reference, we make up the phase difference of the received signal at m-th antenna by multiplying $e^{-j2\pi \times [(m-1)d \times cos(\theta)/c] \times f}$ to the received signal, and the compensation operation can be denoted as:

$$Q(\omega) = \begin{bmatrix} 1 & \Phi(\theta) & ... & \Phi(\theta)^{M-1} \end{bmatrix}^T \cdot C(\omega) \tag{5}$$

$$C(\omega) = \begin{bmatrix} 1 & e^{-j2\pi \times d \times cos(\omega)/c \times f} & ... & e^{-j2\pi \times (M-1)d \times cos(\omega)/c \times f} \end{bmatrix} \tag{6}$$

where ω ranges from $0°$ to $180°$, and k is the number of each antenna in the linear array. The phase compensation for each antenna is equivalent to compensate the ToF of signal by rotating the linear array in clockwise direction, as shown in Fig. 2.

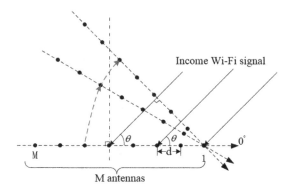

Fig. 2. The antenna array rotates clockwise until it is perpendicular to the incident signal, where the phase difference between the incident signal and the different antennas is smallest.

With the angle rotation, the compensated phase on each antenna and the phase difference of any two antennas change. As ω approaches to the true incidence angle, the linear array will be gradually perpendicular to the incident signal and the phase differences among different antennas will become smaller. When ω equals to the expected AoA, the linear array becomes perpendicular to the signal direction and the ToF at all antennas is the same. Thus the phase shift is formulated into:

$$f(\omega) = 1 / \sqrt{\frac{1}{M} \sum_{n=0}^{M-1} (\Phi(\theta)^n \times e^{-j2\pi \times n \times d \times cos(\omega)/c \times f} - \bar{Q})^2} \qquad (7)$$

where $\bar{Q}$ refers to the mean of elements from $Q(\omega)$. For each rotation angle, we use Eq. (7) to measure the dispersion degree of the phase values from all antennas. For instance, we uses 3 antennas to estimate a signal with an angle of arrival of 90°. When the antenna array begins to rotate clockwise, rotation angle ω changes from 0° to 180°, the phases dispersion degree of three antennas changes from -6 to 6 as shown in Fig. 3. Construct a compensation signal with the same structure as the original compensated signal by using the parameter ω, calculate the variance between the compensate signal and the mean of the original compensated signal. We will find that when $\omega = 90°$, the signal phase difference between the compensated signal and the original compensated signal reach a minimum value of 0, and the variance of the phase difference between the compensated signal and the original compensated signal is also a minimum value, the reciprocal of the variance $f(\omega)$ reaches the highest value. Therefore, We can get the angle of arrival according to the angle corresponding to the maximum value and the angle of compensated.

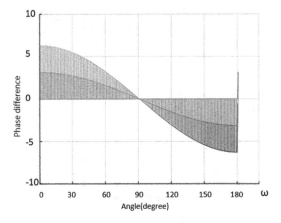

Fig. 3. When the phase compensation angle is equal to the angle of incidence, the phase different between all antennas is 0 and the signal phase from all antennas will be the same.

3   Experimental Results

In this section, first, we explore the estimation accuracy of proposed algorithm with linear array and compare it with SpotFi. Then, case studies are performed in a typical indoor environment and performance comparisons are made with SpotFi under different parameter settings.

3.1   Experiment Based on Linear Array

We set 4 Access Points (AP) with three antennas at a height of 2 m operating as the signal receivers. The central frequency is 5.2G and we use only 30 of the subcarriers and single carrier modulation with signal noise ratio (SNR) $\xi = 10\,\mathrm{dB}$. We compare the performance of proposed AoA estimation algorithm with SpotFi.

We chose SpotFi with three antennas as the comparison point because among recently proposed designs it is the best performing system which can be deployed without any hardware or firmware modifications at the APs. First, we compare the performance of the proposed algorithm and SpotFi with incoherent signal. As can be seen from Fig. 4, SpotFi is more accurate with error of 60% less than 4° compared to 5° in the same case with the proposed algorithm. Under this circumstance, by phase compensation, the proposed system works effectively without smoothing between carriers although the accuracy of proposed algorithm is slightly lower than SpotFi. For coherent signals, however, its performance is superior to SpotFi. We will explain this in the following experiments. In addition, the proposed algorithm can calculate the incident angles of coherent signals without smoothing, and it only operates on signal phase without matrix decomposition which is the main reason for complexity reduction.

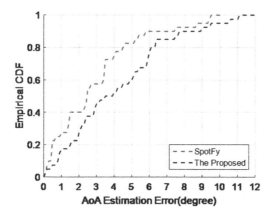

Fig. 4. SpotFi is more accurate with error of 60% less than 4° and the proposed algorithm is more accurate with error of 60% about 5° in the same time.

For coherent signal, we conduct case study in a typical indoor environment to verify the capability of the proposed algorithm. There are 3 columns, each of which has 9 test points. 27 test points are uniformly calibrated with every two adjacent points spacing 0.6 m in each column and the distance interval between the neighboring columns of test points is about 3 m.

The results of the experiment are as follows Fig. 5. From Fig. 5(a), we can see that although both SpotFi and the proposed algorithm contain some large estimation errors due to the complex indoor environment, the proposed algorithm can guarantee a satisfactory estimate accuracy. The proposed algorithm is more

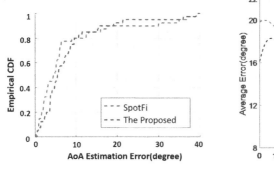
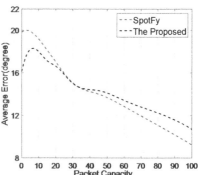

(a) The performance of the AoA estimation error

(b) The performance of packet capacity

Fig. 5. (a) The performance of the AoA estimation error of SpotFi and the proposed algorithm is compared. (b) The effect of the number of packets on the accuracy of angle estimation is compared, and the proposed algorithm is more accurate with less than 25 packet.

accurate when the AoA estimation error is more than 10. However, as shown in the Fig. 5(a), SpotFi is more accurate than the proposed algorithm when the AoA estimation error is less than 10. Because of the influence of environment and other factors, there will be some errors in the experimental results of the measured data. At the same time, we study the influence of the packet number on the angle estimation accuracy in Fig. 5(b). As can be seen from Fig. 5(b), the proposed algorithm is more accurate with less than 25 packets. As the number of packets increases, the accuracy gradually rises. This is because SpotFi needs to use incoherent data in a large number of packets to perform operations. When the number of packets is small, the useful information in the packets is less so that the estimation accuracy is low. The proposed algorithm can use both coherent and incoherent signals to calculate at the same time, and the estimation accuracy is higher when the number of packets is small. Meanwhile, the proposed algorithm does not need matrix decomposition, thus reducing the complexity of the algorithm.

4   Conclusion

In this paper, we present a novel algorithm to estimate the incident signal angle based on phase compensation. By phase compensation for each antenna in the antenna array, the antenna array rotates perpendicular to the incident signal, the phase different between all antennas reaches the lowest and the AoA is estimated. Therefore, the proposed algorithm can deal with multipath and coherent signals effectively, the AoA estimation is more accuracy than SpotFi and the complexity is greatly reduced since there is no complex matrix decomposition and coherent signal processing involved.

References

1. Gjengset, J., Xiong, J., Mcphillips, G., et al.: Phaser: enabling phased array signal processing on commodity WiFi access points. In: International Conference on Mobile Computing and Networking, pp. 153–164. ACM (2014)
2. Youssef, M., Rieger, C., Rieger, C., et al.: PinPoint: an asynchronous time-based location determination system. In: International Conference on Mobile Systems, Applications and Services, pp. 165–176. ACM (2006)
3. Wu, Y., Chen, H., Chen, Y.: A method of 2-D DOA estimation of coherent signals based on uniform circular array via spatial smoothing. In: IEEE CIE International Conference on Radar, pp. 312–314. IEEE (2012)
4. Golden, S.A., Bateman, S.S.: Sensor measurements for Wi-Fi location with emphasis on time-of-arrival ranging. In: IEEE Educational Activities Department, pp. 1185–1198 (2007)
5. Lanzisera, S., Zats, D., Pister, K.S.J.: Radio frequency time-of-flight distance measurement for low-cost wireless sensor localization. IEEE Sens. J. **11**, 837–845 (2011)
6. Xiong, J., Sundaresan, K., Jamieson, K.: ToneTrack: leveraging frequency-agile radios for time-based indoor wireless localization. In: International Conference on Mobile Computing and Networking, pp. 537–549. ACM (2015)

7. Jia, M., Gu, X., Guo, Q., Xiang, W., Zhang, N.: Broadband hybrid satellite-terrestrial communication systems based on cognitive radio toward 5G. IEEE Wirel. Commun. **23**, 96–106 (2016)
8. Jia, M., Liu, X., Gu, X., Guo, Q.: Joint cooperative spectrum sensing and channel selection optimization for satellite communication systems based on cognitive radio. Int. J. Satell. Commun. Netw. **35**, 139–150 (2017)
9. Jia, M., Liu, X., Yin, Z., Guo, Q., Gu, X.: Joint cooperative spectrum sensing and spectrum opportunity for satellite cluster communication networks. Ad Hoc Netw. **58**, 231–238 (2016)
10. Xiong, J., Jamieson, K.: ArrayTrack: a fine-grained indoor location system. In: USENIX Conference on Networked Systems Design and Implementation, pp. 71–84. USENIX Association (2013)
11. Kotaru, M., Joshi, K., Bharadia, D., et al.: SpotFi: decimeter level localization using WiFi. In: SIGCOMM 2015 - Proceedings of the 2015 ACM Conference on Special Interest Group on Data Communication, pp. 269–282 (2015)
12. Gezici, S., Tian, Z., Giannakis, G.B., et al.: Localization via ultra-wideband radios: a look at positioning aspects for future sensor networks. IEEE Signal Process. Mag. **22**, 70–84 (2005)

Design and Implementation of a RF Transceiver Front-End for UHF RFID Localization System

WenJun Lv$^{(\boxtimes)}$, LiangBo Xie, LingXia Li, Yi Chen, and Bin Luo

School of Communications and Information Engineering,
Chongqing University of Posts and Telecommunications,
Chongqing 400065, China
513534668@qq.com

Abstract. Current RFID readers have a narrow operating bandwidth and not suitable for carrier-phase based RFID localization system requirements. To solve this problem, this paper designs a hardware circuit of the transceiver front-end of ultra-high frequency (UHF) radio frequency identification (RFID) system with wideband operating frequency range. The proposed front-end includes DDS module, transmission module and reception module. Benefiting from the fast switching frequency and wideband output frequency range of DDS, this system can achieve fast frequency hopping within a wide operating bandwidth, which satisfies the requirements of carrier-phase based localization. The results show that the whole hardware system can work correctly within the bandwidth of 700 MHz to 1 GHz, which can meet the design requirements of UHF RFID transceiver front-end.

Keywords: UHF RFID · FPGA chip · DDS chip · Transceiver front-end

1 Introduction

RFID is a wireless communication technology, a complete RFID system consists of readers, antennas, electronic tags [1]. The basic working principle is that the electronic tag enters the magnetic field after reader transmits the signals of specific frequency, the tag sends out a signal by the energy obtained of induced current (Passive tag), or the tag actively sends a signal of a certain frequency (Active tag) [2, 3], then reader obtains the information from the signal and decodes it.

There have already matured RFID chips and readers on the market, such as chips from Texas Instruments and Cypress, Speedway readers from IMPINJ [4] and so on, which comply with EPC global UHF Gen2 (ISO 18000-6C) international standards [5, 6]. The commercial readers also integrate FPGA, modem, power amplification and other modules with good sensitivity and stability. These special chips and readers which have characteristics of reduced development difficulty, easy debugging ability and guaranteed stability, are suitable for RFID system. However, there have more advantages of broadband communication system in localization [7–9], the

M. Jia et al. (Eds.): WiSATS 2019, LNICST 280, pp. 187–193, 2019.
https://doi.org/10.1007/978-3-030-19153-5_18

shortcomings of these commercial readers are I/Q data is unavailable and the working bandwidth is so narrow, which cannot be applied in UHF RFID localization system.

To solve these issues, this paper proposes a transceiver to use DDS as its local oscillator to achieve a wide working bandwidth and fast frequency hopping. The receiving front-end can also obtain the I/Q two-way data directly.

2   System Structure of RFID Transceiver

Commercial readers currently on the market have a narrow working bandwidth, result in limited location and distance estimation accuracy. The localization accuracy is related to the bandwidth [10], so the wider bandwidth it has, the higher accuracy can get. This system designs a hardware transceiver front-end using DDS technology, which can achieve a wider working bandwidth to satisfy UHF RFID localization requirement.

2.1   System Structure

System structure diagram is shown in Fig. 1. The system is mainly divided into three modules, DDS module, transmission module and reception module. DDS module is used to provide a local oscillator frequency source for the transmission module and reception module. The modulator up-converts the baseband signal generated by DAC with the local oscillator source, and the output signal of modulator is amplified by a three-stage amplifier. Reception module receives the RF signal through the circularly polarized antenna, amplifies the echo signal by a low noise amplifier, then down-converts with the local oscillator source to get I/Q signals, these I/Q signals is amplified and filtered by the variable gain amplifier and low-pass filter for baseband processing. The system is designed to be one-path transmission and three-path reception. The three-path reception link can make the obtained data more accurate. For simplicity, only one reception-path is shown here. All reception-paths are consistent in structure.

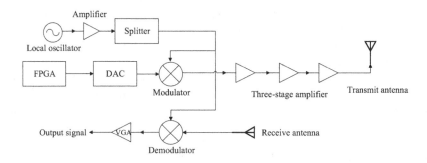

Fig. 1. System structure diagram

3   Circuit Design

3.1   DDS Module Design

The DDS structure diagram is shown in Fig. 2. The DDS module selects AD9914 chip of Analog Devices (ADI) as local oscillator source, the chip can be driven by a 3.5 GHz external clock frequency and have the fast frequency hopping feature [11]. It can generate stable signal that satisfies the operating frequency range. In this system, the AD9914 is controlled by the FPGA chip.

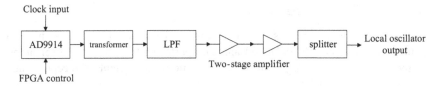

Fig. 2. DDS structure diagram

The differential signal generated by the DDS chip convert to single-ended output by the RF transformer structure, and a low-pass filter is cascade to filter out the out-of-band noise through. This module needs to provide local oscillator for the transmission module and multi-channel reception module. The output of DDS is amplified by two-stage amplifier to satisfy the frequency mixer input power requirements of local oscillator.

3.2   Transmission Module Design

The transmitter structure diagram is illustrated in Fig. 3. The main control chip of this module is EP3C16Q240C8 N (Altera's hurricane triple-series FPGA chip), AD9122 is the DAC (Digital to analog converter) chip of ADI, AD9156 is the clock chip of ADI. The FPGA chip controls AD9516 to generate the desired clock frequency for DAC chip. FPGA controls the DAC internal register through a 16-bit differential cable, the digital signals received by the input-end are converted into analog signals. The modulator mixes the output signals with the local frequency source and then pass a three-stage amplifier. The three-stage amplifier includes the RF gain module, the RF digital control VGA (Variable Gain Amplifier), the RF amplifier. As the required transmit power is large, multistage amplifier circuit needs to be designed. However, the input signal of the third stage amplifier has power limitation, so the second stage amplifier adopts digital control VGA. If the second level amplifier's output signal power exceeds the input power rating of the next stage amplifier, it can be attenuated by the FPGA chip.

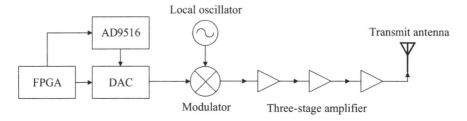

Fig. 3. Transmitter structure diagram

3.3   Reception Module Design

The receiver structure diagram is shown in Fig. 4. This module receives the echo signals through the circularly polarized antenna, performs the primary power amplification by the low-noise amplifier to control the noise coefficient of reception link. Then the I/Q signals can be obtained by down-conversion with the local oscillator frequency source, the output powers of the demodulator output signals can be adjusted by VGA chip. Then the signals pass through the low-pass filter and for processing.

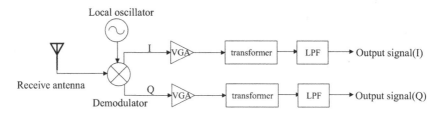

Fig. 4. One of the receiver structure diagram

4   System Test Results

Figure 5 shows the system test environment and Fig. 6 shows the hardware platform.

Fig. 5. System test environment

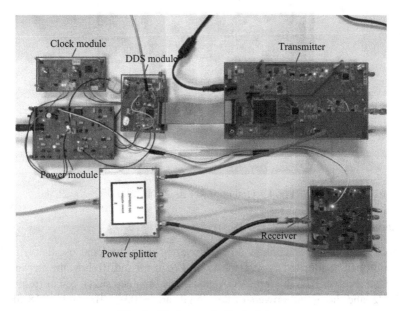

Fig. 6. Hardware physical picture

4.1 Transmitter Test Result

The transmitter uses the local oscillator to up-convert with the signal generated by ADC, then the amplified signal is transmitted to the air through the antenna. The output power of the transmitter in the bandwidth of 700 MHz to 1 GHz is shown in Fig. 7, and the spectrogram of output power near 900 MHz is shown in Fig. 8. The result shows that this transmitter has good performance within the entire operating frequency range.

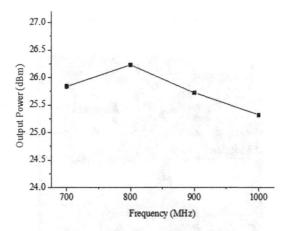

Fig. 7. Transmitter output signal power

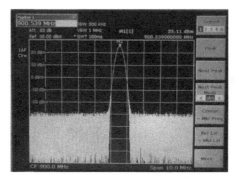

Fig. 8. Output power near 900 MHz

4.2 Receiver Test Result

The signal received by antenna is down-converted with the local oscillator, and the output power can be adjusted through the VGA. Figures 9 and 10 show the measurement results of the receiver with different VGA gains. The obtained signal center frequency is 4.246 MHz, and the output powers of the signals are −10.95 dBm and −1.18 dBm.

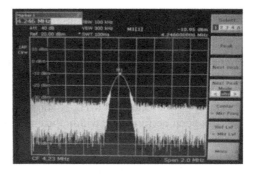

Fig. 9. Baseband amplifier output power

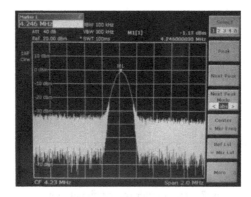

Fig. 10. Baseband amplifier output power

5 Conclusion

This paper designs a UHF RFID transceiver front-end based on discrete components, which utilizes the advantages of DDS technology for fast frequency switch and multi-frequency point output. Using the fast frequency hopping technology in a wide bandwidth of DDS, the system can achieve a high accuracy and high stability local oscillator signal output. The measured results show that the system basically satisfies the design requirements of UHF RFID transceiver front-end for localization, which verifies the correctness and rationality.

Acknowledgement. This work was supported partly by the Scientific and Technological Research Foundation of Chongqing Municipal Education Commission under grant KJ1704083, the National Natural Science Foundation of China under 61704015, the Fundamental and Frontier Research Project of Chongqing under grant cstc2017jcyjAX0380.

References

1. Lin, X., Wang, J., Zhang, C.: Design of an UHF RFID interrogator based on ISO/IEC 18000-6C. Semicond. Technol. **33**(9), 817–820 (2008)
2. Chen, D.: Design and Research of RFID Middleware in Building JMX. Science Mosaic (2013)
3. Du, H.: Research on indoor positioning technology based on RFID. In: Tan, H. (ed.) Knowledge Discovery and Data Mining, pp. 109–115. Springer, Heidelberg (2012). https://doi.org/10.1007/978-3-642-27708-5_15
4. Li, H., Long, X., Tan, H.: Overview on Control Processing Module Hardware Design of UHF RFID System Reader. Shanxi Electronic Technology (2015)
5. Sun, X.: The Development Status of RFID Technology and Industry. Cards World (2007)
6. Shen, J., Wang, X., Liu, S.: Design and implementation of an ultra-low power passive UHF RFID tag. J. Semicond. **33**(11), 115011 (2013)
7. Jia, M., Gu, X., Guo, Q.: Broadband hybrid satellite-terrestrial communication systems based on cognitive radio toward 5G. IEEE Wirel. Commun. **23**(6), 96–106 (2016)
8. Jia, M., Liu, X., Gu, X.: Joint cooperative spectrum sensing and channel selection optimization for satellite communication systems based on cognitive radio. Int. J. Satell. Commun. Netwo. **35**(2), 139–150 (2017)
9. Jia, M., Liu, X., Yin, Z.: Joint cooperative spectrum sensing and spectrum opportunity for satellite cluster communication networks. Ad Hoc Netw. **58**(C), 231–238 (2016)
10. Ma, Y., Selby, N., Adib, F.: Minding the Billions: Ultra-wideband Localization for Deployed RFID Tags. Massachusetts Institute of Technology (2017)
11. Deng, Y.P., Xiao, T.J.: Design and implementation of parallel DDS signal generator based on FPGA. Comput. Eng. Des. **32**(7), 2319–2323 (2011)

Rough Set Reduction Aided Cost-Efficient Indoor WLAN Localization

Hui Yuan[1]([✉]), Mu Zhou[1], Zhian Deng[2], Liangbo Xie[1], Yong Wang[1], and Xiaolong Yang[1]

[1] School of Communication and Information Engineering,
Chongqing University of Posts and Telecommunications, Chongqing 400065, China
`yuanhui0128@foxmail.com`
[2] College of Information and Communication Engineering,
Harbin Engineering University, Harbin 150001, China

Abstract. Due to the popularity of Wireless Local Area Networks (WLAN) applications, more and more access points (APs) are connected to the public network. Therefore, indoor localization technology based on public networks has a predominant development prospect. However, localization in the public network faces a lot of problems, and the excessive number of the APs in one of the most serious problems. Based on this, this paper proposes an indoor localization method based on rough set reduction. In this paper, the Received Signal Strength (RSS) signal strength from APs is used as the condition attribute of the rough set, and the optimal attribute reduction is obtained by the neighborhood rough set operation. After the rough set reduction operation, the number of APs in this paper's data set has been reduced from 520 to 4 or 5, and the location fingerprint database has been greatly reduced. Finally, this paper applies the reduced fingerprint database for indoor localization and estimates the location of each test point.

Keywords: Rough set · Received Signal Strength · AP reduction

1 Introduction

Due to the increasing popularity of wireless networks and smart terminals, Location-based Services (LBSs) [1] based applications are becoming more widespread. In the field of indoor localization, the fingerprint localization approach, as a classic algorithm based on RSS [2], has been emphasized in academic research.

In general, fingerprint localization involves two phases, offline phase and online phase [3]. In the offline phase, a radio map is created, which contains a large number of fingerprint data of RSS from all APs collected at some Reference Points (RPs). In the online phase, some appropriate matching algorithm will be applied to match the fingerprints collected online and the fingerprint database offline.

© ICST Institute for Computer Sciences, Social Informatics and Telecommunications Engineering 2019
Published by Springer Nature Switzerland AG 2019. All Rights Reserved
M. Jia et al. (Eds.): WiSATS 2019, LNICST 280, pp. 194–200, 2019.
https://doi.org/10.1007/978-3-030-19153-5_19

In order to reduce the workload of deploying APs in the offline phase, we used a public network to collect fingerprint data. However, there are a large number of APs in the public network, and some APs have very weak signals, which are not even enough to be displayed on the WLAN list of our mobile phones. Such a large number of APs will not only lead to an increase in the overhead of building a fingerprint database in the offline phase, but also affect the real-time characteristics of online phase localization. To solve this problem, we studied a rough set-based AP screening approach, which greatly reduces the number of APs and improves the localization efficiency in the online phase.

2   Related Work

For the problem of too many APs, scholars have also done a lot of research. Some scholars screen APs by evaluating the importance of APs [4]. Some machine learning dimensionality reduction algorithms, such as Principal Component Analysis (PCA), are also used for AP reduction. In addition, feature extraction of the fingerprint library can also effectively reduce the overhead [5,6].

In this paper, we use rough set reduction to reduce AP, which is an effective method for solving many decision-making problems with many influencing factors [7]. Before localization, we divide the target area into 4 sub-areas. Then, we treat different APs as factors that influence the localization results. After reducing the AP, we apply the K-Nearest Neighbor (KNN) algorithm to estimate the specific coordinates of each test point.

3   Reduced Fingerprint Database Construction

3.1   Positive Set Calculation and AP Reduction

In order to solve the problem of excessive number of APs in an indoor WLAN environment, we propose a method based on rough set attribute reduction to reduce the number of APs. Given N-dimensional real signal space Ω, $\Delta = R^N \times R^N \to R$, and treat Δ as a distance on R^N. We select the Euclidean distance to measure the distance between any two elements x_i and x_j in the signal space, as calculated in Eq. (1).

$$\Delta(x_i, x_j) = \sqrt{\sum_{k=1}^{N}(x_{ik} - x_{jk})^2} \tag{1}$$

We define that the RSS collected at all RPs in real signal space Ω constitutes a non-empty finite set $U = \{x_1, x_2, \cdots, x_s\}$ where s is the number of RPs and δ-neighborhood of any x_i as $\delta(x_i)$.

$$\delta(x_i) = \{x | x \in U, \Delta(x, x_i) \le \delta\}, \ \delta \ge 0 \tag{2}$$

Define the neighborhood decision system $NDS = (U, A \cup D)$, where we treat RSS from each as the condition attribute $A = (ap_1, ap_2, \cdots, ap_k)$ of the rough set, where k is the number of APs. At the same time, we divide the target area of the localization into several sub-areas and use the result of the area division as the decision attribute of the decision system NDS. That is to say, the decision attribute D divides the domain U into c equivalence classes $(X_1, X_2, \cdots, X_c)$. For A, the upper and lower approximation sets of the decision attribute D with respect to A are shown in Eqs. (3) and (4) respectively.

$$N_A X^U = \{x_i | \delta_A(x_i) \cap X \neq \Phi, x_i \in U\} \tag{3}$$

$$N_A X^D = \{x_i | \delta_A(x_i) \subseteq X, x_i \in U\} \tag{4}$$

The boundary domain set of the decision system NDS can also be obtained as shown in Eq. (5).

$$BN(D) = N_A X^U - N_A X^D \tag{5}$$

The positive and negative domains of the decision system NDS are shown in Eqs. (6) and (7).

$$\mathrm{Pos}_A(D) = N_A X^D \tag{6}$$

$$\mathrm{Neg}_A(D) = U - N_A X^U \tag{7}$$

The dependence of the decision attribute D on the condition attribute set A can be obtained as Eq. (8), where $|\cdot|$ stands for the number of elements in a set.

$$\gamma_A(D) = \frac{|\mathrm{Pos}_A(D)|}{|U|} \tag{8}$$

$\forall ap_l \in A$, if ap_l is removed from condition attribute A, the dependency of decision attribute D on condition attribute set A is unchanged, then the significance of ap_l is 0 and ap_l is a redundant attribute, which should be deleted in rough set reduction. On the contrary, if ap_l is removed and the dependency of D on A is changed, then the significance of ap_l is greater than 0. We assume that the dependency of the decision attribute D on the conditional attribute set A with ap_l removed is $\gamma_A^l(D)$, the significance of ap_l is $|\gamma_A^l(D) - \gamma_A(D)|$, where $|\cdot|$ stands for absolute value. By calculating the proportion of difference conditional attributes' significance, we obtain the weights of different conditional attributes, that is, the weights of different APs. We reserve the APs with the weights greater than 0 and delete the remaining APs. The AP weight is calculated as shown in Eq. (9), where w_l is the wight of l-th AP.

$$w_l = \frac{|\gamma_A^l(D) - \gamma_A(D)|}{\sum\limits_{j=1}^{a} |\gamma_A^j(D) - \gamma_A(D)|} \tag{9}$$

Then we find APs with their weight greater than 0, and the remaining APs are deleted as useless APs. After the useless AP is deleted, the storage overhead of the fingerprint database is greatly reduced. The reduction of the fingerprint database in the offline phase provides a good prerequisite for the location estimation of the online phase.

4   Location Estimate

In the online phase we chose the KNN positioning algorithm to estimate the position of each test point. Since the previous step, we have divided the target area into four sub-areas, before applying the KNN algorithm in this step, we need to divide the test points into their own areas. In order to classify test points, we still use a δ neighborhood-based classification method. We need to find all RPs in the δ neighborhood of each test point. Then we calculate the RPs in the neighborhood of each test point separately, and select the area with the most RPs. We treat the area selected as the area to which the test point belongs.

Next we apply the KNN algorithm to locate in the selected area. This article sets $K = 3$. Therefore, we select the three points closest to the test point in the selected area, and then calculate the average of the coordinates of the three points, which is the estimated coordinates of the test point.

5   Experiments

In order to verify the validation of rough set reduction, we conducted experiments in this section. As a result, we obtained the localization results of the test points and analyze them.

5.1   Setup

The main contribution of this paper is the reduction of AP's number. Therefore, we apply the UJI data set [8] published online, which contains thousands of fingerprints from 520 APs. We selected fingerprint training data and test data from Building 2, 0 to 3 floors in this data set. The layout of target building is shown in Figs. 1 and 2.

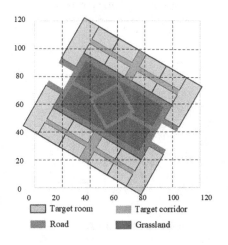

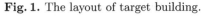

Fig. 1. The layout of target building.

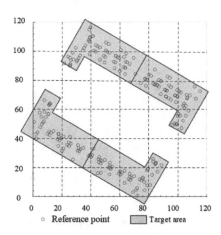

Fig. 2. Target area division and RPs distribution.

5.2 Validation of Rough Set Reduction

First, based on the division of the target area, we classify the test points and get the sub-area to which each test point belongs. Then, the fingerprint database reduction method based on rough set reduction proposed in this paper is applied to reduce the original fingerprint database. After the reduction of AP's number, there are 4 to 5 APs left on each floor for indoor localization. The remaining APs on each floor are shown in Table 1.

Table 1. Remaining APs on each floor.

Floor ID	Remaining AP ID
0	204, 501, 332, 59, 67
1	121, 98, 70, 74, 61
2	132, 62, 77, 60
3	11, 83, 61, 65

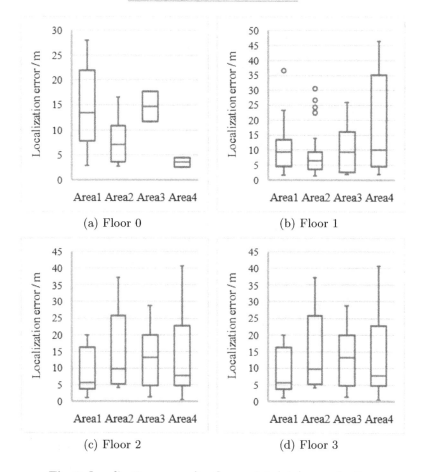

Fig. 3. Localization error after fingerprint database reduction.

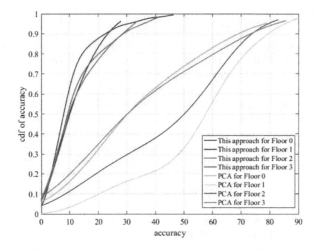

Fig. 4. CDF of localization error after fingerprint database reduction.

Retain the RSS data from the APs in Table 1 and delete the rest of the RSS data in the original fingerprint database. From this we get the reduced position fingerprint database. Finally, we apply the KNN method to the test points in each sub-area of the four floors for position estimation. The localization error of the sub-areas is shown in Fig. 3. To verify the effectiveness of the approach, we compared this method with PCA. The CDF (Cumulative Distribution Function) of localization error on each floor is shown in Fig. 4.

6   Conclusion

In this paper, the correlation operation of the neighborhood rough set is used to reduce the location fingerprint database collected in the public network, which greatly reduces the storage overhead of the location fingerprint database. In the experimental part, we applied the KNN algorithm for indoor localization based on the reduced position fingerprint database, and obtained good experimental results.

Acknowledgment. This work is supported in part by the National Natural Science Foundation of China (61771083, 61704015), Program for Changjiang Scholars and Innovative Research Team in University (IRT1299), Special Fund of Chongqing Key Laboratory (CSTC), Fundamental Science and Frontier Technology Research Project of Chongqing (cstc2017jcyjAX0380, cstc2015jcyjBX0065), Scientific and Technological Research Foundation of Chongqing Municipal Education Commission (KJ1704083), and University Outstanding Achievement Transformation Project of Chongqing (KJZH17117).

References

1. Ali, K., Javed, T., Hassanein, H., Oteafy, S.: Non-audible acoustic communication and its application in indoor location-based services. In: IEEE Wireless Communications and Networking Conference, pp. 1–6 (2016)
2. Han, C., Kieffer, M., Lambert, A.: Guaranteed confidence region characterization for source localization using RSS measurements. Signal Process. **152**, 104–117 (2016)
3. Pu, Y., You, P.: Indoor positioning system based on BLE location fingerprinting with classification approach. Appl. Math. Model. **62**, 654–663 (2018)
4. Byrne, D., Kozlowski, M., Raul, S., Piechocki, R.: Residential wearable RSSI and accelerometer measurements with detailed location annotations. Multi-Discipl. Sci. **5** (2018)
5. Fang, S., Lin, T.: Principal component localization in indoor WLAN environments. IEEE Trans. Mob. Comput. **11**(1), 100–110 (2012)
6. Lee, M., Han, D.: Dimensionality reduction of radio map with nonlinear autoencoder. Electron. Lett. **48**(11), 655–657 (2012)
7. Yuan, Z., Zhang, X., Feng, S.: Hybrid data-driven outlier detection based on neighborhood information entropy and its developmental measures. Expert Syst. Appl. **112**, 243–257 (2018)
8. Torres-Sospedra, J., Montoliu, R., Martinez-Uso, A., et al.: UJIIndoorLoc: a new multi-building and multi-floor database for WLAN fingerprint-based indoor localization problems. In: International Conference on Indoor Positioning and Indoor Navigation, pp. 261–270 (2014)

Device-Free Stationary Human Detection with WiFi in Through-the-Wall Scenarios

Zhengwu Yuan, Shiming Wu$^{(\boxtimes)}$, Xiaolong Yang, and Ailin He

School of Communication and Information Engineering,
Chongqing University of Posts and Telecommunications,
Chongqing 400065, China
2812940421@qq.com

Abstract. Human detection plays an important role in smart home and health monitoring. WiFi-based device-free detection schemes are widely proposed. The current WiFi-based device-free through-the-wall human detection system can detect moving human behind wall by the theory that RF signals would fluctuate remarkably when objects move within the area of interests, and remain stable in the case of no motion interference. However, stationary human detection is still an open issue, because it is hard to capture the fluctuate of signal caused by the weak movements (such as breathing, writing, etc.) of stationary human behind wall. In order to solve this problem, this paper proposes a novel system which extracts more delicate features for detection. The proposed system extracts features from time of fly (ToF) of signal, and then trains a neural network to classify these features to determine if a stationary human behind the wall. Our experiment shows that the detection accuracy of proposed system can reach 87.7% in typical office environment.

Keywords: Device-free · WiFi · Stationary human detection · Channel state information

1 Introduction

Different from conventional device-based schemes, recent development in wireless techniques have spurred an emerging development of device-free sensing techniques, which utilize pervasive WiFi signal to sense human state without attaching any device to users. Device-free means that detect human in the area of interests without attaching any device to them, which is closer to the actual application in our daily life. The typical applications include indoor localization [1], activity recognition [2], even gesture recognition [3], etc. Existing human detection schemes can be divided into two types: wall-through and wall-free. In [4], a unified framework for simultaneous detection of moving and stationary people proposed. The moving and stationary human are detected by using correlation of signals in the time domain and exploiting chest motions of human breathing as an intrinsic indicator. However, the through-the-wall scenario is not considered. In [5], different from utilizing the correlation of channel state information (CSI) in the time dimension, the correlation of the WiFi signal subcarriers is used to detect the moving human behind wall, which is not available for

M. Jia et al. (Eds.): WiSATS 2019, LNICST 280, pp. 201–208, 2019.
https://doi.org/10.1007/978-3-030-19153-5_20

stationary humans. Based on all the references above-mentioned, stationary human detection in the through-the-wall scenario is not considered for two main reasons: (1) the signal-to-noise ratio becomes lower when signal going through the wall; (2) the fluctuate of signal caused by stationary human is too week to capture.

In order to overcome these challenges, this paper proposes a novel detection system. At first, we introduce a linear transformation to reduce the noise of phase. Then, based on the available phase information, we estimate time of fly (ToF) of signal by using the smooth MUSIC algorithm, and calculate the variance of ToF of each path over a period of time as a feature. Finally, we trained a neural network classifier to classify the extracted features effectively. Experimental results show that the proposed system can achieve an overall recognition accuracy of 87.7%.

2   Stationary Human Detection System

2.1   Overview of System

The proposed system is a device-free system that can detect stationary human behind wall by using ubiquitous off-the-shelf Wi-Fi devices, which consists of a transmitter with one antenna and a receiver with three antennas. The transmitter and receiver are separated by a wall. The data processing flow of our system is shown in Fig. 1. At first, after receiving CSI from transmitter, the receiver will provide the CSI to data processing module, where a linear transformation will be implemented to reduce the noise of phase. Then, the processed CSI are used to estimate ToF, from which features are extracted for stationary human detection. Finally, we use neural networks to classify the extracted features to identify the stationary person behind wall. The details of each module will be introduced in the following sections.

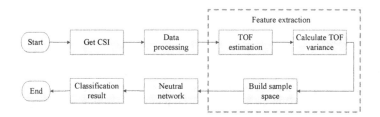

Fig. 1.   The data processing flow of system.

2.2   Data Processing

In this section, we introduce a linear transformation which can reduce the noise of phase. Each packet consists of CSIs from 30 subcarriers, whose structure is shown as:

$$H = [H(f_1), H(f_2), H(f_3), \ldots, H(f_{30})] \tag{1}$$

Each CSI describes the amplitude and phase information of a subcarrier, which is expressed as:

$$H(f_i) = \|H(f_i)\|e^{j\sin\{\angle H(f_i)\}}, \ i \in [1, 30] \tag{2}$$

where $H(f_i)$ represents the CSI of ith subcarrier which the central frequency is f_i, and $\angle H(f_i)$ represents the phase of each subcarrier. Synchronization error between transmitter and receiver cannot be eliminated completely and the existence of synchronization error has a great influence on the phase. Thus, the phase can be represented as:

$$\tilde{\Phi}_j = \Phi_j + 2\pi \frac{j}{k} \varphi_\varepsilon + \beta \tag{3}$$

where φ_ε is the clock synchronization error, and k represents the total number of subcarriers. β is the constant phase error. $\tilde{\Phi}_j$ and Φ_j represents the measured value of phase and the real phase, respectively. We employed one kind of linear transformation to eliminate the clock synchronization error and phase shift [6].

In order to eliminate φ_ε and β, we calculate the approximate slope and intercept of phase. After eliminating φ_ε and β, the phase can be written as:

$$\hat{\Phi}_{ji} = \tilde{\Phi}_{ji} - (ak_i + b) \tag{4}$$

where a is the slope and b is the intercept. When the subcarrier index is symmetric, the sum of subcarriers is zero. Then, the phase after transformation is shown as:

$$\hat{\Phi}_{ji} = \Phi_{ji} - ji\frac{\Phi_{jn} - \Phi_{j1}}{jn - j1} - \frac{1}{n}\sum_{k=1}^{n}\Phi_{jk} \tag{5}$$

where n is the number of subcarriers. After this process, we can obtain the approximate and available phase for next section.

2.3   Feature Extraction

A multipath channel model can be established for each subcarrier by utilizing the CSI measurement matrix obtained on one receive antenna, shown as:

$$\begin{bmatrix} csi_1 \\ csi_2 \\ csi_3 \\ \vdots \\ csi_{30} \end{bmatrix} = \begin{bmatrix} e^{-j2\pi f_1 \tau_1} & e^{-j2\pi f_1 \tau_2} & \cdots & e^{-j2\pi f_1 \tau_L} \\ e^{-j2\pi(f_1 + \Delta f)\tau_1} & e^{-j2\pi(f_1 + \Delta f)\tau_2} & \cdots & e^{-j2\pi(f_1 + \Delta f)\tau_L} \\ e^{-j2\pi(f_1 + 2\Delta f)\tau_1} & e^{-j2\pi(f_1 + 2\Delta f)\tau_2} & \cdots & e^{-j2\pi(f_1 + 2\Delta f)\tau_L} \\ \vdots & \vdots & \ddots & \vdots \\ e^{-j2\pi(f_1 + 29\Delta f)\tau_1} & e^{-j2\pi(f_1 + 29\Delta f)\tau_2} & \cdots & e^{-j2\pi(f_1 + 29\Delta f)\tau_L} \end{bmatrix} \begin{bmatrix} \alpha_1 \\ \alpha_2 \\ \alpha_3 \\ \vdots \\ \alpha_L \end{bmatrix} \tag{6}$$

where csi_k, $k \in [1, 30]$ is the kth subcarrier of the received signal, f_1 is the frequency of the first subcarrier, and L represents the total number of signal propagation paths. Δf is carrier spacing. τ_i, $i \in [1, L]$ and α_i, $i \in [1, L]$ represent the ToF and path coefficients of the ith path arriving at the antenna, respectively.

Let $\mathbf{X} = \begin{bmatrix} csi_1 & csi_2 & \cdots & csi_{30} \end{bmatrix}^T$, and the smooth MUSIC algorithm [7] is used to complete the estimation of TOF. The autocorrelation matrix of the matrix $\mathbf{X}$ can be expressed as:

$$\mathbf{R_{xx}} = E(\mathbf{XX^H}) \tag{7}$$

Assume that the real data matrix is statistically uncorrelated with the noise matrix. Then the matrix $\mathbf{R_{xx}}$ can be divided into signal subspace and noise subspace. Define spectral functions as:

$$p(\tau) = \frac{1}{\mathbf{a^H}(\tau)\mathbf{GG^H}\mathbf{a}(\tau)} \tag{8}$$

where $\mathbf{a}(\tau) = \begin{bmatrix} 1 & e^{-j2\pi\Delta f\tau} & e^{-j2\pi 2\Delta f\tau} & \cdots & e^{-j2\pi 29\Delta f\tau} \end{bmatrix}^T$ denotes the steering matrix and $\mathbf{G}$ stands for the eigenvectors corresponding to noise subspace.

For combating the coherent signals, smoothing on $\mathbf{XX^H}$ is performed before decomposition, as shown in Fig. 2. We assume that the total number of subcarriers is M and the number of subcarriers in the subarray is N, then the number of subarrays is $M - N + 1$. After smoothing, autocorrelation matrix can be expressed as:

$$\mathbf{R}_{smooth} = \frac{1}{N - M + 1} \sum_{i=1}^{N-M+1} \mathbf{R}_i \tag{9}$$

Then, we can get the spectral function by $\mathbf{R}_{smooth}$. Perform a traversal search on τ. When the search τ is equal to the ToF of the signal propagation path, a peak will appear on the spectrum. In fact, due to the existence of packet detection delay (PDD), all paths generate a common additional delay, which is much larger than the TOF of normal indoor signals. It has no effect on feature extraction, although the estimated ToF is not the true value. Because we use the stability of ToF over a period of time as feature.

Select the ToF of the four paths with the strongest energy to represent the TOF of all paths between the transceivers, and calculate the variance of each path over a period of time (2 s) as a feature. There are three receive antennas, and a total of twelve feature can be obtained.

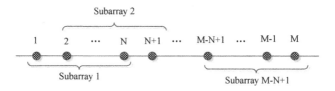

Fig. 2. There is a total of M subcarriers, and each subarray has N subcarriers. After smoothing, $M - N + 1$ subarrays can be obtained.

2.4   Neural Networks Based Detection

Based on the obtained features, a trained neural network is used to complete the recognition. Neural network consists of three parts: input layer, hidden layer, and output layer. Input layer neurons are used to receive external input, Hidden layer and output layer neurons process the signal, and the final result is output by the output layer neurons. The learning process of neural network is to adjust the connection weight between neurons, and change the threshold of each function neuron according to train data. When the appropriate connection weigh and threshold are obtained, the learning process will converge [8].

In our system, after parameter tuning, we design a 3-layer neural network with ten hidden layer neurons. We use the twelve features mentioned above as the input features of the samples. Two features, nobody behind the wall and stationary people behind wall, are used as output features. Our network structure is shown in Fig. 3. We randomly select 60% of the samples as training samples to train a classifier, then use remaining samples as test samples to verify the accuracy of the classification.

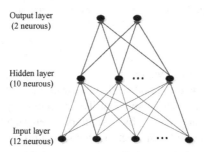

Output layer
(2 neurous)

Hidden layer
(10 neurous)

Input layer
(12 neurous)

Fig. 3. The designed 3-layer neural network has 12 neurons in input layer, 10 neurons in hidden layer, and 2 neurons in output layer.

3   Experiments Evaluation

3.1   Implementation

The proposed system contains a transmitter and a receiver both equipped with the Intel 5300 wireless NIC, and the parameters setting is shown in Table 1.

Table 1. Parameters setting.

Parameters	Transmitting AP	Receiving AP
Mode	Injection	Monitor
Channel number	149 (5.745 GHz)	
Bandwidth	40 MHz	
Channel sample rate	500 times per second	
Number of subcarriers	30	
Index of subcarriers	[−58, 54, …, 54, 58]	
Transmit power	15 dBm	

The transmitter has one antenna and the receiver equipped with three antennas. Meanwhile, in order to reduce the noise interference, we accomplish the experiments with the help of directional antenna at the transmitter. All the experiments are conducted in a typical office as shown in Fig. 4. A volunteer is located at the position marked by pentagram in the picture in experiments. We collect data of two categories: no human in the monitored room and stationary human in the monitored room.

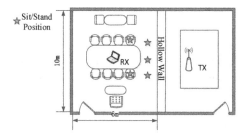

Fig. 4. Floor plan of the experimental areas.

3.2   Spectrum Analysis

In this section, we analyze the value of ToF over time domain. Figure 5 shows the change of ToF over time when nobody is behind wall and stationary human is behind wall. It can be observed that the change of ToF is relatively stable when no one is behind wall, while there are many obvious jitters when stationary human is behind wall. This difference is caused by the fact that the signal propagation paths is relatively stable when there is no man in the room. When a stationary human in the room, the slight action (such as breathing, writing, etc.) will interfere the signal propagation paths, and then changes the propagation time of the signal on the paths.

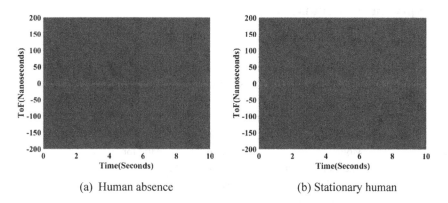

(a) Human absence   (b) Stationary human

Fig. 5. The change of ToF over time. (a) shows the change of ToF over time when no one is behind the wall. (b) shows the change of ToF with time when there is a stationary person behind the wall.

3.3 Detection Accuracy Analysis

We obtain a total of 3867 samples, including 1786 no human samples and 2081 stationary human samples. Stratified sampling is used to randomly select 60% of the samples from the total samples as the training data of the neural network, and the remaining 40% of the samples are used as the test samples.

The detection accuracy of the test samples is shown in Table 2. As seen, most human absence samples are accurately categorized as human absence and only small portion of 7.8% is labelled as stationary human. 85.0% of stationary human samples are correctly classified. The overall recognition accuracy is 87.7%. This accuracy rate is satisfactory, indicating that the proposed system is an effective solution to detect stationary human in through-the-wall scenarios.

Table 2. Detection accuracy.

Output class	Target class	
	Stationary human	Human absence
Stationary human	92.2% (523 samples)	7.8% (44 samples)
Human absence	15.0% (129 samples)	85.0% (732 samples)

4 Conclusion

In this paper, we propose a device-free through-the-wall stationary human detection system based on channel state information. First, we introduce a linear transformation to reduce the noise of phase. Then, we estimate the ToF of the signal using the smooth MUSIC algorithm, and calculate the variance of ToF of each path over a period of time (2 s) as a feature. Finally, a trained neural network is used to complete the recognition. Experimental results show that the proposed system can achieve an overall recognition accuracy of 87.7%, which makes it possible to detect stationary people in through-the-wall scenarios, and expands the application range of WiFi-based device-free detection system.

Acknowledgment. Supported by the Science and Technology Research Program of Chongqing Municipal Education Commission (Grant No. KJQN201800625).

References

1. Seifeldin, M., Saeed, A., Kosba, A.E.: Nuzzer: a large-scale device-free passive localization system for wireless environments. IEEE Trans. Mob. Comput. **12**(7), 1321–1334 (2013)
2. Wang, W., Liu, A.X., Shahzad, M.: Understanding and modeling of WiFi signal based human activity recognition. In: 21st Annual International Conference on Mobile Computing and Networking, MobiCom 2015, Paris, France, pp. 65–76 (2015)
3. Pu, Q.F., Jiang, S.Y., Gollakota, S.: Whole-home gesture recognition using wireless signals (Demo). ACM SIGCOMM Comput. Commun. Rev. **43**(4), 485–486 (2013)

4. Wu, C., Yang, Z., Zhou, Z.: Non-Invasive detection of moving and stationary human with WiFi. IEEE J. Sel. Areas Commun. **33**(11), 2329–2342 (2015)
5. Zhu, H., Xiao, F., Sun, L.: R-TTWD: robust device-free through-the-wall detection of moving human with WiFi. IEEE J. Sel. Areas Commun. **35**(5), 1090–1103 (2017)
6. Qian, K., Wu, C., Yang, Z.: PADS: passive detection of moving targets with dynamic speed using PHY layer information. In: 2014 20th IEEE International Conference on Parallel and Distributed Systems, Hsinchu, Taiwan, pp. 1–8 (2014)
7. Shan, T.-J., Wax, M., Kailath, T.: On spatial smoothing for direction-of-arrival estimation of coherent signals. IEEE Trans. Acoust. Speech Signal Process. **33**(4), 806–811 (1985)
8. Bradley, F., Janette, B.S.: Neural networks: a comprehensive foundation. Inf. Process. Manag. **31**(5), 71–80 (1995)
9. Jia, M., Gu, X., Guo, Q.: Broadband hybrid satellite-terrestrial communication systems based on cognitive radio toward 5G. IEEE Wirel. Commun. **23**(6), 96–106 (2016)
10. Jia, M., Liu, X., Gu, X.: Joint cooperative spectrum sensing and channel selection optimization for satellite communication systems based on cognitive radio. Int. J. Satell. Commun. Network. **35**(2), 139–150 (2017)
11. Jia, M., Liu, X., Yin, Z.: Joint cooperative spectrum sensing and spectrum opportunity for satellite cluster communication networks. Ad Hoc Netw. **58**(C), 231–238 (2016)

Through-the-Wall Human Behavior Recognition Algorithm with Commercial Wi-Fi Devices

Zhenhua Yang$^{(\boxtimes)}$, Xiaolong Yang, Mu Zhou, and Shiming Wu

Chongqing Key Lab of Mobile Communications Technology,
Chongqing University of Posts and Telecommunications,
Chongqing 400065, China
871742538@qq.com

Abstract. Wi-Fi-based human behavior recognition technology is one of the research hotspots in the field of wireless sensing. However, the traditional Wi-Fi-based human behavior recognition algorithm does not consider the attenuation of Wi-Fi signals in the condition of wall barrier under complex indoor environments. As a result, the robustness of the Wi-Fi indoor human behavior recognition system is poor. In order to solve this problem, this paper proposes a Wi-Fi based behavior recognition algorithm through the wall. Firstly, the Wi-Fi signal distribution is analyzed according to the Wi-Fi signal model. Then, according to the distribution characteristics of different Wi-Fi signals, the principal component analysis (PCA) algorithm is used to reconstruct the signal to complete the de-nosing processing of the Wi-Fi signal. Finally, feature extraction and feature classification in the time-frequency domain is performed to complete the human behavior recognition. The experimental results show that the proposed algorithm has higher recognition accuracy in terms of walking and running than the traditional Wi-Fi based indoor recognition algorithms.

Keywords: Behavior recognition · Wi-Fi · Indoor environment ·
Principal component analysis (PCA) · Channel state information (CSI)

1 Introduction

In recent years, human behavior recognition technology has attracted much attention to monitor human behavior in indoor areas. Specific applications include health monitoring and fall detection for older people, scene detection, smart home and many other Internet-based of things (IoT) application. Human behavior recognition systems with different auxiliary equipment are mainly divided into three categories. The first category is a sensor-based human behavior recognition system [4], which requires the identified target to wear special equipment such as motion sensors, extracts the features of the data acquired by the sensor, and then uses the supervised learning algorithm to classify the characteristics of different behaviors. The system recognizes sleeping, sitting, walking, running, etc., with an accuracy rate of 90%. However, the identified target needs to carry the device at any time, so that the application range and recognition ability of the system are limited. In particular, in the case of the elderly forgetting

© ICST Institute for Computer Sciences, Social Informatics and Telecommunications Engineering 2019
Published by Springer Nature Switzerland AG 2019. All Rights Reserved
M. Jia et al. (Eds.): WiSATS 2019, LNICST 280, pp. 209–217, 2019.
https://doi.org/10.1007/978-3-030-19153-5_21

to wear equipment, the consequences are unimaginable. The second category is a camera-based human behavior recognition system [1, 2], which performs well, but the main limitation is that behavior recognition must be performed under Line Of Sight (LOS) conditions. What's worse, the use environment of camera-based target behavior recognition systems is greatly limited due to sensitivity to light and privacy concerns. The third category is a passive detection system based on wireless signals [3, 5]. By extracting the characteristics of echo signals and constructing classifiers, the system realizes the behavior recognition of the identified targets, overcomes the safety hazards and limitations of scenarios of the first two types of human behavior recognition systems. It has obvious advantages in the field of human behavior recognition.

At present, as an important part of wireless signal-based passive detection system, the research of Wi-Fi-based behavior recognition system has been the focus of attention. Such systems include Wi-Fi access points (APs) and one or several receiving devices that support Wi-Fi protocols (such as 802.11n/ac) and are arranged in separate environments. When a person is active in the detection area, his or her behavior will have a certain degree of influence on the transmission environment of the Wi-Fi signal, and the channel state information (CSI) can finely record the change of the Wi-Fi signal. The system monitors the CSI information of the echo signals and extracts the signal characteristics of different actions, and then constructs the classifier to classify the behavior. Currently, the Wi-Fi-based behavior recognition system can identify walking, running, squatting and standing up and other actions, equipment cost is low, versatility, and recognition accuracy can reach 85%. But the environment has a greater impact on the system, especially in complex indoor environments with wall, cabinet and table, resulting in misjudgment of behavior.

For overcoming system stability degradation due to the complex indoor environment, this paper designs a Wi-Fi based through-wall human behavior recognition system, which filter out the interference caused by the wall, then the time and frequency domain characteristics of echo signal is extracted from the CSI information during the activity of the human body. Finally, the calculated behavior characteristics are used to construct the activity classifier to complete the behavioral judgment of the human behind the wall.

2   System Model

2.1   Channel State Information

Currently, CSI can be obtained by the NIC 5300 [6, 7]. CSI information can record the changes of Wi-Fi signals in a fine-grained manner. It has been widely used in human activity sensing areas such as personnel detection [13], behavior recognition [8–10], indoor positioning [14, 15], fall detection [12], etc. In addition, CSI can also be applied to micro-motion recognition. Perceptions of micro-actions such as gestures, lip movements [16], keystrokes [8], and heartbeats [18].

2.2   System Model

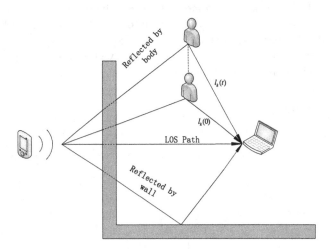

Fig. 1. A multipath signal model caused by human motion.

As shown as the Fig. 1, Wi-Fi signals have multipath effects in indoor environments and can propagate through multiple paths, including the LOS path and the path reflected by surrounding objects [11]. Assuming that the number of propagation paths is N, in the case of ignoring additive noise, different path gain $H(f,t)$ can be given as follows:

$$H(f,t) = e^{-j2\pi\Delta ft} \sum_{k=1}^{N} a_k(f,t) e^{-j2\pi f \tau_k(t)} \qquad (1)$$

where $e^{-j2\pi f\tau_k(t)}$ represents the delay $\tau_k(t)$ of the Wi-Fi signal on the kth path, and $e^{-j2\pi\Delta ft}$ is the phase due to the carrier frequency offset (CFO), $a_k(f,t)$ represents the initial gain of the kth path, the initial gain of the signal will experience an inestimable attenuation after passing through the wall:

$$a_k(f,t) = \sigma_k b_k(f,t) \qquad (2)$$

In the above formula, we ignore the phase offset caused by the sampling frequency offset, because we can effectively eliminate such errors in the subsequent noise reduction processing.

Changes in the length of a path lead to the changes in the phase of the Wi-Fi signal on the corresponding path. Consider the scenario in Fig. 1, where the Wi-Fi signal is reflected by the human body through the kth path. When the human moves by a small distance, the length of the kth path changes from $l_k(0)$ to $l_k(t)$. The delay of the kth path, denoted as $\tau_k(t)$, can be written as: $\tau_k(t) = d_k/c$, where c is the speed of light. Thus, the phase shift $e^{-j2\pi f\tau_k(t)}$ can be written as $e^{-j2\pi f d_k(t)/\lambda}$.

Theoretically, it is possible to accurately measure phase changes due to path changes, such as RFID systems [19], when receiving full synchronization. However, commercial Wi-Fi has a non-negligible CFO due to hardware defects and environmental changes. The center frequency drift is up to 100 kHz under the IEEE 802.11n protocol, and this frequency drift results in a fast CSI phase change. We observe that the CSI amplitude is not subject to severe interference with respect to phase, so we will use the CSI amplitude in subsequent work.

2.3   CSI De-nosing

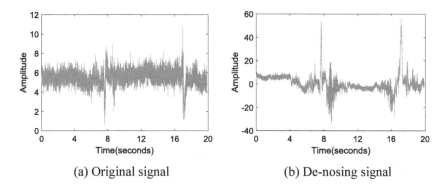

(a) Original signal   (b) De-nosing signal

Fig. 2. CSI de-nosing based on PCA

In the complex indoor environment, due to the influence of obstacles such as walls, the CSI amplitude information and phase information will be interfered, and the signal changes caused by the human body are relatively weak, so it is impossible to directly extract the signal variation characteristics caused by human activities such as Fig. 2(a). Therefore, this paper uses the PCA algorithm to cancel the interference, which caused by the hardware and wall in CSI information.

First, the CSI stream in the current sliding window is centered to eliminate the static components of the signal:

$$x_i = x_i - \frac{1}{n}\sum_{j=1}^{n} x_j \tag{3}$$

Then, the covariance matrix of the CSI stream is calculated and eigenvalue decomposition on the covariance matrix is performed to obtain the eigenvector of the covariance matrix. Finally, a new projection matrix is calculated by dimensional transformation to complete the target motion signal reconstruction:

$$Z_i = X^T w_i \tag{4}$$

where w_i and Z_i are the ith eigenvector and the main component of the ith signal.

3 Behavior Recognition Through-the-Wall

3.1 Behavior Feature Extraction Based on Short Time Fourier Transform

Short-time Fourier transform (STFT) algorithm adds time domain window based on Fourier transform to avoid the shortage of traditional Fourier transform time domain information. Therefore, The choice of window is important because a shorter duration window will retain high frequency components and vice versa. In addition, since the window function value is typically very small or zero nearby its boundary, a portion of the windowed signal is ignored. Therefore, it is necessary to overlap these segments. The percentage of overlap depends on the window function. In general, 50% is a common value for overlap, and Fig. 3 shows the STFT spectrum of the two target activities of walking and sitting. The sampling frequency is 40 Hz, overlap 50%, and the window function uses the Hanning window function. The test time for walking and sitting is 60 s and 30 s, respectively. The test plan for walking is to walk for every 10 s, and the test plan for sitting is to sit every 5 s. It can be seen from the figure that the spectral frequency of walking is between 0 and 5 Hz, and the spectral frequency range of sitting is significantly smaller, ranging from about 0 to 2 Hz.

Therefore, we extract a spectrum with a length of 3 s, a frequency range of 10 Hz, and a total length of 210 as behavioral features.

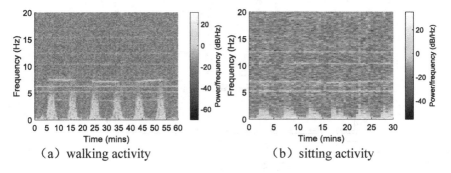

（a）walking activity   （b）sitting activity

Fig. 3. Spectrum of human activities

3.2 Behavior Classification

First, we use random forest with 100 trees for classification of activities. To have a feature vector that contains enough information about an activity, the modified STFT bins are stacked together in a vector for every 3 s of activity. Hence, every feature vector will be of length 210. We also implement other techniques such as SVM, logistic regression, and decision tree; however, the random forest outperforms these techniques. We observe that decent performance can be obtained for some of the activities, but not for activities such as "Sit down" and "Stand up".

4 Implementation and Evaluation

4.1 Implementation

We use a Mini PC with an Intel 5300 Wi-Fi card as the receiver and transmitter. The CSI values obtained from the regular data frames are sent by the AP, and we install the CSI tool developed by Halperin et al. All experiments in the 5.5 GHz band with channels, the bandwidth is 20 MHz. We choose the 5.5 GHz band for two reasons: first, the 5.5 GHz band has shorter wavelengths, which results in better range resolution; second, it has less line interference than the 2.4 GHz band.

We collect training samples for eight different activities in the lab environment with 6.5 m in length and 7 m in width, shown in Fig. 4. Our activity data contains 420 samples performed by 6 volunteers who are 4 male and 2 female graduate/undergraduate students. The specific behavior is shown in Table 1.

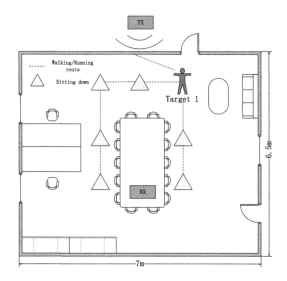

Fig. 4. Test environment

Table 1. Activity dataset

Activities	Training samples	Test samples
(R) Running	105	85
(W) Walking	120	95
(SD) Sitting down	75	60
(SU) Standing up	75	60

4.2   Evaluation

The experimental results are shown in Fig. 5. Among them, the two movements of walking and running can reach the accuracy of more than 90%, but the recognition accuracy of the two movements of standing up and sitting down is not ideal. At the same time, the experimental results show that the Wi-Fi-based behavior recognition through the wall method is effective.

	Walk	Run	Sit down	Stand up
Walk	0.95	0.04	0.01	0
Run	0.06	0.92	0.01	0.01
Sit down	0.02	0.03	0.68	0.27
Stand up	0.04	0.02	0.31	0.63

Fig. 5. Confusion matrix

5   Conclusion

Aiming at the problem of signal attenuation caused by wall blockage in Wi-Fi signal in complex indoor environment, this paper proposes a Wi-Fi based post-wall target behavior recognition method. Firstly, the PCA algorithm is used to eliminate the interference caused by the wall and hardware. Then, the behavior characteristics are extracted by STFT algorithm. Finally, the classification of target behavior is completed according to the random forest algorithm. However, although the proposed behavior recognition method can effectively improve the accuracy and stability of Wi-Fi indoor identification, how to solve the problem of distinguishing similar actions will be considered in the future.

Acknowledgement. This work is supported by the Science and Technology Research Program of Chongqing Municipal Education Commission (Grant No. KJQN201800625).

References

1. Kinect - Windows app development. http://www.microsoft.com/en-us/kinectforwindows/. Accessed 22 Sept 2016
2. Aggarwal, J.K., Ryoo, M.S.: Human activity analysis: a review. ACM Comput. Surv. **43**(3), 16 (2011)
3. Ertin, E., et al.: AutoSense: unobtrusively wearable sensor suite for inferring the onset, causality, and consequences of stress in the field. In: Proceedings of the ACM Sensys, pp. 274–287 (2011)
4. Lien, J., et al.: Soli: ubiquitous gesture sensing with millimeter wave radar. ACM Trans. Graph. **35**(4), 142 (2016)
5. Yatani, K., Truong, K.N.: BodyScope: a wearable acoustic sensor for activity recognition. In: Proceedings of the ACM UbiComp, pp. 341–350 (2012)
6. Halperin, D., Hu, W., Sheth, A., Wetherall, D.: Tool release: gathering 802.11n traces with channel state information. ACM SIGCOMM Comput. Commun. Rev. **41**(1), 53 (2011)
7. Xie, Y., Li, Z., Li, M.: Precise power delay profiling with commodity wifi. In: Proceedings of the ACM MobiCom, pp. 53–64 (2015)
8. Ali, K., Liu, A.X., Wang, W., Shahzad, M.: Keystroke recognition using WiFi signals. In: Proceedings of the ACM MobiCom, pp. 90–102 (2015)
9. Wang, Y., Liu, J., Chen, Y., Gruteser, M., Yang, J., Liu, H.: E-eyes: device-free location-oriented activity identification using fine-grained wifi signatures. In: Proceedings of the ACM MobiCom, pp. 617–628 (2015)
10. Xi, W., et al.: Electronic frog eye: counting crowd using WiFi. In: Proceedings of the IEEE INFOCOM, pp. 361–369 (2014)
11. Han, C., Wu, K., Wang, Y., Ni, L.M.: WiFall: device-free fall detection by wireless networks. In: Proceedings of the IEEE INFOCOM, pp. 271–279 (2014)
12. Wang, W., et al.: Understanding and modelling of WiFi signal based human activity recognition. In: Proceedings of the 21st Annual International Conference on Mobile Computing and Networking, pp. 65–76 (2015)
13. Zhou, Z., Yang, Z., Wu, C., Shangguan, L., Liu, Y.: Towards omnidirectional passive human detection. In: Proceedings of the IEEE INFOCOM, pp. 3057–3065 (2013)
14. Sen, S., Lee, J., Kim, K.-H., Congdon, P.: Avoiding multipath to revive inbuilding WiFi localization. In: Proceedings of the ACM MobiSys, p. 249–262 (2013)
15. Yang, Z., Zhou, Z., Liu, Y.: From RSSI to CSI: indoor localization via channel response. ACM Comput. Surv. **46**(2), 25 (2013)
16. Wang, G., Zou, Y., Zhou, Z., Wu, K., Ni, L.M.: We can hear you with Wi-Fi! In: Proceedings of the ACM MobiCom, pp. 2907–2920 (2014)
17. Qiao, Y., Zhang, O., Zhou, W., Srinivasan, K., Arora, A.: PhyCloak: obfuscating sensing from communication signals. In: Proceedings of the Usenix NSDI, pp. 685–699 (2016)
18. Zhao, M., Adib, F., Katabi, D.: Emotion recognition using wireless signals. In: Proceedings of the ACM MobiCom, pp. 95–108 (2016)
19. Yang, L., Chen, Y., Li, X.-Y., Xiao, C., Li, M., Liu, Y.: Tagoram: real-time tracking of mobile RFID tags to high precision using cots devices. In: Proceedings of the ACM MobiCom, pp. 237–248 (2014)
20. Jia, M., Gu, X., Guo, Q., Xiang, W., Zhang, N.: Broadband hybrid satellite-terrestrial communication systems based on cognitive radio toward 5G. IEEE Wirel. Commun. **23**(6), 96–106 (2016)

21. Jia, M., Liu, X., Gu, X., Guo, Q.: Joint cooperative spectrum sensing and channel selection optimization for satellite communication systems based on cognitive radio. Int. J. Satell. Commun. Netw. **35**(2), 139–150 (2017)
22. Jia, M., Liu, X., Yin, Z., Guo, Q., Gu, X.: Joint cooperative spectrum sensing and spectrum opportunity for satellite cluster communication networks. Ad Hoc Netw. **58**(1), 231–238 (2016)

A Pseudorange Difference Positioning Algorithm for Automatic Driving

Yi Chen[(⊠)], Yong Wang, Wei He, Qing Jiang, and Mu Zhou

School of Communications and Information Engineering,
Chongqing University of Posts and Telecommunications, Chongqing, China
751796746@qq.com

Abstract. Real-time and accurate positioning is very important for automatic driving. Traditional positioning methods, such as radar and inertial sensor, have limitations in universality and accuracy. Therefore, this paper proposes a pseudorange difference positioning algorithm, which combines Global Positioning System (GPS) receiver with reference station. The proposed algorithm achieves sub-meter positioning accuracy that providing a guarantee for automatic driving. The feasibility of the proposed algorithm is verified in static and dynamic environments, respectively. The results show that the positioning error is less than one meter.

Keywords: Automatic driving · Pseudorange difference positioning · Reference station

1 Introduction

Automatic driving is an inevitable trend of human development and progress that will lead us into a new era. In the process, lots of difficulties need to be solved. A serious problem is how to achieve high accuracy and real-time positioning when car is running. Another one is how to achieve the ability of compatibility and adaptation for various complex environments. Although researchers in this field have made great efforts, there are still so many worth works need to be done. Li et al. in [1] study the problem of positioning latency for real-time position. Zhang et al. in [2] analyze the precise point positioning(PPP) of Global Positioning System (GPS). Misra et al. in [3] and Parkinson et al. in [4] analyze the pseudorange difference positioning in detail. The authors in [5] and [6] discuss various high-precise positioning methods of GPS. Satellite-terrestrial communication systems, joint cooperative spectrum sensing and channel selection optimization have been proposed in [7–9]. However, the above mentioned works cannot solve the problem of how to apply their positioning algorithm in practice and how to achieve the high accuracy with sub-meter even sub-centimeter.

Therefore, this paper proposes a pseudorange difference positioning algorithm for automatic driving. Firstly, a car terminal collects the observation pseudorange data of GPS receiver and reference station simultaneously. Then, by using the proposed algorithm to build the trilateration localization equations with pseudorange difference positioning model, we can obtain the positioning results. Experiments show that the proposed algorithm gives a positioning accuracy with error less than one meter. The

M. Jia et al. (Eds.): WiSATS 2019, LNICST 280, pp. 218–225, 2019.
https://doi.org/10.1007/978-3-030-19153-5_22

rest of the paper is organized as follows. In Sect. 2, we describe the whole system framework of pseudorange difference positioning. The experiment results show the static and dynamic positioning accuracy in Sect. 3. And Sect. 4 concludes this paper.

2   System Description

The pseudorange difference positioning system framework is shown in Fig. 1, which can be divided into three parts: car terminal, reference station and the pseudorange difference model. Firstly, pseudorange observations of GPS satellites and ephemeris data including the satellite position information, can be obtained through GPS car terminal. At the same time, the car terminal needs use public network to obtain the observation and location of reference station through the NTRIP protocol. Finally, the pseudorange difference model is utilized to obtain the real-time position of car terminal with the pseudorange observation of reference station and car terminal.

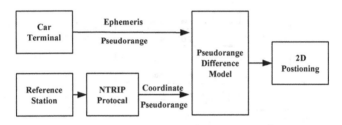

Fig. 1. System framework

2.1   Reference Station Data

Data Collection
Since Pseudorange difference positioning algorithm requires a reference station to provide real-time pseudorange observation data, we can use the strong spatial correlation between the car terminal and reference station to eliminate various errors such as satellite clock error, ionospheric delay and tropospheric delay. Generally speaking, the service of reference station is provided by professional location service companies (such as QianXun), which can provide many benefits, such as reducing the cost of difference positioning and the complexity of achieving high-precision positioning, or increasing the widespread use of difference positioning [10].

As shown in Fig. 2, the observation data of reference station follows an NTRIP protocol. The NTRIP protocol is built on the HTTP protocol and is specified for difference positioning. The car terminal establishes communication connection with the reference station using the public network. The detailed communication process can be divided into three steps which is given as follows.

- Step 1: The car terminal sends a request connection to obtain difference data sources. The reference station gives concrete parameters of data source table, such as mount point, difference data type and transmit frequency.
- Step 2: According to the concrete parameters, the car terminal selects a mount point with professional account and password to request login operation. The "ICY 200 OK" message will be responded after confirming that the account information is correct.
- Step 3: After receiving the confirmation information, the car terminal sends a GPGGA message, which includes imprecise location information of car terminal, to get the reference station location and real-time pseudorange observation data for solving car terminal position.

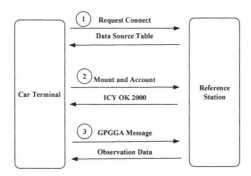

Fig. 2. NTRIP communication process.

Data Decode

The difference data acquired by the car terminal through the NTRIP protocol conforms to the RTCM32 standard, which is an internationally common standard difference data format. The data format [11] consisting of five parts is shown in Table 1.

Table 1. Data format

Guide words (8 bit)	Reserved (6 bit)	Msg length (10 bit)	Var length (0–1023 byte)	CRC (24 bit)
11010011 (0XD3)	000000	Msg size	Msg content	G(X)

The difference data is mainly derived from message 1005 and message 1074 after decoding the reference station data. The message type can be obtained by the first 12 bits of the variable length part. Message 1005 mainly contains the location information of reference station in the WGS84 coordinate system, whose concrete data protocol definition can be further explained in the document RTCM STANDARD 3.2 [12]. Message 1074, containing the real-time pseudorange observation information of reference station for GPS satellites, can be divided into three parts: message header, satellite data and signal data. Message header includes GPS epoch information of the observation satellite, the number of observation satellites and the type of observation data at the current time. Satellite data includes the number of integer milliseconds in GPS satellite rough range and GPS satellite rough range modulo 1 ms. Signal data mainly contains the precise pseudorange observation and signal-to-noise ratio. The accurate pseudorange measurement can be obtained by using above data, and the calculation formula can be expressed as

$$P = \left(Nms + \frac{Roughrange}{1024} + 2^{-24} \times Fine\_Pseudorange \right) \times c/1000, \qquad (1)$$

where P is the pseudorange and $c = 299792458 \text{m/s}$ is the speed of light. Nms is the number of integer milliseconds in GPS satellite rough ranges, $Roughrange$ is the GPS satellite rough ranges modulo 1 ms, $Fine\_Pseudorange$ is the measurement part with more high accuracy.

2.2 Pseudorange Difference Positioning Algorithm

Positioning Principle
According to the trilateration localization theory, the car terminal needs to solve the specific location of each visible satellite and the precise distance between the satellite and the car terminal. The satellites position and the distance between satellites and the car terminal are the key factors to solve car terminal position. GPS satellites will broadcast ephemeris data every two hours which can be used to calculate the real-time position of every satellite. And the pseudorange observed by the car terminal is used to approximate the actual distance. Therefore, the single point positioning algorithm actually solves the following nonlinear equations:

$$\sqrt{(x^1 - x)^2 + (y^1 - y)^2 + (z^1 - z)^2} = \rho^1$$

$$\sqrt{(x^2 - x)^2 + (y^2 - y)^2 + (z^2 - z)^2} = \rho^2 \qquad (2)$$

$$\sqrt{(x^3 - x)^2 + (y^3 - y)^2 + (z^3 - z)^2} = \rho^3,$$

where $X = [x, y, z]^T$ is the unknown car terminal position, $X^n = [x^n, y^n, z^n]^T, n = 1, 2, 3$ is the position of satellite, ρ^n is the pseudorange between satellite n and the car terminal. Obviously, ρ^n is not very accurate on standing for the actual distance because of the various errors, resulting in the poor positioning accuracy.

Pseudorange Difference Model
Assume that the pseudorange measurement of reference station from satellite n is p_r^n, which can be modeled as

$$\rho_r^n = R_r^n + c(\delta_{t_r} - \delta_{t^n}) + I^n + T^n + \varepsilon^n, \tag{3}$$

where R_r^n is the actual distance between reference station and satellite n, δ_{t_r} and δ_{t^n} are the receiver and satellite n clock error, respectively, I^n and T^n are the ionospheric and troposphere propagation delays, respectively, ε^n accounts for modeling errors (e.g., satellite clock modeling error and orbit prediction error) and other effects(e.g., receiver noise and multipath) [10]. Due to the strong spatial correlation between the car terminal and the reference station, the pseudorange difference positioning model can eliminate these errors, which ensures sub-meter accuracy on positioning.

In the WGS84 coordinate system, the real position (x^n, y^n, z^n) of satellite n can be obtained in real-time through the ephemeris data and the real position of reference station is (x_r, y_r, z_r). So the true geometric distance from satellite n to reference station r is

$$R_r^n = \sqrt{(x^n - x_r)^2 + (y^n - y_r)^2 + (z^n - z_r)^2}. \tag{4}$$

Obviously, the difference correction between the pseudorange observation ρ_r^n and actual real distance R_r^n is denoted as

$$\Delta p^n = \rho_r^n - R_r^n, \tag{5}$$

where Δp^n is the difference correction including various errors. Substituting Eq. (3) into Eq. (5), we can obtain

$$\Delta p^n = c(\delta_{t_r} - \delta_{t^n}) + I^n + T^n + \varepsilon^n. \tag{6}$$

So the pseudorange observation of the car terminal after difference correction is

$$\rho = \rho_i^n - \Delta \rho^n. \tag{7}$$

The corrected pseudorange can be substituted into Eq. (2) to solve the precise position of car terminal.

3   Experiment Results

In order to verify the feasibility of the proposed algorithm, we first collect data of the car terminal and reference station simultaneously, and then test the positioning error of static and dynamic environments in the roof of a building with latitude 29.5316° and longitude 106.5849°.

3.1   Static Positioning Test

In the static environment, the GPS receiver is installed in the car terminal and the car is static. We collect the observation data of GPS receiver and reference station simultaneously. The datasets are divided into three groups for positioning error comparison of the proposed algorithm. The results are shown in Figs. 3, 4 and 5.

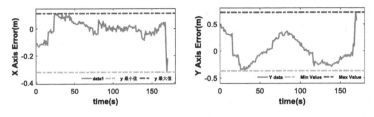

Fig. 3. Group 1

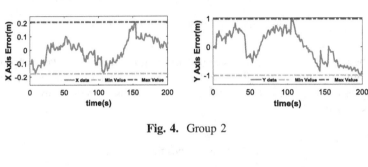

Fig. 4. Group 2

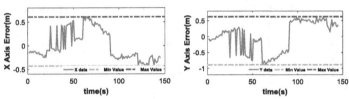

Fig. 5. Group 3

We can observe from Figs. 3, 4 and 5 that group 1 shows X axis error is −0.3 m–0.1 m, and Y axis error is −0.4 m–0.6 m. For group 2, X axis and Y axis error is −0.18 m–0.2 m and −0.91 m–0.92 m, respectively. Similarly, for group 3, X axis error is −0.45 m–0.55 m and Y axis error is from −0.9 m–0.6 m.

Through the above positioning error analysis, we can see that the positioning error of X axis and Y axis for all data sets are less than 0.55 m and 0.92 m, respectively. It is obvious that the static results can prove our theoretical analysis accuracy with positioning error is less than 1 m.

3.2 Dynamic Positioning Test

Dynamic positioning accuracy cannot directly be measured since there is no standard anchor in this case. So this paper adopts an idea of relative positioning for measuring positioning error. Specifically, we first design the car driving trajectory as shown in Fig. 6(a) and make the car drive straightly. The straight line length is 50 m and each line is spaced by 1 m or 0.5 m. Then, we use difference positioning algorithm to test the real driving trajectory. The results are shown in Fig. 6(b).

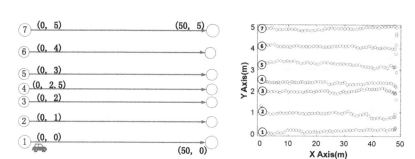

(a) Design trajectory   (b) Positioning trajectory

Fig. 6. Experiment result (Color figure online)

It can be seen from Fig. 6(b) that the positioning trajectories are very approximate to the design trajectories (red lines in Fig. 6(a)). In order to analyze the dynamic positioning error, we calculate the difference of Y axis among various positioning trajectories in Table 2.

Table 2. Dynamic positioning error

Trajectory diff	Real interval (m)	Positioning interval (m)	Error (m)
1–2	1	0.45	0.55
2–3	1	1.96	0.96
3–4	0.5	0.24	0.26
4–5	1	1.62	0.62
5–6	1	1.37	0.37
6–7	1	0.38	0.62

We can see from Table 2 that the difference between straight lines at intervals of 1 m is obvious with the errors of all trajectories no more than 0.96 m. As for the straight lines with 0.5 m interval, the difference is also clear with 0.26 m positioning error. Therefore, the results demonstrate that positioning accuracy of the proposed algorithm satisfies the theoretical sub-meter accuracy even under dynamic positioning situation.

4 Conclusions

This paper proposes a pseudorange difference positioning algorithm for automatic driving. Combined observation data of car terminal with reference station data, the positioning results could be obtained by the proposed algorithm. By combining observation data of car terminal with reference station data and utilizing the proposed algorithm, we can obtain the positioning results. And the results demonstrated that the positioning error is no more than 0.92 m and 0.96 m in static and dynamic environment, respectively. Therefore, the proposed positioning algorithm could achieve sub-meter positioning accuracy.

References

1. Li, B., Yao, D.: Calculation of vehicle real-time position overcoming the GPS positioning latency with MEMS INS. In: IEEE International Conference on Service Operations and Logistics, and Informatics, pp. 248–254. IEEE (2014)
2. Zhang, X., Pan, L., Pan, Y.: Comparison of BDS/GPS precision single point positioning convergence time and positioning accuracy. J. Surv. Mapp. **44**(03), 250–256 (2015)
3. Misra, P., Enge, P.: Golbal Positioning System-Signals measurements and Perforemance, 2nd edn. Ganga-Jamuna Press, Lincoln (2004)
4. Parkinson, B.W., Spilker Jr., J.J.: Global Positioning System: Theory and Application (Volume II). American Institute of Aeronautics and Astronautics, Reston (1996)
5. Lan, X., Zhang, B., Huang, J., Huang, X.: Experimental study on GPS pseudo-distance differential positioning technology. J. Hohai Univ. (Nat. Sci. Ed.) 300–303 (2004)
6. Jie, Y., Zhang, F.: Comparative study of high-precision GPS differential positioning technology. Mob. Commun. **38**(02), 54–58 (2014)
7. Jia, M., Gu, X., Guo, Q., Xiang, W., Zhang, N.: Broadband hybrid satellite-terrestrial communication systems based on cognitive radio toward 5G. IEEE Wirel. Commun. **23**(6), 96–106 (2016)
8. Jia, M., Liu, X., Gu, X., Guo, Q.: Joint cooperative spectrum sensing and channel selection optimization for satellite communication systems based on cognitive radio. Int. J. Satell. Commun. Netw. **35**(2), 139–150 (2017)
9. Jia, M., Liu, X., Yin, Z., Guo, Q., Gu, X.: Joint cooperative spectrum sensing and spectrum opportunity for satellite cluster communication networks. Ad Hoc Netw. **58**(C), 231–238 (2016)
10. Huang, Y., Shi, J.: Analysis of real-time observation data decoding and positioning performance under the chixun beidou foundation reinforcement network. Bull. Surv. Mapp. 11–14 (2017)
11. Yu, X., Lu, Z., Wang, B.: Introduction and decoding of DGNSS data transmission format RTCM3.2. Global Position. Syst. **40**(03), 37–41 (2015)
12. RTCM: RTCM special committee no. 104. RTCM standard 10403.2 for differential GNSS. Radio Technical Commission for Maritime Services, Arlington (2013)

Two Dimensional Parameters Based Hand Gesture Recognition Algorithm for FMCW Radar Systems

Yong Wang[✉], Zedong Zhao, Mu Zhou, and Jinjun Wu

School of Communications and Information Engineering, Chongqing University
of Posts and Telecommunications, Chongqing 400065, China
yongwang@cqupt.edu.cn

Abstract. In recent years, hand gesture recognition has increasingly become important in the field of human-computer interaction. This paper proposes a two-dimension parameter based hand gesture recognition method using frequency modulated continuous wave (FMCW) radar. Specifically, we analyze the time domain of the radar signal and estimate the radial distance and angle parameters of hand gestures, and then construct the parameter dataset. The dataset is fed into an improved convolutional neural network to extract features. Finally, the extracted features are fused and then classified by the full connection layer. Experimental results show that the recognition accuracy of the proposed approach is significantly higher than that of the single-parameter ones.

Keywords: Hand gesture recognition · FMCW radar · Convolutional neural network

1 Introduction

With the development of human-computer interaction, as one of the most important parts, hand gesture recognition influences in various fields of our life, such as home entertainment and intelligent drive. In the hand gesture recognition technology, the data sources are mainly divided into optical camera and wireless equipments. The former one uses cameras to collect the dataset, constructs a model based on the changes of the images and the motion trajectory of the hand gestures. Then, the features are extracted using machine learning methods such as neural network [1], k-Nearest Neighbor (KNN) [2] and Support Vector Machine (SVM) [3] for recognition. The latter one mainly adopts wireless equipment to collect the hand gesture signals, and then the frequency domain is analyzed through signal processing. The motion parameters are extracted and identified through clustering [4] or dynamic time regulation [5] or hidden Markov model [6]. The signal sources of the above-mentioned methods mainly include radar, ultra-wide Band (UWB) and wireless channel state information.

Motived by the above analysis, this paper proposes a Frequency Modulation Continuous Wave (FMCW) radar [7] based hand gesture recognition method. The hand gestures of the radial range and angle are calculated, and they are mapped to namely the range-time map (R-TM) and point of angle-time map (A-TM). Then, we design the

M. Jia et al. (Eds.): WiSATS 2019, LNICST 280, pp. 226–234, 2019.
https://doi.org/10.1007/978-3-030-19153-5_23

convolutional neural network to extract the features of R-TM and A-TM. The extracted features are fused and then classified using the classifier function. Finally, by dividing the dataset into training and testing ones, we use training dataset to train the confused convolutional neural network (CNN), and then use the testing dataset for hand gesture classification.

2   Signal Model of FMCW Radar

2.1   IF Signal Model

FMCW radar transmits high-frequency continuous signal, and the frequency of the transmitted triangle signal changes linearly with time. To obtain the intermediate frequency signal of the FMCW radar, the transmitting and receiving signal are input into the mixer. The high-frequency part is filtered by a low-pass filter. The intermediate frequency signal is finally obtained by sampling. The FMCW radar prototype is shown in Fig. 1.

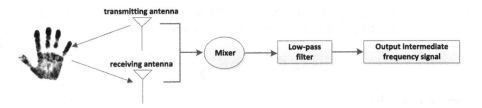

Fig. 1. FMCW radar prototype.

Both transmitting and receiving signals of radar are sawtooth wave, and there exists a fixed delay Δt_{delay} in the receiving signals. The concrete form is shown in Fig. 2.

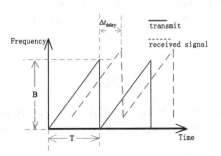

Fig. 2. Correlation curve between transmitted and received signals.

where T is the pulse width of the sawtooth signal, B is the bandwidth of the radar signal.

According to [7], the emission signal of FMCW radar can be expressed as

$$s_T(t) = A_T \cos 2\pi \left[f_c t + \int_0^t f_T(\tau) d\tau \right] \tag{1}$$

where f_c is the central frequency of the carrier, $f_T(\tau)$ denotes the frequency of the transmitted signal in a period of time with length T and T is the pulse width of the sawtooth signal, A_T denotes the amplitude of the transmitting signal.

Due to the influence of flight delay of radar echo signal and doppler frequency shift of the hand gesture, the frequency of radar echo signal is

$$f_R(t) = s(t - \Delta t_{\text{delay}}) + \Delta f_{doppler} \tag{2}$$

where Δt_{delay} is a flight delay between the sending signal and the receiving echo signal, $\Delta f_{doppler}$ denotes the Doppler shift. The echo signal can be obtained by substituting Eqs. (2) into (1):

$$s_R(t) = A_R \cos 2\pi \left[f_c(t - \Delta t_{\text{delay}}) + \int_0^t f_R(\tau) d\tau \right] \tag{3}$$

where A_R is the amplitude of an echo signal. By mixing $s_R(t)$ and $s_T(t)$, we get the intermediate frequency signal $s_{IF}(t)$ using a low frequency filter:

$$s_{IF}(t) = f_{LPF}\{s_T(t)s_R(t)\} = \frac{1}{2} A_T A_R \cos \varphi \tag{4}$$

where φ is the phase.

2.2 Range and Angle Dataset Establishment

When the gesture is not moving, the intermediate frequency (IF) signal should be a sinusoidal signal with a constant frequency. Otherwise, the frequency of the IF signals change with the range between the hand gesture and the radar. In this paper, the intermediate frequency of each frame contains 128 pulses. Because Δt_{delay} is very small in actual measurement, so:

$$\frac{B}{T} = \frac{f_{IF}}{\Delta t_{\text{delay}}} \tag{5}$$

where B is the bandwidth of the radar signal, f_{IF} is frequency point of IF signal.

The corresponding relation between range estimation R and frequency point f_{IF} of IF signal is obtained

$$R = \frac{cT}{2B} f_{IF} \tag{6}$$

The distance-doppler map was obtained by 2D-FFT analysis based on one frame. Therefore, the range can be obtained according to the relationship between the range estimation and the frequency point of the intermediate frequency signal.

Assuming that K hand gesture exists in front of the FMCW radar, the IF signal of the radar is expressed as

$$s_{IF}(t) = \sum_{k=1}^{K} A^{(k)} e^{j2\pi \left[f_c \Delta t_{\text{delay}}^{(k)} + \left(f_{IF}^{(k)} - \Delta f_{\text{doppler}}^{(k)} \right) t \right]} \tag{7}$$

where k represents the target corresponding to the k-th distance unit in the FMCW radar range.

In this paper, the radar has $N_T = 2$ transmitting antennas and $N_R = 4$ receiving antennas. There are 8 virtual receiving antennas. Considering that the radar signals are affected by noise, the signal model is

$$s(m, t) = s_{IF}(m, t) + n(m, t) \tag{8}$$

where $m = 1, 2, \ldots, 8$ is different antenna arrays, $s_{IF}(m, t)$ and $n(m, t)$ represents the signal component and noise component of route m. According to Eqs. (7) and (8), discrete signal $s(m, l)$ is obtained after sampling $s(m, t)$ with the sampling rate F_s, and it can be expressed as

$$s(m, l) = \sum_{k=1}^{K} A^{(k)} e^{j2\pi \left[f_c \cdot \Delta t_{\text{delay}}^{(k)} - \frac{l}{F_s} \cdot \Delta f_{\text{doppler}}^{(k)} + f_{IF}^{(k)} \right]} + n(l) \tag{9}$$

where $l = 0, 1, 2, \ldots, L - 1$ satisfies the relations $L = T \cdot F_s$. Then, we can construct the signal vector matrix S as

$$S = \left\{ \begin{matrix} s(1,1) & \cdots & s(1,l) & \cdots & s(1,L) \\ \vdots & \ddots & \vdots & \ddots & \vdots \\ s(m,1) & \cdots & s(m,l) & \cdots & s(m,L) \\ \vdots & \ddots & \vdots & \ddots & \vdots \\ s(N_T N_R, 1) & \cdots & s(N_T N_R, l) & \cdots & s(N_T N_R, L) \end{matrix} \right\} \tag{10}$$

The corresponding angle is then obtained by searching the spectral peak of the spatial spectral function.

3 Proposed Fusion Neural Network Based Gesture Recognition

3.1 Range and Angle Feature Extraction

The work of this chapter is to extract feature values by using improved neural network. In R-TM and A-TM, the aim is to extract the continuous position change information in the sequence according to the dimension information of the sequence. According to the network structure of literature [8] and VGG-16 [9], the network is setting as 5 convolution pooling layers. Since the R-TM and A-TM of gesture movement have great differences, the network is a single-parameter network improved by VGG-16-Net. The entire network consists of 5 convolution pooling layers and 2 full connection layers. In the first and second convolutional pooling layers, the input was convoluted twice and pooled once, and the latter three convoluted and pooled once. After the last pooling of the full connection layer, the last input softmax [10] layer was classified, as shown in Fig. 3.

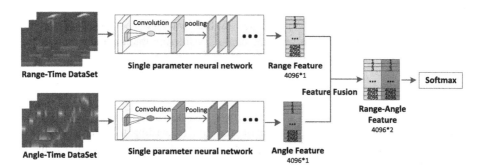

Fig. 3. R-AM schematic.

By using convolution and pooling for R-TM and A-TM, the continuous frames of feature graph are obtained. Then, the range and angle feature vectors are obtained through the full connection layer of the two layers. In this model, there are 5 convolution and pooling modules. The size of the eigenvalue output to the full connection layer through the single-parameter network is 4096×1, and the size of the fused eigenvalue is 4096×2.

3.2   Training Model

After extracting the features of the hand gesture, we add the full connection layer to map the gestures to the specimen marker space. As the final fusion feature is generated by different networks, normalization is carried out before the full connection layer. Finally, the eigenvector $\mathbf{z}$ input into the normalized exponential function for classification, as:

$$\text{softmax}(\mathbf{z}) = \frac{\exp(\theta_i^{\mathrm{T}} z_i)}{\sum_{j=1}^{k} \exp(\theta_j^{\mathrm{T}} z_j)} \qquad (11)$$

where i represents the gesture of class i, k represents the type of hand gestures, in this paper, $k = 6$ represents the i-th element of feature vector $\mathbf{z}$, and θ_i represents the corresponding weight of z_i.

In the training, the initial learning rate is setting to a fixed value 0.009. With the iterative tuning of the model, the error is gradually reduced. When the parameter is close to the optimal value, too much update could make the parameter jitter near the optimal value, and too little update will slow down the learning rate. Therefore, in this paper, the exponential decay method is adopted to select a larger learning rate in the initial stage of training, so that the loss value of the network converges to a smaller value more quickly, and the loss value of the network model gradually becomes stable with the exponential reduction of the learning rate.

4 Experimental Results and Analysis

4.1 Experimental Platform

In this paper, the radar platform is a single chip FMCW sensor of Texas instruments AWR1642, which is equipped with two transmitting antennas and four receiving antennas. The slope of the FMCW sawtooth wave signal is 105 MHz/us, and the bandwidth is 4 GHz. In the experiment, hand gesture data from the radar sensor is collected and transmitted to PC, and signal processing is carried out using Matlab software. Then we use Tensorflow deep learning framework for training on the server configured with Intel-6700K processor and NVIDIA-GTX1080 graphics card.

4.2 Experimental Data

Because there are few samples in the gesture dataset of radar signals, the self-built gesture signal data set is verified in the study of establishing deep learning network for feature extraction. This paper designs six types of gestures, including scroll left, scroll right, push forward, pull backward, scroll left-right and push-pull. Each type of gesture was repeated 200 times, with a total of 1200 gesture radar data. In this paper, the platform is placed in a relatively empty indoor environment. The gesture testers repeat the dynamic gestures continuously when the radar transmitted signals to ensure sufficient experimental data collection.

In this paper, each data acquisition contains 32 frames, and each frame contains 128 sawtooth pulses. The parameter graphs are obtained by calculating the range and angle. After data processing, datasets are divided into training sets and test sets, which input into neural network for training and testing.

4.3 Experimental Results

4.3.1 Network Training

In order to compare the performance of the proposed network, this paper carries out model training under different initial learning rates. Figure 4 shows the accuracy rate of different initial learning rates. According to the test results, the network does not converge when the initial learning rate is 0.3. When the initial learning rate is 0.03 and 0.006, each update range is too large to obtain the global optimal solution. When the initial learning rates are 0.001 and 0.0009, the network weight update is too slow.

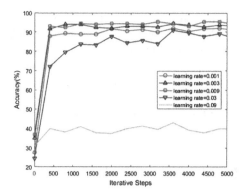

Fig. 4. Accuracy of R-AM under different initial learning rates.

When the learning rate was 0.009, the recognition effect was the best, and the accuracy rate reaches to 95%.

4.3.2 Analysis of Gesture Recognition Results

The accuracy curves of convolutional neural network training reflect the variation of network model accuracy with iterative steps. In this paper, the R-TM and A-TM training and test sets have the same data sources for single-parameter network validation. Each dataset contains 900 and 300 samples respectively. Batch_size is the amount of data required for each iteration, and it is set to 32. This model adopts the optimization strategy of stochastic gradient descent, the maximum number of iterative steps is 5000 and the initial learning rate is 0.003. The study rate attenuation strategy adopts the exponential attenuation method. The attenuation interval is 3 epochs and the attenuation rate is 0.99.

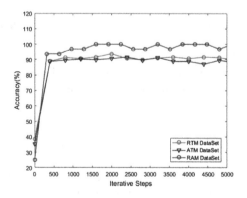

Fig. 5. R-TM, A-TM and R-AM accuracy curve.

Figure 5 compares the accuracy curve of R-AM and single-parameter network when separately trained on R-TM and D-TM data sets. The results show that compared with the single-parameter gesture recognition approach, the proposed one has significantly improved the recognition accuracy by 5%.

This paper designs six types of gestures, including push forward, pull backward, scroll left, scroll right, push-pull and scroll left-right, the test set of each gesture has 50 data, the correct number of data predicted is 46, 49, 48, 47, 46 and 48 in R-AM's confusion matrix. In R-TM and A-TM confusion matrix, the test set of each gesture has 50 data, too. Figure 6 shows the confusion matrix of R-AM, R-TM and A-TM. It can be seen from the figure that the accuracy of R-AM network on the test set reaches 94.7%. The average accuracy rates of R-TM and A-TM were 91.8% and 90.0%. In Table 1 compared with the single-parameter network and the single-parameter data set, the method in this paper has improved the accuracy of gesture recognition by about 5%.

(a) R-AM

	push forward	pull backward	scroll left	scroll right	push-pull	scroll left-right
push forward	92	0	4	0	0	4
pull backward	0	98	0	0	2	0
scroll left	0	0	96	2	0	2
scroll right	0	2	0	94	2	2
push-pull	2	2	0	2	92	2
scroll left-right	0	0	2	2	0	96

(b) R-TM

	push forward	pull backward	scroll left	scroll right	push-pull	scroll left-right
push forward	94	2	0	0	0	4
pull backward	4	92	0	2	0	2
scroll left	0	0	88	8	0	4
scroll right	0	2	6	86	0	6
push-pull	2	0	0	0	98	0
scroll left-right	0	0	0	0	8	92

(c) A-TM

	push forward	pull backward	scroll left	scroll right	push-pull	scroll left-right
push forward	84	6	0	0	10	0
pull backward	4	88	0	0	8	0
scroll left	0	0	92	2	2	4
scroll right	0	0	2	96	0	2
push-pull	2	10	0	0	88	0
scroll left-right	0	0	4	4	0	92

Fig. 6. R-AM, R-TM and A-TM confusion matrix.

Table 1. Comparison results of accuracy of different methods.

Network structure and data sets	Accuracy (%)
One parameter network+R-TM	91.7
One parameter network+A-TM	90.0
This article's fusion network+R-TM/A-TM	94.7

5   Conclusion

This paper proposed an improved convolutional neural network gesture recognition method based on two-parameter estimation of FMCW radar. Firstly, the radial distance and angle parameters of the forward hand gestures were obtained. Secondly, range and angle information were accumulated in time domain to construct the datasets of R-TM and A-TM. Then, the dataset were sent to the proposed CNN based hand gesture recognition system for training and testing. The results showed that compared with the single-parameter gesture recognition approach, the proposed one has significantly improved the recognition accuracy by about 5%.

Acknowledgments. This work was supported in part by the National Natural Science Foundation of China (61771083, 61704015), Program for Changjiang Scholars and Innovative Research Team in University (IRT1299), Special Fund of Chongqing Key Laboratory (CSTC),

Fundamental and Frontier Research Project of Chongqing (cstc2017jcyjAX0380, cstc2015j-cyjBX0065), University Outstanding Achievement Transformation Project of Chongqing (KJZH17117), and Postgraduate Scienti_cResearch and Innovation Project of Chongqing (CYS17221).

References

1. Coelho, Y.L., Salomao, J.M., Kulitz, H.R.: Intelligent hand posture recognition system integrated to process control. IEEE Lat. Am. Trans. **15**(6), 1144–1153 (2017)
2. Salunke, T.P., Bharkad, S.D.: Power point control using hand gesture recognition based on hog feature extraction and K-NN classification. In: 2017 International Conference on Computing Methodologies and Communication (ICCMC), pp. 1151–1155. IEEE (2017)
3. Pai, N.S., Hong, J.H., Chen, P.Y., et al.: Application of design of image tracking by combining SURF and TLD and SVM-based posture recognition system in robbery pre-alert system. Multimed. Tools Appl. **76**(23), 25321–25342 (2017)
4. Park, J., Cho, S.H.: IR-UWB radar sensor for human gesture recognition by using machine learning. In: IEEE, International Conference on High PERFORMANCE Computing and Communications; IEEE, International Conference on Smart City; IEEE, International Conference on Data Science and Systems. pp. 1246–1249. IEEE (2017)
5. Zhou, Z., Cao, Z., Pi, Y.: Dynamic gesture recognition with a terahertz radar based on range profile sequences and doppler signatures. Sensors **18**(1), 1–15 (2018)
6. Wang, W., Liu, A.X., Shahzad, M., et al.: Device-free human activity recognition using commercial WiFi devices. IEEE J. Sel. Areas Commun. **35**(5), 1118–1131 (2017)
7. Li, G., Zhang, R., Ritchie, M., et al.: Sparsity-based dynamic hand gesture recognition using micro-Doppler signatures. In: 2017 IEEE Radar Conference (RadarConf), pp. 0928–0931. IEEE (2017)
8. Winkler, V.: Range Doppler detection for automotive FMCW radars. In: Microwave Conference, European, pp. 1445–1448. IEEE (2007)
9. Pan, H., Zhang, F., Shi, C., et al.: High-precision frequency estimation for frequency modulated continuous wave laser ranging using the multiple signal classification method. Appl. Opt. **56**(24), 6956–6961 (2017)
10. Vamplew, P., Dazeley, R., Foale, C.: Softmax exploration strategies for multiobjective reinforcement learning. Neurocomputing **263**, 74–86 (2017)

WLAN Indoor Passive Intrusion Detection Method Based on SVDD

Yong Wang, Xiaoya Zhang$^{(\boxtimes)}$, Luoying Gao, Mu Zhou, and Lingxia Li

School of Communication and Information Engineering,
Chongqing University of Posts and Telecommunications, Chongqing 400065, China
xiaoyazhang0@163.com

Abstract. The existing passive intrusion detection technology has poor adaptability under different monitoring environments and low detection performance, this paper proposes a wireless local area network (WLAN) indoor passive intrusion detection method based on Support Vector Domain Description (SVDD). A-distance is adopted to evaluate multiple features to correctly distinguish the average contribution of the two states of silence and intrusion, screening the extreme difference and variance as the characteristic quantity of the signal change. Then, the paper introduces the single classification method SVDD to train the hypersphere anomaly detection boundary in the high dimensional feature space. We can achieve accurate anomaly detection by determining whether the current sample point is within the hypersphere. In a typical indoor environment, compared with the existing detection algorithms, the proposed method achieves better detection performance under low overhead conditions. F1-measure which is the system evaluation index increased by nearly 4%.

Keywords: WLAN · Passive intrusion detection · SVDD

1 Introduction

Passive intrusion detection means that the detected target does not carry any signal transmitting and receiving equipments, and detects the intrusion target via the radio wave [1]. Its potential application range from smart home and elderly guardianship to police security [2].

Our work proposes a WLAN indoor passive intrusion detection algorithm based on Support Vector Domain Description (SVDD). This paper uses A-distance to evaluate multiple features to correctly distinguish the average contribution of the two states of silence and intrusion. Silence stage selects the two features with the highest contribution to construct the feature matrix that trains the SVDD [3–5] model. This paper verifies the effectiveness of the proposed algorithm in the home environment. The results show that the F1-measure of the proposed algorithm can reach 96%, which is much better than the existing WLAN-based passive intrusion detection technology.

© ICST Institute for Computer Sciences, Social Informatics and Telecommunications Engineering 2019
Published by Springer Nature Switzerland AG 2019. All Rights Reserved
M. Jia et al. (Eds.): WiSATS 2019, LNICST 280, pp. 235–241, 2019.
https://doi.org/10.1007/978-3-030-19153-5_24

2   System Model

The proposed indoor intrusion detection system of this paper consists of two phases: offline training phase and online detection phase. The framework is in Fig. 1.

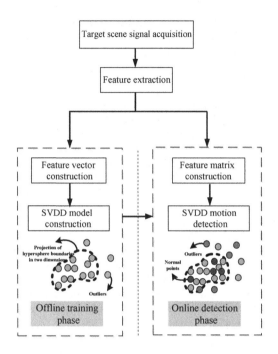

Fig. 1. System model.

2.1   Offline Training Phase

Collecting silent data to build an intrusion detection model for detecting abnormalities in the environment. At this stage, no activity in the sensing area, the receiving devices collect the parameters of received signal strength of each link. Then, we extract the corresponding feature values of each link and constructs a feature matrix based on the collected multi-link signal features. Finally, the SVDD intrusion detection model is trained by the feature matrix.

(a) Characteristic distribution analysis
   In order to select features effectively, we use A-distance to evaluate the different distribution of each feature in the state of silence and walking, and select the feature with clear distribution difference to construct the detection model. Then, we use a decision tree as a linear classifier, the A-distance can

be described as $d^{\mathcal{A}}(D_s, D_t) = 2(1 - 2E(h))$, where D_s and D_t are two data sets for constructing the second classifier, $E(h)$ represents the loss of the classifier.

This paper proposes t o design a passive intrusion detection system based on the feature and select the extreme difference and variance as two detection features.

(b) Feature matrix construction

Let k be the number of wireless links in the system. k is equal to the number of signal transmitting devices, multiplied by the number of signal receiving devices. The receiving frequency of receivers is 1 time/second. We use sliding window function (sliding window length is L) to extract signal characteristics $\mathbf{s}_{t,j}$ corresponding to each link j at time t. $\mathbf{s}_{t,j} = [s_{t,j}^1, s_{t,j}^2]$, $s_{t,j}^1$ is the extreme difference and $s_{t,j}^2$ is the variance. Feature vector $\mathbf{S}_t = [\mathbf{s}_{t,1} \cdots \mathbf{s}_{t,j} \cdots \mathbf{s}_{t,k}]$, j represents the wireless links in the system. After acquiring the signals of T moments, $T - L + 1$ feature vectors are obtained, and the feature matrix $\mathbf{S} = [\mathbf{S}_1 \cdots \mathbf{S}_t \cdots \mathbf{S}_N]$ is constructed by the feature vectors, $N = T - L + 1$.

(c) Construction of SVDD passive intrusion detection model

In the SVDD intrusion detection model is trained by using the feature matrix $\mathbf{S}$. The goal of SVDD is to find the smallest sphere in a high-dimensional space that contains all or most of the training samples. In order to avoid the influence outliers effect, a slack variable $\xi_i \geq 0$ is introduced for each training sample point, allowing some points to be outside the hypersphere. Multiplying the penalty parameter C for each slack variable ξ_i, making the system has certain anti-noise performance. The objective function is:

$$\begin{aligned} &\min_{R,\mathbf{a},\xi_i} R^2 + C \sum_i \xi_i, \\ &s.t. \ \|\mathbf{S}_i - \mathbf{a}\|^2 \leq R^2 + \xi_i, \xi_i \geq 0, i = 1, \ldots, N. \end{aligned} \tag{1}$$

Lagrangian function can be constructed according to Eq. (2).

$$L = R^2 + C \sum_i \xi_i - \sum_i \alpha_i \left\{ R^2 + \xi_i - \|\mathbf{S}_i - \mathbf{a}\|^2 \right\} - \sum_i \gamma_i \xi_i. \tag{2}$$

The Lagrange multiplier $\alpha_i \geq 0$, $\gamma_i \geq 0$.

$$\begin{cases} \partial L / \partial \mathbf{a} = 2R(1 - \sum_i \alpha_i) = 0 \Rightarrow \sum_i \alpha_i = 1, \\ \partial L / \partial R = 2 \sum_i \alpha_i (\mathbf{S}_i - \mathbf{a}) = 0 \Rightarrow \mathbf{a} = \sum_i \alpha_i \mathbf{S}_i, \\ \partial L / \partial \xi_i = C - \alpha_i - \gamma_i = 0 \Rightarrow C = \alpha_i + \gamma_i, \end{cases} \tag{3}$$

where $\alpha_i \geq 0$ and $\gamma_i \geq 0$, we can get $0 \leq \alpha_i \leq C$.

According to the Lagrangian duality, the minimum value problem of Eq. (2) equals to a maximum value problem of its dual problem. We introduce Gaussian kernel functions $K(\mathbf{S}_i, \mathbf{S}_j)$ to implement nonlinear mapping from low-dimensional input space to high-dimensional feature space. The following optimization problem is given by:

$$\max_{\alpha} L = \sum_i \alpha_i K(\mathbf{S}_i, \mathbf{S}_i) - \sum_{i,j} \alpha_i \alpha_j K(\mathbf{S}_i, \mathbf{S}_j),$$
$$s.t. \sum_i \alpha_i = 1, 0 \le \alpha_i \le C i = 1, 2, \dots, N. \tag{4}$$

The optimal solution α_i can be obtained by using Sequential Minimal Optimization (SMO) [6]. When $\alpha_i = 0$, it indicates that the corresponding sample point is located inside the hypersphere; when $\alpha_i = C$, it indicates that the corresponding sample point is outside the hypersphere, which is the limited support vector; when $0 < \alpha_i < C$, it indicates the corresponding sample. The point is on the hypersphere, which is the support vector, and the set of support vectors is represented as $\{V_q, q = 1, 2, \dots, n\}$. The radius R of the sphere can be found by the distance from any support vector V_q on the hypersphere to the center of the sphere $\mathbf{a}$.

$$R^2 = \|V_q - \mathbf{a}\|^2 = K(V_q, V_q) - 2\sum_{i=1} \alpha_i K(V_q, \mathbf{S}_i) + \sum_{i,j=1} \alpha_i \alpha_j K(\mathbf{S}_i, \mathbf{S}_j). \tag{5}$$

In most cases, the hypersphere boundary trained by the Gaussian kernel function is better for describing the sample, so the Gaussian kernel function $K_G(\mathbf{S}_i, \mathbf{S}_j) = \exp(-\|\mathbf{S}_i - \mathbf{S}_j\|^2 / \sigma^2)$ is chosen in this paper, and the Eqs. (4) and (5) become:

$$L = 1 - \sum_i \alpha_i^2 - \sum_{i \ne j} \alpha_i \alpha_j K_G(\mathbf{S}_i, \mathbf{S}_j). \tag{6}$$

$$R^2 = 1 - 2\sum_{i=1} \alpha_i K_G(V_q, \mathbf{S}_i) + \sum_{i,j=1} \alpha_i \alpha_j K_G(\mathbf{S}_i, \mathbf{S}_j). \tag{7}$$

2.2   Online Monitoring Phase

At this stage, we extract the characteristic matrix of signal strength to construct a feature vector $\mathbf{S}_{t_{on}} = [\mathbf{s}_{t_{on},1} \cdots \mathbf{s}_{t_{on},j} \cdots \mathbf{s}_{t_{on},k}]$ at time t_{on}. Then we use the formula $m_{t_{on}} = \|S_{t_{on}} - \mathbf{a}\|^2 / R^2$ to detect environmental anomaly degree, $m_{t_{on}} > 1$ indicates someone invaded. Otherwise, there is no activity in the current perceived environment.

3   Experiment Results

We verify performance in a typical indoor environment which area is $59.48\,\mathrm{m}^2$. We uses Huawei glory router (WS851) as the access point AP. Samsung mobile phones (MP1: GT-I9308 and MP2: GT-S7568) as monitoring points MP. Figure 2 shows the indoor scenario, which is arranged with 4 APs and 1 MP. Firstly, we perform silent data collection for 25 min and train the SVDD intrusion detection model. Then, the detection model is tested in a test environment.

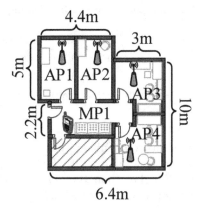

Fig. 2. Indoor scene.

In order to explore influence of penalty factor C and Gaussian kernel width factor σ on the detection performance of the system, we use FP (False Positive), FN (False Positive) and $F1 - measure$ in the experimental scene. The results are shown in Fig. 3.

As can be seen from Fig. 3, a smaller penalty factor $C(< 2^{-9})$ leads to a higher false alarm rates FP. However, as C increases, the false alarm rate FP and $F1 - measure$ gradually increase. When $C > 2^{-7}$, impact on the system is negligible. But, during actual deployment, excessive abnormal points can make the radius too large, and the FN too high in the training data. C should not be too large, therefore, we set $C = 2^{-4}$. The Gaussian kernel width factor σ is too small($\sigma < 1$) or too large ($\sigma > 2^6$), the false alarm rate FP will be higher. $F1 - measure$ shows a trend of rising first and then falling. In the scene, the most optimal $\sigma_{opt} = (2^{0.3} + 2^{5.05})/2 \approx 17.18$.

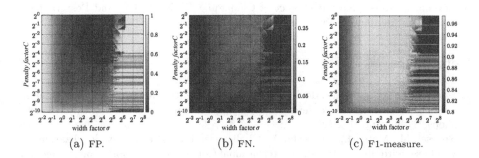

(a) FP.   (b) FN.   (c) F1-measure.

Fig. 3. Effect of C and σ on detection performance in indoor scene.

In this section, the performance of the proposed method is compared with other passive RSSI-based passive intrusion detection techniques. The results are

Table 1. Comparison of detection performance with existing detection technologies.

Performance		MA	MV	Ichnaea	SVDD
Indoor scene	FN	0.110	0.119	0.093	0.054
	FP	0.103	0.097	0.095	0.040
	F1-measure	0.017	0.891	0.906	0.960

given in Table 1. It can be seen from Table 1 that the proposed method has a certain degree of reduction in false alarm rate FP and missed detection rate FN, which is more than 4% higher than the classical Ichnaea system, which proves the effectiveness of the proposed algorithm.

4   Conclusion

In order to achieve human activity detection in a real wireless environment. This paper proposes a WLAN indoor passive intrusion detection algorithm based on SVDD. The algorithm extracts the salient features of the signal. In this paper, the extreme difference and variance are used to train the SVDD passive intrusion detection model to identify the normal state and the abnormal state. Accuracy is significantly improved. FN and FP are lower than 5% and 9%, respectively. $F1-measure$ is higher than 96%, compared with algorithms based on statistical properties, it has improved by nearly 4%, which proves our system has better performance.

Acknowledgments. This work was supported in part by the National Natural Science Foundation of China (61771083,61704015), Program for Changjiang Scholars and Innovative Research Team in University (IRT1299), Special Fund of Chongqing Key Laboratory (CSTC), Fundamental and Frontier Research Project of Chongqing (cstc2017jcyjAX0380, cstc2015jcyjBX0065), University Outstanding Achievement Transformation Project of Chongqing (KJZH17117), and Postgraduate Scientific Research and Innovation Project of Chongqing (CYS17221).

References

1. Moustafa, Y.: Challenges: device-free passive localization for wireless environments. In: IEEE International Conference on Pervasive Computing Communication Workshops, Sydney, pp. 1–2 (2016)
2. Youssef, M., Mah, M., Agrawala, A.: Challenges: device-free passive localization for wireless environments. In: ACM International Conference on Mobile Computing and NETWORKING, Canada, pp. 222–229 (2007)
3. Tax, D.M.J., Duin, R.P.W., Agrawala, A.: Support vector domain description. Pattern Recognit. Lett. **20**(11–13), 1191–1199 (1999)
4. Jinhong, Y., Tingquan, D.: A one-cluster Kernel PCM based SVDD method for outlier detection. Acta Electron. Sin. **45**(4), 813–819 (2017)

5. Long, L., Zheng, L.: Identifier for Radar ground target based on distribution of space of training features. J. Electron. Inf. Technol. **38**(4), 950–957 (2016)
6. Keerthi, S., Gilbert, E.: Convergence of a generalized SMO algorithm for SVM classifier design. Mach. Learn. **46**(1–3), 351–360 (2002)

The Gesture Detection Algorithm Based on 3-DCGAN Range Estimation in FMCW Radar System

Xiuqian Jia[✉], Yong Wang, Mu Zhou, and Zengshan Tian

Chongqing Key Lab of Mobile Communications Technology, Chongqing
University of Posts and Telecommunications, Chongqing 400065, China
1506894146@qq.com

Abstract. Recently, hand gesture detection has gradually become a research hotspot. We propose a Region-based Faster Convolutional Neural Network (F-RCNN) gesture detection method based on Frequency Modulated Continuous Wave (FMCW) radar using 3-Dimensions Deep Convolutional Generative Adversarial Networks (3-DCGAN). Specifically, this paper adopts FMCW radar for hand gesture data acquisition, and estimates the distance of the hand gesture using the regularity of the change of echo frequency and emission frequency of radar signals. Then the semantic label maps of the generated images of distance are sent to the 3-DCGAN to extend datasets. After that, the original images and the images generated by the 3-DCGAN are simultaneously sent to F-RCNN for training. The results show that the proposed approach increases the mAP by 3% compared to the baseline F-RCNN. Besides, the proposed method not only effectively solves the problem of small amount of hand gesture data, but also the manpower and material resources consumed by collecting data.

Keywords: F-RCNN · FMCW radar · Gesture detection

1 Introduction

With the rapid development of computer radio in 5 Generation [1–3] and human-computer interaction, the use of gesture detection methods to replace traditional mechanical keyboards and mice has gradually become a research hotspot [4–7]. The traditional gesture detection method is mainly based on the processing method of the camera [4, 5]. After the scene is taken by the camera, a static image is obtained, and then the image content is detected by a computer graphics algorithm [4]. The camera method is divided into an optical sensor method and a depth sensor method [6]. Although the optical sensor camera method can provide accurate detection, it is susceptible to illumination conditions [6, 7], and can't effectively provide accurate depth information, and the optical camera method has a great trouble for people's privacy. For depth sensor cameras, performance is greatly reduced during outdoor measurements due to sun damage. Compared with the camera method, the gesture detection method based on radar can effectively overcome the above shortcomings and has been widely used [8–11]. Using radar for gesture detection, the hand is modeled as a single

M. Jia et al. (Eds.): WiSATS 2019, LNICST 280, pp. 242–250, 2019.
https://doi.org/10.1007/978-3-030-19153-5_25

hard object [8, 10], in fact, it can scatter the signal from the radar. The Frequency Modulated Continuous Wave (FMCW) radar can perceive the hand as a multi-scattering object and captures its local microscopic motion [12–14]. Therefore, the hand is modeled as a non-rigid object. In the context of dynamic gesture detection, gestures produce multiple reflections from different parts of the hand, with different ranges values vary over time. In [15], the FMCW radar is used to estimate the distance-Doppler map of the radar to detect the gesture signal, and the 3-Dimension (3D) spatial position of the gesture is estimated by the radar. Since the frequency difference is determined by the frequency aspect ratio of the FMCW signal, in order to accurately estimate the distance information of the gesture, a highly linear frequency aspect ratio can be adopted to improve the ranging accuracy [16]. Besides, the Region-based Faster Convolutional Neural Network (F-RCNN) method [17] selects the feature candidate boxes in the picture and uses the classifier to discriminate, and the gesture detection accuracy is improved.

Based on the above analysis, this paper proposes a gesture detection method for 3-Dimensions Deep Convolutional Generative Adversarial Networks (3-DCGAN) range estimation based on FMCW radar. Firstly, the FMCW radar is used for gesture data acquisition. According to the law of the echo frequency and the transmission frequency of the radar signal, we can calculate the distance of the gesture. Secondly, we send the semantic label maps of the Range-Time-Map (RTM) images into the 3-DCGAN network model to extend the dataset. Thirdly, the original range images and the images generated by the 3-DCGAN model are simultaneously sent to F-RCNN for jointly training. We adopt 3-DCGAN model in our paper, and 3-DCGAN extracts both high resolution and low resolution features to improve the dimensional information of the original image. Since high resolution and low resolution features are sensitive in the process of feature extraction, the detection performance of the generated images of 3-DCGAN will better. Besides, the 3-DCGAN model are used to extend the datasets, the experimental results show that the proposed method not only effectively solves the problem of small amount of hand gesture data, but also the manpower and material resources consumed by collecting data, and greatly improves the accuracy of hand gesture detection.

2   FMCW Radar

This paper adopts FMCW radar sensor for hand gesture data acquisition. FMCW radar transmits high-frequency continuous signal, and the frequency of the transmitted tri-angle signal changes linearly with time. The echo frequency of the radar signal has the same regularity as the change of the transmission frequency, and they only differ by one time difference. The FMCW radar prototype used for hand gesture data acquisition is shown in Fig. 1.

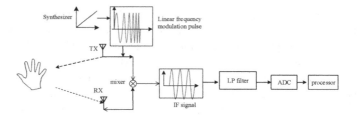

Fig. 1. The process of acquiring gesture data by FMCW radar.

It is observed from Fig. 1 that FMCW radar generates a chirp signal (linear frequency modulation pulse) through a synthesizer, and transmitted signal encounters an obstacle (such as a hand) for reflection, and the receiving antenna (RX) captures a reflected signal. With a mixer, the differential signal (intermediate frequency (IF)) of the transmitted and received signals is obtained. Then the IF signal passes through a low-pass filter and is digitized by the analog-to-digital converter (ADC). The ADC sample rate is commensurate with the largest range. Then the digital data is for Fast Fourier Transform (FFT) processing.

In general, the frequency of the transmitted signal can be expressed as:

$$f_T(t) = f_0 - B/2 + Bt/T \tag{1}$$

where f_0 is the center frequency of the transmitted signal, T is the signal period, and B is the bandwidth of the transmitted signal, then the transmitted signal can be expressed as

$$V_T(t) = A_T \cos\left(2\pi \int_0^t f_T(t)dt\right)$$
$$= A_T \cos\left(2\pi(f_0 - \frac{B}{2})t + \frac{\pi B}{T}t^2\right) \tag{2}$$

where A_T is the amplitude of the transmitted signal. Assuming that the range from the radar to the gesture is R, the delay of the received signal obtained by the radar relative to the transmitted signal is t_d, $\Delta\varphi$ is the Doppler phase shift, and c is the speed of light, then $t_d = 2R/c$. So the received signal can be expressed as

$$V_R(t) = A_R \cos\left(2\pi(f_0 - \frac{B}{2})(t - t_d) + \frac{\pi B}{T}(t - t_d)^2 + \Delta\varphi\right) \tag{3}$$

where A_R is the amplitude of the received signal. When the transmitted signal is mixed with the received signal and passed through a low-pass filter, the IF signal is obtained

$$S(t) = \frac{A_R A_T}{4} \cos\left(2\pi t_d(f_0 - \frac{B}{2})\right) \cos\left(\frac{\pi B}{T}t_d^2 - \frac{2\pi B}{T}t_d t + \Delta\varphi\right) \tag{4}$$

The frequency of the IF signal is

$$f_{IF} = Bt_d/T \tag{5}$$

The correspondence relationship between the estimated range R of the gesture and the frequency f_{IF} of the IF signal can express as

$$R = \frac{cT}{2B}f_{IF} \tag{6}$$

where B/T is the slope of the chirp signal.

This paper mainly analyzes the fast time domain (one sweep time) of the FMCW radar signal. In the fast time domain, according to the FFT analysis of the frequency sweep signal, the spectrum of the IF signal can be obtained, and then the frequency point corresponding to the gesture target is obtained according to the spectral peak search.

The parameter information of one frame (128 sweep time) of data can be obtained by using the distance estimation methods of the gesture. Since the time of one frame of data is only 40 ms, the change of the gesture target is almost negligible in one frame. This paper has set the observation duration to 32 frames by some experiments. Therefore, we use the FMCW radar equipment to analyze the obtained data as described above, and the distance of the gesture signal can be obtained respectively, as shown in Fig. 2.

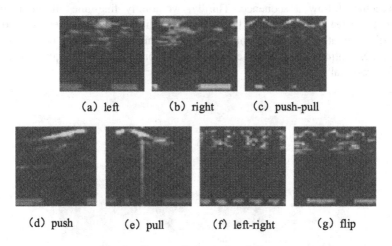

(a) left   (b) right   (c) push-pull

(d) push   (e) pull   (f) left-right   (g) flip

Fig. 2. Gesture distance signal diagram

3 Model Description

3.1 3-DCGAN Model

In our paper, we adopt a 3-Dimension generator, a multi-scale discriminator architecture and a robust adversarial learning objective function, named 3-DCGAN.

Because 3-DCGAN can extract both high resolution and low resolution features, and they are sensitive in the process of feature extraction. Now we will introduce it in detail.

Firstly, we collect the data through the FMCW radar board, and the data is pre-processed to obtain range, speed, and angle maps of different gestures. Then we get the semantic label maps of the three kinds of gestures. We describe our generator into four sub-networks: G1, G2, G3 and G4. In our model, G1, G2, G3 are represented the high-resolution, low-resolution and the original feature maps, respectively. And G4 represents the residual blocks. G1 and G2 are extracted from the original images, and the residual network G3 is trained on the original images. Then the different dimensional features G1, G2 and the original image features G3 are merged. Finally, the fusion feature is input into the residual network G4 for image generation. The resolution of image G1 is 4 times the previous output size G1 ($2\times$ along each image dimension) and the resolution of image G2 is 1/4 times of the previous output size G1.

In our paper, our original generator G3 is adopted the model by Johnson et al. [5], which includes a convolutional front-end G_3^F, a set of residual blocks G_3^R [6], and a transposed convolutional back-end G_3^B. G_1 and G_2 can only include a convolutional front-end G_1^F and G_2^F G_4 is composed of a set of residual blocks G_4^R and a transposed convolutional back-end G_4^B. In our model, G_4^R is different from G_3, which is the element-wise sum of three feature maps: the output feature map of G_1^F, the output feature map of G_2^F, and the last feature map of the G_3^B.

In order to improve the resolutions and to extract gesture image features effectively. During training, we train G_3 generator firstly. Secondly, we train the remaining network structure follow a sequence. Thirdly, we jointly fine-tune all the networks together. This idea can be found in [18, 19] and conditional image generation [20, 21]. As for discriminator, we adopt multi-scale discriminators in [22]. The 3-DCGAN generator description can be observed in Fig. 3. Among them, black square dotted line represents residual blocks.

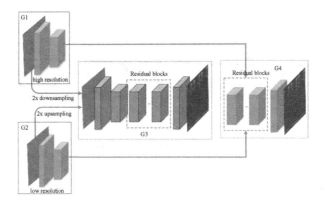

Fig. 3. 3-DCGAN generator network structure.

3.2 F-RCNN Model

The F-RCNN consists of two modules: the region proposal network (RPN) candidate extraction module and Fast R-CNN detection module. The RPN is a full convolutional neural network that is adopted for extracting candidate regions. Then, Fast R-CNN detects and identifies targets based on the extracted RPN proposal. To infer the hand gesture location, the more advanced hand gesture detection network needs to use the regional recommendation algorithm. Although SPP-net [23] and Fast R-CNN network have reduced the detection time, the calculation of area recommendation is still time-consuming. As a result, RPN is proposed to extract the interest area. Since RPN shares the convolution feature of the whole image with the entire detection network, the area recommendation time is largely reduced. The F-RCNN diagram for hand gesture detection is shown in Fig. 4.

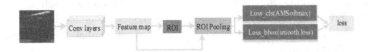

Fig. 4. The F-RCNN based hand gesture detection diagram

4 Experiment Results

4.1 mAP Performance Comparison

In this paper, the initial baseline mAP of F-RCNN is 69.5%. When adopting the 3-DCGAN model to generate images, the mAP rises to 72.9%. In addition, the performance of left-right gesture detection is best, and the mAP is 85.9%. This is because when the radar captures the gesture data with the hand slides left-right, the distance information of the gesture are processed and the image features are obvious, as shown in Fig. 5 and Table 1.

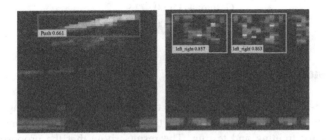

Fig. 5. The detection effect in F-RCNN model.

Table 1. Detection effect for different gestures (%).

Method	Avg	Left	Right	Push-pull	Push	Pull	Left-right	Flip
F-RCNN [14]	69.5	65.5	60.7	60.1	62.9	74.5	86.2	76.7
F-RCNN + 3-DCGAN	72.9	68.4	62.9	66.5	65.8	78.2	85.9	82.9

4.2   Impact of Generated Images

In order to evaluate the proposed method effectively, Table 2 shows the results of comparing the different numbers of 3-DCGAN generated images with the original images in this paper. Among them, 0 (basel) means the number of the original image is 7000 without the 3-DCGAN generated images. Gesture-7000 means only 7000 3-DCGAN generated images are used. Gesture + 7000 represents 7000 3-DCGAN generated images plus the 7000 original images. When the original 7000 gesture images and the 7000 3-DCGAN generated images are simultaneously fed into the F-RCNN model for training, the mAP is 71.8%. Compared with the baseline, the mAP is increased by 2.3%. This shows that training with images generated by the 3-DCGAN model perform better than the original images, indicating that the effectiveness of training 3-DCGAN model.

We continue to increase the number of 3-DCGAN generated images, when the original images and the number of 2 × 3-DCGAN images are sent to F-RCNN, the mAP reaches a maximum of 72.9%. However, we furtherly increase the 3-DCGAN generated images for training, the detection accuracy is reduced. This is because the learning machine tends to assign a uniform prediction probability to all training samples when there are too many 3-DCGAN images.

Table 2. The comparison of adding different numbers of 3-DCGAN generated images and the original images.

3-DCGAN	mAP(%)
0 (basel)	69.5
Gesture − 7000	71.2
Gesture + 7000	71.8
Gesture + 15000	72.9
Gesture + 21000	72.1

5   Conclusion

In this paper, 3-DCGAN is firstly presented to generate high quality images to expand the hand gesture dataset. Then, we adopt the generated and the original images to Faster RCNN for training and testing. The results show that the proposed approach increases the mAP by 3% compared to the baseline F-RCNN. We adopt 3-DCGAN model in our paper, and 3-DCGAN extracts both high resolution and low resolution features to improve the dimensional information of the original image. Since high resolution and low resolution features are sensitive in the process of feature extraction, the detection performance of the generated images of 3-DCGAN will better. Besides, the 3-DCGAN model are used to extend the datasets, the experimental results show that the proposed method not only effectively solves the problem of small amount of hand gesture data, but also the manpower and material resources consumed by collecting data, and greatly improves the accuracy of hand gesture detection.

References

1. Jia, M., Gu, X., Guo, Q., Xiang, W., Zhang, N.: Broadband hybrid satellite-terrestrial communication systems based on cognitive radio toward 5G. IEEE Wirel. Commun. **23**(6), 96–106 (2016)
2. Jia, M., Liu, X., Gu, X., Guo, Q.: Joint cooperative spectrum sensing and channel selection optimization for satellite communication systems based on cognitive radio. Int. J. Satell. Commun. Network. **35**(2), 139–150 (2017)
3. Jia, M., Liu, X., Yin, Z., Guo, Q., Gu, X.: Joint cooperative spectrum sensing and spectrum opportunity for satellite cluster communication networks. Ad Hoc Netw. **58**, 231–238 (2016)
4. Hjelmas, E., Low, B.K.: Face detection: a survey. Comput. Vis. Image Underst. **83**(3), 236–274 (2001)
5. Mitra, S., Acharya, T.: Gesture recognition: a survey. IEEE Trans. Syst. Man Cybern. Part C: Appl. Rev. **37**(3), 311–324 (2007)
6. Zhao, W., Chellappa, R., Phillips, P.J., Rosenfeld, A.: Face recognition: a reference survey. ACM Comput. Surv. (CSUR) **35**(4), 399–458 (2003)
7. Gavrila, D.M.: The visual analysis of human movement: a survey. Comput. Vis. Image Underst. **73**(1), 82–98 (1999)
8. Raj, B., Kalgaonkar, K., Harrison, C., Dietz, P.: Ultrasonic doppler sensing in HCI. IEEE Pervasive Comput. **11**(2), 24–29 (2012)
9. Wan, Q., Li, Y., Li, C., Pal, R.: Gesture recognition for smart home applications using portable radar sensors. In: IEEE Conference on Engineering in Medicine and Biology Society, pp. 6414–6417, August 2014
10. Molchanov, P., Gupta, S., Kim, K., Pulli, K.: Multi-sensor system for driver's hand-gesture recognition. In: 2015 11th IEEE International Conference and Workshops on Automatic Face and Gesture Recognition (FG), vol. 1, pp. 1–8. IEEE (2015)
11. Molchanov, P., Gupta, S., Kim, K., et al.: Short-range FMCW monopulse radar for hand-gesture sensing. In: 2015 IEEE Radar Conference (RadarCon), pp. 1491–1496. IEEE (2015)
12. Molchanov, P., Gupta, S., Kim, K., et al.: Multi-sensor system for driver's hand-gesture recognition. In: 2015 11th IEEE International Conference and Workshops on Automatic Face and Gesture Recognition (FG), vol. 1, pp. 1–8. IEEE (2015)
13. Wang, S., Song, J., Lien, J., Poupyrev, I., Hilliges, O.: Interacting with soli: exploring fine-grained dynamic gesture recognition in the radio-frequency spectrum. In: Proceedings of the 29th Annual Symposium on User Interface Software and Technology, pp. 851–860. ACM (2016)
14. Molchanov, P., Gupta, S., Kim, K., et al.: Short-range FMCW monopulse radar for hand-gesture sensing. In: 2015 IEEE Radar Conference (RadarCon) on Automatic Face and Gesture Recognition (FG), vol. 5, pp. 1–6. IEEE (2015)
15. Piper, S.O.: Homodyne FMCW radar range resolution effects with sinusoidal nonlinearities in the frequency sweep. In: Proceedings of IEEE International Radar Conference, pp. 563–567 (1995)

16. Molchanov, P., Gupta, S., Kim, K., Pulli, K.: Multi-sensor system for driver's hand-gesture recognition. In: AFGR (2015)
17. Ren, S., He, K., Girshick, R., Sun, J.: Faster R-CNN: towards real-time object detection with region proposal networks. IEEE Trans. Pattern Anal. Mach. Intell. (2016)
18. Denton, E., Chintala, S., Szlam, A., Fergus, R.: Deep generative image models using a Laplacian pyramid of adversarial networks. In: Advances in Neural Information Processing Systems (NIPS) (2015)
19. Huang, X., Li, Y., Poursaeed, O., Hopcroft, J., Belongie, S.: Stacked generative adversarial networks. In: IEEE Conference on Computer Vision and Pattern Recognition (CVPR) (2017)
20. Chen, Q., Koltun, V.: Photographic image synthesis with cascaded refinement networks. In: IEEE International Conference on Computer Vision (ICCV) (2017)
21. Zhang, H., et al.: StackGAN: text to photo-realistic image synthesis with stacked generative adversarial networks. In: IEEE Conference on Computer Vision and Pattern Recognition (CVPR) (2017)
22. Wang, T., Liu, M., Zhu, J., Tao, A., Kautz, J., Catanzaro, B.: High-resolution image synthesis and semantic manipulation with conditional GANs. In: European Conference on Computer Vision (ECCV) (2017)
23. He, K., Zhang, X., Ren, S., Sun, J.: Spatial pyramid pooling in deep convolutional networks for visual recognition. IEEE Trans. Pattern Anal. Mach. Intell. (TPAMI) 37, 1904–1916 (2015)

Optimization Methods of Motion Recognition System Based on CSI

Hongtao Zhu[1], Dezhi Li[1], Zhenyong Wang[1,2(✉)], Qing Guo[1],
and Zhenbang Wang[1]

[1] School of Electronics and Information Engineering,
Harbin Institute of Technology, Harbin, Heilongjiang, China
zhuhongtao@stu.hit.edu.cn,
{lidezhi,ZYWang,QGuo}@hit.edu.cn, zhenbangw@163.com
[2] Shenzhen Academy of Aerospace Technology, Shenzhen, Guangdong, China

Abstract. Motion recognition system based on WiFi overcomes the limitations of the system based on vision and wearable sensor in the past, it's the most ideal design for the implementation of this technology. On the basis of realizing the motion recognition system based on CSI amplitude, a joint optimization algorithm based on CSI amplitude and phase difference is proposed in this paper. Through linear transformation and continuation compensation of CSI phase, the problem that phase distribution error can't be used is overcome. The amplitude of CSI value of received motion signal is obtained. It is combined with the phase difference of multiple antennas at the receiving end as the basis signal. In order to solve the problem of high complexity of the system, an optimization algorithm based on amplitude distribution variance is proposed. The experimental results show that the system can recognize three different motions with high accuracy, and after using the optimization algorithm, the average recognition accuracy of the system is increased by 4.7%, and the distinguishing rate between static and motion behavior is greatly improved, which has a certain universality.

Keywords: Motion recognition · CSI · Phase difference of multiple antennas · Variance of amplitude distribution

1 Introduction

With the rapid progress and popularization of high-speed processing chip, communication technology and network technology, human-computer interaction (HCI) technology [1] plays an important role in all aspects of people's lives. In many applications of human-computer interaction technology, motion recognition, as an important component of smart city and smart home, has attracted wide attention from academia and industry. According to the channels of motion data acquisition, the existing motion recognition systems can be divided into three categories: motion recognition based on wearable sensors, motion recognition based on vision and motion recognition based on WiFi signals. Radio signals have the advantages of strong penetration, wide sensing range, no recording of sensitive information involving privacy, and no need to carry additional devices to measure. More importantly, with the development of communication

M. Jia et al. (Eds.): WiSATS 2019, LNICST 280, pp. 251–264, 2019.
https://doi.org/10.1007/978-3-030-19153-5_26

technology, WiFi infrastructure is everywhere. Therefore, the use of radio signal detection motion is the most ideal form at present. As early as 2013, Nuzzer, a motion research system based on Received Signal Strength (RSS), first appeared in the literature [2]. The system uses Bayesian formula to locate people whose indoor positioning error is less than 2 m, and judges whether there is human movement in the room according to the variance of the received signal. In [3], WiGest motion recognition system is proposed to extract three basic changes from the influence of different gestures on RSS waveforms, namely, rising, falling and pausing. By combining the three changes with the change of RSS amplitude to detect different gestures, the average recognition accuracy is 86%. Document [4] presents a motion recognition system WiSee for indoor environment on USRP. By observing the instantaneous Doppler frequency shift caused by the movement of people, the system can judge the different motion states of human body, and the recognition accuracy of 9 different behaviors is 94% on average. However, given the number of transmit and receive antennas, the system can only realize single user motion recognition with no more than three interference in the environment. Reference [5] presents a representative E-eyes behavior recognition system, which uses WiFi commercial equipment to statistics CSI amplitude distribution information, uniquely identifies walking and in-situ activities, and achieves an average real case rate of over 96% and a false positive case rate of less than 1% in two different environments. However, the system needs to work in a more stable environment, which limits the use of indoor environment where other users or large pets often exercise. [6] The amplitude of CSI from the same access point (AP) is measured simultaneously by multiple receiving devices. Three data fusion methods, namely majority voting fusion, possibility fusion and feature fusion, are used to select communication links with less interference and higher quality to identify different behaviors. Compared with E-eyes, this method identifies the environment in which multiple users coexist simultaneously. The rate increased by 8%.

Through the analysis of previous work, the behavior recognition system based on WiFi signal can distinguish different motion behavior by observing the changes of CSI of WiFi signal. Therefore, this paper improves the motion recognition system from two directions. Firstly, most of the existing systems only extract the amplitude of CSI, which wastes the phase information that CSI can provide. In this paper, a joint basis signal optimization algorithm based on the amplitude and phase difference of CSI is proposed. By comparing the amplitude of the received signal at the receiving end of the system and designing the processing algorithm of phase linear transformation and phase continuation compensation, the solution is given. The influence of singularity on signal recognition accuracy and the application of CSI phase can't be applied. Secondly, the existing motion recognition system directly uses the traditional classification algorithm to distinguish different behaviors. In the process of matching the behavior to be identified and the existing behavior template, it needs to compare the similarity of the behavior one by one, which has high complexity. In this paper, an optimization algorithm based on the variance of the amplitude distribution of subcarriers is proposed. By comparing the variance of the amplitude of CSI signals between adjacent packets with the variance of the distribution of subcarriers, the severity of the motion is defined, and the fast distinction between the motion and the static behavior is realized, which saves the training time of the static behavior data and reduces the overall complexity of the system.

The remainder of the article is structure as follows: in the Sect. 2, and the system model based on CSI motion recognition is introduced. In the Sect. 3, the continuation compensation algorithm and the joint optimization algorithm based on amplitude and phase difference are designed to realize the use of two basic signals. At the same time, the optimization algorithm based on amplitude distribution variance is designed to optimize the system. Section 4 compares the performance of the improved model with the original model, and the optimization results are compared with the results of related literatures. Section 5 concludes the paper.

2   System Architecture Based on CSI Motion Recognition

2.1   CSI

Wireless channel is usually modeled by channel impact response (Channel Impulse Response, CIR) [7]. CIR can be expressed as:

$$h(\tau) = \sum_{i=1}^{N} \alpha_i e^{-j\theta_i} \delta(\tau - \tau_i) \tag{1}$$

Where α_i, θ_i and τ_i represent amplitude attenuation, phase shift and time delay of I path respectively.

Similarly, when converted to frequency domain, multipath propagation can be characterized by channel frequency response (CFR), which includes amplitude-frequency response and phase-frequency response.

Similarly, when converted to frequency domain, multipath propagation can be characterized by channel frequency response (CFR), which includes amplitude-frequency response and phase-frequency response.

Using the wireless network card, a set of CSIs can be obtained from the wireless signal packets received at each time. Each CSI is based on the sub-carrier frequency difference as the frequency sampling interval. The CFR samples on 30 OFDM sub-carriers in the bandwidth can be collected. The CSI corresponding to each sub-carrier is:

$$CSI_k = \frac{1}{K} \sum_{k=1}^{K} \frac{f_k}{f_0} \times \|H_k\|, \quad k \in (-15, 15) \tag{2}$$

Where f_0 is the center frequency and f_k is he frequency of sub carrier K.

2.2   System Architecture

Based on the principle of WiFi signal behavior recognition, this paper designs a complete system structure, which is shown in Fig. 1. The system consists of two parts: hardware module and software module. The left dotted wire frame is mainly composed of the hardware part and the right is mainly composed of the software module. The system is mainly used to identify and distinguish three different behaviors, including one static behavior and two moving behaviors. For convenience, this paper uses motion 1 to express the behavior of repeated movement after entering the environment, motion 2 to express the behavior of leaving immediately after a short stay in the environment, and motion 3 to express the behavior of not entering the environment.

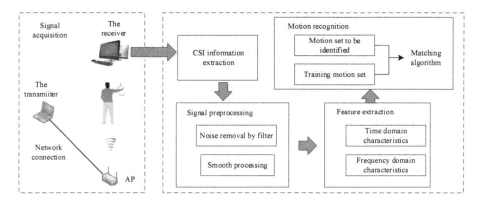

Fig. 1. Structure of motion recognition system based on CSI.

The software module designed in this paper consists of four parts: CSI signal collection, signal pre-processing, feature extraction and motion recognition. After collecting the motion data, the receiver extracts the CSI information. Because the wireless signal is affected by the external environment and various factors within the system, it is necessary to pre-process the data signal, and remove the sudden change data with the help of smoothing algorithm while filtering the noise. The processed signal enters the feature extraction step. In this paper, the features of different wireless signals are extracted in time domain and frequency domain and sent to SVM for training, thus forming the feature data set. Finally, the data set is divided into training set and testing set by cross validation method, and the optimal training template is determined by grid search method. When the test identifies different motions, the motion to be identified is matched with the training motion template to realize the system function.

3   Improved Optimization Algorithms

3.1   Joint Optimization Algorithm Based on Amplitude and Phase Difference

Linear Transformation Processing of Phase. Due to the Clock out of sync and random noise between the receiver and the transmitter, the phase information obtained directly is very random and can't distinguish different behavior. In order to avoid wasting valuable phase information provided by CSI, the existing phase must be corrected. The phase calibration algorithm is introduced to deal with the phase.

Assuming that the phase of the i-th sub carrier of the measured CSI data is A, so the phase can be expressed as follow:

$$\hat{\phi}_i = \phi_i - 2\pi \frac{k_i}{N} \delta + \beta + Z \tag{3}$$

Where ϕ_i is the true phase; δ is the time offset between the receiver and the transmitter, which is the main factor causing the phase error; β is the unknown phase offset; Z is the noise introduced into the measurement process; k_i is the subcarrier index of the subcarrier i; N is the FFT point number.

In order to eliminate the influence of δ and β, two variable a and b are defined.

$$a = \frac{\hat{\phi}_n - \hat{\phi}_1}{k_n - k_1} = \frac{\phi_n - \phi_1}{k_n - k_1} - \frac{2\pi}{N} \delta \tag{4}$$

$$b = \frac{1}{n} \sum_{j=1}^{n} \hat{\phi}_j = \frac{1}{n} \sum_{j=1}^{n} \phi_j - \frac{2\pi\delta}{nN} \sum_{j=1}^{n} k_j + \beta \tag{5}$$

Assume that the frequency of the subcarriers is completely symmetrical. b can be expressed as follows:

$$b = \frac{1}{n} \sum_{j=1}^{n} \hat{\phi}_j = \frac{1}{n} \sum_{j=1}^{n} \phi_j - \frac{2\pi\delta}{nN} \sum_{j=1}^{n} k_j + \beta \tag{6}$$

By subtracting the linear variable $ak_i + b$ from the measured phase, the linear combination of the true phase for removing the random phase offset is obtained. And it is shown as Eq. 7.

$$\tilde{\phi}_i = \hat{\phi}_i - ak_i - b = \phi_i - \frac{\phi_n - \phi_1}{k_n - k_1} k_i - \frac{1}{n} \sum_{j=1}^{n} \phi_j \tag{7}$$

At this time, the error term of random noise is no longer included in the phase signal. The phase obtained by linear calibration is not the real CSI phase, but the linear transformation value of the real phase. Suppose A is frequency independent and identically distributed, then:

$$\sigma_{\tilde{\phi}_i}^2 = c_i \sigma_{\hat{\phi}_i}^2, \quad c_i = 1 + 2\frac{k_i^2}{(k_n - k_1)^2} + \frac{1}{n} \tag{8}$$

This means that the difference between the calibrated phase variance and the true phase variance is only a constant multiple related to frequency. That is to say, the change trend of the calibrated phase signal can be used to reflect the fluctuation of the real phase, which solves the problem that the phase can't be used because of the random distribution of the real phase in theory.

Joint Optimization Algorithm. This paper considers the combination of amplitude and phase of the receiver's multiple antennas as the base signal. The phase difference between the two antennas at the receiving end is used as a new basic signal, which not only utilizes the phase information, but also takes into account the spatial characteristics of the signal. The feasibility of phase difference as a base signal is proved theoretically.

Because amplitude can be used to distinguish different behaviors in the form of curve fluctuation, phase difference can enhance the recognition ability of wireless signals in different directions in different environments and improve the recognition accuracy in complex environments. Therefore, combining amplitude and phase difference, a joint optimization algorithm based on amplitude and phase difference of CSI is proposed to further improve the accuracy of CSI. By comparing the amplitudes of CSI signals received by three antennas at the receiving end, the two items with the largest amplitudes are selected, and the phase difference of the corresponding CSI signals is calculated. If the amplitudes of the received signals of three receiving antennas are identical, two of them are arbitrarily selected to calculate the phase difference; if the amplitudes of the signals of two of the three antennas are equal, the phase difference of the antennas is calculated directly; otherwise, the two antennas corresponding to the two maximal amplitudes of CSI are selected directly. Then the continuation compensation and linear transformation processing of the calculated phase difference are processed.

3.2 Classification Optimization Algorithm Based on Variance of Amplitude Distribution

Distinction Between Motion and Static Behavior. The traditional classification and recognition algorithm only uses SVM to train and test the data feature set. This method takes a long time in the training process, making the whole system more complex. This section designs an optimization algorithm from the state of motion to achieve a quick distinction between different behaviors. Firstly, motion and static behavior are distinguished from the perspective of signal characteristics. The obvious difference between static and motion behavior is that the amplitude of the collected CSI signal fluctuates sharply in the time domain. Obviously, the motion behavior must have more obvious fluctuations. Compared with the static behavior, the variance of the amplitude of the signal is larger. Comparing with the first sub-carrier of the three motions in the non-interference experimental environment, the amplitude of the signal is larger. The amplitude of the CSI signal is shown in the Fig. 2.

Observation of Fig. 2 shows that compared with motion 3, motion 1 and motion 2 have larger amplitude of CSI and more obvious signal fluctuation. Therefore, the variance of signal fluctuation can be used to measure the stability of CSI amplitude distribution. At the same time, the variance of signal distribution considering subcarrier

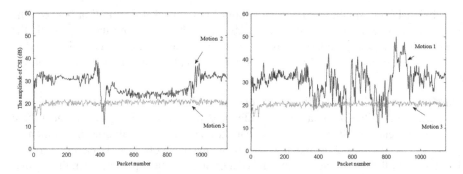

Fig. 2. CSI amplitude of movement and rest behavior changes with time.

variation is used to further distinguish between motion and static behavior. The distribution of the CSI amplitude of the three movements in the frequency domain is compared, and the result is shown in Fig. 3.

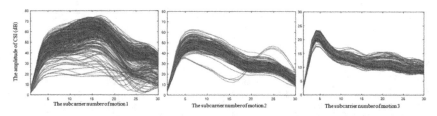

Fig. 3. The CSI amplitude distribution of motion and static behavior varies with sub carrier and time.

Figure 3 shows that the amplitude distribution of CSI in frequency domain is different for different motions. Compared with static motion, the amplitude distribution of motion 1 and motion 2 is more scattered and less stable. Therefore, in the frequency domain, the degree of compactness of the distribution between the curvilinear shapes at different times. That means variance can be used to measure the signal stability. From the point of view of mathematical deduction, a new variable is given: the variance of amplitude distribution, then the variance of CSI amplitude difference of adjacent time signal data is shown as:

$$S_j = \frac{1}{n}\sum_{i=1}^{n}\left[\left(d_i - \overline{d}\right)^2\right] \tag{9}$$

Where d_i is the difference between the amplitude of the current j signal and that of the previous time signal CSI signal on the i-th subcarrier, $\overline{d}$ is the mean of the amplitude difference of the current time signal under all subcarriers, and N represents 30 subcarriers.

Obviously, the smaller S is, the more compact the packet distribution between the time and the previous time is, the more stable the behavior is, and the more static the behavior is; otherwise, the larger S is, the closer the behavior is. The changing trend of CSI signal distribution stability can be obtained by calculating the variance of all the moments.

Classification and Recognition Optimization Algorithm. Figure 4 compares and simulates the distribution of amplitude difference in the whole time domain under three different sub-carriers. It can be found that the variance of amplitude distribution of motion 1 and motion 2 is much larger than that of motion 3. Even the variance distribution of the beginning and the end of motion 3 can be separated from the former. Therefore, the corresponding threshold can be set to distinguish static and dynamic behavior. Now, the optimization algorithm based on the variance of amplitude distribution is no longer necessary to carry out large-scale experimental tests on static behavior. It omits the process of pretreatment, feature extraction and feature set establishment. Theoretically, the algorithm complexity of classification and recognition can be reduced.

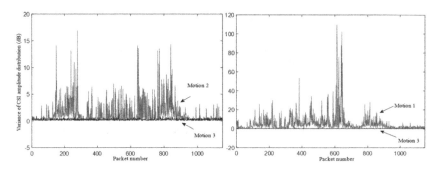

Fig. 4. Comparison results of amplitude distribution variance.

Considering that the optimized system adds a new basic signal of phase difference, in addition to amplitude characteristics, phase characteristics should be introduced in the process of building feature data sets. The eigenvalue of phase difference distribution variance can be used as the eigenvalue of multi-antenna phase difference. The features selected by amplitude can reflect the characteristics of signal distribution. Adding the eigenvalues of the variance of phase difference distribution in time domain can reflect the characteristics of signal more fully, and improve the accuracy of CSI signal acquisition. Compare the variance of phase difference between motion 1 and motion 2, and the result is shown in Fig. 5. The phase difference distribution of different motions is different. Extracting the features can help distinguish different motions. Combining with the amplitude features, it can fully reflect the changes of certain motions and obtain high-precision CSI information recognition.

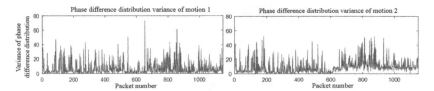

Fig. 5. Comparison of variance of phase distribution of different motions.

4 Experimental Results and Analysis

4.1 System Performance in Strong Interference Environment

In this paper, strong interference environment refers to the experimental environment in which no more than 10 WiFi networks are covered and no more than two unrelated experimenters with small amplitude of motion are involved. The strong interference environment in this paper is shown in Fig. 6.

Fig. 6. Strong interference experimental environment

There are many routers inside and around the environment. There are usually eight WiFi networks covered, and there are not more than two unrelated experimenters in the environment whose mobility is not obvious. Outside the glass door, there are unrelated experimenters who can move freely. Under this environment, the system can move freely. The same frequency interference and multipath interference may be caused.

In order to verify the effectiveness of the optimization algorithm, the optimization algorithm introduced in this paper is used to optimize the system in the strong interference experimental environment. Figure 7 is the confusion matrix obtained from the recognition results of three motions.

Figure 6 shows the accuracy of motion recognition before and after system optimization in strong jamming environment. The experiment shows that in strong jamming environment, compared with the original system before optimization, the recognition accuracy of each motion after optimization has been improved, and the average recognition accuracy has been increased by 4.6%.

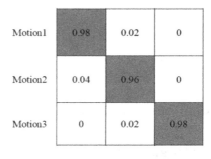

	Motion1	Motion2	Motion3
Motion1	0.98	0.02	0
Motion2	0.04	0.96	0
Motion3	0	0.02	0.98

Fig. 7. Confusion matrix of optimization results in strong interference environment

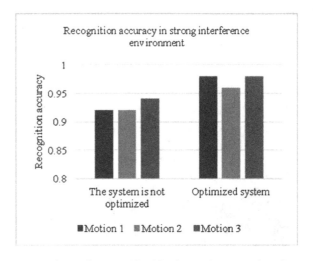

Fig. 8. Accuracy comparison of system identification under strong interference environment.

Figure 7 shows the accuracy of motion recognition before and after system optimization in strong jamming environment. The experiment shows that in strong jamming environment, compared with the original system before optimization, the recognition accuracy of each motion after optimization has been improved, and the average recognition accuracy has been increased by 4.6%.

Table 1 is the time of motion recognition before and after system optimization under strong interference. The comparison shows that the recognition time of motion 1 and motion 2 increases slightly after optimization, which is due to the introduction of the optimization algorithm to complete the distinction between motion and static behavior first, and then to recognize motion 1 and motion 2; but at the same time, the recognition efficiency of motion 3 is significantly improved, the distinction between static behavior. The speed increase is more than half, which has obtained strong system performance.

Table 1. Time of motion recognition under strong interference

	Motion 1	Motion 2	Motion 3
Not optimized	30.04	26.74	10.67
Optimization	31.63	30.63	4.66

4.2 System Performance in Weak Interference Environment

In this paper, the weak interference environment refers to the experimental environment in which no more than five WiFi networks are covered, and there is no unrelated experimenters. The strong interference environment in this paper is shown in Fig. 9.

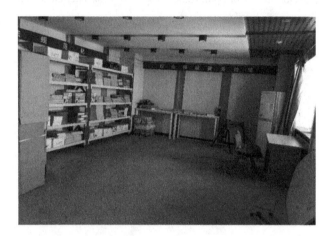

Fig. 9. Weak interference experimental environment

The number of routers in and around the environment is very small, usually covering two WiFi networks, and there is only one experimenter in the environment for each test. There are no glass doors and other items in the environment, and there is a wall between the external corridor and the environment.

In order to verify the optimization system in weak interference can also realize the function of the system under the experimental environment, using the above optimization algorithm is introduced to optimize the design of system identification, Fig. 10 is a confusion matrix obtained from the recognition results of three actions.

Figure 11 shows the accuracy of motion recognition before and after system optimization in strong jamming environment. The recognition accuracy of the optimized system is 98%, 98% and 100% respectively, and the average recognition accuracy is 98.7%. The highest recognition rate is static motion. Compared with the non-optimized system under the same environment, the average recognition accuracy is improved by 4.7%, which can basically achieve error-free recognition. Compared with the optimization system in strong jamming environment, the average recognition

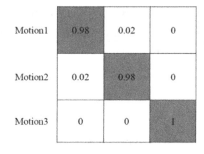

Fig. 10. Confusion matrix of optimization results in weak interference environment

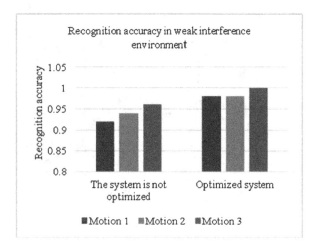

Fig. 11. Accuracy comparison of system identification under weak interference environment.

accuracy in weak jamming environment is improved by 1.4% due to the reduction of obstacles in the environment.

Table 2 is the time of motion recognition before and after system optimization under weak interference. Compared with the recognition time, the recognition time of motion 1 and motion 2 increases slightly due to the introduction of optimization algorithm, and the new system spends a certain amount of complexity to separate motion and static behavior. Therefore, the recognition efficiency of motion 3 is improved significantly, and the recognition time is saved by 56.1% on average and improves the overall performance.

In this paper, the recognition time and accuracy of the optimized system are compared with those of similar systems in reference [6]. The results are shown in Fig. 8. As can be seen from Fig. 12, the system in this paper has a certain advantage in fast recognition of static behavior, but the recognition of dynamic behavior is slightly inferior to that in reference [6]. This is due to the preferential use of optimization

Table 2. Time of motion recognition under weak interference

	Motion 1	Motion 2	Motion 3
Not optimized	24.87	23.16	9.16
Optimization	27.80	26.05	4.02

algorithm to distinguish motion. Although the recognition time of two kinds of motion behavior has slightly increased, the overall performance has been greatly improved. The validity of the fast discrimination algorithm for static and motional behavior is proved.

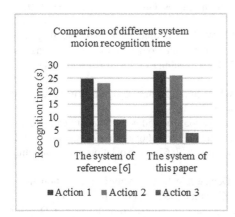
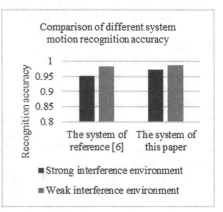

Fig. 12. Comparison of different system motion recognition accuracy.

5   Conclusion

In this paper, we use WIFI signal to design a motion recognition system based on CSI, and propose two optimization algorithms. Two representative experimental scenarios, strong interference environment and weak interference environment, were selected to complete the behavior recognition before and after the system optimization in the two environments, and the recognition accuracy, accuracy and recognition time of the three motions were compared. The experimental results show that the recognition accuracy of the optimized system has been improved to a certain extent, and the recognition accuracy has been improved by 4.6% and 4.7% respectively in strong and weak interference environment. Although the introduction of the optimization algorithm makes the system spend a certain amount of time to establish the phase feature set, making the recognition time of the first two behaviors slightly increased, but compared with motion 3 recognition speed as high as 56.1%. At the same time, the performance of the system is compared with similar systems in reference [6], and the comparative experiments fully prove the robustness of the design system and the effectiveness of the optimization algorithm.

Acknowledgment. This work was supported by National Natural Science Foundation of China (Grant Nos. 61601147, 61571316) and Fundamental Research Funds of Shenzhen Innovation of Science and Technology Committee (Grant No. JCYJ20160331141634788).

References

1. Agarwal, S., Pandey, G.N.: Human computer interaction design for intensive care unit monitors. In: 4th International Conference on Intelligent Human Computer Interaction: Advancing Technology for Humanity, IHCI 2012, pp. 5–8. IEEE Computer Society, Kharagpur (2012)
2. Seifeldin, M., Youssef, M.: A large-scale device-free passive localization system for wireless environments. In: 3rd International Conference on Pervasive Technologies Related to Assistive Environments, PETRA 2010, Pythagorion, Samos, Greece, pp. 1321–1334 (2013). IEEE Transactions on Mobile Computing
3. Abdelnasser, H., Youssef, M., Harras, K.A.: WiGest: a ubiquitous WiFi-based gesture recognition system. In: 34th IEEE Annual Conference on Computer Communications and Networks, IEEE INFOCOM 2015, pp. 1472–1480. Institute of Electrical and Electronics Engineers Inc., Hong Kong (2015)
4. Pu, Q.F., Sidhant, G., Shyamnath, G., et al.: Whole-home gesture recognition using wireless signals. Comput. Commun. Rev. **43**(4), 485–486 (2013)
5. Wang, Y., Liu, J., Chen, Y., et al.: Device-free location-oriented activity identification using fine-grained WiFi signatures. In: 20th ACM Annual International Conference on Mobile Computing and Networking, MobiCom 2014, pp. 617–628. Association for Computing Machinery, Maui (2014)
6. Wang, W., Liu, A.X., Shahzad, M., et al.: Device-free human activity recognition using commercial WiFi devices. IEEE J. Sel. Areas Commun. **35**(5), 1118–1131 (2017)
7. Wang, Y.L., Zhang, Y.Y., Zhu, Y.X.: A novel channel estimation algorithm based on DFT for LTE-a system. In: 2014 International Conference on Electronic Engineering and Information Science, ICEEIS 2014, pp. 59–62. Trans Tech Publications Ltd., Harbin (2014)

WiFi CSI Fingerprinting Positioning Based on User Rotation

Jiahao Zhang[1], Ming Zhang[1], Zuoliang Yin[2], Zhian Deng[1(✉)], and Weijian Si[1]

[1] College of Information and Communications Engineering, Harbin Engineering University, Harbin 150001, China
dengzhian@hrbeu.edu.cn
[2] School of Electronics and Information, Qingdao University, Qingdao 266000, China

Abstract. This paper studies the indoor fingerprinting positioning using Channel State Information (CSI) in commercial WiFi network environment. In this paper, we improve the existing indoor fingerprinting positioning method by considering the influence of human body absorption on CSI signal amplitude and collecting CSI data with user rotation at each reference location. The whole positioning process includes two stage: offline stage and online stage. In the offline stage, we extract features from the filtered CSI data of three APs at each reference location to construct CSI fingerprints. In the online stage, we first compare the feature vectors of filtered CSI data with fingerprints, and then calculate the Euclidean distance between the online CSI feature vector and fingerprints. Finally, user location will be obtained by the K Nearest Neighbor (KNN) algorithm. Experiments proved the performance improvement of the proposed CSI fingerprinting positioning method.

Keywords: Indoor positioning · CSI · Fingerprint · KNN

1 Introduction

With the popularity of location-based services in our lives, the demand for positioning and navigation is increasing. Although the Global Positioning System (GPS) performs well in outdoor positioning, it doesn't work effectively in indoor environments [1]. In daily life, we need to acquire the location information of indoor targets, such as in-door location information of large venues, and real-time location information of workers in high-risk working environment. Due to the widespread deployment of WiFi infrastructures, research on WiFi indoor positioning has become a hot spot, since its cost is relatively low and easy to implement.

Currently, research on WiFi indoor fingerprinting positioning begin to shift to using CSI instead of RSS [2]. Existing CSI indoor fingerprinting positioning method research shows that using CSI instead of RSS as the positioning signal source can further improve the positioning accuracy [3, 4]. Traditional CSI fingerprinting positioning method only considers the CSI signal amplitude information in specific directions at each reference location [5, 6]. In fact, during online stage, CSI data may be collected by

M. Jia et al. (Eds.): WiSATS 2019, LNICST 280, pp. 265–271, 2019.
https://doi.org/10.1007/978-3-030-19153-5_27

users face arbitrary directions. This may render mismatch between offline constructed fingerprints and online collected CSI data [7].

Considering the shortcomings of traditional CSI fingerprinting positioning method, we propose WiFi CSI fingerprinting positioning based on user rotation. Firstly, in the process of CSI data collection, the influence of human body absorption on the CSI signal amplitude is taken into account, and the CSI data is collected by the user turning around at each reference location. Secondly, in the process of online matching with fingerprints, different statistical features are selected to form the feature vectors for matching. Thirdly, we use the CSI from different APs to build a fingerprinting database and compare the impact of the number of APs on the positioning accuracy. Finally, the effectiveness of our method is verified by experiments. Compared with the traditional CSI fingerprinting positioning method, the CSI fingerprinting positioning system proposed in this paper has higher positioning accuracy and better stability.

The proposed positioning method is described in Sect. 2. Section 3 presents the experimental results and related discussions. Section 4 summarizes this paper.

2   Method Design

2.1   Fingerprinting Positioning Principle

Fingerprinting positioning method matches the online CSI feature vector with fingerprints, the method has two stages: offline stage and online stage, as shown in Fig. 1.

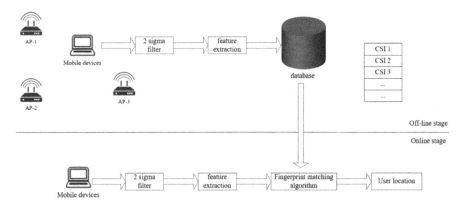

Fig. 1. Fingerprinting positioning principle.

In offline stage, we firstly divide the room area into n reference location, and collect CSI data at each reference location from m APs. Then, we extract the CSI signal amplitude from the collected CSI data, and use a filter to eliminate the disturbed CSI values. Finally, the statistical features of the filtered CSI signal amplitude are extracted to construct feature vectors. The feature vectors and related reference location coordinates are used to form a fingerprint. We use the *sigma* filter to eliminate disturbed CSI values. For the extraction of statistical features, we choose the minimum value, the median value, the maximum value, the arithmetic mean value, the geometric mean value, and the harmonic mean value and standard deviation.

When collect data in the online stage, indoor environment must ensure is same as the fingerprint generate. We collect CSI data at user location. We eliminate the perturbation value and extract statistical features to form an online feature vector, and calculate the Euclidean distance with fingerprints. This can be obtained by the Euclidean distance formula (1):

$$dist_{ij} = \sum_{n=1}^{N_{ant}*N_{sub}} \sqrt{\mathbf{x}_i - \mathbf{x}_j} \tag{1}$$

Where $dist_{ij}$ is the Euclidean distance from the i-th user location to the j-th reference location in the fingerprint. $\mathbf{x}$ denotes a feature vector, N_{ant} is the antennas number for collected CSI data, and N_{sub} is the subcarriers number of CSI data.

2.2 Fingerprint Matching Algorithm

In online stage, we use KNN algorithm to fingerprint matching positioning. The KNN algorithm is an improvement on the nearest neighbor (NN) algorithm. The first step of the KNN algorithm is to calculate the Euclidean distance from the user location CSI feature vectors with fingerprints. The second step is to sort the Euclidean distance from small to large (the smaller Euclidean distance, the higher similarity). The third step is to select the top K ($K \geq 2$) sorted Euclidean distance, and find the coordinate of the selected data. Finally, as shown in the formula (2), we will get user location by compute the mean of the coordinates corresponding to the K selected data.

$$(x, y) = \frac{1}{k} \sum_{i=0}^{k} (x_i, y_i) \tag{2}$$

Where (x_i, y_i) is the i-th selected reference location coordinate using KNN algorithm, and (x, y) is the result user location coordinate.

3 Experiment

3.1 Experimental Setup

In order to get CSI data, we chose Ubuntu 14.04.4 system notebook with Intel 5300 NIC. According to the MIMO protocol, subcarriers between antennas don't interfere with each other, therefore, 30 subcarriers can be combined as experimental data. In the experiment of this paper, we chose a 70 m^2 room. According to the actual environment in the room (table location, whether the CSI data is convenient to collect), we set twenty-four reference locations, ten user locations and three APs. Figure 2 shows the indoor environment layout.

We collect CSI data using two methods, the proposed method in this paper and the traditional method. In the proposed method, we consider the influence of human body absorption on CSI signal amplitude, and collect CSI data by user rotation in each reference location. In the traditional method, we collect CSI data in four directions (0°, 90°, 180°, 270°) at each reference location.

3.2 CSI Data Analysis

Through the study of CSI signal amplitude feature vectors, we found that the CSI signal amplitude is related to location and direction. In theory, the line-of-sight (LOS) path wireless signal have a large signal strength, and the CSI signal amplitude is low. On the contrary, the non-line-of-sight (NLOS) path wireless signal strength is small, and the CSI signal amplitude is high. When the user holds the notebook in front of the chest to receive CSI data, the CSI signal amplitude will change with different directions because of the influence of human body absorption on CSI signal amplitude.

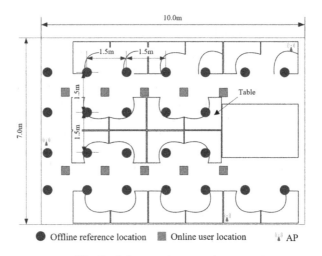

● Offline reference location   ■ Online user location   AP

Fig. 2. Indoor environment layout.

We collect CSI data by user rotates three times in one location. It can be seen from Fig. 3 that the CSI signal amplitude periodically change three times during the user rotation three times. Figure 3(a) show the raw CSI signal amplitude. We can be seen that there are some disturbed value, so we use 2 sigma filter to process raw data. The filtered data is shown in Fig. 3(b).

3.3 Positioning Accuracy Comparison

According to the experiment setup in Sect. 3.1. Using our method, we collect CSI data from three AP in each reference location to generate a fingerprint. In online stage, we use KNN algorithm to estimate the location of twenty online samples. Then analyze mean positioning errors by using different AP numbers, we can get that the mean positioning error using one AP is 2.34 m, using two APs is 2.04 m and using three APs is 1.58 m.

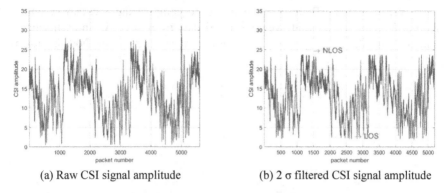

(a) Raw CSI signal amplitude   (b) 2 σ filtered CSI signal amplitude

Fig. 3. CSI single amplitude variations of user rotation three times.

As shown in Fig. 4, it can be seen that the positioning accuracy is significantly improved as the number of AP increases. The reason is that when use one or two APs collecting CSI data, the positioning error may occur at the same radius around the AP. In Fig. 4, we can also see the influence of the parameter K on the positioning accuracy. We use KNN algorithm to choose the K location with the smallest Euclidean distance as the user location neighborhood cluster. Finding the mean of the coordinates corresponding as the user location. As the parameter K increases, it can be seen that the KNN algorithm positioning accuracy first becomes higher and then becomes lower. When K is equal to four, the positioning error is the smallest, and equal to 1.58 m.

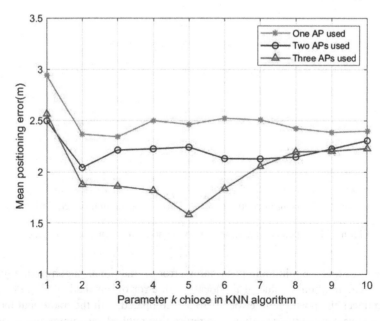

Fig. 4. Positioning error of the user rotating fingerprint under different AP numbers.

Now we use three APs positioning results to compare the accuracy. Using our method and traditional method, we collect CSI data from three AP in each reference location to generate two fingerprints. The positioning error of two methods is shown in Fig. 5.

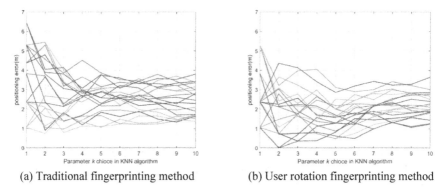

(a) Traditional fingerprinting method   (b) User rotation fingerprinting method

Fig. 5. Positioning error of two methods for twenty test samples.

Figure 5(a) shows the positioning results of the Traditional fingerprinting method. It can be seen that the positioning error of twenty test samples is 2–4 m. Figure 5(b) shows the positioning results of our method. We can see that the positioning error of twenty test samples distribute at 0.5–3 m. The mean positioning error of twenty samples is shown in Fig. 6.

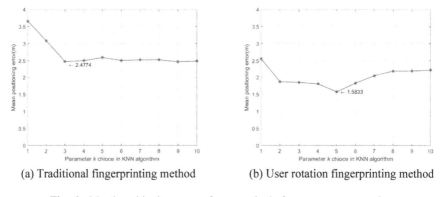

(a) Traditional fingerprinting method   (b) User rotation fingerprinting method

Fig. 6. Mead positioning error of two methods for twenty test samples.

We can see that the minimum positioning error of traditional fingerprinting method is 2.48 m. The minimum value of the local mean error of our method is 1.58 m. Our method reduces the positioning error by 36.3% compared with the traditional method. In Fig. 6(a), we can see that traditional fingerprinting method has minimum positioning error when K value is three, and in Fig. 6(a) when the *K* value is five our method has minimum positioning error. By analyzing the positioning results of the two methods and selecting the K value with the highest positioning accuracy, we can obtain Table 1.

Table 1. Comparison of positioning errors between two methods.

	Traditional method	Proposed method	Error reduction rate
Max error (m)	4.14	3.13	24.4%
Mean error (m)	2.48	1.58	36.3%
Media error (m)	2.32	1.57	32.3%
Min error (m)	0.79	0.48	39.2%

It can be seen from Table 1 that compared with the traditional method, the proposed method of this paper reduces the maximum positioning error by 24.4%, the mean error by 36.3%, the median positioning error by 32.3% and the minimum positioning error by 39.2%. In addition to some large positioning errors caused by some environmental factors, the positioning accuracy of our method is significantly improved.

4 Conclusions

In this paper, we introduce a CSI fingerprinting positioning method, which considers the influence of human body absorption on CSI signal amplitude. We collect CSI data by user rotation in each CSI collected location. The positioning results indicate that compared with the traditional method, the proposed method in this paper reduces the mean positioning error by 39.1%.

References

1. Wang, Z., Chen, Y., Wang, H.: Sequence-based indoor localization with channel status information. IEEE Sens. J. **18**(6), 1817 (2018)
2. Deng, Z.A., Hu, Y., Yu, J., et al.: Extended Kalman filter for real time indoor localization by fusing WiFi and smartphone inertial sensors. Micromachines **6**(4), 523–543 (2015)
3. Fang, S.H., et al.: Channel state reconstruction using multilevel discrete wavelet transform for improved fingerprinting-based indoor localization. IEEE Sens. J. **16**(21), 7784–7791 (2016)
4. Wang, X., Gao, L., Mao, S., et al.: CSI-based fingerprinting for indoor localization: a deep learning approach. IEEE Trans. Veh. Technol. **66**(1), 763–776 (2017)
5. Shi, S., et al.: Accurate location tracking from CSI-based passive device-free probabilistic fingerprinting. IEEE Trans. Vehic. Technol. **PP**(99), 1 (2018)
6. Song, Q., et al.: CSI signal amplitude fingerprinting based NB-IoT indoor localization. IEEE Internet Things J. **5**(3), 1494–1504 (2018)
7. Zhou, M., Tang, Y., Nie, W., et al.: GrassMA: graph-based semi-supervised manifold alignment for indoor WLAN localization. IEEE Sens. J. **17**(21), 7086–7095 (2017)

International Workshop on Integrated Space and Onboard Networks (ISON)

A Method of Automatic Code Generation for Spacecraft OBDH Software

Hongjun Zhang$^{(\boxtimes)}$, Li Pan, and Mengmeng Yu

Beijing Institute of Spacecraft System Engineering, Beijing 100094, China
zhanghongjunbuaa@sina.com

Abstract. The numerous interfaces of spacecraft OBDH software and frequent changes in requirements, resulting in the low efficiency and reliability of the manual coding of OBDH software. An automatic code generation method based on electronic data sheet (EDS) is proposed. The EDS system is introduced, and the output of the EDS system can be used to generate OBDH software code automatically, which improves the efficiency of software development. An structure of OBDH software is designed, which separates the logical code from the parameter code. Due to the EDS system data source is unique, and software code is automatically generated by tools, which avoids the mistakes of coding manually and promotes the reliability of OBDH software and even the reliability of spacecraft is improved.

Keywords: Spacecraft · OBDH software · Automatic code generation

1 Introduction

OBDH subsystem is the information management center of spacecraft. It is responsible for data acquisition, transmission and processing within the spacecraft, between spacecraft and ground station, between spacecrafts. It is also the key to improve the spacecraft efficiency [1]. OBDH software completes the above services with the support of hardware equipment. Therefore, the efficiency and quality of the development of OBDH software greatly affects the development progress and reliability of the spacecraft.

The role of OBDH subsystem in spacecraft determines that it has data transmission interface with all the subsystems in spacecraft that generate data information, as shown in Fig. 1. After the delivery of OBDH subsystem, the spacecraft AIT test will begin. This requires the earliest delivery of OBDH subsystem, which greatly reduces the development cycle of OBDH software. Because of so many interfaces, requirements of OBDH software vary greatly, which leads to the large number and high frequency of changes in the development process.

M. Jia et al. (Eds.): WiSATS 2019, LNICST 280, pp. 275–282, 2019.
https://doi.org/10.1007/978-3-030-19153-5_28

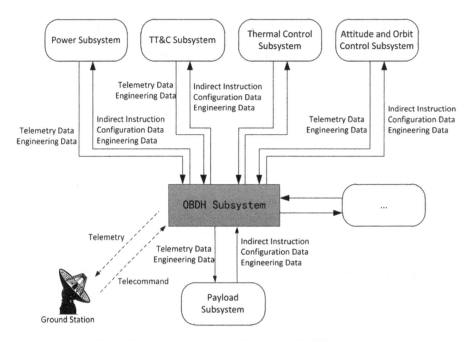

Fig. 1. The external interface diagram of OBDH subsystem

The requirements of OBDH software are mainly Microsoft Word documents, whose content are described by natural language, and the inherent semantic fuzziness of natural language may lead to the ambiguity in requirement description [2]. A large number of spacecraft data input and output interfaces, data formats, communication protocols, etc., are embedded in Word documents in the form of tables. Due to the complex format constraints in Word tables, the process of transforming these contents into software code by manual coding in the past is inefficient and error-prone. A large part of OBDH software function requirements are configuration parameters, and the change of configuration parameters are frequent. Logic and parameters are strongly coupled in common software architecture, this makes the parameter part changes when would inevitably cause logical parts changes, this leads to changes in the risk of unnecessary mistakes.

In this paper, an automatic code generation method based on electronic data sheet (EDS) is proposed. The requirements are provided in the form of EDS. EDS is used to format spacecraft data source, data channel, data format and transmission protocol. Programmers can use special tool to convert the output of EDS into software code, greatly reducing the time of manual coding. Because the spacecraft data source is managed uniformly in EDS, the inevitable error rate during the manual input process is greatly reduced.

2 Design Status of OBDH Software

2.1 Information Processing Function of OBDH Software

OBDH software is responsible for the information processing of the spacecraft, the efficient and reliable management and control of the spacecraft information flow, the monitoring of the status of each subsystem, and the completion of in-orbit tasks and parameters configuration with the payload, so as to achieve the predetermined objectives and meet the mission requirements. OBDH subsystem adopts the bus mechanism to connect each subsystem organically and realize the exchange and sharing of information and data to complete the management, control and task scheduling.

The information processing function of OBDH software includes:

(1) Telemetry function: collecting telemetry data of OBDH and other subsystems, and then process and store them. It is formatted according to the constraint, and transmitted to the ground via the telemetry downlink radio frequency channel.
(2) Remote control function: receiving remote control commands and uplink data from the ground station, decoding, verifying, distributing and executing them, and output remote control commands for other subsystems.
(3) Bus management function: at present, most spacecraft adopt 1553B bus or CAN bus, and OBDH software completes the communication management between the subsystems attached to the data bus, controls the data transmission between the subsystems, and completes the spacecraft mission.

Other functions of OBDH software, such as program control function, housekeep function, autonomous management and autonomous operation function, etc., are not described in this paper.

2.2 Structure of OBDH Software

Most of the requirements for the information processing function of OBDH software come from various protocol tables, which are generally given in the form of Microsoft Word documents. Programmers copy the required protocol information from the Word documents and forms the software code after symbol and format conversion, which is generally expressed as various parameters. In the current software structure, logic and parameters code have high coupling, as show in Fig. 2.

When the parameter part of the code needs to be changed, programmers need to copy the data from the new version of the protocol table, after conversion, the software code is formed. Due to the coupling between the logic code and the parameter code, the logic code may be changed when changing the software parameters, thus causing software exceptions.

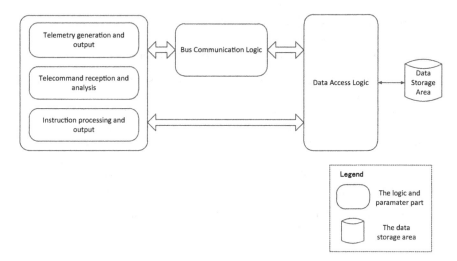

Fig. 2. A software structure coupled with logic and parameters

3 Automatic Generation of Software Code

3.1 Software Structure that Separates Logic from Parameters

Since the requirements of OBDH software have changed a lot and the changes are mostly related to information flow, the software changes caused by these changes are mainly the modifications of configuration parameters, which basically do not involve the changes of software logic. Therefore, a software structure that separates logic from parameters is designed, as shown in Fig. 3. The logic part designs the standard interface, calls various constraints of the parameter part, and completes the acquisition and processing of spacecraft information flow.

The logic part according to the constraint relation of the parameter part, completes the corresponding data acquisition, processing and transmission. For example, the logic part completes the bus communication control according to the bus communication protocol agreed in the parameter part, the acquisition of telemetry data is completed according to the telemetry parameter acquisition channel agreed in the parameter part, the generation of telemetry packages is completed according to the configuration of telemetry packages and the type of parameters agreed in the parameter part, the instructions output is completed according to the instruction format agreed in the parameter part.

The logic part uses mature code, so the spacecraft development process does not need to re-develop the logic part of OBDH software. The parameter part is generated automatically by converting the output of EDS system.

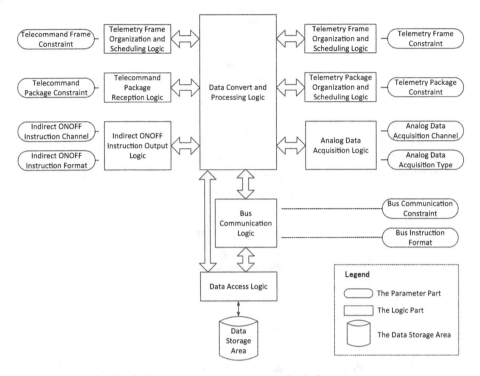

Fig. 3. Software structure that separates logic from parameters

3.2 EDS System

EDS is short for electronic data sheet. It can realize the full-cycle management of the spacecraft electronic information system design. It satisfies the coordinated design and transmission of information overall, OBDH subsystem, single device, AIT, operation control, etc.

EDS integrates the input and output data sources of spacecraft information overall to form a unified basic data source of spacecraft. Data classification and hierarchical management are realized, and data association related to information flow at the spacecraft system level, subsystem level and configuration item level is realized. This ensures the spacecraft in the overall information design, software development, measurement, operation control, simulation and verification and ground testing phase of effective synchronization, as shown in Fig. 4. In this paper, the management parameters provided by EDS are used for OBDH software development, as shown in the dotted line box in the figure.

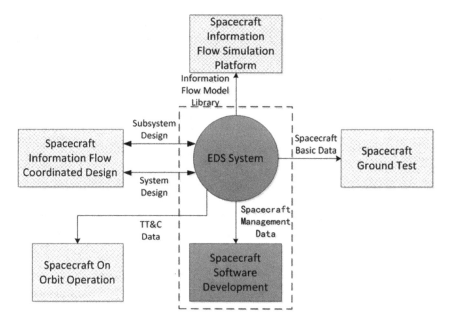

Fig. 4. EDS interface diagram.

The data that EDS can output includes telemetry parameter acquisition channels, remote command channels, telemetry package, telemetry frame, virtual channels, telemetry packet scheduling strategy, telemetry frame scheduling strategy, bus transmission protocol and so on. Here are two typical data constraints to illustrate (Tables 1 and 2).

Table 1. Analog telemetry acquisition constraints

Parameter name	Instructions
Telemetry parameter code	Uniquely identifies telemetry parameter
Telemetry parameter name	Description of telemetry parameter
Telemetry parameter type	Including analog, temperature and BL
Acquisition device ID	Identifies the device that collects remote data
Acquisition channel	Identifies the acquisition channel of telemetry data
Acquisition length	Indicates the length of current telemetry data

Table 2. 1553B bus protocol constraints and examples

Sub address	Word count/mode code	T/R	Communication mode	Transmission cycle(s)	Service request	Data content
7	32	1	RT -> BC	1	0	Telemetry Data1
8	32	1	RT -> BC	1	0	Telemetry Data2
20	32	1	RT -> BC	1	0	GPS original observation data
21	128	1	RT -> RT	0.5	0	Orbital measurement data
24	32	0	BC -> RT	–	1	GPS import data
31	17	0	BC -> RT	–	0	Synchronization word

3.3   EDS Output Conversion

XML (Extensible Markup Language), was founded in 1998 by the main design organization the W3C (the World Wide Web Consortium) of the world wide web. It is a Markup Language, its format to describe the structure and semantic clarified. It is a plain text, non-proprietary format, and you can use any editor to edit, can display in a variety of devices [3]. It is effective to avoid the Word document is limited by a proprietary format.

The EDS system outputs XML files in uniform format, including analog telemetry acquisition type and channel, indirect ONOFF instruction output format and channel, bus instruction format, bus communication protocol, telemetry packet format and content, telemetry packet scheduling strategy, telemetry frame format, telemetry frame scheduling strategy, virtual channel allocation, etc. As it comes from EDS system, the changing process is selected and completed in EDS system. Taking it as the requirement input for the development of OBDH software, it can effectively guarantee the uniqueness of data source and avoid the error caused by inconsistent document versions.

Programmers dedicated conversion tool converts the XML files to the software code, this part of the software code stored in a separate c file, after the follow-up requirement change also change the c file only, do not change the software logic code section, reduces the possibility of software failure caused by accidental modification of the logic code when modifying the parameter code.

Take telemetry package format as an example to illustrate the software code generated by the output of EDS system.

```
struct tm_packet_struct
{
    unsigned int tm_index;
    unsigned char tm_type;        /*Three types: byte type,  double level type
and bit type*/
    unsigned int tm_length;       /*Telemetry parameter length in bits*/
    unsigned char bit_pos_in_byte; /*The start position of a bit-type telemetry
parameter in a byte*/
};
```

4 Conclusion

Due to the numerous external interfaces of spacecraft OBDH subsystem and frequent changes in requirements, the manual coding of OBDH software is low efficient and reliable. An automatic code generation method is proposed based on EDS. The software development process is illustrated. This method can more significantly reduce the duplication of work caused by frequent changes in requirements, avoid the software failure caused by manual coding errors, and improve the reliability of OBDH subsystem and even the spacecraft.

References

1. Weichi, T.A.N., Yingqi, G.U.: Space Data System, pp. 8–9. China Scientific and Technology Press, Beijing (2004)
2. Xiong, Q., Yang, H.: Application of detects seeking for evaluating the ambiguity in software requirements documents (SRS). Wirel. Commun. Technol. (2), 38–42
3. Yuan, Y., Liang, S.: A brief introduction to XML Extensible Markup Language. Comput. Knowl. Technol. 6(20), 5523–5526 (2010)

An Improved RTEMS Supporting Real-Time Detection of Stack Overflow

Rui Zhang[1,3(✉)], Yan Du[2,3], Tao Zhang[1,3], Qi Qiu[1,3], Liang Mao[1,3], and Jiaxiang Niu[1,3]

[1] Beijing Institute of Spacecraft System Engineering, Beijing, China
299542@qq.com
[2] Institute 706, Second Academy of China
Aerospace Science and Industry Corporation, Beijing, China
[3] Science and Technology on Communication Networks Laboratory,
Shijiazhuang, China

Abstract. Aiming at the common problem of stack overflow in satellite software, this paper improves the RTEMS operating system which is supporting real-time stack use depth and overflow detection. Taking the on-board software based on TSC690F processor as an example, the accessible area and unaccessible area are set for each thread stack by using the memory access protection mechanism provided by the processor. The improved RTEMS shared the access protection mechanism among threads through context switching. A trap handler is designed to take over write protection error traps, calculate stack usage depth, and monitor stack overflow in real time. The core module performance test and stack detection instance verification show that the improved RTEMS has little effect on the software performance, so that the software can detect the stack depth online and real-time. By using this method, the software is still manageable in case of stack overflow, rather than runaway crash, and the reliability of the software is improved.

Keywords: Improved RTEMS · On-board software · Stack used depth · Stack overflow

1 Introduction

RTEMS (Real Time Executive for Multiprocessor System) is a multi-processor embedded real-time operating system which was developed in the 1980s [1]. It was a free open source software supported by the U.S. military and first applied to the missile control system. RTEMS has the characteristic of good real-time and stability, and it is widely used in the field of aerospace. On-board software is a typical embedded software. With the support of RTEMS operating system, on-board software runs stably on space-borne equipment. The Aerospace Orbit Control System (AOCS) software and On-Board Data Handling (OBDH) software are the two typical on-board embedded software. The OBDH software is mainly responsible for the data management, telecommand and telemetry service for the satellite [2]. The AOCS software mainly

© ICST Institute for Computer Sciences, Social Informatics and Telecommunications Engineering 2019
Published by Springer Nature Switzerland AG 2019. All Rights Reserved
M. Jia et al. (Eds.): WiSATS 2019, LNICST 280, pp. 283–293, 2019.
https://doi.org/10.1007/978-3-030-19153-5_29

controls the attitude of satellites. This two software is classified as the key level software, and its function is very critical to the satellite.

The stack is one of the most important resources in the software running process. It not only stores the parameters and return address of the calling function, but also stores the local variables of the function. The usage of the stack depends on the running software which is dynamic, then it is not easily for the verification whether the allocation of the stack is enough for the software running. Of course, the overwhelming allocation will result in the waste of on-board computer resources.

For stack depth detection, static test method and dynamic test method are usually used [3, 4]. Static testing methods are generally supported by specialized tools, such as Stack Analyzer tools developed by AbsInt. This tool is not widely used, because of the cost, and the analysis process does not support function pointers, recursive logic analysis and so on. Dynamic testing method is to test the software stack during system running. For example, the RTInsight tool developed by Shanghai Chuangjing Company can be used for dynamic testing of the stack after matching the interface of the target system. Dynamic testing methods has higher requirement for the design of test case. If the deepest function call path on the stack cannot be analyzed, even if the program runs for a long time, the maximum use depth of the stack cannot be obtained, and the stack overflow problem cannot be avoided during the running of the software. StackGuard and StackSheild are widely used in stack overflow protection technology [5]. The principle is to add some code to each function to create a "guard" when it is called, and compare when it is returned. Because each function call and return must run these codes, the efficiency of software operation is greatly affected. It is difficult to satisfy the real-time requirement of on-board software.

In summary, the use of on-board software stack has the following problems. ① Designers unable to obtain the actual use of stacks and margins, and always create the stack space by experience. Generally, it is a margin insufficiency or waste. ② Stack depth detection is difficult. Static testing is more dependent on tools, and dynamic testing is more dependent on test case design. Both of them are unsatisfactory. ③ software cannot be prevented before stack overflow, and it cannot provide alert alarm or protection measures. ④ After the stack overflow, the running position of the program when the software crashes are generally not near the overflow code, and the hysteresis characteristic of the fault makes it difficult to solve the problem [6, 7]. ⑤ The behavior after software collapse is unpredictable, and there is a risk of secondary failures. In addition, it is also difficult to design targeted protective measures.

In view of the above problems, we have improved the RTEMS. The improved RTEMS has the ability of real-time stack overflow detection. It mainly supports SPARC series processors. This paper introduces the implementation principle of RTEMS which supports real-time stack overflow detection, taking the TSC695F processors commonly used in spaceborne equipment as an example. The principle is also applicable to the SPARC series processors such as TSC697 and BM3803.

2 Introduction of TSC695F Processor

2.1 Access Protection Mechanism

The Rad Hard 32-bit SPARC Embedded Processor (TSC695F), ERC32 Single-chip, is a highly integrated, high-performance 32-bit RISC embedded processor implementing the SPARC architecture V7 specification. It has been developed with the support of the ESA (European Space Agency), and offers a full development environment for embedded space applications.

TSC695F processor can be programmed to detect and mask write accesses in any part of the RAM [8]. The programmable write access protection is segment based. A segment defines an area where write cycles are allowed. Any write cycle outside a segment is trapped and does not change the memory contents. Two segments are implemented. Each segment is implemented with two registers: The Segment Base Register and the Segment End Register. The segment base register contains the start address of the segment, and enabling bits for supervisor/user mode (SE/UE). The segment end register contains the first address outside the segment, i.e. last address of segment plus one word. The start address of segment is a low memory address than the end address. Only word aligned addresses are supported. The segments are only active during RAM access, i.e. they can only be mapped to the RAM area. There are two modes of the access protection. In normal mode, a memory exception is generated only if both segments indicated a write protection error. In block protect mode, a memory exception is generated if any of the segments indicate a write protection error. Fig. 1 is shown difference of two mode. The memory exception will force the IU to vector to a data access exception, then the IU enters the corresponding trap (trap type 9).

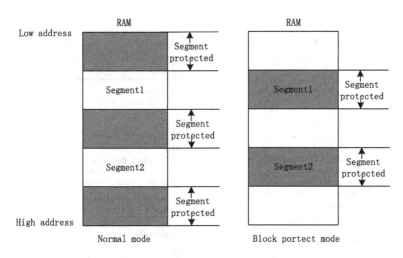

Fig. 1. Access protection mechanism

2.2 Stack Introduction

When satellite onboard software is running, the code and data are divided into text section, data section and bss section. The remaining space in memory is allocated to the heap space and stack space, which are generally uniformly allocated and managed by the operating system. Figure 2 is a schematic diagram of the memory allocation of the satellite onboard software.

TSC695F is widely used in spacecraft because of its EDAC (Error Detection and Correction) protection mechanism. The EDAC detects any two bits error and corrects any single bit data error on the 40-bit bus. The processor has eight sets of window registers, each of them consists of eight input registers (i_0–i_7), eight local registers and eight output registers (o_0–o_7). The input and output registers are mainly used to pass parameters to the function and receive the return value of the function. The output register o6 saves the stack pointer (sp), which points to the top of the current stack. Therefore, the output register can pass 6 parameters at most, and more parameters shall be passed through the stack. The input register i6 keeps the heap pointer (fp), which points to the bottom of the current stack. The stack consists of heap pointer and stack pointer, and the stack grows from high address to low address direction. The stack space occupied by each function is called a stack frame. For example, function A calls function B, function B then calls function C, and their stacksare shown in Fig. 3.

With the support of the operating system, the functions of on-board software are usually divided into several threads. The stack of each thread is allocated from the stack space in Fig. 2. In this paper, the start address of stack is a high memory address than the end address of stack, because stack grows direction shown in Fig. 2. When the stack of one thread overflows, it might overwrite the stack of another thread which will cause an error when another thread ready and runs.

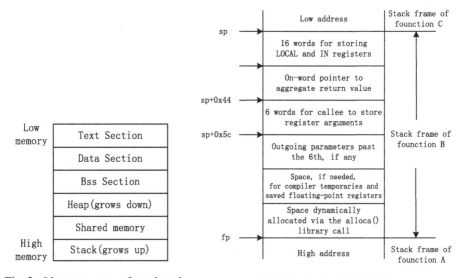

Fig. 2. Memory map of on-board software

Fig. 3. Stack of TSC695F

3 Improvement and Implementation

3.1 Principle Introduction

Considering the problems discussed above, this paper proposes a method which protects the stack of different threads and provide the detection of the stack depth and overflows. This method bases on the memory access protection mechanism of processor. The improved RTEMS use the block protect mode of memory access protection mechanism.

The detection principle is: adding the definition of access protection register as variable in RTEMS thread control block (TCB), that is, expanding the definition of thread context, so that a single thread can exclusively use the access protection register of the processor when it is running. Different threads share the access protection mechanism of the processor by switching the thread context. The thread stack is divided into the initial accessible and unaccessible areas during initialization. With the growth of the stack, when the stack exceeds the initial accessible area and attempts to write data to the unaccessible area, the processor will produce a trap (type 0x9) immediately. By hooking the corresponding trap handler, the software resets the thread unaccessible stack area to extend the accessible area. This method can meet the stack growth and make sure the software keeps running normally. The software can calculate the depth of the current stack according to the expansion of the accessible area. As the stack grows, when the software triggers the trap and finds that the unaccessible area is less than or equal to 1 K bytes, it is assumed that the thread stack is about to overflow. At this time, the software can design specific recovery measures from stack overflow, such as thread restart, software reset, switch to backup computer work, etc. Figure 4 shows an example of the growth of thread stack changes using this RTEMS.

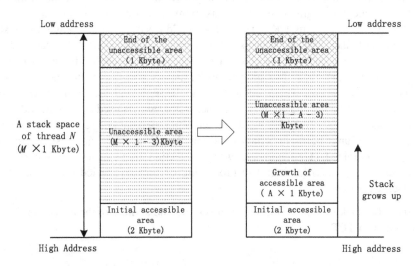

Fig. 4. An instance for growth of stack

The above detection principle requires the following improvements to RTEMS:

(a)   Modify the definition of the thread control block (TCB) and add access protection registers as variables in thread context.
(b)   Modify the stack initialization module of RTEMS (function _Stack Initialize). After the thread stack is created, the initial accessible area and unaccessible area of the thread stack are calculated and set. The start and end addresses of the unaccessible area are saved as thread context in the thread control block.
(c)   Modify the thread context switch module of RTEMS (function _Thread Dispatch) to switch the write protection area of the stack when different threads are running. When context switching occurs, the value of the current access protection register is stored in the suspended thread control block, and the value recorded in the TCB of the thread to be run is written to the access protection register.
(d)   Add the corresponding trap processing module to achieve the re-setup of the unaccessible area of the stack, and detect the stack depth and process the overflow in real time.

3.2   Stack Initialization Module

When a thread is created, the size of its stack is generally need to be specified. After RTEMS allocate the stack to the thread, the initial start address and depth of the stack are recorded in TCB. It can also be assigned with other unit lengths. This paper takes 1 Kbyte as an example to illustrate.

The stack space of a thread is divided into the following 2 parts, as shown in the left half of Fig. 4.

(a)   Accessible area: the initial size is 2 Kbyte. This area is a stack area allowed for normal operation by software. With the growth of the stack, the scope of the area can be increased gradually. The maximum accessible space equals the stack allocation space minus 1 K bytes. The start address of this area is equal to the start address of stack. the end address is a low memory address than the start address.
(b)   Unaccessible area: the scope of this area is located at the end of the accessible area to the end of the stack. The end address of the stack is used as the start address of the unaccessible area which would be set to the segment base register when thread is running. And the end address of the accessible area is used as the end address of the unaccessible area which would be set to the segment end register. As the stack grows, the area becomes smaller and smaller. When the unaccessible area has been minimized (1 K bytes), a write protection trap occurs and the stack is thought to be overflowing. The processing of traps is carried out according to stack overflow.

When the stack initializes, the start address and end address of the unaccessible area are recorded to TCB.

3.3   Context Switch Module

When the software runs, the CPU switching to another thread needs to save the state of the current thread and restore the state of another thread, which is called context switching. Context switch includes saving the running environment of the current thread and restoring the running environment of the thread that will run. In RTEMS, the running environment of the thread includes window register, floating point register, PC counter and so on. In improved RTEMS, segment base register and segment end register are added to the context definition of threads.

The module has very little modification, only a small amount of assembler code needs to be added. When context switching occurs, the value of the current access protection register is stored in the suspended thread control block, and the value recorded in the TCB of the thread to be run is written to the access protection register. In this way, different threads can share processor access protection mechanism.

3.4   Trap Handler

After all threads have been created, the software starts running normally. As the stack grows gradually, and its use depth extends to low addresses. When it exceeds the accessible area (initial 2 Kbyte), it enters the unaccessible area. Due to the existence of processor access protection mechanism, the program running on the unaccessible area cannot operate write operations. Any write operation will immediately trigger processor exceptions, resulting in a 0x9 trap. The flow of trap handler is shown as Fig. 5.

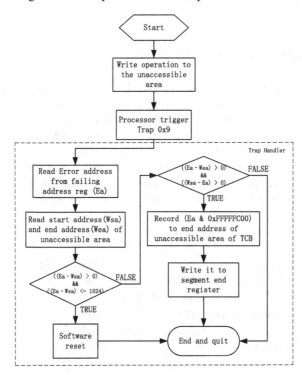

Fig. 5. Flow of trap processing

After the software enters the trap handler, it gets the error address of the trap by reading the failing address register. Comparing the error address with the access protection address range set by the current processor determines whether it is in a thread stack area. If the error address falls within the scope of a thread stack unaccessible area, the error address is compared with the start address of the unaccessible area for the corresponding thread. If the error address minus the starting address of the unaccessible area is less than 1 Kbyte, it is considered the thread stack will overflow soon. If it is greater than 1 Kbyte, the stack is considered to grow normally. The following operations are performed for this error:

① Logical AND operation is performed for the error address and 0xFFFFFC00, and the result is used as the end address of unaccessible Area and saved to TCB, which enlarges the accessible area and makes the wrong address in the accessible area.

② Write the end address of the unaccessible area to the processor write protection end register.

3.5 The Use Depth of Stack

While the software runs, the depth of use of each thread stack can be calculated by accessing the unaccessible protection area end address of each thread (The stack depth equals the stack start address minus the unaccessible protection area end address, accurate to 1 Kbyte). Stack occupancy equals the stack depth divided by the allocation depth, multiplied by 100%.

4 Improvement and Implementation

The performance and accuracy of the improved RTEMS are tested and verified on the target hardware platform. The target system processor uses TSC695F platform and the main frequency is set to 10 MHz. The performance of initialization module, context switching module and trap processing module are tested respectively. The test results are shown in Table 1. From the performance test results, it can be seen that the delay of initialization module and context switching module modified by this method almost does not increase. The processing delay of the new trap processing module is also very small, so the processing time of 30us has little effect on the system performance.

Table 1. Module performance test

Module		Performance(us)
Initial stack	RTEMS	4.89
	Improved RTEMS	9.12
Context switch	RTEMS	72.32
	Improved RTEMS	76.27
Trap handler	New	30.15

Taking an on-board software of the integrated electronic system as the test object, the stack usage of eight threads created by the improved RTEMS is tested, and the test results are compared with those using dynamic testing tools. The test results are shown in Table 2.

Table 2. An instance for stack used depth detection

Thread id	Start address of stack	Stack space (Kbyte)	Dynamic test tools		Improved RTEMS	
			Use depth (Kbyte)	Margin (%)	Use depth (Kbyte)	Margin (%)
1	0x023eb858	32	8.564	73.2	9.000	71.8
2	0x023e1708	10	1.886	81.1	2.000	80.0
3	0x0243ea30	20	4.004	80.0	5.000	80.0
4	0x0243bf98	10	1.742	82.6	2.000	80.0
5	0x023e45a0	6	0.704	88.3	2.000	66.7
6	0x023f6b00	8	1.124	86.0	2.000	80.0
7	0x02444450	8	2.450	69.4	3.000	62.5
8	0x0244ff90	12	3.670	69.4	4.000	66.7

In the above test case, thread 5th is selected to illustrate how thread stack overflow can be detected, through calling the following C function.

```
void foo(void)
{
inttest_array[1200];
test_array[1199] = 0;
return;
}
```

The trap of the test program may suspend the stack overflow thread and print out the memory address of the trap, program pointer by the Serial port. The results of the above test case are shown in Fig. 6. The program pointer address is 0x02015488 which points to the function foo. The trap was trigger at memory address 0x023E3020, which is the address is the last 1 Kbyte of the thread 5th and cannot be accessed by the thread. As soon as the trap was triggered, the thread 5th will be suspended.

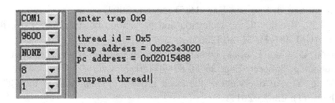

Fig. 6. Output of test result

The test results show that the stack depth can be obtained by using the improved RTEMS and accuracy is 1 Kbyte. The accuracy is not as high as that measured by dynamic testing tools, but it can meet the requirements for stack margin observation. In addition, this method is the same as most dynamic testing methods, and measuring the maximum depth of stack usage depends on the test case. But different from this method, the stack usage depth can be obtained online and real-time, and the key information (including the overflow address, thread ID and program counter) can be recorded before the stack overflow, which is very important for the subsequent fault detection.

5   Conclusion

Satellite On-board software is difficult to sense the growth process of the stack during its operation. It is not sure whether the usage margin is sufficient, and also it is difficult to allocate the stack overflow fault. This paper improves the RTEMS by using the processor memory access protection mechanism, and proposes a real-time stack overflow detection method. Taking the on-board software running on the TSC695F processor as an example, the software is set by setting the access protection area in the stack, and it has ability to sense stack dynamic growth and calculate stack size in real time. By checking the minimum scope of the access protected area, the improved RTEMS have the ability to forecast the stack overflow in advance. The improved RTEMS has the advantage that operation system can obtain the stack depth of every thread (accuracy to 1 Kbyte) in real time; the principle is simple and easy to implement, and the software can detect online and in real time after the implementation, and the performance of improved RTEMS is almost unchanged. With the RTEMS improved in the paper, once the stack overflow happens, the trap handler will take over the following up task, which effectively eliminate the uncertainty of software behavior after stack crash, greatly simplify the design of system fault handling countermeasures and improve software reliability.

References

1. Li, H., Yin, C.: Analysis and improvement of RTEMS memory management. In: CONFERENCE 2009 First International Workshop on Education Technology and Computer Science (2009)
2. He, X., Sun, Y.: Engineering realization of software in central terminal unit of satellite data management system. J. Spacecr. Eng. **16**(5), 47–53 (2007)
3. Kuperman, B.A., Brodley, C.E.: Detection and prevention of stack buffer overflow attacks. J. Commun. ACM **48**(11), 51–56 (2005)
4. Dong, Z., Hou, C., Guo, J., et al.: Dynamic detection method of spacecraft software process stack used depth. J. Spacecr. Eng. **26**(1), 85–90 (2017)
5. Cao, Y., Wang, Y.: An overview of the stack protection techniques in the GCC compiler. J. Inf. Technol. (7), 23–25(2017)

6. Pan, Q., Wang, C., Yang, Y.: Analysis and prevention of the stack overflow attacking. J. Shanghai Jiaotong Univ. **36**(9), 1346–1350 (2002)
7. Sun, H., Xu, L., Yang, H.: The principle and detection of buffer overflow attack. J. Comput. Eng. **27**(1), 127–128 (2001)
8. ATMEL Corporation: TSC695FSPARC 32-bit Space Processor User Manual

MPTCP Based Load Balancing Mechanism in Software Defined Satellite Networks

Ziyi Ma[1,2], Xiaoqiang Di[1,2(✉)], Jinqing Li[1,2], Ligang Cong[1,2], and Ping Li[1]

[1] School of Computer Science and Technology,
Changchun University of Science and Technology, Changchun, China
dixiaoqiang@cust.edu.cn
[2] Jilin Province Key Laboratory of Network and Information Security,
Changchun, China

Abstract. The instability of satellite network links, unbalanced user distribution, and limited resources have caused severe network congestion and load imbalance. To address this problem, we propose a load balancing mechanism based on Multipath TCP (MPTCP) and apply it to software defined satellite networks (SDSN). This mechanism obtains the topology and the state of the whole network through the monitoring function of controller, and then selects k shortest paths from all available paths. It first divides the flow into several subflows according to the cost of different paths, and then establishes the MPTCP connection. To improve the efficiency of the network, we install OpenFlow rules to each switch. In the end, we conduct experiments in the Mininet simulation platform. The results show that the proposed mechanism can achieve load balancing of different links and improve the throughput while reducing delay.

Keywords: Multipath TCP · SDSN · Load balancing

1 Introduction

Satellite networks have many advantages such as flexible networking, wide coverage, convenience, and it can also provide various communication services regardless of geographical environment and climatic conditions. It is especially suitable for remote regions where the ground communication coverage is imperfect. The Starlink project currently being developed by SpaceX aims to build a constellation of thousands of satellites that can beam the Internet to the entire globe, including remote regions that currently do not have Internet access [1]. SES's SaT5G project covers geostationary earth orbit (GEO) and medium earth orbit (MEO) satellites to achieve satellite integration and improve the efficiency of 5G services [2]. This shows that the new trend of satellite networking is quantity and multilayer. Due to the high speed of the satellite, the link connection is unstable. When the link is interrupted, the redesign of the route is required. In addition, the Internet users are imbalanced distributed, resulting in congestion on local networks. What is more, satellite resources are relatively limited, so it is difficult to meet the QoS requirements of newly added services. The problems such

M. Jia et al. (Eds.): WiSATS 2019, LNICST 280, pp. 294–302, 2019.
https://doi.org/10.1007/978-3-030-19153-5_30

as the increase of delay and packet loss ratio, also pose a great impact on the communication quality of satellite networks. Therefore, it is important to choose the proper path for data transmission in order to balance the load of the entire network.

Considering the characteristics of the satellite networks mentioned above, multipath TCP (MPTCP) is very suitable for data transmission in satellite networks [3]. MPTCP is an extension of TCP that enables two applications to communicate over a reliable byte stream while utilizing one or more paths. A regular TCP connection can only communicate through one interface, but MPTCP can send data through multiple interfaces simultaneously. This can improve the reliability of parallel transmission for high-bandwidth data streams in a satellite network, and provide users efficient service.

The architecture design of satellite network has been imitating the layered design of terrestrial network, where each layer has different protocols to realize various functions. Unlike the terrestrial network, the satellites move at high speed in the air. So when the satellite network protocols need to be updated, it is more difficult than terrestrial network. Thus, this paper proposes a new type of satellite network architecture, which is based on software-defined networking (SDN). Considering the performance of MPTCP over software defined satellite networks (SDSN) [4], this architecture contains a centralized controller, which provides a platform for planning route of the ground control center in the MPTCP research of the satellite network. The protocol used between the switch and the controller is OpenFlow in this architecture. Subflows on each path are forwarded based on this protocol. In this paper, we first collect topology information and monitor link state in the controller, and then make MPTCP decision to select k shortest paths. Secondly, according to the path cost, we carry out the load balancing strategy, and select different paths for the subflows. Finally, we install these paths to each switch. We teach the switches to make decisions themselves. So the switch does not have to ask the controller what to do every time a packet arrives to the switch.

The rest of the paper is organized as follows. The second part discusses the related work of MPTCP and SDN in satellite networks. In the third part, we analyzes the specific implementation of the MPTCP routing decision in the satellite network. The fourth part introduces the software-defined satellite networks. The fifth part covers the experimental results and performance analysis of the proposed solution. Finally, the sixth part summarizes this paper.

2   Related Work

MPTCP splits the dataflow into separate subflows. Each subflow establishes a regular TCP connection, but the process of handshake contains specific MPTCP options, such as MP_CAPABLE and MP_JOIN. The MP_CAPABLE option is exchanged between the two hosts that establish the connection to indicate that both parties support MPTCP, after which both parties can create a subflow through the SYN packet with the MP_JOIN flag. The main advantage of using MPTCP in satellite networks is to avoid the impact of link disruption on data transmission and to make better use of the available link capacity in the presence of multiple available satellite links. Hwang and Yoo proposed another packet scheduling method [5]. When the difference of delay between slow and fast paths is large, the slow path will be frozen. It facilitates the transmission of small amount of data on the fast path. Singh et al. [6] compared two solutions of Dynamic Window Coupling and Opportunistic Linked Increase Algorithm. Both schemes can maintain fairness over traditional protocols such as TCP and SCTP in a crowded environment while increasing link throughput under different bottlenecks. The strategy for adding or removing subflows in MPTCP has been studied in many papers, but there are still some problems in effective identification of the available paths between source hosts and destination hosts. It is still a challenge to consider the network status and routing to select the best path. Krupakaran et al. [7] determined the set of paths that exist between the source hosts and destination hosts, and made decisions based on the number of subflows. Baidya et al. [8] used the MPTCP-based slow path adaptation (SPA) to monitor the quality of the path. If the data transmission is slow, MPTCP-SPA will change a path. MPTCP is usually combined with Equal-Cost Multi-Path Routing (ECMP). ECMP uses random hashing to assign subflows to different paths [9]. Different subflows may share the same path, so this method is not ideal. Zannettou et al. [10] adopted an SDN controller supporting MPTCP. Considering both FatTree and Jellyfish topologies, the controller calculates the shortest path and the disjoint path between two hosts. The above works did not take the impact of link load on subflow transmission. Therefore, our focus is on the impact of load balancing on the overall performance of the network.

Due to the limited costs of updating network services and the limited resources of satellite nodes, many new algorithms and protocols cannot be deployed to satellite networks. This limits the implementation of new technologies and makes it difficult to meet the diverse need of the users. In this case, SDN is introduced into the satellite networks, and new application functions can be achieved [11]. In [12], the author proposed a multi-layer satellite network architecture based on SDN. GEO controls the forwarding of dataflow in the data plane of the LEO/MEO according to commands given by the network operation and control center on the ground. SERvICE [13] used SDN to carry out QoS-oriented routing and bandwidth allocation algorithm to ensure the QoS requirements of multiple users. [14] explored SDN and NFV technologies to provide further innovative services and flexible operations for satellite networks. The difference with the above papers in that we pay more attention to the use of MPTCP to optimize network load between SDN and the terminal host.

3   The MPTCP-SDN Architecture Design

Our MPTCP-based path load balancing strategy applies to the software-defined satellite network architecture. This architecture, which is shown in Fig. 1, is characterized by the separation of the control plane and the data plane. Load balancing is achieved across multiple paths between the source node and the destination node. At the same time, network resources should be made full use of to ensure the correctness of the path. Therefore, the controller selects k shortest paths by using the topology discovery module and the traffic state monitoring module. This helps balance load when transmitting subflow links.

3.1   Topology Collection and Traffic Monitoring

The topology discovery module of the controller is used to obtain the location of the terminal host in the global network. The controller sends LLDP packets to all switches by sending a Packet_out message. After receiving the packets, the switch sends LLDP packets to all of its ports. If an OpenFlow switch receives these outgoing LLDP packets, it will send the link information between the two switches to the controller through the Packet in message. After the controller collects the link information of its own management area, it can build the network topology based on these information. The traffic statistics module is used to periodically collect the number of packets and bytes forwarded by the OpenFlow switch port. It can also record the forwarding rate of each stream on each port, get the total capacity of the port and the available bandwidth.

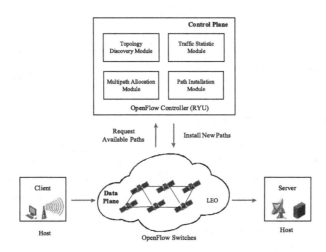

Fig. 1. Architecture of our proposed mechanism.

3.2   Multipath Allocation Module

Subflow path selection scheme plays an important role in satellite transmission performance. Here we analyze the routing strategy of load balancing between links based on k shortest paths. We consider the topology shown in Fig. 2, where the hosts at both ends communicate through satellite nodes such as switches s1 and s2.

There are multiple paths between two user nodes in the network. If there are too many optional paths, choosing the best path can be too inefficient. We use the Depth First Search path find algorithm to get all the paths. The basic principle is as follows: Record the relationship of connection between all nodes in the adjacency matrix. Before backtracking, find the deepest node in the graph first, and then find other possible nodes through the stack. Finally, return a list of all possible paths. Since the DFS algorithm returns an unweighted path list, we need to measure the cost of the path to allocate the subflows to achieve load balancing. We set a MAX_PATHS to indicate the number of the selected the k shortest paths, which is also the number of paths of the subflow. We calculate the link cost by polling the corresponding switch port using the OSPF mechanism. We use the following cost formula. This formula uses the above-mentioned OSPF mechanism to obtain the link cost. For a path i, bw represents the weight of the bucket, $0 \leq$ bw(p) < 10. The pw represents the path cost and n represents the total number of available paths. When it comes to path cost, we ideally want to find the optimal path first, and then choose the suboptimal one. Correspondingly, the priority of the bucket in the OpenFlow Group table is sorted according to the weight of the bucket. Through this formula, we can predict that the lower the path cost is, the higher the bucket weight will be. We divide the subflow according to the weight of the bucket to achieve the load balancing effect of the path.

$$bw(i) = \left(1 - \frac{pw(i)}{\sum_{j<n}^{j=0} pw(j)}\right) \times 10 \tag{1}$$

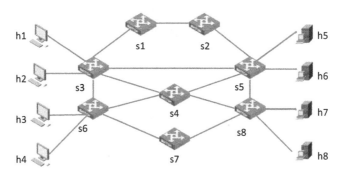

Fig. 2. Topology of switches and hosts.

Algorithm 1 K Shortest Paths Based Load Balancing Algorithm (mptcp-klb)

Input: k, bandwidth, Reference bandwidth
Output: a weight for each path t∈k

1: J is the total paths from S to T
2: For each j in {1,2,..., J}
3:     For each i in j nodes
4:         cost[j]= Reference bandwidth/ bandwidth(i, i+1)
5:     End For
6: End For
7: Get the k shorted paths from Sorted(J, key=lambda x: cost[x])
8: For each t in k
9:     return Weights[t]=1-cost[t]/ $\sum_k^1 cost[t]$
10: End For

3.3   Path Installation Module

The forwarding rule is generated by the controller according to the results of the multipath allocation module. When the user sends a request to the switch, if the switch sends a request message to the controller every time, enabling the controller to make a routing decision and then returns to the switch, the network performance will get lower. We consider letting the switch itself make a decision that installs OpenFlow rules on the switch by itself, so that the switch will directly forward network traffic [15]. At the same time, we must also consider the continual change of network traffic and topology. As a result, the flow table needs to be dynamically updated to meet the load balancing of the path. When a new flow arrives or the network topology changes, select the best path for the subflow and install the path to the corresponding switch through the previously described module. At the same time, the control network collects global information and updates the flow table configuration in time.

4   Performance Evaluation

In order to evaluate the path load balancing strategy based on MPTCP, we simulate the network topology and communicate with the controller in the Mininet [16] platform, the topology is shown in Fig. 2. Mininet creates virtual networks quickly, running hosts, switches and network links on a single computer. All switches in Mininet are software-based OpenFlow switches. The version of OpenFlow is 1.3. All modules in the controller are implemented on Ryu [17] and all of the softwares listed above run in the VMware virtual machine. Our routing algorithm runs on the Ryu controller. We also implemented k-shortest-paths (mptcp-ksp) [18] and single-path routing (single-tcp) algorithms in Ryu, so that it is easy to compare them with the performance of our algorithm.

We set the link delay between two satellites at 20 ms and bandwidth at 25 Mbps [19]. The link delay and bandwidth between the terminal host and the satellite are respectively set to 5 ms and 15 Mbps. The connection status of the network device is shown in Fig. 2. We assume that the weight of each link is 1. h1 and h7 are selected as observation objects. Firstly, the k-shortest-path algorithm is used to select the three optimal paths, and then the sub-flows are distributed in proportion through the path bw to achieve load balancing. h1 sends TCP packets to h7. For all of the path sets from h1 to h7, we select three paths for transmission. Considering that the paths should be shortest and disjoint, we select three paths, path 1, path 2, and path 3. The bw of them is proportionally allocated as 7:7:6. As is shown in Fig. 3, we test the total number of packets transmitted on three paths with different number of parallel clients. It can be seen that as the number of clients increases, the number of packets forwarded on the three paths all increases accordingly. The proportion of the number of packets transmitted in each path is close to the proportion of bw.

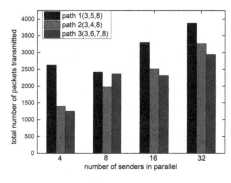

Fig. 3. Total number of packets transmitted with different sender number

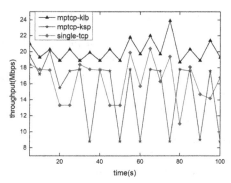

Fig. 4. Sender h1's total throughput

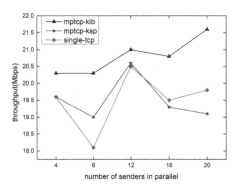

Fig. 5. Sender h1's total throughput with different sender number

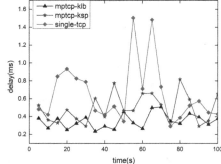

Fig. 6. Delay performance of three algorithms

In Fig. 4, the total throughput of the sender h1 is plotted in the context of using three different algorithms. Because mptcp-ksp and single-tcp do not take the path load into account, the throughput of the system has a certain fluctuation. Mptcp-ksp focus on path selection without congestion control, so it may be more unstable than single-tcp in large number of packets. The overall throughput of mptcp-lb is compared with the other two algorithms. Figure 5 shows the throughput performance of the three algorithms with different number of parallel clients. As we can see, the throughput of the mptcp-ksp and single-tcp schemes rise rapidly when there are 12 parallel clients, and then remain relatively low. This is because the distribution of traffic on the path is not considered, resulting in congestion of the path. Since mptcp-lb allocates subflows according to the load capacity of the path, the throughput of sender h1 has shown an upward trend.

Figure 6 shows the delay performance of the three algorithms. Single-tcp is a single path transmission. Affected by link congestion, its delay performance fluctuates greatly. Relatively speaking, mptcp-lb and mptcp-ksp utilize multipath transmission, so the delay performance of packet transmission can be improved effectively. mptcp-lb has lower latency than mptcp-ksp, which proved that mptcp-lb can realize the rationality of subflow routing arrangement under load balancing.

5   Conclusion

In this paper, we proposed an MPTCP-based load balancing strategy to solve the problem of transmitting data flow in satellite networks. Applying the SDN architecture to the satellite network can obtain the real-time global network topology and state, which improves the utilization and reliability of the path. This strategy can effectively balance the link bandwidth by considering the path cost. We, and proved that the proposed scheme can effectively divide and forward subflow in comparison with other schemes. The simulation results verify that the total system throughput and delay are improved.

Acknowledgements. This research is partially supported by research grants from Science and Technology Project of Jilin province (20180414024GH), and the project in the Education Department of Jilin Province (JJKH20170630KJ).

References

1. SpaceX. https://en.wikipedia.org/wiki/SpaceX
2. SES S.A. https://en.wikipedia.org/wiki/SES_S.A
3. Ford, A., Raiciu, C., Handley, M., et al.: TCP extensions for multipath operation with multiple addresses (2013)
4. Du, P., Nazari, S., Mena, J., et al.: Multipath TCP in SDN-enabled LEO satellite networks. In: 2016 IEEE Military Communications Conference, MILCOM 2016, pp. 354–359. IEEE (2016)
5. Hwang, J., Yoo, J.: Packet scheduling for multipath TCP. In: 2015 Seventh International Conference on IEEE Ubiquitous and Future Networks (ICUFN), pp. 177–179. IEEE (2015). https://doi.org/10.1109/ICUFN.2015.7182529
6. Singh, A., Xiang, M., Konsgen, A., et al.: Enhancing fairness and congestion control in multipath TCP. In: 2013 6th Joint IFIP Wireless and Mobile Networking Conference (WMNC), pp. 1–8. IEEE (2013). https://doi.org/10.1109/WMNC.2013.6549059
7. Krupakaran, K., Sridharan, A.P., Venkatesan, S.M.: Optimized multipath TCP subflows using traceflow, April 2015
8. Baidya, S.H., Prakash, R.: Improving the performance of multipath TCP over heterogeneous paths using slow path adaptation. In: 2014 IEEE International Conference on Communications (ICC), pp. 3222–3227. IEEE (2014). https://doi.org/10.1109/ICC.2014.6883817
9. Raiciu, C., Barre, S., Pluntke, C., et al.: Improving datacenter performance and robustness with multipath TCP. ACM SIGCOMM Comput. Commun. Rev. **41**(4), 266–277 (2011)

10. Zannettou, S., Sirivianos, M., Papadopoulos, F.: Exploiting path diversity in datacenters using MPTCP-aware SDN. In: 2016 IEEE Symposium on Computers and Communication (ISCC), pp. 539–546. IEEE (2016)
11. Rossi, T., De Sanctis, M., Cianca, E., et al.: Future space-based communications infrastructures based on high throughput satellites and software defined networking. In: 2015 IEEE International Symposium on Systems Engineering (ISSE), pp. 332–337. IEEE (2015)
12. Bao, J., Zhao, B., Yu, W., et al.: OpenSAN: a software-defined satellite network architecture. ACM SIGCOMM Comput. Commun. Rev. **44**(4), 347–348 (2014). https://doi.org/10.1145/2619239.2631454
13. Li, T., Zhou, H., Luo, H., et al.: SERvICE: a software defined framework for integrated space-terrestrial satellite communication. IEEE Trans. Mob. Comput. **17**(3), 703–716 (2018)
14. Ferrs, R., Koumaras, H., Sallent, O., et al.: SDN/NFV-enabled satellite communications networks: opportunities, scenarios and challenges. Phys. Commun. **18**, 95–112 (2016)
15. Giotis, K., Argyropoulos, C., Androulidakis, G., et al.: Combining OpenFlow and sFlow for an effective and scalable anomaly detection and mitigation mechanism on SDN environments. Comput. Netw. **62**, 122–136 (2014)
16. Mininet. http://mininet.org/. Accessed 4 Oct 2017
17. Ryu controller. http://osrg.github.io/ryu/. Accessed 4 Oct 2017
18. Zannettou, S., Sirivianos, M., Papadopoulos, F.: Exploiting path diversity in datacenters using MPTCP-aware SDN. In: 2016 IEEE Symposium on Computers and Communication (ISCC), pp. 539–546. IEEE (2016)
19. Taleb, T., Mashimo, D., Jamalipour, A., et al.: Explicit load balancing technique for NGEO satellite IP networks with on-board processing capabilities. IEEE/ACM Trans. Netw. **17**(1), 281–293 (2009)

A Novel Dynamic Multi-source Multi-sink Flow Algorithm over the Satellite Networks

Peng Wang, Hongyan Li$^{(\boxtimes)}$, Tao Zhang, Shun Zhang, and Keyi Shi

State Key Laboratory of Integrated Service Networks, Xidian University,
Xi'an 710071, China
hyli@xidian.edu.cn

Abstract. The multi-source multi-sink maximum flow problem can be of great significance in guiding network optimization, service scheduling, and capacity analysis. With intermittent connectivity and time-dependence characteristics of satellite networks, the existing flow algorithms for multi-source multi-sink without temporal dimension involvement can no longer maintain high efficiency in satellite networks. To overcome the problem, we propose a novel dynamic multi-source multi-sink flow algorithm. Specially, the storage time-aggregated graph (STAG) is adopted to depict the time-varying properties of satellite networks. Then, a novel dynamic multi-source multi-sink flow (DMMF) algorithm is proposed to enhance the satellite networks' resource utilization. At last, the simulation is conducted, and the results with obvious network performance gain verifies our proposed DMMF algorithm.

Keywords: Storage time-aggregated graph ·
Dynamic multi-source multi-sink flow · Satellite networks

1 Introduction

The multi-source multi-sink maximum flow problem can effectively represent the maximum transmission ability of networks and assign data flow, and has great guiding value in network optimization, capacity analysis and service scheduling [2]. However, with the time-varying topology and no persistent paths for source-destination nodes in satellite networks [3], it will be more difficult to find efficient dynamic multi-source multi-sink flow in satellite networks with temporal-dimension involved. As shown in Fig. 1, without precise description of time-varying satellite network resources (i.e. transmission resources, storage resources), static-graph based maximum flow algorithm can no longer keep efficient [1,4,5]. To be more specific, with the network topology shown in Fig. 1 and $\{\{\mathbb{S},\mathbb{D}\},\{\mathbb{A},\mathbb{B}\}\}$ being the two source-sink node pairs, the maximum flow calculated by the static-graph based algorithm [4] for $\{\mathbb{S},\mathbb{D}\}$ is 3 and for $\{\mathbb{A},\mathbb{B}\}$ is 0. In fact, with storage

---

Supported by organization x.

M. Jia et al. (Eds.): WiSATS 2019, LNICST 280, pp. 303–311, 2019.
https://doi.org/10.1007/978-3-030-19153-5_31

resources involved and considerate analysis of the relationship between the two flows, the maximum flow for $\{\mathbb{S}, \mathbb{D}\}, \{\mathbb{A}, \mathbb{B}\}$ can be 3 respectively.

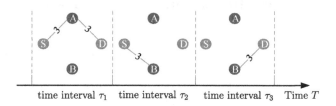

time interval τ_1 time interval τ_2 time interval τ_3 Time T

Fig. 1. A simple illustration of satellite network topology within 3 time intervals

Hence, we will propose a novel dynamic multi-source multi-sink algorithms for satellite networks to enhance the transmission capacity of satellite networks. First, the storage time aggregated graph based on our previous work [7] is adopted to depict the network topology of satellite networks with temporal-dimension involvement. Then the feasibilities of flows with different source-node pairs are carefully considered and the special constraints are derived. Then based on the dynamic two-commodity maximum combined flow in our previous work [9], we propose the heuristic novel DMMF algorithm, which can effectively increase the network transmission ability among different source-sink node pairs compared with the existing algorithms. For completeness and clearness, one virtual satellite network with time-vary topology is constructed, and the performance of our proposed DMMF algorithm is verified by comparing with other flow assignment algorithms.

2   Satellite Networks Model

With the trajectories of satellites predictable, the communication windows among satellites could be precisely obtained. Based on the predictable feature and reasonable assumptions, we adopted storage-time aggregated graph [7] to model the time-varying resources (i.e. satellites' storage resources, communication windows, data transmission capacity of links) of satellite networks.

Specifically, given time horizon $T = [t_0, t_n]$, and the specific satellites which the satellite networks consist of, the communication windows between satellites can be predicted from STK. With the communication time windows among satellites obtained and reasonable assumptions, the undirected $\text{STAG} = \{T, \mathcal{V}, \mathcal{E}, \mathcal{C}_{u,v}(T), \mathcal{N}_v(T), \mathcal{S}_\mathcal{V} | u \in \mathcal{V}, v \in \mathcal{V}, (u,v) \in \mathcal{E}\}$ is assorted to model the satellite networks:

- $T = [t_0, t_n]$, a time horizon of the satellite networks, which is not the life time of satellite networks. We split $[t_0, t_n]$ into n small time intervals $\{\tau_1, ..., \tau_p, ..., \tau_n\}$, where $\tau_p = (t_{p-1}, t_p]$ and during each small time interval τ, the topology of the satellite network is fixed.

- $\mathcal{V}$, the set of the nodes (satellites).
- $\mathcal{E}$, the set of undirected edges, where $(u, v) \in \mathcal{E}$ holds if and only if the contact time window between satellite u and v during T is nonzero.
- $\mathcal{C}_{u,v}(T) = \{c_{u,v}(\tau_1), ..., c_{u,v}(\tau_p), ..., c_{u,v}(\tau_n)\}$, is a capacity time series set for each link $(u, v) \in \mathcal{E}$, where $c_{u,v}(\tau_p) = \int_{t_{p-1}}^{t_p} w_{u,v}(t)dt$, and $w_{u,v}(t)$ depict the link capacity of edge (u, v) at time instant t. Note that even if links of satellite works are not directional, flows themselves are directional.
- $\mathcal{N}_v(T) = \{N_v(\tau_1, \tau_2), ..., N_v(\tau_p, \tau_{p+1}), ..., N_v(\tau_{n-1,n})\}$, a node storage time series set, where $N_v(\tau_p, \tau_{p+1})$ records the storage resources utilization of each node $v \in \mathcal{V}$ from τ_p to τ_{p+1}. And the storage resources correspond to maximum amount of data one node can store from one small time interval to the adjacent one.
- $\mathcal{S}_\mathcal{V}$, a storage resource set, where the storage resources of each satellite $v \in \mathcal{V}$ at time instant t_0 is denoted as s_v.

To be more explicit, one simple satellite network (S, D, B, A) within 3 time intervals is depicted by undirected STAG shown in Fig. 2 as further illustration.

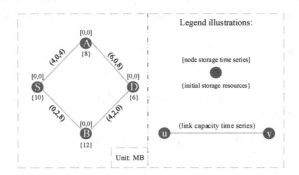

Fig. 2. Satellite network modeled by undirected STAG within 3 time intervals

3   Feasible Multi-source Multi-sink Flow Definitions in STAG

Unlike the static flow definitions with the links' directed capacity determined and just considered in networks with fixed topology, there are some remarkable differences here for the feasible and dynamic multi-source multi-sink flow in the undirected $\text{STAG} = \{T, \mathcal{V}, \mathcal{E}, \mathcal{C}_{u,v}(T), \mathcal{N}_v(T), \mathcal{S}_\mathcal{V} | u \in \mathcal{V}, v \in \mathcal{V}, (u, v) \in \mathcal{E}\}$ without loops and parallel edges. With $\{\mathbb{S}_k, \mathbb{D}_k\}$ being the k_{th} source-sink node pair, then the flow of the k_{th} source-sink node pair from u to v within T can be noted as:

$$f_{u,v}^k(T) = \sum_{q=1}^{n} f_{u,v}^k(\tau_q), \tag{1}$$

where $f_{u,v}^k(\tau_q)$ means the flow of k_{th} source-sink nodes from u to v within τ_q. Then with the h source-sink nodes given as $\{(\mathbb{S}_1, \mathbb{D}_1), ..., (\mathbb{S}_k, \mathbb{D}_k), ..., (\mathbb{S}_h, \mathbb{D}_h)\}$, the total flow of the h source-sink nodes is:

$$sum = F_{\mathbb{S}_1,\mathbb{D}_1}^1(T) + ... + F_{\mathbb{S}_k,\mathbb{D}_k}^k(T) + ... + F_{\mathbb{S}_h,\mathbb{D}_h}^h(T), \tag{2}$$

where the total flow of the k_{th} source-sink nodes is:

$$F_{\mathbb{S}_k,\mathbb{D}_k}^k(T) = \sum_{v\in V} f_{\mathbb{S}_k,v}^k(T) - \sum_{v\in V} f_{v,\mathbb{S}_k}^k(T). \tag{3}$$

With the definitions given above, the specific constraints for h source-sink node pairs in the undirected STAG should be satisfied as follows:

Capacity Constraints: Note that the speciality of the undirected graph is that flow assignment of each source-sink node pairs between two nodes can only be single directed. To be more explicit:

$$|f_{u,v}^k(\tau_p)| \times |f_{v,u}^k(\tau_p)| = 0, \forall p \in [1,n], \forall k \in [1,h], \tag{4}$$

where the flow assignment $f_{u,v}^k(\tau_p)$ and $f_{v,u}^k(\tau_p)$ should be non-negative. And with the direction rule of each source-sink flow assignment, in undirected STAG:

$$0 \le \sum_{k=1}^h f_{u,v}^k(\tau_p) + \sum_{k=1}^h f_{v,u}^k(\tau_p) \le c_{u,v}^{\tau_p}, \forall p \in [1,n]. \tag{5}$$

Node Storage Transfer Constraints: For k_{th} source-sink determined flow ($\forall k \in [1,h]$), within τ_1:

$$\sum_{v\in V} f_{v,u}^k(\tau_1) - \sum_{v\in V} f_{u,v}^k(\tau_1) = N_u^k(\tau_1, \tau_2). \tag{6}$$

Naturally, during the next time intervals $\forall p \in [2, n-1]$:

$$\sum_{v\in V} f_{v,u}^k(\tau_p) + N_u^k(\tau_{p-1}, \tau_p) - \sum_{v\in V} f_{u,v}^k(\tau_p) = N_u^k(\tau_p, \tau_{p+1}). \tag{7}$$

With simple mathematical operations, the storage transfer constraints within T can be easily obtained as:

$$\sum_{p=1}^q \sum_{v\in V} f_{v,u}^k(\tau_p) - \sum_{p=1}^q \sum_{v\in V} f_{v,u}^k(\tau_p) = \begin{cases} N_u^k(\tau_p, \tau_{p+1}), q \in [1, n-1]. \\ 0, q = n. \end{cases} \tag{8}$$

Storage Resource Constraints: And with the constraints of each source-sink flow satisfied, there exists the following storage resource constraints:

$$\begin{cases} 0 \le N_v^k(\tau_p, \tau_{p+1}) \le s_v, \forall k \in [1,h], \forall p \in [1, n-1]. \\ 0 \le \sum_{k=1}^h N_v^k(\tau_p, \tau_{p+1}) \le s_v, \forall p \in [1, n-1]. \end{cases} \tag{9}$$

Flow Conservation: Then for each source-sink node pair determined flow, there exits the following flow conservation:

$$\sum_{v \in \mathcal{V}} f_{u,v}^{k}(T) - \sum_{v \in \mathcal{V}} f_{v,u}^{k}(T) = \begin{cases} F_{\mathbb{S}_k,\mathbb{D}_k}^{k}(T), u = \mathbb{S}_k, \\ 0, u \neq \mathbb{S}_k, \mathbb{D}_k, \\ -F_{\mathbb{S}_k,\mathbb{D}_k}^{k}(T), u = \mathbb{D}_k. \end{cases} \tag{10}$$

With the above constraints for feasible DMMF in undirected STAG, it's more complicated to obtain a rather-efficient feasible DMMF in undirected STAG compared with the static graph. Mechanical re-conduct of time-varying maximum flow solution can result in severe network resources waste.

4   Heuristic Multi-source Multi-sink Flow Algorithm

The multi-commodity flow algorithm is a NP-hard problem and has been proved in [6], and it will be more difficult to solve in the disruption tolerant satellite networks. To enhance the transmission ability in satellite networks, we have solved the dynamic maximum single-commodity [7,8], two-commodity flow problem [9] in our previous works. To overcome the problem of efficient dynamic multi-source multi-sink flow assignment problem, a heuristic DMMF algorithm is proposed

---

Algorithm 1. The Heuristic Multi-source Multi-sink Flow Algorithm

---

1: **Input:** STAG $= \{T, \mathcal{V}, \mathcal{E}, \mathcal{C}_{u,v}(T), \mathcal{N}_v(T), \mathcal{S}_{\mathcal{V}} | u \in \mathcal{V}, v \in \mathcal{V}, (u, v) \in \mathcal{E}\}$, h source-sink node pairs $\{(\mathbb{S}_1, \mathbb{D}_1), ..., (\mathbb{S}_k, \mathbb{D}_k), ..., (\mathbb{S}_h, \mathbb{D}_h) | h > 2\}$.

2: **Output:** The feasible efficiently dynamic flow assignment of each source-node pair.

3: **Decompose** the original problem of solving the dynamic and efficient feasible flow for h source-sink nodes over the satellite networks into two-commodity maximum dynamic flow problem by inserting two virtual source-sink nodes pairs $\{(\mathbb{S}_1', \mathbb{D}_1'), (\mathbb{S}_2', \mathbb{D}_2')\}$ to $\mathcal{V}$.

4: **Define** j as an integer counter and the initial value of j is 1.

5: **while** $j \leq \lfloor h/2 \rfloor$ **do**

6:    plug virtual link $(\mathbb{S}_1', \mathbb{S}_j)$ and $(\mathbb{D}_j, \mathbb{D}_1')$ into $\mathcal{E}$.

7:    $C_{\mathbb{S}_1', \mathbb{S}_j}(T) = \sum_{v:(\mathbb{S}_j, v) \in \mathcal{E}} C_{\mathbb{S}_j, v}(T), \quad C_{\mathbb{D}_j, \mathbb{D}_1'}(T) = \sum_{v:(\mathbb{D}_j, v) \in \mathcal{E}} C_{\mathbb{D}_j, v}(T).$

8:    increase j by 1.

9: **end while**

10: **while** $j \leq h$ **do**

11:    plug virtual link $(\mathbb{S}_2', \mathbb{S}_j)$ and $(\mathbb{D}_j, \mathbb{D}_2')$ into $\mathcal{E}$.

12:    $C_{\mathbb{S}_2', \mathbb{S}_j}(T) = \sum_{v:(\mathbb{S}_j, v) \in \mathcal{E}} C_{\mathbb{S}_j, v}(T), \quad C_{\mathbb{D}_j, \mathbb{D}_2'}(T) = \sum_{v:(\mathbb{D}_j, v) \in \mathcal{E}} C_{\mathbb{D}_j, v}(T).$

13:    increase j by 1.

14: **end while**

15: **Compute** the logically constructed two-commodity maximum flow assignment with **Algorithm 2**.

16: **while** the flow assignment of each source-sink nodes is not feasible **do**

17:    Repeat this algorithm with input and output updated.

18: **end while**

---

based on the efficiency of the maximum dynamic two-commodity flow, which can be shown in Algorithm 1.

With respect to the dynamic two-commodity maximum flow DCF algorithm, adopted in the same undirected STAG and with extra storage resource constraints involvement, the DCF algorithm can be perfectly transformed here to solve the efficient DMMF assignment problem as following. For completeness and clarity, the maximum dynamic two-commodity algorithm is presented as Algorithm 2. And the detailed construct, perform and adjust process and the corresponding proving process in Algorithm 2 can be found in our previous work [9].

The overall solution for efficient DMMF flow algorithm is to recursively decompose multi-source multi-sink flow problem into logically dynamic two-commodity maximum flow problem.

Algorithm 2. Maximum Dynamic Two-commodity Flow Algorithm

1: **Input:** STAG $= \{T, \mathcal{V}, \mathcal{E}, \mathcal{C}_{u,v}(T), \mathcal{N}_v(T), \mathcal{S}_\mathcal{V} | u \in \mathcal{V}, v \in \mathcal{V}, (u,v) \in \mathcal{E}\}$, 2 source-sink node pairs $\{(\mathbb{S}_1, \mathbb{D}_1), (\mathbb{S}_2, \mathbb{D}_2)\}$.

2: **Define** $f^+_{u,v}(\tau_q)$ the assignment of addition-flow from node u to node v within τ_q. Naturally, the assignment of minus-flow from node u to node v during τ_q is $f^-_{u,v}(\tau_q)$ Besides, For each node v, denote the storage transfer series in addition-flow graph as $N^+_v(T)$, and $N^-_v(T)$ records the storage transfer series in minus-flow graph.

3: **Construct** the addition-flow graph $STAG^+$ and minus-flow graph $STAG^-$, based on which the coupling relationship of two commodity flow can be reduced into two independent ones by setting the single source-sink node pair of the two graphs as $(\{\mathbb{S}_1, \mathbb{S}_2\}, \{\mathbb{D}_1, \mathbb{D}_2\})$ and $(\{\mathbb{S}_1, \mathbb{D}_2\}, \{\mathbb{S}_2, \mathbb{D}_1\})$, respectively.

4: **Perform** the STAG-based maximum flow algorithm in addition-flow graph and minus-flow graph respectively, and note that augmentation path search in $STAG^-$ is different from that in $STAG^+$, which can be explained as follows, to obtain the maximum flow in $STAG^-$, in addition to the normal augmenting flow process from source to sink node, augmenting flow from sink to source node is also necessary.

5: **Adjust** the flow through the nodes in addition-flow graph and minus-flow graph respectively to satisfy the constraint (9).

6: **Output** the nodes' and links' storage and capacity resources allocation for each source-node flow. Explicitly, for $\forall v \in \mathcal{V}$, the storage assignment for $F^1_{\mathbb{S}_1,\mathbb{D}_1}(T)$ is $(N^+_v(T) + N^-_v(T))/2$, and $F^2_{\mathbb{S}_2,\mathbb{D}_2}(T)$ is $(N^+_v(T) - N^-_v(T))/2$. Furthermore, for $\forall (u,v) \in \mathcal{E}$, the assignment for $f^1_{u,v}(T)$ is $(f^+_{u,v}(T) + f^-_{u,v}(T))/2$, and $f^2_{u,v}(T)$ is $(f^+_{u,v}(T) - f^-_{u,v}(T))/2$.

---

5   Simulation

To further verify the performance of our proposed dynamic multi-source multi-sink flow assignment algorithm, we consider one virtual satellite network with 12 satellites and 3 source-sink node pairs during an hour, and the length of each small time interval τ is set as 20 min, which can be seen from Fig. 3(a). Note

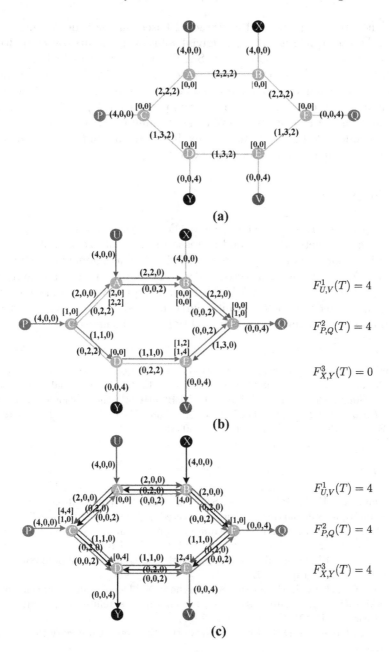

Fig. 3. (a) Topology of the virtual constructed network. (b) Flow assignment of the priority-based single commodity maximum flow algorithm. (c) Flow assignment of our DMMF.

that the network is virtual and constructed based on the time-varying characteristics. As shown in Fig. 3(b), the trivial solution for multi-source multi-sink flow problem is to repeat applying the STAG-based temporal single-commodity algorithm, and the flow result is 8 and there is no flow for the third commodity (X, Y). And with our two-commodity based DMMF algorithm, the flow assignment can increase to 12, and the flow assignment for (X, Y) is also 4, which can be explained as our algorithm involved the coupling relationship between different source-sink node pairs. To be more explicit, the link and node resources are assigned jointly among multi source-sink nodes.

6   Conclusion

In this paper, we propose a STAG-based DMMF for satellite networks to efficiently assign the network flow and increase resource utilization. We construct one effective algorithm of multi-source multi-sink flow assignment, which is based on the efficiency of the undirected STAG and the dynamic maximum two-commodity flow algorithms. With the feasibility of flow assignment carefully considered, we decompose the multi-source multi-sink flow assignment problem into maximum dynamic two-commodity flow problem over the time-varying satellite networks.

Acknowledgments. This work is supported by the National Natural Science Foundation of China (61871456, 91638202, 61401326, 61571351), the National Key Research and Development Program of China (2016YFB0501004), the National S&T Major Project (2015ZX03002006), the 111 Project (B08038), Natural Science Basic Research Plan in Shaanxi Province of China (2016JQ6054).

References

1. Borradaile, G., Klein, P.N., Mozes, S., Nussbaum, Y., Wulff-Nilsen, C.: Multiple-source multiple-sink maximum flow in directed planar graphs in near-linear time. In: 2011 IEEE 52nd Annual Symposium on Foundations of Computer Science, pp. 170–179, October 2011. https://doi.org/10.1109/FOCS.2011.73
2. Borradaile, G.: Planar maximum flow: multiple-source multiple-sink maximum flow in directed planar graphs (2015)
3. Caini, C., Cruickshank, H., Farrell, S., Marchese, M.: Delay- and disruption-tolerant networking (DTN): an alternative solution for future satellite networking applications. Proc. IEEE **99**(11), 1980–1997 (2011)
4. Ford, L.R., Fulkerson, D.R.: Flows in Networks. Princeton University Press, Princeton (1962)
5. Goldberg, A.V., Tarjan, R.E.: Efficient maximum flow algorithms. Commun. ACM **57**(8), 82–89 (2014)
6. Hall, A., Hippler, S., Skutella, M.: Multicommodity flows over time: efficient algorithms and complexity. In: Baeten, J.C.M., Lenstra, J.K., Parrow, J., Woeginger, G.J. (eds.) ICALP 2003. LNCS, vol. 2719, pp. 397–409. Springer, Heidelberg (2003). https://doi.org/10.1007/3-540-45061-0_33

7. Li, H., Zhang, T., Zhang, Y., Wang, K., Li, J.: A maximum flow algorithm based on storage time aggregated graph for delay-tolerant networks. Ad Hoc Netw. **59**, 63–70 (2017)
8. Wang, P., Zhang, X., Zhang, S., Li, H., Zhang, T.: Time-expanded graph based resource allocation over the satellite networks. IEEE Wirel. Commun. Lett. 1 (2018). https://doi.org/10.1109/LWC.2018.2872996
9. Zhang, T., Li, H., Li, J., Zhang, S., Shen, H.: A dynamic combined flow algorithm for the two-commodity max-flow problem over the delay tolerant networks. IEEE Trans. Wirel. Commun. 1 (2018). https://doi.org/10.1109/TWC.2018.2872551

Optimum Layout and Simulation of TT&C Antennas on Lunar Exploration Capsule

Xiaoguang Li[✉] and Baobi Xu

Beijing Institute of Spacecraft System Engineering,
104 Youyi Road, Haidian District, Beijing, China
lixiaoguang1003@163.com

Abstract. In the field of deep space exploration, to optimize the layout of TT&C antennas on space capsule, based on heat flux identification and TT&C condition analysis, we place the TT&C antennas shifted from the traditional position on vertical surface. So the TT&C antennas can avoid the high heat flux identification area due to the second cosmic velocity return of the space capsule. At the same time, known the orbit and the position of the ground station, we use STK to simulate the return phase to promise the TT&C antennas are used within their main lobe. The design method of TT&C antennas layout on deep space capsule is optimized, and is proved by the CE-5T project.

Keywords: Capsule · TT&C antenna · Layout · Simulation

1 Introduction

Up to the present in China, the spacecraft with the function of returning to the earth keeps the tradition of placing the two TT&C antennas exactly up to the sky and down to the earth. As the development of the deep space exploration, the satellite to the moon needs to return to the earth as well. Different from the former returning satellite and spaceship, this capsule comes back at the second cosmic velocity, the thermal environment is much worse, including high heat flux peak, high heat enthalpy, large heat up sum [1, 2]. What's more, the capsule will leap up after entering the atmosphere and enter again, the longer journey causes the heat accumulated to much higher temperature, which brings new requirement of heat insulation design of the antennas. Although the antenna has been redesigned due to the new thermal environment, it still can't bear the heat if being placed in the traditional position. At this time the problem is brought out, is the traditional position suitable for lunar exploration capsule? Is there a position which has better thermal environment as well as good communication condition? In this paper, a new position is found, and is proved to be effective by the successful flight of CE-5T satellite.

© ICST Institute for Computer Sciences, Social Informatics and Telecommunications Engineering 2019
Published by Springer Nature Switzerland AG 2019. All Rights Reserved
M. Jia et al. (Eds.): WiSATS 2019, LNICST 280, pp. 312–319, 2019.
https://doi.org/10.1007/978-3-030-19153-5_32

2 Heat Flux Analysis

2.1 Simulation Results

Take the moon exploration project as an example, the capsule separates form the other part of the satellite at the height of 5000 km from the earth, and keep the flight until the height of 120 km to enter the atmosphere. Later it leaps out and enters the atmosphere again to reduce the speed. 12 points on the surface of the capsule are chosen to analyze the heat flux, including 3 points exactly down to the ground while flying (on the 0° line in the Fig. 1), 3 points shifted 30° aside from the 0° line, 3 points shifted 45° aside from the 0° line, 3 points shifted 60° aside from the 0° line. On each line, the 3 points have different heights as A, B, C shown in the Fig. 1.

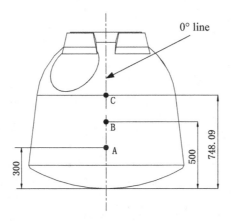

Fig. 1. Sketch map of the calculating point's position (Unit: mm)

Figures 2, 3 and 4 show the curve of the simulation results of the heat flux of each point. Time 0 in the figure refers to the time of entering at the height of 120 km.

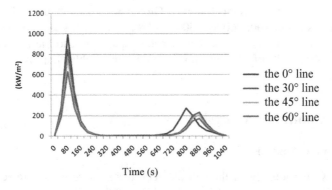

Fig. 2. Heat flux of point A

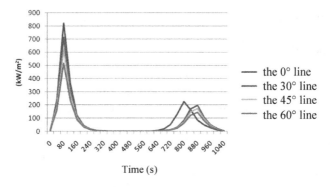

Fig. 3. Heat flux of point B

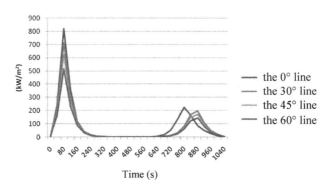

Fig. 4. Heat flux of point C

2.2 Data Analysis

Seen from the data above, the heat flux peak appears at 80 s after the entry. On the $0°$ line, the heat flux of A, B, C is 991.54, 820.89 and 820.42 kW/m^2, respectively. Compared to 223.5 kW/m^2 of the Shenzhou spaceship and 294.4 kW/m^2 of the former returning capsule, the value is much higher. On the $30°$ line, $45°$ line and $60°$ line, the heat flux reduces about 100, 200 and 300 kW/m^2, and it will keep reducing over $60°$ line. Although it's still higher than the Shenzhou spaceship and the former returning capsule, but the shift of the position would remarkably improve the thermal environment.

3   TT&C Condition Analysis

3.1   Qualitative Analysis

Figure 5 shows the journey of the capsule. The black curve is the projection of the journey, the direction is from the Australia to the west, through the Africa to China, and finally to Siziwangqi in China. It's easily to see from the figure that the four ground station of Namibia, Malindi, Karachi and Hetian are all coincidently under or on the left of the projection. In this situation, we can place the to-the-ground antenna shifted to the left side, and the to-the-sky antenna to the right side accordingly, so as to promise the TT&C antenna be used within its mainlobe.

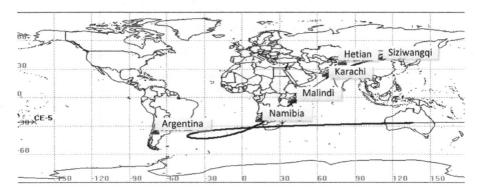

Fig. 5. The projection of the capsule journey

3.2 Quantitative Analysis

The TT&C condition is analyzed based on the actual attitude of the capsule during the entry.

Figures 6 and 7 show the angle between the capsule to the ground station and the point of the antenna VS time, under the situation of antenna being placed on the 0° line and the 45° line. The angle indicates the actual use of the antenna beam pattern [3]. If the angle is larger than 78°, then the line connecting the capsule and the ground station is outside the antenna beam lobe, which means the communication is processed using the interference region of the antenna, and the gain is too low to support the link. So the fundamental rule is to restrict the angle within 78° during the period when the capsule is in sight. The shade part of the figure indicates such period.

For Namibia station in Fig. 6, the insight period starts before the capsule separation and ends 14 min later. During the 14 min the angle gradually decrease from 66° to 20°, then increase up to 55°. In other words, it's always within 78°. As to the station of Malindi, during the 14 min of insight period, the angle gradually decrease from 78° to 31°, then increase up to 74°, also within 78°.

The analysis above is when the antenna is placed exactly down to the earth as traditional way. We can get the conclusion that the TT&C condition is good, although the thermal environment is too strict. To solve this, the following analysis is processed with the antenna placed on the 45° line, as shown in Fig. 7.

For Namibia station in Fig. 7, the insight period starts before the capsule separation and ends 14 min later. During the 14 min the angle gradually decrease from 72° to 35°, then increase up to 58°. As to the station of Malindi, during the 12 min of insight period, the angle gradually decrease from 78° to 31°, then increase up to 78°, also within 78°.

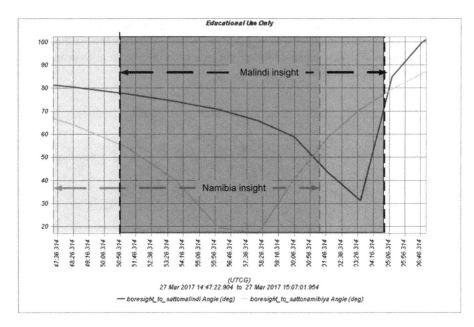

Fig. 6. The angle between the capsule to the ground station and the point of the antenna VS time (the antenna is placed on the 0° line, separation to first entry)

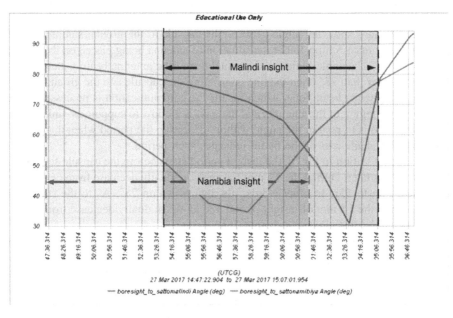

Fig. 7. The angle between the capsule to the ground station and the point of the antenna VS time (the antenna is placed on the 45° line, separation to first entry)

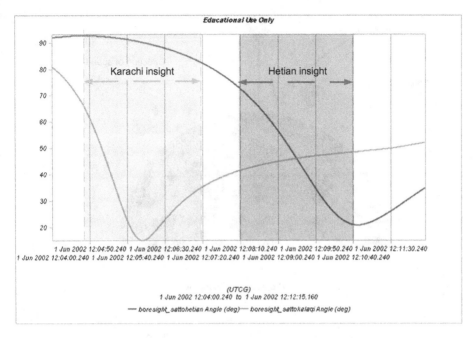

Fig. 8. The angle between the capsule to the ground station and the point of the antenna VS time (the antenna is placed on the 45° line, leap out period)

From the two analyses, the link is always with the main lobe of the antenna. For Namibia station, the TT&C condition is similar. For Malindi station, the insight period is 160 s shorter. But it is due to the delay of the start, at that time Namibia station is already insight, the total time of the two stations keeps the same. So the shift of the antenna does not influence the communication.

After the entry is the continuous blackout, and then comes the leap out period. During this period, under the situation of shifting to 45° of the antenna position, the angle is show in Fig. 8. It can be seen that the angle is less than 78° for both Karachi and Hetian station. The TT&C communication is not affected by the shifting of the antenna.

4 Practical Resolution

Above is the analysis and simulation under ideal condition. Putting into practice, other factors should be considered such as the antenna view, the layout of the capsule and the position of other antennas and umbrella cabin, etc. At last, the TT&C antennas are placed on the 115° line and 295° line, respectively, which is near the side of the capsule. This shift greatly improved the thermal environment of the antenna. The heat flux requirements of the two points are 592 and 300 kW/m2, much lower than before. Figures 9 and 10 show the position sketch map of the capsule and the ground station. The angle illustrates the angle between the capsule to the ground station and the point of the antenna in Figs. 6, 7 and 8.

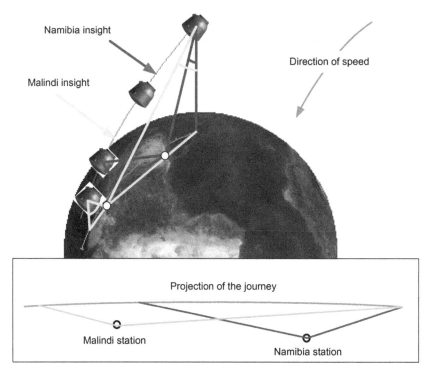

Fig. 9. The position sketch map of the capsule and the ground station (separation to first entry)

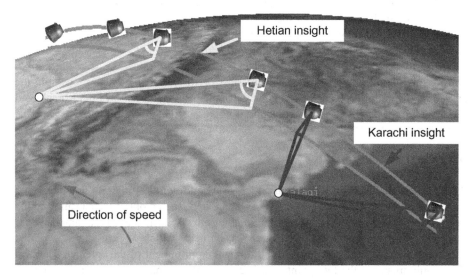

Fig. 10. The position sketch map of the capsule and the ground station (leap out period)

5   Conclusion

Considering both the TT&C link and thermal environment, based on the orbit and the position of ground station, this resolution keeps the link within the main lobe of the antenna and avoids the strict heat area on 0° line. Compared to traditional layout plan, the confliction between the antenna heat endurance and the high heat flux due to the second cosmic velocity is solved.

In the fight of CE-5T satellite in Oct. 2014 [4], the TT&C link was just good after capsule separation, and the antennas endured the burn at the position, which proved the resolution to be effective. The change of the antennas' position performed successfully.

References

1. Ryabak, J.P., Churchill, R.J.: Progress in reentry communications. IEEE Trans. Aerosp. Electron. Syst. **AES-7**(5), 879–894 (1971)
2. Evans, J.S., Huber, P.W., Jr, Schexnayder C.J.: Comparison of theoretical and flight-measured ionization in a blunt body re-entry flowfield. AIAA J. **9**(6), 1154–1162 (1971)
3. Paulat, J.C., Boukhobza, P.: Re-entry flight experiments lessons learned – the atmospheric reentry demonstrator ARD. In: European Aeronautic Defence and Space (EADS ST) LES MUREAUX (FRANCE), ADA476493 (2007)
4. Zong, H.E.: China lunar exploration project stage III achieved fully success. Space Int. **11**, 1–10 (2014)

Data Management Software System Design for Spacelab

Panpan Zhan$^{(\boxtimes)}$, Lan Lu, Xiongwen He, Luyuan Wang,
and Yong Sun

Beijing Institute of Spacecraft System Engineering,
Beijing 100094, People's Republic of China
panpan3210@qq.com

Abstract. The technology of propellant refueling is one of the important technologies of spacelab and cargo ship rendezvous and docking mission. With the data management software system, the function of two aircraft docking bus network is established, and the function of data transmission and control is realized. In the spacelab task, a data management software system for propellant refueling of cargo spaceship was proposed. Firstly, the software requirements and design principles are analyzed. Then, the layered software architecture is designed, and the rendezvous and docking task is expatiated. Finally, the realization of propellant refueling process in spacelab and cargo ship is illustrated. The research results can provide an important basis for the design of the data management system for the propellant refueling on space station.

Keywords: Spacelab · Data management · Rendezvous and docking ·
Propellant refueling

1 Introduction

According to China's manned space engineering development strategy [1], the space laboratory's main task is to verify the rendezvous and docking with various transport spacecraft, and to verify the space laboratory's onboard propellant refueling. It accumulates experience for the space station. In addition to supporting manned spacecraft rendezvous and docking missions, one of the important tasks of the space laboratory is to realize onboard propellant refueling and space-to-ground or ground-to-space transmission of goods with cargo ships.

Data management system is an important platform system in space laboratory. It mainly realizes the functions of telecommand, telemetry, bus network managements, flight program control, flight state management and rendezvous and docking mission. In the process of rendezvous and docking between space laboratory and transport spaceships (manned spaceships or cargo spaceships), the data management system is responsible for establishing the docking bus network between the two spacecraft. It realizes the functions of telecommand, telemetry acquisition and control data bidirectional transmission for the two spacecraft. The data management software system completes the above functions with the hardware cooperation, and realizes the data transmission and control of the propellant refueling data during the rendezvous and docking process with the cargo ship.

The data management software system supporting the propellant refueling with cargo ships is an important control platform of the onboard refueling system. At present, only ISS [2, 3] has applied the space propellant refueling system.

Based on the requirements of rendezvous and docking mission, this paper designs a data management software system for space laboratory, which can support multiple rendezvous and docking modes. It supports propellant refueling functions with cargo ships. The research results in this paper can provide reference for the mission of china's space station several years later.

2   Requirements Analysis and Design Principles

The data management software of the spacelab mainly has the following requirements:

(1) Telemetry management. It includes the functions of telemetry data acquisition, telemetry source packets organization, source packets scheduling, AOS [4] frames generation and downlink.

(2) Telecommand management. It includes the functions of receiving the telecommand data, checking and verifying the format, processing the real-time instructions and forwarding the telecommand data to other applications.

(3) Bus network management. The data management software realizes the functions of data acquisition, instruction sending and data interaction of all devices on the whole satellite bus. The docking 1553B bus is used to realize the data communication function of the spacelab and the cargo ship in the mode of rendezvous and docking. It realizes the data interaction and control function between the spacelab and the cargo ship.

(4) Flight status management. It can identify and control the key contact signals (launch takeoff, separation of vehicle and rocket, emergency shutdown of carrier) and docking signal interfaces (docking and separation signals) of the whole satellite. It realizes the conversion of flight status from ground flying stage to ascending stage and the conversion from ascending stage to normal flying stage. It performs corresponding flight programs in the flight status conversion.

(5) Rendezvous and docking management. It realizes the rendezvous and docking functions with manned ships or cargo ships. It can support the conversion of normal operation mode, docking mode with manned ships or cargo ships. It realizes the telemetry data, telecommand data, propellant refueling data and other control information routing and transmitting after the docking of the two spacecraft and their buses connected with each other.

In view of the complexity of the upper task and the multi-layer of the underlying bus network in the data management software of the spacelab, the software system design is based on the layered method. Combining with the idea of component design, it is organized into a number of software tasks to drive the software's operation. The Spacecraft Onboard Interface Service (SOIS) [5] of the Consultative Committee for Space Data Systems (CCSDS) and the Packet Utilization Standard (PUS) [6] of ESA are fully used in the design of the hierarchy, components and tasks. The main design ideas are as follows:

(1) Design of low level coupling architecture. It aggregated the application tasks, functional modules and underlying drivers to form a single-body system in existing data management software. Errors in one module resulted in errors in other modules. Therefore, the excessive coupling of each module leads to reliability degradation. Data management software of spacelab adopts hierarchical architecture design. Operating system and hardware driver are placed in the bottom layer, and the top layer is the tasks of user application layer. The data management software is divided into application layer, middleware layer and driver layer. The driver layer realizes the driver of each hardware interface. The middleware layer completes the specific functions of each business module. The application layer calls the business module of the middleware layer to realize the task's functions. Hierarchical low-coupling architecture can reduce the coupling between system modules, shield the impact of the replacement of hardware interface and protocol on the upper software, and improve the flexibility and reliability of the system.

(2) Component design. Onboard software component [7] (component for short) refers to a functional module that can be released independently and assembled by a third party. It meets certain spacecraft software requirements and provides services through interfaces. It should have two basic characters. Firstly, component users can assemble components according to established rules. Secondly, it must have specific, one or more functions. It can be called by the user, and run correctly in a predetermined operating environment. In order to improve the universality and adaptability of onboard software, and improve the efficiency and reliability of software development, this paper uses component-based design of transport layer, application support layer and system business layer components to accomplish business function encapsulation and module design.

(3) Multiple flight modes are independent from the rendezvous and docking task. During the flight mode conversion, different exchange and docking management tasks are performed according to the different spacecraft. The functions of independent operation mode, spaceship data management function in docking mode with manned ship, and propellant refueling after docking with cargo ship are realized respectively. Since the flight mode switching states are complex, it is more complex for the rendezvous and docking task to intertwine with it. By separating various flight modes and the rendezvous and docking task independently, the rendezvous and docking task in different docking modes can be realized, which makes the manned ships data management function and cargo ships propellant refueling function independent and definite.

3   Software Architecture Design

In order to improve the reliability and flexibility of the data management software system and to support multiple rendezvous and docking functions such as cargo ship's propellant refueling management, this paper designs the data management of spacelab according to the principles of hierarchical low-coupling architecture and component-based design, and separation of the multiple flight modes and the rendezvous and docking task. The architecture of the spacelab's software system is divided into three layers: driver layer, middleware layer and application layer, as shown in Fig. 1. The middleware layer is divided into transport layer, application support layer and system business layer.

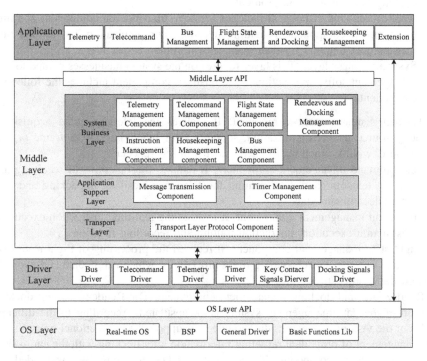

Fig. 1. Data management software architecture of spacelab

3.1   Driver Layer

In order to reduce the dependence of the software on the hardware changes, hardware-related interfaces are encapsulated into hardware drivers, including bus driver, remote control driver, telemetry driver, clock driver, key contact signals driver and docking signals driver. These drivers together with the components of the middleware layer realize the corresponding functions. Driver layer provides hardware-specific drivers for the system, which can shield the differences between hardware platforms and effectively ensure the independence and portability of the middleware layer and application layer.

3.2   Middleware Layer

The middleware layer is a general middle system located between the driver layer and the user application layer. It completes the specific functions of each business module.

It provides standard program interfaces in the form of onboard components. The upper application software can obtain business services independently through the standard business interfaces provided by the middleware. In order to make the middleware have good expansibility and maintainability, the middleware is divided into three layers.

(1) Transport layer. It provides standard interfaces for the upper services. The transport layer protocol implements the 1553B bus transmission protocol and the docking bus transmission protocol.
(2) Application support layer. It includes message transmission component and time management component, providing inter-task communication and unified time management function for data management system respectively.
(3) System business layer. This layer focuses on the system businesses related to data management software functions. The business component includes the following components.

Telemetry management component. It realizes the telemetry data acquisition, telemetry source packet organization, source packet scheduling, AOS frame organization and downlink functions of each systems of the spacelab.

Telecommand management component. It realizes the functions of receiving and checking the telecommand data, routing the telecommand data, unpacking and executing the telecommand data.

Instruction management component. It realizes the real-time instruction execution, delay instruction execution, instruction routing and recording functions.

Flight state management component. It realizes the processing of flight state conversion, and executes corresponding flight procedures, which can update and maintain onboard flight procedures.

Rendezvous and docking management component. The Rendezvous and docking function of the data management system is encapsulated. According to the different modes of the visiting spacecraft, the module can support the bidirectional transmission and management of propellant refueling information after docking with the cargo ship.

Bus management component. The application data of the upper layer is divided into message frames conforming to 1553B bus protocol and sent to the transport layer for processing.

Housekeeping management component. It realizes the functions of housekeeping management and autonomous management of the spacelab, including memory management, onboard maintenance, event reporting and onboard monitoring.

3.3   Application Layer

Application layer is composed of many tasks (or processes). These tasks use the standard interface provided by middleware layer for task-related processing, to complete the tasks specified by the spacelab.

3.4   Rendezvous and Docking Task Design

The manned ship and cargo ship carry out the rendezvous and docking mission with the spacelab respectively. The rendezvous and docking process with the cargo ship is a new and key verification activity, which can realize the important functions of onboard propellant refueling and space-to-ground or ground-to-space transmission of goods. Therefore, the design of rendezvous and docking mission is an important part of the data management software system of spacelab, which can realize the bus interconnection, telecommand, telemetry downlink and data transmission control after docking with spacecraft.

According to the design principles of separation of multiple flight modes and rendezvous and docking task, the rendezvous and docking task is not started when spacelab is flying independently. In this case, the rendezvous and docking task is not performed. The rendezvous and docking task is only started when the flight mode is changed to docking mode with a manned ship or a cargo ship. The rendezvous and docking task completes the rendezvous and docking function with the execution of other tasks. The communication method between these tasks is shown in Fig. 2.

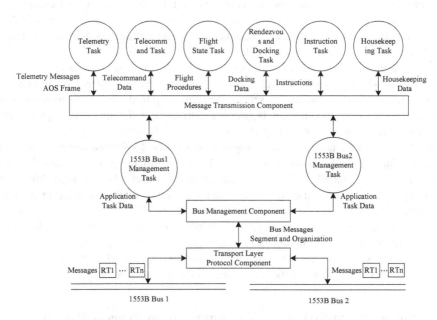

Fig. 2.   Interaction method between multi-tasks

From the view of telecommand data stream and telemetry data stream, the communication process between each task in data management software is explained.

Telecommand data flow design. After receiving telecommand data from ground, telecommand driver sends them to telecommand task through message transmission component. Telecommand task invokes telecommand management component to check and resolve the telecommand data. When the format is correct, if they are the data of other devices on the bus, the telecommand management component sends the data to the remote terminal through the bus. The bus management component and transport layer protocol component are invoked and finally forwarded to the corresponding device through 1553B bus. If the data are sending to the software itself, they are forwarded to other tasks through message transmission component.

Telemetry data stream design: The telemetry data stream is divided into the telemetry data collected from bus and the telemetry data collected by software itself.

The process of the telemetry data collected from bus is that the telemetry task registers the data to be collected to 1553B bus management task, and starts the periodic collection. The 1553B bus management task organizes the bus messages of RT -> BC through the bus management component and the transport layer protocol component, and then starts the task. After the bus messages return, the bus management component sends the message to the telemetry task. The telemetry task will organize telemetry source packet from telemetry data collected on the bus.

The process of telemetry data processing of the software itself is that the telemetry task periodically sends a notification message to each task through the message transmission component. The other tasks send their own telemetry data to the telemetry task after receiving the notification message, and the telemetry task organizes them into a software telemetry source packages. And then, the telemetry source packages of other devices and the software's own source packets are organized into AOS frames. Finally, the AOS frames are sending to ground.

The process of rendezvous and docking management task is shown in Fig. 2. The task runs periodically. Firstly, the telecommand data sent from the telecommand task is processed, the telecommand data is sent to the cargo ship through the bus management task. Then the control command is processed to control the process of propellant refueling. If the propellant refueling process is started, the data of propellant refueling are collected from the propellant refueling manager on the 1553B bus and forwarded to the cargo ship. If it is the docking mode with the cargo ship, the service request for data communication is queried, and the communication data status with the cargo ship is set according to the service requests. The service requests include the cargo ship real-time telemetry service request, delay telemetry service request, advance supplementary management data service request and display parameter service request, etc. If there is a service request, the data communication state is set up. It generates a set of RT -> BC 1553B bus messages, receives the propellant refueling data and telemetry data from the cargo ship, and sends them to the propellant refueling manager in spacelab.

4   Rendezvous and Docking Communication Process Design

The communication process of rendezvous and docking is supported by the data management software system of spacelab and cargo ship after the connection and interconnection of the two 1553B buses. It controls the action of the propellant refueling devices, such as the liquid floating device and compressor, to connect and close the gas-liquid pipeline of the propellant refueling system, so as to realize the propellant refueling process.

After rendezvous and docking, the communication network between the cargo ship and the spacelab establishes a physical connection based on the docking 1553B bus. Under the control of the data management software of the spacelab, the functions of telemetry acquisition, data frames organization, telecommand transmission and propellant refueling of the cargo ship are completed. CTU is the data management center computer and the physical equipment in witch data management software is running. Under the control of software, the two aircraft communicate with each other by transmitting the state information which represents the state of their propellant refueling functions.

Before proceeding with the propellant refueling process, the propellant refueling function of the spacelab data management software is started by executing the propellant refueling starting instruction. The software collects the propellant refueling disposal information and the fault detection information of the propellant refueling manager, sends them to the cargo ship by docking 1553B bus. The data management software of the spacelab collects the service request of data communication, inquires the data of propulsion replenishment sent by the cargo ship, and sends it to the propulsion Replenishment Manager to realize the control of the valve and compressor of the propulsion replenishment system of the space laboratory. After the propulsion refueling is completed, the refueling stopping command is sent through the flight program, and the refueling system valve is closed to stop the transmission of the propellant refueling information between the two spacecraft.

5 Conclusion

Onboard propellant refueling is one of the key technologies in manned space station project. Data management software system, as the information bridge of rendezvous and docking between spacelab and cargo ship, realizes the rendezvous and docking of two spacecraft and the function of propellant refueling. This paper presents the architecture of data management software system for space laboratory, designs the mission of rendezvous and docking management, and gives the process of propellant refueling of spacelab and cargo ship. It can realize the pre-verification of onboard propellant refueling technology for cargo ship and space station.

References

1. He, Y., Yang, H., Bai, M.: Spacelab technology summary and development stratagem. Manned Spacelight 15(3), 10–17 (2009)
2. Zimpfer, D., Kachmar, P., Tuohy, S.: Autonomous rendezvous, capture and in-space assembly: past, present and future. In: AIAA 1st Space Exploration Conference: Continuing the Voyage of Discovery, Orlando, Florida, pp. 321–328 (2005)
3. International Space Station Communications Systems. Washington D.C., USA, pp. 2–17 (2005)
4. Consultative Committee for Space Data System: AOS space data link protocol. CCSDS 732.0-B-2. Recommended Standard, Issue 2, Washington D.C., USA (2006)

5. Consultative Committee for Space Data System: Spacecraft Onboard Interface Services Concepts and Rationale. CCSDS 830.0-G-0.4, Washington D.C., USA (2005)
6. European Cooperation for Space Standardization: Space Engineering: Ground Systems and Operations - Telemetry and Telecommand Packet Utilization. ECSS-E-70-41A (2003)
7. Zhang, Y., Yuan, J., Guo, J.: Design of reconfigurable general TM based on software components. Spacecraft Eng. **22**(4), 62–67 (2013)

A Load-Balancing Based Research on Inter-satellite Link-Building Planning for Navigation Satellite Network

Weisong Jia[1,2(✉)], Liang Qiao[1,2], Lijun Yang[1,2], and Tao Zhang[1,2]

[1] Beijing Institute of Spacecraft System Engineering, Beijing 100094, China
kingarthurjs@163.com
[2] Science and Technology on Communication Networks Laboratory,
Shijiazhuang, China

Abstract. Based on navigation satellite network constituted by phased array inter-satellite links, our research proposes to optimize rapidly changing inter-satellite links topology. In the beginning of our research, we establish the topological model of the navigation satellite constellation dynamic network, and clarify the routing strategy. Then according to the principle that the topology is uniquely determined, our research analyzes the asymmetric traffic characteristics of the navigation satellite network. Furthermore, a topological link optimization method based on predicting load balance is proposed to describe the calculation steps of the link-building optimization method. Moreover, we verify load-balancing performance of inter-satellite link-building optimization method by using average time delay, maximum time delay and cache occupancy as indicators. It is verified through simulation that the load-balancing based inter-satellite link-building optimization method is feasible, at the same time, it is a valuable reference for planning of building inter-satellite links of the global navigation systems.

Keywords: Navigation satellite network · Load-balancing ·
Link-building planning

1 Introduction

Global navigation satellite system applied inter-satellite links in distance measurement for self-contained navigation and communication for operation data, which achieved long-time autonomous running without earth-based station support or managing global satellite navigation system with a small quantity of earth-based stations. Based on phased array antenna, inter-satellite links feature short response time, high precision in link building and long service life. Moreover, it not only provides more inter-satellite distance measurement results, but also forms Delay Tolerant Network (DTN) with rapidly changing topology. Network time-division multiplexing link-building needs to consider the time evolution before and after the inter-satellite link switching in route planning. Targeting the routing problem of DTN, Zhao Yue proposed dynamic

M. Jia et al. (Eds.): WiSATS 2019, LNICST 280, pp. 329–338, 2019.
https://doi.org/10.1007/978-3-030-19153-5_34

planning routing algorithm based on inter-satellite allocation plan constructed by polling link-building mode, and Fraire presented using simulated annealing algorithm to solve link-building planning problem. All these algorithms did not think over load balancing of network flow. Focusing on load balancing, Jain proposed earliest delivery routing algorithm based on local queue and whole network queue, and Yan Hongcheng presented an earliest delivery routing algorithm using subnet queue. However, for above two algorithms, it has great time delay for DTN when queue information interacting between network nodes, so queue information is obsolete easily. In addition, load balancing using queue status should generate routes dynamically with fixed link building topology planning, which cannot guarantee that link building planning is optimal compared with random routing strategy. In navigation satellite network, the visible relationship between satellite and satellite or between satellite and earth-based station is periodically predictable, therefore, optimized link topology of navigation satellite network is also able to be pre-planned. Once network topology is determined, end-to-end shortest path can be calculated by graph routing algorithm, and then the loads of every satellite node are available in advance using path set. This paper premeditates loads of satellite nodes and asymmetry of operation when just starting building links and planning routes, and applies simulated annealing global optimal search algorithm to achieve solving link-building planning with multi-objective optimization which includes average time delay, maximum time delay and load balancing. Through verifying in the navigation constellation network simulation system, it can be revealed that the method proposed by this paper can achieve efficient and balanced transmission of operation information among satellite nodes.

2   Network Model and Optimization Objective

When the navigation satellite carries only one phased array transceiver, each satellite establishes at most one half-duplex inter-satellite link in the planned time slot to form a typical DTN. In order to ensure the fairness of the link building between satellite nodes, that is, the chances of establishing an inter-satellite link between this satellite and other satellite are relatively equal, the navigation constellation operation cycle is divided into several link-building periods T. In each link-building period T, one navigation satellite repeatedly establishes links with different satellites in sequence until satellite visibility changes. The constellation link state within the link-building period T can be considered as a finite state machine, where each state represents the link pairing relationship of the satellites within a certain time slot. Our research divide link-building period T in k time slots, which correspond to k states in the state machine. The followings are graph model of navigation satellite network based on time cost and link-building planning.

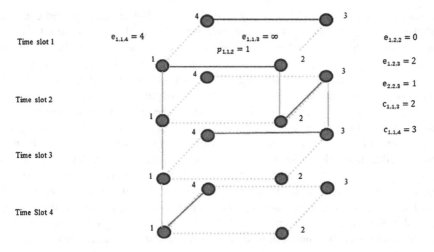

Fig. 1. Simplified model of navigation satellites network

(1) $v_{k,i,j}$ represents the visible relationship between the satellite i and the satellite j in the time slot k, where 1 represents visible and 0 represents invisible;

(2) $p_{k,i,j}$ represents the link-building relationship between the satellite i and the satellite j in the time slot h, where 1 represents linked and 0 represents unlinked;

(3) $e_{k,i,j}$ represents the edge cost between the satellite i and the satellite j in the time slot k, if $p_{k,i,j} = 1$, then $e_{k,i,j} = 1$, or if $p_{k,i,j} = 0$ and $p_{mod(k+t,T),i,j} = 1$, then $e_{k,i,j} = t + 1$, otherwise $e_{k,i,j} = \infty$. That is, if the satellite i and the satellite j are directly linked in the time slot k, the cost of the edge between the node i and the node j in the figure only includes the communication time cost 1; if the satellite i and the satellite j are linked after t time slots, then the cost between the node i and the node j in the figure includes the communication time cost 1 and the delay cost t; if the satellite i and the satellite j are not linked in the link-building period T, then the cost of the edge between the node i and the node j is infinite.

(4) $c_{k,i,j}$ represents the minimum cost between the satellite i and the satellite j in the time slot k.

A simplified network model is shown for ease of description in Fig. 1. The time-varying map structure of the navigation satellite network is described by four satellite nodes. $v_{1,1,2}$ indicates that satellite 1 and satellite 2 are mutually visible in time slot 1, $p_{1,1,2}$ indicates that satellite 1 and satellite 2 are established an inter-satellite link in time slot 1. $e_{1,1,2}$ indicates that the cost of the edge between the satellite 1 and the satellite 2 is 1. $c_{1,1,4}$ indicates that the minimum cost of the edge between satellite 1 and satellite 4 is 3. The shortest path from node i to node j at the time slot k is showed by $l_{k,i,j} = \{(k+t_1, i, u_1)(k+t_2, u_2, u_2)...(k+t_n, u_n, j\}$, where u_n is the intermediate node. And $l_{k+t1+1,u_1,j} = \{(k+t_2, u_2, u_2)...(k+t_n, u_n, j)\} \in l_{k,i,j}$, that is, if the shortest path from the satellite i to the satellite j arrives at the satellite u_1 after t_1 time slots, the shortest path from satellite u_1 to satellite j in time slot $t_1 + 1$ is necessarily same as the shortest path from the satellite i to the satellite j at the time slot k. Therefore, the end-to-end shortest path $l_{k,i,j}$ calculated in any time slot k in a link-building period coincides with the end-to-end shortest path of other time slots, that is, the end-to-end information transmission path in the link-building period T is one and only. When improved Dijkstra algorithm is used to calculate the unique shortest path under the determined link-building plan, the routing strategy of the satellite node for the transferred information is also determined to ensure that all the information in the network can be transmitted along the optimal path. Therefore, under the premise of not considering the sudden asymmetric traffic, the process of routing load balancing to the navigation satellite network is the optimization process of the link-building planning. The navigation satellite network carries the telemetry service, the telecontrol service, and the autonomous navigation service. The telemetry service is forwarded from the non-access satellite through the network to the access satellite and then transferred to the earth-based station. The telecontrol service is uploaded to the access satellite through the earth-based station and then forwarded to the non-access satellite. Both of these make navigation satellite network be characterized of data flow long-term asymmetry. Access satellites are more loaded in the navigation satellite network as the connection hub between satellites and earth-based stations. Set $Z = \{z_1, z_2 \ldots, z_m\}$ as the set of M access satellites. When planning links, it should be preferential satisfied that the end-to-end path delay of one access satellites as the start point or the end point is minimum, which to achieve load balancing based on asymmetric service. In addition, the more times the satellite node u appears in the end-to-end shortest path set R, the greater the probability that the information flows through the satellite node u. So the shortest path set can be adjusted in advance through the link-building re-planning to realize the satellite-node-based load balancing.

3   Method of Link-Building Planning

The problem of satellite network link-building planning based on time-varying graph is essentially a global optimal solution search problem based on multiple optimization objectives. The first thing to do is to set objective function and calculate the optimal value. By continuously adjusting the link-building planning, the simulated annealing algorithm is used to get the global near-optimal solution. The key steps are as follows.

3.1   Determining Evaluating Function Optimization Goal and Parameter Analysis

The objective function for solving the optimal link-building planning is $f(x) = \alpha AD + \beta MD + \gamma AUD + \delta ADD + \varepsilon RMS$.

$AD = \dfrac{\sum_{k=1}^{T} \sum_{i=1}^{N} \sum_{j=1}^{N} c_{k,i,j}}{T \times N \times (N-1)}$ indicates the average end-to-end time delay, where N is the number of satellites in the navigation satellite network.

$MD = \max_{\forall k,i,j} c_{k,i,j}$ indicates the maximum end-to-end time delay.

$$AUD = \frac{\sum_{k=1}^{T}\sum_{i \in Z}\sum_{j \notin Z} c_{k,i,j}}{T \times M \times (N-1)}$$ indicates the average end-to-end time delay in of the uplink telecontrol of the access satellites.

$$ADD = \frac{\sum_{k=1}^{T}\sum_{i \notin Z}\sum_{j \in Z} c_{k,i,j}}{T \times M \times (N-1)}$$ indicates the average end-to-end time delay in of the downlink telemetry of the access satellites.

$$RMS = \frac{\sum_{i=1}^{N} \frac{F_i - F_{avr}}{F_{avr}}}{N}$$ indicates the load mean square deviation of satellite nodes under the optimal path, where F_i is the statistics of satellite i in the end-to-end shortest path set R, and $F_{avr} = \frac{\sum_{i=1}^{N} F_i}{N}$ is the average statistics of all the satellites in set R.

For the weight adjustment factors of each indicator, which includes, $\alpha, \beta, \gamma, \delta$ and ε, when the asymmetric traffic is large, the value γ and δ should be increased, however, when the asymmetric traffic is small, the values should be decreased. In this way, the problem of link-building planning translates into the problem of finding the global minimum of $f(x)$.

3.2   Shortest Path Calculation

In this paper, the Dijkstra algorithm is used to complete the calculation of the end-to-end shortest path from node s to the arbitrary destination node d in the time slot k of the network. The steps of the algorithm are as follows:

(1) Set V as the constellation network nodes set. Q is the shortest path nodes set, in which every element represents whether a satellite node has been included in the shortest path $L = \{l_{k,s,j}, j = 1, 2 \ldots N, j \neq s\}$. T = V − Q shows the nodes that has not been included in the shortest path. Also, the path cost sets $C = c_{k,s,j}, j = 1, 2 \ldots N, j \neq s$.

(2) Initialize the shortest path nodes set Q and the shortest path L, and let Q and L include the source node S. Initialize $c_{k,s,j}$ as ∞.

(3) Find the satellite node u with the shortest distance $c_{k,s,u}$ from s in T = V − Q and add u to set Q and L.

(4) Slacken the path L that the destination satellite node $j \in T$. If $c_{k,s,j} > (e_{k+t,u,j} + c_{k,s,u})$, add node u to $l_{k,s,j}$ and modify $c_{k,s,j}$.

(5) Repeat step (3) and step (4) until all satellite nodes are included in the shortest path node set Q, that is Q = V.

It is different from Dijkstra algorithm in continuous link network topology, due to the time evolution characteristics of the time-varying graph, when the non-optimal path is slackened, the edge cost of the intermediate node u to the destination satellite j should be $e_{k+t,u,j}$ rather than $e_{k,u,j}$, in which the time delay $t = c_{k,s,u}$.

3.3   Link-Building Planning Adjustment

When the results of the objective function are not optimal, it is necessary to make minor adjustments to the link-building planning. This paper adopts the random link exchange method. The steps are as follows:

(1) Generate the time slot k, the source node A of link 1 and the source node C of link 2;
(2) Due to the original link-building planning, our research obtain satellite B pointed by satellite A and satellite D pointed by satellite C;
(3) If B $\neq$ C, $v_{k,a,c} = 1$ and $v_{k,b,d} = 1$, a link should be built between A and C and another link should be built between C and D; if B $\neq$ C, $v_{k,a,d} = 1$ and $v_{k,b,c} = 1$, a link should be built between A and D and another link should be built between B and C, otherwise, go to step (1).

3.4 Simulated Annealing Optimization

Compared with genetic algorithm, it is more efficient to use simulated annealing algorithm to solve optimal path problem based on the characteristics that the network link path genes are only related to time and node data flow. The optimization steps are as follows:

(1) Form initial link-building planning and evaluation function value $f(x_{old})$ with initial temperature T = 1. The number of adjustment times for every temperature T is L;
(2) Adjust and generate new link-building plans;
(3) Recalculate to get new evaluation function value $f(x_{new})$;
(4) Calculate the increment $\Delta f = f(x_{new}) - f(x_{old})$;
(5) If $\Delta f < 0$, we accept the new link-building plan, otherwise, accepting the new plan with the probability $e^{-\frac{\Delta f}{T}}$;
(6) If the link-building plans are not accepted for 20 consecutive times, the algorithm ends. If the adjustment times are less than 20, the process goes to step (2).
(7) T = T $\times$ μ, if T > T_{min}, the process goes to step (2).

The speed of temperature dropping in simulated annealing and the number of adjustment L at each temperature depend on the rate of changing of the evaluation value during the link-building optimization process. If the evaluation function value can converge quickly, and L can be set to a smaller value.

4 Performance Simulation

4.1 The Parameter Setting of Simulation Scene

The navigation satellite network uses the constellation of 24MEO+3GEO+3IGSO, in which the configuration of MEOs is selected walker24/3/1, and each satellite carries one inter-satellite link. The STK simulation scenario is constructed based on the network parameters, and the inter-satellite visibility is obtained to form a link-building planning. The node transmission simulation platform for navigation satellite network is built by MATLAB. And the simulation results are used to compare the average time delay, maximum time delay, satellite cache occupancy and the number of dropped frames (Tables 1 and 2).

Table 1. The parameters of navigation satellite

Parameters	Settings
Number of satellite nodes	30
Number of inter-satellite nodes	1
MEO/IGSO inclination angle	55
Type of constellation	Walker24/3/1
MEO constellation period	7 days
Number of access satellite	6
Number of satellite nodes	30
Number of inter-satellite nodes	1
MEO/IGSO inclination angle	55

Table 2. Simulation parameters of navigation satellite network transmission

Parameters	Settings
Simulation duration (seconds)	3600
Inter-satellite bandwidth (frames/time slot)	50
Autonomous navigation frames generation rate (frames/time slot)	1
Telecontrol frames injection rate (frames/time slot/satellite)	12
Telemetry generation rate (frames/time slot/satellite)	5
Terminal node cache size (frames)	400
Routing node cache size (frames)	800
Maximum hop count	10
Simulation duration (seconds)	3600

4.2 Optimization Objectives Analysis

In the navigation satellite network, the link-building planning method forms link-building configuration Fig. 1. And the setting values of the adjustment factors are shown in Table 3.

Table 3. The adjustment factors of evaluation function indicator weights

Parameters	Settings
α	1
β	1
γ	1
δ	1
ε	10

The minimum average end-to-end time delay is used as the optimization target to form the link-building configuration Fig. 2. The link-building configuration schemes are respectively deployed on the node transmission simulation platform for navigation satellite network, and the simulation results are shown in Figs. 2, 3, 4 and 5.

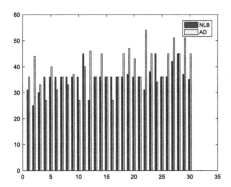

Fig. 2. Time delay comparison of link-building plans

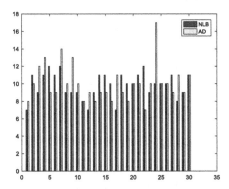

Fig. 3. Node cache occupancy of link-building plans

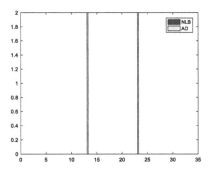

Fig. 4. Dropped frame numbers comparison under full load circumstances

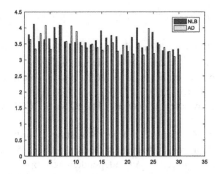

Fig. 5. The average time delay comparison of link-building plans

In the management and control scenario of the traffic asymmetric navigation satellite network, the link-building configuration scheme based on the load-balancing link-building planning method is better than that targeting minimum average end-to-end time delay on the indicators of maximum time delay and the balance of the node cache occupancy. Under full load, the number of dropped frames in the network after load balancing is significantly smaller than that of the non-load-balancing scheme. However, the difference of the average end-to-end time delay between the two schemes is less than 1. In summary, the load balancing based DTN link-building planning scheme effectively achieves the load balancing among the satellite nodes of the navigation satellite network without affecting the average end-to-end time delay.

5 Conclusion

This paper establishes a time-division multiplexed network model for navigation satellite constellation. According to the uniqueness of the optimal routing path under the fixed link-building topology and the asymmetric characteristics of the navigation satellite network service information path, this paper proposes a method to improve the load balancing performance of network routing in topological link-building planning. The simulation results show that the topological link-building optimization method based on load balancing is better than that targeting minimum average end-to-end time delay, which can support the link planning of the inter-satellite links of the global navigation system. The next step in this study will consider more influencing factors in the link-building planning. For instance, satellite visibility changing will lead to the switch of link-building planning, so the optimal path will change during the information transmission process. Under this circumstance, it is necessary to ensure that the network time delay performance will not decrease during link-building planning switching. In addition, autonomous navigation requires more ranging links between navigation satellites, and also requires better geometric accuracy factors. Moreover, when selecting ground access nodes, it is necessary to consider the impacts of satellite elevation angle, satellite-ground connection duration and the number of accessed satellites.

References

1. Yue, Z.: Navigation satellite network routing algorithm based on dynamic programming. In: China Satellite Navigation Academic Annual Meeting (2017)
2. Fraire, J.: Routing-aware fair contact plan design for predictable delay tolerant networks. Ad Hoc Netw. **25**, 303–313 (2015)
3. Jain, S.: Routing in a delay tolerant network. In: ACM SIGCOMM 2004, Portland, USA, pp. 145–157 (2004)
4. Hongcheng, Y., Qingjun, Z., Yong, S.: A novel routing algorithm for navigation satellite network based on partial queues. J. Astronaut. **36**(12), 1444–1452 (2016)
5. Brinkmann, G., Crevals, S., Frye, J.: An independent set approach for the communication network of the GPS III system. Discrete Appl. Math. **161**, 573–579 (2013)
6. Liu, L.: Research on Routing Policy Based on the Graph Model for Tolerant Networks, XIDIAN University (2015)
7. Zixuan, L., Zhibo, Y., Kanglian, Z.: Research on routing algorithm of navigation constellation network. J. Nanjing Univ. **3**, 529–534 (2018)

Design of Spaceborne AIS System

Xiangyu Lin[✉], Dong Yan, Yufei Huang, Fan Bai, Xiongwen He,
and Panpan Zhan

Beijing Institute of Spacecraft System Engineering,
Beijing 100094, People's Republic of China
linxiangyu1981@163.com

Abstract. The AIS communication system is a global positioning aided navigation system, which can improve the safety of ship operation and the reliability of navigation. A spaceborne AIS system can dynamically monitoring ships in the global area. But It has many challenges such as message collision and signal transmission loss. This paper first designed a LEO AIS constellation, analyzed the coverage of this constellation, and then carried out the design of the on board AIS receiving system, including an array antenna and a receiver. Finally, the method of multi-user signal separation and detection was expounded.

Keywords: Spaceborne · AIS · DBF · Message collision

1 Introduction

At the beginning of AIS system design, the global ship monitoring problem was not considered. Therefore, satellite-based AIS system has many challenges. The main problems are message collision, transmission loss of electromagnetic wave, doppler shift phenomenon, transmission delay, and Faraday rotation of signal polarization direction.

Firstly, a low-orbit AIS constellation is designed and its performance is analyzed in this paper. Then, an AIS receiving system is designed, including a polarization diversity array antenna and a receiver. The methods of multi-user signal separation and detection are then described, including digital beam forming technology, frequency and polarization diversity technology.

1.1 Satellite Orbit Design

A spaceborne AIS system needs to have global coverage and to achieve rapid re-access to any maritime target. Moreover, AIS satellites only need the ability to transmit data with ships and base stations in time, so there is no requirement for the return characteristics of satellite orbit.

Considering the factors such as the coverage of the satellite antenna, the length of the single visible segment of the satellite and the information conflict caused by the number of ships in the beam of the satellite antenna, the orbit height of the AIS satellite

M. Jia et al. (Eds.): WiSATS 2019, LNICST 280, pp. 339–347, 2019.
https://doi.org/10.1007/978-3-030-19153-5_35

is about 600 km. Since the mission has no special requirements for the altitude of satellites passing through the earth at different latitudes, in order to reduce the control complexity of the satellite operation, the orbit of the satellite is determined to be a circular orbit (Table 1).

The solar synchronous orbit has the advantage of fixed illumination time, and the design of solar array, thermal control subsystem and power subsystem of the satellite is relatively simple. Therefore, most LEO satellites in China choose this type of orbit. For the sun synchronous orbit with a height of 600 km, the orbit inclination is near 97°, and the distribution of the locus of the satellite is between 83° north and south latitude. The satellite can achieve global coverage, that is, it can provide services for ships operating in various sea areas around the world (Fig. 1).

Table 1. AIS constellation orbit

Satellite number	0	1	2	3	4
Orbit height (Km)	561				
Orbital tilt angle (degree)	97.64				
Eccentricity	0				
Ascension point	0	72	144	216	288
Perigee angle (degree)	0	72	144	216	288
Near point angle (degree)	0				

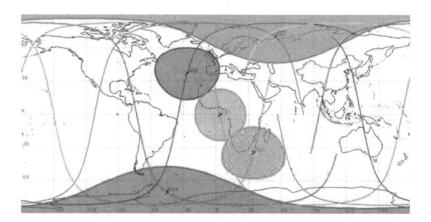

Fig. 1. AIS constellation 2D configuration

1.2   Analysis of Coverage Performance

In order to analyze the coverage performance of AIS constellation, the criterion of judging the coverage performance is to determine the coverage performance. Commonly used coverage performance indicators include global coverage time, maximum revisit time, bandwidth, instantaneous visible area, etc. According to the AIS task requirements, this paper intends to analyze the maximum revisit time and coverage. In the simulation calculation, all the visible areas below the satellite are regarded as "covered".

The revisit time is the time interval between two satellite beams illuminating the same area, that is, the coverage gap. For AIS satellites, the maximum revisit time is the maximum of the time interval between two beams irradiating the same area.

The calculation shows that the AIS constellation composed of 5 satellites in the previous section is the largest revisit time between anywhere from 0.12 h to 1.44 h. With the increase of latitude, the maximum revisit time is gradually shortened. Among them, 84% of the areas had the maximum revisit time of 1–1.5 h,

The ground coverage of AIS constellation increases with latitude. The calculation shows that the AIS constellation composed of 5 satellites in the previous section can achieve 19–30 times per day for 70% of the area, and the coverage of the two level is as high as 60–76 weight/day,

By analysis, 5 satellites operating in 5 orbiting orbit satellites can operate to ensure that the maximum revisit time of the spaceborne AIS system to any area in the world is less than 1.5 h, that is, it can provide updated services for ships in any area of the world less than 1.5 h.

2   Design of the AIS Receiving System

2.1   Design of Spaceborne AIS Antenna

Aiming at the fading characteristics of the AIS signal transmitted to the 600 km height and the polarization mismatch caused by Faraday rotation, a polarization diversity receiving antenna is designed to improve the reception quality of the signal. At the same time, in order to solve the problem of signal separation, array antennas should be used. Because the wavelength of the signal is 1.85 m, the size of the antenna array is also limited. Designing a better antenna system that can be carried on the satellite is one of the keys of the whole system.

Therefore, taking into account the needs of spaceborne AIS system and the available resources of the satellite platform, taking full account of the radiation unit, geometry structure and DBF processing technology of the antenna, the spaceborne AIS antenna is designed as a two element array antenna consisting of three orthogonal crossed half wave oscillator, and its intention is shown in Fig. 2. In the figure, the Z direction is the local direction, the Y direction is the satellite flight direction, and the X direction realizes the DBF beam scanning to expand the coverage area (Fig. 3).

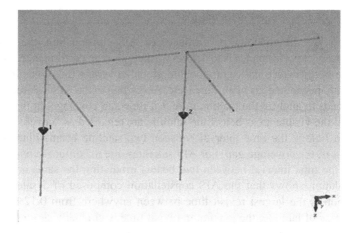

Fig. 2. Antenna array for satellite borne AIS system

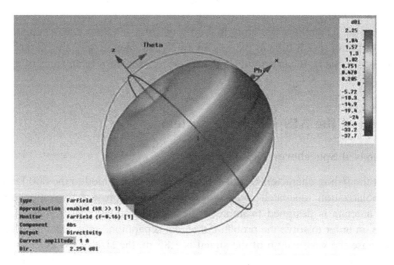

Fig. 3. Antenna 3D radiation pattern

2.2   Design of Spaceborne AIS Receiver

The task of the receiver is to select the weak high-frequency signal received by the antenna from the accompanying noise and interference by proper filtering, and then send it to the signal processor and other equipment after amplification and demodulation.

The spaceborne AIS receiver adopts direct frequency conversion receiver technology. Because it works in the VHF band, it can be regarded as if signal. Therefore, in order to guarantee the sensitivity index, an amplifier is added after the LNA. The receiver mainly includes limiter, band-pass filter, low noise amplifier, broadband amplifier, variable gain amplifier, automatic gain control unit, mixer, demodulator and other modules.

Therefore, the scheme of spaceborne AIS receiver is to receive the signals of three orthogonal antenna antennas in each antenna array separately when receiving the AIS signal. The dual frequency signal of AIS is separated by band-pass filter, and the baseband sampling method is adopted for A/D acquisition, and the block diagram is shown in Fig. 4.

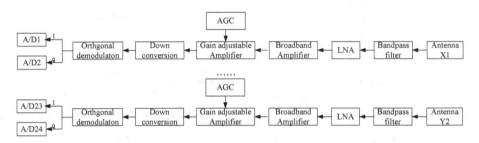

Fig. 4. Scheme of AIS receiver

Because each antenna oscillator channel has two frequency points, each frequency point data acquisition is divided into I and Q orthogonal two channels. The spaceborne AIS system adopts 3 cross oscillator array, so 24 channels of data acquisition are needed.

Because the signal bandwidth of AIS system is 12.5 kHz or 25 kHz, plus Doppler frequency shift + 4 kHz, it is considered that more than 8 times the sampling rate should be adopted, and the quantization bits should be more than 14 bits. Therefore, the sampling rate above 240 kHz can be satisfied, and the core chip with a sampling frequency of 250 kHz is initially selected, and the quantization bits are 16 bit, which can meet the requirements.

Due to the need for buffering, parallel conversion and other data processing before multiple storage data is collected, considering the system data processing speed and IO pin requirements, Xilinx Virtex IV series XQR4VSX55 is selected.

The real-time data unit processes the collected signal data in real time, detects the ship information, and sends it to the data storage unit for storing the data to the ground receiving station. The real-time data processing unit and its relationship with other stand-alone computers are shown in Fig. 5.

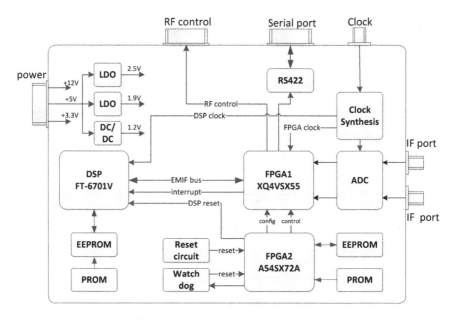

Fig. 5. Real-time data processing unit

3 Multiuser Signal Detection

3.1 Multiuser Signal Detection Overall Scheme

On the two central frequencies of 161.975 MHz and 162.025 MHz channels, the bandwidth of the standard signal is 25 kHz and the Doppler shift frequency is + 4 kHz, so the bandwidth of the two channels is 33 kHz. After the RF front-end processing, the I/Q branch is formed, and then the digital baseband signals of AIS1 and AIS2 are formed by 8 times bandwidth sampling.

As shown in Fig. 6, each channel is processed by digital beam forming of six channels (corresponding to six antenna units), and then the beam diversity of the received data is carried out. Then, the ship information detection based on the frequency diversity is carried out.

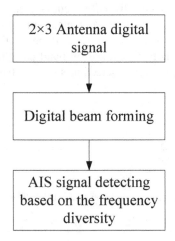

Fig. 6. Overall digital processing scheme on satellite (AIS1 and AIS2 have the same processing scheme)

3.2 Digital Beamforming Scheme

The basic digital baseband I and Q signals need to be synthesized into complex baseband signals in digital processing. As shown in Fig. 7, the y-polarized signal digitally forms two beams, and the x-polarized and z-polarized beams form four beams, respectively.

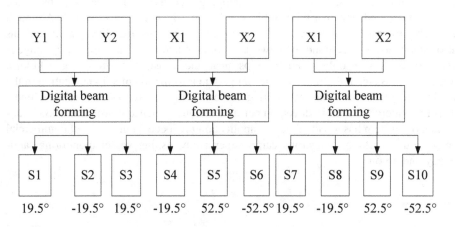

Fig. 7. Beam forming structure diagram

3.3 Multiuser Signal Detection

Due to the Doppler shift and multi-user signals, the bandwidth of each beam signal exceeds the bandwidth of a single user without frequency offset signal, which is close to 8 kHz, which brings great difficulties to frequency offset estimation and ship information detection. The mixed signal in the wideband can be divided into several narrow band signals by frequency diversity method, which can reduce the dynamic range of the frequency offset estimation parameters, improve the estimation accuracy, reduce the number of multi-user signals, and improve the detection rate of ship information. Frequency diversity is realized by band-pass filters. The frequency division parameter estimation and signal detection structure based on the band filter are shown in Fig. 8

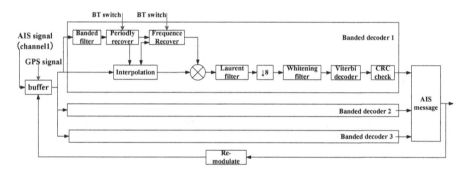

Fig. 8. Block diagram of demodulation based on frequency diversity method (single channel)

4 Conclusion

The research and application of spaceborne AIS has been developing abroad for many years. With the development of China's shipping industry, the number of ships on the sea has increased and maritime traffic has become increasingly crowded. Although China has established a relatively complete shore based universal AIS system, and has also established a corresponding network in some inland rivers, its monitoring range is very small. It can only monitor ships near the coast (not exceeding 100 km). Receiving AIS signal through satellite can get the information of ship navigation in the world, and carry out safety monitoring for our ships, so as to better serve China's maritime safety, economic development and national defense construction. Satellite-borne AIS system has a wide range of application prospects in the areas of commercial vessel route tracking, dangerous cargo supervision, fishing vessel monitoring, anti-piracy and so on.

References

1. Zhong, J., Wang, H.S., Zheng, L.: Analysis and simulation of ship detection probability of space-based AIS. Telecommun. Eng. **50**, 6–11 (2010)
2. Wang, C., Zhu, S., Jiang, W., Meng, X.: Demodulation algorithm based on Laurent decomposition for satellite-based AIS signals. J. Spacecraft TT&C Technol. (10) (2012)
3. I.-R.M. 1371-2: Technical characteristics for an universal automatic identification system using time division multiple access in the vhf maritime mobile band (1998-2001-2006)
4. Dahl, O.F.H.: Space-based AIS receiver for maritime traffic monitoring using interference cancellation (2006). http://ntnu.divaportal.org/smash/record.jsf?pid=diva2:121772
5. Scorzolini, A.: European enhanced space-based AIS system study. In: 2010 5th Advanced Satellite Multimedia Systems Conference and the 11th Signal Processing for Space Communications Workshop (2010)
6. te Hennepe, F.: Space-based detection of AIS signals. In: 2010 5th Advanced Satellite Multimedia Systems Conference and the 11th Signal Processing for Space Communications Workshop (2010)
7. International Telecommunication Union: Technical Characteristics for a Universal Shipborne Automatic Identification System Using Time Division Multiple Access in the VHF Maritime Mobile Band, ITUR.M.1371-2, September 2007
8. Miguel, A., Cervera, M.A., Ginesi, A., Eckstein, K.: Satellite-based vessel automatic identification system: a feasibility and performance analysis. Int. J. Satell. Commun. Netw. **29** (2), 117–142 (2011)

An Energy Efficient Multicast Algorithm for Temporal Networks

Keyi Shi, Hongyan Li$^{(\boxtimes)}$, Peng Wang, and Tao Zhang

State Key Laboratory of Integrated Service Networks, Xidian University,
Xian 710071, China
hyli@xidian.edu.cn

Abstract. Investigating the energy efficient multicast problem in space-ground integrated network (SGIN) is of vital importance for saving satellites transmission resources. However, the time-varying feature of network topology and resources poses great challenges to energy efficient multicast in SGIN. In this paper, we propose an approximation algorithm based on the modified time-expanded graph to minimize energy consumption while completing multicast transmission. At first, the SGIN is depicted by traditional time-expanded graph to capture the correlations between time-varying network resources. Then, to characterize the energy efficient multicast problem for temporal networks, we extend such graph to the Time Expanded Graph for Multicast (TEGM) by adding auxiliary aggregated destination vertices and aggregating edges. Finally, according to TEGM, an approximation algorithm for energy efficient multicast problem is proposed on the basis of the approach presented by Watel to solve the corresponding Directed Steiner Tree problem (DST). Besides, simulation results are conducted to illustrate the superiority of proposed algorithm over that based on dynamic trees.

Keywords: Energy efficient multicast ·
Space-ground integrated network · Temporal network

1 Introduction

Recently, multicast has gained more and more attentions in wireless communications due to its natural advantage in reducing the spectrum demand and energy consumption [2]. Multicast can be widely used for various applications, e.g., video conference, corporate communication, distance learning and software distribution [5]. In particular, multicast is also with broad application prospects in SGIN. For example, a remote sensing satellite could multicast the observation data to multiple terrestrial sites to save resources of satellite networks. SGIN is a typical temporal network, characterized by long delays, predictable/periodical topology, intermittent connectivity and link disruptions [1]. The time-varying

---

Supported by organization x.

M. Jia et al. (Eds.): WiSATS 2019, LNICST 280, pp. 348–355, 2019.
https://doi.org/10.1007/978-3-030-19153-5_36

feature of SGIN poses a great challenge to enable energy efficient multicast. Therefore, it is prerequisite to construct a precise graph model to characterize the energy efficient multicast problem in SGIN, with the time-varying feature involved. Then, based on such graph model, a Minimum Energy Multicast Tree (MEMT) is constructed to minimize energy consumption.

There have been some works on energy efficient multicast problem in wireless networks and multicast in delay-and disruption-tolerant network (DTN) in the literature. For static wireless networks, the authors in [4] defined the energy efficient multicast problem for the first time. Besides, they proposed a greedy-based heuristic algorithm to generate a multicast tree with the minimum number of transmissions. For DTN, the authors in [7] regarded DTN as a series of snapshots and developed the Dynamic Tree-Based Routing (DTBR) algorithm. Through constructing associated multicast tree in each snapshot, smaller delays and better message delivery ratios can be acquired. Although such approach takes into account the time-varying feature, it ignores the correlations between time-varying resources, which would cause the unavailability of some network resources.

In this paper, we propose an energy efficient multicast approach for temporal networks (e.g., SGIN) to minimize energy consumption. First, in order to characterize the correlations between time-varying network resources, we leverage the traditional time-expanded graph (TEG) [3] to model the temporal network. Then, through adding some corresponding aggregated destination vertices and aggregating edges on the legacy TEG, the Time Expanded Graph for Multicast (TEGM) is proposed to characterize the Energy Efficient Multicast problem (EEM) for temporal networks. Next, on the basis of the TEMG, we present an approximation algorithm based on the approach to solve the corresponding DST to minimize energy consumption. Finally, an instance without loss of generality is given to illustrate that our proposed algorithm can further reduce energy consumption when completing the multicast transmission.

2   System Model

Due to satellites definite orbital movement, the topology of SGIN is time-varying and predictable. The planning horizon $[0, T)$ can be divided into m time intervals. Assume that the topology remains fixed during each interval τ_i, but changes immediately between intervals. As shown in Fig. 1, we use a series of snapshots to describe the system as:

- *Source vertex sv*, representing the remote sensing satellite, which can transmit observation data.
- *Destination vertices* $DV = \{dv_1, dv_2, ...dv_n...\}$, representing multiple terrestrial sites, which receive observation data.
- *Optional vertices* $OV = \{ov_1, ov_2, ...ov_n...\}$, representing other satellites in the network, which can be selected to relay observation data when generating multicast routes.

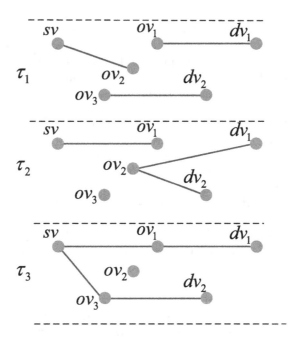

Fig. 1. System described by snapshot with 3 time intervals.

Besides, the edges between different vertices in each time interval indicate that they can transmit data to each other.

In Fig. 1, sv starts a multicast session at $t = 0$, and needs to send the observation data to all vertices in emphDV by multicast. We do not consider multipath transmission and assume that a vertex would consume a certain amount of energy whenever it forwards data. Therefore, to enable the minimum-energy multicast, it is of vital importance to select relay nodes and then build the multicast tree with the minimum number of transmissions.

3   Problem Formulation

3.1   Time Expanded Graph for Multicast

In this subsection, we develop the traditional TEG to the TEGM so as to utilize the correlation between time-varying resources and solve the multiple duplicates of the same destination node in the graph. TEGM is shown in Fig. 2, denoted by $G(V, E, W)$ as:

- V is the set of vertices, the components ($V_{sv} = \{sv^i\}$, $V_{dv} = \{dv_n^i\}$ and $V_{ov} = \{ov_n^i\}$) of which correspond to the duplicates of the sv, DV and OV in each time interval. We add *aggregated destination vertices* $ADV = \{adv_1, adv_2, ..., adv_n, ...\}$ to abstract and aggregate the duplicates of each

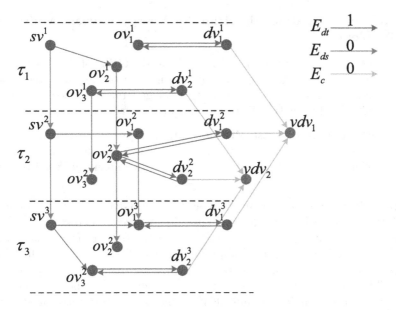

Fig. 2. TEGM.

destination node. The reason is that multiple duplicates of the same destination node in the traditional TEG, would make it difficult to ensure that each destination node only receives multicast data once. Therefore, $V = V_{sv} \cup V_{dv} \cup V_{ov} \cup ADV$.

- E, a set of directed edges, consists of *data transmission edges*, *data storage edges* and *aggregating edges*. The *data transmission edges* $E_{dt} = \{(v_k^i, v_n^i)|v_k^i \in V_{sv} \cup V_{ov}, v_n^i \in V_{dv} \cup V_{ov}\}$ exist between different vertices in the same time interval, indicating that these vertices can transmit data to each other. The *data storage edges* lie between two duplicates of the same vertices at adjacent intervals, which can be denoted as $E_{ds} = \{(v_n^i, v_n^{i+1})|v_n^i, v_n^{i+1} \in V_{sv} \cup V_{ov}\}$. Considering that the remaining storage resources of satellites are limited, the *data storage edges* between duplicates of some vertices at adjacent intervals are not available. The *data storage edges* could characterize the ability of vertices to cache data, which is quite important for correlating network resources in adjacent time intervals. Specially, we add *aggregating edges* $E_a = \{(dv_n^i, vdn_n)|dv_n^i \in V_{dv}\}$ to associate the duplicates of destination vertices in each time interval with their corresponding virtual destination vertices.

- M, a set of metrics, indicate different types of edges in E. The corresponding metric M_{dt} for *data transmission edges* is set to 1, indicating that a vertex has to transmit once when sending data to its neighbors. For *data storage edges*, the element in can be written as M_{ds}. Since caching data does not consume the transmission energy of vertices, M_{ds} is equal to 0. In addition, since the *aggregating edges* are virtual links, their corresponding metric M_a is also set to 0.

3.2   An Approximation Algorithm for Energy Efficient Multicast Problem

In this subsection, with the proposed TEGM, the definition of EEM is presented. In addition, inspired by the approach of solving Directed Steiner Tree problem [6], we propose an approximation algorithm for generating a feasible Minimum Energy Multicast Tree (MEMT) to minimize the energy consumption.

Energy Efficient Multicast Problem in Temporal Networks: Given a TEGM, generate a directed tree $G(V, E, W)$ with the minimum number of transmissions, which is rooted at $sv^1 \in V_{sv} \subseteq V$ and spans all vertices within $VDV \subseteq V$.

Directed Steiner Tree Problem over TEGM: Given a TEGM, denoted as $G(V, E, W)$, we aim to find a minimum *cost* directed tree rooted at $sv^1 \in V_{sv} \subseteq V$ spanning all elements in $VDV \subseteq V$, with *cost* as the sum of weights on all edges.

Assume $T(V^*, E^*, W)$ is an approximate MEMT for corresponding EEM. Note that, not all vertices in V^* have to transmit data. Since some vertices in the original TEGM have no associated *data storage edges*, it can be considered that the number of transmissions is equivalent to that of *data transmission edges* in T. Nevertheless, the number of *data transmission edges* equals the sum of weights on all edges in E^*, i.e. *cost*. Therefore, through solving the corresponding DST over TEGM, we can find a feasible MEMT.

Algorithm 1. An approximation algorithm for EEM.

1: **Input:** A given TEGM $G(V, E, W)$.

2: **Output:** A feasible MEMT T.

3: **Construct** the complete digraph $G'(V', E', W')$ from G such that $V' = sv^1 \cup VDV$, and each element in E corresponds to a directed shortest path in G'. Besides, W' represents the distance of directed shortest path between any two vertices in V', or is set to 0 if such path is not available.

4: **Construct** the minimal directed spanning tree T' rooted at of sv^1 of G'. (Whenever there are several minimal directed spanning trees, pick an arbitrary one.)

5: **Develop** the directed subgraph G_s' of G' by replacing each edge in T' to its corresponding directed shortest path in G'. (When there are several directed subgraphs, select the one with the minimal sum of edge weights.)

6: **Find** the minimal directed spanning tree T rooted at sv^1 from G_s' (When there are several minimal directed spanning trees, pick an arbitrary one.), which is an approximate Minimum Energy Multicast Tree.

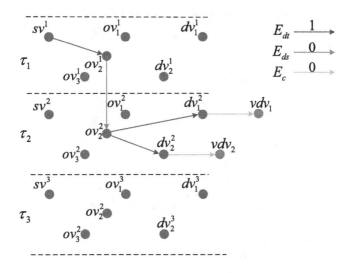

Fig. 3. MEMT for the SGIN.

4   Simulation

In this section, on the basis of the SGIN in Fig. 1, we separately apply the proposed approximation algorithm and DTBR algorithm to solve EEM. Through comparing the number of transmissions (i.e., energy consumption) and that of time intervals (i.e., delay) required to enable energy efficient multicast, the superiority of our algorithm can be verified.

The MEMT constructed by our algorithm in shown in Fig. 3. To accomplish the multicast transmission with the minimum energy consumption, data needs to be transmitted from sv to ov_2 during τ_1. ov_2 would cache the data until τ_2, and then distributes it to dv_1 and dv_2 in a single transmission.

A series of dynamic trees generated by the DTBR algorithm are shown in Fig. 4. Note that, the only available dynamic tree lies in the third snapchat. Therefore, within τ_3, data would be transmitted from sv to ov_1 and ov_3, and be relayed to dv_1 and dv_2 respectively.

Figure 5 shows the number of transmissions and time intervals required to complete multicast transmission. It is obvious that our algorithm can acquire less energy consumption and smaller delays than the DTBR algorithm.

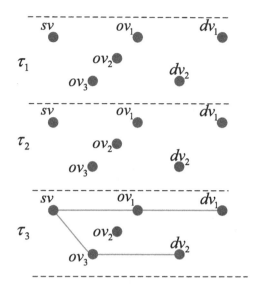

Fig. 4. Dynamic trees constructed by DTBR algorithm.

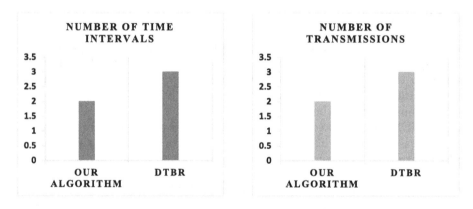

Fig. 5. Number of transmissions and time intervals.

5   Conclusion

In this paper, we propose an approximation algorithm for the energy efficient multicast problem in temporal networks based on the modified TEG to minimize the energy consumption. Specially, the modified TEG is constructed by adding some corresponding *aggregated destination vertices* and *aggregating edges* in the traditional TEG. Simulation results illustrate that our proposed algorithm can achieve less energy consumption and smaller delays compared to the DTBR.

Acknowledgments. This work is supported by the National Natural Science Foundation of China (61871456, 91638202, 61401326, 61571351), the National Key Research and Development Program of China (2016YFB0501004), the National S&T Major Project (2015ZX03002006), the 111 Project (B08038), Natural Science Basic Research Plan in Shaanxi Province of China (2016JQ6054).

References

1. Caini, C., Cruickshank, H., Farrell, S., Marchese, M.: Delay- and disruption-tolerant networking (DTN): an alternative solution for future satellite networking applications. Proc. IEEE **99**(11), 1980–1997 (2011)
2. Chiti, F., Fantacci, R., Tassi, A.: An efficient harq scheme for applications in multicast communication systems. Wirel. Commun. Mob. Comput. **15**(7), 1131–1141 (2015)
3. Ford, L.R., Fulkerson, D.R.: Flows in Networks. Princeton University Press, Princeton (1962)
4. Ruiz, P.M., Gomez-Skarmeta, A.F.: Approximating optimal multicast trees in wireless multihop networks. In: 2005 IEEE Symposium on Computers and Communications, ISCC 2005, Proceedings, pp. 686–691 (2005)
5. Seok, Y.: Device and method for multicast in wireless local access network (2009)
6. Watel, D., Weisser, M.A.: A practical greedy approximation for the directed steiner tree problem. J. Comb. Optim. **32**(4), 1327–1370 (2016)
7. Zhao, W., Ammar, M., Zegura, E.: Multicasting in delay tolerant networks: semantic models and routing algorithms. In: ACM SIGCOMM Workshop on Delay-Tolerant Networking, pp. 268–275 (2006)

The Application Design of SOIS Electronic Data Sheets in Onboard Integrated Electronic System

Lijun Yang[1(⊠)], Xiongwen He[1], Bohan Chen[2], Yan Du[3], Luming Li[1], and Liang Mao[1]

[1] Beijing Institute of Spacecraft System Engineering, Beijing 100094, China
yanglijun87@126.com
[2] Institute of Manned Spacecraft System Engineering,
China Academy of Space Technology, Beijing 100094, China
[3] Institute 706, Second Academy of China Aerospace Science and Industry
Corporation, Beijing, China

Abstract. This paper analyzes the concept and research status of SEDS (SOIS Electronic Data Sheets) in the field of Spacecraft Onboard Interface Services (SOIS) of Consultative Committee for Space Data Systems (CCSDS). In order to achieve fast integration and testing of the onboard software, this paper discusses how to apply the SEDS standard in the onboard integrated electronic system of Chinese spacecraft. This paper shows the structure of the onboard integrated electronic system, the stratification of the structure, and the functions, services, protocols, and components of each layer. Based on the architecture of the system, the top-level application design of SEDS in the process of the development of onboard integrated electronic systems is presented, Taking the remote sensing and acquisition function of spacecraft as an example, the design and application examples of SEDS and the subsequent expansion methods of SEDS are given. The SEDS is used as input in the development and testing of spacecraft integrated electronic system software. The results show that the application of SEDS is helpful to realize the standardization of onboard interface and promote the spaceborne integrated electronic system and even the whole spacecraft research through automatic code generation and electronic data reuse. Shorten the system cycle.

Keywords: SOIS · Electronic Data Sheets · CCSDS

1 Introduction

Founded in 1982, the Consultative Committee for Space Data Systems (CCSDS) is the most authoritative organization in the field of space data systems. At present, there are 11 member organizations and 32 observer organizations, mainly responsible for the development of international standards for space data systems. It includes six fields, such as satellite interface, space link, space Internet, task operation and information management, interactive support, system engineering, etc. Up to now, CCSDS series standards have been implemented and applied on more than 800 spacecrafts worldwide.

M. Jia et al. (Eds.): WiSATS 2019, LNICST 280, pp. 356–364, 2019.
https://doi.org/10.1007/978-3-030-19153-5_37

Current work in the Spacecraft Onboard Interface Services (SOIS) field of CCSDS is focused on SEDS (SOIS Electronic Data Sheet). Aiming at the requirement of fast integration and testing of on-board software, SEDS can describe the device information and services interface information, and automatically generate on-board software, test cases and related documents by tools, the software, test cases and related documents are automatically generated by the tools, so that the integration, test and maintenance time of the software on board is reduced and the consistency of the data in each development stage is guaranteed. The implementation and application of this standard is beneficial to shorten the development cycle of Onboard Integrated Electronic System and reduce the development risk and cost. In this paper, the SEDS standard and foreign research and application status are analyzed, the Onboard Integrated Electronic System is studied and designed, and the application of SEDS is designed and verified based on this system.

2   Overview

In SOIS architecture, EDS (Electronic Data Sheet) is mainly used to describe device information and business interface information, called SEDS. It contains the following contents: the interface of bidirectional data exchange between SOIS protocol layers; the instructions and parameters that constitute the above interfaces; the component services that implement the mapping between two sets of interfaces; the state machine, variables, and behaviors that make up the components; and the types, variables, codes, and terminology that serve as the above references.

Besides describing the devices, SEDS can also be used to describe the interface of services, the connection relationship between services, the configuration parameters of services, and the configuration parameters of the system. In addition, SEDS has many other uses. For example, the ground operator can convert the SEDS of the device by tools, and automatically generate the task database, which is convenient to generate the control instructions for the device and to analyze the telemetry data of the device. For applications such as the space station, if astronauts connect a new device to the system network of the station, when the device stores its own SEDS inside the device, the device can be automatically identified and its data and SEDS information can be published in the space station by plug-and-play mechanism, and astronauts can subscribe to the device through a computer. Astronauts can subscribe to the device's data and SEDS through a notebook, through the SEDS parser tool to analyze the device's data, you can view the data in the interface.

Onboard software codes, test cases, interface control documents, telecontrol instructions, telemetry parsing files generated by SEDS can reduce the uncertainty and inconsistency of documents and avoid modifying a large number of documents when the requirements change. At present, the electronic data sheets used in ground test is described by CCSDS XTCE standard. It mainly focuses on telecontrol and telemetry data. After extending the description of onboard service interface to adopt SEDS standard, SEDS and XTCE can be converted by tools. The advantages of SEDS and XTCE are integrated to realize the electronic data sheets of the entire spacecraft interface software and documents.

3   Current Status of Foreign Research

At present, NASA and ESA are the first ones to launch SEDS in the international field. NASA's Goddard Flight Center implements SEDS applications in its cFE core flight software architecture; ESA is currently using JAVA development tools to support the generation and analysis of SEDS.

3.1   NASA Research Status

NASA core software system cFE has been used in many models to communicate messages between software components based on software bus, and a matching component configuration tool has been developed. Its source code is open, not only for spacecraft, but also for unmanned aerial vehicles and other systems. NASA plans to further refine the software architecture by referring to the interfaces defined by the SOIS architecture to suit the SOIS architecture. In NASA's cFE core flight software architecture, SEDS technology is used to automatically generate software configuration information to facilitate software on-demand configuration and assembly. SEDS can define the interface of the device, and can also define the interfaces of all software components. The SEDS is generated with the help of tool scanning header file. After modifying the SEDS, the new code can be regenerated. At the same time, the tele-control instructions for testing can be generated by SEDS and the telemetry data can be parsed. NASA has developed a tool that takes software component SEDS and task configuration files as input and generates C header files. Header files contain message definitions and transformation of engineering units. At present, the tool is integrated in the cFS (core flight system) creation system, and is used by several NASA centers.

3.2   ESA Research Status

SCISYS from Europe has been researching EDS for many years and is developing tools to support SEDS generation and parsing. The tool is developed by JAVA and can automatically generate onboard software code according to SEDS. The generation and use of SEDS are as follows: in the early stage of development, the SEDS file is generated by the parameters of the device, and the relevant documents can be generated and verified by the SEDS file of the tool. At this time, the generated SEDS file can generate some onboard components, such as device drivers, and also generate input for simulation. In the process of project development, SEDS can be updated directly when the parameters of new device or device change; the model or data of the system can also generate SEDS; when the system data or device data changes, they can influence each other through EDS to modify the data, and the modified SEDS file automatically updates the document by tools. In comprehensive testing, EDS can be used directly as its input without documentation, because SEDS directly contains all its documentation data.

4 SEDS Application Design

4.1 Onboard Integrated Electronic System Architecture

The Onboard Integrated Electronic System architecture is a layered architecture [1] based on SOIS. Each layer contains a variety of services and protocols. In this architecture, on the one hand, the SOIS standard services and protocol are mapped into reusable software components, on the other hand, the software components are divided into middleware layer, and together with the operating system layer and application layer, the Onboard Integrated Electronic System software is composed. The core of the architecture is the middleware layer, which contains a variety of standard protocols of CCSDS and ECSS, and provides services to the application layer through standardized interfaces, as shown in Fig. 1.

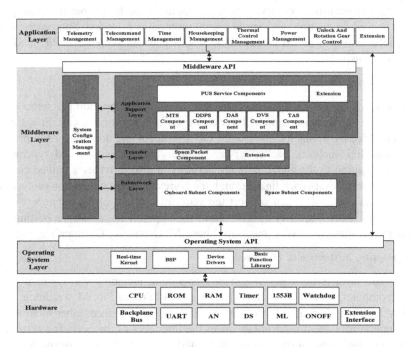

Fig. 1. Spacecraft onboard integrated electronic system architecture

(1) *Application Layer*

The application layer includes top-level functions such as telecontrol, telemetry, time management, housekeeping, thermal control management, energy management, load management and other extended applications. The services provided by the bottom layer can be used to generate different application processes by instantiating these services.

(2) *Application Support Layer*

The application support layer includes command and data acquisition service (including device access service, data pool service, device virtualization service), application programs accessing onboard devices, file and packet storage service for transferring files in the computer file systems within and between spacecraft, and time access service for acquisition. Spacecraft take time; message transfer service is used for message transfer between two applications on board the satellite; standard service defined by PUS basically covers the general functions of current Onboard Integrated Electronic System.

(3) *Transfer Layer*

Transfer/network layer is generally used only when there are multiple subnets and the applications between subnets need to communicate with each other. It provides end-to-end data transmission service between applications. In this paper, Space packet protocol is used for routing, and Space packet protocol is extended. Source/destination address information is added to its sub-header, which can support UDP/IP and other protocols extensively.

(4) *Subnetwork Layer*

Subnetwork layer includes space link and satellite link, providing a series of services for upper application support layer and transfer layer service call. Space link is mainly provided by uplink TC protocol, COP-1 protocol and downlink AOS protocol. The satellite link includes packet service, memory access service and synchronous service. In addition to the above standard services, it also provides a unified common bus interface services, in each link, through the corresponding aggregation protocol and data link layer protocol, it can support the standard services of the subnetwork, thus shielding the different underlying links from the upper. The current supporting links include 1553B bus, SpaceWire bus, serial port, ML interface, DS interface, etc.

(5) *Operating Systems and Hardware*

Hardware layer is the basis of software operation, including various hardware of satellite computer, mainly including CPU, RAM, ROM, EEPROM watchdog, timer, telemetry interface, telecontrol interface, serial port, bus interface, other interfaces.

The operating system layer encapsulates the interfaces of the operating system and provides a unified application programming interface. As long as any operating system supports a unified access interface in this structure, it can be applied in the Onboard Integrated Electronic System. Therefore, it can support the update of the operating system. Its composition includes real-time operating system, device driver, board-level support package (BSP), basic function library and so on.

4.2 SEDS Application Design

The application of SEDS can run through the lifecycle of Onboard Integrated Electronic System development, as shown in Fig. 2. In the software design and development stage, SEDS is generated by the designer; SEDS is divided into two types: one is the existing software component or model, which can be generated directly by the tool; the other is the new software component which can be generated by writing and can be used as the input of component model. In the software testing phase, these SEDS generated above can be read as the input of the simulation test through the tools to ensure the correctness while reducing the test configuration work; in the later test phase and the spacecraft flight ground control phase, these electronic data sheets can also be generated through the ground system tools database. The database can also be used for developer testing, third party testing, and on orbit testing. In short, once the electronic data sheets is formed, its application runs through all stages of project development and operation.

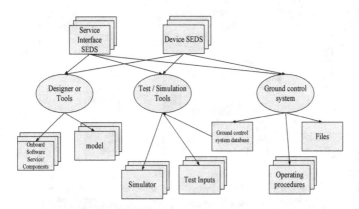

Fig. 2. Top level design for SEDS application

4.3 SEDS Application Example

Figure 3 is an example of telemetry acquisition in satellite software. sheets left to right, it corresponds to hardware, subnetwork layer, transfer layer, application support layer and application layer of satellite Onboard Integrated Electronic System in turn. The left D1, D2, D3 are different devices, D1, D2 are connected to RTU1 (remote unit) through RS422, CSB bus, RTU1 through 1553B and Onboard Integrated Electronic System central management unit (SUM); D2 is directly connected to SUM through 1553B. To collect the telemetry data of these devices, the telemetry acquisition and organization are completed by 1553B and serial port convergence protocol, and the spatial packet is formed. The packet is sent to the application support layer by the spatial packet protocol. The message transmission primitive of the message transmission service transmits the telemetry to the telemetry processing module of the application layer. Spread over the space link to the ground.

In this process, SEDS begins with the device. Because different devices support different data when describing device information, SEDS includes device access interface, device functional interface, device access protocol, device virtual control steps, and subnetwork layer usage information, such as SEDS1, SEDS2, SEDS3, etc. With the layering of Onboard Integrated Electronic System architecture, the higher the level of convergence, the less the number of SEDS devices, such as SEDS5, which aggregates the relevant information of SEDS1 and SEDS2, and then adds 1553B aggregated access interface. SEDS describes the services interface, mainly describes the two-way data exchange interface between services, including business/component parameters (can be input or output), commands, services primitives, the mapping relationship between the three and the state machine that represents the relationship between services.

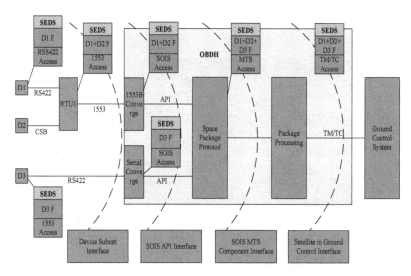

Fig. 3. SEDS describes the device, business interface

4.4   SEDS Application Extension

At present, the electronic data used in ground integrated test system, launching base data system and flight control center data system are described by CCSDS XTCE standard, mainly focusing on telecontrol and telemetry formats, and their applications are mainly for data annotation and Analysis on the ground. The description of the onboard services interface/device is based on SEDS standard, and the subsequent conversion between SEDS and XTCE can be done by the tool, as shown in Fig. 4. With the input of onboard service interface/device SEDS and task configuration file, XTCE standard database is generated, and different mission systems are provided to use the conversion to facilitate the connection between onboard data and ground data. SEDS can be used not only in the various life cycle of onboard software development, but also in ground system.

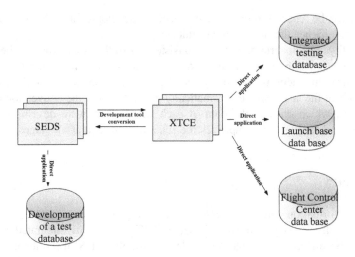

Fig. 4. Conversion of SEDS to XTCE

5 Design Verification

Based on 43 software components of SMU, which include CCSDS spatial link protocol, nine SOIS standard services and protocols, space Internet domain protocol, 1553B protocol, and 12 services, convergence protocol and driver in the PES protocol of ECSS, 43 SEDS of service interfaces are developed for devices with SMU interfaces. 15 SEDS of devices were developed. In the software development stage, debugging and testing stage, unit testing, assembly testing and confirmation testing stage, SEDS was used as the test input. According to statistics, in the development and testing phase of the Onboard Integrated Electronic System, the time is saved about 35%, and the automatic generation part of the integrated code accounts for 62%. At the same time, there is no inconsistent interface state caused by file problems. Through SEDS development, testing in the rapid integration, reusability, reliability has a prominent role, mainly reflected in:

(1) Rapid integration testing. Because SEDS describes the configuration parameters, interfaces, and connections between services, after selecting the relevant software components according to the requirements, the call relationships between these components can be described by SEDS, and the calling codes can be generated by the tools, which can realize the rapid integration within the Onboard Integrated Electronic System. Plug and play is realized through SEDS in the development and testing phase and the whole satellite testing phase, which greatly reduces the configuration work and shortens the testing period.

(2) Reusability. At present, the software components are all stored in the data base, and the SEDS corresponding to the interface is also stored in the data base. For the same component used in different fields, because its parameters, interfaces and invocation relations are fixed, the SEDS of the service interface can be reused. For the same device, when the communication protocol is fixed, the SEDS of the

device can be reused throughout the spacecraft development cycle. The higher the reuse, the higher the development efficiency.

(3) Reliability. The uncertainties and inconsistencies of the documents can be reduced by generating onboard software codes, test cases, interface control documents, telecontrol instructions, telemetry parsing files and so on through SEDS. The database of the tasks can be automatically generated after the conversion of SEDS by tools, which ensures the data of each stage of software development, integration and testing. This improves the reliability of data at all stages.

6 Summary

The device information and service interface information are described by SEDS, and the onboard software is generated automatically. The Onboard Integrated Electronic System can be quickly integrated and tested. Through SEDS, the onboard software code, test cases, interface control documents, telecontrol instructions, telemetry and parsing software can be automatically generated, which can reduce the uncertainty and inconsistency of documents and avoid modifying a large number of documents when the requirements change. At the same time, by extending the automatic conversion between SEDS and ground XTCE, flexible and reliable data exchange among software developers, integrated testing, flight control center and equipment producers can be realized. While SEDS achieves rapid integration and testing, its reusability and reliability help to improve development efficiency and shorten the entire spacecraft development cycle.

References

1. He, X.: Design and implementation of spacecraft avionics software architecture based on spacecraft onboard interface services an packet utilization standard. In: IAF 66th International Astronautical Congress (2015)
2. Spacecraft Onboard Interface Services—XML Specification for Electronic Data Sheets CCSDS 876.0-R-3. CCSDS, Washington, D.C. (2018)
3. SOIS XML EDS Prototyping Test Plan & Report. CCSDS 876.1-Y-1. CCSDS, Washington, D.C. (2018)
4. Spacecraft Onboard Interface Service. CCSDS.850.0-G-2. CCSDS, Washington, D.C. (2013)
5. Spacecraft Onboard Interface Service—Specification for Dictionary of Terms For Electronic Data Sheets for Onboard Components. CCSDS 876.1-R-1. CCSDS, Washington, D.C. (2013)
6. Electronic Data Sheets and Common Dictionary of Terms for Onboard Devices and Components. CCSDS TBD.0-G-0. CCSDS, Washington, D.C. (2013)
7. Zhao, Y.: XML-based satellite plug-and-play interface module design-academy of device. J. 4 (2012)

Research on Wireless Networks
for Intra-spacecraft

Cuitao Zhang[✉], Xiongwen He, Dong Zhou, Panpan Zhan,
Zheng Qi, and Yong Xu

Beijing Institute of Spacecraft System Engineering, Beijing, China
zct259@163.com

Abstract. With the rapid development of onboard avionic technology, there are increasing requirements for internetworking, modularization and non-cable of spacecrafts. The onboard wireless networks technology provides one of the most important foundation to enable communication among intelligent nodes inside a spacecraft. This paper studies the application of wireless sensor networks for spacecraft. Wireless networks technology has significant advantages in reducing the weight of spacecraft, saving time in spacecraft integration. Based on wireless sensor networks, a scheme for spacecraft avionic system is put forward. The avionic system overall networks are a combination of wired and wireless networks. The block diagram and key interface design of the spacecraft overall networks are given. The design proposal of the wireless node and the data flow of the spacecraft are also analyzed. The results show that the application of wireless networks scheme is reasonable and feasible. The onboard wireless networks technology can meet the new requirements of the spacecraft in internetworking, modularization and non-cable.

Keywords: Wireless networks · Spacecraft · Research and application

1 Introduction

With the development of space technology, wireless communications technology in the spacecraft plays an increasingly important and even irreplaceable role to meet the networking, modular and cableless requirements and other new demands [1]. Wireless communications technology gets more and more attention. The CCSDS (The Consultative Committee for Space Data Systems) has accelerated the research on wireless communications technology in recent years on the basis of years of wireless communications study and tracking. At present, several wireless communications standards have been developed for the application field of aerospace [2–4]. For spacecraft environmental monitoring and control, CCSDS recommends the use of the wireless sensor networks standard IEEE 802.15.4 [5]. IEEE 802.15.4 standard is intended to be used in low-speed wireless personal area networks (PAN). The key objectives are to achieve low power consumption and low cost. The CCSDS has defined the MAC (Medium Access Control) layer and PHY (Physical layer) layer protocol, but the network layer and higher layer are not defined. Based on the CCSDS standard, this

M. Jia et al. (Eds.): WiSATS 2019, LNICST 280, pp. 365–370, 2019.
https://doi.org/10.1007/978-3-030-19153-5_38

paper studies the application of wireless sensor networks in spacecraft environment monitoring and control.

2   Advantages of Wireless Communications Technology

In the field of spacecraft environmental monitoring and control, a large number of spacecraft test data and health data need to be collected. These data are generally required to be collected through a dedicated cable for capture and transmission. The demands for this type of transmission cables on spacecraft are generally very high, and the connections between the cables are often very complex. Thus the spacecraft assembly is usually very cumbersome, time-consuming, inefficient and error-prone. These inconveniences prompt spacecraft engineers to concern about the use of wireless communications technology to replace the traditional cables. The use of wireless communications technology can not only achieve cableless data transmission and reduce the weight of the satellites, but also facilitate the modular design of spacecraft equipment, realize information network transmission, and improve the flexibility of spacecraft design, test and assembly. Due to structural reasons places where traditional wired way can not cover are easily covered by wireless way. At the same time, the convenience of the wireless connection is conducive to the realization of spacecraft structure functional innovation.

3   Applications of Wireless Networks on Spacecraft

3.1   Application Situations

The CCSDS standard points out that the wireless communications technology based on IEEE 802.15.4 is used to build wireless personal area network (PAN). The network coverage is generally about 10 m, within the spacecraft size. The data transfer rate is about 250 kbps, almost equal to the data amount of spacecraft telemetry and tele-control. It is very suitable for the spacecraft environmental monitoring and control identified by the CCSDS recommendation. This paper focuses on the application of wireless sensor networks standard in spacecraft telemetry and remote control.

3.2   Design of Spacecraft Networks

In the wireless personal area network based on IEEE 802.15.4, the network topology is a star topology. The gateway node can communicate with the spacecraft backbone network. The wireless node can communicate with the gateway node. A block diagram of the spacecraft networks based on PAN networks are shown in Fig. 1.

In Fig. 1, each compartment of the spacecraft establishes a separate PAN network. Each PAN network can cover a communication distance of 10 m, supporting the number of wireless nodes in 10–100. Each PAN network has a separate gateway connected to the cable backbone network, and can communicate with the backbone network. The spacecraft backbone network can be a conventional 1553B bus, a CAN bus or

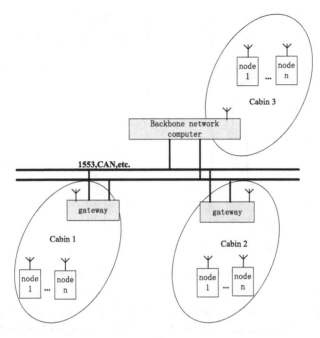

Fig. 1. Block diagram of spacecraft networks based on PAN networks.

other bus. In each cabin, the wireless nodes can only communicate with the gateway nodes, and can not communicate directly with each other. If they need to communicate with each other, they should first communicate with the gateway node, their messages should be exchanged though the gateway node. Wireless nodes have the basic telemetry acquisition, instruction output and other similar functions. The wireless transmitter transmission power is in the range of −15 dBm–10 dBm. Considering the electromagnetic compatibility, radio radiation, interference and other issues, the specific distribution of the RF nodes on the spacecraft should be paid special attention to.

3.3 Wireless Node Design

The design of wireless node needs to consider the reliability of the node itself. One of the byproducts of using wireless technologies in space systems is the extra flexibility introduced when implementing wireless fault-tolerance and redundancy schemes. The redundant design of the wireless interface compared to the traditional cable connection is much easier to achieve well effect. The design is simple, as shown in Fig. 2.

The left of Fig. 2 shows the traditional cable connection implementing the cross redundant backup design. Each device's main and backup is connected to another device's main and backup through two sets of cables. Cable connections are relatively complex outside the devices. The right side in the figure shows the wireless way of cross redundant backup design. The main and backup of each device are connected to two wireless communication modules respectively inside the equipment. No connections are required outside the equipments to realize the cross redundant backup design.

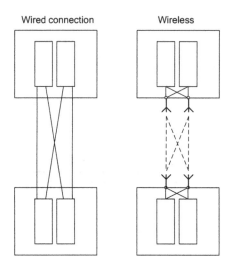

Fig. 2. Redundancy wireless interface design

Wireless communications technology effectively reduces the weight of spacecraft, and makes it easy to achieve networking, modular, cableless design of spacecraft.

Although the wireless communications technology has the above advantages, in practical applications there are many problems to be solved, such as EMC, EMI, RF radiation and other issues [6–8]. The solutions of these problems have a great relationship with the specific structure of the spacecraft. Different structures often require for different solutions. In addition, the advantages of wireless communications lie in the design of wireless nodes. The principle of wireless node design is to simplify the spacecraft cable connection, shorten the spacecraft assembly time, reduce the spacecraft cable weight, and achieve spacecraft modular assembly.

At present, in the field of industrial control, a wide range of complete wireless communications protocols such as ZigBee, based on IEEE 802.15.4 PHY layer and MAC layer protocol, implement higher-level network layer protocol. These protocols not only realize the CCSDS defined single-hop competition access and single-hop scheduling access, but also realize multi-hop relay communications. The user can configure the required communication functions. Texas Instruments also offers a dedicated monolithic solution CC2530. The chip integrates the ZigBee complete protocol stacks and RF transceiver functions. The MAC layer and PHY layer protocol are compatible with IEEE 802.15.4 specification. It can work in the 2.4 GHz frequency band, and is compatible with CCSDS standards. This chip also integrates a 8051 microprocessor and an ADC, SPI/UART ports, GPIO ports and other peripherals. Its power consumption is very low. It consumes only 0.4 μA current in the idle state. In the working state, It consumes about 24–29 mA current. The supply voltage is 3.3 V, assuming 10% duty cycle operating conditions, the average power consumption is only

8.3 mW, meets the CCSDS proposal of less than 10 mW. The wireless node (or gateway node) design based on this chip is shown in Fig. 3.

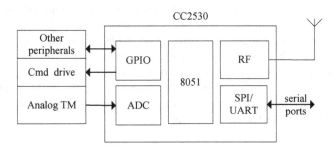

Fig. 3. Wireless node design

Based on the design of wireless node above, traditional devices of the spacecraft only need to add a few small components (such as command-drive chips, multi-channel analog multiplexers, etc. according to the specific requirements of the single device) so as to discard the heavy cables for telemetry and telecontrol. In this way, it is very easy to extend more than 10-channels of command-drive and telemetry acquisition channels for each device. The channel number is enough for each device. Gateway nodes need to use the serial ports to communicate with the spacecraft backbone network through the gateway computer. This scheme easily meets the spacecraft common equipment requirements for remote control and telemetry. And the cost is very low. For each device, the weight of the new added wireless node is much lighter than the weight of external cables. The advantages of wireless communications technology are fully reflected. Low-speed wireless communications technology not only reduces the weight of spacecraft, but also reduces the time cost in spacecraft assembly. Spacecraft testing is also simplified. Improving efficiency is the purpose and real reason to apply wireless communications technology on spacecraft.

3.4   TC and TM Data Flows

For the TC data flow, if the spacecraft receives direct commands from the ground, the TC data flow is the same as the original wired connection. This article will not describe. For indirect commands or data injection, the backbone network computer will first send the received data to the corresponding gateway computer, the gateway computer will then transfer the information to the gateway node through the serial ports interface, and finally the gateway node will send the data wirelessly to the target wireless node. If the wireless node receives the TC information, it will execute the commands directly.

For the TM data flow, each wireless node sends their telemetry data to the gateway node of the PAN network. The gateway node collects the data and then transfers the data to the gateway computer through the serial ports. The gateway computer then processes the data and then sends the data to the backbone network. The backbone network computer groups the data into packages and sends them down to the ground.

4   Conclusion

Based on the analysis of the CCSDS standard of wireless networks, this paper summarizes the advantages of wireless communications technology applying on spacecraft, and puts forward an application example of wireless networks for spacecraft environment monitoring and control. The paper gives the block diagram of the spacecraft networks and the key interface reliability design. It also gives the design suggestions of the wireless nodes, analyzes the feasibility of the design scheme, and points out the problems that need to be solved urgently. Wireless networks technology can meet the spacecraft demands in networking, modularization and non-cable, and is a very promising technology for future spacecraft.

References

1. Zhou, L., Cao, S.: Application of wireless sensor networks for environmental monitoring in spacecraft. Chin. J. Space Sci. **32**(6), 846–848 (2012)
2. CCSDS. Wireless network communications overview for space mission operations. CCSDS 880.0-G-1. CCSDS, Washington, D.C. (2010)
3. Zhou, Y.: Overview of standardization in CCSDS spacecraft onboard interface services. J. Spacecraft TT&C Technol. **30**(z1) (2011)
4. CCSDS. CCSDS 850.0-G-2, Spacecraft Onboard Interface Services. CCSDS, Washington, D.C., USA (2013)
5. CCSDS. Spacecraft onboard interface systems-low data-rate wireless communications for spacecraft monitoring and control. CCSDS 882.0-M-1, Magenta Book. CCSDS, Washington, D.C. (2013)
6. Intanagonwiwat, C., Govindan, R., Estrin, D., Heidemann, J., Silva, F.: Directed diffusion for wireless sensor networking. IEEE/ACM Trans. Netw. **11**, 2–16 (2002)
7. Wang, J., Yao, Y.: Application of WSN technology on parameter monitoring in spacecraft and campaign with more missile. Navig. Control **15**(2) (2016)
8. Liu, Y., Zhang, S., Sun, B.: Prediction of wireless communication interruption between spacecraft. Spacecraft Eng. **22**(6) (2013)

Design and Implementation of Multi-partition Paralleled Image Storage Hardware File System for MARS Rover

Yong Xu[1(✉)], Cuilian Wang[1], Lei Zhao[1], Pangfeng Wu[2], and Wenjuan Li[1]

[1] Beijing Institute of Spacecraft System Engineering, Beijing 10094, China
andrexu@163.com
[2] Shandong Aerospace Electro-Technology Institute, Yantai 264670, China

Abstract. Mars rover mission carried many types of cameras, which need to complete complex science exploration and research task, it's hard to meet the demands of image paralleled storage and access operations using the traditional Chang-E's multiplex and storage scheme. Due to the speed and memory size limitation of on-board highly reliable radiation-hardened computer, the ground computer file system cannot be realized. This paper designed a FPGA based hardware paralleled image file system to meet the requirement of image data storage management in the Mars rover explore task. In addition the multi-type and multi-camera data file storage system of MARS rover is implemented in the actual rover's computer which provided multi-partition paralleled reading and writing of multi-image files and on demand addressing and copying functions while ensuring high reliability.

Keywords: MARS rover · Paralleled image storage · Hardware file system

1 Preface

Mars is the closest planet to Earth in the outer orbit of the solar system, and the cost of human exploration of Mars is relatively low. And because of Mars special space position, many of its features are similar to Earth, which makes it most possible for humans to develop a second home in the universe. At the same time, studying Mars can help us understand some of the mysteries of the birth and evolution of the solar system. Among all kinds of information obtained by the Deep Space Exploration Research Institute, image information is the most intuitive and core information. Mars Exploration Rovers (MERs), the Spirit and Opportunity rovers that landed on Mars on January 4 and 25, 2004, respectively, have traveled tens of kilometers on Mars and sent back more than 100,000 photographs, including precious exotic photographs of meteors, sunsets, eclipses and cyclones. Among them, the May 19, 2005 "courage" captured the scene of the sunset of Mars. In January 2007, NASA was named the best picture of Mars in the public election. What is more significant is that they not only found evidence of volcanic eruptions on Mars, but also found silica (May 2007), adding new evidence to the Martian theory of life, and the strongest evidence of water

M. Jia et al. (Eds.): WiSATS 2019, LNICST 280, pp. 371–379, 2019.
https://doi.org/10.1007/978-3-030-19153-5_39

on Mars so far [1]. As a result, deep space probes usually carry multiple sets of cameras. Take the identical designs of Courage and Opportunity for example, each has nine visible-light cameras, while Curiosity has up to 17 cameras, including mast cameras, obstacle avoidance cameras, landing cameras, chemical analysis cameras, and mechanical arm cameras. Machine and so on. Multi-type camera, multi-imaging system, multi-resolution, multi-camera and other factors pose new challenges to the storage and management of Mars Rover image data. Generally speaking, because the onboard computer needs to withstand the examination of long-term harsh space irradiation environment, the performance of the electronic components of the selected space-level computer is rather limited, and it is impossible to deploy the more mature file system similar to NTFS and YAFFS [2] on the ground. Therefore, the traditional remote sensing satellite and the Chang'e Lunar Exploration Series before our country can not be deployed. The on-orbit image data storage of the measuring task is based on the multiplexing storage scheme of FPGA [3]. After multiplexing, the task data is sequentially stored in NandFLASH chip according to VCDU format, and read and write sequentially by recording and playback. Data storage scheme based on multiplexing storage [4] is more suitable for sequential recording and playback of data similar to tape recorders, and can not meet the data management requirements of Mars Rover multi-camera, multi-partition, multi-resolution, multi-system image flexible storage and access and image processing on the Mars surface. Under the premise that it is impossible to improve the performance and memory of the irradiation-resistant computer on board, a hardware file system based on FPGA architecture is designed to meet the requirements of large-capacity storage management, high-speed parallel storage of multi-type camera data, flexible data access and on-orbit data processing.

According to the data characteristics of Mars exploration mission and camera image data, this paper designs a hardware-only image partitioning parallel storage and management file system, which includes a set of bad block table management, partitioning management, image file data storage management and access mechanism of Nand-FLASH high-capacity memory, and designs a scheme based on the system. The hardware file system of Mars Rover image storage is realized. In addition to Nand-FLASH data memory, the MRAM is used as bad block information management and file structure management memory. The file system management mechanism is implemented based on FPGA, and a set of hardware-only partitions is implemented. Parallel, fast and highly reliable Rover image management system.

2 Design of Image File Storage System

In the Mars rover, the image file storage and processing system is located in the onboard computer, which mainly completes the storage and management of image data sent by each camera, the engineering load multiplexing storage, image compression, compressed bit stream organization transmission, telemetry/playback data download, and data communication with the central processing control module. The image file storage and processing system adopts A/B dual-machine cold backup mode. The single component block diagram is shown as follows, mainly including the following functional components (Fig. 1):

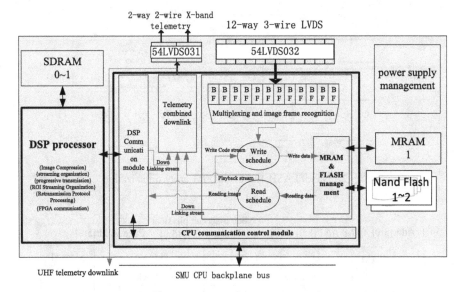

Fig. 1. Block diagram of data storage & processing module

(1) LVDS interface module: completes the function of high-speed differential interface between receiving load data and downloading data to data transmitter.

(2) FPGA chip module: 3 million gate anti-irradiation FPGA is used to realize CPU communication, image data reception and NandFLASH file system, MRAM and NandFLASH interface and redundant fault-tolerant management.

(3) MRAM & FLASH Memory Array Module: MRAM stores all kinds of non-volatile information, including bad block table, read-write address, etc. NandFLASH is used to store large capacity data.

4) DSP & SDRAM processing component: used for image compression algorithm, bit stream organization and downlink control. DSP uses an anti-irradiation space-level DSP processor, and two SDRAM buffers are added to provide the computational buffers needed by the image compression algorithm.

(5) Power management: module power supply, power on reset, voltage conversion and so on, generating 3.3 V, 1.5 V and 1.8 V voltage.

3 File System Data Management Mechanism Design

In order to meet the requirement of miniaturization of the Mars rover, the memory array uses two 3-D stacked NDFLASH chips [5] (eight K9F8G08U0M substrates) with 64 Gbits per chip, so the total on-board physical capacity is 64 Gb * 2 = 128 Gb = 16 GB (Figs. 2 and 3).

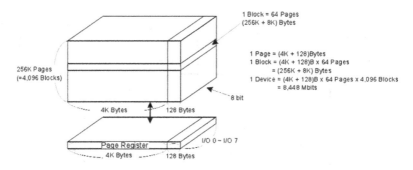

Fig. 2. NandFLASH K9F8G08U0M array organization

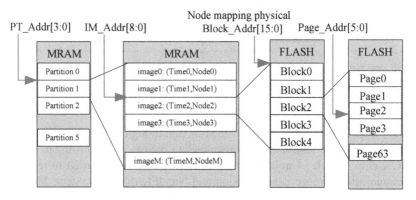

Fig. 3. Organization of panchromatic image data in MRAM

As shown above, each K9F8G08U0M substrate contains 4096 Block, and each Block contains 64 pages, 4096 Byte per page. Therefore, each board has a total storage space of 4194304 pages, 65536 blocks, and block address range 0x0000–0xFFFF. In order to support parallel storage in random access by camera and by image frame, the image storage system is divided into 11 partitions and the storage space is allocated according to the block as shown in the following table (Table 1):

Data organization in MRAM is shown in the figure above. The initial allocation of 32bit * 2K logical space in MRAM stores the bad block information of the whole Nandflash, and then allocates 6K * 32bit space to store the node information of image files in each partition. The node information of each file includes 32bit time and some 32bit node physical address information. To store the above information, a magneto-electric memory (MRAM) with a capacity of 8 Mb (32 * 256K) is mounted on the board. All the data stored in MRAM is stored in three addresses and accessed according to TMR. The logical space is 32bit * 85K. Besides the 32bit * 8K space analyzed above, there is a surplus of 32bit * 77K left for storage others in formation.

Table 1. Image storage partition address allocation table

Partition	Type data	Block address range	Capacity
1	Camera1	0x0000–0x0FFF	512 MB
2	Camera2	0x1000–0x1FFF	512 MB
3	Camera3	0x2000–0x2FFF	512 MB
4	Camera4	0x3000–0x3FFF	512 MB
5	Camera5	0x4000–0x4FFF	512 MB
6	Camera6	0x5000–0x5FFF	512 MB
7	Engineering telemetry	0x6000–0xBFFF	≥ 5 GB
8	Internal use cache 1	0xC000–0xCFFF	512 MB
9	Internal use cache 2	0xD000–0xDFFF	512 MB
10	Alternate partition 1	0xE000–0xEFFF	512 MB
11	Alternate partition 2	0xF000–0xFFFF	512 MB

4   FPGA Design Implementation of File System

It mainly includes five modules: image receiving and writing module, DSP image access module, image node information initialization module, MRAM controller, FLASH access control module (Fig. 4).

(1) Image Receiving and Writing Module: Create image file: Use the way that the nodes in the partition are sequentially used backward. When the image is created, the MRAM access module reads the current image count n of the corresponding partition; then the newly created file uses n + 1 image and writes the current timestamp; read the corresponding n + 1 node address in MRAM. Return to the image data receiving module; update the partition node count to N + 1, write back the current image count of the corresponding partition in MRAM; write to the image file: image data is received after image creation; every page of data received, call FLASH control module to write to FLASH. Close the image file: After receiving the image file close command, the remaining less than 1 page of data, fill a full page, write to FLASH (Fig. 5).

(2) DSP image access module complete the random access of image files, when we need to read and write the image; take the first logical address of the P partition in MRAM, access the inner block address (physical address), with the physical address to NandFLASH to continuously access five blocks of data content. The first page of the first node of each image is the Affiliated Information page, which stores the relevant time, camera parameters and other parameters. After the first page of the first node is accessed back to a total of 298 data pages, an image data is obtained.

(3) Image node information initialization module establishes the image node information by erasing the partition from the partition start address Bi to the end block address Ei, and updating the failed block information to the bad block table; and searching from the partition start block address to the end block. The first block address of the consecutive block is the starting address of the node; the storage

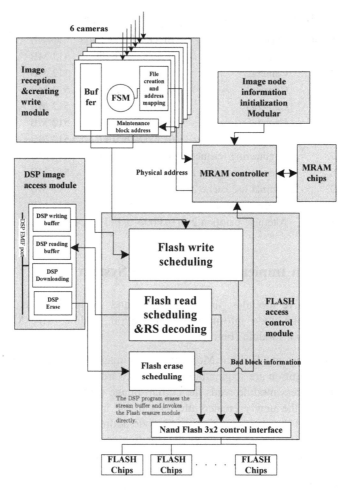

Fig. 4. Top-level architecture design of the FPGA files system

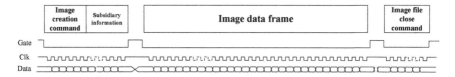

Fig. 5. Image files creation and write operation initialed by camera

mapping is related to the first node address of the partition in MRAM; if enough 512 nodes are established or queried to the end address of the partition. Clear the number of images stored, indicating that the partition is empty.

(4) MRAM controller which manages one piece of MRAM, provides five independent MRAM access ports, and five ports can access MRAM at any time. Three

physical addresses P_A0~2 are converted from one logical address L_A by cyclic priority processing the access requests of each port.

(5) FLASH Access Control Module realize the universal operation control of Nand-FLASH, including the detection of bad block information of FLASH, and control the operation with block as the unit. FLASH erase, erase in block units; FLASH programming, write one page of data per programming unit; FLASH read, read data in page units.

5 Design Result Analysis

In order to adapt to the long-term work of deep space exploration interstellar navigation and the system reliability under harsh space irradiation environment, the file system FPGA is designed and implemented with a space-level anti-irradiation 3 million gate FPGA. The design is based on VHDL language, and its design hierarchy tree is shown in the image below. There are 19 top-level modules (Fig. 6).

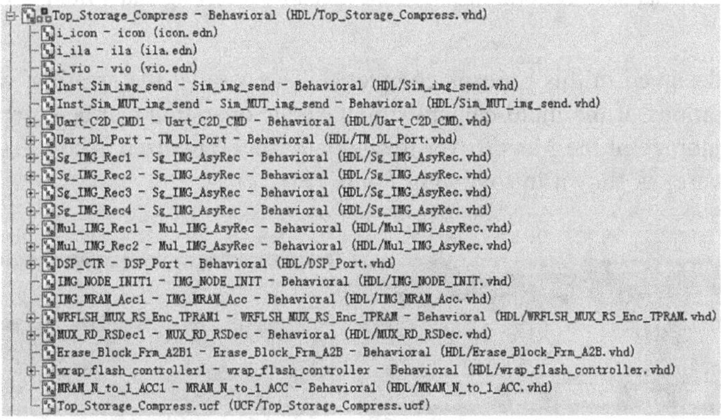

Fig. 6. Hierarchy tree of FPGA design

Each module is implemented by a secure state machine, and three modular redundancy (TMR) design is adopted on key registers and critical control paths, supplemented by [6] on orbit scrubbing, which can effectively resist the effects of single particle interruption in space environment and ensure the reliability of the rover in the mission process. The design is finally synthesised by ISE9.2 XST tool. The design resources are shown in the following table (Table 2):

ModelsimSE 6.4 is used to simulate the design. Peripheral camera interface, NandFLASH and other devices test bed and test records are compiled. Image files are created, received and accessed are simulated. Some simulation results are as follows (Fig. 7):

This research designs a 1:1 verification board for the on-board file storage system of the Mars rover. As shown in the following figure, the on-board verification of proposed

Table 2. Resources utility in XQR2V3000 (−4) FPGA

Logical resources	Used	Available	Utilization
Slice	3832	14336	26%
4-LUT	6821	28672	23%
FF register	4216	28672	14%
BRAMs	53	96	55%
Highest frequency		66.878 MHz	

Fig. 7. Simulation waveform of image file creation, receiving and writing operation

file system designed in this paper is completed. The parallel file creation, writing and closing operations of the multi-camera simultaneous operation can be completed, and the flexible storage of the Mars Rover image data can be realized. The file system test master software, as shown in following figure (Fig. 8).

Fig. 8. Evaluation board (left) and Monitor software (right) for image file storage and compression system

6 Conclusion

In Mars exploration mission, Mars Rover carries many kinds of exploration cameras, which need to complete complex scientific exploration and exploration tasks on the surface of Mars. The multiplex storage scheme of traditional satellite can not meet the flexible and parallel storage and access requirements of image data. Due to the highly reliable anti-irradiation satellite-borne computer, the main frequency and memory of the controller are very small, so that the existing computer file system on the ground can not be realized. In this paper, a parallel image file system based on FPGA is designed to meet the requirements of image file storage and management in Mars exploration mission. The parallel image file system is implemented by FPGA, which takes into account the characteristics of high speed, high reliability and high flexibility, and resists by adopting various measures such as RS encoding and so on. Multi-type, multi-camera data file storage and management, while ensuring high reliability, provides multi-partition, multi-image file parallel read-write and on-demand addressing functions, effectively solving the traditional multiplexing storage equipment in the image data parallel storage and Mars surface image processing on-demand access problems.

References

1. Xu, X.: MERs Deep-space Imagery Compression on—board. J. Test Meas. Technol. **21** (2007)
2. Charles Manning: Introducing YAFFS, the first NAND-specific flash file system. http://www.linuxdevice.com/articles/AT9680239525.html
3. Pei, N., Li, K., Zhao, L.: Rate adaptive image extraction method based on FPGA. Modern Electron. Tech. **36**(19) (2013)
4. Wu, Z.: Research of on-board date routing multiplexing and srorage. Harbin Institute of Technology (2016)
5. 3D-Plus Co. Memory Module Flash Nand 4Gx16-SOP 3DFN64G16VS8477, November 2012
6. Yin, M.: SEU-tolerant design of SRAM FPGA for space use. Spacecraft Environ. Eng. **28**(6) (2011)

Research for Data Communications Based on IPv6 in Integrated Space-Ground Network

Panpan Zhan[(✉)], Xiongwen He, ZhiGang Liu, Zheng Qi, Ming Gu,
Cuitao Zhang, and Dong Yan

Beijing Institute of Spacecraft System Engineering, Beijing 100094,
People's Republic of China
panpan3210@qq.com

Abstract. The integrated space-ground network and its architecture are the focus and difficulty in research. Aiming at the problems of the incompatibility between satellite networks, satellite networks and ground networks, and the insufficiency of space network address resources, we propose an integrated space-ground network architecture based on the next generation Internet protocol IPv6. It combines the space communication protocols defined by CCSDS. The network layer protocol based on IPv6 is the foundation of the architecture. It ensures the interconnection and interoperability among inter-satellite networks and intra-satellite networks. The protocol of each layer in the architecture is designed. The IPv6 protocol, inter-satellite and intra-satellite transmission format, inter-satellite routing and intra-satellite communications are analyzed and designed. The experimental results show that the designed satellite router realizes the network communication and routing of IPv6 packets in intra-satellite and inter-satellite networks. It shields the differences between the satellite and ground network systems at the protocol level. It makes the satellite networks have good scalability and adaptability as with as the ground networks.

Keywords: Satellite network · Inter-satellite routing ·
Intra-satellite communication

1 Introduction

With the rapid development of aerospace industry and the advantages of space network in Civil Communications and military fields, integrated space-ground network has become a hot research topic and key project in China. In recent years, the construction of information network has made rapid progress and achieved remarkable results. However, the development of China's space information network and ground Internet is very imbalanced, showing the characteristics of "the space information network is weak and ground Internet is strong". In the space information network, China has initially built communication relay systems, navigation and positioning systems, earth observation systems and other systems. However, each satellite system is built independently, the number of satellites is seriously insufficient, and the type of satellite is relatively simple. What is more prominent is that satellites do not have a space network and cannot have a comprehensive efficiency. The planning and designs are not efficient

M. Jia et al. (Eds.): WiSATS 2019, LNICST 280, pp. 380–391, 2019.
https://doi.org/10.1007/978-3-030-19153-5_40

in integrated space-ground network, the advantages of the integration of space and earth has not been realized, and the information service capability of the integrated space-ground network has not been formed [1–4].

The International Maritime Satellite (INMARSAT) has 11 GEO communication satellites in orbit, which can provide global mobile communication and IP access services. The United States and other countries have established satellite communication systems with space networking such as Iridium and AEHF. The idea of integrated space-ground network such as Interplanetary Network (IPN) and transitional communication satellite system (TSAT) is proposed. A series of space technology experiments, including space router (IRIS) are carried out [5–9].

The construction of space network and the engineering realization are still needed to be strengthened. Although there are nearly 100 satellites such as remote sensing satellites, navigation satellites and communication satellites on orbit, the satellites have the following problems:

(1) Most of these satellites are working independently and are unable to communicate and connect with one another.
(2) Communication protocols between satellites are not uniform and inconsistent with international standards. As a result, they can't communicate with each other. Even if there are individual satellites that can communicate with each other, they are still isolated from most satellites. The other satellites are difficult to access and communicate with them.
(3) The number of ground stations is insufficient. One single satellite operation mode is difficult to interact with the ground, and can't be integrated into a unified network with the ground network.

Similar to the initial stage of the development of ground network, the development of space technology has put forward higher requirements for the framework of space communication [10]. It is necessary to guarantee the integration of space information system and ground information network through network technology. The ground Internet technology based on IP network provides an effective means for the integration of space network and ground network. At present, the global IPv4 address resources have been basically exhausted, and the address resources allocated to our country are very few, which can not meet the needs of the space network for address resources. However, the next generation Internet protocol IPv6 has a huge amount of address resources, which can solve that problem. At present, IPv6 is the only core protocol that can replace IPv4 in the next generation of Internet. It has been widely recognized and applied in the field of Internet [11].

Therefore, based on the next generation Internet protocol (IPv6), this paper designs the data Communications in Integrated Space-ground Network. It shields the differences between different systems at the protocol level, and provides users with cross-system services and applications that do not need to distinguish between space and ground. It provides design schemes and technical reference for the implementation of integrated space-ground Network.

2 Communication Protocol Architecture Design

The integrated space-ground network consists of the ground network and space network. It uses a unified technical framework, unified technical system and unified standards. Space network consists of space-based backbone network, space-based access network and ground node network. Ground network is more mature, so this paper focuses on the space network, including inter-satellite communication (including satellite-to-ground communication) and intra-satellite communication.

In order to realize the communications in integrated space-ground network, the design of space network communication protocol architecture follows the following principles:

(1) Integration and standardization principles. The space network and ground network are considered as a whole networks, the network can be interconnected and interoperable, and the network protocols meet uniformed standards.
(2) Efficient adaptability and scalability principles. The space network is required to be as scalable and adaptable as the ground network, with flexible network expansion and access modes.
(3) Minimum Cost Principle. It is designed to avoid the problem of extra overhead caused by multiple protocol transformations to adapt to different communication protocols, so that the network communication performance is optimal.

Based on the above principles, the satellite network adopts IP packet forwarding mode in the network layer which is the same with the ground network, and puts the IP network above the physical layer and the data link layer of the satellite network. When interconnecting with the ground network, the satellite network can be regarded as an independent subnet, which assigns IP addresses to each satellite node, and carries out network access and routing through the satellite router to shield the changes of network topology. The space network topology based on IP is shown in Fig. 1.

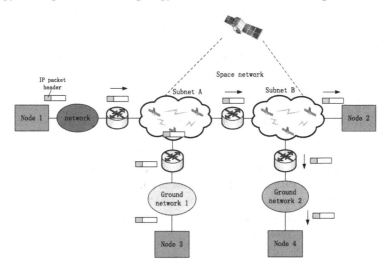

Fig. 1. Space network topology based on IP

The lower layer of IP network layer mainly completes the data transfer function between nodes of a certain data link. When it needs to transmit across multiple data links and networks, IP network layer can realize the data transmission from node to node in different satellite networks or ground networks. In Fig. 1, the network packet switching and routing control are implemented by satellite routers between the satellite sub-networks and between the satellite sub-networks and ground networks. By satellite router, when node 1 communicates with node 2 in satellite subnet B, it sends IP packets to subnet A and routes to node 2 via two hops. When node 1 communicates with node 4 on the ground, it transmits to ground network 2 after several routes. It completes point-to-point communication with node 4 across inter-satellite network and ground network.

The adoption of IP network in satellite networks has the following advantages:

(1) The interconnection of multiple heterogeneous subnets is realized. IP network layer can shield the differences between different networks, including satellite networks and ground networks, realize data transmission across multiple networks, and enable communication between space networks and any nodes in the ground network, so as to achieve the purpose of space-ground integration and interconnection.

(2) It is compatible with ground network. As one or more sub-networks, satellite networks can directly use IP packets to communicate with ground networks, which reduces the cost of protocol conversion.

(3) The network has good reliability and flexibility. Due to the packets forwarding, when a satellite communication link is disconnected, the satellite network can reflect the change of the satellite network topology in real time. The routing table can be modified to forward packets to the destination satellite node through other links. It is suitable for the satellite network environment with changing network topology.

The design of inter-satellite network and intra-satellite network communication protocol is the key problem in integrated space-ground network. Although the CCSDS protocol is relatively perfect in space application, it can not be directly used to communicate with the ground network and has the problem of protocol conversion. In order to realize the interconnection between satellite network and ground network, the ground network protocols are applied to satellite network. Combined with the IPv6 protocol of ground network, the space communication protocols defined by CCSDS, the integrated space-ground network communication protocol architecture as shown in Fig. 2 is established. The network layer protocol based on IPv6 is the foundation of the architecture. It ensures the interconnection and interoperability among the inter-satellite networks and the intra-satellite networks.

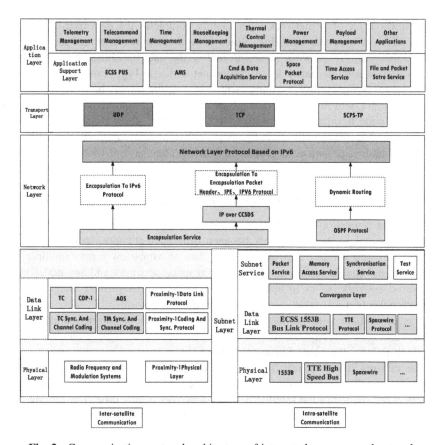

Fig. 2. Communication protocol architecture of integrated space-ground network

2.1 Physical Layer

According to the different communication links of satellite network, the physical layer is divided into the inter-satellite communication physical layer and the intra-satellite communication physical layer. The physical layer of inter-satellite communication includes radio frequency modulation system and Proximity-1 physical layer. The physical layer of inter-satellite communication includes 1553B bus, TTE high speed bus, spacewire bus and so on.

2.2 Data Link Layer

The data link layer is responsible for data transmission between nodes directly connected to physical links. In the data link layer, the inter-satellite communication protocol uses CCSDS defined Telecommand space data link protocol (TC), Advanced Orbiting System (AOS), COP-1, Proximity-1 spatial link protocol, remote control synchronization and channel coding, telemetry synchronization and channel coding, Proximity-1 coding and synchronization sub-layer protocol. According to the different communication media, the intra-satellite communication protocol can adopt five kinds of standard services: 1553B communication protocol, TTE communication protocol, spacewire communication protocol, convergence layer protocol and subnet services.

2.3 Network Layer

Based on IPV6, the network layer provides the upper layer users with a unified addressing and routing service in inter-satellite network and intra-satellite network, which is the core of the whole architecture. The network layer includes IPV6 protocol, packaging service, IP Over CCSDS protocol and OSPF protocol. The IP packets are encapsulated by IP Over CCSDS, and the IPE header is added. Then the IP packet is encapsulated by the encapsulation of the encapsulated services, which can be transmitted through the inter-satellite link.

2.4 Transport Layer

The transport layer provides end to end data transmission services for the upper users and plays a reliable role in transmission. The layer is processed only on communication nodes without processing on the router. The specification of space communication protocol – Transport Protocol (SCPS-TP) defined by CCSDS, can be used as a transport layer protocol. Because IPV6 protocol is applied in the network layer, TCP and UDP can be used directly in the transport layer. The packets generated by them can be transmitted directly to IPV6 protocol in the network layer for processing. The communication protocol and process are not different from those of the ground network, which facilitates the efficient integration of space network and ground network.

2.5 Application Layer

The application layer is mainly related to the spacecraft platform and load application, which can be divided into application support layer. In the application support layer, this protocol architecture provides standard services for satellite-ground operations, remote operations between spacecrafts and intra-satellite data transmission through PUS protocols and application support layer services of SOIS. The PUS standards are part of the European space standards organization ECSS's standard series, which defines 16 types of operations to meet the needs of ground operations. The standards describe in detail how these businesses are used by the ground for standardized operations, and define in detail the data formats for business requests (remote packages) and business reports (telemetry packages).

3   Integrated Design of Inter-satellite and Intra-satellite Communications

3.1   IPv6 Protocol

Although both are in IP network layers, IPv6 and IPv4 are very different in protocol format. IPv4 has a fixed header length and a larger number of fields. These fields need to be filled in regardless of whether they are used in the communication process, which wastes and consumes network bandwidth and routing performance greatly. In order to reduce the burden of the router, IPv6 protocol omits the checksum field of the packet header, so the router no longer calculates the checksum, thus improving the efficiency of data routing, and part of the identification code becomes an option to re-optimize the packet format.

One IPv6 address consists of 16 bytes and can effectively provide almost unlimited network address space, so the IPv6 address resources used by spatial networks are no longer restricted.

The second major improvement to IPv6 is simplification of the header, which consists of seven domains (13 domains in IPv4) with a fixed length (40 bytes). This improvement enables routers to process packets more quickly, thus improving router throughput and shortening latency.

The third major improvement is to support the optional functions. This is essential for the new header, because the previously required domains have now become optional domains, allowing routers to simply skip options that are not relevant to it. This improvement speeds up the packets processing [12].

3.2   Inter-satellite and Intra-satellite Transmission Format Design

According to the integrated communication protocol architecture, the conversion between satellite-to-ground and inter-satellite protocols is minimized. KA or laser high-speed physical links are used for satellite-to-ground and inter-satellite's communications in physical layer. AOS protocol is used in this layer. IPv6 protocol, encapsulation service and IP Over CCSDS protocol are used in network layer. UDP protocol is used in transport layer. Space packet protocol or other extended protocols are used in application layer. Inter package protocol or other extension protocol.

Between satellites, complete data with synchronous header and LDPC encoding is transmitted in physical layer. The data link layer uses CCSDS AOS protocol, encapsulates AOS header, insertion domain, MPDU header and other data domains. The network layer uses encapsulation header and IPv6 format to carry out routing processing based on IPv6. The transmission layer uses UDP packet, while the application layer uses space packet or user defined data.

The processing of each layer in the inter-satellite and intra-satellite integrated communication protocol architecture is shown in Fig. 3. When the data is transmitted, the protocol header and the data of the application itself are appended to the data. All packets received from the upper layer are passed to the underlying layer by encapsulating the protocol header of the layer. The encapsulation header and IPE header are removed by the satellite router, and then sent to the receiver. After each protocol layer, there will be information identifying the sender and receiver of the packet. The data link layer is identified by the spacecraft ID in AOS. The network layer has an IPv6 address. The transport layer uses the port number as the address to identify the two end nodes, and the application layer uses the APID of the space packet as the address of the application.

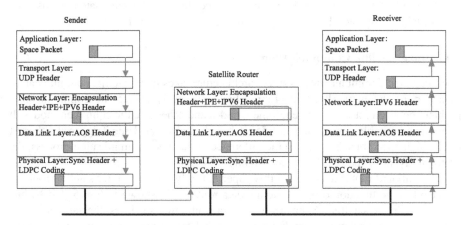

Fig. 3. Processing of each layer in integrated communication protocol architecture

3.3 Inter-satellite Routing

To make the satellite networks to be interconnected, the problem of inter-satellite routing must be solved first.

Although the routing problem has been well solved and applied in ground networks, there are still many difficulties in satellite network. In performing inter-satellite routing, the following main characteristics of satellite networks should be considered:

(1) Limited capacity for on-board processing and storage;
(2) Longer time delay and higher error rate;
(3) Highly dynamic network topology.

In view of the fact that many dynamic routing algorithms require high computing and storage resources, and the processing capacity of satellite router is still low, in order to solve the above problems, this paper uses static routing design, through hardware and software cooperation, in a less overhead way to achieve inter-satellite routing function. The operation of routing table is the key part of the whole routing protocol. It records the routing information of the whole network. It has a direct effect on the efficiency of routing. Therefore, a hardware routing table is designed, which contains IPv6 address, next hop address and inter-satellite port information. The inter-satellite routing table is designed in Fig. 4.

After receiving the inter-satellite data, FPGA parses the network layer and gets the next hop address and inter-satellite communication port by looking up the table according to the destination IPv6 address. If they are the other satellite's data, it sends

| Destination IPv6 Address | IPv6 Address of Next Hop | Inter-satellite communication Port |

Fig. 4. Structure of inter-satellite routing table

them to that satellite through the inter-satellite link port. If they are the local satellite's data, it sends them to the local satellite's device through the intra-satellite bus. The routing table is updated by injecting routing tables through software.

3.4   Intra-satellite Communication

The integrated communication protocol architecture takes intra-satellite communication as a part of the network architecture, which effectively solves the communication problem between intra-satellite equipment nodes and other satellite equipment nodes. It is not only suitable for traditional 1553B bus, but also for Time-Triggered Ethernet (TTE) high-speed bus. Because of the difference of the bus communication process, the protocol layers of the two buses are slightly different.

The onboard router designed in this paper not only serves as inter-satellite routing, but also has the function of intra-satellite data routing. As shown in Fig. 5, 1553B bus is used inside the satellite. After receiving data from other satellites, the satellite router parses the space packet and sends them to 1553B bus through the space packet protocol, packet service and data link aggregation protocol. And then the RT address of the device in 1553B bus is generated according to the APID (application layer address) in the space packet. The space packet is routed to the destination bus device in 1553B bus.

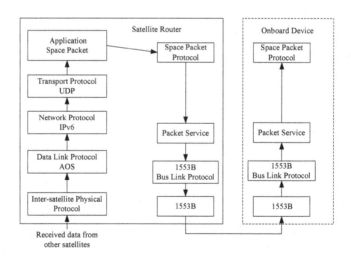

Fig. 5. Communication process of intra-satellite 1553B bus

As shown in Fig. 6, a TTE high-speed bus is used in the satellite. After receiving data from other satellites, the satellite router knows that the data needs to be processed by itself after judgement by software. The data in network layer is transmitted downward to the data link layer. Then the data is sent to TTE bus as the data link layer data by adding the MAC header of the TTE network. After receiving the data, the device on the TTE bus can get the application data and process it after parsing UDP/IPv6 packets. It can be seen that the process is interconnected with the ground network.

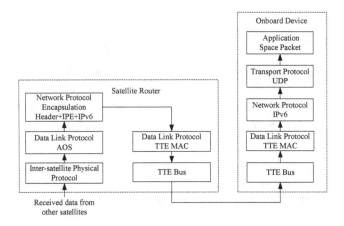

Fig. 6. Communication process of intra-satellite TTE bus

4   Implementation and Verification

This paper tests and verifies the satellite router based on IPv6, which realizes inter-satellite communication and intra-satellite data routing. In hardware configuration, a four-core anti-irradiation processor S698PM with main frequency up to 600 MHz is used, a FPGA chip XC5VFX130T is used, and a six-channel high-speed TLK2711 interface is used in inter-satellite data communication. The inter-satellite links are established with six satellites (or ground stations) through laser or KA antennas, and the peak rate of receiving and receiving can reach 1 Gbps per interface. A high-efficient time-triggered Ethernet TTE is used in intra-satellite bus communication to realize high-speed data communication of various devices in the satellite, and the data transmission rate can reach up to 1 Gbps.

The data from other satellites is sent to TLK2711 interface 1 by ground test equipment. After judging that the data will be sent to the other satellite by IP address, the satellite router queries the routing table and sends it to the destination satellite through TLK2711 interface 2. In this way, the inter-satellite communication function is verified.

The satellite data is sent to TLK2711 interface 1 of the satellite router through the ground test equipment. After judging that the data will be processed by the satellite's SMU (System Management Unit) device by IP address, the satellite router sends it to SMU via TTE bus. As shown in Fig. 7, The IPv6 packets communicated through TTE bus are monitored by the network monitoring tool WireShark. The satellite router is the transmitter, its IPv6 address is fd01:: A, and the receiving address is fd01:: 6. The satellite router receives the local satellite's IPv6 packet and routes it to the other device in the local satellite. In this way, the intra-satellite communication function based on IPv6 is verified, which indicates that the IPv6 packet can be transmitted directly in the intra-satellite network.

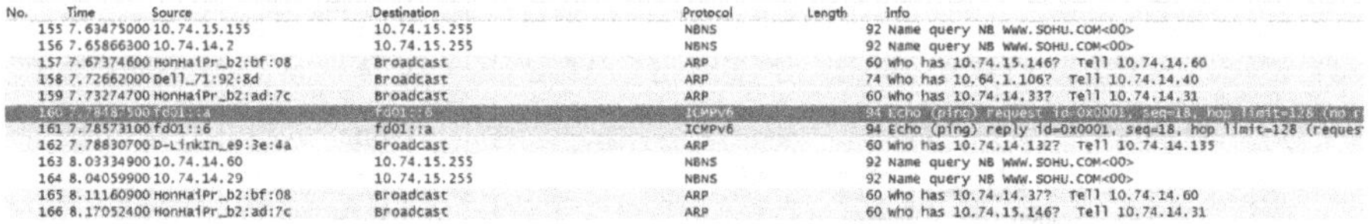

No.	Time	Source	Destination	Protocol	Length	Info
155	7.63475000	10.74.15.155	10.74.15.255	NBNS	92	Name query NB WWW.SOHU.COM<00>
156	7.65866300	10.74.14.2	10.74.15.255	NBNS	92	Name query NB WWW.SOHU.COM<00>
157	7.67374600	HonHaiPr_b2:bf:08	Broadcast	ARP	60	Who has 10.74.15.146? Tell 10.74.14.60
158	7.72662000	Dell_71:92:8d	Broadcast	ARP	74	Who has 10.64.1.106? Tell 10.74.14.40
159	7.73274700	HonHaiPr_b2:ad:7c	Broadcast	ARP	60	Who has 10.74.14.33? Tell 10.74.14.31
160	7.84133100	fd01::6	fd01::a	ICMPv6	94	Echo (ping) request id=0x0001, seq=18, hop limit=128 (no r
161	7.78573100	fd01::6	fd01::a	ICMPv6	94	Echo (ping) reply id=0x0001, seq=18, hop limit=128 (reques
162	7.78630700	D-LinkIn_e9:3e:4a	Broadcast	ARP	60	Who has 10.74.14.132? Tell 10.74.14.135
163	8.03334900	10.74.14.60	10.74.15.255	NBNS	92	Name query NB WWW.SOHU.COM<00>
164	8.04059900	10.74.14.29	10.74.15.255	NBNS	92	Name query NB WWW.SOHU.COM<00>
165	8.11160900	HonHaiPr_b2:bf:08	Broadcast	ARP	60	Who has 10.74.14.37? Tell 10.74.14.60
166	8.17052400	HonHaiPr_b2:ad:7c	Broadcast	ARP	60	Who has 10.74.15.146? Tell 10.74.14.31

Fig. 7. IPv6 packets from satellite router to SMU

The experimental results show that the designed satellite router realizes the whole network communication and routing of IPv6 packets in intra-satellite, inter-satellite and ground network. It ensures the whole network access with the minimum protocol overhead.

5 Conclusion

The integrated space-ground network is one of the important designs of the system engineering. The implementation of the integrated space-ground network will push the top-level design of information system and the integration of space and ground to a new height, and will realize the leap-forward improvement of the service ability of information system in China [13]. Aiming at the present situation and requirement of integrated space-ground network, this paper presents the design of integrated space-ground network communication protocol architecture based on IPv6, and analyzes and designs IPv6 protocol, inter-satellite communication format based on UDP/IPv6 and CCSDS protocol, inter-satellite routing, inter-satellite communication and so on. Finally, it gives the experimental verification. It provides technical support for the construction and engineering implementation of integrated space-ground network.

References

1. Wu, M., Wu, W., Zhou, B., et al.: Some thoughts of integrated space-ground network architecture. Satell. Netw. **10**(3), 30–36 (2016)
2. Jia, M., Gu, X., Guo, Q., Xiang, W., Zhang, N.: Broadband hybrid satellite-terrestrial communication systems based on cognitive radio toward 5G. IEEE Wirel. Commun. **23**(6), 96–106 (2016)
3. Jia, M., Liu, X., Gu, X., Guo, Q.: Joint cooperative spectrum sensing and channel selection optimization for satellite communication systems based on cognitive radio. Int. J. Satell. Commun. Netw. **35**(2), 139–150 (2017)
4. Jia, M., Liu, X., Yin, Z., Guo, Q., Gu, X.: Joint cooperative spectrum sensing and spectrum opportunity for satellite cluster communication networks. Ad Hoc Netw. **58**(C), 231–238 (2016)
5. Florio, M.A., Fisher, S.J., Mittal, S., et al.: Internet routing in space. In: Prospects and Challenges of the IRIS JCTD. In: Proceedings of IEEE Military Communications Conference, Orlando, FL, pp. 1–6 (2007)
6. Pulliam, J., Zambre, Y., Karmarkar, A., et al.: TSAT network architecture. In: Proceedings of IEEE Military Communications Conference, San Diego, CA, pp. 1–7 (2008)
7. Johnson, J.D., Connary, J.A., Thompson, J., et al.: Internet routing in space NMS architecture. In: Proceedings of IEEE Aerospace Conference, Big Sky, MT, pp. 1–11 (2009)
8. Cuevas, E.G., Esiely-Barrera, H.A., Kim, H.W., Tang, Z.: Assessment of the internet protocol routing in space-joint capability technology demonstration. Johns Hopkins APL Tech. Digest **30**(2), 89–102 (2016)
9. Shen, J.: Some thoughts of chinese integrated space-ground network system. Eng. Sci. **8**(10), 19–30 (2006)
10. Zhang, N., Zhao, K., Liu, G.: Thought on constructing the integrated space-terrestrial information network. J. China Acad. Electron. Inf. Technol. **10**(3), 223–230 (2015)
11. Wu, J., Wu, Q., Xu, K.: Research and exploration of next-generation internet architecture. Chin. J. Comput. **31**(9), 1536–1548 (2008)
12. Tanenbaum, A.S.: Computer Networks, 2nd edn. Pearson Education, New York (2003)
13. Sun, C.: Research status and problems for space-based transmission network and space-ground integrated information network. Radio Eng. **47**(1), 1–6 (2017)

Integration Design of IPv6 and Time-Triggered Ethernet on Spacecraft

Ming Gu[✉], Panpan Zhan, Xiongwen He, and Dong Yan

Institute of Spacecraft Engineering System, Beijing 100094, China
gumingnr@163.com

Abstract. Internet protocol (IP) and time-triggered Ethernet (TTE) are two important emerging technologies for spacecraft information systems and networks. How the TCP/IP protocol stack, including the IPv6 protocol and the TTE be integrated into the integrated electronic system of spacecraft is introduced. In particular, it is studied that the implementation method of using IPv6 protocol on the time-triggered Ethernet. The problem that the embedded TTE network card does not have the built-in IPv6 protocol and cannot directly support IPv6 is solved. The integration and application of TTE and IPv6 are realized in the spacecraft integrated electronic software architecture. The experiments and tests can indicate its correctness and the effectiveness.

Keywords: Onboard networks · IPv6 · TTE

1 Introduction

In recent years, the functions and performances of spacecraft have been continuously developed and strengthened. Especially, the information system of spacecraft is becoming more and more informational, networked, standardized and intelligent.

There are many kinds of information and large amount of data generated and interacted on the new generation spacecrafts. The number of applications involved in information exchange is large, and the relationships are very complex. It is necessary to evolve from a traditional onboard data bus to a multi-node multi-source information network. The highly integrated onboard electronic information system has also replaced the traditional separate isolated buses and data links with integrated high-speed, high-reliability networks. With a unified network to meet the platform's high-reliability control and large-capacity transmission requirements [1], it is modular and scalable, avoiding the sharp increase in complexity and reliability, and thus better adapt to the enhancement of spacecraft electronic information system functions. The Time Triggered Ethernet (TTE) [2] is a promising solution.

There are more and more information interaction requirements among multiple spacecraft and ground user nodes. Space information network and space-terrestrial integrated information network are the focus of current research work. Extending the widely used IP network technology to the space has become the mainstream research direction in recent years [3]. Especially, the application of IPv6 technology on spacecraft, which has broader development prospect, large address capacity and good

Published by Springer Nature Switzerland AG 2019. All Rights Reserved
M. Jia et al. (Eds.): WiSATS 2019, LNICST 280, pp. 392–400, 2019.
https://doi.org/10.1007/978-3-030-19153-5_41

adaptability for network dynamic, is an important key technology of future space-terrestrial integrated network [4].

In response to these development trends and needs, research and experimentation are required to integrate the IP protocol system (especially the IPv6 protocol) on the new type spacecraft bus and network. This paper presents the design scheme and implementation method of integrating TTE and IPv6 on spacecraft integrated electronic equipment in engineering experiments, including the solved technical problems.

2 Onboard TTE Network

Time-Triggered Ethernet is a new type network which integrates synchronous clock and time-triggered protocol to the widely used standard Ethernet, and can realize high-precision time synchronization and real-time performance of the whole network. TTE can be compatible with standard Ethernet event-triggered communication and real time time-triggered communication. It can meet the requirements of high reliability and real time data transmission and large capacity, random burst data transmission on the same network at the same time. The transmission rate of TTE can reach 1 Gbps, which can meet the requirement of communication capability as the onboard backbone network. TTE has perfect redundancy and fault-tolerant structure and mechanism, can provide high reliability and security, and meet the security and reliability requirements of critical scenarios.

Because of these characteristics and capabilities, TTE has been widely used in automotive network, industrial control, avionics systems, and began to be used in spacecraft electronic information systems. NASA has developed a new generation of manned spacecraft "Orion", in which the TTE-based data transmission network has been adopted after research and comparison [5].

The TTE network includes TTE terminal nodes and switches. In order to implement a TTE network on the spacecraft, besides adding the onboard TTE switch, embedded TTE ES (end system) cards and corresponding drivers are integrated into electronic information equipments which need to work as TTE terminal nodes. The configuration of TTE ES card and its interface with the bottom board conform to the general module board specifications of spacecraft electronic products and meet the following requirements:

(1) Conforming to the TTE1.0 specification;
(2) Comply with IEEE802.3 Ethernet specification
(3) Support the full duplex Ethernet link of 10/100/1000 Mbps;
(4) Support time schedule table loading function.

In view of the spacecraft embedded software environment that TTE ES card works in, it is necessary to design the TTE ES card driver suitable for the software environment, which mainly includes two parts: the initialization program of TTE ES card and the port reading and writing data operation program according to TTE network configuration.

TTE networks support three types of communication: time-triggered (TT), rate-constrained (RC), best-effort (BE), i.e. standard Ethernet communications. TT messages are used in time-triggered applications and are sent to the network in pre-determined cycles with the highest priority and the accuracy below 1 microsecond. RC messages guarantee bandwidth resources and limited delay and delay jitter. BE messages have the lowest priority according to the ordinary Ethernet communication mode. For TTE-based spacecraft information network, it is necessary to design time scheduling plan according to the specific quality of service requirements of whole network data transmission, including periodicity, delay tolerance limits, data amount, and importance and so on, and specify the ports and link types of the end systems. If it needs to mix the TTE device with the normal Ethernet device, then the TTE device should be configured to BE mode to work as the standard Ethernet.

TTE ES card has a built in network protocol architecture. In addition to being compatible with IEEE 802.3 standard Ethernet protocol, they also have a time-triggered synchronization protocol (SAE AS6802), and a network layer IP protocol (IPv4) and a transport layer protocol, UDP, built on top of the data link layer. In this way, the onboard system integrated with TTE ES card can provide the following usage mode for upper application in some scenarios without deploying external network protocol stack.

(1) Using UDP/IPv4 protocols, upper application provides user data unit, IPv4 address and port number to TTE driver software, and communicates with UDP Com mode.
(2) Using IPv4 protocol, the upper application provides user data unit and IPv4 address to TTE driver software, and communicates with IP Com mode.
(3) Without using the build in UDP/IP protocols, the upper application organizes the protocol data unit by itself and submits it to the TTE ES card in RAW Com mode for transmission in TTE network.

However, if need to use more complex network protocol functions or algorithms, or use protocols other than UDP and IPv4, we can not rely solely on the TTE ES card built-in protocol processing functions. Some expert protocol stack should be deployed on top of the TTE according to the task requirements.

3   Embedded IP Protocol Stack Transplantation

Theoretical research on space information network theories, architecture, protocols and specific algorithms has been carried out for many years. There are more than one kind of proposals and schemes for space network protocol system. This paper focuses on the implementation of IP protocol stack on spacecraft.

TCP/IP is a mature protocol system widely used in terrestrial networks. There are many specific software versions. Considering the type of processor, the limitation of computing and storage capacity, and the operating system environment of the electronic information equipment on the spacecraft, the embedded protocol stack software should be selected to meet the needs of the network function and the characteristics of the space network, which is relatively suitable for the software and hardware environment on the spacecraft. On this basis, software transplantation is carried out according to the specific interface requirements of the software architecture inside the onboard computer. If the transplanted object contains more functions that are not needed in the spacecraft network, in order to avoid occupying too much storage space on the spacecraft and affecting the processing speed, it is necessary to move the "redundant" software functions and modules off, leaving only the simplest parts that do not affect the predetermined mission requirements. After the tailoring and porting adaptation are completed, the configurable parameters in the embedded network protocol stack should be configured according to the requirements and working mode before putting them into operation.

With the networking of embedded systems, many kinds of embedded network protocol stack have appeared. According to the preceding principles, the lightweight IP stack LwIP (Lightweight TCP/IP protocol stack) is selected. LwIP is derived from the classical BSD TCP/IP stack [6]. It reduces memory usage and code size while maintaining the main functions of TCP/IP protocol, so as to adapt to the embedded environment with limited resources [7]. LwIP can be ported to a variety of embedded operating system software environments.

At present, the IPv4 protocol has been serving for many years in the ground network, facing the problem of IP address space constraints, and the newer IPv6 technology is emerging. The selection of IPv6 on the spacecraft network rather than the current more popular Ipv4 is mainly for the following reasons:

(1) The address capacity of IPv6 is sufficient.
(2) IPv6 has the ability of neighbor discovery and automatic address placement, and is more suitable for high dynamic space network [8].
(3) The development of IPv6 is more extensive. The newly developed spacecraft information system should have some technological foresight.

LwIP has IPv6 related protocols from version 2.0. Around the core function of the spacecraft network protocol stack, IPv6 and TTE technologies need to be integrated to form a new generation of spacecraft high-speed integrated information network platform, which is tailored and transplanted on the basis of LwIP (version 2.02). To this end, the most basic core content of LwIP, namely IPv4, IPv6 and UDP protocol related software modules are retained, and other protocol functions are deleted. The number of original source code .C files of LwIP is reduced from 122 to about 35, and most of the files in the directories of "core", "ipv4", "ipv6", "netif" and "drv" are retained. In the tailoring implementation phase, an embedded experimental software engineering with the same software environment as the onboard target system can be established for debugging, compiling and experimenting when code deletion and pre-compiling switches and configuration parameters are adjusted. After the original spacecraft integrated electronic system software integrates the simplified LwIP code, the object file (.o file) after compilation will increase less than 600 kB.

4   Integration Implementation in Onboard Software Architecture

Because IPv6 protocol is needed, UDP/IPv4 protocol stack built in TTE ES card can not be used directly, but LwIP protocol stack and TTE need to be integrated into onboard integrated electronic equipment.

In terms of hardware, TTE ES card can connect to the general backplane of spacecraft integrated electronic equipment through PCI-CPCI transfer, and can be accessed its internal address space by CPU. In terms of software, it is necessary to integrate the driver of TTE ES card and LwIP protocol stack software into the software system of onboard integrated electronic equipment.

Spacecraft integrated electronic software architecture is an open, hierarchical structure, and the service function modules are flexibly combined in the form of software components, so it has better scalability. The software architecture is the integrated implementation and application of several standards in CCSDS SOIS, SLS and SIS, as well as the standards of PUS and 1553B of ECSS. It realizes the standardization, modularization and reusability of spacecraft integrated electronic software, and can be used as the basic platform of spacecraft software [9]. Figure 1 is the onboard integrated electronic software architecture before the integration of IP protocol stack and TTE network.

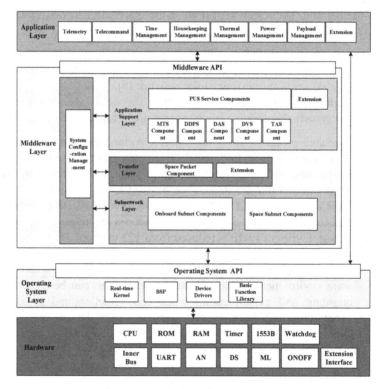

Fig. 1. Onboard integrated electronic software architecture.

As can be seen from the figure, the core of the architecture is the software middleware under the application layer and above the embedded operating system. The software middleware structure is divided into application support layer, transport layer and sub network layer. The application support layer provides supporting standard business with spacecraft platform applications. The transfer layer includes the transport layer and the network layer, which are used to process data transmission and distribution. The subnetwork layer provides a unified software interface to the upper layer, and operates different kinds of underlying data links.

The onboard integrated electronic software architecture provides good support for expanding or replacing new service functions and equipment through layered structure and component. The TTE network and its driver software and the tailored LwIP protocol stack can be integrated according to the structure and interface requirements of the architecture without affecting other original functions. The combination of TTE and IPv6 protocol can be realized to provide communication services for the upper services.

After the UDP, IPv6 and IPv4 codes in LwIP stack are processed and encapsulated as software components, they can be added to the architecture as an extension module of the transfer layer. A UDP access interface is designed for the upper layer to provide data service for sending and receiving. Mac processor and network card driver in LwIP stack need to dock with TTE ES card driver, and access operator to TTE is used as the underlying input and output interface of network card driver, as an extension module of subnetwork layer. The specific method is to modify the "ethernetif.c" file that processes the NIC driver in LwIP, including:

(1) In the network card initialization function low_level_init() defined by LwIP, the Mac address specified by the TTE ES card is configured and the initialization program of the TTE ES card is invoked.
(2) In the low_level_output() function defined by LwIP, the port selection and output operation program of TTE ES card are invoked.
(3) Call the data receiving and reading program of TTE ES card in the low_level_input () function defined by LwIP.
(4) Call the network card receiving function ethernetif_input() defined by LwIP in a TTE interrupt or background periodic software task.

Figure 2 is the relationship between LwIP and TTE protocol architecture. In the dotted frame on the right is the TTE ES card built-in processing protocol, and in the dotted frame on the left is the LwIP stack, both of which cross the transfer layer and the subnetwork layer. If only need to use UDP/IPv4 mode, it can communicate directly using UDP Com type ports provided by TTE ES cards. However, when IPv6 or other protocols are needed, the embedded LwIP stack in the system is needed to process the generated Mac frames, and then the generated Mac frames are handed over to the Mac Com or Mac Raw interface provided by the TTE ES card for transmission.

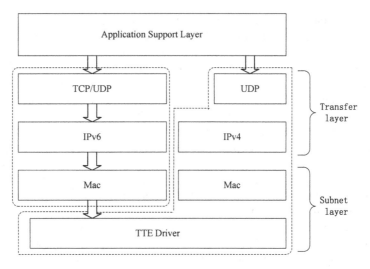

Fig. 2. TTE and LwIP protocol stacks structure.

5 Experiments and Verification

The whole TTE and LwIP integration test, as well as the construction of onboard TTE network and the experimental verification of IPv6 running on TTE, is divided into the following stages step by step:

(1) The first is the integration of TTE ES card and the driver debugging. The main work is the initialization of TTE ES card and data receiving and receiving, using the TTE network card which has been configured in the ground equipment (a PC with PCIE TTE network card and Windows TTE driver and transceiver software) as the other side. A straight-through experiment between the two TTE terminals verifies the correctness of the TTE ES card driver design and the integration in spacecraft equipment. At this stage TTE communication can use the RC mode.

(2) Secondly, the TTE ES card is used as the underlying network card of the LwIP stack. After initializing the LwIP stack and UDP interface, UDP packages are invoked from the upper layer to test the process of data transfer and output to TTE network.

(3) Then perform debugging and experimentation of IPv6 based on TTE network. One terminal is an onboard integrated electronic device that has integrated LwIP and TTE, the other is still a ground device, using the IPv6 protocol stack in Windows 7 system, and equipped with Ethernet packet monitoring tools. IPv6 addresses and UDP port numbers of both sides are specified. UDP packets are sent from TTE terminal to ground terminal. ICMP and UDP packets are observed in ground monitoring tools. The main purpose is to debug the IPv6 neighbor discovery protocol (ND) of LwIP in the onboard software. This phase is mainly to verify that the IPv6 protocol of the tailored LwIP can work properly. In this stage the TTE must use BE mode.

(4) After the software system integrated with TTE driver and LwIP protocol stack has been debugged and verified, the design and function of the TTE network carrying IPv6 protocol are tested between the two onboard equipments. Communication between TTE terminals can use RC mode or BE mode.

(5) After the direct connection experiments of the two TTE terminal devices are passed, the TTE switch is added for the farther experiments. The network configuration needs to be generated in the TTE network planning tool and loaded into the TTE switch. With the TTE switch, the TT mode network communication experiment can be carried out through corresponding planning and configuration.

(6) Finally, the network scale expansion experiment is carried out, and the number of terminals connected to the TTE switch is increased to more than 3. Each terminal uses UDP/IPv6 protocol to communicate with each other. In turn, an IPv6 communication experiment on a hybrid network composed of a TTE network and a standard Ethernet can be performed.

Expected results are obtained from the debugging tests and experimental verification conducted in the above order, which verify the correctness and effectiveness of the technical solutions and implementation methods introduced in this paper.

6   Conclusion

It is a new attempt to apply IP network protocol system and time trigger technology to spacecraft, especially to run IPv6 protocol on TTE network, which has technical value and application prospect. On the basis of integrating embedded TTE ES card hardware into spacecraft integrated electronic equipment, the embedded LwIP protocol stack software is tailored and integrated by using the layered and modular extensible framework of spacecraft integrated electronic software architecture. The transport layer, network layer and mac layer protocols are combined with the Raw Com method of the TTE ES card to enable simultaneous integration of IPv6 and time-triggered technologies on the spacecraft information network. Running IPv6 protocol system on TTE network can realize powerful and perfect network, which is easy to realize platform and payload network integration, inter- and intra- network integration, space and terrestrial expansion network integration, and ensure high reliability and real-time performance of large-capacity information transmission of spacecraft.

This paper is not a theoretical study of network protocols, but a solution to the practical technical problems of the implementation of new network technologies in aerospace engineering. The introduced design principle, implementation method and verification results can provide reference for the design and application of spacecraft information system and network using IP network protocol and time triggering technology.

References

1. Grams, P.R.: Ethernet for Aerospace Applications. NASA Report 20150011061 (2015)
2. Loveless A.: TTEthernet for Integrated Spacecraft Networks. NASA Report 20150002995 (2015)
3. Ivancic, W., Stewart, D., Wood, L.: IPv6 and IPsec Tests of a Space-Based Asset. the Cisco Router in Low Earth Orbit. NASA Report 20080022425 (2008)
4. Jaff, E., Pillai, P., Yim, H.: IP multicast receiver mobility support using PMIPv6 in a global satellite network. IEEE Commun. Mag. **53**(3), 30–37 (2015)
5. Scott, D.N.: Orion project status. In: AIAA SPACE 2013 Conference and Exposition (2013)
6. Zoican, S., Vochin, M.: LwIP stack protocol for embedded sensors network. In: 2012 9th International Conference on Communications, COMM 2012, pp. 221–224 (2012)
7. Yuan, Z., Lu, Y.: Analysis and optimization of lightweight TCP/IP protocol stack mechanism. Comput. Eng. **41**(2), 317–321 (2015)
8. Daniel, M.: Satellite Systems Engineering in an IPv6 Environment. CRC Press, New York (2009)
9. Xiongwen, H., Bowen, C., Dong, Y., Jianbing, Z., Ming, G.: Design and implementation of spacecraft avionics software architecture based on spacecraft onboard interface services and packet utilization standard. In: IAF 66th International Astronautical Congress (2015)

Study on Autonomous Mission Management Method for Remote Sensing Satellites

Lu Chao[✉] and Ren Fang

Beijing Institute of Spacecraft System Engineering, Beijing 100094, China
doggiez@sina.com

Abstract. A remote sensing satellite is an earth observation satellite that acquires ground image information in space. It plays an important role in various areas such as resource surveying, environment monitoring and geological mapping. As the number of satellites increases, observation missions become more diverse and complicated as well as growing rapidly. Current implementations of remote sensing satellite observation missions still greatly depend on the ground operation control system. Multi-satellite and multi-function mission management, planning and uplink control also complicate the use of satellites by users. A key problem is how to improve the intelligence level and observation efficiency of on-orbit remote sensing satellites, while developing the overall efficiency of the satellite system for the convenience of users and also reducing the on-orbit operational cost. This article proposes an autonomous mission management strategy, which is based on the traditional mission management mode used by low-orbit remote sensing satellites. An implementation method for on-orbit mission rationality judgment, decoupling and instruction sequence generation is also established. This strategy aims to improve the intelligence level of remote sensing satellites and provide reference and guidance for future mission implementation of mission-oriented remote sensing satellites.

Keywords: Remote sensing satellite · Mission management · Autonomous

1 Introduction

A remote sensing satellite is an earth observation satellite that acquires ground image information from a spaceborne payload. It is currently the most widely-used and most typical satellite type and comprises the largest number of satellites launched worldwide [1]. The function and on-orbit working mode of early models were relatively simple. The design was based on a command-oriented mode, which meant that the ground operation control system had to implement mission planning, plan generation, mission instruction set scheduling and code injection for each observation before the satellite could initialize execution of various operating modes using the loaded instruction set. In these models, the implementation of satellite observation missions greatly relied on the ground operation control system [2].

In recent years, the increasing demand for remote sensing images by various industries and the continuous development of remote sensing technology have created a dramatic increase in the number of remote sensing satellites and have led to a constant

M. Jia et al. (Eds.): WiSATS 2019, LNICST 280, pp. 401–411, 2019.
https://doi.org/10.1007/978-3-030-19153-5_42

improvement of satellite functions, giving rise to new problems in satellite mission planning and the implementation process [3]. Multi-satellite and multi-function mission management, planning, uplink control and collaboration methods have imposed higher and higher pressures on ground operation control systems, making the functionality required by ground operation control systems more complex. Therefore, there is an imminent requirement for intelligent implementation of satellite missions to meet the growing needs of satellite users [4].

2   Research Status Review

A surge of research into autonomous management technology took place in the 1990s as the concept of autonomous spacecraft management became popular. Now the United States has successfully applied autonomous management technology in spacecraft such as Deep Space 1(DS-1), Earth Observer 1(EO-1) [5] and Mars Exploration Rovers and space shuttles. The technology has played an important role in guaranteeing the reliability of spacecraft. In comparison, spacecraft in Europe mostly adopt autonomous management technology based on the FDIR system of analytical model and safe mode, such as SMART-1 and SPACEBUS 4000.

In China, autonomous management technology has been studied both in the fields of remote sensing satellites and deep-space exploration. The directed graph method [6] has helped develop algorithm research for on-orbit mission instruction generation, but the logic used in the algorithms is still complex and difficult to realize.

3   Autonomous Mission Management Process

3.1   Definition of Typical Operating Mode

Earth observation missions with remote sensing satellites use imaging and data transmission. The typical operating modes [7] can be defined as follows:

1. Imaging real-time transmission mode: The satellite flies within the visual range of the earth station (visible when the angle of elevation is greater than 5) with a normal flight attitude or side flight attitude, which means that the satellite swings around the motor shaft through a range of angles. After a certain period of stable flight, the payload starts up and starts taking images of the earth [8]. The data processing and transmission system on the satellite implements real-time processing, formatting, channel coding, modulation, amplification and filtering of the observation data and then sends the data to the earth station via a data transmission antenna.
2. Imaging recording mode: The satellite flies through the area of interest with a normal flight or side flight attitude. After a certain period of stable flight, the payload starts up and starts taking images of the earth. The data processing and transmission system on the satellite implements real-time processing and formatting of the observation data. The data is then sent to an on-board data storage unit and transmitted to the earth station at a later stage, when the satellite is flying within the earth station's visual range.

3. Data transmission mode: The satellite flies within the visual range of the earth station with a normal flight attitude. The data is processed with channel coding and transmitted from the on-board data storage unit to the data transmission RF channel. Modulation, amplification and filtering processes are implemented and the data is sent to the earth station via the data transmission antenna [9].

The direction of data flow under each different operating mode is shown in Fig. 1.

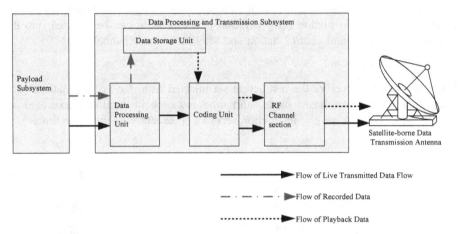

Fig. 1. Direction of data flow under different operating modes

3.2   Implementation Process of Mission Management

The implementation of mission management in remote sensing satellites generally can be divided into scientific planning, mission planning, sequence generation and spacecraft execution, as shown in Fig. 2.

1. Scientific planning

This is usually performed by satellite users based on the requirements of the earth observation mission. The area for the mission is mainly determined based on hot spots, emergency events, resource surveying and mapping requirements.

2. Mission planning

This step is completed by the ground operation control system based on analysis of the scientific planning requirements. Based on the satellite orbit information, weather information, observation target area [10], etc., the scientific planning mission can be translated into an observation mission plan for the particular planning period. Information elements, including the start time of the observation or transmission, the duration, attitude angle and other relevant information for each observation mission, are output to form the mission plan.

3. Sequence generation

The ground operation control system chooses the operating mode for each mission based on the mission plan and observation information elements, and implements the instruction set scheduling and generation for the mode based on the template provided by the satellite provider. The instruction set is composed of several individual instructions and each individual instruction or a combination of several single instructions can control the satellite to fulfil certain functions, such as satellite platform side-sway, data transmission antenna rotation, data processing initialization and camera imaging. Once the instruction set generation is complete, it can be injected into the satellite from the ground control station and satellite control channel.

4. Spacecraft execution

When the satellite receives the instruction set injected from the ground station, each instruction set executes based on its start time and each instruction is executed sequentially. In general, several instruction sets can be executed at the same time.

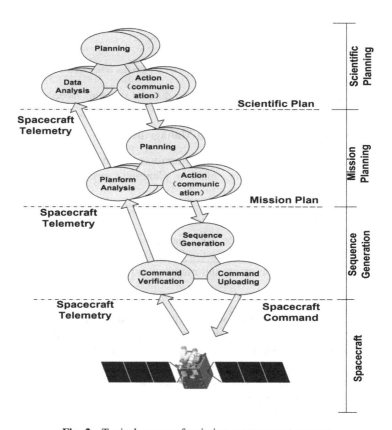

Fig. 2. Typical spacecraft mission management process

This demonstrates that the implementation of the first three processes all need ground control, i.e. mission planning, instruction set generation based on a template and code injection all need to be completed on the ground. This implementation method causes the following problems for users of an on-orbit service:

- As the number of on-orbit satellites increases, users have to undertake a large volume of work related to on-orbit management and planning, meaning that their missions require an increased level of augmentation.
- Instruction scheduling and rule generation are complex processes, and require the instructions to be regularly injected into the satellite. The information interaction process between the satellite and the ground station is tedious and consumes a lot of measurement and control resources.

Optimization of the current operating mode of the satellite is required, and the on-orbit intelligence level also needs to be improved to enhance user experience. Additionally, the interaction process between the satellite and the ground station needs to be simplified, and the user cost needs to be reduced. A spacecraft with autonomous mission management integrates mission planning, sequence generation and instruction implementation into a satellite-borne computer processing mission. The specific process is shown in Fig. 3.

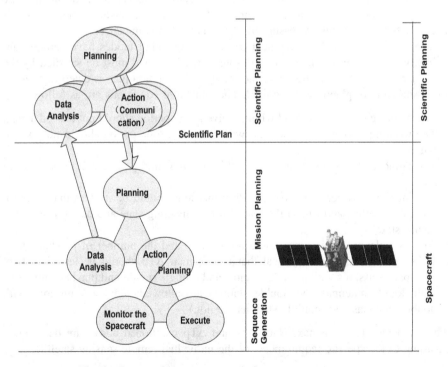

Fig. 3. Spacecraft autonomous mission management process

4   Implementation Strategies for Autonomous Mission Management

The complexity and variability between different operating modes of remote sensing satellites mean that autonomous mission management of spacecraft cannot be expressed as a single algorithm for each data model. Since different remote sensing satellites usually have different operating modes, it is necessary to determine a method which can abstract, simplify and decompose the complex operating modes. Additionally, the complexity of the user interface should be reduced as much as possible to enhance user experience.

A multithread autonomous mission management method is presented in this article that will autonomously manage a spacecraft through three separate processes: mission rationality judgment, mission decoupling and mission instruction generation. This method can transform a complex satellite mission into several simple satellite missions and then process each of these simple missions individually.

4.1   Mission Rationality Judgment

The influence of mission planning on satellite safety should be first taken into consideration, since the process of mission planning is undertaken autonomously by the satellite. In order to ensure that the mission requirements received by the satellite are correct and that the implementation is practical, a mission rationality judgment step is necessary before mission processing by the satellite can commence.

The combination and arrangement of various operating modes have certain constraints, which are set by the satellite design restrictions, and must be satisfied by the planning results. If the constraints cannot be met, the mission plan is determined to be not feasible and re-planning is required. The constraint conditions are as follows:

- The working hours of the load within a given time period should not exceed Tmax.
- The working frequency of the load within a given time period should not exceed Nmax.
- The number of attitude maneuvers within a given time period should not exceed Natt.
- The interval between any two recording missions should be no less than ΔTr (in order to establish and cancel the reserved load imaging state and data transmission record state)
- Any two playback missions should not overlap and the number of playback missions with a continuous interval that is less than ΔTp should be less than two. (Playback missions with a single antenna and a single station and playback missions with double antennas and double stations are allowed; playback missions with double antennas and multiple stations are not.)

The parameters Tmax, Nmax, Natt, ΔTr and ΔTp mentioned above are determined according to the specific requirements of the individual remote sensing satellite.

4.2 Mission Decoupling

Mission decoupling aims to modify and improve the injected mission parameters in combination with the actual execution mode of the satellite. It can control the satellite so that it will execute layer by layer subsequently based on a unified strategy, in order to avoid any conflicts between two individual missions in the implementation process. There are generally two objects that require mission decoupling: the first is the "playback missions with double antennas and double stations" mode, which has a short interval between two data playbacks. The second is the "recording and playback" mode, which means the data recording mode is implemented at the same time as the playback mode.

Mission decoupling is necessary because analysis has found that when a satellite executes recording and playback simultaneously, there may be timing sequence conflicts during the following scenarios:

- The satellite is executing side-sway in preparation for recording while executing the playback mode. If the angle-velocity of the side-sway is too large and exceeds the maximum capability of the angle-velocity of the data transmission antenna, the antenna will not be able to track the ground station effectively.
- Some stand-alone devices for data transmission (such as a data processor and solid-state memory) may have conflicts when switching over between single recording, single playback and recording and playback.
- Some stand-alone devices for data transmission (such as a data processor and solid-state memory) may have instruction conflicts when they are powered up or down during the process of establishing and canceling an operating mode.

As an example of the first point, assume that the satellite executes an attitude maneuver along the X axis, with a capacity of 32°/600 s, and that the curve of the angle and angle-velocity in the attitude maneuver of the X axis is as shown in Fig. 4.

As seen in Fig. 4, the maximum angle-velocity of the X axis under side-sway is approximately 0.15°/s. The angle-velocity of the antenna tracking ground station will be superimposed on the angle-velocity of the X axis. If the side-sway of the whole satellite is not considered, the angle-velocity of antenna X axis in the tracking process is very small, generally no more than 0.05°/s. Based on this, the angle-velocity of the X axis is superimposed and the total angle-velocity is less than 0.2°/s. Now the maximum biaxial rotation capacity of antenna is 1.1°/s, which can satisfy the angle-velocity requirement on tracking the ground station under side-sway. Similarly, it also does not affect the data transmission antenna tracking the ground station during backswing of the whole satellite.

In relation to the second point, when the data processor executes in data recording mode, the internal "AOS routing module" is working, and when it executes in playback mode, the internal "coding module" is working. The two modes can be executed simultaneously or successively without conflict even during mode switchover. The solid-state memory now can realize both recording and playback functions on existing satellites, which is sufficient to maintain an instruction time interval between the two switchovers in the order of seconds.

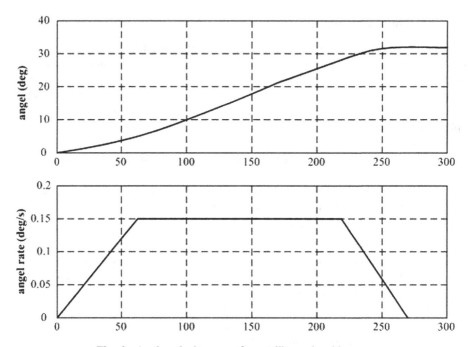

Fig. 4. Angle-velocity curve for satellite under side-sway

For the third point, when the recording and playback overlap, the instructions of the "data processor boot" and the "solid-state memory boot" may be sent repeatedly, but they will not affect the operating state of the subsystem and stand-alone devices. The instructions of "data processor shutdown" and "solid-state memory shutdown" will influence the operating state of the subsystem and the stand-alone devices, and therefore overlapping between the recording and playback states should be identified. If there is an overlap, the last mission should be selected as the target and the instructions of "data processor shutdown" and "solid-state memory shutdown" should be sent.

4.3 Mission Instruction Generation

After mission decoupling, the operating mode can be divided into an "imaging sub-mission" and a "playback sub-mission", which can be combined and arranged into a sequence to realize any complex operating mode. The mission instruction generation actually becomes a combination of a finite number of states. Depending on the design state of different satellite payloads, the corresponding mission instruction sequences of the "imaging sub-mission" and the "playback sub-mission" can be stored in the satellite-borne computer, as shown in Fig. 5. The parameters in the figure can be calculated by the following methods:

- Imaging parameter setting: TgaP = Ts − dTset
- The control unit power up: TonCtrl = Ts − dTset − dTon
- Payload simulator image data unit power up: TonData = TonCtrl + 30
- Payload simulator image data unit power down: ToffData = Te + 1

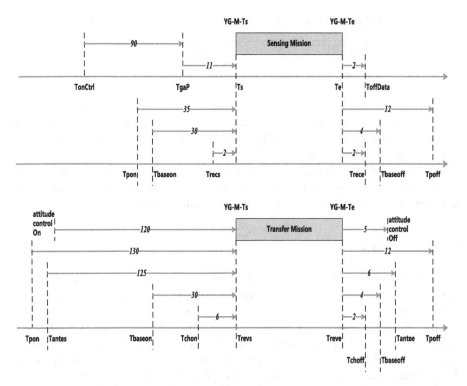

Fig. 5. Timing sequence of instruction sequence generation

Depending on the factors involved in the process of mission decoupling, the sub-mission generating complex mission algorithm will be obtained and the mission instructions will be generated.

5 Application Effect

Traditional satellite mission command block is composed of every commands of on-board equipment.

Table 1. Traditional satellite mission command block

1	Data processing parameter	11	Camera on 3
2	Data processing mode	12	Camera on 4
3	Satellite attitude set	13	Camera off 4
4	Mapping parameter	14	Camera off 3
5	Antenna parameter	15	Camera off 2
6	Antenna on	16	Camera off 1
7	Modulator on	17	Coding unit off
8	Coding unit on	18	Modulator off
9	Camera on 1	19	Antenna off
10	Camera on 2	20	Satellite attitude set

Table 2. Autonomous mission management command block

1	Data processing parameter	4	Time for mapping
2	Data processing mode	5	Mapping parameter
3	Satellite attitude set	6	Antenna parameter

As seen in Tables 1 and 2, Traditional satellite mission command block should be composed of 200 Bytes. Now, satellite users can send only 20 Bytes to complete the same mission by using Autonomous mission management function.

As seen in Table 1, satellite users also need to know how to operate the satellite and the operation steps in traditional satellite mission. Now, only mission parameters are necessary. Therefore, the user's operations are greatly simplified.

6   Conclusions

This article discussed the function and definition of satellite autonomous mission management, based on the traditional mission management mode of remote sensing satellites, and proposed a management method for remote sensing satellites. Our study focused on the implementation strategies of on-orbit autonomous mission rationality judgment, decoupling and instruction generation, and aimed to improve the on-orbit intelligence level and simplify the control and use of satellites. Additionally, it also should reduce ground operation costs and improve the efficiency of on-orbit image acquisition, thus laying the foundation for future satellite-borne mission management designs of mission-oriented intelligent satellites.

References

1. Davies, A.G., Chien, S., Doggett, T., et al.: Improving mission survivability and science return with onboard autonomy. In: Proceedings of the 4th International Planetary Probe Workshop, Calary. CASI (2006)
2. Pang, X., Yu, B., Jiang, W.: The weekly task scheduling model and solving algorithm of imagining satellites. J. Nat. Univ. Defense Technol. **35**, 44–51 (2013)
3. Kuchinskis, F.N., Ferreira, M.G.V.: Planning on-board satellites for the goal-based operations for space missions. IEEE Latin Am. Trans. **11**(4), 1110–1120 (2013)
4. Tian, Z., Cui, X., Zheng, G., et al.: Remote sensing satellite autonomous command sequences generation based on digraph-model. Spacecraft Eng. **23**(6), 54–60 (2014)
5. Thompson, D.R., Bornstein, B.J., Chien, S.A., et al.: Ausonomous spectral discovery and mapping onboard the EO-1 spacecraft. IEEE Trans. Geosci. Remote Sens. **51**(6), 3567–3579 (2013)
6. He, R., Li, J., Yao, F., et al.: Models, algorithms and applications to the mission planning system of imaging satellites. Syst. Eng. **31**, 411–422 (2011)
7. Walton, J.: Models for the management of satellite based sensors, Massachusetts Institute of Technology (1993)

8. Jeremin, P., Sylvain, J., Patxi, O.: Autonomous mission planning in space: mission benefit and real-time performance. In: Proceedings of the Embedded Real Time Software and Systems, Toulouse, Paris. CNES (2014)
9. Gabrel, V., Murat, C.: Mathematical programming for earth observation satellite mission planning. In: Ciriani, T.A., Fasano, G., Gliozzi, S., Tadei, R. (eds.) Operations Research in Space and Air Applied Optimization, vol. 79, pp. 10–122. Springer, Boston (2003). https://doi.org/10.1007/978-1-4757-3752-3_7
10. Lemaître, M., Verfaillie, G.: Selecting and scheduling observations of agile satellites. Aerosp. Sci. Technol. 6, 367–381 (2002)

Towards High Energy Efficiency Contact Plan Design in Collaborative Data Offloading in Space Information Network

Xianfeng Liu[(⊠)], Lei Yang, Chengguang Fan, Shuai Wu,
Jianming Guo, and Quan Chen

College of Aerospace Science and Engineering,
National University of Defense Technology, Changsha 410073, China
Liuxianfeng_edu@163.com

Abstract. Space information network (SIN) consisting of communication satellites plays an important role in information acquisition and transmission. An increasing volume of data produced by different space missions is forwarded by satellites to ground stations (GSs), which leads to satellites that are responsible for forwarding being overload and data cannot be timely downloaded to GS. Moreover the dynamic and complex SIN operating environment deteriorates the performance of data downloading. Thus, for improving data downloading, it is a key to realize data load balance. That means extra data is offloaded to other satellites having extra downloading capacity with an effective scheduling method. To this end, we modeled collaborative data offloading problem as multi-objective mixed integer nonlinear programming (MOMINLP) problems based on developing time-evolving graph (TEG) and contact plan. Due to its computational complexity, we proposed a heuristic approach with phasing based on contact plan, i.e., phased offloading algorithm (POA) operating on a slot-by-slot basis, to jointly schedule data offloading among the satellites and data downloading from satellites to the GS. Simulation results demonstrate that, in many cases, the proposed algorithms can guarantee relatively high data downloading throughput and low energy consumption produced by data offloading.

Keywords: Space information networks · Data offloading ·
Contact plan design · Optimization

1 Introduction

Recently, with deep exploration of space, space information network (SIN) gradually attracts human's attention and becomes hot research field [1]. A SIN may consist of many satellites or satellite constellations at different orbits. These satellites separately or cooperatively accomplish different space missions, such as earth observation, scientific measurement and so on [2]. And a large volume of data would be generated (e.g., the NASA Earth observing system is able to totally collect 27.9 TB/day data from diverse observing missions [3]). Through the SIN, these data from different space missions can be real-timely transmitted to ground stations (GSs) and processed on orbit with cooperative mechanisms. It is well-known that Low Earth Orbit (LEO) satellites

© ICST Institute for Computer Sciences, Social Informatics and Telecommunications Engineering 2019
Published by Springer Nature Switzerland AG 2019. All Rights Reserved
M. Jia et al. (Eds.): WiSATS 2019, LNICST 280, pp. 412–424, 2019.
https://doi.org/10.1007/978-3-030-19153-5_43

are significant part of SIN for this reason that they have many advantages of shorter propagation and better signal quality [4]. However, LEO satellite's downlink contact time is limited. For instance, a typical LEO satellite can access a certain GSs location for less than 10 min within the system period of approximately 100 min [5]. The problem of data offloading during data downloading can be regard as a transmission scheduling problem that focus on data exchanging from satellite nodes to one or more GSs. Most of the existing work pays attention to scheduling algorithms to schedule data exchanging (or download) from satellites to a single or multiple GSs. In literature [6], the concept of Satellite Range Scheduling (SRS) is first proposed to describe the problem of scheduling data communication. Usually, satellites have limited resources such as data buffer, energy buffer and so on. Based on the resource constraints, Gooley et al. modeled this problem using Mixed Integer Programming (MIP), and designed a heuristic algorithm to solve it. In literature [7], Barbulescu et al. firstly analyzed Single-Resource Range Scheduling (SiRRS) problem and proved that it is NP-complete. Then they studied the Multi-Resource Range Scheduling (MuRRS) problem, a genetic algorithm is proposed to find near-optimal solutions. From inspiration of the contact graph routing (CGR) scheme, an event-driven time-expanded graph (EDTEG) is employed to characterize multi-resource variations over the dynamic space environment [8]. And based on the EDTEG, observation resource and transmission resource are jointly considered, and an integer linear programming optimization problem is formulated to maximize the sum priorities of successfully scheduled tasks. However, above research work hardly consider the inter-plane links (ISLs) to improve the performance of data downloading. In [9], Jia et al. designed a collaborative scheme that allows satellites to offload data among themselves using inter-satellite links (ISLs). And simulations based on cooperated simulated software were carried out. The simulation results showed that their scheme can promote the performance of data downloading significantly. However, their work for the problem of data downloading has no generic mathematical model and they only consider the data downloading throughput without energy consumption from data offloading. To sum up, for data downloading, existing work hardly consider ISLs helping data downloading to the GS meanwhile considering energy consumption.

The main contributions of this paper are summarized as follows. Firstly, based on contact plan and time-expanded graph, we formulate a offloading data problem with the aim of maximizing network throughput and minimizing energy consumption produced by data offloading coupling multiple time slots as a multi-objective mixed-integer linear programming (MOMINLP). Secondly, by exploiting the predictable mobility of satellites, we design a heuristic approach to improve data throughput and meanwhile reduce energy consumption.

The remainder of this paper is organized as follows. Section 2 describes the system model. An offloading data problem is formulated as a multi-objective optimization problem on the contact plan to trade off throughput and energy consumption in Sect. 3. Then in Sect. 4, we analyze structure of optimization problem and characteristics of offloading in SIN. We design a heuristic algorithm to improve performance of offloading under the limited resources network. Section 5 presents a series of simulation and analysis results. Finally, conclusions are drawn in Sect. 6.

2   System Model

2.1   Network Model

As shown in Fig. 1, some users (aircrafts, satellites et al.) utilize the relay satellite network to indirectly deliver their information to GSs which are defined as $G = \{g_1, g_2 \ldots, g_n\}$. The relay satellite network consists of a set of satellites $S = \{s_1, s_2 \ldots, s_n\}$, which have ability of high speed communication and data transmission. These space missions are modeled in data traffic, which is defined as $F = \{f_1, f_2 \ldots, f_n\}$. We mainly focus on data offloading during data downloading. Satellites download data only when they move into the coverage of the GSs. Besides the establishment of ISLs also need satisfying some conditions [10]. Due to dynamic and predictive motion of satellite, we exploit Time-Evolving Graph (TEG) [11] to characterize network resources and capture the topology evolution of the network duration data offloading.

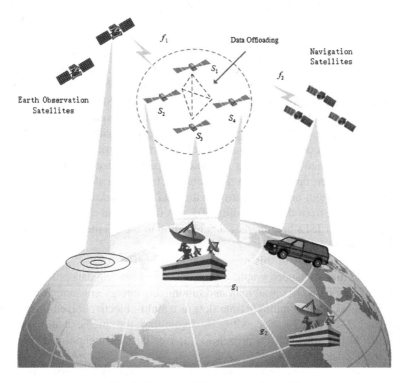

Fig. 1. Space backbone network model

2.2   Graph Model

The TEG consists of T layers which represent consecutive time slots indexed by $t \in \Gamma = \{1, 2 \ldots k \ldots T\}$. The time of data offloading lasts T slots. Each time slot lasts duration of τ and in every slot network states is regard to keep unchanged. We donate the TEG as $G(V^t, E^t)$, where V^t and E^t represent the set of vertices and edges in t-th layer. Figure 2 shows data offloading and downloading in terms of TEG.

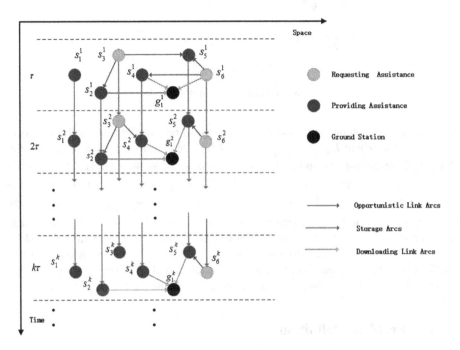

Fig. 2. Time-evolving graph (Color figure online)

For each slot, the vertices of correspond to the replicas of satellites and GSs denoted as $V = V_s \cup V_g$, where $V_s = \{s_i^t | s_i \in S, 1 \leq t \leq T\}$ and $V_g = \{g_i^t | g_i \in G, 1 \leq t \leq T\}$. These vertices representing satellites have two states depending on the mismatching level of data volume being downloaded and downloading capacity. Actually, each satellite contacts with the GS with limited time. The length of contact window represents its downloading capacity under a certain downloading data rate. Whether the satellite providing assistance helping data offloading or not depends on its data load when the satellite accesses to a station ground (e.g., when the data volume carried in the satellite exceeds the downloading capacity, the satellite offloads data to other satellite with lighter data load). Thus satellites keeping in coverage of GS have two states: one is called 'Requesting Assistance' where $V_{s-r}^t = \{s_i^t | s_i \in S, 1 \leq t \leq T\}$, s_i^t requests to offload their data in the t-th slot; another is 'Providing Assistance' where $V_{s-p}^t = \{s_i^t | s_i \in S, 1 \leq t \leq T\}$, s_i^t can help other satellites offloading data in the t-th slot. These satellites will form a bipartite graph shown in Fig. 3. During data offloading, satellites in V_{s-r}^t may form a pair with those in V_{s-p}^t in each slot.

In Fig. 2, there are three kinds of arcs, i.e., opportunistic link arcs (blue arcs), downloading link arcs (red arcs) and storage arcs (brown arcs). Opportunistic link arcs

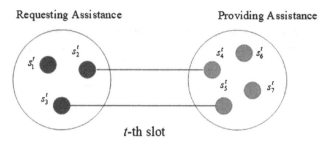

Requesting Assistance   Providing Assistance

t-th slot

Fig. 3. Bipartite graph in the *t*-th slot

are potential communication links among satellites, i.e., satellite to satellite (S2S) in each time slot, where $E_{ss} = \{(s_i^t, s_j^t)|1 \leq t \leq T\}$, s_i^t and s_j^t can establish an ISL in *t*-th slot}. And the weight of opportunistic link arcs denoted as $W = \{w_{ij}^t|1 \leq t \leq T\}$ w_{ij}^t is transmission cost from s_i^t to s_j^t, $s_i^t \in V_{s-r}^t, s_j^t \in V_{s-p}^t\}$ represents the cost of transmitting data. The downloading link arcs are denoted as $E_{sg} = \{(s_i^t, g_j^t)|1 \leq t \leq T\}$, s_i^t is in the coverage of g_i in the *t*-th slot. Denoted as $E_d = \{(s_i^t, s_i^{t+1})|s_i^t \in V_s, 1 \leq t \leq T\}$, storage arcs represent the ability of satellites to store data between the consecutive time slots. According to the work [12], discussion in later sections is based the assumption that satellites have two transponders for other one satellite and a GS respectively. And the GS can establish links within a certain number of satellites at the same time.

3   The Problem Definition

In data downloading, we formulate the data offloading problem to maximize downloading data and minimize energy consumption under constraints of data buffer, transponders and satellite' orbiting movement as an optimization problem.

Contact Constraints: In each slot, a satellite has a chance to establish several potential ISLs with other satellites. However, according to Sect. 2, each satellite has only one transponder for ISL in one slot. Thus, concerning with data offloading among satellites, we introduce a set of boolean variables

$$x(s_i^t, s_j^t) = \{0, 1\}, (s_i^t, s_j^t) \in E_{ss} \tag{1}$$

$x(s_i^t, s_j^t)$ is equal to 1 if and only if link (s_i^t, s_j^t) is active in *t*-th time slot and 0 otherwise. Due to the fact that each satellite connects other one satellite, we impose

$$\sum_{s_j^t \in V_{s-p}^t} x(s_i^t, s_j^t) \leq 1 \quad \forall \quad s_i^t \in V_{s-r}^t \tag{2}$$

$$\sum_{s_j^t \in V_{s-r}^t} x(s_j^t, s_i^t) \leq 1 \quad \forall \quad s_j^t \in V_{s-p}^t \tag{3}$$

And for restricting bi-directionality on the contact selection of satellite to satellite links, we have

$$x(s_i^t, s_j^t) = x(s_j^t, s_i^t) \tag{4}$$

Transmission Constraints: Signal transmitted is affected by the attenuation, ambient noise, transmission power and so on. Assuming additive white Gaussian noise (AWGN) channel, Shannon's capacity formula provides the achievable transmission rate [13] as

$$R = W \log_2\left(1 + \frac{P_{ij}^t h_{ij}^t}{\sigma^2}\right) \tag{5}$$

Where W is the bandwidth and σ^2 is the noise power. P_{ij}^t and h_{ij}^t are the transmission power and the channel gain between the satellite i and j respectively in t-th time slot. h_{ij}^t is a function of, free-space attenuation, sensitivity of receiver and antenna gain. In this paper, we mainly consider contribution of free-space attenuation to transmission power.

For simplifying problem, based on the formula (5), we utilize transmission power P_{ij}^t to control the volume of delivering data in each slot. Moreover, on the condition of limited resource, we consider each satellite joining offloading has a limited data buffer which is equal to itself downloading capacity $C_s = C_{s-r} \cup C_{s-p}$ where C_{s-r} and C_{s-p} correspond to state of 'Requesting Assistance' and 'Providing Assistance' defined in Sect. 2.

$$\sum_{s_i^t \in V_{s-r}, (s_i^t, s_j^t) \in E_{ss}}^{T} x(s_i^t, s_j^t) * \tau * \log_2\left(1 + \frac{P_{ij}^t h_{ij}^t}{\sigma^2}\right) \leq C_{s-p} \quad \forall \quad s_j^t \in V_{s-p} \tag{6}$$

$$\sum_{s_j^t \in V_{s-p}, (s_i^t, s_j^t) \in E_{ss}}^{T} x(s_i^t, s_j^t) * \tau * \log_2\left(1 + \frac{P_{ij}^t h_{ij}^t}{\sigma^2}\right) \geq \beta_i C_{s-r} \quad \forall \quad s_i^t \in V_{s-r} \tag{7}$$

Where τ is length of a slot. Satellites' capacity of receiving data is varying with time. During the offloading process, we are deserved to forbid data overflow in each satellite from V_{s-p} shown in constraint (6). The constraint (7) denotes that satellites from V_{s-r} need to guarantee a certain volume of data to offload to others, where β_i is scale factor.

Optimization Problem Formulation: According to the above depicted constrains, we formulate the effectively collaborative data offloading problem based on TEG. The problem is to select and schedule a subset of satellites to balance data load in energy-efficient slot window so that data can be download to GSs as much as possible. Two objectives are proposed: one is to maximize throughput of downloading data; another is to minimize energy consumption produced by offloading data. The throughput maximization and energy consumption minimization (TMEMP) can be formulated as follows:

$$\max \sum_{\substack{(s_i^t, s_j^t) \in E_{ss}}}^{T} x(s_i^t, s_j^t) * \tau * W * \log_2(1 + \frac{P_{ij}^t h_{ij}^t}{\sigma^2})$$

$$\min \sum_{\substack{(s_i^t, s_j^t) \in E_{ss}}}^{T} x(s_i^t, s_j^t) P_{ij}^t \tau \qquad (8)$$

$$s.t \quad (1) - (7)$$

From the formulation (8), we can observe that the problem falls into the category of multi-objective mixed integer nonlinear programming (MOMINLP) problems [14] which is computationally intractable. It's well known that MOMINLP is a NP-hard problem whose computational complexity depends on the number of integer variables [15]. Based on TEG and contact window, multi-phase collaborative scheduling is applied to data offloading, which can decrease the computational complexity.

4 Algorithm

The data offloading algorithm runs on the TEG and the bipartite graph. In reality, the GS does not know the data load of each satellite until it accesses to the GS. We limit the offloading operation occurring in a set of satellites which are contacting with GS and within one hop [9]. And data should be offloaded as soon as possible. Based on above assumptions, we can divide the contact window graph during time T into several phases (numbering these from 1 to n) so as to efficiently balance data load and conform to reality. The dividing criterion is that, the moment of each satellite accessing GS is set as beginning moment of each phase shown in Fig. 4.

In every phase, we introduce to a bipartite graph as discussed in Sect. 3 to reflect that satellites can join data offloading. For every satellite, we need to keep track of its initial load state at the beginning of each phase. For the phase $m \in [1, n]$, we introduce the following notations summarized in Table 1:

At the beginning of each phase, satellites would report these load state F_i^m to GS. And then the GS put satellites into different groups as described in Fig. 3. When $F_i^m > C_i^m$, v_i^m is belongs to V_{s-r}^m; When $F_i^m < C_i^m$, $v_i^m \in V_{s-p}^m$ means having more download time to help others. After insuring the scope of satellites joining in offloading data, in each phase, we exploit to hybrid particle swarm optimization (HPSO) [16] combining with penalty function to solve MOMINLP. Due to the fact that the multi-objective optimization problem involves maximizing data throughput and minimizing total energy consumption produced by offloading data, we utilize energy efficiency to choose ideal solutions.

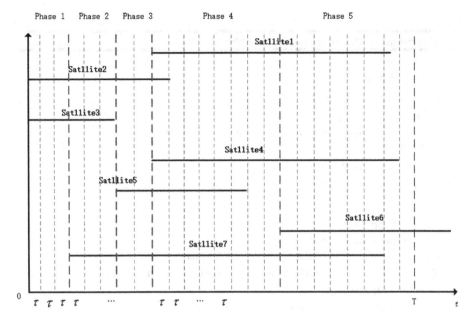

Fig. 4. Phasing of data offloading

Table 1. I Notations used in our algorithm

Symbol	Definition
v_i^m	Satellite i in phase m
V_{gs}	Subset of V_s that have contact with the GS $V_{gs} = \{V_{gs}^1, \ldots, V_{gs}^n\}$ and $V_{gs}^m = \{v_1^m, \ldots, v_j^m\}$ in phase m
V_{s-r}^m	Subset of V which request to offload data to others in phase m
V_{s-p}^m	Subset of V which help other satellites offloading data in phase m
V_{s-n}^m	Subset of V do not participate in data offloading in phase m
T^m	Period of phase m
F_i^m	Amount of remaining data of S_i at beginning of phase m
C_i^m	Downloading capacity in phase m

$$\eta^m = \frac{E^m}{O^m} \tag{9}$$

Where E^m and O^m are energy consumption produced by offloading data and offloading data volume respectively. The algorithm is described as followed

---
Algorithm 1 Phased Offloading Algorithm (POA)

// Initialization

1: **for** $s_i \in S$ do

2:   Initial allocation of F_i ;

3: **end**

// Insure the scope of satellites joining in offloading data

4: **for** $m<n$ do

5:   **For** $v_i^m \in V_{gs}^m$ do

6:     Classify v_i^m into V_{s-r}^m or V_{s-p}^m

7:   **end**

//data offloading

8: Construct Time-Evolving Graph.

9: Construct a bipartite graph for node sets for phase m

10: Solve the TMEMP, and obtain the solutions $x^m(t)$ and $P^m(t)$ based on maximum energy efficiency.

11: Update F_i^{m+1}, $\forall$ $v_i^{m+1} \in V_{gs}^{m+1}$;

12: m=m+1

13: **end**

---

5   Simulation Results

Our simulations are conducted on the Globalstar constellation [9] with 8 orbital planes and 6 satellites each. The inter-plane is 60°. And satellite orbit height is 1414 km with an orbit inclination angle of 52°. We assign bandwidths of 16.5 MHz and 33 MHz for ISL communication and satellite-ground communication respectively. The GS is set at Xi'an (34°N, 108°E). We build up Globalstar constellation based on STK that can produce a contact plan. And the optimization algorithm operated in MATLAB is used to find the solutions of scheduling problem. The time slot period τ is set as 10 s. And we choose a period from 19 Jul, 2018 at 04:00:00 UTC to 19 Jul, 2018 at 04:30:00 UTC as simulation time. The data in satellites is collected in advance. Besides, we normalize data load as a ratio of receiving capacity of GS and fix data downloading rate of each satellite. Thus, we defined the volume of which excessive data can be downloaded to GS successfully as downloading throughput concisely called throughput

$$Throughput = \sum_{i=1}^{N} (F_i^o - \hat{F}_i^o)/ \sum_{i=1}^{N} F_i^o \tag{10}$$

Where, for the satellite s_i, F_i^o is data volume excessing its downloading capacity before scheduling corresponding to that $\hat{F}_i^o$ after scheduling. And during the period of simulation, we randomly choose some satellites as those needing to offload data to others. The data volume is set at 80–100% of downloading capacity of satellites. According to the simulation results, this process of data offloading lasts six phases. Some feasible solutions of each phase shown in Fig. 5

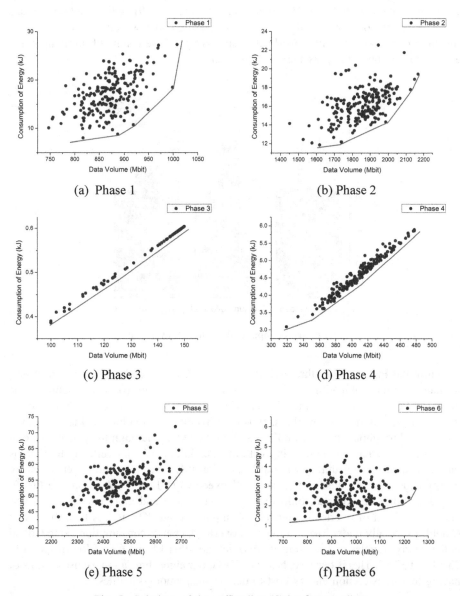

(a) Phase 1

(b) Phase 2

(c) Phase 3

(d) Phase 4

(e) Phase 5

(f) Phase 6

Fig. 5. Solutions of data offloading (Color figure online)

Due to the fact that the data offloading problem is MOMINLP, there exists trade-off between transmitting data volume and energy consumption during the period of data offloading. For each phase, the different length of scheduling time decides on the difference of the number of optimization variables. And our developing HPSO with penalty function can effectively find the Pareto Fronts [14] of TMEMP in each phase shown as red line in Fig. 5. In each phase, the choosing of ideal solution is based on max energy efficiency. Moreover, to evaluate the performance of the proposed POA, we compare them with the CoDld proposed in the literature [9] on the condition of data load which are 30%, 60% and 90% of downloading capacity called 'low overload', 'medium overload' and 'high overload' respectively. These results of throughput and energy consumption are presented in Figs. 6 and 7.

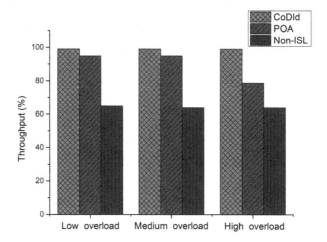

Fig. 6. Throughput under different overloads

From the Fig. 6, under three levels of overload, the CoDld method has best performance of data offloading which can nearly approach to 100% throughput. The proposed POA can help satellites downloading almost 90% overload data to GS under low overload and medium overload. When the overload data volume is high (reaching 90%), the throughput still reach 80% based on the POA. Although the performance of the POA has a small gap comparing with the CoDld under high overload, the POA is far better than the scheduling without ISLs (Non-ISL). Actually, the target of saving energy should be responsible for the gap between CoDld and POA. From the Fig. 7, with increasing of overload, offloading data need more and more energy. However, under each level of overload, energy consumption using POA is less than that using CoDld. Especially under low and medium overload, energy consumption using CoDld is the nearly double of that using POA,which are 45.4 kJ and 67.6 kJ correspond to 23 kJ and 32 kJ. This is because, based on TEG, our algorithm can make use of slots of having low transmission energy cost to deliver data among satellites.

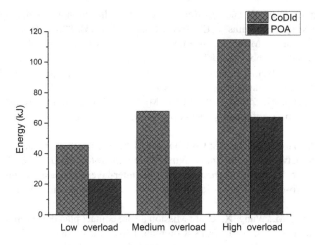

Fig. 7. Energy consumption under different overloads

6 Conclusion

In this paper, we investigate the problem of data offloading during the period of data downloading, such that satellites carrying a large number of data will offload data to these with low data load according to the length of their contact time with GS. The target is that the throughput of data downloading will increase and meanwhile energy consumption will be reduced as much as possible. We combine phasing based on contact plan and a heuristic approach, i.e., POA operating on a slot-by-slot basis, to achieve high performance of data offloading. Extensive simulations have been conducted evaluate to newly proposed POA based on Satellites Took Kit (STK) and MATLAB. Comparing with CoDld and data downloading without ISLs, the POA can guarantee relatively high throughput and low energy consumption produced by data offloading.

Acknowledgement. This paper is supported by program 'National Key R&D Program of China' (2016YFB0502402).

References

1. Du, J., Jiang, C., Guo, Q., et al.: Cooperative earth observation through complex space information networks. IEEE Wirel. Commun. **23**(2), 136–144 (2016)
2. Sheng, M., Wang, Y., Li, J., et al.: Toward a flexible and reconfigurable broadband satellite network: resource management architecture and strategies. IEEE Wirel. Commun. **24**(4), 127–133 (2017)
3. The role and evolution of NASA' s earth science data systems [EB/OL]. http://ntrs.nasa.gov. Accessed 21 June 2018
4. Jian, Y., Yuan, Z., Zhigang, C.: Reverse detection based QoS routing algorithm for LEO satellite constellation networks. Tsinghua Sci. Technol. **16**(4), 358–363 (2011)

5. Du, J., Jiang, C., Qian, Y., Han, Z., Ren, Y.: Resource allocation with video traffic prediction in cloud-based space systems. IEEE Trans. Multimed. **18**(5), 820–830 (2016)
6. Gooley, T., Borsi, J., Moore, J.: Automating air force satellite control network (AFSCN) scheduling. Math. Comput. Model. **24**(2), 91–101 (1996)
7. Barbulescu, L., Watson, J.P., Whitley, L.D., et al.: Scheduling space-ground communications for the air force satellite control network. J. Sched. **7**(1), 7–34 (2004)
8. Wang, Y., Sheng, M., Zhuang, W., et al.: Multi-resource coordinate scheduling for earth observation in space information networks. IEEE J. Sel. Areas Commun. **36**(2), 268–279 (2018)
9. Jia, X., Lv, T., He, F., Huang, H.: Collaborative data downloading by using-satellite links in LEO satellite networks. IEEE Trans. Wirel. Commun. **16**(3), 1523–1532 (2017)
10. Wu, T.Y., Wu, S.Q.: Performance analysis of the inter-layer inter-satellite link establishment strategies in two-tier LEO/MEO satellite networks. J. Electron. Inf. Technol. **30**(1), 67–71 (2008)
11. Zhou, D., Sheng, M., Wang, X., et al.: Mission aware contact plan design in resource-limited small satellite networks. IEEE Trans. Commun. **65**(6), 2451–2466 (2017)
12. Sandau, R., Roeser, H.P., Valenzuela, A.: Small Satellite Missions for Earth Observation. Springer, Heidelberg (2010). https://doi.org/10.1007/978-3-642-03501-2
13. Alagoz, F., Gur, G.: Energy efficiency and satellite networking a holistic overview. Proc. IEEE **99**(11), 1954–1979 (2011)
14. Mela, K., Koski, J., Silvennoinen, R.: Algorithm for generating the pareto optimal set of multiobjective nonlinear mixed-integer optimization problems. In: Aiaa/asme/asce/ahs/asc Structures, Structural Dynamics, and Materials Conference (2007)
15. Zhu, R., Wang, H., Gao, Y., Yi, S., Zhu, F.: Energy saving and load balancing for SDN based on multi-objective particle swarm optimization. In: Wang, G., Zomaya, A., Perez, G. M., Li, K. (eds.) ICA3PP 2015. LNCS, vol. 9530, pp. 176–189. Springer, Cham (2015). https://doi.org/10.1007/978-3-319-27137-8_14
16. He, Y.J., Chen, D.Z.: Hybrid particle swarm optimization algorithm for mixed_-integer nonlinear programming. J. Zhejiang Univ. (Eng. Sci.) **42**(5), 747–751 (2008)

Target Evaluation of Remote Sensing Image Based on Scene Context Guidance

Wenjuan Li[1(✉)], Shunan Shang[2], and Ling Tong[1]

[1] Beijing Institute of Spacecraft System Engineering, Beijing 10094, China
`wjolee@126.com`
[2] Institute of Telecommunication Satellite, CAST, Beijing 10094, China

Abstract. The correlation between scenes and targets in remote sensing images can provide useful and important information and guidance for satellite to achieve onboard targets evaluation in order to find valuable targets to image. The relationship between the target and the scene, as well as the spatial location association it contains, determines what the system should "focus on" and "what areas to focus on" in different scenarios. Referring to the guiding role of context information in the visual system, this paper studies how to identify potential targets through the scene context information, and a saliency model based on the task context information to achieve the target evaluation under different scenarios is proposed. At the end of the paper, a simulation experiment is given. It can be seen from the experiment that through scene context guidance, different parameters can be loaded in different scenarios to realize the evaluation and discrimination of different targets.

Keywords: Context · Saliency model · Target detection

1 Preface

In the case of complex targets and backgrounds, the human visual system can still quickly identify and classify a large number of targets, and has very good adaptability to the illumination, attitude, texture, deformation and occlusion of the target imaging. In addition, the human brain has powerful learning and reasoning ability to identify targets which have never been seen by observing a set of targets. This is because when humans recognize objects in the real world, other surrounding objects and specific environments provide a rich contextual connection to the visual system. Targets appear in consistent or common scenarios, making detection and recognition tasks more accurate and faster than appearing in uncoordinated scenarios. The broad connection between the target and its environment is called context information. Studies in the human visual system [1–8], cognitive neuroscience [9–13], and computer vision [14–16] have shown that context information plays an important role in the target classification of the human brain. In fact, the human brain using context information during feature analysis. Inspired by the recognition goals of human cognitive system, many scholars imitate the human visual system to improve the performance of computer recognition systems. Some new methods consider the context information of the target,

M. Jia et al. (Eds.): WiSATS 2019, LNICST 280, pp. 425–436, 2019.
https://doi.org/10.1007/978-3-030-19153-5_44

and introduce the scene information and the mutual constraints between the targets into the target classification task to improve the performance and eliminating the uncertainty.

2 Context Feature

2.1 Definition

Cognitive psychology believes that perception and human knowledge and experience are inseparable. The impact of experience knowledge on vision is multifaceted, and the most striking one is the role of context information. The human visual process can be viewed as being guided and planned under context information. Thus, context information is an important reminder when humans are performing target detection and recognition. Context information can indicate what is worth noting and what is negligible, which greatly reduces the processing burden of the visual system and reduces processing time. Biederman et al. have pointed out that when humans detect targets, the prompts that violate the context information not only increase the processing time, but also make them more error prone. The MRI results also confirmed the use of context information when human brain is detecting and identifying man-made targets. If the human body is the evolution of the visual upper and lower information, then context information is an effective way to understand the visual world. Thus, it can be inferred that context information is also beneficial to machine cognitive systems.

In practical applications, the scene configuration in which the target is located or the structure inside the target is often highly structured. The context information of the target can be defined as information contained in the scene or the entire scene information for detecting and identifying the target. In a general sense, the context is about the surrounding environment in which the objects are located. In a natural image, there is a strong specific relationship between the target and the scene, and the context is to describe it. Generally, context information can be divided into the following three categories.

(1) Local context. The image to be detected contains many local regions, each of them have a relationship with their surroundings. The information describing the relationship is called a local context feature. It includes the neighborhood context of the local region and the geometric relationships between the local regions.
(2) Target context. The target to be detected has a certain relationship with the surrounding targets, including whether these targets appear, and the location and scale relationship between them. This information is called the target context.
(3) Scene context. The targets are in a certain scene, and the scene in which the targets are located is very helpful for the detection and recognition of the target. This scene information is called the scene context.

2.2 Detection and Recognition Methods Based on Context Features

Context in computer vision can be defined as all information related to the target but not the apparent description of the target itself. To some extent, this reveals to some extent the "connotation" of the target. Computer vision uses context information from three different levels, namely: local context feature layer, target context target layer, and scene context scene layer. The local context includes a location relationship between the context based on the neighborhood and the local region of the geometric context.

(1) Local context

At present, the mainstream target detection and recognition method is based on local features. It is simple, easy to calculate, insensitive to affine transformation, and also has certain resistance to occlusion, illumination and intra-class changes. The Bag of Features (BoF) model is a very hot model in recent years, and the target detection and recognition effect is very good. However, the model does not consider the positional relationship between local features, which is very important, because the target is a whole, and the local regions which constitute the target are not unrelated, but organized according to certain rules. Recently, some researchers have proposed a method to add rough spatial positional relations to a local feature model, such as embedding spatial information into the BoF model. This method needs to balance discriminative ability and generalization ability, which needs to be considered from two aspects of feature quantization and spatial feature extraction.

In addition, the local context also includes the neighborhood context of the local area. The neighborhood context information is mainly used in image labeling. When labeling an area, the information of the surrounding area is considered, and the labeling of the area is constrained to improve the accuracy of labeling. Even in unsupervised cases, tags based on neighborhood contexts also have good results. The models describing this neighborhood context constraint are mainly random fields, including Markov Random Field (MRF), Discriminative Random Fields (DRF), multi-scale conditional random fields (mCRF) [17].

(2) Target context

The target context refers to the co-occurrence relationship and location relationship between the target and other objects in the scene. There is no doubt that other objects in the scene can be very helpful in detecting and identifying the target object. There are many target recognition methods based on target context in computer vision. However, based on the target context method, a condition is also required, that is, the identification of other objects is relatively accurate. If you use some very unreliable information to infer, the results will not be very good. In order to solve this problem, the commonly used target context-based detection and recognition method is implemented by iteration, using the most reliable target recognition result to infer other targets, and then repeating the process until convergence. For example, Finks proposes a method to detect local features of targets and other targets using cascaded target detection structures [18]. All the interdependencies are calculated in an iterative manner. Torralba et al. also proposed a similar framework that using boosting and graph networks to learn the possibility of co-occurrence and related locations of targets [19]. In addition, the method must have multi-target information in the training. If the object to be identified is the only target in the database, then the target context information cannot be learned, and the target context cannot be used [20].

(3) Scene context

In the research of computer vision, the most commonly used method of scene classification is target based method. There are some fixed and obvious signs in some scenes. The object-based scene classification method identifies the scene by recognizing these marks. But these methods also include some intermediate steps, such as segmentation, feature organization and target recognition, which are also the key problems in computer vision. On the other hand, the human vision system performs very well in scene classification, far surpassing the computer vision system. Human beings start from the whole in scene recognition, because of this, there are some recent research methods analyzing the whole scene to achieve the classification tasks and the results are very good. There are two main methods based on scene context features: the first is to add rough context relations to the model based on local features. For example, Lazebnik et al. put forward a Beyond Bag of Features (BBoF) model, which uses spatial pyramid structure to extract the spatial relationship of local features. And then it is added to the BoF model, referred to as the "BBoFs" model. The second is based on the spatial distribution of multi-scale and multi-directional filters, which is called "gist" model. Extracting more robust and semantically explicit scene context features is very important for scene classification. But since the first model only aims at local features and the second model is based on filter features, it is necessary to extend the two models so that they can be applied to both features. Moreover, the combination of multiple features can make the scene representation more robust. Recent studies have shown that low dimensional statistics of low-level features can be used as a description of the context of the scene. As it contains certain semantic information, which can be used to predict the target in the scene, including the probability, location and scales of the target etc. Many traditional methods are based on local features, but high-level semantic descriptions are more stable, so the semantic description of adding context can fill the gap between low-level features and high-level semantics.

In this paper the context information is added to the saliency model trying to imitate the prior knowledge guidance in human cognitive system, which will be used to load different algorithms to realize onboard target evaluation in difference satellite scenarios such as the sea, deserts, etc.

3 Scene Context Guidance Based Target Evaluation

3.1 Scene-Target Context

The context relationship between the targets in the scene of the remote sensing image includes the relative position, scale size and panoramic spatial relationship of the target and the surrounding environment. A thorough understanding of these relationships can increase or decrease the probability of different targets appearing in different scenarios and can be used to guide the system in selecting the appropriate target evaluation method. For example, the possibility of an airport around a city increases; the possibility of ships and islands in the ocean is high.

For Earth observation, there is a mapping relationship between the flight orbit of the remote sensing satellite and the geographical location of its imaging area: the observation field can be determined according to the width of the imaging field, flight orbit and flight time. Figure 1 shows the relationship between the strip number, line number and administrative division, latitude and longitude of the Landsat satellite using the global reference system WRS2 in China. From this mapping relationship, scene semantic information of the current observation area of the satellite can be obtained, such as mountains, cities, oceans, ports, and so on.

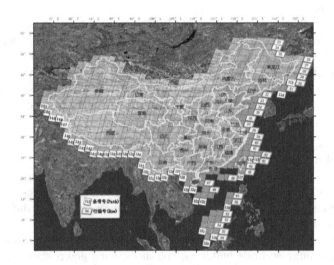

Fig. 1. The WRS2 of China for Landsat imaging [figure is obtained from internet]

For the realization of the onboard target evaluation, the scene semantic information not only contains the scene feature, but also the information of the potential valuable targets. The scene feature gives a characterization of the scene, and the potential valuable targets information can determine the observation targets, thereby guiding the system to "where/what to pay attention to" in the scene. The scene semantic information also reveals the relationship between the target and the scene. For example, the airport is usually built on the suburbs of the city, so it can be inferred that the probability of the aircraft appearing in that scene is high. It can be seen that the analysis of the scene semantics not only provides the general information and features of the scene, but also determines the probability of potential targets appearing in the scene.

3.2 Model

In order to realize the onboard target evaluation, it is necessary to analyze the scene semantics, based on the parsed information, and select appropriate parameters of the payload to determine the salient features of the potential targets and other corresponding parameters, such as the size range, length-width ratio of the target etc. According to the analyzed scene information and potential targets, the appropriate saliency detection method is selected to realize the targets evaluation, and the valuable targets and their regions are determined, which can guide the satellite to select image and provide basis for further detailed observation of other satellites. In this paper, a framework for target evaluation based on scene information is proposed. In order to verify the validity of the model, several simple application scenarios are designed. By inputting scene semantic information, the model can independently select the corresponding algorithm to complete the target evaluation and detection of the scenario. The more detailed scene division, the more precise the constraint relationship between the target and the scene, and the more accurate the result of the target evaluation and detection can be.

According to the types of terrain, it can be simply divided into three categories: sea area, sea-land junction and lands, of which the lands can also be subdivided. From the perspective of remote sensing images target evaluation application can be divided into: man-made targets detection, natural disasters and scientific phenomena detection, and hot spot change detection. Considering the scene and the application point of view, the scene and the targets or events that may need to be observed are divided as follows, and are listed in Table 1.

(1) Sea: ships, islands, air planes.
(2) Sea-land junction: vessels, nuclear power plants, airports.
(3) According to characteristics of land features, lands can be roughly divided into: mountains, deserts, plains, fields, cities, woodlands, rivers, lakes, and glaciers. And the targets and events that may need to be observed in these different surface types are divided as follows:
    (a) Desert and Gobi: oasis, man-made buildings, winds power stations;
    (b) Mountain: man-made buildings, volcanoes, wind power stations;
    (c) Plain land: man-made buildings;
    (d) Rivers: dams and bridges, ships, floods;
    (e) Fields: man-made buildings;
    (f) Cities: special buildings or designated buildings, airports;
    (g) Woodlands: man-made buildings, fires.

Table 1. The example of the potential targets in different scenes

Scene		Potential valuable targets
Sea-land junction	Sea	Ship, island, air plane
	Land	Port, vessels, nuclear power plants, airport
Lands	Desert, Gobi	Oasis, man-made buildings, winds power stations, roads
	Mountain	Man-made buildings, volcanoes, wind power stations
	Plain land	Man-made buildings, airports
	Rivers	Dams, bridges, ships
	Fields	Man-made buildings, waters
	Cities	Special buildings or designated buildings, airports, waters
	Woodlands	Man-made buildings, waters

Applying saliency detection features combined with the image data and its potential targets, this paper proposes a saliency model for targets evaluation to achieve valuable targets detection guided by scene semantic information. Firstly, in the process of top-down attention mechanism, the potential targets are derived from the scene context information of the scene semantic analysis, such as searching for ships, man-made buildings, etc. in the remote sensing image. Meanwhile, in the process of bottom-up visual simulation, the appropriate scale and method are selected according to the analyzed scene information, and the feature maps of the image are calculated according to the selected method, and the saliency detection of the valuable targets are realized according to the saliency features of the scene at last. In this process, the scene context information introduces "attention" into the region of interest driven by the task, and combines the top-down information with the data-driven saliency map to achieve the valuable target detection without human involved. The model is shown in Fig. 2.

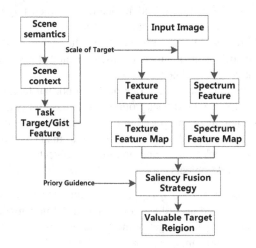

Fig. 2. The schematic diagram of the target evaluation model

As can be seen from Fig. 2, the scene context information provides task target information and gist features that guide the extraction of the scene, which provide prior knowledge as attention guidance information. Under the guidance of the target information, it is first necessary to extract the features of the image, and provide the basis for distinguishing the significant target and the background in different scenarios. The extracted features are mainly as follows:

(1) Texture features. As a form of perception representation of an object in the human visual system, the image texture features refer to the gray-scale or color change of the pixel points in the image and the regular pattern of variation distribution. The texture features reflect the surface roughness, certain regularity and directionality of the object. Different objects have different texture features. It is one of the causes of human visual difference and an important basis for distinguishing

different objects. Texture is also important information of remote sensing images. It not only reflects the brightness statistics of the image, but also the relationship between the structural features and the spatial arrangement of the object itself. The texture features are composed of local texture information and global texture information, wherein the local texture feature is represented by the gray level or color distribution of the pixel and its surrounding spatial neighborhood; and the global texture feature is repeated by different degrees of the local texture. Therefore, image texture features can be used to characterize different scenes contained in the image, such as deserts, grasslands and so on. Their extraction methods are divided into various types such as gray level co-occurrence matrix, LBP, etc. And the extracted texture features reflect the characteristics of objects or features from different angles, and the feature maps $S_{texture}$ are obtained.

(2) Spectrum features. Fourier transform is a typical spectral feature extraction method. The spectrum of different frequency bands corresponds to different features in the image. Therefore, the identification between target and background can also be realized by spectrum analysis. Similar to the extraction of texture features, the different scale spectrum features of the image are extracted according to the spectral distribution quantization method, and the spectrum feature map $S_{spetral}$ of the image is calculated.

(3) Fractal features. Fractal features are one of the important features that distinguish man-made targets from natural backgrounds. A method for calculating multi-scale fractal dimension features is proposed in [21]. The difference of multi-scale fractal dimension between natural background and man-made is obvious, which can distinguish natural background and man-made objects, and beneficial to the detection of man-made objects.

Thus, three feature maps $S_{texture}$, S_{frac}, and $S_{spetral}$ are obtained. Finally, the saliency map of the image is calculated according to the task target information and Eq. 1, and the salient object is the high-value target in the scene. Where, the exponents α_1, α_2 and α_3 are weighting factors, and satisfy $\alpha_1 + \alpha_2 + \alpha_3 = 1$.

$$SM = S_{texture}^{\alpha_1} \cdot S_{frac}^{\alpha_2} \cdot S_{spetral}^{\alpha_3} \tag{1}$$

Table 1 lists potential targets in different scenarios of remote sensing images. As mentioned above, different targets constitute a scene, and a scene contains various targets. It is assumed that scene A contains target C. And if scene X is determined to be the scene A, the scene-target context infers that the probability of occurrence of target C is relatively high. The probability of the same target appears in different scenes varies. For example, the probability of a road appearing in a city or a desert is different, and can be expressed as p_1 and p_2 respectively. Therefore, the probability can be used to represent the relationship between the target and the scene. Set S to be the scene, T is the target, $P(T = T_j | S = S_i)$ indicating the probability of occurrence of the target T_j under the scene S_i. The value of the probability determines the value of the weighting factor, so that the most effective target evaluation method in the scene can be selected according to the scene semantics. And the scene context information also provides the gist feature of background for the algorithm as a reference, and the size of the target to select the appropriate scale for calculation. Take the sea scenario for example, the multi-scale fractal dimension method has a large weighting factor due to the high probability of the ship appearing, and then the multi-scale fractal dimension method is selected to realize the ship detection. In the mountain background, the detection of man-made buildings can also be achieved by multi-scale fractal dimension. However, due to the different dimensions of the building and the ship target and the different background gist features, it is necessary to change the settings of the parameters such as the scale, weighting factors to realize the detection of man-made buildings in the mountain background. Thus, the corresponding effective methods and parameters are selected according to different scenarios and potential targets to realize the target evaluation under the scenario.

4   Experiment

In order to illustrate the target evaluation in different scenarios under the framework of this model, this paper builds an experimental environment using MATLAB, in which the image to be processed and the scene type of the image can be selected, as shown in Fig. 3. Each type of scene corresponds to the known and stetted context information of the scene, including: size range of potential valuable targets, the extracted features, gist features of the scene, the probability of the potential targets. And the probability of the potential valuable targets determines the weighting factors, which are used to select the effective features of the targets in the scene. As the scene classification is refined, the information of the scene will be more and more detailed, and the parameters for guiding, such as weighting factors, will be more and more precise, and the result of the target evaluation will become more and more accurate.

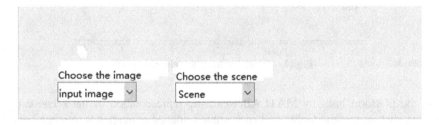

Fig. 3. The Menu of image and scene selection

   By analyzing the semantic information of the regional scene, and comparing the context information between the scene and the target, it is possible to select appropriate features and target evaluation method for the region. Further, the scene estimation of the future observation area may be performed in advance according to the flight orbit of the satellite, and an appropriate method is selected according to the method to achieve the target evaluation. Defining the scene semantics of the image into a format as $\{Scene, Target, Scale, Feature, Summary\ Information\}$. The 'target' represents the potential targets in the scene; some features of the target are mostly presented as local saliency, and the 'scale' is based on potential targets to determine the size of the target area in order to highlight the targets, as well as determining the scale range of different size targets in a scene to achieve multi-target multi-scale target evaluation; 'features' is to select the effective features of the target in the scene; 'gist information' is a feature representing the scene, as a reference of the potential targets saliency. The parsing of the scene semantic information and the pseudo code selected by the target evaluation algorithm are shown in Fig. 4.

```
IF Scene = S₁ THEN Target = {T₁, T₂};  end
IF Scene = S₁ and Target = T₁
THEN
    scale = wᵢ;
    feature = F{f₁, f₂, f₃};
    gist ={f_gist1, f_gist2, f_gist3};
    P(S₁|T₁) = p₁
    IF P(S₁|T₁)= p₁ THEN  weight ={α₁, α₂, α₃};  end
end
IF Scene = S₁ and Target = T₂
THEN
    scale = wⱼ;
    feature = F{f₁, f₃};
    gist = {f_gist1, f_gist3};
    P(S₁|T₂)=p₂
    IF P(S₁|T₂)=p₂ THEN weight = {β₁, β₂, β₃};  end
end
IF Scene = S₁and Target = {T₁, T₂}
THEN
    Method  = Model1;
end
```

Fig. 4. Pseudo code of the algorithm

From the platform built by MATLAB, semantic representation of the scene can be selected, such as sea and Gobi. And each scene semantic corresponds to scene context information contains features, setting parameters of targets and the scene, which can guide the selection of appropriate methods to complete the target evaluation under the scene. Figure 5 shows the result of the target evaluation of the image according to the selected scene. The simulation experiment selects the scene of the image by manual selection. While onboard the semantic description of the scene needs to be obtained according to the mapping relationship between the actual observed field and the geographical location. Each scene corresponds to an algorithm configuration file, and the corresponding parameters of the algorithm in the configuration file can be improved by experiments to make the system continuously self-learning and correcting.

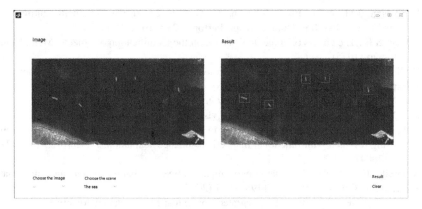

Fig. 5. The processing result of an image with sea background

5 Conclusion

The scene context information in the remote sensing image provides useful and important information and guidance for the satellite to achieve onboard target evaluation. The guiding role of context information in the visual system is taken as the entry point, and the potential target in different scenes through the scene context information has been studied. Thus a novel integrated saliency model has been proposed, in which the analyzing the parameters corresponding to the scene context information and the target feature information has been introduced. In the model, the guiding system selects the appropriate method to achieve the target evaluation in different scenarios. In order to verify its validity, the experiment was carried out by using MATLAB to set up the experimental environment. Selecting the preset scene to call its configuration file, and read the information in it to realize the target evaluation under the certain scene. And the scene context guided valuable target detection is simulated and realized.

Acknowledgment. The project was supported is the independent research and development project in China Academy of Space Technology.

References

1. Auckland, M.E., et al.: Non-target objects can influence perceptual processes during object recognition. Psychon. Bull. Rev. **14**, 332–337 (2007)
2. Biederman, I., et al.: Scene perception: detecting and judging objects undergoing relational violations. Cognit. Psychol. **14**, 143–177 (1982)
3. Davenport, J.L., Potter, M.C.: Scene consistency in objects and background perception. Psychol. Sci. **15**, 559–564 (2004)
4. Friedman, A.: Framing pictures: the role of knowledge in automatized encoding and memory of gist. J. Exp. Psychol. Gen. **108**, 316–355 (1979)
5. Gordon, R.D.: Attentional allocation during the perception of scenes. J. Exp. Psychol. Hum. Percept. Perform. **30**, 760–777 (2004)

6. Henderson, J.M., et al.: Effects of semantic consistency on eye movements during scene viewing. J. Exp. Psychol. Hum. Percept. Perform. **25**, 210–228 (1999)
7. Palmer, S.E.: The effects of contextual scenes on the identification of objects. Mem. Cognit. **3**, 519–526 (1975)
8. Hollingworth, A., Henderson, J.M.: Does consistent scene context facilitate object detection. J. Exp. Psychol. Gen. **127**, 398–415 (1998)
9. Bar, M.: Visual objects in context. Nat. Rev. Neurosci. **5**, 617–629 (2004)
10. Bar, M., Aminoff, E.: Cortical analysis of visual context. Neuron **38**, 347–358 (2003)
11. Goh, J., et al.: Cortical areas involved in object, background, and object-background processing revealed with functional magnetic resonance adaptation. J. Neurosci. **24**, 10223–10228 (2004)
12. Aminoff, E., et al.: The parahippocampal cortex mediates spatial and non-spatial associations. Cereb. Cortex **27**, 1493–1503 (2007)
13. Gronau, N., Neta, M., Bar, M.: Integrated contextual representation for objects' identities and their locations. J. Cogn. Neurosci. **20**(3), 371–388 (2008)
14. Murray, N., Vanrell, M., Otazu, X., et al.: Saliency estimation using a non-parametric low-level vision model. In: IEEE Conference on Computer Vision and Pattern Recognition, pp. 433–440 (2011)
15. Torralba, A., et al.: Contextual guidance of attention in natural scenes: the role of global features on object search. Psychol. Rev. **113**, 766–786 (2006)
16. Hoiem, D., et al.: Putting objects in perspective. Proc. IEEE Comp. Vis. Pattern Recog. **2**, 2137–2144 (2006)
17. He, X., Zemel, R.S., Carreira-Perpiñán, M.Á.: Multiscale conditional random fields for image labeling. In: CVPR 2004, vol. 2, pp. II-695–II-702 (2004)
18. Viola, P., Jones, M.: Robust real-time face detection. Int. J. Comput. Vis. **57**(2), 137–154 (2004)
19. Torralba, A., Murphy, K.P., Freeman, W.T.: Contextual models for object detection using boosted random fields. In: Nips, pp. 1401–1408 (2004)
20. Wolf, L., Bileschi, S.: A critical view of context. Int. J. Comput. Vis. **69**(2), 251–261 (2006)
21. Li, W.J., Zhao, H.P., Guo, J., et al.: A multi-scale fractal dimension based onboard ship saliency detection algorithm. In: 2016 IEEE 13th International Conference on Signal Processing (ICSP), pp. 628–633 (2016)

Information Centric Networking for Future Deep Space Networks

Yongqi Zhou$^{(\boxtimes)}$ ⓘ, Wenfeng Li ⓘ, and Kanglian Zhao ⓘ

Nanjing University, Nanjing, China
nju_zhou@foxmail.com

Abstract. With the flourish of the space sensing technology, various space information systems are playing an irreplaceable role in space exploration. Delay-Tolerant Networking (DTN) has been proposed to cope with the harsh transmission conditions and it provides a store-forward mechanism to push scientific data to Earth. However, in the future, Deep Space Networking (DSN) is bound to be more richer, while the volume of data transmission will rise considerably and communication services will also be diversified including both push-traffic and pull-traffic. In this way, we think DTN still needs to be improved while Content-Centric Networking (CCN) may be another candidate for these challenges. CCN [14] is a novel networking paradigm which has been used for terrestrial network and it provides both push-traffic and pull traffic for different scenes. Besides of it, cache mechanism can effectively reduce the influence arising from increase in data transmission. Therefore, we think CCN may be a better solution for future Deep Space Networking.

Keywords: Push-traffic · Pull-traffic · Cache · CCN

1 Introduction

Currently, the Deep Space Networking (DSN) has been researched extensively for scientific exploration. It provides a necessary communication system to receive commands from Earth to the spacecraft and to return scientific data. To date, Deep Space Networking (DSN) only consists of several relay orbiters and bound assets e.g., landers, rovers, probes, which presents a uncomplicated structure. Thus, deep space missions are traditional robotic missions [7] and scientific data collected by robot are directly pushed to Earth. Besides, DSN works in a harsh transmission conditions including long propagation delays, high loss of data, frequent link disruptions, dynamic changes of the network infrastructure, etc. In this way, Delay-Tolerant Networking (DTN) [15] has been proposed, which provides a store-forward mechanism in this environment.

DTN is a network architecture that supports significant delays or disruptions between data search and data receive phases. In this architecture, Bundle protocol (BP) plays a pretty significant role in which data units, termed bundles, can

© ICST Institute for Computer Sciences, Social Informatics and Telecommunications Engineering 2019
Published by Springer Nature Switzerland AG 2019. All Rights Reserved
M. Jia et al. (Eds.): WiSATS 2019, LNICST 280, pp. 437–448, 2019.
https://doi.org/10.1007/978-3-030-19153-5_45

be temporarily stored at intermediate nodes until an appropriate receiver can be found. Additionally, BP also provides custody transfer option to improve the reliability of transmission. When this function is opened, sender will not delete this bundle in local storage and resend it until receiving an acknowledgement from the next hop node. Therefore, DTN is useful for coping with disrupted links, long delays and intermittent connectivity. During this decade, DTN has been modified in many ways and it seems that DTN is pretty suitable for current Deep Space Networking.

However, with the flourish of the space sensing technology, more and more satellites and space probes will be put into operation for communication, broadcasting, Earth observation, navigation, and deep-space exploration, etc. More types of data including audio, video, new in-situ relay services for communications and navigation services will appear in the future DSN. What's more, interoperability and cross-support will be necessary to achieve the connectivity goals of the Mars Relay Network (MRN) in the human Mars era [10]. The communication connection fabric is bound to be richer: robotic sensors will push scientific data to Earth continuously while astronauts also need request some specific message from other nodes. Data transfer will no longer be limited to the single pathway between deep space and Earth, but all the entities will be interconnected and exchange data each other. Thus, future deep space network capabilities and services are based on a service oriented architecture and must be able to provide both push and pull transmission so that it can meet the diversified communication services. Additionally, it is necessary that the candidate architecture also have an effective measure to deal with the increase of data transmission. In this way, we think that DTN which is designed only for push traffic still need to be improved due to these predictable changes in future DSN.

Therefore, in this paper, we present an information-centric approach to meet aforementioned challenges. Information-Centric Networking (ICN) is a novel networking paradigm which is not based on the point-to-point scenario. Instead of the conventional host-centric, content is considered to be the first element in ICN and each of them has a unique name as the identifier. Several ICN architecture proposals have emerged from research communities and Content-Centric Networking (CCN) is one of these proposals. In CCN, each node has three important data structure, namely the content store (CS), the pending interest table (PIT) and the forwarding information base (FIB) [5]. CS caches data transmitted through it. When some interest is coming, PIT records its incoming interface. Then, the table is checked when the content message returns to forward it. FIB is just like the IP routing table. It forwards the incoming interest message by names prefix. The CCN paradigm is the ideal candidate architecture for the implementation of that space internetworking.

Generally, there are several benefits that CCN could provide.

1.1   In-network Storage

In CCN, all hosts have CS. When receiving some content message, they decide whether to cache the content message according to the corresponding mechanism. In this way, many hosts have the duplicate, and thus, when consumer requests the same content, the interest message will be responded quickly. There-fore, it reduces both of distance and latency in transmission and improves the quality of service [9, 12]. It is worth mentioning that in space networking, power constraint is a prominent problem and communications consume more power than other activities, so cache mechanism also contributes to saving devices power partly.

1.2 Data-Centric Security

CCN provides a security mechanism based on the message, which is totally different from the host-based mechanism in IP [6]. Three entities are included in it and interrelated with each other, as shown in Fig. 1. Real World Identity (RWI) means real identity of satellites or space probes in the space and Name represents content name. Then producer associates a public key with a private key. When receiving a content message, consumer verifies whether the producer does publish this content. This mechanism is directly built on message to ensure the reliability of the content source.

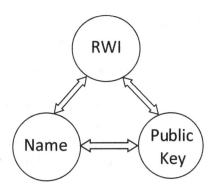

Fig. 1. Entities in security mechanism.

1.3 Handing Mobility

CCN supports mobility inherently [4]. When a consumer moved for a long dis-tance, it can resend the unsatisfied interest message and wait for the respond. Besides, consumer can use different interfaces to forward or send message due to the native support of host multi-homing. It is complex when producer moves because FIB of neighbor nodes need to be updated slowly, which brings latency. However, thanks to its in-networking and multi-homing, the influence of pro-ducer mobility is weakened to some degree.

Besides of these, we identity four primary points of common characteristics between CCN and DTN [16]:

- Network Storage: Both architectures rely on in-network storage.
- Late Binding: Both approaches espouse the late binding of names to locations.
- Data Longevity: Both approaches make the units of network interaction (ICN data objects, DTN bundles) into long-term entities in comparison to traditional IP packets.
- Flexible Routing: Both approaches relax traditional constraints on routing and transport (loop free, multi-homing), making richer routing substrates possible.

These similar capabilities or elements seem to indicate that CCN, like DTN, can also be an alternative solution for DSN, and we will compare these two architectures in different scenarios as follows.

2   Comparisons Between CCN and DTN for Future DSN

In [8], Kevin Fall has made a comparison between Information Centric and Delay Tolerant Networking as shown in Table 1.

Table 1. Comparison between ICN and DTN

Feature	DTN	ICN
Push model	Yes	No but "preplacing" content - similar
Interest	Recent	Yes
Storage	Persistent	Transient (persistent is add-on)
Custodian	Integral	Separate
Node IDs	Yes	Varies [No (NDN)/Yes (Netinf)]
Conv.Layer	Yes	Yes (Netinf - explicit)/Yes (CCN - effectively)
Lifetimes	Yes	Yes (on data and on interests)
Names	Regex on strings (URI)	Prefix-based names (CCN); flat names (Netinf)

We can see that many specifics have been mentioned in this table. Firstly, DTN names endpoints, groups or predicates with URI-based format while ICN names data and matches data to interest. Secondly, DTN uses storage to primarily for persistence and disruption tolerance, but storage in ICN mainly acts as a cache. Security models are also different because DTN provides security of channels and ICN pays more attention to content security. Besides of these, to make more distinct comparisons between CCN and DTN in deep space environment, we analyse these two architectures in future Mars-Earth system, as illustrated in Fig. 2.

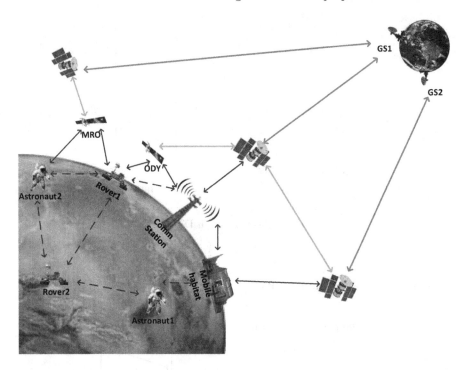

Fig. 2. Connectivity in future DSN.

2.1   Push-Traffic

Forwarding data to Earth without being requested (Push-traffic) is the basic mission in deep space exploration and DTN is just designed for this scene. We simplify the Mars-Earth system as shown in Fig. 3 and assume that node-A need to push data to node-B. Then, this mission is divided into two processes: data transmission and reply of ACK as shown in Fig. 3.

Correspondingly, CCN also provides a mechanism to support push-traffic: Long-Lived Interest [3,13] depicted in Fig. 4. In the beginning, consumer sends a long-live interest message to producer. Different from standard interest message, it has a very long lifetime. Producer receives such request and waits for the generation of corresponding content. Once the corresponding sensors collect a set of information, they push matched content to respond the request. Then, the lifetime is refreshed to wait for the next periodic content. So, the long-lived interest maintains a state of waiting for being responded in producers. Due to the high loss of data in transmission, if consumer fails to receive the content within vRTO (equal to lifetime), it resends this long-lived Interest. vRTO is a little larger than the interval between data generation. During this process, pull-based transmission is normally running. In this way, we omit the process of requests transmission and achieve the push-traffic of periodic data.

Therefore, in terms of push-traffic, both CCN and DTN perform well.

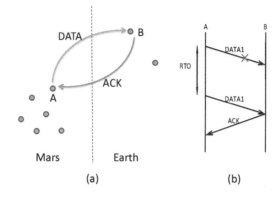

Fig. 3. Push-traffic in DTN.

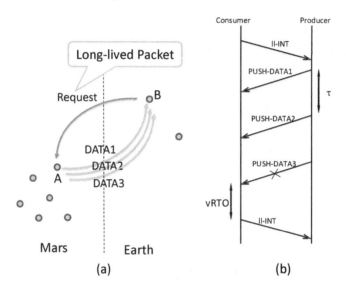

Fig. 4. Push-traffic in CCN.

2.2 Pull-Traffic

Due to the increase of nodes and human activities in DSN, communication services wouldn't be limited to push-traffic any more. Sometimes, we also need to request some specific data that we urgently need. In this way, request-respond transmission (Pull traffic) is necessary while DTN didn't take this scenario into consideration. So it is complicated to finish this process as depicted in Fig. 5. Firstly, nodeA will forwards a message containing its request to the network. After receiving it, nodeB responds an ACK and then sends the corresponding data to nodeA. Finally, nodeA gets the data it needs and sends an ACK to complete this request-respond transmission. From these processes, we can see that it is really complicated to implement this function in DTN while it also consumes more resources and time.

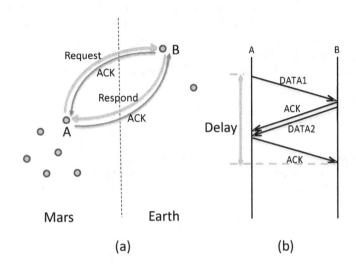

Fig. 5. Pull-traffic in DTN.

However, CCN provides pull-traffic inherently. In Fig. 6, nodeA just forwards an interest package to the network and any node could respond if they have these content in their local content store. These processes are pretty simple and multi-homing can effectively reduce the transmission latency. So, we can see that in the scenario of pull-traffic, CCN has a better performance than DTN does.

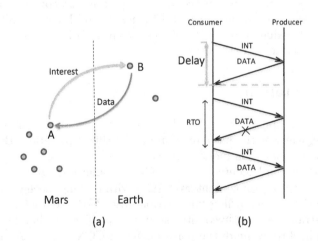

Fig. 6. Pull-traffic in CCN.

2.3 Cache

As mentioned in Sect. 1, some nodes in DSN may have content store to cache important data, such as communication station, mobile habitat, etc. In Fig. 7, node1 and node7 completed a data transmission and in this process, node6 cached this message. After that, another request of this data can be responded directly by node6. In this way, part of the requested data may be directly responded by nodes on Martian surface. Through this mechanism, we can avoid the transmission in inter-satellite links and reduce the latency, while DTN don't provide this function.

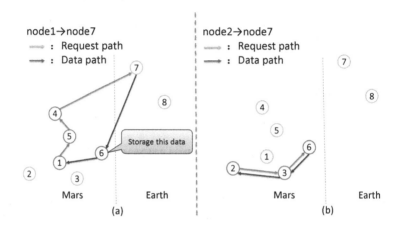

Fig. 7. Cache in CCN.

Through these comparisons, we come to the preliminary conclusion that CCN can basically realize the function of DTN, namely push-traffic. What's more, CCN also provide request-respond mechanism conveniently to support diversified communication services in the future.

3 Implementation

In this section, we apply CCN to Mars-Earth system to verify the implementation of push traffic, which is the basic mission in scientific exploration. Besides of it, we achieve the transmission mode of request-respond in another experiment.

To this end, we implemented modified CCN simulator in OPNET [11], which includes data structures of content store (CS) with caching mechanism, pending interest table (PIT), forwarding information base (FIB), contact graph routing (CGR), push-traffic by long-lived interest and so on. Then we build this scenario as shown in Fig. 8 to evaluate the performance of CCN. There are six nodes in this scenario with two astronauts (EVA1, EVA2), two grand stations (GS1, GS2) and two relay orbiters (MRO, ODY) [1].

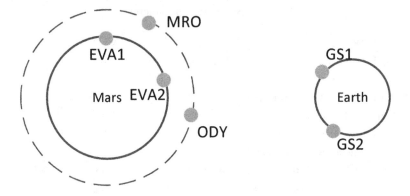

Fig. 8. Experimental scene.

Figure 9 depicts the contact plan exported from STK. The horizontal axis shows the time divided into equal one hour intervals and the vertical axis represents the moment that two nodes are in contact with each other [2]. Simulation parameters are set as represented in Table 2.

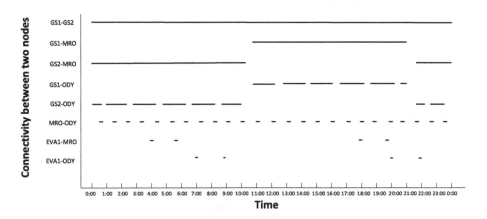

Fig. 9. Contact plan.

3.1 Push

In this scenario, we expect that EVA1 will forward scientific data to GS1 continuously without being requested. Then, GS1 firstly send a long-lived interest to EVA1 and this interest will be stored in EVA1 forever even if it once responded to it.

In Fig. 9, we can see that from 4 o'clock, EVA1 generate corresponding message every one hour and send it to GS1. As the link between EVA1 and satellite

Table 2. Simulation parameters

Scenario type	CCN
Link Data Rate (EVA-Satellite) (Mbps)	100
Link Data Rate (Satellite-Ground Station) (Mbps)	10
Latency (EVA-Satellite) (sec)	0.012
Latency (Satellite-Ground Station) (sec)	750
Interest Packet Size (byte)	80
Data Packet Size (Mbyte)	5
Interest Packet Inter-arrival time (sec)	Constants (3600)
Data Packet Inter-arrival time (sec)	Constants (3600)
Length of Simulation Run (sec)	86400

is frequently disrupted between 4 o'clock and 9 o'clock, transmission delay in this interim would be unstable but in a small range. After 9 o'clock, EVA1 can connect with neither MRO nor ODY until 18 o'clock. Thus, there will be a huge latency over nine hours when transmissions start during this period. Figure 10 shows the simulation result that accord with the above description.

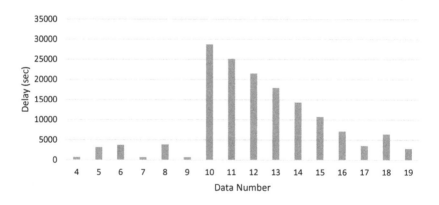

Fig. 10. Push-traffic

It is worth to mention that the path will be recalculated every time before EVA1 replies, instead of following the record in PIT according to the original CCN. In this way, we realize the push-traffic in CCN which is similar with DTN.

3.2 Pull

In this experiment, EVA1 requests data storing in GS1 every hour and waits for the corresponding data. If EVA1 receives a packet that has been requested,

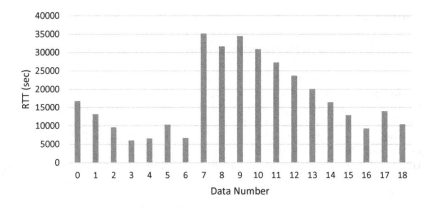

Fig. 11. Pull-traffic

it will record the time of forwarding and receiving. After seven thousands seconds of simulation, we stop this pull-traffic and print the transmission record as illustrated in Fig. 11.

To verify the correctness of these result, we can focus on the relevance of Figs. 9 and 11. In the beginning, requests before 4 o'clock would be stored in cache until the connection between Mars and relay orbiter is established. So, the latency before 4 o'clock presents a downtrend due to the different start time of requests. After 7 o'clock, although we can send request packet by a short-time link between EVA and ODY, data return would still be put back because the corresponding paths are unavailable until 18 o'clock.

4 Conclusion and Future Work

Currently, Delay-Tolerant Networking provides a store-forward mechanism to support push-traffic of scientific data in DSN. However, due to the increase of data transmission and diversification of communication services, we think CCN may be a candidate solution for these challenges, while it inherently provides both of pull-traffic and push-traffic. Further, cache can help to reduce the effects caused by the increased data transmission.

Therefore, in this paper, we implement modified CCN in OPNET including three data structures, contact graph routing, push-traffic, pull-traffic and so on. Then we apply it to Mars-Earth system to preliminarily evaluate the performance in DSN. Finally, we realized our idea in this scenario.

However, in this paper, we only preliminarily verified the feasibility of applying CCN to future DSN. Some aspects still remain to be researched. For example, cache can effectively reduce the transmission latency, but almost all the nodes in DSN don't have enough space to store these content. Our future work will be devoted to the verification of cache mechanism.

References

1. Alaoui, S.E., Palusa, S., Ramamurthy, B.: The interplanetary internet implemented on the geni testbed. In: 2015 IEEE Global Communications Conference (GLOBE-COM), pp. 1–6, December 2015. https://doi.org/10.1109/GLOCOM.2015.7417313
2. El Alaoui, S.: Routing optimization in interplanetary networks (2015)
3. Amadeo, M., Campolo, C., Molinaro, A.: Internet of Things via named data networking: the support of push traffic. In: 2014 International Conference and Workshop on the Network of the Future (NOF), pp. 1–5, December 2014. https://doi.org/10.1109/NOF.2014.7119766
4. Amadeo, M., et al.: Information-centric networking for the Internet of Things: challenges and opportunities. IEEE Netw. **30**(2), 92–100 (2016). https://doi.org/10.1109/MNET.2016.7437030
5. Amadeo, M., Campolo, C., Molinaro, A.: Information-centric networking for connected vehicles: a survey and future perspectives. IEEE Commun. Mag. **54**(2), 98–104 (2016)
6. Baccelli, E., Mehlis, C., Hahm, O., Schmidt, T.C.: Information centric networking in the IoT: experiments with NDN in the wild, pp. 77–86 (2014)
7. Cola, T.D., Paolini, E., Liva, G., Calzolari, G.P.: Reliability options for data communications in the future deep-space missions. Proc. IEEE **99**(11), 2056–2074 (2011)
8. Fall, K.: Comparing information-centric and delay-tolerant networking. In: IEEE Conference on Local Computer Networks, p. xxxiii (2012)
9. Fall, K.: A message-switched architecture for challenged internets, October 2018
10. Kazz, G., Burleigh, S.C., Cheung, K.M., Shah, B.: Evolution of the mars relay network end-to-end information system in the mars human era (2030–2040). In: International Conference on Space Operations (2016)
11. Kim, S., Kim, K., Choi, S., Kim, B., Roh, B.H.: An implementation of content-centric network, using OPNET modeler. In: Opnetwork (2012)
12. Lindgren, A., Abdesslem, F.B., Ahlgren, B., Schelén, O., Malik, A.M.: Design choices for the IoT in information-centric networks. In: 2016 13th IEEE Annual Consumer Communications Networking Conference (CCNC), pp. 882–888, January 2016. https://doi.org/10.1109/CCNC.2016.7444905
13. Majeed, M.F., Ahmed, S.H., Dailey, M.N.: Enabling push-based critical data forwarding in vehicular named data networks. IEEE Commun. Lett. **21**(4), 873–876 (2017). https://doi.org/10.1109/LCOMM.2016.2642194
14. Rubenstein, D., Misra, V., Feng, H., Martin, M.C.: Content centric networking (2014)
15. Torgerson, L., et al.: Delay-tolerant networking architecture. RFC 4838 (2007). https://doi.org/10.17487/RFC4838
16. Tyson, G., Bigham, J., Bodanese, E.: Towards an information-centric delay-tolerant network. In: 2013 IEEE Conference on Computer Communications Workshops (INFOCOM WKSHPS), pp. 387–392, April 2013. https://doi.org/10.1109/INFCOMW.2013.6970723

A Weighted Set Cover Model for Task Planning of Earth Observation Satellites

Pengyun Li, Hongyan Li$^{(\boxtimes)}$, and Jun Chang

State Key Laboratory of Integrated Service Networks, Xidian University,
Xian 710071, China
hyli@xidian.edu.cn

Abstract. Due to the diversification of observation missions and the differentiation of satellite resources, the task scheduling of Earth observation satellites has always been an NP-hard problem. In this paper, aiming at multi-load Earth observation satellite mission scheduling, considering multi-satellite coordinated observation, facing regional target mission and point target mission, a weighted set cover model is proposed to represent the coupling relationship between multi-satellite and multi-task. The classical greedy approximation algorithm is used to optimize the sum of satellite observation time windows. The model-based algorithm can effectively save satellite storage resources and sensor resources, and realize multi-satellite coordinated observation task scheduling.

Keywords: Task planning · Set cover model ·
Greedy approximation algorithm

1 Introduction

As an effective tool for the exploring of the earth's resources, the earth observation satellites (EOS) have been widely used in the fields of the agricultural monitoring, the natural disaster warning, the large-scale infrastructure construction and the ground military target identification [12]. However, with the increase of the number of observing tasks and the diversification of observational demands, the scarce resources on the star become more and more valuable. How to maximize the resource utilization through reasonable scheduling has become an important issue to be solved urgently.

For example, when it is necessary to observe a large range of targets, or to make continuous observations on a hot-spot area, it will take a long time or cannot complete at all depending on the periodic motion of one single satellite, where the joint observation of multiple satellites and the splitting-aggregation of multiple tasks will greatly shorten the observation delay and save the satellite resources.

Supported by organization x.

M. Jia et al. (Eds.): WiSATS 2019, LNICST 280, pp. 449–455, 2019.
https://doi.org/10.1007/978-3-030-19153-5_46

The task scheduling of the earth observation satellites is a typical NP-Hard problem. In the process of multi-satellite coordinated observation, due to the different geographic locations and the different requirements in time delay and resolution of the observation tasks, as well as the limited time windows of the remote sensing satellites flying upon the observation tasks, the optimal matching method of satellite resources and tasks is difficult to find.

The existing scheduling models include integer linear programming model [4,6], backpack model [5], graph theory model [1,9,10], etc. The related algorithms are mostly heuristic algorithms such as simulated annealing algorithm and tabu search algorithm [9]. These algorithms have uncertain time complexity and cannot give approximate optimal solutions of NP-hard problems in polynomial time, resulting in high task acquisition delay and low utilization of satellite observation resources and energy resources.

In this paper, we will focus on the graph model representation of multi-satellite multi-task scenario in the earth observation process. Firstly, we will present the satellite observation scenario. Then, the weighted set cover modeling process will be introduced, followed by a greedy approximation algorithm, proved to be the optimal approximation algorithm in polynomial time for the minimum cost in our model.

2   WSC Model

2.1   Observation Scenario

Figure 1 shows the expansion diagram of multi-observation satellite flight around the earth over a period of time. The colored lines represent the satellite's flight paths, and the elliptic colored part represents the to-be-observed tasks.

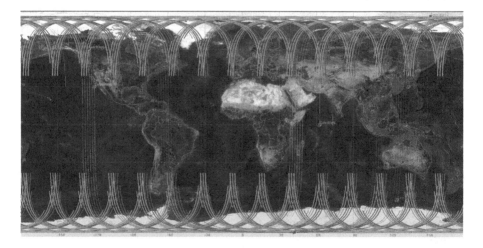

Fig. 1. The expansion diagram of multi-observation satellite flight around the earth over a period of time.

2.2   Modeling Process

Since the satellite trajectory is periodic, we consider the situation in which resources and tasks are predictable. In addition, due to the principle of fairness, the priority of observation tasks is not considered. Based on these principles, we model satellite observation scenarios.

Definition 1. *The parameters used in the following are defined as follows.*

- m_i: *The identification number of the original task,* $i = 1, 2, ...;$
- m_{ij}: *The identification number of the sub task split from* m_i, $j = 1, 2, ...;$
- $\mathcal{M}$: *The set of all sub tasks,* $\mathcal{M} = \{m_{ij} | i, j = 1, 2, ...\};$
- T: *The total period of time considered;*
- τ_k: *The k-th discrete time slot;*
- sat_p: *The identification number of the satellite,* $p = 1, 2, ...;$
- $\mathcal{S}_{sat_p}^{\tau_k}$: *The collection set of the sub tasks which can be observed by* sat_p *within time slot* τ_k;
- $G_{\mathcal{S}_{sat_p}^{\tau_k}}$: *The gain of the set* $\mathcal{S}_{sat_p}^{\tau_k}$, *which is defined as the number of the elements in the set* $\mathcal{S}_{sat_p}^{\tau_k}$;
- $w_{\mathcal{S}_{sat_p}^{\tau_k}}$: *The wight of the set* $\mathcal{S}_{sat_p}^{\tau_k}$, *which is defined as the time window size required to observe all sub tasks in the set* $\mathcal{S}_{sat_p}^{\tau_k}$;

Firstly, the original tasks $m_i(i = 1, 2, ...)$ are split into sub tasks $m_{ij}(j = 1, 2, ...)$ of the same size according to experience or learning, satisfying $|m_i| = \bigcup_j |m_{ij}|$, where $|*|$ represents the geographic location of task $*$, as shown in Fig. 2(a) the task1.

Then, the total period of time we considered T is sliced into n time slots, donated in order as $\tau_1, \tau_2, ..., \tau_n$.

In each time slots, we model the collection of the sub tasks covered by each satellite as a set. The gain of each set can be expressed by the number of elements in the set, that is, the number of subtasks observed. In addition, a cost factor is attached to each set, defined here as the time required for all elements in the set to be covered, i.e. the length of time window required by the satellite to observe these subtasks.

For example, Fig. 2(b) shows the trajectory coverage of satellite sat_1 and satellite sat_2 in the same time slot τ_1, and the shaded parts represent subtasks m_{11} and m_{12}, then we get $\mathcal{S}_{sat_1}^{\tau_1} = \{m_{11}, m_{12}\}$, $G_{\mathcal{S}_{sat_1}^{\tau_1}} = 2$, $w_{\mathcal{S}_{sat_1}^{\tau_1}} = 1$, and $\mathcal{S}_{sat_2}^{\tau_1} = \{m_{12}\}$, $G_{\mathcal{S}_{sat_2}^{\tau_1}} = 1$, $w_{\mathcal{S}_{sat_2}^{\tau_1}} = 1$. That is, the two sets have the same cost, but the set $\mathcal{S}_{sat_1}^{\tau_1}$ covers more elements and the gain is larger, so the set $\mathcal{S}_{sat_1}^{\tau_1}$ is better than the set $\mathcal{S}_{sat_2}^{\tau_1}$. In addition, intuitively from Fig. 2 that storage resources will be wasted to observe non-target areas if satellite sat_2 were utilized in this area. The specific planning algorithm will be mentioned in Sect. 3.

According to the above modeling method, we construct the multi-satellite multi-task observation scenario as a weighted set cover model. Next we discuss the way of minimizing the cost on the premise of all tasks can be observed.

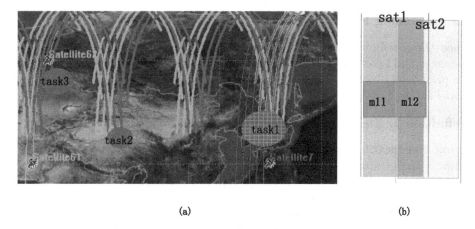

Fig. 2. (a) Task splitting diagram (b) the example schematic diagram of flight paths of satellite sat_1 and satellite sat_2 in time slot τ_1

3   Approximate Greedy Algorithm

A large number of scholars have studied the degree of approximation of the set cover algorithm. The set cover was first proved to be NP-Complete by Karp [3], and Johnson [7] gave a polynomial time greedy approximation algorithm with an approximate ratio of $\ln n$. Chvatal [8] extended the algorithm to the weighted set cover problem. Feige et al. [2] proved that there is no polynomial time approximation algorithm better than approximation ratio $(1 - \varepsilon)\ln X$, $(\varepsilon > 0)$, unless $NP \subseteq DTIME\left(n^{O(\log \log n)}\right)$. Zhang et al. [11] gave a greedy algorithm of $\ln(|X| + 1)$-approximation to the weighted set cover problem, according to Feige [2], this algorithm is optimal approximation algorithm in polynomial time.

Based on the proposed weighted set cover model, drawing on the classic greedy approximation algorithm, by adding the constraints of remote sensing satellite observation, an optimal approximation algorithm in polynomial time is given to optimize the time window of remote sensing satellite observation to save the remote sensing resources.

3.1   Constraints

The total on-off duration of each sensor on the satellite is limited by the satellite storage capacity, i.e., the formula below needs to be always established,

$$\sum_{k=1}^{n} \left\| \mathcal{S}_{sat_p}^{\tau_k} \right\| \leq C_{sat_p} \tag{1}$$

where $\left\| \mathcal{S}_{sat_p}^{\tau_k} \right\|$ represents the data sum of the subtask observation in the set, and C_{sat_p} represents the storage capacity of the satellite sat_p.

If the total data amount of the subtasks covered by satellite sat_p in all time slots exceeds the satellite storage capacity, the last overflow subtasks will be discarded according to the algorithm execution order.

3.2 Algorithm Flow

This paper draws on the thought of greedy algorithm proposed by Zhang [11], and considering the constraints of satellite scenario, the following approximate greedy algorithm suitable for the satellite scenario is given.

Algorithm 1. Approximate Greedy Algorithm

1: **Input:** $\mathcal{M}, S_{sat_p}^{\tau_k}, w_{S_{sat_p}^{\tau_k}}, C_{sat_p} (k = 1, 2, ..., n; p = 1, 2, ...)$
2: **Output:** a series of ordered sets $\mathcal{O} = \{\mathcal{O}_{sat_j}^{\tau_i} | i, j = 1, 2, ...\}$
3: $\mathcal{O} \leftarrow \phi$;
4: $\mathcal{V} \leftarrow \mathcal{M}$;
5: **while** $\mathcal{V} \neq \phi$ **do**
6:    Select the $S_{sat_j}^{\tau_i}$ such that $\dfrac{w_{S_{sat_j}^{\tau_i}}}{G_{S_{sat_j}^{\tau_i} \cap \mathcal{V}}}$ is the smallest;
7:    **if** $\left\| \mathcal{O}_{sat_j} \cup S_{sat_j}^{\tau_i} \right\| \leq C_{sat_j}$ **then**
8:        $\mathcal{V} = \mathcal{V} - S_{sat_j}^{\tau_i}$;
9:        $\mathcal{O} = \mathcal{O} \cup S_{sat_j}^{\tau_i}$;
10:    **else**
11:        $\mathcal{V} = \mathcal{V} - \sum\limits_{i=1}^{n} S_{sat_j}^{\tau_i}$;
12:    **end if**
13:    Output the set $\mathcal{O}$;
14: **end while**

The algorithm is a greedy algorithm. Each loop selects the smallest set of $\dfrac{w_{S_{sat_j}^{\tau_i}}}{G_{S_{sat_j}^{\tau_i} \cap \mathcal{V}}}$ from the remaining sets while ensuring that the observation data sum of each satellite does not exceed its total storage, until all subtasks are covered, where $G_{S_{sat_j}^{\tau_i} \cap \mathcal{V}}$ represents the number of subtasks selected for the first time in the set S_{sat_j}, and $w_{S_{sat_j}^{\tau_i}}$ represents the cost (time window size) required to cover the set S_{sat_j}. The algorithm returns the selected collection $\mathcal{O}$ in order of execution.

4   Approximate Analysis of the Greedy Algorithm

Theorem 1. *The approximation of the greedy algorithm proposed is lnn+O(1)-approximation of the optimal solution.*

Proof. We analyze the approximation of this algorithm briefly. In the greedy algorithm, the cost of selecting a set is $w_{\mathcal{S}^{\tau_i}_{sat_j}}$, and there are $G_{\mathcal{S}^{\tau_i}_{sat_j} \cap \mathcal{V}}$ subtasks that are covered for the first time in the set. So in this step, the cost of each node being covered is

$$cost(x_i) = \frac{w_{\mathcal{S}^{\tau_i}_{sat_j}}}{G_{\mathcal{S}^{\tau_i}_{sat_j} \cap \mathcal{V}}}. \tag{2}$$

Obviously, the total cost of all subtasks in the algorithm is

$$apx = \sum_i cost(x_i), \tag{3}$$

where apx is the cost of the greedy algorithm.

Now we consider the optimal solution. Suppose that at a certain step, the uncovered elements are $x_i, ..., x_n$, and the selected element is x_i, with another c_i elements selected, that is, the number of uncovered elements are at most c_i. The set cost is $w_{\mathcal{S}_i}$, so the following inequality holds,

$$opt \geq \frac{n-i+1}{c_i} * w_{\mathcal{S}_i}, \tag{4}$$

summing the left and right sides of the inequality respectively, we have

$$apx \leq opt * \sum_{i=1}^{n} \frac{1}{n-i+1}, \tag{5}$$

where $\sum\limits_{i=1}^{n} \frac{1}{n-i+1} = \sum\limits_{i=1}^{n} \frac{1}{i} = \ln n + c$, c is an Euler constant with a value of 0.6 approximately, i.e.,

$$apx \leq opt * (\ln n + O(1)). \tag{6}$$

According to Feige et al.'s proof at [2], the algorithm is the optimal polynomial time approximation algorithm for the weighted set cover model in the EOS scenarios.

5   Conclusion

In this paper, a weighted set cover model was proposed to characterize the matching of the tasks and the resource for the multi-satellite multi-task scenario. We put up one approximate greedy algorithm based on the model, where the constraint of satellite cache resources was considered, and the approximation of the algorithm to the optimal solution was analyzed.

Acknowledgments. This work is supported by the National Natural Science Foundation of China (91638202,61871456,61401326,61571351), the National Key Research and Development Program of China (2016YFB0501004), the National S & T Major Project (2015ZX03002006), the 111 Project (B08038), Natural Science Basic Research Plan in Shaanxi Province of China (2016JQ6054).

References

1. Gabrel, V., Vanderpooten, D.: Enumeration and interactive selection of efficient paths in a multiple criteria graph for scheduling an earth observing satellite. Eur. J. Oper. Res. **139**, 533–542 (2002)
2. Feige, U.: A threshold of ln n for approximating set cover 1 introduction. J. ACM **45**(4), 314–318 (1999)
3. Karp, R.M.: Reducibility among combinatorial problems. In: Miller, R.E., Thatcher, J.W., Bohlinger, J.D. (eds.) Complexity of Computer Computations. The IBM Research Symposia Series, pp. 85–103. Springer, Boston (1972). https://doi.org/10.1007/978-1-4684-2001-2_9
4. Lin, W.C., Liao, D.Y., Liu, C.Y., Lee, Y.Y.: Daily imaging scheduling of an earth observation satellite. IEEE Trans. Syst. Man Cybern. - Part A: Syst. Hum. **35**(2), 213–223 (2005)
5. Shamna, T.P., Praveen, P.N.: Data acquisition and delay optimization in WSN using knapsack algorithm in presence of transfaulty nodes. In: 2017 International Conference on Intelligent Computing and Control (I2C2), pp. 1–5, June 2017
6. Sindhu, S., Sen, G.: An optimal scheduling policy for satellite constellation deployment. In: 2017 IEEE International Conference on Industrial Engineering and Engineering Management (IEEM), pp. 100–104, December 2017
7. Johnson, D.S.: Approximation algorithms for combinatorial problems. J. Comput. Syst. Sci. **9**, 256–278 (1974)
8. Chvatal, V.: A greedy heuristic for the set-covering problem. Math. Oper. Res. **4**, 233–235 (1979)
9. Wu, G.H., Ma, M., Wang, H., Qiu, D.: Multi satellite observation scheduling based on task clustering. Acta Aeronautica et Astronautica Sinica **32**, 1275–1282 (2011)
10. Xu, Y.L., Xu, P.D., Wang, H.L., Peng, Y.H.: Clustering of imaging reconnaissance tasks based on clique partition. Oper. Res. Manag. Sci. **19**, 143–149 (2010)
11. Zhang, X.D., Luo, L.: Approximation algorithm for weighted set cover problem. J. Wenzhou Univ. Nat. Sci. **29**(6), 46–48 (2008)
12. Zhu, Y., Sheng, M., Li, J., Liu, R., Liu, J.: Modelling for data acquisition, storage and transmission of EOS. In: 2017 IEEE 28th Annual International Symposium on Personal, Indoor, and Mobile Radio Communications (PIMRC), pp. 1–6, October 2017

Information Flow Design and Verification for Networked Satellite Systems

Jia Guo[1]([⊠]) and Nuo Xu[2]

[1] Institute of Spacecraft System Engineering,
China Academy of Space Technology, Beijing 100094, China
guojia_email@163.com
[2] Institute of Telecommunication Satellite,
China Academy of Space Technology, Beijing 100094, China

Abstract. For efficient information sharing and timely processing, networked satellite constellation with the feature of space and terrestrial network integration will be constructed. Information flow design and verification is necessary for networked satellites with complex information interfaces. This paper describes and analyzes information feature classification, information flow based network architecture design, and information flow functionality validation and performance evaluation for networked satellite systems. We also propose design strategy analysis of information transmission, processing and storage as reference and suggestion. Furthermore, an instance of information flow performance evaluation is introduced.

Keywords: Networked satellite · Information flow · Network architecture

1 Introduction

Along with Space-Ground integrated development, networked satellite systems will be of great benefit to efficient sharing and integrated processing of space information, also to promoting system service quality, expanding service area and exploring user requirement. For instance, navigation satellite constellation with multi-interface to ground and space has multiform information and complex information transmission routes involved with system-system, satellite-satellite and equipment-equipment information interaction [1–3]. Telecommunication satellite and remote sensing satellite systems have similar characteristics. Information flow integrated design and verification is necessary for networked satellite systems. Based on demand analysis of networked satellite systems, compatibility and interoperability across the network should be considered in the architecture design, which are beneficial to terrestrial users and application efficiency.

We study on information flow integrated design towards the application background of networked satellite systems. This paper proposes several design guidelines and key elements. Based on functionality operation analysis of information type, quantity, transmission and processing, communication channel planning, information feature classification, network architecture design and information flow evaluation are conducted.

© ICST Institute for Computer Sciences, Social Informatics and Telecommunications Engineering 2019
Published by Springer Nature Switzerland AG 2019. All Rights Reserved
M. Jia et al. (Eds.): WiSATS 2019, LNICST 280, pp. 456–465, 2019.
https://doi.org/10.1007/978-3-030-19153-5_47

The remainder of the paper is structured as follows. Section 2 presents networked satellite system information classification. In Sect. 3, we describe information flow network architecture design. The analysis of information flow functionality validation and performance evaluation is presented in Sect. 4. Section 5 introduces an instance of information flow performance evaluation. We conclude in Sect. 6.

2 Networked Satellite System Information Classification

2.1 Information Classification

Information classification based on functionality, purpose and characteristics is useful for designing corresponding information transport and process strategy towards multiplex requirements.

Information classification based on functionality and purpose:

- Control information includes telecommand, operating parameters, constellation network configuration data and on-orbit reconfiguration data.
- Monitor information includes telemetry, anomaly data, command response, attitude data, space environment measurement data, dynamic environment measurement data and memory download data.
- Operation information includes data generated by satellite payloads.

Information classification based on characteristics:

- Periodicity data can be modelled by periodic function. For instance, satellite equipment health monitoring data are generally collected with fixed cycle.
- Stochastic data can be modelled by stochastic process. For instance, satellite command response and fault data are triggered by specific event randomly.

Based on information characteristics analysis, fusion-model can be constructed for information flow design simulation.

2.2 Transmission Channel

Networked satellite system information interactive transmission is based on Ground-Satellite Link (GSL) and Inter-Satellite Link (ISL). Furthermore, ISL is one of the symbols of networked satellite system [4].

- Wireless communications and measurements between satellite and terrestrial station are supported by GSLs for satellite control, monitor and data transport. GSLs upload commands for satellite operating, and download telemetry and payload data for health monitoring and data collection.
- Wireless communications and measurements between satellite and satellite are supported by ISLs for satellite control, monitor and data transport of invisible satellite, also for inter-satellite ranging and time synchronization.

3 Information Flow Based Network Architecture Design

3.1 Network Architecture Design Elements

Several design elements should be considered for information flow based architecture design as followed.

- **Reliability.** Design to guarantee normal or degraded running when failure occurs. Based on distributed information flow network with multi-controller, information processing centre can be alternate in particular situation to insure information management basically. Redundant information transport channels and equipment are adopted both on-board and externally. Isolation and redundancy of information node shared parts are adopted to avoid single-point failure. Information interface switch is supported for redundancy. Appropriate margin of information network capacity and bandwidth are reserved to avoid congestion.
- **Safety.** Design to avoid local breakdown for system safety. Information sources which affect safety should be identified. Safety of storage and process of important information sources should be enhanced with distributed redundancy. Important control commands should be multi-level authenticated to avoid abnormal execution. Appropriate selection strategy should be adopted to avoid information competition when multiple information flow channels link to node.
- **Efficiency.** Design to promote information management efficiency based on reliability and safety. Information management resources should be allocated and scheduled with trade-off among reliability, safety and efficiency. Equipment hardware and software and information coupling should be reduced for simplified system scheme. Layered-network architecture should be designed to reduce network complexity, also for flexibility. Standard or validated products should be selected for maturity.

3.2 Information System Architecture Design

Distributed and composite architecture is designed for networked satellite information system generally, for graded process in system, sub-system, equipment and assembly, also reduce information flow complexity. Master node is always the system-mission computer. Slave node is always the intelligent processing unit which has single functionality. Slave node can be designed for updating as master node due to management. Satellite information system information flow network backbone structure is generally based on the on-board data bus. Information flows in the on-board data bus.

An instance of layered information system architecture is shown in Fig. 1, which consists of information processing layer, digital signal processing layer, signal preprocessing layer and antenna layer. Information always flows in the upper layer while signals always transmit in the lower layers.

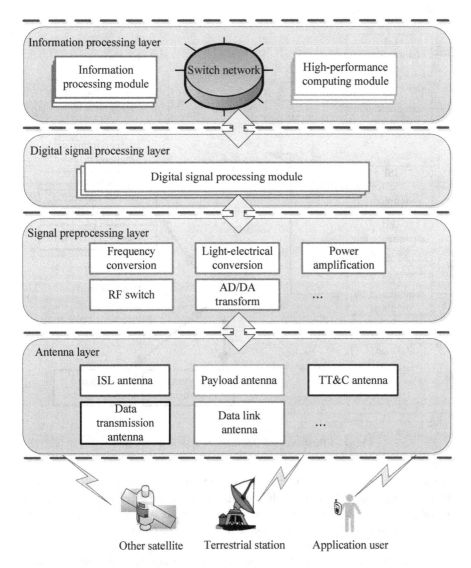

Fig. 1. Block diagram of layered information system architecture

With the improvement of on-board computing power, storage capacity, and space communication capabilities, networked satellite system based on integrated space-terrestrial routing could be introduced in the future. Considering compatibility with terrestrial IP networks, the network layer of satellite information system architecture should involve IP. Figure 2 shows an instance of Ethernet-based information system architecture with switching network linked by on-board equipment, which has great flexibility.

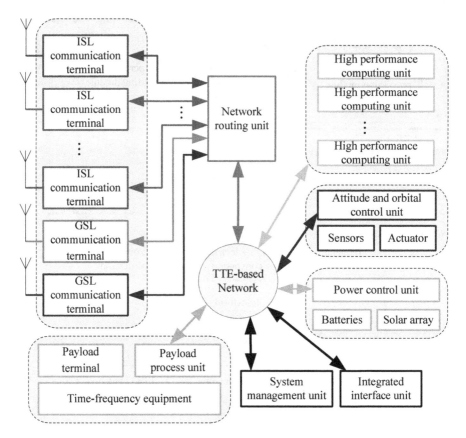

Fig. 2. Ethernet-based information system architecture

Time Triggered Ethernet is adopted to support time-triggered services to solve the problem that traditional Ethernet is difficult to guarantee the time certainty of satellite information system. The switch with redundant backup is the core of the information system, and each satellite device is connected to the corresponding port of the switch. The quantity of ports and switches can be expanded corresponding to the number of nodes accessing the network with extensibility. The information system task can be assigned by each node with flexible and adaptable configuration, which is beneficial to realize system-level resource dynamic management and reconstruction.

3.3   Information Transport and Process Strategy

Information Flow Network Protocol. Information flow network architecture should be layered to reduce the coupling between layers with standard protocols.

Application layer protocol should be designed according to the specific task. Transport layer, network layer, data link layer, physical layer protocol should refer to the relevant standard design or implementation. For the data types that require high reliability of information transmission, such as telecommand data and operation control data, reliable data transfer services with standardized definition should be provided.

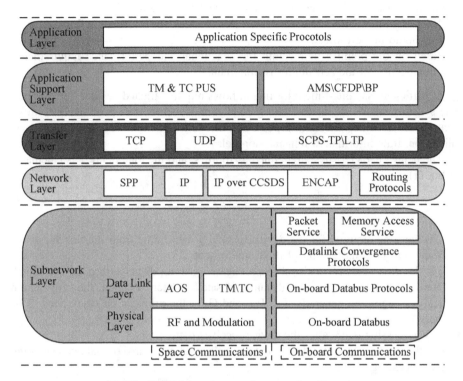

Fig. 3. CCSDS-based network protocol architecture

GSL and ISL information flow protocols should be designed with consideration of compatibility and interoperability, technology evolution to support ground segment and space segment constellation seamless transmission of information across the network. The system should provide unified control interface for terrestrial users, simplify the format conversion between ground and space, also reduce the handling complexity of terrestrial users, and improve the efficiency. Figure 3 shows an instance of CCSDS-based network protocol architecture [5].

Information Flow Integrated Application. Based on information sharing in the satellite information flow network, system functions, performance, reliability and safety can be improved. For instance, energy, thermal, attitude, orbit and other key feature data shared for integrated application. Interactive support for transmission should be provided in multiple information flow channels.

Information Flow Scheduling. Several design guidelines of information flow scheduling are proposed generally to ensure the processing logic among network nodes.

- The sequence of response events of information flow in each node should meet the design logic requirements.
- Scheduling relationships should be adapted to the performance changes of communication interfaces over the full life cycle of the satellite.
- When any information flow node interfaces changes, the information flow matching test should be performed.
- Based on the premise of meeting the functional and performance requirements, simplification of the scheduling is important.

In particular, satellite-time information flows require targeted design. For instance, time synchronization of satellite and ground, time synchronization of satellite equipment should consider the starting point of time, time synchronization accuracy, time calibration, time information transmission delay.

The delay characteristics are defined as follows, and the total delay T is calculated by Eq. (1).

$$T = t_s + t_t + t_p + t_q \tag{1}$$

- t_s is the time required for the device to send a data frame from the first bit of the frame sent until the last bit of the frame is sent.
- t_t is the time takes for a signal to propagate a certain distance through a channel. Due to the short propagation distance of satellite internal signal, the propagation delay is negligible generally. For ISL and GSL, the propagation delay need to be included.
- t_p is processing delay after the device receives data.
- t_q is the time occupied for data in the device's input queue and output queue waiting for processing.

4 Information Flow Functionality Validation and Performance Evaluation

After functional validation and performance evaluation, information flow design results can be optimized by comparing with the design requirements and iterative design.

4.1 Information Flow Evaluation

Information flow evaluation indicators include completeness, accuracy, and timeliness.

- Completeness represents that the difference between the design result and the real situation of object types, quantities and parameter range in the information flow.
- Accuracy indicates the difference between the parameter value and the actual value of the objects in the information flow.
- Timeliness represents that the length of time of information flow generation, transmission and processing.

From the perspective of information flow network, for network managers and users, technical indicators that evaluate the performance of information flow network include throughput, capacity, bandwidth utilization, response time, delay, etc.

4.2 Information Flow Simulation

Through mathematical and semi-physical modeling, simulation and analysis of information flow design should be implemented by software and sample data, which could provide the basis for the information flow design and improvement. Information flow simulation generally covers all kinds of information flow channel function, analysis of the actual capacity of information flow network, obtain information system performance evaluation result. It can also cover untestable projects in information flow design or verify high-cost items, examine multiple information paths, multiple simultaneous events, etc.

4.3 Information Flow Test

The main purpose of information flow test is to inspect the satellite information transmission process. Through checking and solving the problems, the test should verify that the information flow network operation meets satellite design and application requirements, which ensures correct function, system coordination and qualified performance parameters.

Information flow test should generally be included in the equipment, sub-system, system tests and special tests level by level. The main purpose of information flow test includes:

- Verify the correctness, consistency and adaptation of the satellite information flow design.
- Check the correctness and adaptation of the satellite information network nodes.
- Verify the correctness and adaptation of the satellite external information interface.

5 Instance of Information Flow Performance Evaluation

The BDS-3 space constellation is chosen as the evaluation object. The basic constellation consists of 3 GEO satellites, 3 IGSO satellites, and 24 MEO satellites [6]. Based on the assumption that the semiduplex ISLs rate is 100kbps with CCSDS AOS protocol data frame [7, 8], the information flow performance evaluations which include network throughput and bandwidth utilization are presented. Different information types are simulated including control information, monitor information, and operation information with periodicity or stochastic characteristics, which flow in the network.

Figure 4 shows the total throughput of the network. Throughput is defined as: the amount of data successfully transmitted in a unit of time [9].

T_i is the throughput of satellite No.i, Calculate the total throughput of the network as:

$$T = \sum_{i=1}^{30} T_i \qquad (2)$$

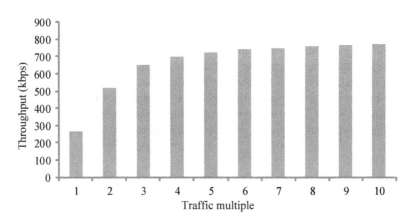

Fig. 4. Total throughput evaluation

Along with the information traffic increases, the value of the network throughput increases. When the information traffic increases to six times the initial value, the network throughput increases very little, this could be considered as the maximum network throughput.

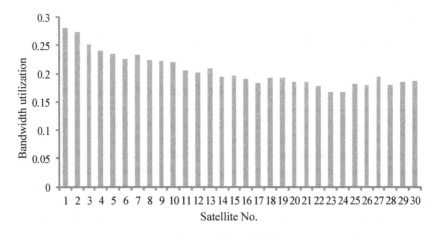

Fig. 5. Bandwidth utilization evaluation

Figure 5 shows the bandwidth utilization of 30 satellite nodes in the network. Bandwidth utilization is defined as: Link layer effective transmission bandwidth divided by Total bandwidth [10].

η_i is the bandwidth utilization of satellite No.i, Calculate the average bandwidth utilization as:

$$\bar{\eta} = \frac{\sum_{i=1}^{30} \eta_i}{30} \approx 0.206 \tag{3}$$

For demonstration, the results are reasonable due to the vacant bandwidth which is not occupied by the default setting of information traffic.

6 Conclusion

This paper studies on networked satellite information flow integrated design and verification with instance of evaluation for reliability, maturity and accuracy to guarantee stable and efficient operation of networked satellite systems. With the advancing Space-Ground integrated development, the connotation and extension of networked satellite system information flow design will be further expanded.

References

1. Maine, K., Anderson, P., Bayuk, F.: Communication architecture for GPS III. In: IEEE Aerospace Conference Proceedings 2004, pp. 1532–1539 (2004)
2. Luba, O., Boyd, L., Gower, A., Crum, J.: GPS III system operations concepts. IEEE Aerospace Electron. Syst. Mag. **20**(1), 10–18 (2005)
3. Jun, X.: Beidou navigation satellite technology development and prospect. Aerospace China **3**, 7–11 (2013)
4. Fernandez, A.: Inter-satellite ranging and inter-satellite communication links for enhancing GNSS satellite broadcast navigation data. Adv. Space Res. **47**, 786–801 (2011)
5. CCSDS Secretariat: CCSDS 130.0-G-3 overview of space communications protocols, CCSDS, pp. 18–20 (2014)
6. China Satellite Navigation Office: Beidou navigation satellite system signal in space interface control document open service signal B3I version 1.0. BDS-SIS-ICD, pp. 1–2 (2018)
7. Li, Z., He, S., Liu, C., et al.: An topology design method of navigation satellite constellation inter-satellite links. Spacecraft Eng. **20**(3), 32–37 (2011)
8. Yan, H., Zhang, Q., Sun, Y.: A novel routing algorithm for navigation satellite network based on partial queues. J. Astronaut. **36**(12), 1444–1452 (2015)
9. Morgan, H., Wiswell, E., et al.: Throughput analysis of satellite network architectures. In: AIAA International Communications Satellite Systems Conference and Exhibit 2000, pp. 602–612 (2000)
10. Pavarangkoon, P., Murata, K.T., et al.: Bandwidth utilization enhancement using high-performance and flexible protocol for INTELSAT satellite network. In: IEEE Information Technology, Electronics and Mobile Communication Conference 2016, pp. 1–7 (2016)

Design and Realization of Onboard Router Based on IPv6 and SPP with Software

Zheng Qi$^{(\boxtimes)}$, Xiongwen He, Panpan Zhan, Cuitao Zhang, Ming Gu, and Dong Yan

Beijing Institute of Spacecraft System Engineering,
Beijing 100094, People's Republic of China
qzqz365@126.com

Abstract. For the purpose of Spacecraft Networking, considering the factor of the deployment of SPP within SOIS protocol system and the deployment of IPv6 in ground network with its development in the future, we present a set of scheme about design and realization, with software, of onboard router based on IPv6 and SPP. The design and realization of onboard router provides a new idea on constructing the Integrated Space-Ground Network, establishing the foundation of Spacecraft Networking in the future.

Keywords: IPv6 · SPP · SOIS · Route · Spacecraft Networking

1 Introduction

Along with the proposal of constructing Integrated Space-Ground Network, some domestic enterprises and universities have already researched in relative fields of Integrated Space-Ground Network and have obtained pretty good results [1]. Among the fields, spacecraft networking is considered as a very important theme, worthy of being deeply researched.

Until now, onboard equipment of traditional spacecraft has deployed SOIS protocol system of CCSDS, and treats the SPP of transport layer as the routing protocol within spacecraft [2]. Besides, for the purpose of taking good advantage of networking and routing technology, unifying message format and protocol between equipment, improving equipment's versatility and flexibility, decreasing development cost, IPv6 protocol [3] has been deployed in a part of modern spacecraft for networking between spacecraft.

Although IPv6 and SPP can resolve the problem of data routing, but SPP is originally developed to resolve the routing problem intra-spacecraft, not inter-spacecraft. Considering the deployment of SPP within SOIS protocol system, it is unrealistic or difficult to deploy IPv6 protocol on all onboard equipment in the near future at least [2]. So, how to use IPv6 and SPP to realize spacecraft networking, more specifically, end-to-end communication between equipment of different spacecraft, is the key point of this paper.

In this paper, we briefly analyze the feature of IPv6 and SPP and propose a reasonable scheme about design and realization of onboard router with software based

M. Jia et al. (Eds.): WiSATS 2019, LNICST 280, pp. 466–474, 2019.
https://doi.org/10.1007/978-3-030-19153-5_48

on IPv6 and SPP. Besides, we present a typical topology or scenario to verify the rationality of the scheme, establishing the foundation of Spacecraft Networking in the future.

2 Protocol Analysis

2.1 IPv6

IPv6, version 6 of Internet Protocol, is used to expand IPv4 for reasons of address space, simplification, etc. Due to reasonable fields of IPv6 packet format, IPv6 has been proved reasonable and reliable in Terrestrial Internet and can satisfy the demand for constructing global network and local network among IPv6 equipments, even IPv4 equipments with tunnel. Besides, because of kinds of address types, described in following chapter, it is possible and realistic to use IPv6 in spacecraft to construct network in space.

However, IPv6 has not been deployed in traditional spacecraft owning to user's requirement and even though it is used in some modern spacecraft, it also can't be compatible with SPP of SOIS till now, even taking the place of SPP in spacecrafts.

So, it's still difficult to deploy IPv6 on all onboard equipments to resolve the problem of constructing network and routing within spacecraft, even with other spacecrafts [3].

2.2 SPP

The SPP in SOIS communication protocol system, has been proved feasible and reliable to resolve the problem of constructing network and routing within spacecraft, using Destination APID, etc. However, the APID and other identifier used in SOIS only has local meaning and don't have global meaning, just like local IP address.

Besides, considering that the era and background of this protocol, we didn't expect to construct network among spacecrafts, just between earth and spacecraft. But, this should have been taken into account.

So, for SPP, it is not suitable for construct network among spacecrafts [4, 5].

3 Routing Scheme

For the above-mentioned contents, if we want to realize the routing for the onboard equipment of different spacecraft, IPv6 and SPP need to be changed and merged.

3.1 IPv6

As the following figure shows, the customization of IPv6 protocol is IPv6 address format [6] (Fig. 1).

The meaning of every field of this format is shown below (Table 1).

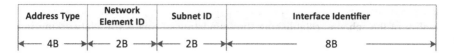

Fig. 1. Customization on IPv6 address format

Table 1. Field meaning

Name	Meaning
Address Type	Type of IPv6 address (Unicast, Multicast, etc.)
Network Element ID	Spacecraft ID or ground equipment ID
Subnet ID	The subnet ID of onboard gateway interface
Interface Identifier	Same as the Interface Identifier of normal IPv6 address

It is easy to identify every IPv6 equipment in every spacecraft with the format and it is compatible for this format with normal IPv6 address format.

3.2   SPP

The customization of SPP is mainly focused on its payload, Application Management Layer (AML) Service. As shown below, it's useful to carry two fields ahead of the valid data field (Fig. 2).

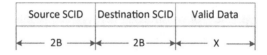

Fig. 2. AML service format

The meaning of every field of the format is shown below (Table 2).

Table 2. Field meaning

Name	Meaning
Source SCID	Source spacecraft ID of current message
Destination SCID	Destination spacecraft ID of current message
Valid Data	Real application data

Besides the payload, when receives space packet, SPP firstly judges the destination of current message whether is current spacecraft by "Destination SCID" field, then transfers SPP to IPv6. IPv6 can realize the communication between onboard equipment of different spacecraft.

3.3 Protocol Information Map

The conversion of transferring SPP to IPv6 is established on the mapping information as shown below (Table 3).

Table 3. Protocol information map

Network Element ID	Address Type	Subnet ID	APID
0xAA	0xFD000000	1	0x4AD
			0x44A
			0x9BD
		...	...
			0xB21

The map, calling PIM below, can be initialized by ground control unit and later updated. Besides, after the built of spacecraft, every field associated with the spacecraft in the map can be fixed and the "Network Element ID" field has global meaning for networking.

The routing scheme or packet handling process is based on the three points mentioned above and is described in the following chapter for the reason of content arrangement of this paper.

4 Gateway Equipment

The two routing protocols' transformation needs to be done by a kind of gateway unit. In this paper, we designed an onboard router to do it. The software of the router, calling CPU below, needs to support the two protocols. If the message needs to be transmitted to other spacecraft or other link subnet within spacecraft, SPP will be encapsulated in IPv6 packet as payload which is same as the tunnel scheme between IPv4 and IPv6 [7].

The protocol stack of the onboard router is shown below (Fig. 3).

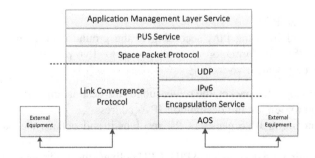

Fig. 3. Protocol stack diagram within router

In this paper, router's job is mainly focused on the part of the dash line above. We can see that the SPP can be the routing protocol within SOIS and also be the payload of IPv6 packet. Because the router executes the routing scheme in the chapter above, the flow chart about processing IPv6 packet and space packet in router is shown below (Fig. 4).

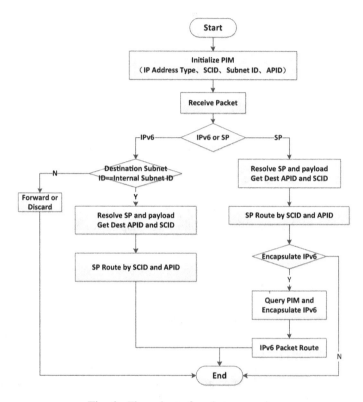

Fig. 4. Flow chart of packet processing

Step 1. Initialize PIM
Router firstly initializes the PIM according to the ground control unit's command, convenient for the transformation of space packet to IPv6 packet.
  Step 2. Routing from IPv6 to SPP

(1) After receiving IPv6 packet, the router judges the destination port according to the address prefix length and destination IPv6 address.
(2) For the incoming IPv6 packet, CPU resolves it and obtains the payload, space packet.
(3) After obtaining the destination APID, CPU delivers the space packet to the SPP of transfer layer to route to other link subnet.

Step 3. Routing from SPP to IPv6

(1) After receiving space packet, the router extracts the destination APID from space packet and destination SCID from AML Service.
(2) (According to the SCID, the router firstly determines whether to route using SPP. If SCID doesn't equal to current spacecraft's SCID, router queries the PIM, encapsulates IPv6 packet and routes packet to outside by queries routing table; Otherwise, goes to 3).
(3) Routing space packet. If the destination link type is Ethernet, router also transfers space packet to IPv6 packet, transmit the packet to destination equipment by IP route. Otherwise, router encapsulates space packet into Packet Service and then to destination link subnet base on space packet routing [2].

5   Systematic Verification

The scheme, presented in this paper, can be verified in typical topology and has been realized in physical onboard router. The typical topology is shown below (Fig. 5).

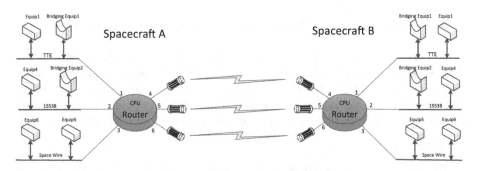

Fig. 5. Typical network topology diagram

As shown above, onboard router is equipped as spacecraft's gateway and connects three different links via interface 1–3 inside of spacecraft. Equipment 1 and bridging equipment 1, equipped on TTE, belong to subnet 1. Equipment 4 and bridging equipment 2, equipped on 1553B bus, belong to subnet 2. Equipment 5 and 6, equipped on Space Wire, belong to subnet 3. Meanwhile, router connects three laser terminals. Every interface belongs to a subnet. Besides, the router of spacecraft A connects to the router of spacecraft B with inter-spacecraft link. The connection between routers will be changed along with spacecraft's movement.

The typical topology above can support two end-to-end route scenarios shown below.

- Intra-Spacecraft

According to this paper's focus, we only describe the end-to-end route between equipment A linked by 1553B and equipment B linked by Ethernet. The system protocol configuration is shown below (Fig. 6).

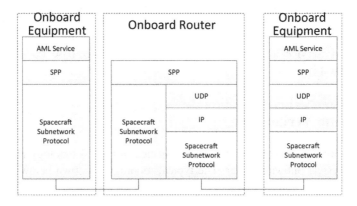

Fig. 6. Intra-spacecraft end-to-end route system protocol configuration

As shown above, Ethernet link can also be fitted into scope of Subnetwork Layer of SOIS. Equipment A encapsulates AML Service via PUS Service, space packet, Packet Service and routes it to the router by space packet routing. Router extracts destination APID from space packet and destination SCID from AML Service and finally routes the space packet to destination link, encapsulating space packet via UDP, IPv6, MAC [7].

- Inter-Spacecraft

The end-to-end route system protocol configuration between equipment of different spacecraft is shown below (Fig. 7).

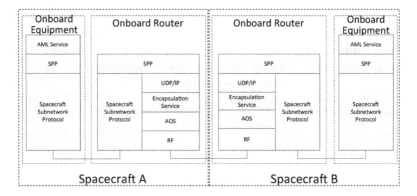

Fig. 7. Inter-spacecraft end-to-end route system protocol configuration (direct connection)

As shown above, equipment within spacecraft A encapsulates AML Service via PUS Service, space packet, Packet Service and routes it to the router by space packet routing. Router extracts destination APID from space packet and destination SCID from AML Service and finally routes the space packet to spacecraft B via UDP, IPv6, ES (Encapsulation Service), AOS and RF. The router of spacecraft B routes IPv6 packet into spacecraft B by querying IP routing table, extracts space packet and routes space packet to destination link by space packet routing. Finally, equipment within spacecraft B receives packet and extracts message from Packet Service, space packet, PUS Service, realizing the end-to-end communication [8–10].

Besides, if the end-to-end route between source spacecraft and destination space-craft needs to be relayed by relay spacecraft, the system protocol can be configured as the following figure shows (Fig. 8).

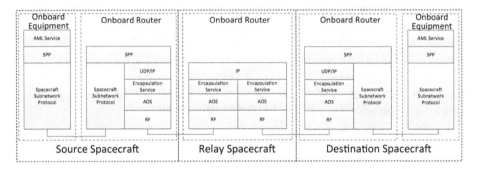

Fig. 8. System protocol configuration of relay system

Under the current circumstances, the relay spacecraft only needs to forward IPv6 packet by querying routing table, no additional operation like analyzing space packet.

6   Conclusion

In this paper, we firstly analyzed the feature of IPv6 and SPP and then introduced a reasonable scheme about design and realization of onboard router with software. By means of combining this two routing protocols, the scheme both meet the requirement of data routing intra-spacecraft and inter-spacecraft. Although the scheme has been proved reasonable and feasible, it's necessary to deploy the scheme in much more systems. The proposal of the scheme establishes the foundation of Spacecraft Net-working in the future.

References

1. Manqing, W., Wei, W., Zhou, B., et al.: Some thoughts of integrated space-ground network architecture. Satell. Netw. **10**(3), 30–36 (2016)
2. Zhao, H., He, X., Liu, C.: Space Data System, 1st edn. Beijing University of Technology Press, Beijing (2018)
3. Hinden, R., Deering, S.: RFC 2460, Internet Protocol, Version 6 (IPv6) Specification, Network Working Group (1998)
4. CCSDS: CCSDS 850.0-G-2, Spacecraft Onboard Interface Services, Washington, D.C., USA, CCSDS (2013)
5. CCSDS: CCSDS 133.0-B-1, Space Packet Protocol, Washington, D.C., USA, CCSDS Secretariat (2003)
6. Hinden, R., Deering, S.: RFC 3513, IP Version 6 Addressing Architecture, Network Working Group, 4 (2003)
7. Andrew, S.: Tanenbaum: Computer Networks, 4th edn. TsingHua University Press, Beijing (2004)
8. CCSDS: CCSDS 133.1-B-2, Encapsulation Service, Washington, D.C., USA, CCSDS Secretariat (2009)
9. CCSDS: CCSDS 732.0-B-3, AOS Space Data Link Protocol. Washington, D.C., USA, CCSDS Secretariat (2015)
10. CCSDS: CCSDS 851.0-M-1, Spacecraft Onboard Interface Services-Subnetwork Packet Service, Washington, D.C., USA, CCSDS Secretariat (2009)

Adaptive Subcarrier-Bandwidth Multiple Access (ABMA) for High-Mobility Environments

Jionghui Li[✉], Xiongwen He, Xiaofeng Zhang, and Fan Bai

Beijing Institute of Spacecraft System Engineering, Beijing 100094, China
lijionghui@126.com

Abstract. In this paper, adaptive subcarrier-bandwidth multiple access (ABMA) is proposed as a novel downlink multi-user access scheme to support robust wireless communications in the high-mobility environments with different kinds of high-speed receivers. The proposed ABMA allows flexible spectrum resource allocation and subcarrier bandwidth adaptation according to mobile receivers' velocities. Resource band is used as the unit for spectrum resource allocation. Well-localized bandpass filters are applied on each resource band, in order to control the multiple access interference and achieve coexistence of different subcarrier bandwidth. Universal receiver structure with low implementation complexity is described as part of the scheme. Theoretical and numerical results show that the ABMA scheme is effective in repelling the impact of high-range Doppler effects and performs high robustness in the high-mobility environments.

Keywords: Adaptive subcarrier-bandwidth multiple access ·
High-mobility · Doppler effects

1 Introduction

With the development of integrated space-ground networks and internet of things (IoT), future space links should provide communication services for different kinds of ground users, including planes, vessels, high-speed trains, ground vehicles and individual pedestrians. Therefore, future space-ground network is expected significant improvement over current space links on peak data rate and high scalability. This requires the space-ground downlink transmission system to support a wide range of user velocities over 500 km/h (for civil aviation and high-speed train). Additionally, future integrated space-ground networks are targeted to unified transmission systems for ground and space as well as better spectral efficiency to support high volumes of signaling and data transmission. These bring challenges to current orthogonal frequency-division multiple access (OFDMA) systems, since the OFDM signal is sensitive to inter-carrier interference (ICI) caused by the Doppler effects with the high-speed relative movement.

© ICST Institute for Computer Sciences, Social Informatics and Telecommunications Engineering 2019
Published by Springer Nature Switzerland AG 2019. All Rights Reserved
M. Jia et al. (Eds.): WiSATS 2019, LNICST 280, pp. 475–486, 2019.
https://doi.org/10.1007/978-3-030-19153-5_49

Regarding to a large scale of users with different channel conditions and time-varying moving velocities, downlink transmission signal should be robust and flexible for user-specific environments in order to serve such large-scale multi-user access in the high-mobility environments, providing a supportive technique for future development of integrated space-ground networks and IoT. Universal-filtered multicarrier (UFMC) [1] and filtered-OFDM (f-OFDM) [2] are developed as subband-based filtered waveforms which provide better spectrum localization compared to conventional OFDM and keep relatively balance with time localization compared with filter band multi-carrier (FBMC). Although subband-based spectrum localization helps to reduce multiple access interference (MAI) from other subbands, the improvement on the overall inter-carrier interference (ICI) is still limited, since the ICI mainly comes from the adjacent subcarriers within the subband. ICI is proportional to the maximum Doppler shift, whereas it is inversely proportional to the subcarrier bandwidth. Therefore, subcarrier bandwidth is proposed to be considered as a system freedom. [3] discusses different subcarrier bandwidths for OFDMA systems over fast fading channel. [4] and [5] have highlighted user-specific subcarrier spacings with UF-OFDM to improve low latency and high Doppler use cases in an uplink model, allowing users to pick up different settings for its signal. Compared to UFMC, Filtered-OFDM has even lower out-of-band emission (OOBE). Therefore, filtered-OFDM waveform allows for a minimum number of guard tones between each subband [2], making it flexible for coexistence of different settings in each subband to acquire frequency domain quasi-orthogonality. A downlink transceiver structure of filtered-OFDMA is introduced in [6], which applies user-specific subcarrier spacing, cyclic prefix (CP) length, transmission time interval (TTI) duration and spectrum shaping filters. Further considering the time-varying cases, Doppler frequency shift becomes hard to estimate ahead of time. Therefore, to ensure the multi-user downlink transmission robustness, spectrum resource adaptive allocation should be applied based on the feedback of channel and users' information. The current multi-user access schemes are designed with constant parameters, which are not flexible enough to support the time-varying scenarios. Hence, a new multi-carrier access with flexible spectrum resource allocation and subcarrier bandwidth adaptation is demanded for downlink multiuser transmissions, to serve high scale users in time-varying high-mobility environments. In this paper, we target at time-varying environments where users are moving with a large range of velocities and propose a downlink multi-user access scheme based on filtered-OFDM waveform, named adaptive subcarrier-bandwidth multiple access, ABMA. The targeted problem is addressed in Sect. 2. ABMA scheme and corresponding signal model are introduced in Sect. 3, including the time-spectrum resource allocation, transceiver structure with universal receiver and ICI analysis. Based on the proposed scheme, the numerical results in Sect. 4 prove the high transmission robustness of ABMA system with time-varying Doppler spread in the high-mobility environments. We conclude the paper in Sect. 5.

2   Problem Statement

The average moving velocity of civil aviation aircraft is about 500–1000 km/h. And the average velocities are about 500–600 km/h for vessels, about 300–500 km/h for speed train, 30–200 km/h for cars and up to 10 km/h for pedestrians. Future integrated space-ground networks and IoT are target to support users with such a wide range of velocities. Therefore, Doppler spread is rising compared to that with current settings. The Doppler frequency shift is also time-varying, making it hard to estimate ahead of time. Therefore, signal with higher robustness and less sensitivity to the Doppler effects becomes highly preferred.

For an OFDM-based symbol, the symbol period T follows

$$T = \frac{N + L_{cp}}{B} = \left(1 + \frac{L_{cp}}{N}\right)\frac{N}{B} = (1 + \alpha_{cp})f_s \tag{1}$$

where L_{cp} is the length of CP used in OFDMA symbol for ISI elimination, α_{cp} denotes the ratio of CP compared with N, B is the signal bandwidth and the subcarrier spacing $f_s = B/N$.

Then, as derived in [7], in the time-varying Rayleigh fading channel, the ICI power with unit average transmitted signal power is bounded with

$$\begin{aligned} P_{ICI} &\geq \frac{\alpha_1}{12}(2\pi f_m T)^2 - \frac{\alpha_2}{360}(2\pi f_m T)^4 \\ &= \frac{\alpha_1}{12}\left[2\pi(1 + \alpha_{cp})\frac{f_m}{f_s}\right]^2 - \frac{\alpha_2}{360}\left[2\pi(1 + \alpha_{cp})\frac{f_m}{f_s}\right]^4 \end{aligned} \tag{2}$$

$$P_{ICI} \leq \frac{\alpha_1}{12}(2\pi f_m T)^2 = \frac{\alpha_1}{12}\left[2\pi(1 + \alpha_{cp})\frac{f_m}{f_s}\right]^2 \tag{3}$$

where f_m is the maximum Doppler frequency with $f_m = \frac{v}{c}f_c$. v is the mobile UE velocity, c is the speed of light and f_c is the RF carrier frequency.

Therefore, from (2)–(3), ICI resulting from Doppler spread is determined by f_m/f_s. We define

$$f_\delta = \frac{f_m}{f_s} \tag{4}$$

as normalized Doppler carrier frequency offset (D-CFO), which is proportional to f_m and inversely proportional to f_s.

Assuming Rayleigh fading channel following Jakes model, $\alpha_1 = 1/2$ and $\alpha_2 = 3/8$ in (2)–(3). Accordingly, for $f_c = 6$ GHz, the ICI power with different receiver velocities is shown in Fig. 1.

Regarding to the downlink transmission, each user may have different time-varying velocities and receive the same transmitted signal with different channel impacts. If the entire OFDM signal parameters are adaptively changed, all the serving users in the cell have to make adjustments accordingly, which is

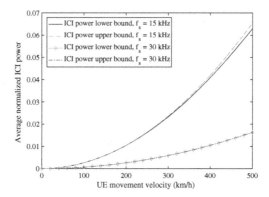

Fig. 1. Comparison of ICI power bounds with different subcarrier spacings at different velocities.

unnecessary for most of the users. Therefore, an efficient adaptation should be conducted on a user basis, instead of on the entire signal setting. In order to satisfy the transmission quality for a large amount of users with temporal channel variations, we need an adaptive scheme that allows dynamic coexistence of different subcarrier bandwidths in one transmitted multi-carrier symbol. The rest of the paper will introduce the proposed novel downlink multi-user access scheme, ABMA, targeting on this issue.

3 Downlink Adaptive Numerology Filtered Multi-carrier Access Scheme

We assume that perfect feedback of the channel state information (CSI) is available at the base station (BS). The BS obtains users' GPS information, including the velocities to decide the spectrum resource allocation.

The subcarrier bandwidth is regarded as $2f_s$. The existing of subcarriers with different bandwidth breaks the orthogonality. Thanks to filtered-OFDM waveform [6], spectrum side lobes are suppressed with subband-based filtering to achieve quasi-orthogonality in the frequency domain, allowing different bandwidths. ABMA scheme is designed based on filtered OFDM waveform. However, as a multiple access scheme, ABMA is different from the filtered-OFDMA [2] in the following aspects:

1. In filtered-OFDMA scheme, user data are allocated on a subband basis. With different subcarrier spacing, the number of subcarriers in each subband varies to keep a relative constant subband width. To differentiate from the concept of subband, in the ABMA scheme, we use the concept of "resource band (Rb)" as the unit of filtering and user resource allocation. For reception and allocation convenience with the adaptive scheme, each resource band loads a fixed number of subcarriers, while the signal bandwidth of the resource band varies with difference subcarrier spacing settings.

2. The resource allocation and parameters setting can be variable for each TTI in ABMA, while filtered-OFDMA applies the constant settings.
3. In order to minimize the transmission overhead and guard tones, in each time unit, BS pre-allocates the resource bands into groups based on the bandwidth. In each group, consistent parameters is applied.
4. In the proposed ABMA scheme, each receiver-end is able to locate the resource band based on the adaption control information and to demodulate the user data with an universal structure, instead of using matched filters as filter-OFDMA. The filter banks are avoided for better supporting the adaptation with reasonable implementation complexity.

3.1   Time-Spectrum Resource Adaptive Allocation

The time-spectrum resource adaptive allocation is illustrated in Fig. 2. As mentioned above, resource band is defined as the spectrum allocation unit. And the transmission time interval (TTI) is the time unit for the adaptation. The waveform setting remains consistent within one TTI.

Each user's data takes one resource band with fixed number of subcarriers, N_s. The resource band allocation for each user is based on the feedback of CSI and the user's GPS information.

The LTE setting with subcarrier spacing, $f_{s1} = 15\,\text{kHz}$, is used as a baseline [4]. Resource bands with baseline setting are used to serve stationary and slow-moving users. With higher velocities, users' are able to request an increment of subcarrier spacing to reduce the ICI caused by Doppler carrier frequency offset (D-CFO). In order to pack all users data into the downlink transmission frame, the adjusted subcarrier spacing should be an integer times of the baseline spacing, i.e. $f_{sz} = r_z \cdot f_{s1}$, where $r_z = 2^{z-1}, z \in \mathbb{Z}^+$. z denotes group index, and r_z is named adjust order.

Receivers depend on the adaptive control information to locate the allocated resource band. In order to minimize the control information overhead and reduce inter-band interference, in each TTI, resource bands are allocated into groups. Each resource band can be defined with three indices, which are resource band index I_b, in-group index I_g and group index z. I_b denotes the order of the resource band regarding to the whole spectrum; I_g reveals the position of the resource band in its group; and z decides the adjust order r_z of the group.

In the example shown in Fig. 2, two subcarrier spacings are applied, which are the baseline spacing $f_{s1} = 15\,\text{kHz}$, and the adjusted spacing $f_{s2} = 30\,\text{kHz}$. At the TTI t_1, $N_{g1}^{t_1}$ number of resource bands keep the baseline spacing and $N_{g2}^{t_1}$ number of resource bands are adjusted to 30 kHz. A slow-moving user, as denoted as U_1 requires downlink transmission. The BS allocates the resource band with $I_b = i$ to transmit the data to U_1. As shown in the figure, it is also the last resource band in the baseline setting group. Therefore, at TTI, t_1, the resource band for U_1 can be defined by $I_b^{t_1} = i$, $I_g^{t_1} = N_{g1}^{t_1}$, and $z = 1$.

At the TTI, t_2, with time-varying motion, the velocity of U_1 is assumed to exceed a pre-settled threshold, ϕ_v. Then, according to the user's GPS information, BS decides to use the adjusted spacing for U_1 data. Thus, the resource band

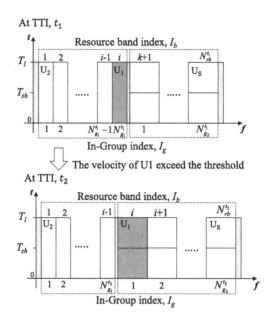

Fig. 2. Illustration of resource band adaptive allocation in two different TTI.

is re-allocated as shown in Fig. 2. The resource band is in one adjusted group, defined by $I_b^{t_2} = k$ and $I_g^{t_2} = 1$. With the same sampling rate, the duration of multi-carrier modulated symbol to U_1 is shortened from T_l to T_{sh}. Guard tones are inserted between each two groups to eliminate inter-band interference.

With the information of z, I_b and I_g, resource bands can be located by calculating the digital domain offset as

$$S_{I_b} = (I_g - 1)N_s + S_{GT} \cdot (z - 1) + \left\lceil \frac{S_{GB} + (I_b - I_g)N_s}{r_z} \right\rceil \tag{5}$$

where S_{GB} denotes the null subcarriers offset as guard bands before the first resource band, and S_{GT} is the offset of guard tones inserted before groups.

With larger subcarrier spacing, the transmitted signal takes more bandwidth resource. In order to keep the scalability with limited bandwidth and keep the long-term balance, the subcarrier spacing should return to baseline once the adjustment is no longer required.

3.2   Downlink Transmitter Structure and Signal Model

Figure 3 depicts the downlink transmitter structure of the proposed ABMA scheme at the TTI t_1, matched with the example shown in Fig. 2.

Mapping to the digital domain, the subcarrier bandwidth/spacing is decided by the length of IFFT. As shown in Fig. 3, let N_1 denote the IFFT length of baseline setting. Then with the adjusted setting, the IFFT length is $N_z = N_1/r_z$.

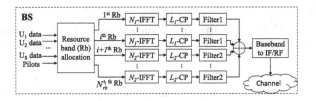

Fig. 3. Downlink transceiver structure at TTI t_1. Baseline setting and one adjusted setting are applied, i.e. $z = 1, 2$.

Regarding to the TTI t_1, if resource band, $I_b = k$, is in the baseline group ($z = 1$) with subcarrier spacing f_{s1}, let $\boldsymbol{X}^k = [X_0^k, X_1^k, \ldots, X_{N_s-1}^k]$ denotes the complex mapped data symbols (including pilots) that will be demodulated into this resource band, then the time-domain output of the IFFT is

$$x^k[n] = \frac{1}{\sqrt{N_1}} \sum_{l=0}^{N_s-1} X_l^k e^{j2\pi(l+S_k)n/N_1} \tag{6}$$

where $S_k + N_s \leq N_1$. The baseline setting of CP length is denoted as L_1. CP is inserted to $\boldsymbol{x}^k$ for ISI elimination and filter tails treatment. Thus, in (6), $-L_1 \leq n \leq N_1 - 1$.

Then the time-domain signal $\boldsymbol{x}^k$ is filtered by a L_{f1}-length FIR-filter, $\boldsymbol{p}_1^k$ to suppress the spectrum side lobes. The output signal can be expressed as

$$s^k = x^k * p_1^k \tag{7}$$

where $*$ denotes the linear convolution. $\boldsymbol{p}_1^k$ fits to the baseline resource band bandwidth and matches with the central frequency of the resource band.

If resource band $I_b = k$ is in an adjusted group with subcarrier spacing f_{sz}, where $z \neq 1$, The frequency-domain complex mapped data symbols is defined as $\boldsymbol{X}^k = [X_{1,0}^k, X_{1,1}^k, \ldots, X_{1,N_s-1}^k \cdots X_{z,0}^k, X_{z,1}^k, \ldots, X_{z,N_s-1}^k]$. The time-domain output signal is denoted as $\boldsymbol{x}^k = [\boldsymbol{x}_1^k, \ldots, \boldsymbol{x}_z^k]$, where

$$x_z^k[n] = \frac{1}{\sqrt{N_z}} \sum_{l=0}^{N_s-1} X_l^k e^{j2\pi(l+S_k)n/N_z} \tag{8}$$

with $-L_z + (z-1) \cdot (N_z - 1) \leq n \leq z \cdot (N_z - 1)$, where $N_z = N_1/r_z$. Then, the output signal is

$$s^k = [x_1^k * p_z^k, \ldots, x_z^k * p_z^k] \tag{9}$$

where $\boldsymbol{p}_z^k$ is the L_z-length FIR filter that fits to the adjusted resource band width and matches with the central frequency of the resource band k.

In order to be compatible with transmission frame structure, we desire that $L_z = L_1/r_z$. Therefore, to keep performance of filter tails treatment, the length of the FIR filter, L_{fz}, is desired to follow $L_{fz} = L_{f1}/r_z$. This is one of the reasons to adjust the bandwidth of resource bands, instead of the subcarrier number within the resource band. With larger passband width, FIR filter can be designed with shorter length to match with the time-domain requirement. Therefore, the transmitted multi-carrier symbol is the superposition of the time-domain modulated symbols corresponding to all of the resource bands, which can be written as

$$s_t[n] = \sum_{k=1}^{N_{rb}^{t_1}} s^k[n], \quad -L_1 \le n \le N_1 - 1 \tag{10}$$

where $N_{rb}^{t_1}$ denotes the total number of the allocated resource bands in the TTI t_1. It is seen that the length of the transmitted symbol, $s_t[n]$, is determined by the baseline setting.

3.3   Universal Receiver Structure and Received Signal

To achieve adaption, at the TTI t_1, a certain user, denoted as U_1, should be able to demodulate its data with a universal structure. Parameters can be adjusted according to adaption control information, $(z, I_g^{t_1}, I_b^{t_1})$. Note $I_b^{t_1} = i$. As shown in Fig. 4, at the receiver-end, after down-conversion, synchronization and A/D sampling, CP is discarded and the discrete signal is demodulated by FFT according to the knowledge of z. And based on the information of S_i, corresponding resource band can be located to obtain the U_1 data. S_i can be calculated by (5). Filtering distortion is further compensated by equalization.

Assuming ideal carrier synchronization and sampling rate, the received baseband discrete signal can be written as

$$y[n] = \sum_{\gamma=0}^{\Gamma-1} h[n, \gamma] s_t[n - \gamma] + w[n] \tag{11}$$

where $w[n]$ is additive white Gaussian noise (AWGN) with variance of σ_n^2, and $h[n, \gamma]$ is the channel impulse response of the lth path at sampling time n.

z number of modulated symbols can be successively demodulated from one transmitted symbol. For each modulated symbol, the lth subcarrier within the resource band i can be obtained by FFT as

$$Y_l^i = \frac{1}{\sqrt{N_z}} \sum_{n=0}^{N_s-1} y[n] e^{-j2\pi n(l+S_i)/N_z} \tag{12}$$

$$= \frac{1}{N_z} X_l^i P_r^i[l] \sum_{n=0}^{N_z-1} H_{l+S_i}[n] + I^i[l] + W^i[l] \tag{13}$$

where P_r^k is the frequency response of FIR filter p_r^i and $W^i[l]$ is the FFT of noise $w[n]$. $I^i[l]$ is the intra-band ICI and inter-band interference. With the filtering,

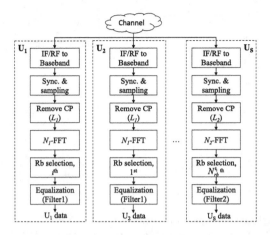

Fig. 4. Downlink receiver structure at TTI t_1. Baseline setting and one adjusted setting are applied, i.e. $z = 1, 2$. Data to U_1 and U_2 are modulated to baseline resource bands $I_b = i$ and $I_b = 1$ respectively, with $z = 1$; and data to U_3 are modulated to the last resource band, $I_b = N_{rb}^{t_1}$, in the adjusted group ($z = 2$).

inter-band interference is negligible compared with intra-band ICI. So, $I^i[l]$ can be written as

$$I^i[l] = \frac{1}{N_z} \sum_{m=0, m \neq l}^{N_s - 1} X_m^i P_r^i[m] \sum_{n=0}^{N_z - 1} H_{m+S_i}[n] e^{j2\pi n(m-l)/N_z} \tag{14}$$

Considering the time-varying Rayleigh fading channel following classical Jakes model, we have [8]

$$E\{H[n]H^*[m]\} = J_0 \left(2\pi f_m T_z (n - m)/N_z\right) \tag{15}$$

$$= J_0 \left(2\pi(1 + \alpha_{cp}) \frac{f_m}{f_{sz}} (n - m)/N\right) \tag{16}$$

where $J_0(\cdot)$ is the zeroth-order Bessel function of the first kind, $T_z = (1 + \alpha_{cp}) f_{sz}$ is the modulated symbol duration. Therefore, with $E\{|X_m^i|^2\} = 1$, the average power of ICI is [8]

$$E \left\{ |I^i[l]|^2 \right\}$$

$$= \frac{1}{N_z^2} \sum_{m=0, m \neq l}^{N_s - 1} \left[N_z + 2 \sum_{n=1}^{N_z - 1} (N_z - n) J_0 \left(2\pi f_m T_s n\right) \right.$$

$$\left. \cdot \cos\left(\frac{2\pi n(m - l)}{N_z}\right) \right] \tag{17}$$

Figure 5 shows the signal-to-ICI ratio (SIR) under different user movement velocities. A comparison is made between baseline OFDMA and ABMA with $z = 1, 2, 3$.

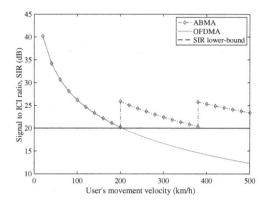

Fig. 5. Signal-to-ICI ratio comparison between baseline OFDMA and ABMA. Subcarrier spacings of ABMA switch among three settings with $z = 1, 2, 3$ to ensure the SIR above the required lower-bound.

For illustration purpose, we set a required SIR lower-bound to 20 dB. It is seen from Fig. 5 that only 200 km/h can be supported with SIR above the lower-bound by baseline OFDMA. While with ABMA, it is able to remain the SIR above the required SIR by its adaptive structure. Thus, ABMA can be much more robust than OFDMA in the time-varying mobility environments with high-range velocities.

4   Numerical System Evaluation

In this section, we present the numerical system evaluation. RF carrier frequency is set to be 6 GHz. Users' velocities are time-varying in the range of 0 to 500 km/h with uniform distribution. Perfect CSI and users' GPS information is assumed to be available at the BS. One adjusted numerology setting is applied, i.e. $z = 1$ or 2, as summarized in Table 1. For simulation purpose, set the pre-settled velocity threshold, $\phi_v = 260$ km/h. Considering the balance of frequency-time localization, soft-truncated sinc filters with Hanning window [6] is used as the prototype of FIR bandpass filters for each resource band. Guard tones between the two groups is 4×30 kHz. Figure 6 shows the BER performance

Table 1. Simulation parameters of ABMA.

Parameter	Baseline setting	Adjusted setting
Resource band size, N_s	60	60
Subcarrier spacing	$f_{s1} = 15$ kHz	$f_{s2} = 30$ kHz
Length of IFFT/FFT	$N_1 = 2048$	$N_2 = 1024$
Filter length	$L_{f1} = 200$ samples	$L_{f2} = 100$ samples
CP length	$L_1 = 160$ samples	$L_2 = 80$ samples

with QPSK data symbols in Rayleigh channel following classical Jakes model and a line-of-sight transmission, under OFDMA and proposed ABMA respectively. Zero-forcing equalization is used to compensate the filtering distortion. Three pilots are inserted in each resource band for phase tracking.

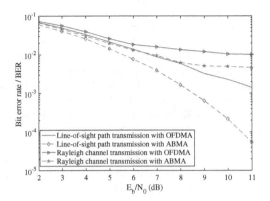

Fig. 6. BER performance of ABMA and OFDMA in time-varying mobility environment, with $z = 1, 2$; $\phi_v = 260$ km/h.

Compared to baseline setting OFDMA, ABMA brings 3 dB E_b/N_0 gain for BER $= 10^{-3}$ regarding to the line-of-sight path transmission as well as lower BER platform with Rayleigh channel. The results prove that ABMA enhances the transmission robustness in time-varying mobility environment with high-range velocities. Regarding to salability with fixed bandwidth resource, because of the user request-orientated adaptive subcarrier bandwidth adjustment, ABMA is the compromise of baseline OFDMA ($f_s = 15$ kHz) and adjusted subcarrier bandwidth OFDMA (f_s is fully switched to 30 kHz).

5   Conclusion

In this paper, we propose a downlink multi-user access scheme based on filtered-OFDM waveform, named adaptive subcarrier-bandwidth multiple access (ABMA), targeting at high-mobility environment with different kinds of high-speed receivers. ABMA allows coexistence of difference sizes of subcarrier bandwidth. Frequency-domain quasi-orthogonality is obtained by resource band based filtering. With the time-varying change of user velocities, BS is able to adaptively allocate the spectrum locations and parameters of the resource bands. Adaptation control information is designed, with consideration of adaption flexibility and overhead minimization. With ABMA, ICI power caused by Doppler spread can be limited in a certain range. Simulation results prove the significant gain in BER performance to support a wide range of users with time-varying velocities.

References

1. Schaich, F., Wild, T., Chen, Y.: Waveform contenders for 5G-suitability for short packet and low latency transmissions. In: Proceedings of the 79th Vehicular Technology Conference (VTC Spring), pp. 1–5. IEEE (2014)
2. Abdoli, J., Jia, M., Ma, J.: Filtered OFDM: a new waveform for future wireless systems. In: Proceedings of the 16th International Workshop on Signal Processing Advances in Wireless Communications (SPAWC), pp. 66–70. IEEE (2015)
3. Dong, Z., Fan, P., Hu, Q., Gunther, J., Lei, X.: Filtered OFDM: a new waveform for future wireless systems. IEEE Trans. Veh. Technol. **65**(8), 6038–6050 (2015)
4. Schaich, F., Wild, T.: Subcarrier spacing-a neglected degree of freedom?. In: Proceedings of the 16th International Workshop on Signal Processing Advances in Wireless Communications (SPAWC), pp. 56–60. IEEE (2015)
5. Schaich, F., Wild, T., Ahmed, R.: Subcarrier spacing-how to make use of this degree of freedom. In: Proceedings of the Vehicular Technology Conference (VTC Spring), pp. 1–6, IEEE (2016)
6. Zhang, X., Jia, M., Chen, L., Ma, J., Qiu, J.: Filtered-OFDM-enabler for flexible waveform in the 5th generation cellular networks. In: Proceedings of the Global Communications Conference (GLOBECOM), pp. 1–6. IEEE (2015)
7. Li, Y., Cimini, L.J.: Bounds on the interchannel interference of OFDM in time-varying impairments. IEEE Trans. Commun. **49**(3), 401–404 (2001)
8. Choi, Y., Voltz, P.J., Cassara, F.A.: On channel estimation and detection for multi-carrier signals in fast and selective Rayleigh fading channels. IEEE Trans. Commun. **49**(8), 1375–1387 (2001)

Intelligent Signal Processing, Wireless Communications and Networks

R/I-Capon for Low-Complexity Direction of Arrival Estimation with Real-Valued Computation

Xiang Li⑩, Feng-Gang Yan$^{(\boxtimes)}$⑩, Shuai Liu⑩, and Ming Jin⑩

School of Information Science and Engineering,
Harbin Institute of Technology at Weihai, Weihai, China
yfglion@163.com

Abstract. The problem of low-complexity direction-of-arrival (DOA) estimation without knowing sources number is addressed. Real/imaginary-part of array covariance matrix (ACM) can be remodeled as a whole ACM of signal received by virtual array aimed at fast DOA estimate. Based on such a virtual signal model, a novel real/imaginary-part Capon (R/I-Capon) involving the inverse of only the real/imaginary-part of the estimated ACM (EACM) is derived. In-depth insights are provided to prove that the rank of real/imaginary-part of EACM is always equal or greater than that of whole EACM, which indicates that R/I-Capon exceeds conventional Capon under the circumstance with small numbers of snapshots. Further discussion indicates that R/I-Capon is also capable of decreasing about 75% complexity with any array structures, which shows an enforcement advantage over state-of-the-art prototype methods. Simulations are finally conducted to verify theoretical analysis and to show practicability of proposed algorithm.

Keywords: Orthogonal projection · Cumulative sum ·
Cumulative multiplication · Singular value decomposition · Intersection

1 Introduction

Subspace-based direction of arrival (DOA) algorithms including MUSIC [2,3], root-MUSIC [4,5] and ESPRIT [6] generally desire number of sources to be detected in advance or to be known [7], when sources number is misjudged, performance of those estimators can get deteriorated signally [8]. Beamforming techniques such as Capon [9] can be applied for DOA estimation without knowing sources number, but they have to compute inverse of estimated array covariance matrix (EACM) as well as complex product of steering vector, which involve higher complexity than MUSIC. Unitary techniques with real-valued

This work is supported by National Natural Science Foundation of China under granted numbers 61501142 and 61871149.

computation are able to decrease complexity by a quarter as compared to their complex-valued versions [10,11]. Unfortunately, those algorithms are based upon centro-symmetrical arrays (CSAs), [13].

This paper aims for solving problem of low-complexity DOA estimation without knowing sources number, in which real-valued computation is attempted to be implemented with arbitrary array structures. To this end, the real/imaginary-part of the EACM is used instead of the whole EACM to simplify the optimization problem by a new real/imaginary-part Capon (R/I-Capon). Theoretical analysis and numerical simulations show that R/I-Capon is able to decrease about 75% complexity with improved precision in the condition of small numbers of snapshots.

2   Signal Models and Conventional Capon

Consider a linear array with M antennas placed at $\mathbb{X} = [x_1, x_2, \ldots, x_M]$, where $\mathbb{X}$ is arbitrary array[1] including uniform linear array and sparse array, but is assumed to own rank-$(M-1)$ ambiguity restriction [14]. Assume $K, K < M$ uncorrelated narrow-band signals with DOAs $\boldsymbol{\theta} = [\theta_1, \theta_2, \ldots, \theta_K]$ impinging on array, and the output of array at $t, t \in [1, T]$ is expressed as [1–13]

$$\mathbf{x}(t) = \mathbf{A}(\boldsymbol{\theta})\mathbf{s}(t) + \mathbf{n}(t), \tag{1}$$

where $\mathbf{s}(t)$ is $K \times 1$ signal, $\mathbf{n}(t) \sim \mathcal{CN}\left(\mathbf{0}, \sigma_n^2 \mathbf{I}_M\right)$ is $M \times 1$ additive noise, σ_n^2 is noise power, $\mathbf{I}_M$ is $M \times M$ identity matrix, $\mathbf{A}(\boldsymbol{\theta}) = [\mathbf{a}(\theta_1), \mathbf{a}(\theta_2), \ldots, \mathbf{a}(\theta_K)]$ is $M \times K$ array manifold with

$$\mathbf{a}(\theta_k) = \left[e^{j\frac{2\pi}{\lambda}x_1 \sin\theta_k}, e^{j\frac{2\pi}{\lambda}x_2 \sin\theta_k}, \cdots, e^{j\frac{2\pi}{\lambda}x_M \sin\theta_k}\right]^T \tag{2}$$

denoting $M \times 1$ steering vector, where $(\cdot)^T$ is transpose. The $M \times M$ array covariance matrix (ACM) is given by

$$\mathbf{R}_{xx} = \mathrm{E}\left[\mathbf{x}(t)\mathbf{x}^H(t)\right] = \mathbf{A}(\boldsymbol{\theta})\mathbf{R}_{ss}\mathbf{A}^H(\boldsymbol{\theta}) + \sigma_n^2 \mathbf{I}_M, \tag{3}$$

where $(\cdot)^H$ is conjugate transpose and $\mathbf{R}_{ss} = \mathrm{E}\left[\mathbf{s}(t)\mathbf{s}^H(t)\right]$ is the $K \times K$ source covariance matrix. Note that $\mathbf{R}_{ss}$ is a real diagonal matrix as $\mathbf{s}(t)$ is uncorrelated. In practice, ACM is estimated by EACM from T snapshots of observed data as

$$\widehat{\mathbf{R}}_{xx} = \frac{1}{T}\sum_{t=1}^{T}\mathbf{x}(t)\mathbf{x}^H(t). \tag{4}$$

When K is known by signal number detection methods [15] in advance, subspace-based methods utilize eigenvalue decomposition (EVD) and obtain

---

[1] The new method can be easily extended to arbitrary plane array for two-dimensional DOA estimate by introducing two electrical DOAs [13].

signal-noise orthogonal matrix to find DOAs. However, performance of subspace-based methods will get deteriorated without the correct K [8].

Instead of detecting signal number K, Capon [9] suggests a weighted output of array $\mathbf{y}(t) = \mathbf{w}^H \mathbf{x}(t)$ and searches DOAs by minimizing power of $\mathbf{y}(t)$ as

$$\min_{\mathbf{w}} \ \mathrm{E}\big[\mathbf{y}(t)\,\mathbf{y}^H(t)\big] = \mathbf{w}^H \mathbf{R}_{xx} \mathbf{w} \quad \text{s.t. } \mathbf{w}^H \mathbf{a}(\theta) = 1. \tag{5}$$

By solving (5), DOAs can be estimated over $[-\pi/2, \pi/2]$ by seeking peaks of

$$f_{\mathrm{Capon}}(\theta) = \frac{1}{\mathbf{a}^H(\theta)\,\widehat{\mathbf{R}}_{xx}^{-1}\mathbf{a}(\theta)} \tag{6}$$

The sources number and DOAs can be obtained by peak number of $f_{\mathrm{Capon}}(\theta)$ and their locations.

3 Proposed R/I-Capon Algorithm

3.1 Virtual Signal Models

It can be shown that real- and imaginary-parts of ACM contain virtual signal models can be used for DOA estimate. Using $\mathrm{Re}(\mathbf{R}_{xx}) = \frac{1}{2}(\mathbf{R} + \mathbf{R}^*)$ as well as (3), we have

$$\mathrm{Re}(\mathbf{R}_{xx}) = \frac{1}{2}\big[\mathbf{A}(\boldsymbol{\theta})\,\mathbf{R}_{ss}\mathbf{A}^H(\boldsymbol{\theta}) + \mathbf{A}^*(\boldsymbol{\theta})\,\mathbf{R}_{ss}\mathbf{A}^T(\boldsymbol{\theta})\big] + \sigma_n^2 \mathbf{I}_M$$

$$= \underbrace{\big[\mathbf{A}(\boldsymbol{\theta})\ \mathbf{A}^*(\boldsymbol{\theta})\big]}_{M \times 2K} \times \underbrace{\frac{1}{2}\begin{bmatrix}\mathbf{R}_{ss} & \mathbf{0} \\ \mathbf{0} & \mathbf{R}_{ss}\end{bmatrix}}_{2K \times 2K} \times \underbrace{\begin{bmatrix}\mathbf{A}^H(\boldsymbol{\theta}) \\ \mathbf{A}^T(\boldsymbol{\theta})\end{bmatrix}}_{2K \times M} + \sigma_n^2 \mathbf{I}_M$$

$$= \mathbf{A}_1(\boldsymbol{\theta}) \mathcal{R}_{ss,1} \mathbf{A}_1^H(\boldsymbol{\theta}) + \sigma_n^2 \mathbf{I}_M, \tag{7}$$

where $\mathbf{0}$ is a $K \times K$ matrix with all zero elements, $\mathcal{R}_{ss,1}$ and matrix $\mathbf{A}_1(\boldsymbol{\theta})$ are defined as

$$\mathcal{R}_{ss,1} = \frac{1}{2}\begin{bmatrix}\mathbf{R}_{ss} & \mathbf{0} \\ \mathbf{0} & \mathbf{R}_{ss}\end{bmatrix} \in \mathbb{C}^{2K \times 2K} \tag{8-1}$$

$$\mathbf{A}_1(\boldsymbol{\theta}) = \big[\mathbf{A}(\boldsymbol{\theta})\ \mathbf{A}^*(\boldsymbol{\theta})\big] \in \mathbb{C}^{M \times 2K}. \tag{8-2}$$

Using $\mathrm{E}\big[\mathbf{s}(t)\mathbf{s}^H(t)\big] = \mathbf{R}_{ss}$ and $\mathrm{E}\big[\mathbf{s}(t)\mathbf{s}^T(t)\big] = 0$, $\mathcal{R}_{ss,1}$ can be rewritten as

$$\mathcal{R}_{ss,1} = \mathrm{E}\left\{\underbrace{\begin{bmatrix}\mathbf{s}(t) \\ \mathbf{s}^*(t)\end{bmatrix}}_{2K \times 1} \times \underbrace{\big[\mathbf{s}^H(t)\ \mathbf{s}^T(t)\big]}_{1 \times 2K}\right\}$$

$$= \mathrm{E}[\mathbf{s}_1(t)\mathbf{s}_1^H(t)], \tag{9}$$

where $\mathbf{s}_1(t) = \begin{bmatrix} \mathbf{s}(t) \\ \mathbf{s}^*(t) \end{bmatrix}$ is a $2K \times 1$ vector. Inserting (9) into (7) and using $\mathrm{E}[\mathbf{n}(t)\mathbf{n}^H(t)] = \sigma_n^2 \mathbf{I}_M$ leads to

$$
\begin{aligned}
\mathrm{Re}(\mathbf{R}_{xx}) &= \mathbf{A}_1(\boldsymbol{\theta})\mathcal{R}_{ss,1}\mathbf{A}_1^H(\boldsymbol{\theta}) + \sigma_n^2 \mathbf{I}_M \\
&= \mathbf{A}_1(\boldsymbol{\theta})\mathrm{E}[\mathbf{s}_1(t)\mathbf{s}_1^H(t)]\mathbf{A}_1(\boldsymbol{\theta})^H + \mathrm{E}[\mathbf{n}(t)\mathbf{n}^H(t)] \\
&= \mathrm{E}\left\{ [\mathbf{A}_1(\boldsymbol{\theta})\mathbf{s}_1(t) + \mathbf{n}(t)] \times [\mathbf{A}_1(\boldsymbol{\theta})\mathbf{s}_1(t) + \mathbf{n}(t)]^H \right\} \\
&= \mathrm{E}[\mathbf{x}_1(t)\mathbf{x}_1^H(t)],
\end{aligned}
\tag{10}
$$

where $\mathbf{x}_1(t)$ is a $2K \times 1$ vector, given by

$$
\mathbf{x}_1(t) = \mathbf{A}_1(\boldsymbol{\theta})\mathbf{s}_1(t) + \mathbf{n}(t).
\tag{11}
$$

Comparing (11) with (1) and (10) with (3), we can conclude that real-part of ACM can be completely treated as the whole ACM with a virtual manifold $\mathbf{A}_1(\boldsymbol{\theta})$ [16]. $\mathbf{x}_1(t)$ and $\mathbf{s}_1(t)$ are observed data and incident signal via this virtual array, respectively. Signal covariance matrix are noted as $\mathcal{R}_{ss,1}$.

Likewise defining

$$
\mathcal{R}_{ss,2} = \frac{j}{2} \begin{bmatrix} \mathbf{R}_{ss} & \mathbf{0} \\ \mathbf{0} & -\mathbf{R}_{ss} \end{bmatrix} \in \mathbb{C}^{2K \times 2K}
\tag{12-1}
$$

$$
\mathbf{A}_2(\boldsymbol{\theta}) = [\mathbf{A}^*(\boldsymbol{\theta}) \quad \mathbf{A}(\boldsymbol{\theta})] \in \mathbb{C}^{M \times 2K}
\tag{12-2}
$$

$$
\mathbf{s}_2(t) = \frac{1}{2} \begin{bmatrix} (1+j)\mathbf{s}(t) \\ (1-j)\mathbf{s}^*(t) \end{bmatrix} \in \mathbb{C}^{2K \times 1}
\tag{12-3}
$$

$$
\mathbf{x}_2(t) = \mathbf{A}_2(\boldsymbol{\theta})\mathbf{s}_2(t) + \mathbf{n}(t) \in \mathbb{C}^{2K \times 1},
\tag{12-4}
$$

and using $\mathrm{Im}(\mathbf{R}_{xx}) = \frac{j}{2}(\mathbf{R}^* - \mathbf{R})$, one can easily obtain

$$
\mathrm{Im}(\mathbf{R}_{xx}) + \sigma_n^2 \mathbf{I}_M = \mathrm{E}[\mathbf{x}_2(t)\mathbf{x}_2^H(t)].
\tag{13}
$$

Hence, $\mathrm{Im}(\mathbf{R}_{xx}) + \sigma_n^2 \mathbf{I}_M$ can be also regarded as the whole ACM and those manifold is $\mathbf{A}_2(\boldsymbol{\theta})$. Similarly, $\mathbf{x}_2(t)$ and $\mathbf{s}_2(t)$ are severally observed data and incident signal as well as its covariance matrix noted as $\mathcal{R}_{ss,2}$.

3.2 Proposed R/I-Capon Algorithm

Defining a new weighted array output $\mathbf{y}_1(t) = \mathbf{w}^H \mathbf{x}_1(t)$ using (11) on virtual array, optimization problem is shown as

$$
\min_{\mathbf{w}} \; \mathrm{E}[\mathbf{y}_1(t)\mathbf{y}_1^H(t)] = \mathbf{w}^H \mathrm{Re}(\mathbf{R}_{xx})\mathbf{w}
\tag{14-1}
$$

$$
\text{s.t.} \quad \mathbf{w}^H \mathbf{a}_1(\theta) = 1,
\tag{14-2}
$$

where $\mathbf{a}_1(\theta)$ is virtual steering vector composing $\mathbf{A}_1(\boldsymbol{\theta})$. Noting $\forall \boldsymbol{\theta}$, $\mathbf{A}^*(\boldsymbol{\theta}) = \mathbf{A}(-\boldsymbol{\theta})$ holds, thus $\mathbf{A}_1(\boldsymbol{\theta}) = [\mathbf{A}(\boldsymbol{\theta}) \quad \mathbf{A}(-\boldsymbol{\theta})]$ and $\mathbf{A}_1(\boldsymbol{\theta})$ can be treated as new manifold combined with $\mathbf{A}(\theta)$ and $\mathbf{A}(-\theta)$. Equally, $\mathbf{a}_1(\theta)$ can be treated as new steering vector combined with $\mathbf{a}(\theta)$ and $\mathbf{a}(-\theta)$. Then, (19-1) and (19-2) can be simplified as[2]

$$\min_{\mathbf{w}} \mathbf{w}^H \mathrm{Re}(\mathbf{R}_{xx})\mathbf{w} \quad \text{s.t.} \quad \mathbf{w}^H \mathbf{a}(\theta) = 1. \tag{15}$$

Now, adopting Lagrange multiplier technique, we have

$$h(\mathbf{w}) = \mathbf{w}^H \mathrm{Re}(\mathbf{R}_{xx})\mathbf{w} - \mu \left[\mathbf{w}^H \mathbf{a}(\theta) - 1 \right], \tag{16}$$

where μ is Lagrange multiplier. By making $\partial h_1(\mathbf{w})/\partial\mathbf{w} = 0$, (16) can be simplified as

$$\mathbf{w}_{\mathrm{opt}} = \frac{\mathrm{Re}^{-1}(\mathbf{R}_{xx})\mathbf{a}(\theta)}{\mathbf{a}^H(\theta)\,\mathrm{Re}^{-1}(\mathbf{R}_{xx})\mathbf{a}(\theta)}. \tag{17}$$

Combining (17) and $\mathbf{w}^H \mathrm{Re}(\mathbf{R}_{xx})\mathbf{w}$, the problem can be solved as

$$f_{R/I\text{-Capon}}(\theta) = \frac{1}{\mathbf{a}^H(\theta)\,\mathrm{Re}^{-1}(\widehat{\mathbf{R}}_{xx})\mathbf{a}(\theta)}. \tag{18}$$

Taking (13) into account, we can get another weighted output $\mathbf{y}_2(t) = \mathbf{w}^H\mathbf{x}_2(t)$ and the optimization problem can be rewrote as

$$\min_{\mathbf{w}} \mathrm{E}\left[\mathbf{y}_2(t)\mathbf{y}_2^H(t)\right] = \mathbf{w}^H \left[\mathrm{Im}(\mathbf{R}_{xx}) + \sigma_n^2\mathbf{I}_M\right]\mathbf{w}$$

$$= \mathbf{w}^H\mathrm{Im}(\mathbf{R}_{xx})\mathbf{w} + \sigma_n^2\|\mathbf{w}\|^2 \tag{19-1}$$

$$\text{s.t.} \quad \mathbf{w}^H\mathbf{a}_2(\theta) = 1, \tag{19-2}$$

Since $\mathbf{a}_2(\theta)$ covers both $\mathbf{a}(\theta)$ and $\mathbf{a}(-\theta)$, (19-1) and (19-2) can be simplified as

$$\min_{\mathbf{w}} \mathbf{w}^H\mathrm{Im}(\mathbf{R}_{xx})\mathbf{w} + \sigma_n^2\|\mathbf{w}\|^2 \quad \text{s.t.} \quad \mathbf{w}^H\mathbf{a}(\theta) = 1. \tag{20}$$

By applying Lagrange multiplier technique to solve (20), proposed R/I-Capon can be equivalently given by[3]

$$f_{R/I\text{-Capon}}(\theta) = \frac{1}{\mathbf{a}^H(\theta)\left[\mathrm{Im}(\widehat{\mathbf{R}}_{xx}) + \widehat{\sigma}_n^2\mathbf{I}_M\right]^{-1}\mathbf{a}(\theta)}. \tag{21}$$

Considering $\widehat{\theta}$ varies over $[0, \pi/2]$ and $f_{R/I\text{-Capon}}(-\widehat{\theta}) = f_{R/I\text{-Capon}}(-\widehat{\theta})$, $\widehat{\theta} \in [-\pi/2, 0]$ could also be true DOAs. Moreover, $\widehat{\theta}$ and $-\widehat{\theta}$ could be both true DOAs when two sources come from $\widehat{\theta}$ and $-\widehat{\theta}$ incidentally. To deal with ambiguity problem, conventional beamformer (CBF) [1] is appropriate for selecting true DOA by maximizing $\|\mathbf{a}^H(\theta)\widehat{\mathbf{R}}_{xx}\mathbf{a}(\theta)\|$.

Detailed steps of proposed algorithm are summarized in Table 1.

---

[2] The simplification leads to an estimation ambiguity problem, which is analyzed and solved at the end of this subsection.

[3] It is suggested to use (18) rather than (21) in practice since (21) contains a noise part $\widehat{\sigma}_n^2\mathbf{I}_M$ which should be estimated in advance.

Table 1. Detailed steps of R/I-Capon algorithm

• **Step 1**	Compute $\widehat{\mathbf{R}}_{xx} = \frac{1}{T}\sum_{t=1}^{T}\mathbf{x}(t)\mathbf{x}^{H}(t)$ and obtain $\mathrm{Re}(\widehat{\mathbf{R}}_{xx})$
• **Step 2**	Search peaks of $f_{R/I\text{-Capon}}(\theta) = \frac{1}{\mathbf{a}^{H}(\theta)\mathrm{Re}^{-1}(\widehat{\mathbf{R}}_{xx})\mathbf{a}(\theta)}$ over $[0, \pi/2]$ to obtain the candidate angles $\widehat{\theta}_i, i \in [1, Q], Q \leqslant \lfloor\frac{K}{2}\rfloor$
• **Step 3**	For each $\widehat{\theta}_i, i \in [1, Q]$, select true DOA between $\widehat{\theta}_i$ and $-\widehat{\theta}_i$ from maximization of product $\|\mathbf{a}^{H}(\theta)\widehat{\mathbf{R}}_{xx}\mathbf{a}(\theta)\|$

3.3 Rank Enhancement and Complexity Reduction

Comparing (18) and (21) with (6), it can be predicted that performance of R/I-Capon may behave worse than conventional Capon because of the half-exploitation of the EACM in R/I-Capon. However, simulation shows that new method has a similar performance compared to Capon. Besides, following theorem illustrates the outperformances of R/I-Capon over the conventional Capon in the situation of small numbers of snapshots.

Theorem 1. *Let the EACM be computed using T snapshots data by (4) in practice, the rank of the real/imaginary-part of the EACM is always no less than that of the entire EACM such that*[4]

$$\begin{cases} \mathrm{rank}[\mathrm{Re}(\widehat{\mathbf{R}}_{\mathbf{xx}})] \geqslant \mathrm{rank}(\widehat{\mathbf{R}}_{xx}) \\ \mathrm{rank}[\mathrm{Im}(\widehat{\mathbf{R}}_{\mathbf{xx}}) + \widehat{\sigma}_n^2\mathbf{I}_M] \geqslant \mathrm{rank}(\widehat{\mathbf{R}}_{xx}) \end{cases}. \tag{22}$$

4   Simulation Results

Throughout numerical simulations, 500 independent Monte Carlo trials were used to compare performances between conventional Capon and proposed algorithm[5], where the root mean square error (RMSE) can be defined by

$$\mathrm{RMSE} \triangleq \sqrt{\frac{1}{500}\sum_{k=1}^{K}\sum_{i=1}^{500}\left(\widehat{\theta}_{k,i} - \theta_k\right)^2}, \tag{23}$$

where $\widehat{\theta}_{k,i}$ is the ith estimated value for kth DOA θ_k.

Figure 1 plots the RMSEs against the signal-to-noise ratios (SNRs), and Fig. 2 plots those against T's. Figure 1 shows a similar performance of R/I-Capon compared with conventional Capon over SNR = 0 dB–40 dB. With a moderate SNR = 10 dB, it is observed from Fig. 2 that our method achieves better results than conventional Capon all along different T's, especially in scenario within $T \leqslant 100$.

---

[4] In fact, we also have $\mathrm{rank}[\mathrm{Im}(\widehat{\mathbf{R}}_{\mathbf{xx}})] \geqslant \mathrm{rank}(\widehat{\mathbf{R}}_{xx})$.

[5] A half-wavelength uniform linear array (ULA) with $M = 12$ sensors are used to find $K = 2$ sources at $\theta_1 = 20°$ and $\theta_1 = 30°$, where the standard MUSIC [2] is applied for a common comparison reference.

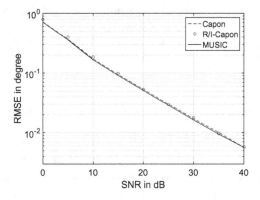

Fig. 1. RMSE against the SNR, $T = 100$ snapshots.

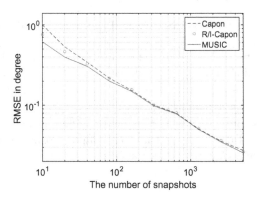

Fig. 2. RMSE against the number of snapshots, SNR $= 10$ dB.

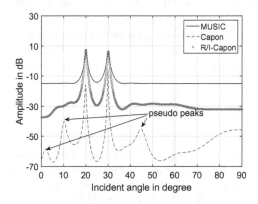

Fig. 3. Direction finding with $T = 20$ snapshots and SNR $= 10$ dB.

To see more clearly performance of new algorithm with small snapshots, Fig. 3 compares spectrums of different algorithms with $T = 20$. From Fig. 3, it is apparent that conventional Capon appears pseudo peaks while R/I-Capon does

Table 2. Matrix rank against small number of snapshots, SNR = 10 dB.

Items	$T = 30$	$T = 25$	$T = 20$	$T = 15$	$T = 10$
rank$(\widehat{\mathbf{R}}_{\mathbf{xx}})$	12	10	10	10	7
rank$[\mathrm{Re}(\widehat{\mathbf{R}}_{\mathbf{xx}})]$	12	12	12	12	9

Table 3. Comparison of CPU time in second, SNR = 10 dB, $T = 100$.

Items	$M = 8$	$M = 12$	$M = 16$	$M = 20$	$M = 24$
Capon	1.8017	3.1400	3.3097	3.2956	3.5283
R/I-Capon	0.5003	0.8121	0.8201	0.8510	0.8806
MUSIC	1.3358	2.5361	2.6361	2.8725	3.0456

not at $T = 20$ snapshots. Moreover, we find the pseudo peak shows repetitively in conventional Capon spectral.

To further verify results observed from Figs. 2 and 3, Table 2 compares rank$(\widehat{\mathbf{R}}_{\mathbf{xx}})$ and rank$[\mathrm{Re}(\widehat{\mathbf{R}}_{\mathbf{xx}})]$ with different small T's. It is shown from the table that $\mathrm{Re}(\widehat{\mathbf{R}}_{\mathbf{xx}})$ does has an enhanced rank as compared to $\widehat{\mathbf{R}}_{\mathbf{xx}}$, which verifies the conclusions of Theorem 1.

Finally, Table 3 compares the CPU times of different algorithms against the number of sensors. Table 3 shows that R/I-Capon costs about 4 times lower simulation times than Capon in expectations.

5   Conclusions

A novel R/I-Capon algorithm for DOA estimation without investigation for number of sources has been proposed. The new algorithm develops only real part of ACM to decrease complexity by a factor about four. It has been demonstrated by Theoretical analysis as well as numerical simulations that R/I-Capon also shows a better property than Capon at small snapshots owing to the rank enhancement of R/I-Capon in comparison to conventional Capon.

References

1. Krim, J., Viberg, M.: Two decades of array signal processing research: the parametric approach. IEEE Signal Process. Mag. **13**(3), 67–94 (1996)
2. Schmidt, R.O.: Multiple emitter location and signal parameter estimation. IEEE Trans. Antennas Propag. **AP-34**(3), 276–280 (1986)
3. Yan, F.G., Jin, M., Qiao, X.L.: Low-complexity DOA estimation based on compressed MUSIC and its performance analysis. IEEE Trans. Signal Process. **61**(8), 1915–1930 (2013)
4. Friedlander, B.: The root-MUSIC algorithm for direction finding with interpolated arrays. Signal Process. **30**, 15–29 (1993)

5. Yan, F.G., Shen, Y., Jin, M., Qiao, X.L.: Computationally efficient direction finding using polynomial rooting with reduced-order and real-valued computations. J Syst. Eng. Electron. **27**(4), 739–745 (2016)
6. Roy, R., Kailath, T.: ESPRIT-estimation of signal parameters via rotational invariance techniques. IEEE Trans. Signal Process. **37**(7), 984–995 (1989)
7. Yan, F.G., Jin, T., Jin, M., Shen, Y.: Subspace-based direction-of-arrival estimation using centro-symmetrical arrays. Eletron. Lett. **27**(11), 1895–1896 (2016)
8. Zhang, Y., Ng, B.P.: MUSIC-like DOA estimation without estimating the number of sources. IEEE Trans. Signal Process. **58**(3), 1668–1676 (2010)
9. Capon, J.: High-resolution frequency-wavenumber spectrum analysis. Proc. IEEE **57**, 1408–1418 (1987)
10. Huarng, K.C., Yeh, C.C.: A unitary transformation method for angle-of-arrival estimation. IEEE Trans. Signal Process. **39**, 975–977 (1991)
11. Yan, F.G., Shen, Y., Jin, M.: Fast DOA estimation based on a split subspace decomposition on the array covariance matrix. Signal Process. **115**, 1–8 (2015)
12. Haardt, M., Nossek, J.A.: Unitary ESPRIT: how to obtain increased estimation accuracy with a reduced computational burden. IEEE Trans. Signal Process. **43**(5), 1232–1242 (1995)
13. Yan, F.G., Jin, M., Liu, S., Qiao, X.L.: Real-valued MUSIC for efficient direction estimation with arbitrary array geometries. IEEE Trans. Signal Process. **62**(6), 1548–1560 (2014)
14. Tan, K.C., Goh, Z.: A detailed derivation of arrays free of higher rank ambiguities. IEEE Trans. Signal Process. **44**(2), 351–359 (1996)
15. Wax, M., Kailath, T.: Detection of signals by information theoretic criteria. IEEE Trans. Acoust. Speech Signal Process. **33**(3), 387–392 (1985)
16. Yan, F.G., Yan, X.W., Shi, J., et al.: MUSIC-like direction of arrival estimation based on virtual array transformation. Signal Process. **139**, 156–164 (2017)
17. Golub, G.H., Van Loan, C.H.: Matirx Computations. The Johns Hopkins University Press, Baltimore (1996)

Energy Efficiency Optimization Based SWIPT in Multiuser OFDM Systems

Shanzhen Fang[1(✉)], Weidang Lu[1], Yu Zhang[1], Bo Li[2], Xin Liu[3], and Zhenyu Na[4]

[1] College of Information Engineering, Zhejiang University of Technology, Hangzhou 310023, China
742430646@qq.com
[2] School of Information and Electrical Engineering, Harbin Institute of Technology, Weihai 264209, China
[3] School of Electronic Information and Electrical Engineering, Dalian University of Technology, Dalian 116024, Liaoning, China
[4] School of Information Science and Technology, Dalian Maritime University, Dalian 116026, China

Abstract. The research on wireless communication has been mainly focused on improving the system rate. However, while achieving the higher rate, it also consumes a lot of power, which leads to a reduction in energy efficiency. Therefore, in this paper, we propose a new algorithm to maximize energy efficiency in multiuser OFDM systems. More specifically, users can transfer information and collect energy simultaneously by using SWIPT technology, and the energy efficiency is maximized by optimizing the subcarrier allocation under some constraints. We formulate the proposed algorithm at first, and the initial optimization problem is non-convex, so we cannot get the optimal resource allocation directly. Later, by transforming the original objective function, the optimal solution is obtained. Finally, we validate the proposed algorithm with simulation results. The results show that the proposed algorithm can indeed improve energy efficiency. We also find that some variables have a huge impact on system energy efficiency.

Keywords: Multiuser system · OFDM · Energy efficiency · SWIPT

1 Introduction

In recent years, the rapid development of wireless networks has been bringing great convenience to our life, but it also brings new challenges, one of which is that the energy consumption is too large, which leads to a reduction in energy efficiency. Therefore, how to improve the energy efficiency of the system becomes very important in wireless networks.

SWIPT technology is an ideal way to improve energy efficiency. And TS (Time switching) and PS (Power splitting) are two most frequently used methods in SWIPT technology. And [1–5] used the PS method to improve energy efficiency. In [1], the authors optimized the PS ratio to achieve maximum secrecy energy efficiency

© ICST Institute for Computer Sciences, Social Informatics and Telecommunications Engineering 2019
Published by Springer Nature Switzerland AG 2019. All Rights Reserved
M. Jia et al. (Eds.): WiSATS 2019, LNICST 280, pp. 498–506, 2019.
https://doi.org/10.1007/978-3-030-19153-5_51

(SEE) where the artificial noise (AN) is also considered. [2] improved the energy efficiency of a MIMO system, in order to maintain the trade-off between the spectral efficiency and energy efficiency of the system, the authors also provided the Quality of Service (QoS) constraints. The authors in [3] studied how to improve energy efficiency of a two-way relay system. In [4], the authors applied SWIPT technology to the Internet of Things (IOT) and studied methods for improving energy efficiency under the case of single IOT device and multiple IOT devices. In [5], the authors used PS to harvest energy for forwarding information in clustered wireless sensor networks and then iterative optimize three variables, i.e., power, PS ratio, and relay selection, to maximize energy efficiency.

And [6, 7] used the TS method to improve energy efficiency. In [6], the authors gave optimal energy efficiency optimization schemes based on TS method. Then the authors also gave a suboptimal algorithm with lower complexity. Maximizing energy efficiency by optimizing time allocation factor and power is investigated in [7].

In the existing literature, PS method or TS method are mainly used for the energy efficiency maximization problem, but these two methods need to provide additional splitter or switcher. However, the method we give does not require splitter or switcher.

2 System Model and Problem Formulation

In this part, we introduce the multiuser OFDM system model and formulate the energy efficiency optimization problem of the system.

2.1 System Model

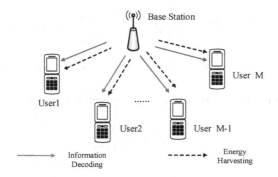

Fig. 1. System model

In a multiuser OFDM system, we consider there are M users and $\mathbf{N} = \{1, 2, \ldots N\}$ denotes the set of subcarriers, as shown in Fig. 1. User m can harvest energy while transmitting information. The set of subcarriers that user m uses to harvest energy can be expressed as S_m^P, and S_m^I represents the subcarriers set for transmitting information. Let $p_{m,n}$ and $h_{m,n}$ denote the power and channel gain of user m on subcarrier $n(n \in \mathbf{N})$ respectively, and the total power transmitted by the base station is set to P. In multiuser systems, interference often occurs. To solve this problem, the subcarriers used for each user for information transmission cannot be the same. We stipulate that each user has a target rate R_m to maintain the trade-off between energy efficiency and system capacity. Thus, we can get the transmission rate of user m on subcarrier $n(n \in S_m^I)$:

$$R_m = \sum_{n \in S_m^I} \log(1 + \frac{h_{m,n} p_{m,n}}{\sigma^2}) \tag{1}$$

where σ^2 is the variance of additive white Gaussian noise (AWGN). The throughput of the system is the sum of the rate transmitted by all users and is given by

$$E(S) = \sum_{m=1}^{M} \sum_{n \in S_m^I} \log(1 + \frac{h_{m,n} p_{m,n}}{\sigma^2}) \tag{2}$$

And the energy harvested by user m on subcarrier $n(n \in S_m^P)$ is given by

$$Q_m = \sum_{n \in S_m^P} (\varepsilon h_{m,n} p_{m,n} + \sigma^2) \tag{3}$$

where ε represents the conversion efficiency. The total power consumption is defined as the power consumed by the system minus the energy harvested by all users, and is shown as follows

$$E_{TP}(S) = P_B + M P_R + \sum_{m=1}^{M} \sum_{n \in \mathbf{N}} p_{m,n} - \sum_{m=1}^{M} \sum_{n \in S_m^P} (\varepsilon h_{m,n} p_{m,n} + \sigma^2) \tag{4}$$

where P_B, P_R represent the fixed power dissipation at base station and users, respectively.

So we can easily get the expression of the system energy efficiency [8]

$$E_{eff}(S) = \frac{E(S)}{E_{TP}(S)} \tag{5}$$

2.2   Problem Formulation

The optimization problem can be formulated as follows

$$\textbf{P1} : \max_{S_m^I, S_m^P} E_{eff}(S)$$

$$s.t. \ \text{C1} : \sum_{n \in S_m^I} \log(1 + \tfrac{h_{m,n} p_{m,n}}{\sigma^2}) \geq R_m, \forall m = 1, 2, \ldots M$$

$$\text{C2:} \ P_B + M P_R + \sum_{m=1}^{M} \sum_{n \in N} p_{m,n} \leq P \tag{6}$$

$$\text{C3:} \ S_{m_1}^I \cap S_{m_2}^I = \emptyset, \forall m_1, m_2 = 1, 2, \ldots M, m_1 \neq m_2$$

$$\text{C4:} \ S_m^I \cap S_m^P = \emptyset$$

where C1 gives the target rate constraints for the users, C2 represents that the power consumed cannot exceed the total power, C3 and C4 are constraints of subcarrier set.

3 Optimal Solution

Since the objective function is a fraction, we cannot get the optimal solution directly. If we use the exhaustive method to solve this problem, the computational complexity is very large, so we apply another method to get the optimal solution. Without loss of generality, we define q^* as the maximum energy efficiency of the system, that is:

$$q^* = \frac{E(S^*)}{E_{TP}(S^*)} = \max_{S_m^I, S_m^P} \frac{E(S)}{E_{TP}(S)} \tag{7}$$

The maximum energy efficiency is obtained only when the following formula is achieved, the proof process can be found in [9, Appendix A].

$$\max_{S_m^I, S_m^P} E(S) - q^* E_{TP}(S)$$

$$= E(S^*) - q^* E_{TP}(S^*) = 0 \tag{8}$$

Inspired by (8), we transform (6) into the following formula.

$$\textbf{P2} : \max_{S_m^I, S_m^P} E(S) - q E_{TP}(S) \tag{9}$$

$$s.t. \ \text{C1}, \text{C2}, \text{C3}, \text{C4}$$

Next we use the Lagrangian algorithm and the Dinkelbach iterative algorithm [10] to get the optimal subcarrier allocation scheme. First given q, and the Lagrange function of **P2** can be written as:

$$L(S, \beta) = \sum_{m=1}^{M} \sum_{n \in S_m^I} \log(1 + \frac{h_{m,n} p_{m,n}}{\sigma^2})$$

$$- q[P_B + M P_R + \sum_{m=1}^{M} \sum_{n \in N} p_{m,n} - \sum_{m=1}^{M} \sum_{n \in S_m^P} (\varepsilon h_{m,n} p_{m,n} + \sigma^2)]$$

$$+ \sum_{m=1}^{M} \beta_{1,m} [\sum_{n \in S_m^I} \log(1 + \frac{h_{m,n} p_{m,n}}{\sigma^2}) - R_m] + \beta_2 [P - \sum_{m=1}^{M} \sum_{n \in N} p_{m,n} - P_B - M P_R]$$

$$(10)$$

Here we equally distribute the power over all subcarriers, i.e., the power on each subcarrier is equal to each other. Next we can rewrite (10) as:

$$L(S, \beta) = \sum_{m=1}^{M} L_m - q(P_B + M P_R) - \sum_{m=1}^{M} \beta_{1,m} R_m + \beta_2 (P - P_B - M P_R) \quad (11)$$

where

$$L_m = \sum_{n \in S_m^I} \log(1 + \frac{h_{m,n} p_{m,n}}{\sigma^2}) - q \sum_{n \in N} p_{m,n} + q \sum_{n \in S_m^P} (\varepsilon h_{m,n} p_{m,n} + \sigma^2)$$

$$+ \beta_{1,m} \sum_{n \in S_m^I} \log(1 + \frac{h_{m,n} p_{m,n}}{\sigma^2}) - \beta_2 \sum_{n \in N} p_{m,n}$$

$$(12)$$

Further, (12) can be also rewritten as:

$$L_m = q \sum_{n \in N} (\varepsilon h_{m,n} p_{m,n} + \sigma^2) + \sum_{n \in S_m^I} F_m - q \sum_{n \in N} p_{m,n} - \beta_2 \sum_{n \in N} p_{m,n} \quad (13)$$

where $F_m = \log(1 + \frac{h_{m,n} p_{m,n}}{\sigma^2}) + \beta_{1,m} \log(1 + \frac{h_{m,n} p_{m,n}}{\sigma^2}) - q(\varepsilon h_{m,n} p_{m,n} + \sigma^2)$
So we can get the optimal subcarrier set S_m^I from F_m, and is given by

$$S_m^{*I} = \arg \max_{S_m^I} \sum_{n \in S_m^I} F_m \quad (14)$$

and the remaining subcarriers belong to S_m^P

$$S_m^{*P} = N - S_m^{*I} \quad (15)$$

The optimal dual variable $\{\beta_{1,m}^*, \beta_2^*\}$ can be derived by the subgradient method [11]. The iterative algorithm we propose can be summarized as the following table.

Algorithm 1 The proposed iterative algorithm

---

1 : **initialize** Fault tolerance range τ

2 : set $q = 0$, $i = 1$

3 : **repeat**

4 : Given q, obtaining $\{S_m{}^P, S_m{}^I\}$ in (14) and (15)

5 : **if** $E(S_m{}^P, S_m{}^I) - qE_{TP}(S_m{}^P, S_m{}^I) < \tau$

6 : return $\{S^*{}_m{}^P, S^*{}_m{}^I\} = \{S_m{}^P, S_m{}^I\}$ and $q^* = \dfrac{E(S_m{}^P, S_m{}^I)}{E_{TP}(S_m{}^P, S_m{}^I)}$

7 : **else**

8 : set $q = \dfrac{E(S_m{}^P, S_m{}^I)}{E_{TP}(S_m{}^P, S_m{}^I)}$ and $i = i + 1$

9 : **end if**

10 : **until** $E(S_m{}^P, S_m{}^I) - qE_{TP}(S_m{}^P, S_m{}^I) < \tau$ is true

---

4 Simulation Results

In this section, we show the simulation results of the proposed algorithm. In the simulation process, we let $N = 32$, $M = 4$ and $\varepsilon = 1$. The fixed power consumption

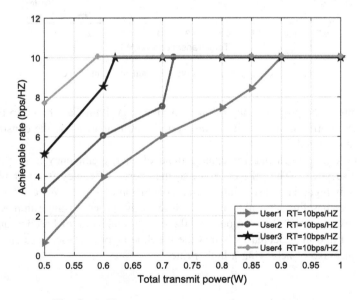

Fig. 2. Achievement rate versus total transmit power

of the transmitter and receiver is set to 0.05 W, i.e., $P_B = P_R = 0.05$ W. We noticed that the energy efficiency reaches its maximum after five iterations.

Figure 2 shows total transmit power versus achievement rate of different users, and we set $R_m = 10(bps/HZ)$. Due to the different channels, the rate trends of different users are also different. And we can see from the figure that the channel of user 4 is the best, while the user 1 has the worst channel.

From Fig. 3, we can see that the energy efficiency increases with the increase of the total transmission power, and then it does not change any more. That means that the system energy efficiency has reached its maximum. Moreover, the noise power also has a significant effect on energy efficiency. If the noise power is increased, the system energy efficiency will be reduced.

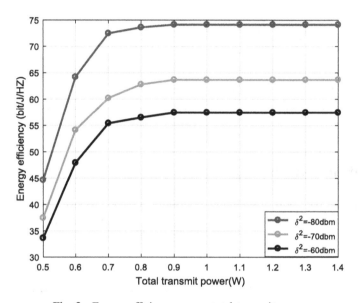

Fig. 3. Energy efficiency versus total transmit power

We compare the proposed algorithm with other algorithms, as shown in Fig. 4.

Baseline algorithm: We maximize the system throughput, while the constraints of **P2** remain unchanged.

It can be clearly seen that the change trend of energy efficiency is similar under different noise power. The difference is that the energy efficiency is lower when the noise power is high. This also validates the conclusion of Fig. 3. We can also see in Fig. 4 that the baseline algorithm is very close to the proposed algorithm when the transmit power is small. The reason why the energy efficiency of baseline algorithm increases first and then decreases is that the baseline algorithm sacrifices energy efficiency for the sake of achieving a higher rate.

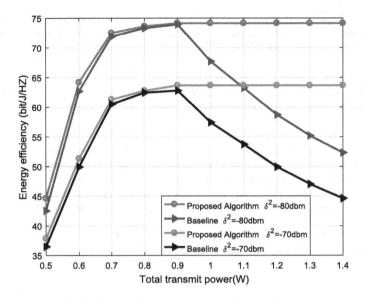

Fig. 4. Energy efficiency versus total transmit power

5 Conclusions

In this paper, we get the optimal subcarrier set to maximize the energy efficiency of multiuser systems. The initial optimization problem is difficult to solve, then we obtain the optimal solution by transforming the objective function. Simulation results show that our proposed algorithm can achieve higher energy efficiency, and we also find that the noise power has an obvious influence on the energy·efficiency of the system.

Acknowledgement. This work was supported in part by the National Natural Science Foundation of China under Grants 61871348 and 61601221, by the Project funded by China Postdoctoral Science Foundation under Grant 2017M612027.

References

1. Mei, W., Chen, Z., Fang, J.: Artificial noise aided energy efficiency optimization in MIMOME system With SWIPT. IEEE Commun. Lett. **21**(8), 1795–1798 (2017)
2. Tan, F., Lv, T., Huang, P.: Global energy efficiency optimization for wireless-powered massive MIMO aided multi-way AF relay networks. IEEE Trans. Sig. Process. **66**(9), 2384–2398 (2018)
3. Zhou, X., Li, Q.: Energy efficiency optimisation for SWIPT AF two-way relay networks. Electron. Lett. **53**(6), 436–438 (2017)
4. Huang, Y., Liu, M., Liu, Y., Chen, Z., Ji, H.: Energy-efficient SWIPT in IoT distributed antenna systems. IEEE Internet Things J. **5**(4), 2646–2656 (2018)

5. Guo, S., Wang, F., Yang, Y., Xiao, B.: Energy-efficient cooperative transmission for simultaneous wireless information and power transfer in clustered wireless sensor networks. IEEE Trans. Commun. **63**(11), 4405–4417 (2015)

6. Sun, Q., Li, L., Mao, J.: Simultaneous information and power transfer scheme for energy efficient MIMO systems. IEEE Commun. Lett. **18**(4), 600–603 (2014)

7. Yang, W., Mou, W., Xu, X., Yang, W., Cai, Y.: Energy efficiency analysis and enhancement for secure transmission in SWIPT systems exploiting full duplex techniques. IET Commun. **10**(14), 1712–1720 (2016)

8. Song, M., Zheng, M.: Energy efficiency optimization for wireless powered sensor networks with non-orthogonal multiple access. IEEE Sens. Lett. **2**(1), 1–4 (2018)

9. Ng, D.W.K., Lo, E.S., Schober, R.: Energy-efficient resource allocation for secure OFDMA systems. IEEE Trans. Veh. Technol. **61**(6), 2572–2585 (2012)

10. Li, S., Ni, Q., Sun, Y., Min, G., Al-Rubaye, S.: Energy-efficient resource allocation for industrial cyber-physical IoT systems in 5G Era. IEEE Trans. Ind. Inf. **14**(6), 2618–2628 (2018)

11. Lobel, I., Ozdaglar, A.: Distributed subgradient methods for convex optimization over random networks. IEEE Trans. Autom. Control **56**(6), 1291–1306 (2011)

Parameter Estimation of Multiple Satellite Signals Based on Cyclic Spectrum

Yu Du[✉], Jingjing Zheng, and Xiaoshuang Jiao

China Academy of Space Technology (Xi'an), Xi'an 710100, China
heidadiangong@163.com

Abstract. The cyclic spectral density function is a linear transformation that satisfies the principle of linear superposition. Based on this property, a new method for parameter estimation of multiple satellite signals is proposed. Firstly, the linear superposition characteristics of the cyclic spectrum are introduced. On the basis of this, the spectral characteristics of the mixed satellite signals are analyzed. According to the corresponding relationship between the cyclic spectrum line of multi-signals and the signal parameters. Finally, the parameter estimation of mixed signals is achieved indirectly through the method of detecting the line in specific cyclic frequency section of cyclic spectrum. The simulation results show that the new method has good performance under Gaussian noise.

Keywords: Satellite signals · Parameter estimation · Cyclic spectrum · Carrier frequency · Symbol rate

1 Introduction

Parameter estimation for signals is widely used in civil and military affairs, especially for space electronic reconnaissance, which is one of its core technologies. In the aspect of aerospace electronic reconnaissance application, the modern battlefield environment is complex and changeable, and the complex background environment, such as enemy interference, weather factors, and electronic interference of multi-type weapon equipment, which makes it possible that the intercepted satellite signals are mixed in two or more signals. Most of the existing signal parameter estimation methods are for single signal, which are no longer applicable for multi-signals, the existing methods of parameter estimation for multi-signals include cycle spectrum, high order cumulant, etc. [1–4], cyclic spectrum is not only insensitive to Gaussian noise [5–8], but also has linear superposition characteristics, which can represent the individual characteristics of this mixed signal very well.

The cyclic spectrum of the signal has discrete spectral lines at its cyclic frequency. By using the correspondence between the cyclic frequency and the signal parameters, the parameters of the signal can be estimated by extracting and analyzing the corresponding cyclic spectral line features. In addition, the cyclic spectrum of the mixed signal is equal to the superposition of the cyclic spectrum of each sub-signal component at the corresponding cyclic frequency. If the spectral line characteristics at the

M. Jia et al. (Eds.): WiSATS 2019, LNICST 280, pp. 507–513, 2019.
https://doi.org/10.1007/978-3-030-19153-5_52

cyclic frequency of the individual signal are analyzed, the other signals are equivalent to noise and will not affect the parameter estimation of the signal.

2 The Cyclic Spectrum Characteristics of Mixed Signals

Cyclic statistics are an effective tool for processing cyclostationary signals and have been widely used in signal processing. The cyclic spectrum is one of the important concepts, which can be used to describe the stationary characteristics of signal circulation while effectively suppressing noise. In addition, cyclic spectrum also has superposition and signal selectivity [9].

If multiple signals are independent of each other, then the cyclic spectrum of the mixed signals of these signals is equal to the sum of the individual signal cyclic spectrum. It is known from the definition of the cyclic spectrum that the cyclic spectral density function is a linear transformation, so it satisfies the principle of linear superposition. Taking the mixing of two signals as an example, the cyclic spectrum formula satisfies:

$$S_{ax_1+bx_2}^{\alpha}(f) = aS_{x_1}^{\alpha}(f) + bS_{x_2}^{\alpha}(f) \tag{1}$$

In the above formula, $S_x^{\alpha}(f)$ represents the cyclic spectrum of signal x, α represents the cyclic frequency, f represents the spectral frequency.

The cyclic spectrum of the signal is not zero only at its own cyclic frequency. Therefore, the cyclic spectrum has signal selectivity, or mixed signals with different cyclic frequencies have separability on the cyclic spectrum. For example, the cyclic frequency of signal x_1 and x_2 are respectively α_1 and α_2, then:

$$\begin{cases} S_{x_1}^{\alpha_2}(f) = 0 \\ S_{x_2}^{\alpha_1}(f) = 0 \end{cases} \tag{2}$$

In addition, considering the cyclic spectrum of the mixed signals after the two signals are superimposed, the following results are obtained:

$$\begin{cases} S_{x_1+x_2}^{\alpha_1}(f) = S_{x_1}^{\alpha_1}(f) + S_{x_2}^{\alpha_1}(f) = S_{x_1}^{\alpha_1}(f) \\ S_{x_1+x_2}^{\alpha_2}(f) = S_{x_1}^{\alpha_2}(f) + S_{x_2}^{\alpha_2}(f) = S_{x_2}^{\alpha_2}(f) \end{cases} \tag{3}$$

The above analysis also has similar conclusions for the superposition form of multiple signals. The above properties of cyclic spectrum make it suitable for multi-signals processing. These properties are also the theoretical basis for the study of satellite multi-signals parameter estimation algorithms based on cyclic spectrum.

Taking the commonly used BPSK and QPSK signals in satellite communication as an example. Assuming that the received signal is a mixed form of these two signals, combined with formula (1–3), the cycle spectrum of the mixed signal can be obtained as follows:

$$
S_{\mathrm{BQ}}^{\alpha}(f) =
\begin{cases}
\frac{E_b}{4T_b}\left[Q_b\left(f - f_{cb} + \frac{\alpha}{2}\right)Q_b^*\left(f - f_{cb} - \frac{\alpha}{2}\right) + \right.\\
\left. Q_b\left(f + f_{cb} + \frac{\alpha}{2}\right)Q_b^*\left(f + f_{cb} - \frac{\alpha}{2}\right)\right], \alpha = \frac{n}{T_b}\\[2mm]
\frac{E_q}{4T_q}\left[Q_q\left(f - f_{cq} + \frac{\alpha}{2}\right)Q_b^*\left(f - f_{cq} - \frac{\alpha}{2}\right) + \right.\\
\left. Q_q\left(f + f_{cq} + \frac{\alpha}{2}\right)Q_b^*\left(f + f_{cq} - \frac{\alpha}{2}\right)\right], \alpha = \frac{n}{T_q}\\[2mm]
\frac{E_b}{4T_b}\left[e^{j2\varphi_{0b}}Q_b\left(f - f_{cb} + \frac{\alpha}{2}\right)Q_b^*\left(f + f_{cb} - \frac{\alpha}{2}\right) + \right.\\
\left. e^{-j2\varphi_{0b}}Q_b\left(f + f_{cb} + \frac{\alpha}{2}\right)Q_b^*\left(f - f_{cb} - \frac{\alpha}{2}\right)\right]\\
\alpha = \pm 2f_{cb} + \frac{n}{T_b}
\end{cases}
\tag{4}
$$

In the above formula, f_{cb} and f_{cq} respectively represent the carrier frequency of BPSK and QPSK; T_b and T_q denotes the symbol period of BPSK and QPSK signals respectively; Q_b and Q_q respectively represent sinc functions corresponding to BPSK and QPSK signals; E_b and E_q respectively represent the average power of BPSK and QPSK signals. Figure 1 gives a more vivid description of the cyclic spectrum characteristics of mixed signals.

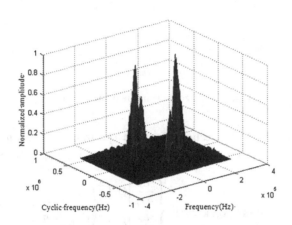

Fig. 1. Cyclic spectrum of mixed signals

In addition, it can be seen from formula (4) and Fig. 1 that the cyclic spectrum of mixed signals has symmetry. In the following paper, for the convenience of calculation and discussion, it only targets at ($\alpha \geq 0, f \geq 0$) region.

In the zero cyclic frequency ($\alpha = 0$) section of the cyclic spectrum, taking into account the common spectral characteristics of these two signals, that is

$$
S_{\mathrm{BPSK + QPSK}}^{\alpha}(f) =
\begin{cases}
\dfrac{E_b}{4T_b}|Q_b(f - f_{cb})|^2, \alpha = 0\\[3mm]
\dfrac{E_q}{4T_q}|Q_q(f - f_{cq})|^2, \alpha = 0
\end{cases}
\tag{5}
$$

As can be seen from the above equation, when $f = f_{cb}$ or $f = f_{cq}$, the above formula obtains the maximum value. Therefore, the peak values are searched at the zero cyclic frequency ($\alpha = 0$) section of the cyclic spectrum, and the frequencies corresponding to the peaks are the carrier frequency estimation values of the two signals, as shown in the Fig. 2.

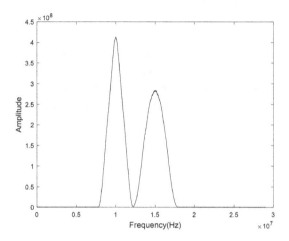

Fig. 2. The zero cyclic frequency section

In the $f = f_{cb}$ or $f = f_{cq}$ section of cyclic spectrum, considering the common spectral characteristics of both signals, formula (4) can be simplified as

$$S_{\text{BPSK}+\text{QPSK}}^{\alpha}(f) = \begin{cases} \dfrac{E_b}{4T_b} \left| Q_b \left(\dfrac{\alpha}{2} \right) \right|^2, \alpha = \dfrac{n}{T_b} \\ \dfrac{E_q}{4T_q} \left| Q_q \left(\dfrac{\alpha}{2} \right) \right|^2, \alpha = \dfrac{n}{T_q} \end{cases} \tag{6}$$

It can be seen from the above formula that, except $\alpha = 0$, the spectral section obtains the maximum value at $\alpha = \frac{1}{T_b}$ and $\alpha = \frac{1}{T_b}$. Therefore, the maximum value is searched in the $f = f_{cb}$ or $f = f_{cq}$ section of cyclic spectrum, and the frequency corresponding to the maximum value is the symbol rate estimation value, as shown in Figs. 3 and 4.

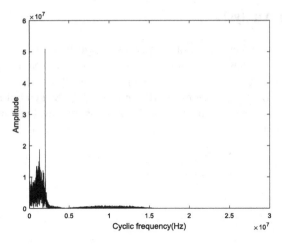

Fig. 3. The $f = f_{cb}$ section of cyclic spectrum

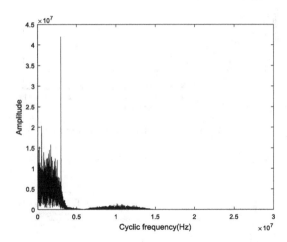

Fig. 4. The $f = f_{cq}$ section of cyclic spectrum

3   Description of Algorithm

According to the above analysis, the parameter estimation steps of the mixed signal are as follows:

(1) Calculate cyclic spectrum of the received signal;
(2) Search for peaks in the zero cyclic frequency section of cyclic spectrum, and frequencies corresponding to peak are the carrier frequency $\widehat{f}_{cb}$ and $\widehat{f}_{cb}$;
(3) Search for the maximum value in the $f = \widehat{f}_{cb}$ and $f = \widehat{f}_{cb}$ section of cyclic spectrum respectively, and the frequencies corresponding to the maximum values are symbol rate $\widehat{R}_{bb}$ and $\widehat{R}_{bq}$.

4 Simulation Analysis

In order to verify the effectiveness of the proposed algorithm, this paper evaluates the performance of the proposed algorithm by using MATLAB. Signal parameters are: sampling frequency is 60 MHz, carrier frequency of BPSK signal is 10 MHz, symbol rate is 2 Mbit/s, carrier frequency of QPSK signal is15 MHz, symbol rate is 3 Mbit/s. The normalized root mean square error is used as the evaluation standard. The parameter estimation results of the mixed signal are as follows (Figs. 5 and 6).

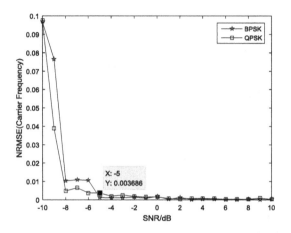

Fig. 5. Estimation results of carrier frequency

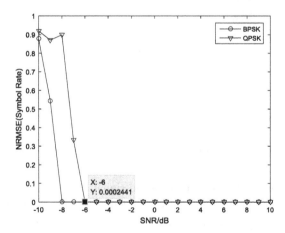

Fig. 6. Estimation results of symbol rate

From the above simulation results, it can be seen that in the whole range of SNR, the carrier frequency estimation is better than 1% when the SNR is larger than −5 dB, and the symbol rate estimation is better than 0.1% when the SNR is larger than −6 dB, indicating that the algorithm has better estimation performance under low SNR. In addition, the symbol rate estimation performance is better than the carrier frequency estimation. The reason is mainly that the symbol rate is estimated in the cyclic frequency domain, and this area is not sensitive to noise.

5 Conclusion

In this paper, a parameter estimation algorithm for mixed satellite signals based on cyclic spectrum is proposed, and the effective parameter estimation of mixed signals is realized by using the linear superposition of cyclic spectrum and the potential correspondence between the spectral lines in different cyclic spectrum sections and signal parameters. The simulation results prove the validity of the method. At the same time, the method in this paper can be extended to multiple signal mixtures, with a wide range of applications.

References

1. Yan, X., Feng, G., Wu, H.C., Xiang, W., Wang, Q.: Innovative robust modulation classification using graph-based cyclic-spectrum analysis. IEEE Commun. Lett. **21**(1), 16–19 (2017)
2. Yang, W.C., Yang, X.Q., Kuang, Y.: Research on parameter estimation of MPSK signals based on the generalized second-order cyclic spectrum. In: 2014 URSI General Assembly and Scientific Symposium (URSI GASS), Beijing, China, pp. 1–4 (2014)
3. Dong, J., Wei, X., Zhang, Q., Zhao, L.: Speech enhancement algorithm based on higher-order cumulants parameter estimation. Int. J. Innov. Comput. Inf. Control **5**(9), 2725–2733 (2009)
4. Kouame, D., Girault, J.M.: Improvement of cumulant-based parameter estimation. In: 2001 IEEE International Conference on Acoustics, Speech, and Signal Processing, Salt Lake City, UT, USA, pp. 3989–3992 (2001)
5. Zhang, W., Li, K., Jiang, W.: Parameter estimation of periodic frequency modulated signal based on cyclic spectrum density and its application on micro-Doppler signatures extraction. In: 2014 International Conference on Information and Communications Technologies, Nanjing, China, pp. 1–7 (2014)
6. Vučić, D., Vukotić, S., Erić, M.: Cyclic spectral analysis of OFDM/OQAM signals. Int. J. Electron. Commun. **73**(3), 139–143 (2017)
7. Peng, J., Han, Z., Sun, J.: A fast cyclic spectrum detection algorithm for MWC based on Lorentzian Norm. In: Sun, G., Liu, S. (eds.) ADHIP 2017. LNICST, vol. 219, pp. 177–188. Springer, Cham (2018). https://doi.org/10.1007/978-3-319-73317-3_22
8. Narieda, S.: Low complexity cyclic auto-correlation function computation for spectrum sensing. IEICE Commun. Express **6**(6), 387–392 (2017)
9. Cohen, D., Pollak, L., Eldar, Y.C.: Carrier frequency and bandwidth estimation of cyclostationary multiband signals. In: 2016 IEEE International Conference on Acoustics, Speech and Signal Processing, Shanghai, China, pp. 3716–3720 (2016)

Repairable Fountain Codes with Unequal Locality for Heterogeneous D2D Data Storage Networks

Yue Li[1], Shushi Gu[1,2(✉)], Ye Wang[1,3], Wei Xiang[2], and Qinyu Zhang[1,3]

[1] Communication Engineering Research Center, Harbin Institute of Technology,
Shenzhen 518055, Guangdong, China
liyue@stu.hit.edu.cn, {gushushi,wangye83,zqy}@hit.edu.cn
[2] Electronic Systems and Internet of Things Engineering, James Cook University,
Cairns, QLD 4878, Australia
wei.xiang@jcu.edu.au
[3] Pengcheng Laboratory, Shenzhen 518055, Guangdong, China

Abstract. In this paper, we consider a problem about a novel distributed erasure code, named repairable fountain code (RFC), used in heterogeneous networks (HetNets) including different micro base station (MBS) coverage areas, for data storage and delivery among the devices connected by D2D links. The system model of three-tier MBS distributed data storage network is presented and the basic principle is also detailed illustrated. Then, the downloading and repairing communication costs of RFC are analyzed based on its rateless, systematic and lower locality properties. Particularly, the unequal repair locality of RFC (URL-RFC) is designed and discussed for the adaption to the different mobilities with the Poisson process of the nodes in three MBS coverages, and to further reduce the energy cost. The simulation results show that, the URL-RFC scheme we proposed can obtain the lowest cost performance in the case of instantaneous repair, and the cost of URL-RFC is larger than that of RFC when the repair interval is also larger, but it will finally approach to the RFC communication cost curve.

Keywords: HetNets · D2D link · Data storage ·
Repairable fountain codes · Locality · Communication cost

1 Introduction

It is predicted that the amount of mobile data will reach 49 exabytes per month in 2021, compared to 32 exabytes per month in 2018. The rapid growth of mobile data has brought tremendous pressure on the storage systems and cellular communication networks. While heterogeneity is a significant feature as we known in the next wireless communication networks (5G) with huge data traffic. Considering the limited connections within small cells and the imbalanced capabilities

M. Jia et al. (Eds.): WiSATS 2019, LNICST 280, pp. 514–528, 2019.
https://doi.org/10.1007/978-3-030-19153-5_53

among different coverages, we can see that for a heterogeneous network (Het-Net) consisting of multi-tier base station (BS) or micro base station (MBS) [1]. While the device-to-device (D2D) communication technique [2,3] is to be widely spread used for lower energy transmission among various classes of low-power nodes (e.g. mobile phone, notebook and tablet). Recently, distributed storage system (DSS) can be established by D2D links in a coverage of BS, to save the power expenditure for large and popular content downloading and sharing continually among different users [4]. Because D2D nodes can replace the MBS and BS for data storage and distribution, this issue is widely studied in some low-energy communication scenes [5].

One serious problem in this topic is the mobility of the users in wireless HetNets, which will make the data stored in various nodes lost, and reduce the availability of DSS composed by unstable D2D links. So the lost data has to be repaired and reconstructed in new coming nodes. Then many literatures focus on some classical redundant error corrections (e.g. replication, MDS codes, regenerating codes [6,7]) used in one BS coverage for wireless content delivery. The instantaneous repair and interval repair are both employed for bring down the downloading and repairing costs [8]. But the essential conditions about sufficient number of helper nodes and bigger storage occupation make the performance gain not outstanding. On the other hand, the influence mechanisms and relationships of the heterogeneity (i.e. power, distances, number of nodes) of the MBSs and devices is difficult to discuss over HetNets. Therefore, some new coding schemes should be attempted to enhance the feasibility and efficiency in D2D HetNets for data restore and delivery.

The Repairable fountain code (RFC) is a new family of fountain codes that can be applied to DSS. RFC has the rateless property, and each encoded symbol is generated independently, so that the encoded symbol can be dynamically added or deleted without recreating the entire encoded process. Because the input symbols are reproduced as systematic symbols in encoding, when there is a requirement to download one data block of the source file, the data block can be directly acquired without decoding. In addition, D2D HetNet systems require frequently data repair under different MBS energy supplies, the RFC can be repaired at a lower bandwidth than MDS code due to its lower repair locality of $O(logk)$ [9]. Therefore, for D2D HetNets, the RFC has some application potential for unequal data reconstruction. Previously, the studies on the unequal error protection of Fountain codes in broadcast transmission have been extensive [10, 11], and the local repairable codes have also been initially studied in terms of unequal failure protection [12].

The contributions of this paper includes two aspects: Firstly, we propose a novel unequal repair locality based on RFC, termed URL-RFC, which trades off heterogeneity of MBS and devices in D2D storage networks. The URL-RFC uses different RFC coding schemes over different MBS coverage areas, and provides different repair localities by allocating unequal input symbols and encoded symbols, thereby reducing the overall communication costs of the system. Secondly, the system model of 3-tier MBS distributed network is presented and the communication costs analysis and formula derivation of 3-tier HetNet system are carried out, and the communication cost of URL-RFC scheme compared with other coding schemes is also analysed.

The structure of this paper: Sect. 2 gives the system model of 3-tier hetero-geneous D2D distributed storage system. Section 3 introduces the construction of the RFC. In Sect. 4, we analyze and compare the communication costs of the replication scheme, RFC scheme, and URL-RFC storage scheme. The simulation results are given in Sect. 5, which prove that the URL-RFC scheme can reduce the costs of heterogeneous D2D systems in some cases. Section 6 summarizes the main research contents of this paper.

2   System Model

We consider a 3-tier heterogeneous D2D distributed storage system, as shown in Fig. 1. This system consists of a macro base station (BS) that covers the entire system area. In order to reduce the power consumption of the base station, the whole coverage area is divided into M identi-cal sub-areas $Area1, Area2, \cdots, AreaM$, and M micro base stations(MBS) $MBS1, MBS2, \cdots, MBSM$ are used. Two adjacent sub-areas can be covered by one MBS to form a layered network structure. The N mobile devices (nodes) in each area can enter and exit the system randomly, subject to the Poisson process. The entry and exit rates of nodes in different areas can be different, and we assume that the departure rate of each node in area m is μ_m, and the rate at which new nodes enter the system is $N\lambda_m$. Mobile devices in the same area can communicate using D2D links to further reduce communication costs.

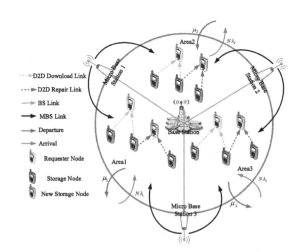

Fig. 1. Three-tier heterogeneous D2D distributed storage system model.

It is noted that only one file exists in the network system and is stored in the MBS and the mobile device, so that all user devices covered by the BS can quickly use the D2D link to cooperate with the MBS for file downloading. If the number of D2D links is insufficient, MBS and BS will be used. At the same time, in order to ensure the availability of the entire network system, it is necessary to perform data repair on the leaving node/new incoming node, which includes D2D link repair and MBS/BS link repair.

The research in this paper is based on the following basic assumptions:

1. Mobile devices in the same area can transmit data through an error-free and delay-free D2D link, which ensures that a theoretically sufficient number of D2D link connections can instantaneously complete file download and data repair.
2. The ρ_{D2Dm}, ρ_{MBS}, and ρ_{BS} represent the energy cost of transmitting 1-bit data between mobile devices in area m, the energy cost of the MBS transmitting 1-bit data, and the energy cost of the BS transmitting 1-bit data, respectively. According to the different pass loss of wireless signals, i.e., lager distance more energy, the average $\rho_{MBS} > \rho_{SBS} > \rho_{D2Dm}$ can be obtained.
3. For simplicity, there is only one file of size F in the BS.
4. Assume $\mu_m = \lambda_m$, that is, the traffic in and out of each area is the same, and the average number of nodes in the area stays constant N. The number of nodes in each area can be described by a $M/M/\infty$ Markov process.
5. The number of encoded symbols n_m for each area satisfies $n_m << N$, hence the probability that the number of nodes in the area is smaller than n_m is negligibly small [13]. Therefore, the file can always be stored in the network.

Data Storage: The file is divided into 3 parts. For any area m, two adjacent MBSs store $fracF3$ files. The remaining $fracF3$ files are stored in the mobile devices(blue mobile phone) called storage nodes through the redundancy strategy of distributed storage. We consider a uniform allocation in our system model. Hence each storage node in area m stores α_m bit data.

Data Repair: When the storage node in the area leaves the area, the data stored in the node will also be lost. In order to ensure that when a user requests to download a file, the file can be obtained by consuming less energy, the lost data needs to be repaired in time and stored on a new node (red mobile phone). If the storage node is repaired immediately when it is lost, it will increase the burden of base station supervision, and this is difficult to implement in practical applications [14]. Therefore, this paper studies a system with a certain repair interval. At the time of repair, if there are enough storage nodes in the area, the data can be repaired through the D2D link, and the repair bandwidth is R, that is, the minimum number of connectable storage nodes required for D2D repair is $\gamma_{D2D} = d\alpha$. Otherwise, it can only be repaired by the BS and the repair bandwidth is $\gamma_{BS} = \alpha$. It should be noted that when $\rho_{D2D}\gamma_{D2D} < \rho_{BS}\gamma_{BS}$, i.e. $d < \frac{\rho_{BS}}{\rho_{D2D}}$, D2D repair is advantageous compared to using BS for repair.

File Download: Assume that the rate of each node requesting a file is ω. When the node in the area requests to download the file, if the number of storage nodes in the area is sufficient, the D2D link can be jointly downloaded with two adjacent MBSs, where the D2D link can provide the data of the $h\alpha$, that is, the number of storage nodes needed to be connected is not less than h, and the two MBSs provide $fracF3$ data, respectively. Otherwise, the download should be jointly performed by the two adjacent MBSs and BS, in which $fracF3$ data is downloaded from each MBS, and the remaining $fracF3$ is downloaded from BS. It should be noted that when $\rho_{D2D}h\alpha < \rho_{BS}\frac{F}{3}$, i.e., $frac3h\alpha F < \frac{\rho_{BS}}{\rho_{D2D}}$, the joint download using D2D and MBSs is superior to the joint download using BS and MBSs.

3   RFC and URL-RFC

3.1   Construction of RFC

Repairable fountain code (RFC) inherits the rateless property of classical fountain codes, so we do not need to pre-determine the number of coded symbols. Unlike classical fountain codes, the RFC is a systematic code and its parity symbols also have logarithmic sparseness [15].

The RFC divides the source file into k packets when encoding, i.e. k input symbols. The input symbols are encoded by the generator matrix of $k \times n$, resulting in n encoded symbols containing a copy of k input symbols and $n - k$ parity symbols. Let the vector v represents the encoded symbol, and the vector u represents the input symbol. The construction method of the RFC can be represented by Fig. 2, each parity symbol is generated by a linear combination of $d(k) = clogk$ input symbols selected uniformly at random. The coefficient ω of the linear combination is selected from the finite field F_q, and c is a constant. Therefore, the generator matrix can be represented as $\mathbf{G} = [\mathbf{I_k}|\mathbf{P}]$, as shown in Fig. 3. The identity part of $\mathbf{G}$ corresponds to the systematic symbols, and the matrix $\mathbf{P}$ corresponds to the parity symbols. Any encoded symbol can be expressed as

$$v_j = u\mathbf{G}(j) = \sum \omega_{ij}u_i, \tag{1}$$

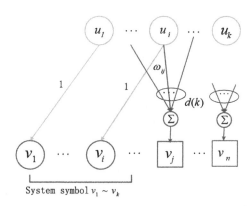

System symbol $v_1 \sim v_k$

Fig. 2. RFC encoding process.

$$\mathbf{G[I_k \mid P]} = \begin{bmatrix} 1 & \cdots & \cdots & 0 & \omega_{1,k+1} & \cdots & \omega_{1,n} \\ \vdots & \ddots & & \vdots & \vdots & & \vdots \\ \vdots & & \ddots & \vdots & \vdots & & \vdots \\ 0 & \cdots & \cdots & 1 & \omega_{k,k+1} & \cdots & \omega_{k,n} \end{bmatrix}$$

k input symbol columns   n-k parity symbol columns

Fig. 3. RFC encoding process.

where $\mathbf{G}(j)$ represents the jth column of the generator matrix $v_j = u\mathbf{G}(j) = \sum \omega_{ij} u_i$.

The encoding process can be expressed as a formula

$$v = u\mathbf{G[I_k \mid P]}. \tag{2}$$

A parity symbol along with the systematic symbols covered by it form a local group. Any symbol in the local group can be reconstructed by the linear combination of other symbols in the local group, and the local group size is $d(k) + 1$. The RFC trades its low locality with its MDS property, but it still possesses near-MDS property. When downloading the entire file, a very small decoding overhead $\varepsilon > 0$ is required, so that any subset of $k' = (1 + \varepsilon)k$ symbols can reconstruction the file. The maximum likelihood decoding method can be used for decoding, which is equivalent to solving the solutions of k' linear equations.

We refer to the set of a parity symbols along with the systematic symbols covered by it as a local group. When repairing a lost encoded symbol, connecting the other encoded symbols in the local group can reconstruct the lost encoded symbols by Eq. (1). The new generator matrix $\mathbf{G_S}$ is composed of the columns of the symbols in the available helper storage nodes, which is a submatrix of G. When decoding, if $\mathbf{G_S}$ is a full rank matrix, the input symbols can be decoded by $u = v\mathbf{G_S}^{-1}$.

It can be seen from the encoding process of the RFC that the local group size is $d(k) + 1$. The RFC exchanges its MDS property for lower locality, but still has the property of near-MDS. When downloading the entire file, a small decoding overhead $\varepsilon > 0$ is required, so that any $k' = (1 + \varepsilon)k$ encoded symbols can reconstruct the source file.

3.2 Unequal Repairing Locality Based on RFC

We consider that the departure rate and the energy cost of transmitting 1-bit data of mobile devices in different areas are different. In order to further reduce the overall communication cost of the HetNet system, we design a repairable fountain code with unequal parameters in different areas based on the RFC, to adapt to the changes in different areas. Therefore, our coding scheme is called Unequal Repair Locality based on RFC (URL-RFC).

Considering the limited space, the coding process is illustrated just in 2-tier HetNet models. Assume that the number of input symbols in the two regions is k_1 and k_2, respectively, u_1 to u_2 represent the input symbols of $Area1$, and the input symbols of $Arae2$ are from u_1' to u_2'. The two sets of input symbols are separately encoded and stored in the nodes of $Area1$ and $Area2$, respectively. As shown in Fig. 4, the encoded symbols of the $Area1$ includes the copy of u_1 to u_2 and a set of parity symbols of degree $d(k_1)$ generated by u_1 to u_2, and the number of encoded symbols is n_1. The encoded symbols of the $Area2$ contains the copy of u_1' to u_2' and a set of parity symbols of degree $d(k_2)$ generated by u_1' to u_2', and the number of encoded symbols is n_2.

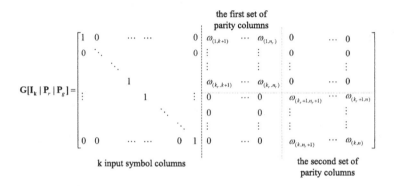

Fig. 4. URL-RFC encoding process.

4   Communication Costs Analysis

In this section we derive the analytical expressions for repair cost $(E(C_r))$, download cost $(E(C_d))$, total communication cost $(E(C))$. The cost is defined in cost units per bit and time unit.

Repair Cost: Within the repair interval Δ, the entire system has i storage nodes leaving, and $0 \leq i \leq Mn$. The probability that any area m leaves i_m storage node obeys the binomial distribution with the parameter (n_m, p_m), and its probability mass function is

$$b_{i_m}(n_m, p_m) = \binom{n_m}{i_m}(1 - p_m)^{i_m} p_m^{n-i_m}, 0 \leq i_m \leq n_m, \tag{3}$$

where, $p_m = e^{-\mu_m \Delta}$, $\sum_{m=1}^{M} i_m = i$.

For any area m, when $0 \leq i_m \leq n_m - d_m$, that is, the number of remaining storage nodes is $l_m \geq d_m$, it can be repaired through the D2D link. Therefore, the probability of repairing through the D2D link is $\sum_{i_m=0}^{n_m-d_m} b_{i_m}(n_m, p_m)$, and the repair cost is $C_{r_m} = i_m \rho_{D2Dm} \gamma_{D2D}$. When $n_m - d_m < i_m \leq n_m$, that is, the number of remaining storage nodes is $l_m < d_m$, it can only be repaired by the BS. The probability of repairing through the BS is $\sum_{i_m = n_m - d_m + 1}^{n_m} b_{i_m}(n_m, p_m)$, and the repair cost is $C_{r_m} = i_m \rho_{BS} \gamma_{BS}$. Therefore, the average repair cost of the area m is

$$
\begin{aligned}
E(C_{r_m}) = \frac{1}{F\Delta} [\rho_{D2Dm} \gamma_{mD2D} \sum_{i_m=0}^{n_m - d_m} i_m b_{i_m}(n_m, p_m) \\
+ \rho_{BS} \gamma_{mBS} \sum_{i_m = n_m - d_m + 1}^{n_m} i_m b_{i_m}(n_m, p_m)]
\end{aligned}
\tag{4}
$$

The total average repair cost of the system is the sum of the repair cost of each area,

$$
E(C_r) = \sum_{m=1}^{M} E(C_{r_m}).
\tag{5}
$$

Download Cost: When there is a node requesting to download the file in any area m, it is also assumed that the number of storage nodes leaving the system is i, and the number of storage nodes leaving in the area m is i_m. When $0 \leq i_m \leq n_m - h_m$, that is, $l_m \geq h_m$, it can be jointly downloaded by D2D and MBSs. The download cost is $C_{d_m} = N\omega(\rho_{D2Dm} h_m \alpha_m + \rho_{MBS} \frac{2F}{3})$, and the probability is

$$
\Pr\{DM\_d\}_m = \frac{1}{\Delta} \sum_{i_m=0}^{n_m - h_m} \frac{1 - p_{m(n-i)}}{u_{m(n-i)}} \prod_{j=0, j \neq i_m}^{n_m - h_m} \frac{n - j}{i_m - j},
\tag{6}
$$

where, $\mu_{m(i)} = i\mu_m$, $p_{m(i)} = e^{-\mu_{m(i)}\Delta}$ [14]. When $n_m - h_m + 1 \leq i_m \leq n_m$, that is, $l_m < h_m$, it can only be downloaded jointly by BS and MBSs. The download cost is $C_{d_m} = N\omega(\rho_{BS} \frac{F}{3} + \rho_{MBS} \frac{2F}{3})$, and the probability is

$$
\Pr\{BM\_d\}_m = 1 - \Pr\{DM\_d\}_m.
\tag{7}
$$

So, the average download cost of the area m is

$$
\begin{aligned}
E(C_{d_m}) &= \frac{N\omega}{F} [(\rho_{MBS} \frac{2F}{3} + \rho_{D2Dm} h_m \alpha_m) \Pr\{DM\_d\}_m \\
&\quad + (\rho_{BS} \frac{F}{3} + \rho_{MBS} \frac{2F}{3}) \Pr\{BM\_d\}_m] \\
&= N\omega[(\frac{h_m \alpha_m}{F} \rho_{D2Dm} - \frac{1}{3}\rho_{BS}) \Pr\{DM\_d\}_m + \frac{2}{3}\rho_{MBS} + \frac{1}{3}\rho_{BS}]
\end{aligned}
\tag{8}
$$

The total average download cost of the system is the sum of the download cost of each area,

$$
E(C_d) = \sum_{m=1}^{M} C_{d_m}.
\tag{9}
$$

The total communication cost of the system is defined as the sum of the average repair cost and the download cost of each area in the system,

$$
E(C) = E(C_r) + E(C_d).
\tag{10}
$$

When the redundancy strategy uses the RFC scheme, the $\frac{F}{3}$ file of each area is decomposed into k data packets (called input symbols). Then use the same RFC with parameter of (n, k, d) to encode the input symbols. Considering uniform allocation, each storage node stores α_{mRFC}-bit data,

$$\alpha_{mRFC} = \frac{F}{3k}. \tag{11}$$

When repairing a node, the number of storage nodes that need to be connected is $d_m RFC = d = c \log(k)$. When downloading the entire file, you need to connect $h_{mRFC} = (1 + \varepsilon)k$ storage nodes, so the amount of information that needs to be transferred when downloading is slightly larger than the file size F.

When the redundancy strategy uses the URL-RFC scheme, the $\frac{F}{3}$ file of each area is decomposed into k_m data packets, which are respectively encoded using the RFC with the parameter (n_m, k_m, d_m). Considering uniform allocation, each storage node stores $\alpha_{mURL-RFC}$-bit data,

$$\alpha_{mURL-RFC} = \frac{F}{3k_m}. \tag{12}$$

When repairing a node, the number of storage nodes that need to be connected is $d_m URL - RFC = d_m = c \log(k_m)$. When downloading the entire file, you need to connect $h_{mURL-RFC} = (1 + \varepsilon)k_m$ storage nodes, so the amount of information that needs to be transferred when downloading is also slightly larger than the file size F.

When the redundancy strategy uses the MDS scheme, the $\frac{F}{3}$ file of each area is decomposed into k data packets. Then use the same MDS with parameter of (n, k) to encode the input symbols. Considering uniform allocation, each storage node stores α_{mMDS}-bit data,

$$\alpha_{mMDS} = \frac{F}{3k}. \tag{13}$$

When repairing a node, the number of storage nodes that need to be connected is $d_m MDS = k$. When downloading the entire file, you need to connect $h_{mMDS} = k$ storage nodes, so the amount of information that needs to be transferred when downloading is equal to the file size F.

When the redundancy strategy uses the n-fold replication scheme, n copies of the $\frac{F}{3}$ file for each area are backed up. Each storage node stores α_{mCopy}-bit data,

$$\alpha_{mCopy} = \frac{F}{3}. \tag{14}$$

When you repair a node, you only need to connect to one storage node,i.e. $d_{mCopy} = 1$.When downloading the entire file, you need to connect $h_{mCopy} = 1$ storage nodes, so the amount of information that needs to be transferred when downloading is equal to the file size F.

5   Simulation and Results

For the purpose of clearer simulation results, and without loss of generality, we set the public parameters $F = 1$, $M = 3$, $N = 50$, and the repair interval Δ takes 0 to 6.

First, in the case of $\omega = 0.02$, the three areas are respectively encoded using the RFC with the parameter (n, k, d) of $(30, 20, 9)$, the MDS code with the parameter (n, k) of $(30, 20)$, and the 3-copy scheme, we observe the change of the simulation curve when $\mu_1 = \mu_2 = \mu_3$ is 1, 3 respectively, as shown in Fig. 5.

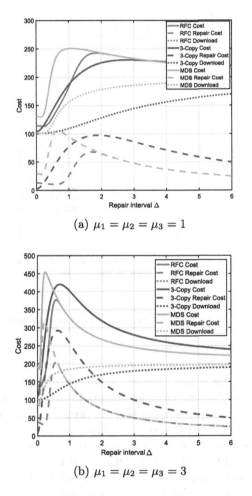

(a) $\mu_1 = \mu_2 = \mu_3 = 1$

(b) $\mu_1 = \mu_2 = \mu_3 = 3$

Fig. 5. Comparison of communication cost when changing nodes departure rate.

In Fig. 5(a) and (b), $\Delta \to 0$ means instantaneous repair, and $\Delta \to \infty$ means no more repair. As the repair interval Δ increases, the total cost increases first

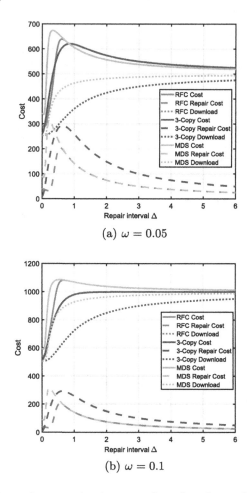

(a) $\omega = 0.05$

(b) $\omega = 0.1$

Fig. 6. Comparison of communication cost when changing nodes download rate.

and then decreases, because our cost calculation formula normalize the repair interval. Initially, as the repair interval increases, the number of nodes to be repaired increases each time, so communication cost increases. As the repair interval increases, more and more nodes are lost, but the total average cost is relatively smaller. The RFC has a small locality, and the bandwidth cost of repairing a node is also small, so it has a small repair cost in most repair intervals. Comparing Fig. 5(a) and (b), it can be found that the node leaving rate increases, the number of nodes to be repaired increases in a certain time interval, and the communication cost also increases.

In the case of $\mu_1 = \mu_2 = \mu_3 = 3$, the same coding scheme as in Fig. 5 is used, and the value of ω is changed. Observe the change of the simulation curve when ω is 0.05 and 0.1 respectively, as shown in Fig. 6(a) and (b). When the increase occurs, the download overhead increases, and the overall communication cost

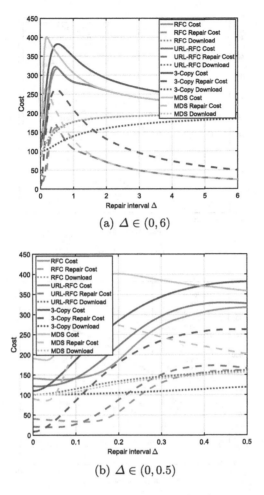

(a) $\Delta \in (0, 6)$

(b) $\Delta \in (0, 0.5)$

Fig. 7. Comparison of communication cost when nodes departure rates are different, $\mu_1 = 1, \mu_2 = 3, \mu_3 = 5$.

also increases. The repair cost relative to the download cost has less impact on the overall system, resulting in a smaller communication cost of the RFC relative 3-copy scheme, but still superior to the MDS code.

The departure rate of node in the above simulation and the energy cost of transmitting 1-bit of mobile devices in each area are the same, but they should be different in different areas in practical applications. In Fig. 7(a) and (b), different departure rates are set for nodes in the three areas, $\mu_1 = 1, \mu_2 = 3, \mu_3 = 5$. In Fig. 8(a) and (b), the energy transfer energy cost between different nodes is set for three areas, $\rho_{D2D1} = 1, \rho_{D2D2} = 3, \rho_{D2D3} = 5$. The URL-RFC communication cost curve is added to the simulation and compared with the RFC scheme.

In Figs. 7 and 8, when the instantaneous repair is performed, the communication cost of the URL-RFC is lower than that of the other schemes except for

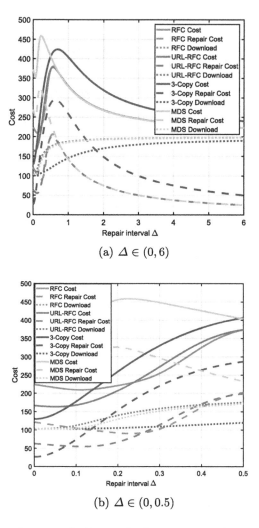

Fig. 8. Comparison of communication cost when energy costs are different, $\rho_{D2D1} = 1, \rho_{D2D2} = 3, \rho_{D2D3} = 5$.

the 3-copy scheme. However, as the repair interval increases, the cost of RFC and URL-RFC is smaller than that of the 3-copy scheme and the MDS scheme. Therefore, in the case of heterogeneous mobile devices of the system, the communication cost is optimal using the URL-RFC and RFC schemes, and the use of URL-RFC communication cost is minimal when the repair interval is small.

6   Conclusions

In this paper, we introduce a new type of distributed storage redundancy strategy called repairable fountain code (RFC). The RFC can be used for heterogeneous networks (HeNets) consisting of D2D links for data storage and delivery between devices within the coverage of different micro base stations (MBS). After giving the 3-tier heterogeneous D2D system model, we analyzed the download and repair communication costs of the RFC scheme, the MDS code scheme and the 3-copy scheme. Furthermore, a RFC scheme with unequal repair locality(URL-RFC) is designed and analyzed to reduce the communication cost of the system for the heterogeneity between multiple areas of the system. The simulation results show that the URL-RFC scheme can obtain the lowest communication cost in the case of instantaneous repair, and when the repair interval is larger, the communication cost is greater than the RFC, but it will finally approach to the RFC communication cost curve.

Acknowledgments. This work is supported by the National Natural Sciences Foundation of China under Grant 61701136, Grant 61831008, and Grant 61525103, China Postdoctoral Science Foundation Grant 2018M630357, Guangdong Science and Technology Planning Project 2018B030322004 and Shenzhen Basic Research Program under Grant JCYJ20170811154233370 and Grant ZDSYS201707280903305.

References

1. Zhao, X., Yuan, P., Chen, Y., Chen, P.: Cooperative D2D for content delivery in heterogeneous networks. In: International Conference on Big Data Computing and Communications, pp. 265–271 (2017)
2. Wang, L., Wu, H., Han, Z.: Wireless distributed storage in socially enabled D2D communications. IEEE Access **4**, 1971–1984 (2017)
3. Paakkonen, J., Hollanti, C., Tirkkonen, O.: Device-to-device data storage for mobile cellular systems. In: GLOBECOM Workshops, pp. 671–676 (2013)
4. Golrezaei, N., Dimakis, A.G., Molisch, A.F.: Wireless device-to-device communications with distributed caching. In: IEEE International Symposium on Information Theory Proceedings, pp. 2781–2785 (2012)
5. Golrezaei, N., Molisch, A.F., Dimakis, A.G., Caire, G.: Femtocaching and device-to-device collaboration: a new architecture for wireless video distribution. IEEE Commun. Mag. **51**(4), 142–149 (2013)
6. Pääkkönen, J., Hollanti, C., Tirkkonen, O.: Device-to-device data storage with regenerating codes. In: International Workshop on Multiple Access Communications, pp. 57–69 (2015)
7. Silberstein, M., Ganesh, L., Wang, Y., Alvisi, L., Dahlin, M.: Lazy means smart: reducing repair bandwidth costs in erasure-coded distributed storage. In: Proceedings of International Conference on Systems and Storage (SYSTOR), Haifa, Israel, pp. 1–7 (2014)
8. Pedersen, J., i Amat, A.G., Andriyanova, I., Brannstrom, F.: Repair scheduling in wireless distributed storage with D2D communication. In: Information Theory Workshop - Fall, pp. 69–73 (2015)

9. Asteris, M., Dimakis, A.G.: Repairable fountain codes. IEEE J. Sel. Areas Commun. **32**(5), 1037–1047 (2014)
10. Luo, Z., Song, L., Zheng, S., Ling, N.: Raptor codes based unequal protection for compressed video according to packet priority. IEEE Trans. Multimedia **15**(8), 2208–2213 (2013)
11. Sejdinovic, D., Vukobratovic, D., Doufexi, A., Ååenk, V., Piechocki, R.J.: Expanding window fountain codes for unequal error protection. IEEE Trans. Commun. **57**(9), 2510–2516 (2009)
12. Hu, Y., et al.: Unequal failure protection coding technique for distributed cloud storage systems. IEEE Trans. Cloud Comput. (2017), Early access. https://doi.org/10.1109/TCC.2017.2785396
13. Miller, S., Childers, D.: Probability and Random Processes, 2nd edn (2012)
14. Pedersen, J., Amat, A.G.I., Andriyanova, I., Brännström, F.: Distributed storage in mobile wireless networks with device-to-device communication. IEEE Trans. Commun. **64**(11), 4862–4878 (2016)
15. Shokrollahi, A.: Raptor codes. IEEE Trans. Inf. Theory **52**(6), 2551–2567 (2006)

Long-Term Object Tracking Method Based on Dimensionality Reduction

Dongfang Zhao, Wenjing Kang$^{(\boxtimes)}$, and Gongliang Liu

School of Information Science and Engineering,
Harbin Institute of Technology, Weihai, China
catmouseand@foxmail.com, {kwjqq,liugl}@hit.edu.cn

Abstract. Long-term object tracking is challenging as target objects often undergo drastic appearance changes over time. Recently, the FDSST algorithm has performed very well which reduces number of the FFT by dimensionality reduction and operates at real-time. But in case of long-term tracking the performance of FDSST degrades, and the existing long-term tracking methods cannot guarantee the accuracy and real-time performance simultaneously. To solve the above problems, we input a set of sample patches of the target appearance to a multi-channel correlation filter to locate the position of the target in a new frame. At the same time, the number of FFTs is reduced by dimensionality reduction, and an online SVM is trained as the detector to ensure the accuracy of target tracking. Finally, we get a method to track long-term object accurately and in real time. To evaluate the method, we did extensive experiments on a benchmark with 100 sequences. The results show that the proposed method performs well both in accuracy and real-time performance and outperforms than the state-of-the-art methods.

Keywords: Long-term tracking · Dimensionality-reduction · Online SVM · Ream-time tracking

1 Introduction

Robust tracking is a fundamental problem in computer vision, with many applications in areas such as robotics, surveillance and human- machine interfaces [1]. Meanwhile, object tracking is challenging due to the large appearance variation caused by deformation, illumination change, heavy occlusion, sudden motion, and target disappearance. Most of the existing tracking algorithms usually could solve one of the problems, they will fail when other problems arise in the same time. Danelljan et al. proposed the FDSST algorithm in 2017 aimed to improve the accuracy and the robustness of the tracker [2]. This novel scale adaptive tracking approach learns separate discriminative correlation and has an outstanding performance when illumination change or the sudden motion occurs. But the FDSST will usually fail even when the object is under slight occlusion.

In the process of long-term object tracking, occlusion often occurs. Therefore, the performance of FDSST is not ideal for long-term tracking. But FDSST is very fast, usually up to 80FPS during the experiment in my computer. In long-term tracking,

M. Jia et al. (Eds.): WiSATS 2019, LNICST 280, pp. 529–536, 2019.
https://doi.org/10.1007/978-3-030-19153-5_54

people generally solve the problem of target tracking failure by adding a detector. In [3], Ma et al. activated an online trained detector to recover the target object. This online detector can effectively solve the problem of target tracking failure caused by occlusion.

In order to solve the problem of low speed in long-term object tracking, we refer to the methods of dimensionality reduction and the online detector, then apply those methods in the long-term object tracking. The experiments show that our method could solve the problem of occlusion very well, and the method can achieve real time results while maintaining accuracy.

2 Related Work

Object tracking is always the most active research topic in computer vision. In this section, we discuss the most closely related approaches. In recent years, the correlation filter has been widely used, because the operator is readily transferred into the Fourier domain, then the algorithm using the correlation filter would own the fastest speed. In 2010, Bolme et al. firstly proposed a Minimum Output Sum of Squared Error filter (MOSSE) [4] that is computationally efficient. Many effort has been made to improve tracking performance since then using correlation filters. In 2012, Henriques, et al. proposed an extension include kernelized correlation filter [5]. In 2013, Galoogahi, et al. proposed a novel framework for learning a multi-channel detector/filter efficiently in the frequency domain. This multi-channel filter is better than the single-channel correlation filters [6]. In 2015, Henriques et al. derive a new Kernelized Correlation Filter (KCF), and based on the KCF, Henriques J F proposed a fast multi-channel extension of linear correlation filters, which called Dual Correlation Filter (DCF) [7]. In the same year, Danelljan et al. proposed Spatially Regularized Discriminative Correlation Filters (SRDCF) for tracking. This filter can be learned on a large number of negative training samples without damaging the positive ones [8].

Recently, long-term visual tracking has received attention. Kalal et al. divided the tracking task into tracking, learning and detection (TLD) [9] where tracking and detection facilitates each other, the results from the tracker provide training data to update the detector. And the detector re- initializes the tracker when it fails. In [10] Supancic et al. proposed a simple and effective system that trains online SVM by learning a large number of negative training examples. The good effect of the system proves the practicability of the above theory in long – term target tracking. In [11], Kang et al. proposed a continuous correlation filter to achieve subpixel object locations in continuous domain. The author learn an online random fern classifier to redetect the target in case of tracking failure. Due to its excellent classification strategy, the CCFT tracker can locate the target with high accuracy.

In this paper, in order to speed up the tracking of long-term target, we adopted the method of dimensionality reduction, which reduced the number of FFT needed to be calculated. By feature dimension reduction, we obtained a higher speed, and the tracking precision is also very high.

3   Proposed Algorithm

3.1   Multi-channel Discriminative Correlation Filters

Our tracking approach is based on FDSST. The FDSST based tracking approaches learn an optimal correlation filter for locating the target in a new frame.

At each location n in a rectangular domain, let target sample f consists of a dimensional feature vector $f(n) \in \mathbb{R}^d$. Then denote feature channel $l \in \{1, \ldots d\}$ of f by f^l. This is achieved by minimizing the L^2 error of the correlation response compared to the desired correlation output g,

$$\varepsilon = ||g - \sum_{l=1}^{d} h^l \odot f^l||^2 + \lambda \sum_{l=1}^{d} ||h^l||^2 \tag{1}$$

The symbol $\odot$ denotes circular correlation. The symbol λ is a weight parameter. Note that the domains of f^l, h^l and g all have the same dimension and size.

Transforming (1) to the Fourier domain using Parseval's formula would solve (1) efficiently. The filter that minimizes (1) is given by,

$$H^l = \frac{\overline{G}F^l}{\sum_{k=1}^{d} F^k\overline{F^k} + \lambda}, l = 1, \ldots, d. \tag{2}$$

Here, the capital letters denote the discrete Fourier transform (DFT) of the corresponding quantities. The bar $\overline{G}$ denotes complex conjugation.

To apply the filter in a new frame t, we extracted a sample z_t from a considered region. We will get the DFT of the correlation scores y_t by computed in the Fourier domain

$$Y_t = \frac{\sum_{l=1}^{d} \overline{A_{t-1}^l} Z_t^l}{B_{t-1} + \lambda} \tag{3}$$

Here, we update the numerator and the denominator of the filter by

$$A_t^l = (1 - \eta)A_{t-1}^l + \eta\overline{G}F_t^l, l = 1, \ldots, d \tag{4}$$

$$B_t = (1 - \eta)B_{t-1} + \eta \sum_{k=1}^{d} \overline{F_t^k}F_t^k \tag{5}$$

Finally, finding the maximum correlation score, we get the estimate of the current target.

3.2   Dimensionality Reduction

To reduce the number of FFT, we employ a dimensionality reduction strategy. We obtain P_t by minimizing the reconstruction error of the target template u_t

$$\varepsilon = \sum_n ||u_t(n) - P_t^T P_t u_t(n)||^2 \qquad (6)$$

We update the u_t by $u_t = (1 - \eta)u_{t-1} + \eta f_t$. When the orthonormality constraint $P_t P_t^T = I$, then the Eq. (7) is minimized. Next we got a solution by performing an eigenvalue decomposition of the auto-correlation matrix

$$C_t = \sum_n u_t(n)u_t(n)^T \qquad (7)$$

We set the rows of P_t to the $\overline{d}$ eigenvectors of C_t corresponding to the largest eigenvalues.

The filter is updated using the compressed training sample $\widetilde{F}_t = \mathcal{F}\{P_t f_t\}$ and compressed target template $\widetilde{U}_t = \mathcal{F}\{P_t u_t\}$ as

$$\widetilde{A}_t^l = \overline{G}\widetilde{U}_t^l, l = 1, \ldots, \widetilde{d} \qquad (8)$$

$$\widetilde{B}_t = (1 - \eta)\widetilde{B}_{t-1} + \eta \sum_{k=1}^{\widetilde{d}} \overline{\widetilde{F}_t^k}\widetilde{F}_t^k \qquad (9)$$

Now, we can do less number of FFT to reduce the computational cost.

The correlation scores at the test sample z_t at the test sample z_t are obtained similarly to Eq. (3) by applying the filter on the compressed sample $\widetilde{Z}_t = \mathcal{F}\{P_{t-1}z_t\}$,

$$Y_t = \frac{\sum_{l=1}^{\widetilde{d}} \overline{\widetilde{A}_{t-1}^l}\widetilde{Z}_t^l}{\widetilde{B}_{t-1} + \lambda} \qquad (10)$$

3.3   Online Detector

A robust tracking algorithm requires a detection module to recover the target from potential tracking failures caused by occlusion. For each tracked target z, we use $y_t = ifft\{Y_t\}$ to be the confidence score. When the confidence score is below a pre-defined threshold, then the algorithm start up the online detector and finds the target back. In our approach, we use an online SVM classifier as the detector, and then we train the SVM classifier by drawing dense training samples around the estimated position. Given a training set $\{(v_i, c_i)|i = 1, 2, \ldots, N\}$ with N samples in a frame, the V_i denotes the feature vector generated by the $i - th$ sample and $c_i \in \{+1, -1\}$ is the class label. In the end, we get the objective function,

$$\min_h \frac{\lambda}{2}||h||^2 + \frac{1}{N}\sum_i \ell(h; (v_i, c_i)) \qquad (11)$$

Where $\ell(h; (v, c)) = \max\{0, 1 - c < h, v > \}$. The notation $< h, v >$ indicates the inner product between h and v. And we apply the passive-aggressive algorithm [12] to update the hyper plane parameters efficiently.

$$h \leftarrow h - \frac{\ell(h; (v, c))}{||\nabla_h \ell(h; (v, c))||^2 + \frac{1}{2\tau}} \nabla_h \ell(h; (v, c)) \tag{12}$$

Where $\nabla_h \ell(h; (v, c))$ is the gradient of the loss function in terms of h and $\tau \in (0, +\infty)$ is a hyper-parameter that controls the update rate of h.

Algorithm: Proposed tracking algorithm: iterate at frame t

Input:

    Image It

    Previous target position p_{t-1} and scale s_{t-1}

    Translation model $A_{t-1,trans}$ and $B_{t-1,trans}$

    Scale model $A_{t-1,scale}$ and $B_{t-1,scale}$

For t= 2:T

    Max response=max(response);

    If Max response< threshold

        Activate detection module.

    End

End

    Until End of the video sequence

Output:

    Estimated target position p_t and scale s_t

    Updated translation mode $A_{t,trans}$, $B_{t,trans}$

    Updated scale model $A_{t,scale}$, $B_{t,trans}$

---

4 Experiment

4.1 Experimental Settings

Datasets. We evaluate the proposed algorithm on a large benchmark dataset [13] that contains 100 videos.

Desktop Configuration. We implement our tracker in MATLAB on an ADM Ryzen-5 3.20 GHz CPU with 16 GB RAM, and use the Vlfeat toolbox.

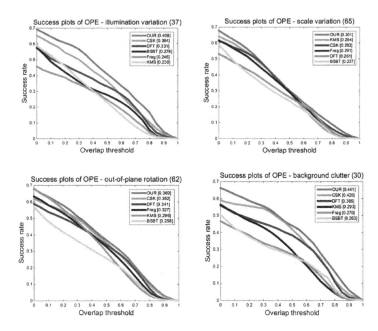

Fig. 1. Overlap success plots over four tracking challenges

Fig. 2. An experiment to track long-term object. The first and second columns prove that our method can effectively recover the target lost due to occlusion and deformation, and the third and fourth columns prove the robustness of our method when tracking the long-term target.

4.2   Comparisons

We compared the proposed algorithm with conventional and state-of-the-art algorithms which are available as source code. They are CSK [14], KMS [15], DFT [16], Frag [17] and BSBT [18]. The parameters for those algorithms are set default.

Figure 1 shows that the tracking results on OTB-100. The results show that our algorithm could track the object accurately. And our algorithm performs better than those Start-of-the-art trackers.

In addition, we tested the robustness of our method in tracking long-term targets. Figure 2 proved that the method we proposed could be a good way to track and reposition the lost object.

In the experiment, our algorithm can reach the speed of 60FPSD. This proves that our method of dimensionality reduction is effective. From Table 1, we could see that our algorithm has a high score than others in DP, OS and CLE. The results show that our algorithm performs better than others.

Table 1. The score of 6 trackers in 6 sequences. (The best results are in italics)

Sequence name		Bird2	Car2	CarDark	Coupon	CarScale	David2
Our tracker	OS (%)	*0.980*	*1.000*	*1.000*	*1.000*	*0.813*	*1.000*
	DP (%)	*0.980*	*1.000*	0.802	*1.000*	*0.516*	0.994
	CLE(%)	9.250	1.370	4.090	2.470	*13.54*	3.26
CSK	OS (%)	0.485	*1.000*	*1.000*	*1.000*	0.651	*1.000*
	DP (%)	0.485	0.797	*0.992*	*1.000*	0.448	*1.000*
	CLE (%)	31.12	10.36	3.23	6.14	83.01	*2.33*
KMS	OS (%)	0.253	0.074	0.275	0.107	0.536	0.337
	DP (%)	0.293	0.074	0.595	0.086	0.298	0.095
	CLE (%)	31.51	121.44	34.12	109.29	39.11	45.53
DFT	OS (%)	0.717	0.278	0.649	1.000	0.647	0.767
	DP (%)	0.707	0.278	0.514	1.000	0.448	0.767
	CLE (%)	27.03	100.64	29.39	5.77	79.95	15.02
BSBT	OS (%)	0.061	0.377	0.700	0.462	0.131	0.156
	DP (%)	0.061	0.377	0.700	0.462	0.131	0.156
	CLE (%)	324.54	129.11	61.69	59.23	220.95	159.44
Frag	OS (%)	0.152	0.380	0.081	0.141	0.631	0.758
	DP (%)	0.141	0.380	0.115	0.141	0.317	0.825
	CLE (%)	66.90	88.10	79.64	72.26	31.07	15.74

5   Conclusion

In this paper, in order to accelerate the speed of the long term object tracking, we use the dimensionality reduction method to reduce the number of FFTs and increase the target tracking speed to 60 FPS. At the same time, we use multi-channel discriminative correlation filters and give this filter a set of sample patches of the target appearance to ensure tracking robustness. In addition, we use an online training SVM to re-track the lost targets. This method successfully solves the problem that the accuracy and speed cannot be maintained simultaneously in long-term object tracking through dimensionally reduction and online SVM detector. Extensive experiment results on a large-scale benchmark demonstrate that our method could track the long-term object at real time and accurately.

References

1. Yilmaz, A., Javed, O., Shah, M.: Object tracking: a survey. ACM Comput. Surv. **38**(4), 13 (2006)
2. Danelljan, M., Häger, G., Khan, F.S., et al.: Discriminative scale space tracking. IEEE Trans. Pattern Anal. Mach. Intell. **39**(8), 1561–1575 (2017)
3. Ma, C., Huang, J.B., Yang, X., et al.: Adaptive correlation filters with long-term and short-term memory for object tracking. Int. J. Comput. Vis. **126**, 771–796 (2018)
4. Bolme, D.S., Beveridge, J.R., Draper, B.A., et al.: Visual object tracking using adaptive correlation filters. In: 2010 IEEE Conference on Computer Vision and Pattern Recognition (CVPR), pp. 2544–2550. IEEE (2010)
5. Henriques, J.F., Caseiro, R., Martins, P., Batista, J.: Exploiting the circulant structure of tracking-by-detection with kernels. In: Proceedings of the European Conference on Computer Vision (2012)
6. Galoogahi, H.K., Sim, T., Lucey, S.: Multi-channel correlation filters. In: Proceedings of IEEE International Conference on Computer Vision (2013)
7. Henriques, J.F., Caseiro, R., Martins, P., et al.: High-speed tracking with kernelized correlation filters. IEEE Trans. Pattern Anal. Mach. Intell. **37**(3), 583–596 (2015)
8. Danelljan, M., Häger, G., Khan, F.S., Felsberg, M.: Learning spatially regularized correlation filters for visual tracking. In: Proceedings of IEEE International Conference on Computer Vision (2015)
9. Kalal, Z., Mikolajczyk, K., Matas, J.: Tracking-learning-detection. IEEE Trans. Pattern Anal. Mach. Intell. **34**(7), 1409 (2012)
10. Supancic, J.S., Ramanan, D.: Self-paced learning for long-term tracking. In: Proceedings of the IEEE Conference on Computer Vision and Pattern Recognition (2013)
11. Kang, W., Li, X., Li, S., Liu, G.: Corrected continuous correlation filter for long-term tracking. IEEE Access **6**, 11959–11969 (2018)
12. Crammer, K., Dekel, O., Keshet, J., Shalev-Shwartz, S., Singer, Y.: Online passive-aggressive algorithms. J. Mach. Learn. Res. **7**, 551–585 (2006)
13. Wu, Y., Lim, J., Yang, M.H.: Object tracking benchmark. TPAMI (2015)
14. Henriques, J.F., Caseiro, R., Martins, P., Batista, J.: Exploiting the circulant structure of tracking-by-detection with kernels. In: Fitzgibbon, A., Lazebnik, S., Perona, P., Sato, Y., Schmid, C. (eds.) ECCV 2012. LNCS, vol. 7575, pp. 702–715. Springer, Heidelberg (2012). https://doi.org/10.1007/978-3-642-33765-9_50
15. Comaniciu, D., Ramesh, V., Meer, P.: Kernel-based object tracking. PAMI **25**(5), 564–577 (2003)
16. Fragkiadaki, K., Shi, J.: Detection free tracking: exploiting motion and topology for segmenting and tracking under entanglement. In: 2011 IEEE Conference on Computer Vision and Pattern Recognition (CVPR), pp. 2073–2080. IEEE (2011)
17. Adam, A., Rivlin, E., Shimshoni, I.: Robust fragments-based tracking using the integral histogram. In: CVPR (2006)
18. Stalder, S., Grabner, H., Van Gool, L.: Beyond semi-supervised tracking: tracking should be as simple as detection, but not simpler than recognition. In: ICCV Workshops, vol. 3 (2009)

Test Scheduling of Interposer-Based 2.5-D ICs Using Enhanced Differential Evolution Algorithm

Deng Libao[1(✉)], Sun Ning[2], and Fu Ning[1]

[1] Harbin Institute of Technology at Weihai, Weihai, China
denglibao_paper@163.com
[2] Harbin Institute of Technology, Harbin, China

Abstract. Interposer-based 2.5-dimensional integrated circuits (2.5D ICs) are seen as an alternative choice and they are rising as a precursor toward 3D integration. However, as the number of dies embedded in the interposer increases, the efficient test of 2.5D ICs becomes more difficult. In the design of test wrapper and test scheduling, both the test-time and the hardware cost have to be take into account. This paper presents an innovative differential evolution algorithm with dynamic subpopulations and adaptive searching strategy for the optimization of 2.5D IC test scheduling and hardware cost control. The whole population are partitioned into subpopulations dynamically using affinity propagation based clustering algorithm. In the subpopulations, a new mutation scheme which is controlled automatically by fitness values and distances between individuals is also presented. Parallelism among subpopulations and the proposed adaptive mutation and rotation crossover strategy can increase the speed of evolution without losing population diversity. Test wrapper scan chain balance design and the test scheduling algorithm, which combine the DE variant algorithm show an excellent performance in optimization ability comparing with the integer linear programming formulation (ILP) and some other configurations. It can make a good balance between the hardware cost and the test-time cost.

Keywords: 2.5D ICs test scheduling · Adaptive mutation mechanism · Dynamic subpopulations · Test cost

1 Introduction

Integrated circuit technology is taking mankind to a better future at an unprecedented rate, and Moore's law, which has been recognized in academia and industry, is potentially and permanently changing our lives. With the increase of the scale of integrated circuits, the characteristic size of IC decreases continuously, while the size of interconnect wire does not decrease in the same proportion. Therefore, the integrated chip is becoming more and more crowded in the traditional two-dimensional (2D) environment, and the proportion of line delay in total delay increases rapidly. In an effort to meet the needs of microelectronics chip development, 3D technology, which can significantly reduce the bottlenecks in IC designs by using TSVs instead of the long global wires and vertically arranging the logic dies, is gradually emerging.

© ICST Institute for Computer Sciences, Social Informatics and Telecommunications Engineering 2019
Published by Springer Nature Switzerland AG 2019. All Rights Reserved
M. Jia et al. (Eds.): WiSATS 2019, LNICST 280, pp. 537–549, 2019.
https://doi.org/10.1007/978-3-030-19153-5_55

However, due to some technical difficulties, the large-scale commercial production of 3D integrated circuit cannot be realized yet. Nowadays, interposer-based 2.5D ICs are emerging and becoming a good transition from 2D to 3D ICs [1].

In 2.5D ICs, the method of stacking multiple active dies vertically is not adopted. Dies are placed abreast on top of the silicon interposer and they are interconnected through the interposer. The silicon interposer can communicate different dies and connect dies with packages. With micro-bumps, the silicon interposer can make dies stack on it. Die-to-die and die-to-package are interconnected through the silicon interposer using TSVs. A number of metal layers of wires and the silicon substrate interposer are included in the interposer. Moreover, there are a cluster of TSVs that provide vertical interconnections between the dies and package in silicon substrate. The top of the silicon interposer are metal layers which can make different dies interconnect horizontally. The processes of fabricating interconnects in multiple metal layers of the interposer is as same as the processes of fabricating interconnects in the silicon dies. Today, high-density I/O ports can be used inside the interposer. Therefore, 2.5D integrated circuits can provide better performance while reducing power consumption [2].

2.5D integrated circuit testability design is an important means to ensure the reliability of its function and performance. The test structure of 2.5D IC consists of three parts: test access mechanism, test package and test scheduling. Due to the difference of design and integrated technology, 2.5D IC testing has new research contents and restrictive factors besides the problems often encountered in 2D testing [3, 4]. In this paper, we describe solutions for two of these challenges in detail, namely test wrapper test chain balance design and test scheduling.

The article is arranged as follows. The related prior work is presented in Sect. 2. Section 3 presents the proposed modified differential evolution algorithm. In Sect. 4, we will give a detail explanation of the test chains balance design. Section 5 presents the test scheduling algorithm for 2.5D ICs which is combined with the proposed DE variant. Simulation results are presented in Sect. 6. Section 7 concludes this paper.

2   Related Prior Work

No matter the 2.5D ICs test or the 3D ICs test, the final implementation is the IP core test. 2.5D IP core test package scan chain balance technology is one of the important methods to reduce the time cost and hardware cost and ensure the high efficiency of IP core test. The existing 2D IP core scanning chain balancing methods have been well developed, ILP algorithm and heuristic algorithm. The rectangular packing model has also been applied to the problem and made good performance [5–8]. However, considering the complex structure and different integration processes of 2.5D ICs, the test wrapper test chain balance methods of 2D ICs IP cores are no longer applicable. As for 3D ICs test wrapper test chain balance design, many attempts have been proposed. Some researchers consider TSV consumption and power consumption as the main factors of 3D scan chain balancing technology, respectively [9, 10]. Moreover, IEEE 1500 wrapper is expanded to 3D space in [11–13]. Some 2D ICs test chain balance algorithms, like BFD, FFD et al. are combined with some revise algorithms to solve problems in 3D ICs [14, 15]. Moreover, the ILP algorithm and heuristic algorithm are also taken into consideration in [16]. However, few publications present algorithms related to 2.5D test package scan chain design. Moreover, comparing with 2D ICs test chain balances design, hardware costs like RDL and TSV consumptions have to be considered.

Due to the limitations of the test pins, conventional test methods is not feasible for the test of 2.5D ICs. In addition, as integration level increases, the test application time and test power consumption of 2.5D ICs increase accordingly. Thus, in the design of 2.5D IC testability, these factors must be taken into account. In order to reduce the test application time and meet the limits of power budget and fault coverage at the same time, a test scheduling and optimization technique for multicast is proposed [17]. Lu et al. combined several dies into one macro die which is connected to other dies to form a daisy chain for testing. At present, researchers have also made some progresses in 3D ICs test scheduling, where different restriction conditions are considered and several optimization methods are adopted [19, 20]. Considering the multilayer stacking structure of 3D integrated circuits, it is more common for many researchers to take temperature as a limiting condition for test scheduling [21]. Moreover, in [22], the physical location of IP core in SOC is taken into consideration and the routing overhead is seen as an important limiting condition. In terms of the optimization methods, the greedy algorithm, simulated annealing and other intelligent algorithms as well as the packing model have also been well applied [19, 23].

3 Modified Differential Evolution Algorithm

Differential evolution (DE), proposed by Price [24] and Storn et al. [25], has been proved to be an effective and simple method to solve optimization problems in practical applications. DE is arguably one of the most powerful and multifunctional evolutionary algorithms. Since its inception in 1995, DE has been successfully applied to diverse fields of real-world optimization problems. Moreover, DE has attracted extensive attention from researchers around the world resulting in a great deal of variants of the basic algorithm with improved accuracy, computational speed, and robustness.

3.1 The Conventional Differential Evolution Algorithm

The classical DE includes four main steps: initialization, mutation, crossover, and selection, and it only need 3 control parameters: the scale factor, the crossover rate and the population size. DE algorithm is a stochastic search method based on population of NP D-dimensional parameter vectors and it aims to minimize the objective function in continuous domains:

$$\vec{X}_{i,G} = \{x_{1,i,G}, x_{2,i,G}, \ldots, x_{D,i,G}\}, i = 1, 2, \ldots, NP \tag{1}$$

Where G ($G = 0, 1, \ldots, G_{\max}$) represents the evolution generation.

Initialization: The initial population is evenly randomized within the search range given the minimum and maximum bounds at the generation $G = 0$:

$$x_{j,i,0} = x_{j,\min} + rand_{i,j}[0, 1] \cdot (x_{j,\max} - x_{j,\min}) \qquad (2)$$

where $rand_{i,j}[0, 1]$ is a uniformly distributed random number ranging from $[0, 1]$.

Mutation: After initialization, a mutant vector $\vec{V}_{i,G} = (v_{1,i,G}, v_{2,i,G}, \ldots, v_{D,i,G})$ is created responding to each population member of target vector $\vec{X}_{i,G}$ in each generation. There are diverse methods for the selection of parents in DE families and the most frequently referred mutation strategy is:

$$\vec{v}_{i,G} = \vec{x}_{r1,G} + F \cdot (\vec{x}_{r2,G} - \vec{x}_{r3,G}) \qquad (3)$$

where the exponents $r1$, $r2$, and $r3$ are different integers randomly selected from the set $\{1, 2, \ldots, NP\}$ and they are all different from i. Parameter F is called scaling factor.

Crossover: There are two kinds of crossover methods: exponential and binomial, in which binomial is more popular.

When the randomly generated number between $[0, 1]$ is less than or equal to the Cr value, it is performed for each D variable. In this case, the number of parameters inherited from the donor has a (nearly) binomial distribution. Formulations below give an explanation of the scheme:

$$u_{j,i,G} = \begin{cases} v_{j,i,G} & \text{if } (rand_{i,j}[0, 1] \leq Cr \quad \text{or } j = j_{rand}) \\ x_{j,i,G} & \text{otherwise.} \end{cases} \qquad (4)$$

Where, $i = 1, 2, \ldots, NP$, $j = 1, 2, \ldots, D$, and $rand_{i,j}[0, 1]$ is a uniformly distributed random number lying between 0 and 1 which is generated for each j, $jrand \in [1, 2, \ldots, D]$. And it is a randomly selected index, which ensures that $\vec{U}_{i,G}$ gets at least one component from $\vec{V}_{i,G}$. It is instantiated once for each vector per generation. The crossover rate $Cr \in [0, 1]$ is the probability of the event that a component of the trial vector will be inherited from the donor vector.

Selection: The one-to-one competition based selection operator between the target vector and trial vector are formulated as follows:

$$\vec{X}_{i,G+1} = \begin{cases} \vec{U}_{i,G}, & \text{if } f\left(\vec{U}_{i,G}\right) \leq f\left(\vec{X}_{i,G}\right) \\ \vec{X}_{i,G}, & \text{otherwise.} \end{cases} \qquad (5)$$

3.2   The Modified Differential Evolution Algorithm

In terms of the mutation strategy of standard DE, on the one hand, the traditional operation of multiplying the difference vector with the scaling factor results in poor local search ability. On the other hand, for multimodal functions, we want to separate out as many peaks (or minimum values) as possible, and search around these peaks or minimum values to increase the search rate, accuracy, and probability of finding a global optimal solution. Based on the above consideration, we raise an innovative differential evolution algorithm with dynamic subpopulations and adaptive searching strategy. The improvement of mutation operation is divided into two parts: subpopulation partition and adaptive mutation strategy.

Subpopulation Partition. The whole population is partitioned into subpopulations dynamically using affinity propagation based clustering algorithm. Messages between data points are passed between individuals in the population until a high-quality set of centers and corresponding clusters gradually emerges.

Adaptive Mutation Strategy. In the subpopulations, a new mutation scheme which is controlled automatically by differences of fitness values and distances between individuals is also presented. Parallelism among subpopulations and the proposed adaptive mutation strategy can increase the speed of evolution without losing population diversity. For composition functions and multimodal optimization, the affinity propagation based clustering method can be used to divide the whole population into several non-overlapping groups. The subpopulation only needs to search around one or a small number of optima and the searching accuracy will be improved dramatically. Moreover, the proposed mutation scheme can be easily applied to mutation strategies of several other variants of DE with small changes. Formulations of the revised mutation scheme are presented as follow:

$$\vec{V}_{i,G} = \vec{X}_{i,G} + S \cdot sym \cdot \left(\vec{X}_{r0,G} - \vec{X}_{i,G} \right) \tag{6}$$

Where S is the individual adjustment distance within the population and *sym* is a symbol denoted to indicate the adjustment direction of the individuals. The adjustment distance S can be described in the following formulation:

$$S = 0.5 + \frac{K}{2K_{max}} \cdot 0.5 \tag{7}$$

Where K_{max} represents the maximum value in the array K, and the range of S is [0.5, 0.75]. K is the adjustment step controlled by individual fitness difference and distance in a group, of which the formulation is presented as follows:

$$K = \frac{\left| f\left(X_{r0,G}\right) - f\left(X_{i,G}\right) \right|}{\frac{1}{sNP} \left(\sum_{r=1}^{sNP} \left(f\left(X_{r,G}\right) - f\left(X_{i,G}\right) \right) \right)} \cdot \frac{dist_{i,r0}}{\frac{1}{sNP} \sum_{r=1}^{sNP} dist_{r,i}} \tag{8}$$

$$dist_{i,r0}\left(\vec{X}_{i,G}, \vec{X}_{r0,G}\right) = \sqrt{\sum_{j=1}^{D} \left(\vec{X}_{i,j,G} - \vec{X}_{i,j,G}\right)} \tag{9}$$

As for the conventional crossover strategy, in the situation where most of the target vectors are similar, difficulties are encountered in finding the search location for the loss of population diversity. On this basis, we try to overcome the defects of the standard binary crossover operator and propose a rotating crossover operator based on multi-angle searching strategy. The program tactically expands the search space and effectively guides the optimal evolution of the population to the overall situation, thereby preventing the population from generating disadvantaged individuals. The final expression for the improved mutation operation is as follows:

$$
u_{i,G} = \begin{cases} \left(R_{i,G} \cdot \left(sym \cdot \left(v_{i,G} - x_{i,G}\right)/2\right)\right) + v_{i,G} & \text{if } (\text{rand}_{i,j}[0,1] \le Cr \quad \text{or } j = j_{rand}) \\ \left(R_{i,G} \cdot \left(sym \cdot \left(v_{i,G} - x_{i,G}\right)/2\right)\right) + x_{i,G} & \text{otherwise.} \end{cases}
$$

(10)

Where G represents the current evolution generation. $R_{i,G}$ is the rotating control vector and the rotating radium decreases as the generation increases, which accelerate the convergence of late evolution. Detail information about the improved crossover scheme can be presented in [26]. Figure 1 gives a detail explanation of the proposed crossover operator. By multiplying the rotation control vector and the differential vector of the target and donor vector, trial vectors are generated in the elliptical region around the donor and target vector. The rotation angle and radius adjust with the modulus and angles of the rotation control vector.

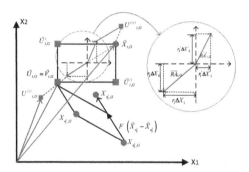

Fig. 1. Detail explanation of rotating crossover operator in 2-D space

4   Optimization Algorithm for Wrapper Scan Chains Balance

Both the 2D SoC and the 2.5D SoC test will eventually be implemented as the IP core test. In order to reduce the test time of a single 2.5D IP core, it is necessary to reduce the length of the longest test encapsulation scan chain in the IP core. 2.5D IP core test encapsulation scan chain balancing technology is one of the important methods to reduce the time cost and ensure the high efficiency of IP core test.

4.1   Scan Chain Balance Design in 2.5D IP Core Test Package

There are three cases of scan chain balance design in 2.5D IP core test package: the IP core is in a single die, the IP core and other IP cores are in one die and the IP core straddles multiple dieses. The first case is consistent with the traditional SoC in scanning chain balance design method; In the second case, it is easy to realize the balanced design of scan chain by drawing on 2D SoC scan chain balance design method and making comprehensive balance design for multiple IP cores with similar test vector data in the same die; For the third case, the balance of the scan chain is related to the number of RDL interconnects, which is the focus of this section. As shown in Figs. 2, 3 and 4 test chains in two dies need to be encapsulated into two scan chains.

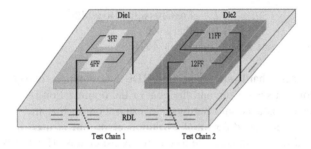

Fig. 2. Example of scan chain balance.

From Fig. 2 we can observe that two internal scan chains in each die are packaged into a scanning chain. It uses four RDL interconnects, with the length of the two scan chains is 7 and 23, respectively.

Two inner scan chains in different dies are packaged into one test chain, and it consumes 8 RDL interconnects with two test chains whose length are all 15 in Fig. 3. The scanning chain balance is realized with the additional 4 interconnections RDL.

In this paper, the proposed differential evolution algorithm is used to assign the best wrapper scan chains and realize the co-operation between the overall test time and hardware overhead.

4.2   Mathematical Model of Wrapper Scan Chain Balance Problem

We assume that the 2.5D IC is consisted of N Dies and M cores namely C_i (i = 1, 2... M). The automatic test equipment (ATE) can provide the maximum bandwidth W_m which can be divided into P parts. The width of each part is known, namely W_k (k = 1, 2...P) is given. CT (C_i, W_j) indicates the test application time for core C_i on the bandwidth W_j. The goal is to determine the cores' allocation for a given width of TAMs, thereby minimizing the total cost of SOC testing, including time and hardware costs. In general, the formula for packaging the scan chain balance problem is as follows.

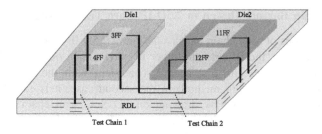

Fig. 3. Example of scan chain imbalance.

The objective function: minimize the maximum value of CT(j), which is the fitness function.

$$x_{i,j} = \begin{cases} k & \text{core } C_j \text{ assigned to width } w_k \\ 0 & \text{otherwise} \end{cases}$$
$$CT(i) = \max(L_{i,k}) + HC \tag{11}$$

Where HC represents hardware connection RDL consumption, $\max(L_{i,k})$ denotes the length of the longest scan chain and the goal of the optimization is to make a balance between test chain balance and hardware consumption so that the test costs can be minimized. The proposed differential evolution algorithm is used to make the best arrangement of the cores in each die to the given test chains. The matrix X represents the possible solutions to the problem.

$$X_{i,j} = \{x_{i,1}, x_{i,2}, x_{i,3}, \cdots, x_{i,M}\}, i = 1, 2, 3, \cdots, NP \tag{12}$$

Where NP is the number of individuals and it also represents the solution number of this problem. $X_{i,j}$ is integer coding ranging from 1 to P, which represents which scan chain these cores belong to. Thus, the initialized result is integer coding rather than real coding. Considering that after mutation and crossover operation, the value of each individual will be real coding, an integer function is needed to convert the real number to an integer. Table 1 gives an example of the integer conversion function which convert real numbers to integers ranging from 1 to 3.

Table 1. The integer conversion function.

Function $[x_{int}] = $ integer(x_{real})
1.Input x_{real};
2.Step=1/3(max(x_{real})-min(x_{real}));
3.x_{int}=zeros;
4.d1= x_{real}<min(x_{real})+Step;
5.d2=(x_{real}<=min(x_{real})+Step&x_{real}<min(x_{real})+2Step);
6.d3= x_{real}>=min(x_{real})+2Step;
7.x_{int}=d1.*ones(NP,Dim)+2d2.*ones(NP,Dim)+3d3.*ones(NP,Dim);
8.return x_{int};

In terms of the fitness evaluation of the individuals, integers representing different scan chains need to be separated to calculate population fitness.

5 Test Scheduling and Optimization

5.1 Test Scheduling Problem

Along with the number of dies embedded in the interposer increases, test scheduling of dies are drawing attention of researchers. In the case that dies are tested in sequence, only one test architecture is needed for the test. In this case, the total test length will be unacceptably high for die testing will be the sum of test lengths of each die. However, if all dies are tested in parallel, the test time will be the test length of the longest die. While the test hardware cost will be very high because every die need to be equipped with the test architecture. Moreover, in the case that all dies are tested simultaneously, it is easy to exceed the power limit. Thus, both the test-time and hardware cost should be taken into account during the die test scheduling design. Hence, multiple test chains are adopted and each test chain has one test structure. Dies arranged in the same test chain have to be tested sequentially [1].

5.2 Mathematical Model of Test Scheduling Optimization

The mathematical model of test scheduling optimization can be described as follows: Given M dies stacked on the interposer of a 2.5D IC, and the cost of test per unit time be a. In addition, assuming that the cost of one test architecture is b, the maximum power that the 2.5D IC can support is P_{max}. The test power consumed by the die is denoted as P_i. Each test chain includes multiple dies, so each die is included in one test chain and the consolidation of all test chains includes all dies. For parallel test dies, their consumption of test power should be under the upper limit. Our goal is to make an optimal configuration that minimizes the cost of the entire test:

$$C = a \cdot \sum_{j=1}^{n} T_j + b \cdot N \tag{13}$$

$$b = area_{BIST} \cdot \cos t_{die} \tag{14}$$

Where variable N and n are respectively the number of test chains and test groups.

6 Simulation Results

The test wrapper scan chain balance design and the test-chain scheduling and optimization problem was solved using MATLAB R2014a.

6.1   Simulation of the Test Wrapper Scan Chain Balance Design

In this part, the balance results for the cores in each die stacked on the interposer are presented. The following describes the experimental results of the ITC'02 SoC benchmark. We chose SoC d695 from Duke University for experimental verification.

Table 2. Scan chain balance results for the test cases.

Die	DE		P1		P2	
	L_{Max}	Cost	L_{Max}	Cost	L_{Max}	Cost
Case 1	**3203**	**3221**	3224	3242	4439	4457
Case 2	**3191**	**3209**	4636	4642	3718	3736
Case 3	**3186**	**3204**	3511	3517	3794	3812
Case 4	**3194**	**3212**	4153	4159	3453	3471
Case 5	**3184**	**3202**	3223	3229	3424	3442
Case 6	**3194**	**3212**	3336	3342	3910	3928

In order to evaluate the above method, we proposed two different test-scan balance configurations. In the first case (P1), cores in the same die are assigned to the same test chain. In the second baseline, cores are randomly assigned to the scan chains. From Table 2 we can observe that scan chain balance design method combining the proposed DE algorithm can minimize the maximum length of test chains and the overall cost.

6.2   Test Scheduling Results

In this section, we will detail the scheduling results. Test lengths and power consumption of each die in test mode can be referred to [1]. The parameter $area_{BIST}$, which is the area of the intest BIST, is 993 μm^2; the parameter c_{die} is $ 4.24 \cdot 10^{-8}/\mu m^2$ [27, 28]; and the test frequency f is 50 MHz

In these experiments, we also took three baselines. In the first case (B11), each die is assigned to different test chains so that all dies can be tested in parallel. However, dies have to be separated into groups because of the limit of P_{max}, and the dies in each group are tested concurrently. In the second case (B12), all dies on the interposer are tested in sequentially in one test chain. Moreover, the ILP algorithm for test scheduling proposed in [1] is also taken into comparison. In these configurations, the test time of B11 is the shortest, but the hardware cost is the largest, and the hardware cost of B12 is the smallest, but the test time is the highest.

In the first baseline, four dies are stacked on a common interposer and there are eight smaller dies in the second baseline. The detail information of the dies can be obtained in [1]. In Table 3, dies on the same line are in the same test chain and commas separate the test groups. Moreover, dies on the two sides of character "‖" are tested concurrently.

From Table 3 we can find that method B11 has the least cost of test time in both of the two cases because of its full parallel strategy. The proposed DE variant cost more time than method B11 while it can make a good balance between test time and

Table 3. Scheduling results for the test cases.

	DE Case1	ILP Case1	B11 Case1	DE Case2	ILP Case2	B11 Case2
Configuration	1,2 4,3	2,4 3,1	2‖3 1‖4	2,5,4 & 7 1,8,3 & 6	1,8,4 & 7 2,5,3 & 6	1 2‖4‖5‖6 3‖7‖8
Test time(s)	**0.206**	**0.206**	0.206	**0.031**	**0.301**	0.028
Test cost($)	**1115**	**1115**	1762	**238**	**238**	477

hardware cost. Considering the small number of dies in the experimental data, the DE algorithm can get similar results of configuration. However, when there are only 8 dies stacked on the interposer in the experiment, the computational speed of DE is 8 times that of ILP. As the number of dies increase, the superiority of DE algorithm compared with ILP algorithm will be more prominent.

Further comparison experiments are presented in Fig. 4. The range of P_{max} is from 2500 μW to 6500 μW, with an interval of 500 μW. The other parameter settings remain unchanged.

From Fig. 4 we can observe that as P_{max} increases, more dies can be tested in parallel and thus the total cost of the test decrease. Although the optimization results of ILP and DE are similar, the running time of these two algorithms is much different. With the value of P_{max} decreases, the optimization difficulty increases, and the calculation time of the ILP algorithm greatly increases.

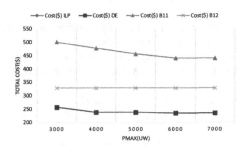

Fig. 4. Total cost with varying P_{max}.

7 Conclusion

In this paper, an improved differential evolution algorithm with dynamic subpopulations and adaptive searching strategy are proposed to solve the 2.5D IC test wrapper scan chain balance and test scheduling problem. The proposed DE variant which consists of adaptive mutation strategy and rotating crossover strategy can increase the speed of evolution without losing population diversity. Test wrapper scan chain balance design method and the test scheduling algorithm, which combine with the proposed DE algorithm show an excellent performance in both optimization ability and convergence rate.

References

1. Wang, R., Chakrabarty, K.: Testing of Interposer-Based 2.5D Integrated Circuits. Springer, Heidelberg (2017). https://doi.org/10.1007/978-3-319-54714-5
2. Wang, R., Chakrabarty, K., Eklow, B.: Scan-based testing of post-bond silicon interposer interconnects in 2.5-D ICs. Comput. Aided Des. Integr. Circ. Syst. **33**(9), 1410–1423 (2014)
3. Wang, R., Chakrabarty, K.: Tackling test challenges for interposer-based 2.5D integrated circuits. IEEE Des. Test **PP**(99), 1 (2017)
4. Huang, S.Y., Zheng, C.C.: Die-to-die clock skew characterization and tuning for 2.5D ICs. In: Asian Test Symposium, pp. 221–226. IEEE (2016)
5. Zou, W., Reddy, S.M., Pomeranz, I., et al.: SOC test scheduling using simulated annealing. In: IEEE VLSI Test Symposium, p. 325. IEEE Computer Society (2003)
6. Iyengar, V., Chakrabarty, K., Marinissen, E.J.: Test wrapper and test access mechanism co-optimization for system-on-chip. J. Electron. Test. **18**(2), 213–230 (2002)
7. Deng, L.B., Zhang, B.Q., Bian, X.L., et al.: Wrapper scan chains balance algorithm based on separation and recombination of integer-float portions. Chin. J. Scientific Instrum. **36**(10), 2363–2371 (2015)
8. Chakrabarty, K.: Test scheduling for core-based systems using mixed-integer linear programming. IEEE Trans. CAD **19**(10), 1163–1174 (2000)
9. Wu, X., Chen, Y., Chakrabarty, K., et al.: Test-access mechanism optimization for core-based three-dimensional SOCs. In: IEEE International Conference on Computer Design, pp. 212–218. IEEE (2008)
10. Jiang, L., Huang, L., Xu, Q.: Test architecture design and optimization for three-dimensional SoCs. In: Design, Automation and Test in Europe Conference and Exhibition, pp. 220–225. IEEE (2009)
11. Noia, B., Chakrabarty, K., Marinissen, E.J.: Optimization methods for post-bond die-internal/external testing in 3D stacked ICs. In: Test Conference, pp. 1–9. IEEE Xplore (2010)
12. Noia, B., Goel, S.K., Chakrabarty, K., et al.: Test-architecture optimization for TSV-based 3D stacked ICs. In: Test Symposium, pp. 24–29. IEEE (2010)
13. Noia, B., Goel, S.K., et al.: Test-architecture optimization and test scheduling for TSV-based 3-D stacked ICs. IEEE Trans. Comput.-Aided Des. Integr. Circ. Syst. **30**(11), 1705–1718 (2011)
14. Lewis, D.L., Panth, S., Zhao, X., et al.: Designing 3D test wrappers for pre-bond and post-bond test of 3D embedded cores. In: IEEE International Conference on Computer Design, pp. 90–95. IEEE (2011)
15. Roy, S.K., Giri, C., Ghosh, S., et al.: Wrapper design of embedded cores for three dimensional system-on-chips (SoC) using available TSVs. In: IEEE International Midwest Symposium on Circuits and Systems, pp. 1–4. IEEE (2011)
16. Noia, B., Chakrabarty, K.: Test-wrapper optimisation for embedded cores in through-silicon via-based three-dimensional system on chips. IET Comput. Digital Tech. **5**(3), 186–197 (2011)
17. Wang, S., Wang, R., Chakrabarty, K., et al.: Multicast test architecture and test scheduling for interposer-based 2.5D ICs. In: Asian Test Symposium, pp. 86–91. IEEE (2016)
18. Lu, S.K., Li, H.M., Hashizume, M., et al.: Efficient test length reduction techniques for interposer-based 2.5D ICs. In: International Symposium on VLSI Design, Automation and Test, pp. 1–4. IEEE (2014)

19. Gupta, B.S., Ingelsson, U., Larsson, E.: Scheduling tests for 3D stacked chips under power constraints. In: Sixth IEEE International Symposium on Electronic Design, Test and Application, pp. 72–77. IEEE Computer Society (2011)
20. Vinay, N.S., Rawaty, I., Larssonz, E., et al.: Thermal aware test scheduling for stacked multi-chip-modules. In: Design and Test Symposium, pp. 343–349. IEEE (2010)
21. Millican, S.K., Saluja, K.K.: Linear programming formulations for thermal-aware test scheduling of 3D-stacked integrated circuits. In: Test Symposium, pp. 37–42. IEEE (2012)
22. Jiang, L., Xu, Q., Chakrabarty, K., et al.: Integrated test-architecture optimization and thermal-aware test scheduling for 3-D SoCs under pre-bond test-pin-count constraint. IEEE Trans. Very Large Scale Integr. Syst. **20**(9), 1621–1633 (2012)
23. Goel, S., Marinissen, E.J., Sehgal, A., et al.: Testing of SoCs with hierarchical cores: common fallacies, test access optimization, and test scheduling. IEEE Trans. Comput. **58**(3), 409–423 (2009)
24. Storn, R., Price, K.V.: Differential evolution–a simple and efficient heuristic for global optimization over continuous spaces. J. Global Optim. **11**(4), 341–359 (1997)
25. Storn, R., Price, K.V., Lampinen, J.: Differential Evolution–A Practical Approach to Global Optimization. Springer, Berlin (2005). https://doi.org/10.1007/3-540-31306-0
26. Deng, L.B., Wang, S., Qiao, L.Y., et al.: DE-RCO: rotating crossover operator with multiangle searching strategy for adaptive differential evolution. IEEE Access **PP**(99), 1 (2017)
27. Chi, C.C., Wu, C.W., Wang, M.J., et al.: 3D-IC interconnect test, diagnosis, and repair. In: VLSI Test Symposium, pp. 1–6. IEEE (2013)
28. Cadix, L.: Lifting the veil on silicon interposer pricing (2012). http://electroiq.com/blog/articles/2012/12/lifting-the-veil-on-silicon-interposer-pricing/

A ICP-Improved Point Cloud Maps Fusion Algorithm with Multi-UAV Collaboration

Hao Li[1], Xiaohan Qi[1], and Zhihua Yang[1,2(✉)]

[1] Communication Engineering Research Center, Harbin Institute of Technology,
Shenzhen, Guangdong, China
lihao_hitsz@163.com, qixiaohan@stu.hit.edu.cn, yangzhihua@hit.edu.cn
[2] Pengcheng Laboratory, Shenzhen, Guangdong, China

Abstract. Using depth sensor devices to obtain 3D reconstruction maps is widely used in robotics and UAVs technology. For instance, large-scale environments reconstruction usually requires multiple or multiple angles to construct local point cloud maps, and then use 3D point cloud fusion technology to obtain global maps. In this paper, we present a complete point cloud fusion system for 3D map reconstruction of indoor environment based on traditional method, including initial fusion and precise fusion. Furthermore, we adopt the method of kd-tree search to match the points in the cloud of two point clouds, and eliminate the wrong matching or the matching point pairs with large error to improve the fusion efficiency. Our experiments show that, the convergence speed of the iterative process is improved, and the time complexity of the whole fusion algorithm is reduced while the final fusion effect achieves the required accuracy.

Keywords: 3D reconstruction · Point cloud map · Map fusion · ICP

1 Introduction

In recent years, with the continuous advancement of image acquisition equipment, it is convenient to obtain massive high-resolution image data using equipment, such as mobile phones, street-view vehicles, and drones. For unmanned vehicles, mobile robots, AR and other agents in a 3D environment, in addition to the understanding of 2D images, the interaction of the 3D environment is also required. In view of the above reasons, the classic problem of constructing a 3D world (image-based 3D modeling) through image data has increasingly become a hot spot for computer vision researchers.

Nowadays, it is of great significance to use computer graphics and computer vision to reconstruct the city building and object model. However, in most cases, we cannot obtain all the data needed for the object or environment to be reconstructed at one time, and it requires multi-angle and multi-time measurement

© ICST Institute for Computer Sciences, Social Informatics and Telecommunications Engineering 2019
Published by Springer Nature Switzerland AG 2019. All Rights Reserved
M. Jia et al. (Eds.): WiSATS 2019, LNICST 280, pp. 550–560, 2019.
https://doi.org/10.1007/978-3-030-19153-5_56

to build local point cloud maps. Therefore, point cloud fusion becomes an indispensable step in 3D reconstruction [1]. The fusion of 3D point cloud is a very important part in the reconstruction of 3D objects. The point cloud registration technology refers to the integration of point clouds in different coordinate systems into the same coordinate system by certain algorithms with the overlapping information of point clouds, to obtain a complete 3D point cloud model of objects or environments. At present, point cloud fusion is mainly divided into three categories: manual fusion, instrument-based fusion, and algorithm-based automatic fusion. In this paper, we study the algorithm-based point cloud fusion technology.

Furthermore, the process can be divided into an *initial fusion* and *precise fusion* [2], which initial fusion is to perform a rough registration transformation of two pieces of point cloud at any position, so that the overlapping regions are roughly in the same position, providing a suitable initial value for precise fusion. Common methods [3] for initial fusion include labeling method, turntable method, principal component analysis method, and curvature analysis and so on. At the same time, precise fusion is to accurately match the point cloud data after initial fusion, optimize the translation matrix and the rotation matrix.

At present, the point cloud registration algorithm is widely used as the *iterative nearest point* (ICP) algorithm proposed by Besl *et al.* [4] in 1992. Then, Magnusson *et al.* [5] used *normal distributions transform* (NDT) to register 3D point cloud. However, the ICP algorithm can fulfill the requirements of our registration task in many cases, there are still some problems. On the one hand, the biggest impact on the ICP algorithm is that the algorithm relies on a better initial registration result. If the initial registration position is poor, the algorithm is simple to fall into local optimization or infinite iteration [6], which greatly affects the convergence speed of the algorithm and increases the time complexity. On the other hand, the traditional ICP algorithm searches for the nearest neighbors at a time cost, and the iterative convergence speed is slow, which is difficult to use in systems that require real-time performance [7]. Because of these limitations, this paper conducts an in-depth study on the point cloud fusion algorithm. We have improved the initial fusion and precise fusion with the matching speed and the time complexity.

The contributions are specified as follow:

(a) we propose the initial fusion of the point clouds with the ISS-based SAC-IA algorithm, which can satisfy the correct matching of the initial matching punctually feature point pair.
(b) we develop the improved ICP with kd-tree to search the nearest neighbors, and propose a method to filter matching point pairs by the normal vector angle to minimize the error iteration.
(c) our experimental results show the feasibility of the algorithm and we analyze the convergence speed, iteration time and fusion error of point cloud fusion.

2   Problem Formulation

2.1   Reference Scenario

Recently, with the need for agents to more accurately locate and construct high-precision 3D maps, a single UAV 3D SLAM algorithm can no longer satisfy the requirements, especially for large-scale 3D reconstruction. It takes a lot of time and generates a large accumulation error, which leads to a significant drop in the accuracy of positioning and mapping. Therefore, we proposed the multi-UAV 3D SLAM algorithm framework that becomes a good solution.

In this paper, the purpose of point cloud fusion is to complete 3D map reconstruction of large-scale environment more efficiently. It is proposed that under the framework of multi-UAV collaboration, multiple UAVs equipped with the same RGB-D sensor are used to reconstruct the local 3D point cloud map using the SLAM algorithm, and we finally obtain the global point cloud map of the environment through the fusion of the map.

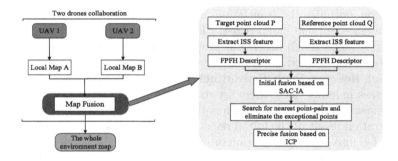

Fig. 1. Collaboration framework and point cloud fusion flow diagram

In Fig. 1, the flow chart of the two-UAVs collaboration is given. Each drone builds its own local point cloud map, and then integrates the map at the back to get the global map. In this paper, we mainly focus on the point cloud fusion part at the back end. The fusion flow diagram is given on the right side of the figure, and the detailed algorithm process is as follows.

2.2   Problem Definition

Suppose we have obtained two point cloud maps with overlapping areas, which are denoted as point cloud $\mathbf{P}$, expressed as $\mathbf{P} = \{p_i | p_i \in \mathbf{R}^3, i = 1, 2, \cdots, N\}$, the number of point clouds is N, and point cloud $\mathbf{Q}$, similarly, expressed as $\mathbf{Q} = \{q_i | q_i \in \mathbf{R}^3, i = 1, 2, \cdots, M\}$, the number of point clouds is M. They are three-dimensional point coordinates in different coordinate systems, where $\mathbf{P}$ is the target point cloud and $\mathbf{Q}$ is the reference point cloud. Our purpose is to unify point cloud $\mathbf{Q}$ through coordinate transformation to the same coordinate system as point cloud $\mathbf{P}$ and merge it into a point cloud map.

The rigid-body transformation can be realized through the following equation when the coordinate transformation of points $\mathbf{P}$ and $\mathbf{Q}$ in two different coordinate systems is carried out

$$q_i'(x, y, z) = \mathbf{R}q_i(x, y, z) + \mathbf{t} \tag{1}$$

In Eq. (1), we fixed the coordinate system of $\mathbf{P}$, and obtained the $q_i'(x, y, z)$ by the rotation and translation transformation of the point $q_i(x, y, z)$ in $\mathbf{Q}$. At this time, we think that $q_i'(x, y, z)$ has been transformed into the coordinate system of $\mathbf{P}$,where $\mathbf{R}$ is the rotation matrix and $\mathbf{t}$ is the translation matrix. They can be expressed as

$$\mathbf{R_{3\times3}} = \begin{bmatrix} 1 & 0 & 0 \\ 0 & cos\alpha & sin\alpha \\ 0 & sin\alpha & cos\alpha \end{bmatrix} \begin{bmatrix} cos\beta & 0 & -sin\beta \\ 0 & 1 & 0 \\ sin\beta & 0 & cos\beta \end{bmatrix} \begin{bmatrix} cos\gamma & sin\gamma & 0 \\ -sin\gamma & cos\gamma & 0 \\ 0 & 0 & 1 \end{bmatrix} \tag{2}$$

and

$$\mathbf{t_{3\times1}} = \begin{bmatrix} t_x & t_y & t_z \end{bmatrix}^T \tag{3}$$

where α, β and γ respectively represent the rotation angles of the point along the x, y and z axes, t_x, t_y and t_z respectively represents the translation of the point along the x, y and z axes.

The rigid-body transformation involves six unknowns $\alpha, \beta, \gamma, t_x, t_y$ and t_z, so at least six linear equations need to be determined. Therefore, three pairs of corresponding point pairs need to be found in the overlapping region of the point cloud to be matched, and cannot be collinear to complete the parameter estimation of the transformation matrix.

Let the rotation transformation matrix be $\mathbf{R}$ and the translation transformation vector be $\mathbf{t}$, and use $f(\mathbf{R}, \mathbf{t})$ to represent the error between the reference point set $\mathbf{Q}$ and the target point set $\mathbf{P}$ under the transformation matrix $(\mathbf{R}, \mathbf{t})$

$$f(\mathbf{R}, \mathbf{t}) = \sum_{i=1}^{M} \| p_i - (\mathbf{R}q_i + \mathbf{t}) \| \tag{4}$$

$$s.t. \triangle f < f_0$$
$$\triangle \mathbf{R} < \delta_1$$
$$\triangle \mathbf{t} < \delta_2$$

where f_0 is the distance error of point cloud registration, δ_1 and δ_2 are defined allowable error quantities, then the problem of solving the optimal transformation matrix can be transformed into solving the optimal solution $(\mathbf{R}, \mathbf{t})$ that satisfies $\min(f(\mathbf{R}, \mathbf{t}))$. Towards this goal, we can get the global fusion map which is formed by the fusion of multiple local point cloud maps.

3   Point Cloud Map Fusion Algorithm

Through the above description of the problem, we want to fuse the point cloud maps in different coordinate systems into a unified coordinate system, which is the process of solving the transformation parameters R and t. First, we need to filter the point cloud data to dry, then find the key points and describe the key points. After doing the above work, we use the initial fusion to obtain the transformation parameters R and t, and finally optimize them by precise fusion.

3.1   ISS Feature Extraction

The method of finding the nearest point of the neighborhood usually uses the ε nearest neighbor or the k nearest neighbor. The former is to search for the points in the sphere with a center point P_i and a radius of ε, and the latter is to search for k points with a minimum geometric distance from the center point P_i. In order to improve the speed of feature point extraction, we improved the ISS (Intrinsic Shape Signatures) algorithm, using k nearest neighbor domain point $N^k(p_i)$.

In the specific search, use the kd-tree search method to find the k nearest neighbor point. For the case where the point cloud of the point cloud has different degrees of density, we set a neighborhood search radius r, and only select k_i points whose distance is less than r. Make it possible to select relatively few points in a sparse area and more points in a dense place. In this way, the point set formed by the nearest point of the k_i neighborhood of each point can obtain the center point c_i

$$c_i = \frac{1}{k_i} \sum_{p_{ij} \in N^k(p_i)} p_{ij} \qquad \|p_i - p_{ij}\| < r \tag{5}$$

where the 3D point cloud is written by $\mathbf{P} = \{p_i\}_{i=1}^N$ and $N^{k_i}(p_i) = \{p_{ij}\}, 1 \leq j \leq k_i$ representatives the k_i nearest neighbor point. Further, solve the correlation matrix C_i

$$\mathbf{C}_i = \sum_{p_{ij} \in N^{k_i}(p_i)} (p_{ij} - c_i)(p_{ij} - c_i)^T \tag{6}$$

Calculate the eigenvalue of the matrix as $\{\lambda_0, \lambda_1, \lambda_2\}, \lambda_0 \leq \lambda_1 \leq \lambda_0$. If p_i satisfies the following formula, it is regarded as a feature point.

$$\frac{\lambda_2}{\lambda_1} < \varepsilon_1, \frac{\lambda_3}{\lambda_2} < \varepsilon_2 \tag{7}$$

where ε_1 and ε_2 are the preset threshold.

3.2   Initial Fusion

Sample consensus initial alignment (SAC-IA) can obtain the corresponding relationship between the feature points after extracting the feature from the point cloud. Then, calculate an initial transformation matrix, so that the two point cloud sets obtain a relatively good initial position.

This algorithm relies on point feature histogram (PFH) to obtain a description of the feature, but in order to reduce the time cost, as far as possible to calculate the descriptor for a small number of point clouds. We use an accelerated description algorithm FPFH that is improved for PFH. Therefore, before the implementation of this algorithm, you should calculate the feature point clouds fast point feature histogram (FPFH) [10].

The steps are described as follows:

Algorithm 1. Initial Fusion of FPFH Feature Description
___
Input: Target point cloud $\mathbf{P}$ and reference point cloud $\mathbf{Q}$
 1: **Begin**
 2: *Set maximum distance threshold d_0 and e_0*
 3: *Calculate the FPFH of point sets of $\mathbf{P}$ and $\mathbf{Q}$*
 4: // Search for match point pairs
 5: **while** $(d > d_0$ and $e > e_0)$ **do**
 6:    *Find points in $\mathbf{P}$ that have similar FPFH characteristics to points in $\mathbf{Q}$*
 7:    *Randomly select n point pairs from these similar points*
 8:    $d = \frac{1}{n} \sum \|p_i - q_i\|$
 9:    *Calculate $p_i = \mathbf{R}q_i + \mathbf{t}$*
10:    $e_i = p_i - (\mathbf{R}q_i + \mathbf{t})$
11: **end while**
12: **End**
Output: Initial transformation matrix $\mathbf{R}$ and $\mathbf{t}$

The ultimate goal of the above registration is to find a set of optimal transforms in all transforms to minimize the value of the error function, and the transformation at this time is the final registration transformation matrix. Then, the registration result can be further obtained with precise fusion.

3.3   Improved ICP Algorithm Based on kd-tree

We complete the precise fusion process by ICP algorithm. However, the classical ICP algorithm that it demands a high relative position between the point clouds and has larger amount of computation. Besides that, the iterative process may not converge to the global optimal solution. In order to improve the matching speed and precision of ICP algorithm, this paper improves the classical ICP algorithm based on kd-tree.

Kd-tree is a data structure used in multi-dimensional data space segmentation. It divides point cloud data in k-dimensional space according to a certain segmentation criterion, and applies the most extensive segmentation criterion to maximum variance segmentation. The point clouds used in this paper are scattered point clouds, so this article uses kd-tree search to implement nearest neighbor queries.

The time complexity of the traditional ICP algorithm is $\mathcal{O}(MN)$, where M and N are the number of two point clouds respectively. However, when the point cloud data is large, it takes a lot of time to search for the nearest point. An improved ICP algorithm based on kd-tree search is used to improve the fusion registration speed of the algorithm. The time complexity of the algorithm can be reduced to $\mathcal{O}(logN)$. Therefore, the kd-tree nearest neighbor search method is used in this paper to accelerate the search of corresponding point pairs. Furthermore, the point pairs are screened out to eliminate the mismatched point pairs so as to improve the convergence speed while ensuring the fusion effect.

Improved algorithm steps are as follows:

Algorithm 2. Improved ICP Algorithm

Input: Point cloud after initial fusion
1: **Begin**
2: *Set $K = 0$, give a series of thresholds $r_0, d_0, f_0, \delta_1, \delta_2$*
3: // Search for match point pairs
4: **for** $i = 1, 2, \cdots, k$ **do**
5:     *Use kd-tree search p_i and $q_i (r < r_0)$*
6:     *Remove the mismatched point pairs*
7:     **if** $d(p_i, q_i) < d_0$ **then**
8:         *Solve the coordinate transformation,get R and t*
9:     **end if**
10: **end for**
11: // Optimized transformation matrix
12: **while** $(\triangle f > f_0 \text{ or } \triangle R > \delta_1 \text{ or } \triangle t > \delta_2)$ **do**
13:     $q_i' = Rq_i + t$
14:     $f(R, t) = \sum_{i=1}^{M} \|p_i - (Rq_i + t)\|$
15:     $K = K + 1$
16: **end while**
17: **End**
Output: Transformation matrix R and t

---

4   Experimental Results

In this experiment, we apply the improved ICP algorithm based on kd-tree to register point cloud maps of indoor environment which are constructed by SLAM algorithm. Experimental device: ubuntu 16.04 LTS, 4 GB, intel Core i5-7500 CPU @3.40 GHz.

According to the algorithm steps described in our paper, we first extract the feature points from the point cloud, and filter the extracted feature points to obtain the feature descriptors. As shown in Fig. 2, on the left is the source point cloud data with the RGB color and on the right is obtained by extracting feature points from the origin cloud map, where the green colors in the picture indicate the extracted feature points.

The experimental results of initial fusion and related data are shown in Table 1. We know the registration score of SAC-IA based on kd-tree is better (where the score represents the Euclidean distance between the corresponding

Fig. 2. Feature detection and description

Table 1. Experimental results of initial fusion

Algorithm	SAC-IA	SAC-IA based on kd-tree
Score	0.236	0.162
Rotation matrix	$\begin{bmatrix} 0.968 & 0.252 & 0.006 \\ -0.252 & 0.869 & -0.007 \\ 0.004 & 0.008 & 1.021 \end{bmatrix}$	$\begin{bmatrix} 1.108 & 0.312 & 0.010 \\ -0.298 & 0.969 & -0.009 \\ 0.006 & 0.019 & 0.954 \end{bmatrix}$
Translation vector	$\begin{bmatrix} 0.230 & 0.252 & 0.423 \end{bmatrix}$	$\begin{bmatrix} 0.243 & 0.265 & 0.419 \end{bmatrix}$

point pairs, and the smaller the better), and transformation matrix is similar. The transformation matrix obtained by SAC-IA is inaccurate, so it can only be used for rough registration. With a large number of points, the feature extraction and calculation of feature descriptors are very time-consuming, making the SAC-IA algorithm inefficient. From the experimental results, the introduction of kd-tree accelerated search can reduce the time cost while ensuring the accuracy of the transformation matrix.

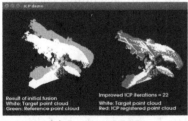
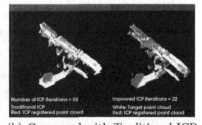

(a) Improved ICP   (b) Compared with Traditional ICP

Fig. 3. ICP iterations results

After initial fusion of two point clouds with overlapping areas, we get the registration result on the left side of Fig. 3. It can be seen that the fusion effect is not very good but acceptable. On this basis, we use the improved ICP algorithm for accurate fusion registration, and the simulation results show the results on the right side of Fig. 3.

Figure 3 shows two images (a) and (b), in which (a), the content shown in the figure on the left is the result of initial fusion, while showing on the right side as a result of precise registration. It can be seen that a better fusion effect can be obtained by using the improved ICP precision registration. In additional, picture (b) shows the comparison between the final fusion map and the real point cloud map. It can be seen that the error of fusion effect is relatively small.

Table 2. Experimental results of precise fusion

Algorithm	ICP	Improved ICP
Time (s)	52.842	20.463
Iterations	50	22

Table 2 describes the time and iterations of the algorithm. The improved ICP algorithm can achieve the required fusion effect with fewer iterations, thus greatly reducing the time cost of the algorithm.

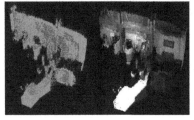 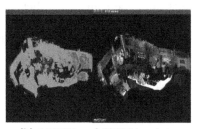

(a) 156575 and 311829 points   (b) 156575 and 870104 points

Fig. 4. Compare the fusion effect of different cloud data

In Fig. 4, the number of point clouds is 156575 and 311829 in (a). In order to study the impact of the huge number of point clouds on the ICP algorithm, we performed two fusions experiments with 156515 and 870104 point clouds shown in (b). When the amount of cloud data is up to hundreds of thousands or even more, the improved algorithm can significantly improve the computational efficiency while maintaining the approximate registration accuracy compared with the traditional algorithm.

In Table 3, we set up 4 sets of experimental data A, B, C and D for comparison of simulation experiments, where P represents target point cloud and Q represents reference point cloud. The evaluation results are shown in Fig. 5, in which A+Improved represents the result of the improved ICP algorithm of the A group data, and A+Traditional represents the result of the traditional ICP

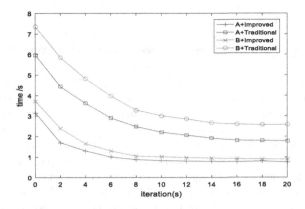

Fig. 5. Time of each iteration

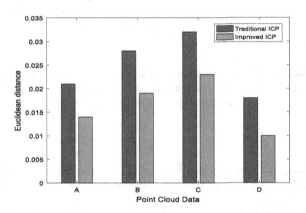

Fig. 6. Error of fusion evalution

Table 3. Point cloud data

Group	A	B	C	D
P	311829	639235	870104	156575
Q	156575	311829	639235	156575

algorithm of the A group data, and the rest are similar. It can be seen from the simulation results, compared with the traditional ICP algorithm, the improved algorithm can reduce the iteration time, shorten the convergence speed, and can achieve higher precision map fusion with fewer iterations. When the point cloud data increases, the time cost of the improved algorithm increases less, which is a big advantage compared to the traditional algorithm. The Fig. 6 shows the fusion result error of four groups of data. We use Euclidean distance to represent the magnitude of the error, it can be seen that the improved algorithm can reduce the fusion error and get better global map.

5   Conclusion

From the above experiments, the proposed collaboration framework is of great help for the 3D reconstruction of large-scale indoor environment, and can be obtained by using local sub-map fusion. Aiming at the shortcomings of traditional initial fusion and slow convergence of ICP algorithm, this paper proposes an improved algorithm based on kd-tree nearest point search. According to the density of the point cloud, feature points can be extracted and the nearest neighbors can be searched effectively. In the same way, the angle threshold of the normal vector is set to eliminate the wrong matching point pair, which can avoid the algorithm to increase the time cost in the wrong direction.

Finally, in this paper, a 3D point cloud maps of indoor environment are constructed by using the intelligent body equipped with the SLAM algorithm for fusion experiments. The results show that for large-scale point cloud data maps, the improved algorithm can improve the convergence speed of ICP algorithm with higher precision, which proves that the study in this paper has certain application value.

Acknowledgments. The authors would like to express their high appreciations to the supports from the National Natural Science Foundation of China (61871426) and Basic Research Project of Shenzhen (JCYJ20170413110004682).

References

1. He, H., Wang, H., Sun, L.: Research on 3D point-cloud registration technology based on Kinect V2 sensor. In: 2018 Chinese Control and Decision Conference (CCDC). IEEE (2018)
2. Salvi, J., Matabosch, C., Fofi, D., Forest, J.: A review of recent range image registration methods with accuracy evaluation. Image Vis. Comput. **25**(5), 578–596 (2007)
3. Qiu, S., Luo, Y.: Point cloud registration based on improved ICP algorithm. Henan Science and Technology (2017)
4. Besl, P.J., Mckay, N.D.: Method for registration of 3-D shapes. In: Sensor Fusion IV: Control Paradigms and Data Structures, pp. 239–256 (1992)
5. Jun, L., Wei, L., Donglai, D., Qiang, S.: Point cloud registration algorithm based on NDT with variable size voxel. In: Control Conference, pp. 3707–3712 (2015)
6. Sharp, G.C., Lee, S.W., Wehe, D.K.: ICP registration using invariant features. IEEE Trans. PAMI **24**(1), 90–102 (2002)
7. Schmuck, P., Chli, M.: Multi-UAV collaborative monocular slam. In: IEEE International Conference on Robotics and Automation, pp. 3863–3870 (2017)
8. Zhong, Y.: Intrinsic shape signatures: a shape descriptor for 3D object recognition. In: IEEE International Conference on Computer Vision Workshops, pp. 689–696 (2010)
9. Mur-Artal, R., Tards, J.D.: ORB-SLAM2: an open-source slam system for monocular, stereo, and RGB-D cameras. IEEE Trans. Rob. **33**(5), 1255–1262 (2017)
10. Rusu, R.B., Blodow, N., Beetz, M.: Fast point feature histograms (FPFH) for 3D registration. In: IEEE International Conference on Robotics and Automation, pp. 3212–3217 (2009)

Capacity Analysis of Panoramic Multi-beam Satellite Telemetry and Command System

Yilun Liu[(⊠)] and Lidong Zhu

National Key Laboratory of Science and Technology on Communications,
UESTC, Chengdu 611731, Sichuan, China
ly16205@163.com, zld@uestc.edu.cn

Abstract. Compared with the Tracking beam satellite Telemetry and Command system, the Panoramic Multi-beam satellite Telemetry and Command system has the advantages that the spacecrafts can be measured and controlled when they enter the coverage area and the system capacity is large. It uses Code-Division Multiple Access (CDMA) to distinguish users. Since the spreading codes are not completely orthogonal, the received signals will introduce Multiple Access Interference (MAI) and affect the system performance. Based on the panoramic multi-beam satellite telemetry and command system, this paper deduces the formula of ranging error in the presence of MAI, and analyzes the system capacity considering the two cases of perfect power control and imperfect power control. The theoretical and simulation results show that the system can support over 500 space-crafts at the same time, but the system performance deteriorates by 1.6 dB when the power control error occurs.

Keywords: Satellite telemetry and command system · Panoramic multi-beam · System capacity · Ranging error · Multiple access interference

1 Introduction

The next generation constellation program represented by the satellite Internet and the Space-terrestrial integrated network has developed rapidly. However, with the rapid increasement in the number of low-orbit spacecraft, the existing tracking beam satellite telemetry and command system, limited by the number of tracking beams, is difficult to meet the telemetry and command requirements of many spacecrafts in the future. Therefore, the concept of a panoramic multi-beam satellite telemetry and command system has been proposed. The beam coverage of the panoramic multi-beam satellite telemetry and command system is unchanged, and the spacecraft can be telemetered within the beam range. Besides, the panoramic multi-beam telemetry and command system uses CDMA to distinguish spacecrafts. Since it is no longer limited by the number of tracking beams, the system capacity will exceed that of satellite telemetry and command system with tracking beams.

This paper is supported by the Foundation of the Ministry (No. 6140518050316).

M. Jia et al. (Eds.): WiSATS 2019, LNICST 280, pp. 561–571, 2019.
https://doi.org/10.1007/978-3-030-19153-5_57

Due to the imperfect orthogonality of the spreading code, the received signal of the telemetry and command system will produce Multiple Access Interference (MAI), which may cause the performance degrading of the telemetry and command system.

Tracking loop performance and multi-beam satellite system capacity have attracted the attention of scholars for long time [1, 2]. In recent years, there have been many new research results [3, 4], but there are few literatures on panoramic multi-beam satellite telemetry and command systems. This paper analyzes the capacity of the telemetry and command system in the presence of MAI. According to the ranging error formula and the bit error rate (BER) formula in the presence of MAI, the system capacity formula under the two limiting factors of ranging accuracy and bit error rate (BER) is deduced. Finally, numerical results show that the system can meet telemetry and command requirements of 500 spacecrafts at the same time.

2   The System Model

This paper is based on the panoramic multi-beam satellite telemetry and command system, as shown in Fig. 1. The system achieves full coverage of 200–2000 km with only three satellites, and the interference between adjacent satellites is small. The interference mainly comes from the interference between adjacent beams of the same satellite and other ones in the same beam.

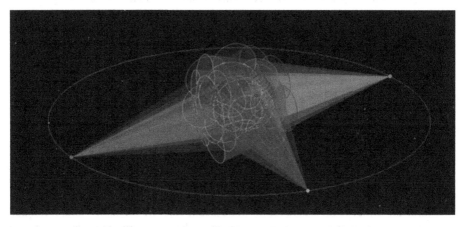

Fig. 1. Schematic diagram of panoramic multi-beam satellite telemetry and command system

The block diagram of the multi-target ranging system using pseudo-code ranging is shown in Fig. 2.

It is known from Fig. 2, the main factor affecting the accuracy of ranging is the synchronization accuracy, which can be divided into acquiring and tracking, and the tracking accuracy is the main factor. This paper analyzes the capacity of the panoramic multi-beam telemetry and command system under the two constraints of ranging accuracy and BER.

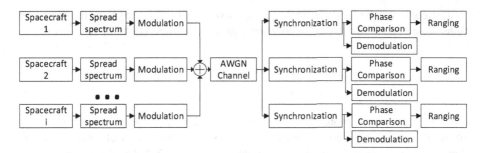

Fig. 2. Block diagram of multi-target ranging system

The parameters of the system are shown in Table 1.

Table 1. System parameters

Parameter	Value
Orbital altitude	35786 km
Number of satellites	3
Orbital position	E176.8°, E77°, E10.6°
Number of single satellite beams	21
Frequency reuse	Three-color frequency reuse
Spacecraft height	200–2000 km
Reverse link rate	10 kbps
Spreading code rate	10.23 M chips/s
S-band center frequency	3 GHz
Modulation	BPSK

3   Capacity Analysis

3.1   SINR

In this part, the power interference of other spacecrafts under the single beam to the target spacecraft is derived, and then the interference of the spacecraft in the other beams to the target spacecraft is analyzed. Assuming the total number of spacecrafts is K, the user power of spacecraft i is $P_{si}(1 < i < K)$. Without loss of generality, if the signal of spacecraft 1 is the target signal, and the power is $P_s = P_{s1} = \min\{P_{si}, 1 < i < K\}$. The Gaussian white noise power is P_n, then the input SINR of the correlator is

$$\left(\frac{S}{I+N}\right)_i = \frac{P_s}{\sum\limits_{j=2}^{K} P_{sj} + P_n} \tag{1}$$

The correlator has a different MAI suppression gain G_{MAI} [5] than the Gaussian white noise suppression gain G_N, as shown in the following equation.

$$G_{MAI-j} = 20 \lg(N_c/R_{j1}(\tau)) \tag{2}$$

$$G_N = 10\lg(R_c/R_b) \tag{3}$$

In Eq. (2), $R_{j1}(\tau)$ represents the cross-correlation function of spacecraft j and spacecraft 1 when the phase difference is τ chips, N_c is the period of spreading code. Therefore, after passing through the correlator, the output SINR will become

$$\left(\frac{S}{I+N}\right)_o = \frac{P_s}{\sum_{j=2}^{K} \frac{P_{sj}}{G_{MAI-j}} + \frac{P_n}{G_N}} = \frac{P_s}{\sum_{j=2}^{K} \frac{G_N P_{sj}}{G_{MAI-j}} + P_n} G_N \tag{4}$$

From Eq. (4), the MAI can be equivalent to Gaussian white noise with an input power of $\sum_{j=2}^{K} G_N P_{sj}/G_{MAI-j}$, which is the basis for analyzing the ranging error and BER later.

Now consider the interference of spacecraft in other beams. It is assumed that the frequency reuse is reasonable, there is no interference between the beams of different frequencies, and only the beams of the same frequency will cause interference. Besides power interference, the received signal power of the interference in other beams is related to the antenna gain. The input SINR of the multi-beam system can be described as the following.

$$SINR = \frac{P_s}{\sum_{i=1}^{M} \frac{G_N}{G_{MAI-i}} f \cdot P_{si} + \sum_{j=2}^{K} \frac{G_N P_{sj}}{G_{MAI-j}} + P_n} \tag{5}$$

In Eq. (5), M is the total number of other beam interference spacecraft, and f is the neighbor cell interference factor to estimate the interference power of other cells, which is defined as

$$f = P_{Ia}/P_{Ie} \tag{6}$$

In Eq. (6), P_{Ia} is the total interference power of "other cells", and P_{Ie} is the total interference power of the "self-cell".

In imperfect power control, the power control error coefficient α_{j1} is introduced, which is define as

$$\alpha_{j1} = P_{sj}/P_s \tag{7}$$

Then, Eq. (5) can be rewritten as follows.

$$
\begin{aligned}
(E_b/N_0)_{eff} = SINR = P_s & \left(\sum_{i=1}^{M} \frac{G_N}{G_{\text{MAI}-i}} f P_{si} + \sum_{j=2}^{K} \frac{G_N P_{sj}}{G_{\text{MAI}-j}} + P_n \right)^{-1} \\
& = \left(\sum_{i=1}^{M} \frac{G_N}{G_{\text{MAI}-i}} f \alpha_{i1} + \sum_{j=2}^{K} \frac{G_N \alpha_{j1}}{G_{\text{MAI}-j}} + P_n \right)^{-1} \qquad (8) \\
& = \left(\sum_{i=1}^{M} \frac{R_{j1}^2(\tau) f \alpha_{i1}}{N_c} + \sum_{j=2}^{K} \frac{R_{j1}^2(\tau) \alpha_{i1}}{N_c} + \frac{N_0}{E_b} \right)^{-1}
\end{aligned}
$$

In Eq. (8), $(E_b/N_0)_{eff}$ is the equivalent E_b/N_0 when MAI exists, and the actual E_b/N_0 is on the right side of the equation.

3.2   Ranging Error and BER

The implementation of the ranging system mainly relies on the phase difference between the ranging signal and the local signal during synchronization. After the acquisition is successful, the code phase difference between the local sequence and that of the received signal is less than half a chip, but it is not enough for the system's requirements of ranging accuracy. For example, if the spreading code rate is 10 M chips/s, then the maximum range error will reach 7.5 m, so it is necessary to enter the tracking phase for better accuracy. The expression of the ranging error is

$$
\Delta = c(T_c \cdot \sigma)/2 \qquad (9)
$$

In Eq. (9), T_c is the time of one chip; σ is the minimum resolution obtained by the synchronization technique, and c is the speed of light. The error of the non-coherent delay-locked loop comes from two aspects: thermal noise error and dynamic stress error, and the total error is less than the threshold. Once the total error of the delay-locked loop is greater than the threshold, then it will be in unlocked state and needs re-acquisition. The relationship between the total error and the threshold is as follows.

$$
3\sigma_{DLL} = 3\sigma_{tDLL} + R_e \leq d \qquad (10)
$$

In Eq. (10), σ_{DLL} is the root mean square error of all errors in the code ring (unit: chip); σ_{tDLL} is the error caused by the loop thermal noise; R_e is the dynamic stress error; d is the threshold, and the value generally is 0.5. In general, the dynamic stress error is negligible.

The classical analysis can get the thermal noise error σ_{tDLL} as follows [6].

$$
\sigma_{tDLL} = \sqrt{\frac{2d^2 B_L}{C/N_0} [2(1-d) + \frac{4d}{TC/N_0}]} \quad (chip) \qquad (11)
$$

In Eq. (11), B_L is the loop equivalent noise bandwidth; T is the pre-detection integration time; C/N_0 is the carrier-to-noise ratio $(dB \cdot Hz)$, which can be calculated as follows [7].

$$C/N_0 = \frac{S}{N} \cdot B_L = \frac{E_b \cdot R_b}{N_0 \cdot B_L} \cdot B_L = \frac{E_b}{N_0} \cdot R_b \qquad (12)$$

The curve of the ranging error as a function of E_b/N_0 can be obtained by the Eqs. (8), (9) and (11). In addition to the ranging error, the BER of the synchronous demodulation under BPSK can be obtained by [4].

$$P_{b-BPSK} = Q(\sqrt{\frac{2E_b}{N_0}}) \qquad (13)$$

In this way, we get the equation of ranging error and bit error rate with E_b/N_0, which is the basis for calculating the capacity.

3.3   The Capacity

It is assumed that the spacecraft is evenly distributed within the satellite coverage. The number of spacecrafts in each beam is equal. The three-color frequency multiplexing is used, and the number of interference beams at the same frequency is L. $R_{j1} = 1$ (Gold sequences are mutually the ideal case for related functions). K is the number of spacecrafts in a single beam. Next, we will analyze the system capacity considering perfect power control and imperfect power control.

In perfect power control, the received signal power of each spacecraft is equal. If the BER is fixed, the system capacity N_{bpsk} per satellite at BPSK modulation can be obtained by Eqs. (8) and (13).

$$N_{BPSK} = 3(L+1)K = \frac{6(L+1)N_c}{fL+1}\left(\frac{1}{Q^{-1}(BER)^2} - \frac{N_0}{2E_b}\right) + 3L + 3 \qquad (14)$$

According to Eqs. (8), (9), (11) and (12), the system capacity N_{DLL} per satellite using the non-coherent delay-locked loop can be obtained.

$$\sigma = \frac{2\Delta}{cT_c} \qquad (15)$$

$$C/N_0 = \frac{4d^2(1-d)B_L + \sqrt{16d^4(1-d)^2B_L^2 + 16d\sigma^2/T}}{2\sigma^2} \qquad (16)$$

$$N_{DLL} = 3(L+1)K = \frac{3(L+1)N_c}{fL+1}\left(\frac{R_b}{(C/N_0)} - \frac{N_0}{E_b}\right) + 3L + 3 \qquad (17)$$

Therefore, the system capacity N per satellite is

$$N = \min\{N_{DLL}, N_{BPSK}\} \tag{18}$$

Compared with the perfect power control, the closed solution of the system capacity in BPSK modulation cannot be obtained because the power control error coefficient α_{j1}. According to Eqs. (8) and (13), the number of users K_{BPSK} in a single beam needs to be satisfied.

$$f \sum_{i=1}^{LK_{BPSK}} \alpha_{i1} + \sum_{j=2}^{K_{BPSK}} \alpha_{j1} \leq 2N_c \left(\frac{1}{Q^{-1}(BER)^2} - \frac{N_0}{2E_b} \right) \tag{19}$$

Equations (15) and (16) are unchanged in the analysis of the existence of power control errors. When the ranging accuracy is constant, the number of users K_{DLL} in a single beam using the non-coherent delay tracking loop needs to be satisfied.

$$f \sum_{i=1}^{LK_{DLL}} \alpha_{i1} + \sum_{j=2}^{K_{DLL}} \alpha_{j1} \leq N_c \left(\frac{R_b}{(C/N_0)} - \frac{N_0}{E_b} \right) \tag{20}$$

Therefore, the system capacity N per satellite is

$$N = \min\{3(L + 1)K_{DLL}, 3(L + 1)K_{BPSK}\} \tag{21}$$

4 Numerical Calculation Results

4.1 Ranging Error in Single Beam Scene

Here we consider the worst case, that is, all spacecrafts are in the same beam, and other beams have no spacecrafts. At this time, the MAI is the strongest and the ranging error is the largest.

Let $R_b = 10$ kbps, $T = 1$ ms, $d = 0.5$, $B_L = 30$ Hz, $R_{j1} = 1$, $\alpha \sim U(0.5, 2)$(dB) [8], K is the number of spacecrafts and it is a parametric variable, and the variation of the ranging error value with E_b/N_0 can be obtained, as shown in Figs. 3 and 4.

It can be seen from Figs. 3 and 4 that the ranging error is less than 1 m when the number of perfect power control and spacecraft is different, as well as power control error exists. When there is power control error, the accuracy of ranging is significantly lower than that of perfect power control. The difference is not so large because $R_{j1} = 1$, which makes the MAI between spacecrafts smaller. In other words, Fig. 4 is the ranging error when the MAI is minimum. Therefore, perfect power control can improve the accuracy of ranging.

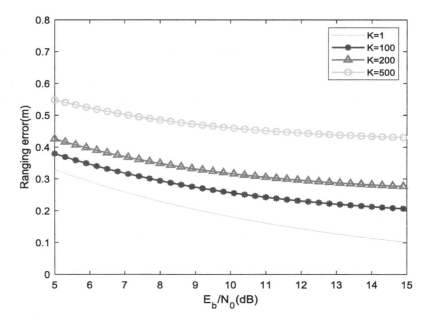

Fig. 3. Ranging error with perfect power control

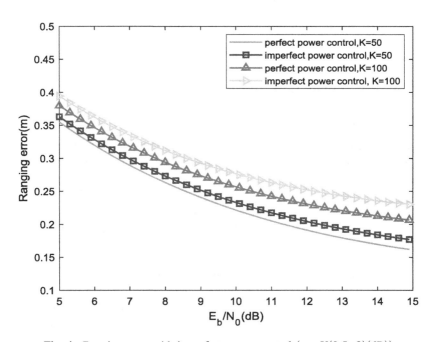

Fig. 4. Ranging error with imperfect power control $(\alpha \sim U(0.5,\ 2)(\text{dB}))$

4.2 The Capacity of the System with Perfect Power Control

Given the BER and ranging accuracy, we can get the curve of capacity per satellite with E_b/N_0. Let $L = 6$, $BER = 10^{-5}$, $\Delta = 0.25$ m, $B_L = 50$ Hz, $N_c = 1023$, $R_c = 10.23$ M chips/s, $R_b = 10$ kbps/s, $f = 0.65$ [9]. The capacity variation curve is shown in Fig. 5.

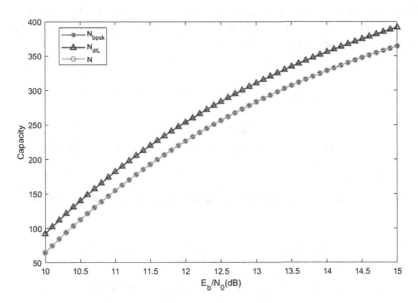

Fig. 5. Capacity with perfect power control

As can be seen from the above figure, the capacity is mainly limited by the BER. Of course, the above result is related to the BER and ranging accuracy. If the accuracy of ranging is improved, the capacity will be mainly limited by the accuracy of ranging. When $E_b/N_0 = 11.4$ dB, the capacity of one satellite is 186, then the total capacity of the three satellites of the panoramic multi-beam satellite telemetry and command System is 558, which meets the needs of 500 targets.

4.3 Capacity with Power Control Error Exists

Since the power error exists, the capacity formula has no closed solution, and the intermediate value is set:

$$V_N = f \sum_{i=1}^{LK} \alpha_{i1} + \sum_{j=2}^{K} \alpha_{j1} \tag{23}$$

$$V_{BPSK} = 2N_c \left(\frac{1}{Q^{-1}(BER)^2} - \frac{N_0}{2E_b} \right) \tag{24}$$

$$V_{DLL} = N_c \left(\frac{R_b}{(C/N_0)} - \frac{N_0}{E_b} \right) \tag{25}$$

Note that in Eqs. (23), (24) and (25), V_N, V_{bpsk}, V_{DLL} is dimensionless. Let $\alpha \sim U(0.5, 2)$(dB), we Simulates 100 times by MATLAB and the numerical calculation result of V_N is shown in Table 2.

Table 2. Numerical calculation result of V_N

Item	Value								
K	3	4	5	6	7	8	9	10	11
V_N	18.33	24.91	31.55	38.07	44.63	51.06	57.74	64.32	70.83

Similarly, the numerical results of V_{BPSK} and V_{DLL} are shown in Table 3.

Table 3. Numerical results of V_{BPSK} and V_{DLL}

Item	Value					
E_b/N_0	10 dB	11 dB	12 dB	13 dB	14 dB	15 dB
V_{BPSK}	10.18	31.22	47.94	61.21	71.76	80.13
V_{DLL}	16.55	37.59	54.30	67.57	78.12	86.49

Therefore, the system of panoramic multi-beam satellite telemetry and command System is shown in Table 4.

Table 4. Numerical result of one satellite capacity

Item	Value					
E_b/N_0	10 dB	11 dB	12 dB	13 dB	14 dB	15 dB
Capacity	<63	84	147	189	231	>231

As can be seen from the above figure, the capacity is mainly limited by the BER. When $E_b/N_0 = 13$ dB, the capacity of one satellite is 189, then the total capacity of the three satellites of the panoramic multi-beam satellite telemetry and command System is 567, which meets the needs of 500 targets and performance deteriorates by 1.6 dB than perfect power control.

5 Conclusion

Based on the panoramic multi-beam satellite measurement and control system, this paper analyzes the ranging error in the presence of MAI, and analyzes the system capacity when the range accuracy and BER are limited. The results show that for perfect power control, MAI will deteriorate the ranging accuracy, but less than 1 m; when power control error occurs, it will be more deteriorated. When the system capacity is 500, the performance of imperfect power error is 1.6 dB worse than the perfect power control.

References

1. Simon, M.: Noncoherent Pseudo-noise code tracking performance of spread spectrum receivers. IEEE Trans. Commun. **25**(3), 327–345 (1977)
2. Fu, H., Bi, G., Arichandran, K.: Performance of multi-beam CDMA-based LEO satellite systems in a Rice-lognormal channel. IEEE Commun. Lett. **3**(4), 88–90 (1999)
3. Tang, Y., Guo, X., Wang, Y.: Research on performance of phase discriminator in code tracking loop inside spaceborne distance measurement transceiver. In: Proceedings 2013 International Conference on Mechatronic Sciences, Electric Engineering and Computer (MEC), Shengyang, pp. 2751–2755 (2013)
4. Colavolpe, G., Modenini, A., Piemontese, A., Ugolini, A.: Multiuser detection in multibeam satellite systems: theoretical analysis and practical schemes. IEEE Trans. Commun. **65**(2), 945–955 (2017)
5. Tian, Z.C.: Spread Spectrum Communication, pp. 57–67. Tsinghua University Press, Beijing (2007)
6. Fu, X.: Research on accuracy of pseudo-ranging under complex channel environment. Master. D. Diss. Harbin Institute of Technology, pp. 26–27 (2010)
7. Li, H.: Principles and Design Methods of Deep Space TT&C system, pp. 195–196. Tsinghua University Press, Beijing (2014)
8. Wu, S.: Uplink multiple access interference and capacity of WCDMA GEO satellite communication system. J. Tsinghua Univ. (Sci. Technol.) **50**(10), 1660–1663 (2010)
9. Zhang, J.: Research on satellite CDMA link performance and system capacity. Master. D. Diss. University of Electronic Science and Technology of China, pp. 47–48 (2005)

Markov Decision Based Optimization on Bundle Size for Halo Orbit-Relay Earth-Lunar DTNs

Yunlai Xu[1,2], Ye Wang[1,2], Zhihua Yang[1,2(✉)], Shushi Gu[1], Yue Li[1], and Peng Yuan[1]

[1] Communication Engineering Research Center, Harbin Institute of Technology, Shenzhen 518055, Guangdong, China
{xuyunlai,liyue}@stu.hit.edu.cn,
{wangye83,yangzhihua,gushushi,yuanpeng}@hit.edu.cn
[2] Pengcheng Laboratory, Shenzhen 518055, Guangdong, China

Abstract. Earth-Lunar communications are important for lunar exploration. Among them, Halo orbit relay satellite communications networks are extremely valuable. However, due to the highly dynamic and long-distance transmission characteristics, Halo Orbit-relay Earth-Lunar Disruption-Tolerant Networks (DTNs) have to endure severe latency. In order to deal with this problem, we propose a new solution that overcomes the impact of transmission characteristics by adjusting bundle size, thereby effectively reducing the latency of the Earth-Lunar relay communication networks. Considering the transmission characteristics and the deep space environment, we derive the delay formula of the Halo Orbit-relay Earth-Lunar DTNs and establish the distance model. In particular, in order to solve this model, we propose a Markov decision method. Finally, the simulation results verify the effectiveness of the Markov decision method.

Keywords: Earth-Lunar communications · Halo orbit · DTN · Markov decision

1 Introduction

With the proposal of the lunar exploration program in various countries, the Earth-Lunar communications have become one of the research hot spots. At present, the use of relay satellites of the Earth-Lunar system (L2) has attracted the interest of numerous countries [1]. Specially, China has carried out flight verification.

Special motion characteristics of the lunar cause an interruption in the communications between the back of the lunar and the earth. Therefore, the deployment of relay satellites has become an effective mean of establishing real-time communications between the earth and the back of the lunar. At this stage, the

M. Jia et al. (Eds.): WiSATS 2019, LNICST 280, pp. 572–586, 2019.
https://doi.org/10.1007/978-3-030-19153-5_58

proposed lunar relay satellites are mainly lunar orbits, including elliptical orbit constellations, polar circular orbit constellations, inclined circular orbit constellations, etc. However, the above methods cannot enable real-time communications between the back of the lunar and the earth. Through recent studies, it is found that L2 point of the earth and lunar has unique geographical and dynamic characteristics. Specially, Halo orbit is completely unaffected by the lunar occlusion under certain conditions. Therefore, it is an ideal location to establish a relay satellite for the earth and the lunar. In summary, we use L2 point Halo orbit as a relay satellite orbit.

In Halo Orbit-relay Earth-Lunar DTNs [2], the relative distances among the earth, satellite and the lunar change instantly with satellites orbital motions, which will cause correspondingly time-varying properties of channel parameters. The authors in [3] use the DTN network to introduce the bundle layer protocol layer, which is located between the application layer and the protocol layer. In general, bundles stored for a long time can be used to overcome frequent link interruptions, long transmission distances, and high bit error rates. Recently, lots of works have studied on the optimization of bundle size in quasi-static scenarios [4], such as wireless sensor networks and social multimedia networks, which almost consider the channel parameters as constant values in the design of bundle delivery [5]. As a result, fixed optimal size of the bundle also leads to inefficiency of link usage and long latency of delivery, due to incapability of filling up different contacts during orbital motions of intermediate nodes. Therefore, we use Markov decision method to optimize the bundle size of Halo Orbit-relay Earth-Lunar DTNs [6]. The general process is shown in Fig. 1.

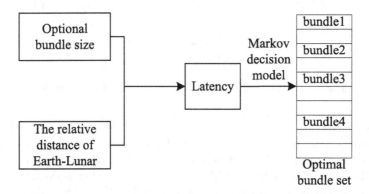

Fig. 1. Acquisition process of optimal bundle set.

The main contributions of this work is to reduce the communications latency of the Earth-Lunar relay communication networks by adjusting bundle size. (a) First, based on the particularity of the earth and the lunar environment, we derive a delay formula that is only related to the bundle size and the distance. (b) Then, we use Halo orbit to establish the distance model of the Earth-Lunar relay communication networks. (c) Finally, the model is solved based on Markov decision to obtain the optimal bundle size.

The rest of the paper is structured as follows: The second part establishes the system model. The third part describes the bundle transmission model and the delay metric, followed by Markov decision model in the fourth part. The simulation results are placed in the fifth part. Finally, the conclusions are given.

2   System Model

2.1   Reference Scenario

We consider the information transmission scenario of the earth to the lunar, in which a relay satellite is configured up to provide communications between the earth and the lunar. In such a scenario, the source node of information is referred to as a source node (SN), such as an earth base station, and a relay node (RN) capable of implementing information forwarding, such as a lunar relay satellite. On the other hand, the recipient of the target file is called a destination node (DN), such as a probe car or base on the back of the lunar. In particular, Earth-Lunar L2 point Halo orbit is periodic, and the relay satellite can be used to achieve full coverage of lunar back, providing real-time uninterrupted communications with the earth.

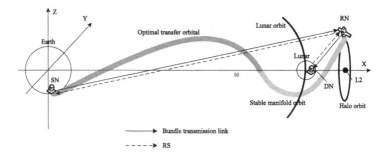

Fig. 2. Earth-lunar Halo orbit relay communication model.

Figure 2 describes the use of L2 point Halo orbit as a relay satellite orbit in communications between the earth and the lunar. The earth base station generates a transmission file as the source node SN, and the file is transmitted to the relay node RN in blocks. After receiving, the relay node RN transmits an acknowledgement signal RS to the source node SN for determining whether the file is successfully transmitted. The relay node RN sends the successfully received file block to the lunar back destination node DN, and at the same time obtains the returned acknowledgement signal RS.

Figure 3 describes the DTN network bundle forwarding flow for Earth-Lunar communications.

In summary, Earth-Lunar two-hop link is highly dynamic, and there is a very large distance difference, which will cause a great delay and reduce the link throughput. Aiming at such problems, we will propose a DTN network bundle size optimization method based on Markov decision.

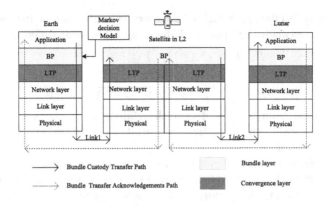

Fig. 3. Bundle forwarding mode.

2.2   Halo Orbit Relay Distance Model

Firstly, it is necessary to establish a distance model of Earth-Lunar communication networks. The direction of the earth and the lunar is the x-axis, the normal direction of the white plane is the y-axis, and the right-handed spiral determines the z-axis. L_{se} indicates the distances between the earth and the relay satellite, and L_{sm} indicates the distances between the lunar and the relay satellite. The specific model diagram is as follows.

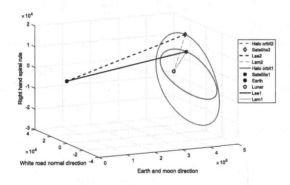

Fig. 4. Earth-Lunar distance model.

As showed in the Fig. 4, the model selects two Halo orbits of different magnitude in the Halo orbital family. At the same time, it is guaranteed that the communications between the relay satellites and the earth in the two Halo orbits are not affected by the lunar mask. In particular, the same set of distance calculation formulas can be used for these two orbits. The coordinates of the relay satellite are represented by $(X(t), Y(t), Z(t))$, and the distance between the earth and the lunar is 384400 km, which can respectively obtain the distance formula of the distance between the lunar and the relay satellite at different times.

$$L_{se}(t) = \sqrt{X(t)^2 + Y(t)^2 + Z(t)^2} \tag{1}$$

and

$$L_{sm}(t) = \sqrt{X(t - 384400)^2 + Y(t)^2 + Z(t)^2} \tag{2}$$

It can be seen from the Fig. 4 that the Halo orbit is the key to the whole model, and the establishment of the Halo orbit needs to be converted from the Earth-Lunar coordinate system to the rotating coordinate system centered on the L2 point. Such a rotating coordinate system can be expressed as $L_2 - \varepsilon\eta\zeta$, and the L2 point is the origin. The direction of the earth pointing to the lunar is the ε axis, the direction of the normal of the white plane is the ζ axis, and the η axis is determined by the right-handed spiral law, and the equation of motion of the satellite is obtained. In particular, we can determine the satellite coordinates by the orbit equation.

$$\begin{cases} \ddot{\varepsilon} - 2\dot{\eta} - (1 + 2c_2)\varepsilon = \frac{\partial}{\partial\varepsilon} \sum_{n\geq3} c_n\rho^n P_n(\frac{\varepsilon}{\rho}) \\ \ddot{\eta} + 2\dot{\varepsilon} - (1 - c_2)\eta = \frac{\partial}{\partial\eta} \sum_{n\geq3} c_n\rho^n P_n(\frac{\varepsilon}{\rho}) \\ \ddot{\zeta} + c_2 = \frac{\partial}{\partial\zeta} \sum_{n\geq3} c_n\rho^n P_n(\frac{\varepsilon}{\rho}) \end{cases} \tag{3}$$

For the L2 point, the c_n in the equation is expressed as follows.

$$\begin{cases} c_2 = \frac{\mu}{\gamma^3} + \frac{(1-\mu)}{(1+\gamma^3)} \\ c_n = \frac{1}{\gamma}[(-1)^n\mu + (-1)^n(1 - \mu)(\frac{\gamma}{1+\gamma^{n+1}})], (n \geq 3) \end{cases} \tag{4}$$

The Richardson third-order approximate solution of the motion equation in this coordinate system is derived by the Lindstedt-Poincare method.

$$\begin{cases} \dot{\varepsilon} = \alpha w cos\tau - 2(a_{23}\alpha^2 - a_{24}\beta^2)w sin2\tau - 3(a_{31}\alpha^3 - a_{32}\alpha\beta^2)w sin3\tau \\ \dot{\eta} = k\alpha w cos\tau + 2(b_{21}\alpha^2 - b_{22}\beta^2)w cos2\tau + 3(b_{31}\alpha^3 - b_{32}\alpha\beta^2)w cos3\tau \\ \dot{\zeta} = -\beta w sin\tau - 2d_{21}\alpha\beta w sin2\tau - 3(d_{32}\beta\alpha^2 - d_{31}\beta^3)w sin3\tau \end{cases} \tag{5}$$

The coefficients in the formula are as follows.

$$\begin{cases} \tau = wt + \varphi \\ w = w_0 + w_1 + w_2 \\ w_0 = \sqrt{(\sqrt{9c_2^2 - 8c_2} - c_2 + 2)/2} \\ w_1 = 0 \\ w_2 = s_1\alpha^2 + s_2\beta^2 \end{cases} \tag{6}$$

The amplitude satisfies the relationship.

$$\begin{cases} l_1\alpha^2 + l_2\beta^2 + (w_0^2 - v_0^2) = 0 \\ l_1 = -\frac{3}{2}c_3(2a_{21} + a_{23} + 5d_{21}) - \frac{3}{8}(12 - k^2) + 2w_0^2 s_1 \\ l_2 = \frac{3}{2}c_3(a_{24} - 2a_{22}) + \frac{9}{8}c_4 + 2w_0^2 s_2 \\ v_0 = \sqrt{c_2} \end{cases} \tag{7}$$

These coefficients constitute a complete third-order analytical solution equation, and the final Halo orbit is obtained by Matlab. The variables are defined as shown in the following table (Table 1).

Table 1. Orbital equation coefficient

Coefficient	Definition
μ	Dimensional lunar mass
γ	L2 point to the lunar distance
ω_0	Linear frequency
α, β	Amplitude in all directions
k	Linear term amplitude ratio
$a_{21} \sim a_{32}$	Constant
$b_{21} \sim b_{35}$	Constant
$d_{21} \sim d_{32}$	Constant

2.3 Problem Definition

In the Earth-Lunar communication scenarios, the delay reduction problem of the two-hop link can be expressed as the bundle size adjustment problem of the DTN network [7]. Abstract formula is as follows.

$$S_l = \arg \min_b RTT_{all} \tag{8}$$

and

$$RTT_{all} = RTT_{se} + RTT_{sm} \tag{9}$$

According to the distance model of the previous part, the distance set L of the Earth-Lunar two-hop link is obtained, and B is a given optional bundle set. In which, $l \in L$ and $b \in B$. As can be seen from the formula, we give a two-hop link distances l, and then select the bundle size that minimizes RTT_{all} from b to form the optimal bundle set. In summary, after derivation, the latency of the two-hop links is only related to the distance and the size of the bundle. After the distance is fixed, the latency can be reduced by adjusting the size of the bundle. Among them, random factors such as an optional bundle set and distance can be characterized by a Markov model, so we model the adjustment of bundle size into a Markov decision process. The specific latency derivation process is explained in the next part.

3 Bundle Delivery Time over Halo Orbit-Relay Two-Hop Link

It can be observed in the figure that the DTN network is used in the Halo orbit two-hop delay system to transmit information through the bundle [8]. Due to the large distance differences between the Earth-Lunar two-hop link, it is necessary to select the optimal bundle size through the change of the distances, adapting to the entire end-to-end Earth-Lunar communication networks, and reducing the latency to improve the throughput [9].

According to the change in the distances between the two-hop link, the two-hop link latency is obtained by the delay calculation formula, and then the Markov decision is used to obtain the optimal bundle size for different distances.

Next, the calculation formula of the single-hop link delay is analyzed. Generally, the propagation delay, the transmission delay of the bundle and ACK, the queuing delay and the random delay are included in one RTT process [10]. The Fig. 5 shows the round trip transmission process of the single-hop bundle.

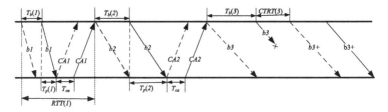

Fig. 5. Bundle delivery time.

In the most ideal communication situation, a bundle is successfully received by the next node after transmission, and no retransmission is required [11]. In this scenario, it can be seen from the above figure that the single-hop link delay is mainly composed of transmission delay $T_b(i)$ and propagation $T_p(i)$ delay. The RTT of a bundle at a certain time t can be expressed as follows.

$$RTT(t) = 2T_p(t) + T_{ca} + T_b(t) + T_{random} \qquad (10)$$

However, the actual situation is not so ideal. Space communication often has a high bit error rate. It can also be seen from the figure that b3 has lost packets during transmission. Once a packet loss occurs, it needs to be retransmitted. The number of transmissions determines the different round-trip time. In this paper, for the sake of analysis, if the packet loss occurs, the round-trip delay of the bundle is equal to the value of the storage timer CTRT confirmed by the bundle set in advance, and the two cases are combined. You can get a general round-trip delays expectation expression [12].

$$RTT_{ev}(t) = (1 - P_{ef}(t)) \cdot RTT(t) + P_{ef}(t) \cdot CTRT(t) \qquad (11)$$

in which

$$CTRT(t) = 2 \cdot T_p(t) + T_{ca} \qquad (12)$$

The packet loss rate $P_{ef}(t)$ is determined by the size of the bundle and the bit error rate.

$$P_{ef}(t) = 1 - (1 - BER(t))^{b \cdot L_{bundle}} \tag{13}$$

Among them, $BER(t)$ is expressed as the bit error rate at time t, and the underlying bit error rate is determined by the modulation technique and the signal-to-noise ratio. In this paper, if BPSK modulation is selected, the bit error rate can be expressed follows.

$$BER(t) = \frac{1}{2} \times erfc(\sqrt{SNR(t)}) \tag{14}$$

$BER(t)$ is the signal-to-noise ratio at link t, and the signal-to-noise ratio is determined by the parameters of the spatial channel. In order to facilitate the analysis, this paper will consider the factor that has less influence on the signal-to-noise ratio as a constant, and use spatial free loss as the main cause of the dynamic change of signal-to-noise ratio.

$$SNR(t) = E_0 - 10lgL_{space}(t) \tag{15}$$

The expected value of the bundle round-trip delay is expressed as follows.

$$RTT_{se}(t) = (1 - \frac{1}{2}erfc(\sqrt{C_0 - 20lgL_{se}(t)}))^{L_{bundle}} \cdot$$
$$(2 \cdot T_p(t) + T_b(t) + T_{ca} + T_{random}) + (1 - (1 - \tag{16}$$
$$\frac{1}{2}erfc(\sqrt{C_0 - 20lgL_{se}(t)}))^{L_{bundle}}) \cdot CTRT(t)$$

and

$$RTT_{sm}(t) = (1 - \frac{1}{2}erfc(\sqrt{C_0 - 20lgL_{se}(t)}))^{L_{bundle}} \cdot$$
$$(2 \cdot T_p(t) + T_b(t) + T_{ca} + T_{random}) + (1 - (1 - \tag{17}$$
$$\frac{1}{2}erfc(\sqrt{C_0 - 20lgL_{sm}(t)}))^{L_{bundle}}) \cdot CTRT(t)$$

The comprehensive delay of the two-hop link between the earth and the lunar is as follows.

$$RTT_{all}(t) = RTT_{se}(t) + RTT_{sm}(t) \tag{18}$$

In summary, the delay is only related to the distance of the two-hop link. The meaning of the parameters used in the formula is shown in the following table (Table 2).

Table 2. Bundle delay calculation parameter

Coefficient	Definitions
T_p	Propagation delay
T_b	Transmission time of bundle
T_{ca}	Transmission time of ACK signal
P_{ef}	Bundle lost probability
P_e	Bit error probability
L_{bundle}	Bundle size
SNR	Signal to noise ratio
E_0	Sum of constant variables
RTT_{all}	End-to-end delay
T_{random}	Random noise

4   Markov Decision

First of all, we have specified the number of retransmissions of the bundle of the Earth-Lunar communications, and found that the next retransmission probability is independent of the previous, satisfying the Markov property. By defining state sets and behavior sets, Markov decision can be used to derive optimal bundle size set from the cost function. The general process is shown in Fig. 6 (Table 3).

Table 3. Bundle delay calculation parameter

Notations	Definitions
M	State set
A	Action set
S_c, S_c'	Current states of the links
p, p'	Maximum number of retransmissions
P_s, P_s'	The probability of successful transmission
B_s	Optional bundle set
B_f	Optimal bundle set
a	Picked bundle size
p_{max}	Maximum number of retransmissions
v, v'	The latency of two links

We set a state set M, which contains two states M_0 and M_1. M_0 indicates that there is no bundle in the storage device of the relay satellite, and M_1 represents that a complete bundle is being stored in the storage device. According to S_c,

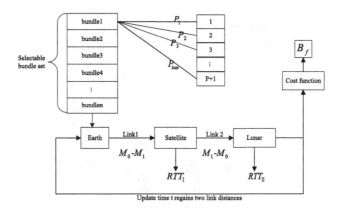

Fig. 6. Markov process.

we can choose different bundle sizes from A, which can minimize the $v + v'$. The probability of successful transmission and the cost function is as follows.

$$P_s = (1 - P_{ef}) \cdot P_{ef}^{p-1} \tag{19}$$

and

$$C = RTT(S_c, A) + (p - 1) \times CTRT(S_c, A) \tag{20}$$

The specific steps of Markov decision are as follows.

Algorithm 1. Markov Decision

Input: M_0, M_1
Output: the optimal bundle set B_f
 1: **for** $S_c, S_c' \in M$ **do**
 2:     $(P_s, p) \leftarrow S_c$;
 3:     $(P_s', p') \leftarrow S_c'$;
 4:     **if** $(p \le p_{max}) \cup (p' \le p_{max})$ **then**
 5:         **for** $a \in A$ **do**
 6:             $C \leftarrow \sum_a P_s \times (r(p, a) + v'(S_n))$;
 7:             $C' \leftarrow \sum_a P_s' \times (r(p', a) + v(S_n))$;
 8:         **end for**
 9:         $B_f \leftarrow \arg\min_a (v + v')$;
10:     **end if**
11:     $Refresh(S_c, S_c')$;
12: **end for**

---

5   Numerical Results

In this part, we compare the performance of the end-to-end latency of the bundle. Through the orbit equation, the satellite coordinates needed to calculate the

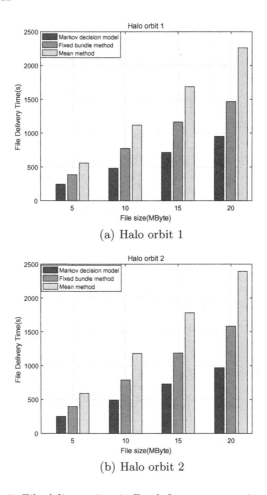

(a) Halo orbit 1

(b) Halo orbit 2

Fig. 7. File delivery time in Earth-Lunar communication.

distance are obtained. In the simulation, we assume that CA_j is a constant, and it takes 7.5 days for the satellite to fly around the Halo orbit. In addition, the number of transmission rounds can be calculated by the bundle loss probability P_{ef}. In general, as the number of transmission rounds increases, the probability of transmission failure decreases exponentially. When the probability of failure is lower than a limit, we believe that the bundle has been successfully transmitted. In this article, we define the threshold to 0.001. So, we can get the number of transmission rounds of a bundle. If the number of transmission rounds is greater than the maximum, we think that such a bundle size is not acceptable.

In Fig. 7, the scene is defined as the Halo orbit relay communication networks with a maximum number of retransmissions of 6. Among them, the amplitude of the Halo orbit selected by the Fig. 7(b) is larger than that of the Fig. 7(a). Then, for two different Halo orbit relay environments, we choose the fixed bundle method and the median method as comparisons respectively. The fixed bundle method is to select an optimal bundle value through a fixed set of link parameters. On the other hand, the media method is to average latency of all optional bundle sizes for the same file size. If the bundle size selected in the current link state cannot be transmitted because of exceeding the maximum number of retransmissions. Therefore, the proposed method is required to wait for the next sampling time to arrive, which results in an additional sampling time in the file transmission latency. Comparing the results of Fig. 7, we can find that facing different Halo orbits, Markov decision can obtain lower delay than the other two methods. At the same time, with the increase in file size, such optimization is more obvious, which is very suitable for Earth-Lunar communications in the future. In particular, we find that the median method has a higher latency growth rate than the fixed bundle method, because in the face of long-distance communication, the extra delay caused by the size of the bundle that cannot be transmitted at all is greatly affected.

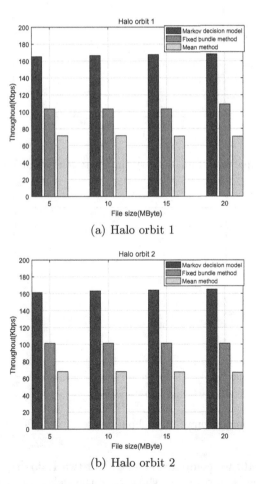

(a) Halo orbit 1

(b) Halo orbit 2

Fig. 8. Throughput in Earth-Lunar communication.

In Fig. 8(a) and (b), we choose the throughput metric to measure the effects of different optimization methods under two scenarios. In Fig. 8(a), the parameters are same as Fig. 7(a), while the scenarios and channel parameters in Fig. 8(b) are same as Fig. 7(b). The results show that using a fixed bundle size or using the median method yields less throughput than using Markov decision. One reason is that the optimal bundle size in the fixed state may be not the optimal size after the changing of the link state. On the other hand, for the median method, the selected bundle size may not be able to transmit at all on this link. Therefore, the extra latency has a higher impact in the Earth-Lunar communication networks, resulting in low throughput.

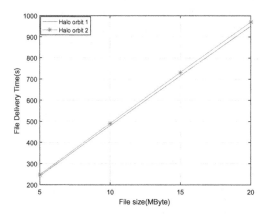

Fig. 9. The comparison of file delivery time between two different Halo orbits.

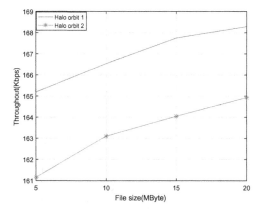

Fig. 10. The comparison of throughput between two different Halo orbits.

In Figs. 9 and 10, we compare the effects of two Halo orbits on latency and throughput. In Fig. 9, the results show that the delay gap increases with the increase in file size. In Fig. 10, the results show that Halo orbit 1 act as a relay orbit with a smooth increase in throughput compared to Halo orbit 2. The reason for the above results is that the distance among Halo orbit 1 and the earth and the lunar is relatively smaller than that of Halo orbit 2, resulting in a smaller transmission loss of the bundle. On the other hand, for files of the same size, low latency can achieve higher throughput.

6   Conclusion

In this paper, we proposed a Markov decision base optimization model to achieve optimal bundle size for bundle end-to-end delivery over the Halo Orbit-relay Earth-Lunar DTNs. For different Earth-Lunar distances, Markov decision will choose different size of the bundle for transmission. Moreover, by comparing Markov decision, fixed bundle method and the mean method respectively, the simulation results show that the disadvantages of other two methods are more and more obvious with the increasing of file size. However, the proposed Markov decision model can effectively reduce file end-to-end latency and increase throughput.

Acknowledgment. The authors would like to express their high appreciations to the supports from the National Natural Sciences Foundation of China (61501140, 61701136, 91538110 and 61831008), and Natural Science Foundation of Guangdong Province (2016A030313661).

References

1. Liu, L., Hu, C., Wang, M., Wang, Y.: Maintenance of earth-moon halo orbit. In: Chinese Control Conference, pp. 5969–5974 (2017)
2. Caini, C., Fiore, V.: Moon to earth DTN communications through lunar relay satellites. In: Advanced Satellite Multimedia Systems Conference, pp. 89–95 (2012)
3. Alfonzo, M., Fraire, J.A., Kocian, E., Alvarez, N.: Development of a DTN bundle protocol convergence layer for spacewire. In: Biennial Congress of Argentina, pp. 770–775 (2014)
4. Yang, Z., Wang, R., Yu, Q., Sun, X.: Analytical characterization of licklider transmission protocol (LTP) in cislunar communications. IEEE Trans. Aerosp. Electron. Syst. **50**(3), 2019–2031 (2014)
5. Yuan, D., Liu, Y., Bai, Y.: A DTN bundle implementation based on UDP in satellite sensor network. In: IEEE International Conference on Communication Technology, pp. 223–226 (2010)
6. Li, Y., Wang, Y., Yuan, P., Yang, Z.: Markov decision based optimization on bundle size for satellite DTN links. IET Commun. **12**(9), 1048–1054 (2018)
7. Magaia, N., et al.: Bundles fragmentation in vehicular delay-tolerant networks. In: EURO-NGI Conference on Next Generation Internet Networks, pp. 1–6 (2011)
8. Scott, K.: Bundle protocol specification. IETF RFC (2007)

9. Wang, W., et al.: DTN-KNCA: a high throughput routing based on contact pattern detection in DTNs. In: IEEE Computer Software and Applications Conference, pp. 926–931 (2018)

10. Yu, Q., et al.: Modeling RTT for DTN protocol over asymmetric cislunar space channels. IEEE Syst. J. **10**(2), 556–567 (2016)

11. Bezirgiannidis, N., Burleigh, S., Tsaoussidis, V.: Delivery time estimation for space bundles. IEEE Trans. Aerosp. Electron. Syst. **49**(3), 1897–1910 (2013)

12. Samaras, C.V., Tsaoussidis, V.: Adjusting transport segmentation policy of DTN bundle protocol under synergy with lower layers. J. Syst. Softw. **84**(2), 226–237 (2011)

A Link-Prediction Based Multi-CDSs Scheduling Mechanism for FANET Topology Maintenance

Xiaohan Qi[1], Xinyi Gu[1], Qinyu Zhang[1], and Zhihua Yang[1,2(✉)]

[1] Communication Engineering Research Center, Harbin Institute of Technology,
Shenzhen 518055, Guangdong, China
yangzhihua@hit.edu.cn
[2] Pengcheng Laboratory, Shenzhen 518055, Guangdong, China

Abstract. In Flying Ad hoc Network (FANET), maintenance of topology is a quite difficult task due to rapid change of connectivity between flight nodes, i.e. unmanned aerial vehicles (UAVs). Aiming to this issue, in this article, we proposed a link prediction-based multiple Connected Dominating Sets (CDSs) scheduling mechanism for stable maintenance of FANET's topology. In particular, a group of candidate CDSs are periodically scheduled for developing a stable backbone subnet of the topology. The proposed mechanism could achieve an early detection of topological changes by employing a Markov chain predicting model on the node's mobility. The simulation results show that the proposed algorithm has a better success rate and less update overheads than the single CDS maintenance method, especially in a typical swarm pattern of UAV team.

Keywords: FANET · Connected dominated set · Link-prediction · Swarm

1 Introduction

Typically, flying ad hoc network (FANET) is a specific category of self-organizing networked systems with a group of swarming unmanned aerial vehicles (UAVs) [1,2], which is widely exploited for remoting sensing, surveillance and emergency communication scenes. With un-even node density, FANET develops a highly dynamic topology with unreliable links due to fast relative motions of UAV nodes, which has caused adverse effects on the maintenance of the network. Currently, virtual backbone network (VBN) is introduced for providing an effective way to maintain the time-related topological stability, i.e. in mobile sensor networks and general ad hoc networks.

At present, constructing methods of VBN are developed into two main categories, such as hierarchically clustering and connected dominating set (CDS). Comparatively, connected dominating set, with less dominating nodes, could provide a smaller scale of backbone network than the clustering method. Therefore,

© ICST Institute for Computer Sciences, Social Informatics and Telecommunications Engineering 2019
Published by Springer Nature Switzerland AG 2019. All Rights Reserved
M. Jia et al. (Eds.): WiSATS 2019, LNICST 280, pp. 587–601, 2019.
https://doi.org/10.1007/978-3-030-19153-5_59

CDS is considered as a preferable candidate solution for constructing a backbone network for FANET. Considering the constrained transmission power of UAV platform, a smaller connected dominating set, thus a slighter scale of VBN, is quite expected for greatly reducing the forwarding overheads of messages during routine communications [3,4]. More heavily, the topology of FANET will change with time due to highly relative motions of nodes, leading to a lower operating efficiency and possible failure of the backbone network. As a result, it is indispensable for constantly monitoring and maintaining the backbone network after the construction of VBN to resist the dynamic of topology. Currently, there exists a lot of works on the topology maintenance of mobile sensor networks [5,6], most of which focus on guaranteeing the connectivity of the backbone network and extend the network lifetime as long as possible. In [7], a k-hop CDS constructing algorithm is proposed, in which the cost and stability of algorithm are closely depending on the value of k without an optimal solution. Mainly, a part of existing maintenance algorithms are dedicated for improving the fault tolerance of the backbone network by a couple of approaches, i.e., adjusting the relationship of nodes and controlling node's transmission power. This type of topology control algorithms with fault-tolerant capability include active and passive modes. Among them, the active algorithm includes power control [8] and network hierarchical partitioning respectively, which mainly consider the fault tolerance of VBN construction. On the other side, the passive topology control algorithm attempt to find a k-connected graph of the topology. In [9], the problem of solving the least cost k-connected graph is proved to be NP-hard, in which the value of k is constrained by the maximum transmission power of node.

Although there are a variety of works discussing on the control and maintenance of topology in diversified scenarios, most of them are aiming to guarantee the connectivity of the backbone network in a relatively quasi-static condition, without considering the dynamic of topology and motion characteristic of in-situ platform. To address this issue, in this paper, we propose a link-prediction based multi-CDSs scheduling mechanism for effective maintenance of FANET topology. The contributions of this paper are as follows: (a) we developed a novel scheduling mechanism of multiple CDSs for constructing a stable VBN. The proposed mechanism could achieve a constantly virtual backbone for the time-changing topology by periodically recruiting a group of candidate CDSs; (b) we proposed a Markov chain-based link-prediction model of connectivity state between nodes by considering the Markovian property of UAV mobility, which could achieve an early detection of topological changes of FANET, especially with a swarming motion pattern. As a result, the proposed maintenance algorithm could obviously reduce the communication overheads and achieve a high success rate with a small time delay.

The remainder of the paper is organized as follows. Section 2 defines the topology model and formulates the problem, the proposed algorithm is detailed in Sect. 3. Section 4 presents the simulation results and Sect. 5 gives the conclusion.

2   Problem Formulation

2.1   Topology Model

For the convenience of analysis, we assume that each UAV node in FANET has the same communication range. Typically, we define an undirected graph $G\left(V^t, E^t\right)$ to represent the network topology at the t-th time slot. In the graph, V^t represents the set of nodes at time t, denoted by $V^t = \{v_1, v_2, v_3, \ldots, v_n\}$, and E^t is the edges with bi-directional connection at time t, denoted by $E^t = \{e_1, e_2, e_3 \ldots e_n\}$, respectively. For less communication overheads, we will adopt a minimum spanning tree based algorithm to obtain a minimum connected dominating set in order to obtain a small scale of VBN. Firstly, we give a group of preliminary definitions of CDS.

Definition 1. Dominating Set (DS). Given graph $G = (V, E)$, V is a DS of $G = (V, E)$, only if $\forall (u, v) \in E$, either $u \in V'$ or $v \in V'$ is true.

Definition 2. Connected Dominating Set (CDS). $C \subseteq V$ is a CDS of G if (1) C is a DS and (2) a graph induced by C is connected.

Definition 3. Degree of node. For node u in graph $G = (V, E)$, the number of neighbors of u is defined as the degree of u, denoted by $D(u)$.

The VBN constructing algorithm is based on the minimum spanning tree and local routing information. The backbone network can achieve a smaller scale and reduce routing overheads through the algorithm. The selection criterion of the nodes in CDS is the weight of nodes. When conflict occurs in weight of nodes, the edge weight is chosen as the new criteria. Therefore, we set the weight definitions of nodes and edges below.

Definition 4. Weigh of node. For node u in graph $G = (V, E)$, the node weight of u is defined as the weighting summation of $D(u)$ and energy of node $E(u)$, denoted by $W(u) = \alpha D(u) + \beta E(u)$, and $\alpha + \beta = 1$.

Definition 5. Weigh of edge. For edge $\langle u, v \rangle$ in graph $G = (V, E)$, the summaion of $D(u)$ and $D(v)$ is defined as the weight of edge, denoted by $W(\langle u, v \rangle)$.

2.2   Problem Formulation

Without loss of generality, we assume that the initial topology graph is connected, which means each node has a reachable path to any other node in the network. The topology will change with intermittent links due to temporal motions of UAV nodes, i.e., join, sojourn and leave the network, leading to a fragile connectivity of backbone network. Typically, three main types of topological changes are frequently encountered during the swarm flight of a FANET, as shown in Fig. 1.

(1) The node of the backbone network is failed.
(2) The link of the backbone is disconnected.
(3) The dominatee exits the network.

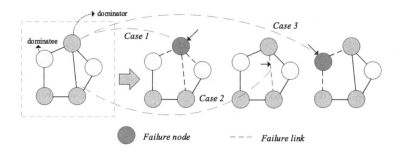

Fig. 1. Topological changes.

As a result, it is scarcely possible for maintaining a stable virtual backbone by only single CDS during a long time. To address this issue, we introduce a novel multiple CDSs based maintenance by reasonably scheduling multiple CDSs in a duration of network operation as long as possible. Firstly, as discussed in the previous section, a smaller connected dominating set is expected since it could easily maintain the connectivity with less communication overheads. In this paper, therefore, we will construct a minimum dominating set with the minimum spanning tree algorithm. The notation employed are illustrated in Table 1.

Moreover, triggering the proposed maintenance algorithm in time is quite indispensable for ensuring the stability of the VBN. The proposed mechanism includes two subsequent phases: the construction of connection dominating sets and the maintenance of VBN. If current VBN is failure, resulting in disconnections of relevant links, the duty backbone cannot guarantee the normal communication connectivity between nodes. Therefore, it is essential to invoke another candidate CDS on duty in time with a feasible schedule, in order to ensure continual effectiveness of the backbone network.

In particular, we define two well-tailored metrics to evaluate the proposed algorithm, i.e., update overhead and successful update rate, respectively.

Update Overhead. The update overheads of CDS is defined as the total overheads of broadcasting messages during the detection and updating phases in a complete working time.

$$T_{cost} = \sum_i P_{t_i}(C_{t_i} \to NC_{t_i}) \tag{1}$$

where $C_{t_i} \to NC_{t_i}$ represents the change of nodes and edges in current CDS on duty at time t_i, in which C_{t_i} represents the status of current CDS on duty, and NC_{t_i} represents the status of CDS to-be-on-duty if the backbone changes, and $P_{t_i}(C_{t_i} \to NC_{t_i})$ is the overheads incurred during the updating phase at i-th time slot, respectively.

Table 1. Notation description

Notation	Representation of the symbol or symbol
S_{cds}	The set of CDSs in the graph
$ESm^{t_c}(S_{cds})$	CDS with maximum energy at time t_c
$Em^{t_c}(cds_i)$	energy of CDS_i
V_{bn}	Nodes in CDS_{ct}
E_{bn}	Links of nodes in CDS_{ct}
$N_1(v)$	Node lists in $v's$ one-hop range
$N_2(v)$	Node lists in $v's$ two-hop range
$v.parent$	Dominator of v
$Nlist(v)$	Neighbor list of v
$Domlist(v)$	Dominator nodes in $N_1(v)$
CDS_{ct}	The CDS of graph at current time
CDS_{bc}	The backup CDS
T_{cost}	Update overheads of the network
P_{srt}	Total successful update rate
p_Θ	Connected probability threshold of the link
$p(u \rightarrow v)$	Predicted connection probability of u and v
K_{TS}	Maximum similarity among CDSs
$MAX\{W\{u\}\}$	The node with maximum weight

Successful Update Rate. It is exactly the percentage of the rounds of successful updates to the total rounds of updates.

$$P_{srt} = \frac{\sum_i S_{t_i}(C_{t_i} \rightarrow NC_{t_i})}{\sum_i R_{t_i}(C_{t_i} \rightarrow NC_{t_i})} \tag{2}$$

in which $S_{t_i}(C_{t_i} \rightarrow NC_{t_i})$ is the amounts of successfully updated nodes at time t_i, and $R_{t_i}(C_{t_i} \rightarrow NC_{t_i})$ is the amounts of failed nodes at time t_i.

In this paper, a Multi-CDSs scheduling algorithm is proposed by employing the minimum spanning tree based on weight of node and maximum similarity criterion, which could maintain the connectivity of topology with lower overheads. In particular, a link prediction algorithm is designed by employing the Markovian property of the mobility model, which could effectively predict node connectivity through calculating one-step transition probability of nodes. The block diagram of the proposed maintenance algorithm is shown in Fig. 2.

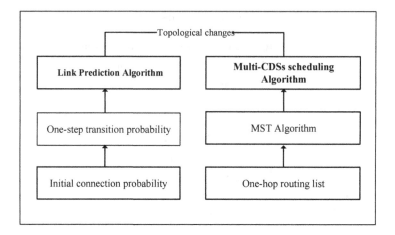

Fig. 2. The block diagram of the proposed mechanism.

3 Algorithms Description

3.1 Link Prediction

In this section, we will propose a Markov chain based link prediction algorithm of FANET topology, which could predict the connectivity state between a pair of nodes. For the convenience of analysis, we employ a SYN-boid model [10] to describe the swarming motions of nodes in FANET. In the model, the velocity of an individual node at the next moment is mainly determined by the previous step, which presents obvious Markovian property.

In specific, in the model, the speed variation is denoted by $v = V_{\max} e^{\beta[syn-1]}$, in which V_{max} is the maximum velocity of UAV nodes, syn is the synchronization coefficient and β is a constant regulating the velocity distribution, respectively. With a given probability density function of syn, expressed as $f_{syn}(syn)$. We can obtain the probability density distribution function of the speed $f_v(v)$ as follows:

$$
\begin{aligned}
f_v(v) &= f_{syn}(syn)\frac{\partial syn}{\partial v} \\
&= \frac{1}{\beta v} f_{syn}(\frac{\ln \frac{v}{v_{\max}}}{\beta} + 1)
\end{aligned}
\tag{3}
$$

in which

$$
syn = \frac{\ln \frac{v}{v_{\max}}}{\beta} + 1
\tag{4}
$$

As shown in Fig. 3(a), for node A and node B, the speeds at the current time are denoted as $\overrightarrow{V_A}$ and $\overrightarrow{V_B}$ respectively, and the relative speed is calculated by

$V_{A \to B} = \overrightarrow{V_A} - \overrightarrow{V_B}$ accordingly. Define Φ as the angle between $\overrightarrow{V_A}$ and $\overrightarrow{V_B}$, then we have

$$|\overrightarrow{V_{A \to B}}| = \sqrt{V_A^2 + V_B^2 - 2V_A V_B \cos \varphi} \tag{5}$$

and

$$\varphi = \arccos \frac{|\overrightarrow{V_A}|^2 + |\overrightarrow{V_B}|^2 - |\overrightarrow{V_{A \to B}}|^2}{2|\overrightarrow{V_A}||\overrightarrow{V_B}|} \tag{6}$$

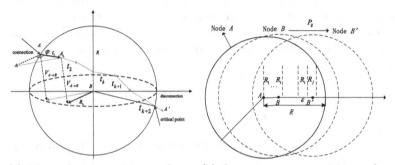

(a) The relative positions of two nodes.

(b) One-step state transition probability.

Fig. 3. Relative movements of two nodes.

In order to conveniently describe changes in connection states of two adjacent nodes, we discrete the relative motion of nodes into a series of individual states. Considering the Markov property of UAV's motion, we proposed a link prediction algorithm for forecasting the VBN changes in advance. Figure 3(b) presents relative positions distribution of node A and B during their motions. Without loss of generality, we fix node A exactly at the center of transmission area with a radius of R. For the convenience of analysis, we dividing the allowed communication range of node i into n segments with equal length ε. In particular, each small segment represents one state of the relative distance l between two nodes, where $l \in [k\varepsilon, (k+1)\varepsilon]$ indicates that the current status is R_k. Therefore, we propose a Markov chain with N states for modeling the variety of relative positions of two nodes. Given **P** as the one-step transition probability matrix, the one-step distance transition probability is

$$\mathbf{P} = \begin{bmatrix} p_{11} & \cdots & p_{1n} \\ & \cdots & \\ p_{n1} & \cdots & p_{nn} \end{bmatrix} = [\mathbf{P}_1 ... \mathbf{P}_k ... \mathbf{P}_n] \tag{7}$$

in which $P_{ij} = \Pr\{l_m \in R_i | l_m \in R_j\}$ is the probability that the relative distance l shifts from the i-th segment to the j-th segment. In particular, the maximum change of transition states should be $N = 2v_{\max}/\varepsilon$. It can be deserved that P_{ij} will be equal to 0 if $|i - j| > N$. Define the probability distribution of the related nodes at the initial time as ρ_{t_0}. In general, the connection probability of the initial state is known, expressed as

$$\rho_{t_0} = [\rho_1 \; \cdots \; \rho_1 \; \cdots \; \rho_n] \tag{8}$$

in which $\rho_{t_0}(k)$ represents the probability that the initial connected state of the node is at R_k. Furthermore, we call the probability that the node locates at certain small segment after m time slots as the m-step transition probability, denoted by ρ_{t_m}. If the initial connected state is at R_k, accordingly, the marginal probability of relative distance after m time slots is derived as

$$\begin{aligned} \rho_{t_m}(k) &= \rho_{t_0}(k)\mathbf{P}^m \\ &= [\rho_{t_0}(1)\mathbf{P_1^m} \cdots \rho_{t_0}(k)\mathbf{P_k^m} \; \cdots \; \rho_{t_0}(n)\mathbf{P_n^m}] \\ &= [0 \cdots \rho_{t_0}(k)\mathbf{P_k^m} \; \cdots \; 0] \end{aligned} \tag{9}$$

in which the one-step state transition probability density function is expressed as

$$P_{ij} = \Pr\{l_m \in R_i | l_m \in R_j\} = \int_{(j-1)\varepsilon}^{j\varepsilon} \int_{(i-1)\varepsilon}^{i\varepsilon} f_{l_m|l_{m-1},v_m}(l_m|l_{m-1})dl_m dl_{m-1} \tag{10}$$

and

$$\begin{aligned} f_{l_m|l_{m-1}}&(l_m|l_{m-1}) \\ &= \int_0^{2v_{\max}} f_{l_m|l_{m-1},v_m}(l_m|l_{m-1},v_m)f_v(v_m)dv_m \\ &= \int_0^{2v_{\max}} \frac{2}{\pi} \cdot \frac{l_m f_v(v_m)dv_m}{\sqrt{4l_{m-1}^2 v_m^2 - (l_{m-1}^2 + v_m^2 - l_m^2)^2}} \\ &= \int_0^{2v_{\max}} \frac{2}{\pi}.T(v_m)f_v(v_m) \end{aligned} \tag{11}$$

In order to ensure that the value of probability distribution is greater than 0, we can further derive the efficient solution, where

$$\begin{aligned} f_{l_m|l_{m-1}}(l_m|l_{m-1}) &= \int_0^{2v_{\max}} f_{l_m|l_{m-1},v_m}(l_m|l_{m-1},v_m)f_v(v_m)dv_m \\ &= \int_{\max\{0,|l_m-l_{m-1}|\}}^{\min\{2v_{\max},|l_m+l_{m-1}|\}} \frac{2}{\pi} \cdot \frac{l_u f_v(v_u)dv_u}{\sqrt{4l_{m-1}^2 v_m^2 - (l_{m-1}^2 + v_m^2 - l_m^2)^2}} \\ &= \int_{\max\{0,|l_m-l_{m-1}|\}}^{\min\{2v_{\max},|l_m+l_{m-1}|\}} \frac{2}{\pi}.T(v_m)f_v(v_m) \end{aligned} \tag{12}$$

According to the speed probability density distribution function in Eq. (3), the one-step state transition probability density function can be further obtained.

$$P_{ij} = \Pr\{l_m \in R_j | l_{m-1} \in R_i\}$$

$$= \int_{(i-1)\varepsilon}^{i\varepsilon} \int_{(j-1)\varepsilon}^{j\varepsilon} \int_{\max\{0,|l_m-l_{m-1}|\}}^{\min\{2v_{\max},|l_m+l_{m-1}|\}} \frac{2}{\pi} \cdot \frac{l_u f_v(v_u) dv_u}{\sqrt{4l_{m-1}^2 v_m^2 - (l_{m-1}^2 + v_m^2 - l_m^2)^2}} dl_m dl_{m-1}$$

$$(13)$$

3.2 Multi-CDS Scheduling

Typically, construction of CDS is a NP-hard problem, in which only approximately effective solutions can be found. In this paper, we design an improved construction algorithm of CDS based on the minimum panning tree (MST) method, by incorporating a series of time-related information. As a result, we can find a most effective CDS at each time slot for a better scheduling. The CDS constructing algorithm is shown in Algorithm 1.

Initially, the CDS with the maximum energy among the constructed CDSs is selected as the current on-duty CDS. With the results of selection, the current CDS on duty is substituted by the to-be-on-duty CDS through replacing the non-common nodes of these two sets, as shown in Fig. 4.

Algorithm 1. MST-CDS

Require: The set of MCDS at t-th time slot, cds
Ensure: $G^t(V^t, E^t), t$
1: Initial Calculate the node weight matrix $\mathbf{W_1}$ and edge weight matrix $\mathbf{W_2}$
2: $\{V_{bn}\} \leftarrow \phi$ //V_{bn} is the set of MCDS at current time slot
3: **for** $num\{V_{bn}\} < N$ //V_{bn} is the number of MCDS **do**
4:    $T \leftarrow \{V_{bn}^k, v_k, W\}$ //v_k is the starting node
5:    $v_m \leftarrow v_k, V_{bn} \leftarrow v_m$
6:    **for** $m \leftarrow num\{N_{node}\} < N$ //N_{node}: node traversal number **do**
7:       SET $U = MAX\{W[u]\}$ //$\{u \in N_1(v_m)\}$
8:       **if** $num\{U\}$ euual to 1 //only one node with maximum weight **then**
9:          $V_{bn} \leftarrow U$
10:      **else**
11:         $V_{bn} \leftarrow MAX\{W(\langle u, v \rangle)\}$
12:      **end if**
13:   **end for**
14: **end for**
15: **if** $V_{bn}^i \not\subset V_{bn}^j$ **then**
16:    DELETE V_{bn}^i
17: **end if**

Here, we define an energy value of each CDS, denoted as $E_{(cds_i)}$, which is exactly a specific value of lowest residual energy of certain node in the

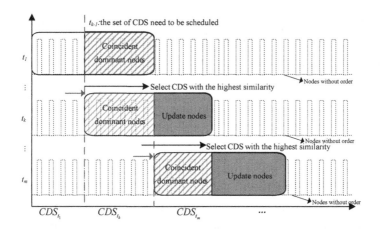

Fig. 4. The scheduling procedure of CDSs.

CDS. In particular, all the backup CDSs will be filtered for being the on-duty CDS according to the energy rule. If there exists imminent disconnections predicted by the proposed Markov model, the scheduling algorithm will find another CDS in the candidate set most similar with the current on-duty CDS. In specific, we define a metric of similarity between two CDSs, denoted by $\frac{CDS_m \cap CDS_{ct}}{CDS_m}$. Furthermore, we define K_{TS} as the maximum similarity between the backup CDS set and the current CDS on duty, expressed as $K_{TS} = Max\{\frac{CDS_1 \cap CDS_{ct}}{CDS_1}, \frac{CDS_2 \cap CDS_{ct}}{CDS_2}, ... \frac{CDS_m \cap CDS_{ct}}{CDS_m}...\}$.

The pseudo-code multi-CDS scheduling algorithm is detailed in Algorithm 2. In particular, $E_{max}\{S_{cds}\}$ represents the certain CDS with the highest energy. Typically, we set two specific rules for triggering the scheduling procedure, respectively as:

(a) a certain type of network changes described in Sect. 2 occurred.
(b) the connection probability of certain edge in $G(V^t, E^t)$ is lower than the pre-determined threshold.

3.3   Communication Scheme

The entire process of constructing and scheduling CDSs requires a sequence of information exchanges, i.e., results of link predictions, identity numbers of CDSs, and routing lists, etc. Once the FANET starts, each node will periodically broadcast its own relevant information and updates the neighbor and dominator lists. In particular, these routing information will be used for constructing CDS and updating the status of local node. As long as the topology changes, the information about neighbor nodes is required to be updated by the local node. The complete procedure of signaling interaction is shown in Fig. 5.

For the dominate node, we propose a specific data structure, including a group of information such as neighbor list, one-hop dominator list and parent node identity, as shown in Fig. 6.

Algorithm 2. Multi-CDS Scheduling

Require: $S_{cds}, G^t\left(V^t, E^t\right)$, t, t_d //detection period
Ensure: Scheduling of S_{cds} and nodes
 1: Broadcast nodes' information to vote CDS_{ct}
 2: $CDS_{ct} \leftarrow E_{\max}\{S_{cds}\}$, $\{ S^{bc}_{cds} \} \leftarrow S_{cds} \backslash CDS_{ct}$
 3: **while** $num\left\{V^t\right\} > 1$ // no nodes in the network **do**
 4:     **DETECT** changes that need to be maintained
 5:     **DETECT** failed CDS in S_{cds}, **UPDATE** S_{cds}
 6:     CASE1: changes in $V\{CDS_{ct}\}$ or $E\{CDS_{ct}\}$ **break**
 7:     **GOTO** 14
 8:     CASE2: $p(u \rightarrow v) < p_\Theta$ // $< u, v > \in E\{CDS_{ct}\}$
 9:     **GOTO** 14
10:     CASE3: domintees leave the network
11:     **GOTO** 18
12:     CASE4: domintee v_i loses connection with $v_i.parent$
13:     **GOTO** 18
14:     **if** $MIN\left\{CDS_{ct} \cap S^{bc}_{cds}\right\} > 1$ **then**
15:         $CDS_{bc} \leftarrow E_{\max}\{MIN\left\{CDS_{ct} \cap S^{bc}_{cds}\right\}\}$
16:         **UPDATE** nodes belong to $CDS_{ct} \cap CDS_{bc}$ **Break**
17:     **end if**
18:     Wait until there are dominators in $N_2 v_i)$
19:     **if** there are dominators in $N_1(v_i)$ **then**
20:         Add $u \leftarrow E_{\max}\{N_1(v_i)\}$ into CDS_{ct} **UPDATE**
21:     **end if**
22:     return S_{cds} CDS_{ct} //Broadcast and update
23: **end while**

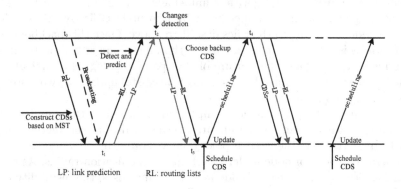

Fig. 5. The signaling sequence.

4 Numerical Analysis

In the simulations, we exploit SYN-boid mobility model for generating a group of topological snapshots in multiple time slots with various number of nodes. The relevant parameters are shown in Table 2, for comparison with the single CDS algorithm (SCDS) in different scenarios.

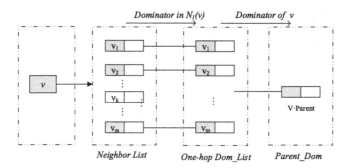

Fig. 6. Data structure.

Table 2. Simulations parameters.

Parameter	Parameter description	Value
N	Number of nodes	10/25/...70/85
T	Total time slots	400
v	Maximum velocity	5/10/15/20 m/s
R_c	Communication radius	90/100/110 m
L_i	Initial position	400 m × 400 m
R_r	Repulsion perception radius	90 m

Typically, a single-CDS algorithm implements the maintenance process in an event-triggered manner. In specific, a backup node is firstly selected for a backbone node according to the rules described above. Once this backbone node fails, its status is updated. However, this method has a non-trivial probability of failure due to the disconnected nature of the sparse topology. In particular, we use the update overheads and the amounts of successful update as two respective metrics for the comparative experiments.

Figure 7 shows the performance comparison of two algorithms under different scenarios with respect to the update overheads during the lifetime of the network. In particular, the used topology is generated by changing the maximum operating speed of node under a certain communication radius. As can be seen in Fig. 7(a), as the speed of node movement increases, the instability duration of topology increases and corresponding update overheads increase, since more nodes are required to be scheduled in order to maintain the normal operation of CDS. Besides, the overheads of proposed algorithm are smaller than the single-CDS (SCDS) algorithm, which indicates that the multi-CDS scheduling algorithm based on link prediction can effectively reduce the update overheads.

Generally, changes of node's communication radius will also affect the topology stability. As the results, we can get the comparison of two algorithms under different communication radium, as shown in the Fig. 7(b). It is seen that the update overheads of the proposed algorithm are significantly less than the SCDS

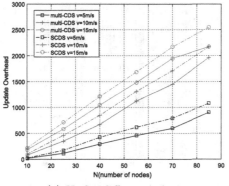

(a) Under different velocity.

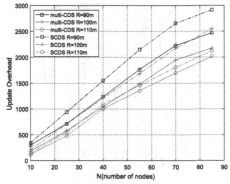

(b) Under different communication radius.

Fig. 7. Update overheads.

algorithm. Combined with the previous simulations, we can conclude that the proposed algorithm has smaller update overheads and smaller impacts on maintaining a highly dynamic network backbone network.

Typically, the success rate (SRT) is directly related to the network connectivity and the success selection of backup node. From Fig. 8(a), it is seen that the success update rates of the proposed algorithm is slightly higher than SCDS, as is apparent under low communication radius. In another word, the proposed algorithm has obvious advantages with heavily topological changes. As the communication radius increases, both algorithms have higher probabilities of successful maintenance.

By changing the maximum velocity of node, we observe the success probability of two algorithms to maintain the backbone network. As can be seen from Fig. 8(b), both algorithms have approximate probabilities of success update with small node's speeds. Once the speed develops to be large, the success rate of the

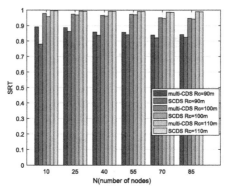

(a) SRTs under communication radius.

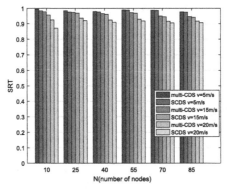

(b) SRTs under different velocity.

Fig. 8. Successful update rates.

proposed algorithm is higher than that of SCDS. Combined with the previous results, we can conclude that the multi-CDS algorithm has advantages in highly dynamic networks.

5   Conclusion

In this paper, we propose a link prediction based multi-CDS scheduling algorithm to maintain the connectivity of the virtual backbone network. The link prediction algorithm could reduce the impact of the maintenance phase on the connectivity. Moreover, the proposed algorithm can maintain the stability of backbone network effectively. Through simulations results, we find that under different motion scenarios, the performance of proposed algorithm is better than SCDS algorithm. We mainly compare two aspects of update overheads and maintenance success rate. The algorithm proposed in this paper has better performance in both aspects.

Acknowledgments. The authors would like to express their high appreciations to the supports from the National Natural Science Foundation of China (61871426) and Basic Research Project of Shenzhen (JCYJ20170413110004682).

References

1. Büchter, K.D.: Availability of airborne ad-hoc communication network in global air traffic simulation. In: International Symposium on Communication Systems, Networks and Digital Signal Processing (2016)
2. Bujari, A., Calafate, C.T., Cano, J.C., Manzoni, P., Palazzi, C.E., Ronzani, D.: Flying ad-hoc network application scenarios and mobility models. Int. J. Distrib. Sens. Netw. **13**(10), 155014771773819 (2017)
3. Kuo, T.W.: On the approximability and hardness of the minimum connected dominating set with routing cost constraint (2017)
4. Ugurlu, O., Tanir, D., Nuri, E.: A better heuristic for the minimum connected dominating set in ad hoc networks. In: IEEE International Conference on Application of Information and Communication Technologies, pp. 1–4 (2017)
5. Dash, D.: Restoring virtual backbone of wireless sensor network on sensor failure. In: International Conference on Recent Advances in Information Technology, pp. 29–34 (2016)
6. Zhu, Q., Zhou, R., Zhang, J.: Connectivity maintenance based on multiple relay UAVs selection scheme in cooperative surveillance. Appl. Sci. **7**(1), 8 (2016)
7. Wang, J., Kodama, E., Takata, T.: Construction and maintenance of K-Hop CDS in mobile ad hoc networks. In: IEEE International Conference on Advanced Information Networking and Applications, pp. 220–227 (2017)
8. Wu, C.H., Chen, H.S., Dai, W.H.: Obstacle-avoiding connectivity restoration based on power adjustment and node's movement in disjoint mobile sensor networks. In:International Conference on Information System and Artificial Intelligence, pp. 115–119 (2017)
9. Chen-Ming, M.A., Wang, W.L., Hong, Z.: Distributed construction for (k, m)-fault tolerant connected dominating set in wireless sensor network. Comput. Sci. (2016)
10. Choi, T.J., Chang, W.A.: Artificial life based on boids model and evolutionary chaotic neural networks for creating artworks. Swarm Evol. Comput. (2017)

The Functional Design of a Multi-protocol Satellite Router

Yushan Wu, Qing Guo, and Mingchuan Yang$^{(\boxtimes)}$

Communication Research Center, Harbin Institute of Technology, Harbin, China
mcyang@hit.edu.cn

Abstract. With the rapid development of Space Information Network and users' demand for communication services, interconnecting heterogeneous space networks becomes a new trend of SIN development. Networks using different protocols, such as TCP/IP, CCSDS and DTN, cannot communicate directly. In order to interconnect heterogeneous networks and face the problems brought by the challenged environment, this paper designs a multi-protocol onboard router which depends on the "store-and-forward" mechanism in DTN network protocol, as a relay with the ability of multi-protocol switching in order to support communication services among heterogeneous networks.

Keywords: Multi-protocol router · DTN protocol · Protocol switching

1 Introduction

Since the 21st century, space technology has developed rapidly and the strategic position of space has become increasingly important. Therefore, all countries are committed to the development of Space Information Network (SIN) [1]. Satellites are an indispensable part of it.

At present, the rapid development of the communication network makes the information no longer experience a simplex environment only during the transmission. Based on the evolution of terrestrial communication network technologies, satellite communication networks improve rapidly. The most obvious difference between the satellite communication network and the terrestrial one is the characteristic of links and channels. The satellite communication network has high bit error rate and asymmetric uplink and downlink bandwidth. Besides, long distance between satellites and terminals leads to long time delay of the traffic transmission. At the same time, the available time duration of links is limited so that the topology of the satellite network changes frequently. Therefore, three types of protocols for space networks are currently formed, named CCSDS (Consultative Committee for Space Data Systems) protocol [2, 3], TCP/IP (Transmission Control Protocol/Internet Protocol) [4], and the DTN (Delay Tolerant Networking) protocol [5].

Heterogeneous networks, using different protocols, bring convenience to human lives. Targeting at different channel conditions, orbital altitudes, and business requirement, different networks are designed to meet the needs of users. However, the heterogeneous network brings difficulties in compatibility and interconnection. In order

© ICST Institute for Computer Sciences, Social Informatics and Telecommunications Engineering 2019
Published by Springer Nature Switzerland AG 2019. All Rights Reserved
M. Jia et al. (Eds.): WiSATS 2019, LNICST 280, pp. 602–611, 2019.
https://doi.org/10.1007/978-3-030-19153-5_60

to satisfy the requirement of multiple service patterns and complex space operation, the communication method that transmitting traffic through the heterogeneous networks cannot be avoided, which exactly the reason that we design a multi-protocol router.

In this context, we put forward the functions of an onboard router which is compatible with CCSDS protocol, TCP/IP protocol and DTN protocol by using the "store-and-forward" mechanism and "bundle layer" protocol in DTN networks, mentioned in Sect. 2. Then, the specific functions of the router are introduced in Sect. 3, including the routing algorithm and the protocol switching method. Besides, a MEO/LEO double layer satellite network model is built for simulation. And finally, the simulation results and the performance analysis are showed in Sect. 5.

2 Traffic Transmission Mechanism and Bundle Layer Protocol in DTN Networks

DTN network protocol is extremely different from other Internet protocols that DTN protocol introduces the concept of a Bundle layer between the application and the transport layer. The comparison between the DTN network architecture and the traditional one is shown in Fig. 1.

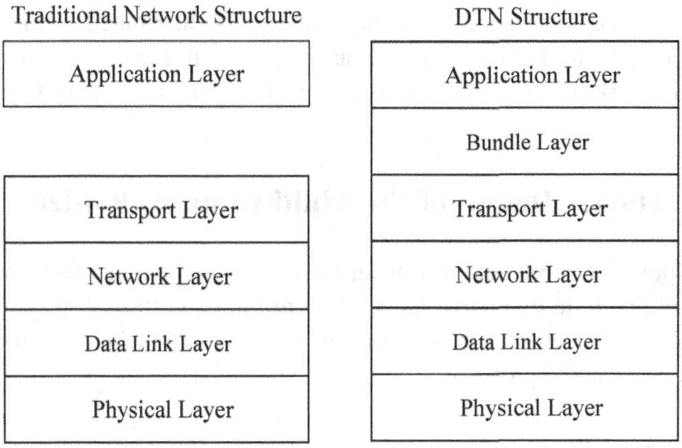

Traditional Network Structure	DTN Structure
Application Layer	Application Layer
	Bundle Layer
Transport Layer	Transport Layer
Network Layer	Network Layer
Data Link Layer	Data Link Layer
Physical Layer	Physical Layer

Fig. 1. The structure comparison between the traditional network and DTN.

The mainly application of DTN is the challenged networks. The main idea is to introduce "Bundle Layer" [6] as a medium of connection among different networks. In addition, traffic transmission in DTN networks is based on store-and-forward mechanism instead of end-to-end transmission paths, shown in Fig. 2.

In the Bundle layer, the part closest to the application layer is called Bundle API [7], which is the application agent of the bundle layer and the interface between the bundle and the application layer, configuring bundle layer according to the services provided by the application layer. In addition, the interface between the bundle layer

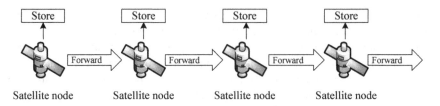

Fig. 2. "Store-and-forward" mechanism of DTN

and the transport layer is the Bundle adaptor, achieving the interconnection and the coordination of various protocols in different networks.

DTN is kind of challenged network with high time delay, which leads to the importance of "store-and-forward" mechanism to ensure the traffic transmission in the communication network with unstable links and long delay. If a DTN node can find out the next hop address of the current data packet, the packet will be transmitted, or else, the packet will be stored in the node and deleted when the packet is successfully sent to the destination. Therefore, a DTN node has permanent storage space to face the challenge of long-time unavailable links, which is one of the differences with the traditional networks.

Two assumptions are required to achieve all the process mentioned above:

1. The storage space of nodes is available and evenly distributed in the network;
2. The space of the storage queue can guarantee certain durability and robustness of the DTN network, in order to support the establishment of the next reliable path.

3   The Functional Design of the Multi-protocol Router

In order to achieve interconnection of heterogeneous satellite networks, the function of the router should include two parts, namely the routing and the gateway function. This section will give the specific routing algorithm and protocol switching procedure of the router based on the DTN protocol.

3.1   Routing Algorithm

Earliest-Delivery (ED) routing algorithm is widely used in DTN networks, details mentioned in [9]. However, ED algorithm is not the optimal routing algorithm for satellite DTN networks. The changing of the topology makes data packets fail to be transmitted according to the originally calculated path. As mentioned above, the topology of the satellite network has uncertain time delay and is interrupted frequently, bringing routing calculation difficulties.

As we all know, the motion of the satellite is cyclical so that the network topology can be obtained by the ephemeris approximately. Therefore, in order to simplify the dynamic topology of the satellite network, the concept of the virtual topology is introduced.

Virtual topology strategy is an efficient way to predigest high-changing-frequency topology [8], which transfers dynamic topology into large amount of static topologies by dividing one period time into several time pieces (or slots), based on the periodicity and predictability of the satellite motion. Concerned that the overhead of ED algorithm is time-varying, the way of time division will directly affect the performance of the ED algorithm. Therefore, the time pieces are divided as follows:

- Take the time that satellite links on/off as the route update time.
- Set a time threshold and when the update interval is less than the threshold, the update time will be merged with the previous one in order to reduce the number of time slice snapshots.

In summary, the specific process of the route calculation strategy is shown in the Fig. 3.

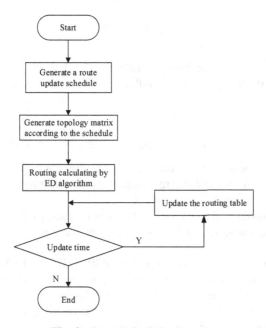

Fig. 3. Route calculation strategy

3.2 Protocol Switching

Another key function of the multi-protocol router is protocol switching. Currently, the commonly used protocols in satellite networks are TCP/IP, DTN, and CCSDS protocol. Therefore, the router designed in this paper will be mainly compatible with these three protocols.

To achieve protocol switching, three steps are required:

1. Identify the protocol used by the received packets.
2. Unpack the data packets.
3. Repack the data according to the protocol of the destination network.

In order to carry out the first step, which is the key point of protocol switching, we put forward a new frame format here, adding an 8-bit frame information part at the beginning of the frame, shows in Fig. 4.

In the 8-bit frame information part, the first 4 bits represent the protocol used in the

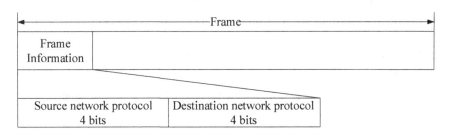

Fig. 4. Frame format

source network protocol and the last 4 bits represent the destination one. Only when the source and the destination protocol are different will the data packets be repacked.

3.3 Summary

The function of the multi-protocol onboard router should include the following points:

- For services in the same subnetwork, the satellite with the router can work as a relay node, in other words, it can forward data packets in each subnetwork under TCP/IP, DTN, and CCSDS protocols respectively.
- To prevent collisions of data packets at the receiver, each satellite networks operates in different frequency, which means 3 different receivers are used in the MEO satellite.
- The router can simultaneously support TCP/IP, DTN, and CCSDS protocol to achieve inter-network transmission, which means the protocol switching.
- As the satellite with router is visible to three different systems, routing tables that this satellite updates are about the whole network, requiring routing tables of three networks. However, networks are not visible to the one using different protocol and their routing calculation is separated from other networks.
- Because of the large business pressure and high time propagation delay, the "storage and forwarding" function of the DTN system is added to ensure packet transmission and low packet loss rate in the satellite communication network.

In this context, we design the operation procedure of the on-board router and divide the procedure into three different parts, as shown in Fig. 5. When the router receives a packet, the protocol of its source and destination should be identified firstly. If the protocols are same, which means two nodes are in the same network, the router will only act as a relay. Or else, the router will repack the data packet according to the protocol used by the destination network and transmit it.

According to the function division in the Fig. 5, we design the router model in OPNET as shown in Fig. 6.

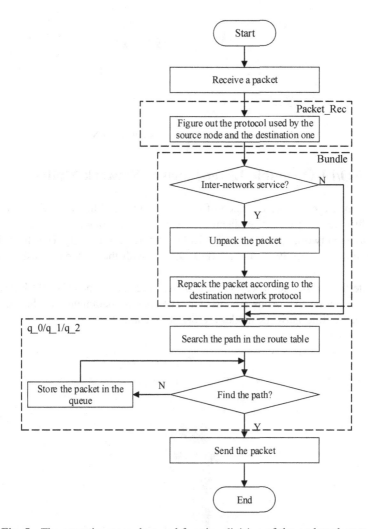

Fig. 5. The operation procedure and function division of the on-board router

The router has 3 independent storage space as queues, corresponding to 3 different networks, saving packets and finding their routes. The router has 3 route searching modules, which are used to find the routes of 3 different networks. The work of these three routing lookup modules is separated from each other and can operate in parallel.

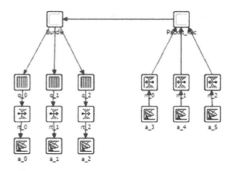

Fig. 6. The on-board router model in OPNET

4   A MEO/LEO Double Layer Satellite Network Model

In order to measure the performance of the router, we establish a MEO/LEO double-layer satellite network as the application scenario of the router, including 3 different LEO satellites network, composed of 3 LEO satellites each, using TCP/IP, DTN and CCSDS protocol respectively and a MEO satellite with the router we designed above on-board.

The satellite constellation we used is shown in Fig. 7, composed of 9 LEO satellites and 1 MEO satellite. All orbits are circular. The specific parameters of the MEO/LEO double layer satellite network model are listed in Table 1.

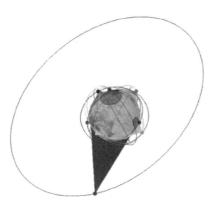

Fig. 7. The MEO/LEO double layer satellite network model

5   Results and Analysis

According to the satellite network mentioned in Sect. 4, we build the MEO/LEO double layer satellite network model in OPNET as the simulation scenario. The performance of the router is simulated by using the storage capacity of the MEO satellite router and the load of the network as variables.

Table 1. Parameters of the network model

Satellite-Protocol	Altitude/km	Inclination/°	RAAN/°
LEO-TCP/IP	1680.8	60	60/180/300
LEO-DTN	2000	60	30/150/270
LEO-CCSDS	1000	60	0/120/240
MEO-ROUTER	20000	55	0

For the routing method, we take the successful packets arrival ratio as a measurement of the performance. As shown in Fig. 8, compared with the traditional ED algorithm, the one using virtual topology strategy has a higher successful transmission ratio. When the storage capacity is not enough, a certain number of packets are dropped due to insufficient storage space. Larger storage capacity brings a better performance.

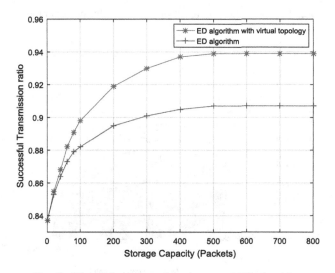

Fig. 8. The performance of the improved ED algorithm

As for the protocol switching part, we take the ratio of packet that the router processes successfully and the end-to-end time delay as the measurements of its capacity. In this context, we consider both of the storage capacity and the network load as variables.

In Fig. 9, we conclude that higher storage capacity allows the router to handle more protocol switching packets correctly. However, the performance of the router does not continue to increase as storage space increases. Network load is another impact factor of the router. The higher the network load, the greater the processing pressure of the router, which causes the decrease of the processing performance.

As shown in Fig. 10, the end-to-end time delay has the same tendency as the performance of the routing processing. Thanks to the improved ED algorithm, the end-to-end time delay of the network is controlled to within 70 ms. What must be

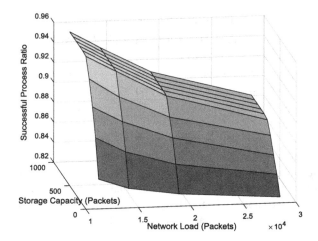

Fig. 9. The simulation result of the successful process ratio

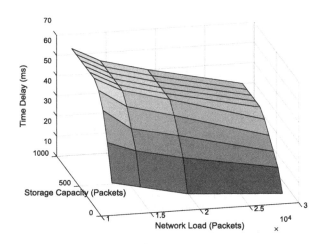

Fig. 10. Average end-to-end time delay

emphasized is that the lower time delay in high network load does not mean a better performance, which is exactly caused by the discarding of a certain number of packets.

6 Conclusion

In this paper, we design a multi-protocol onboard satellite router based on "store-and-forward" mechanism and the bundle layer protocol in DTN network to support TCP/IP, CCSDS and DTN protocol traffic at the same time. In order to simplify the dynamic topology of the satellite network, we apply the virtual topology strategy to improve the ED algorithm. Finally, according to the simulation result in OPNET, we find out the performance of the router is related to its storage space and the network load in a way. However, to realize a further improvement of the performance, a corresponding retransmission method is required, which will be our future work.

Acknowledgements. The paper is sponsored by National Natural Science Foundation of China (No. 91538104; No. 91438205).

References

1. Guo, X.R., Miao, F., Wang, H.J., Du, G.Y.: Initial discussion on the architecture of a new spatial information network service model based on the digital earth. In: 2009 International Conference on Environmental Science and Information Application Technology, Wuhan, pp. 406–410 (2009)
2. Rich, T.M.: A multi-center space data system prototype based on CCSDS standards. In: 2016 IEEE Aerospace Conference, Big Sky, MT, pp. 1–6 (2016)
3. Liu, Y., Cong, B., Li, P., Liu, X., Wang, X.: Discussion on space-earth integration transmission mechanism of space information network based on CCSDS protocols. In: 2016 15th International Conference on Optical Communications and Networks (ICOCN), Hangzhou, pp. 1–3 (2016)
4. Caini, C., Firrincieli, R.: End-to-end TCP enhancements performance on satellite links. In: 11th IEEE Symposium on Computers and Communications (ISCC 2006), pp. 1031–1036 (2006)
5. Fall, K.: A delay-tolerant network architecture for challenged internets. In: Conference on Applications, Technologies, Architectures, and Protocols for Computer Communications, pp. 27–34. ACM (2003)
6. Alfonzo, M., Fraire, J.A., Kocian, E., Alvarez, N.: Development of a DTN bundle protocol convergence layer for SpaceWire. In: 2014 IEEE Biennial Congress of Argentina (ARGENCON), Bariloche, pp. 770–775 (2014)
7. Caini, C., Firrincieli, R.: Application of contact graph routing to LEO satellite DTN communications. In: 2012 IEEE International Conference on Communications (ICC), Ottawa, ON, pp. 3301–3305 (2012)
8. Lu, Y., Sun, F., Zhao, Y.: Virtual topology for LEO satellite networks based on earth-fixed footprint mode. IEEE Commun. Lett. **17**(2), 357–360 (2013)
9. Zhang, L.H., Tang, L.: DTN earliest-delivery routing algorithm based on routing reliability. In: International Conference on Communication Technology, pp. 449–453. IEEE (2013)

Wavelength Routing Assignment of Different Topological Optical Networks Based on Typical LEO Satellite Constellations

Xue Sun[1,2,3(✉)] and Suzhi Cao[2,3]

[1] University of Chinese Academy of Sciences, Beijing 100049, China
sunxue16@mails.ucas.edu.cn
[2] Technology and Engineering Center for Space Utilization,
Chinese Academy of Sciences, Beijing 100094, China
{sunxue16, caosuzhi}@csu.ac.cn
[3] Key Laboratory of Space Utilization, Technology and Engineering Center
for Space Utilization, Chinese Academy of Sciences, Beijing 100094, China

Abstract. Inter-satellite laser communication can fulfill the requirements of huge-capacity transmission of satellite communication. The space-wide all-optical network is a key way to solve problems such as low-latency, huge-capacity transmission and low-cost on-orbit real-time route switching processing through technologies of Wavelength Division Multiplexing (WDM) inter-satellite links (ISLs) and wavelength routing. Then routing and wavelength assignment (RWA) become its core and main technology. Aiming at the RWA issue, this paper takes the typical LEO satellite constellations Iridium and NeLS as examples, establishes a regular ISLs topology, and proposes a simulation model based on the minimum cost routing strategy and wavelength demand. The results of simulations demonstrate that, compared with the link arbitrary topology, the NeLS constellation with regular network topology can save nearly half of the wavelength resource requirement under the condition of slightly sacrificing node connectivity, and the Iridium constellation has the better connectivity with the same wavelength resource demand. Both NeLS and Iridium constellations show a more stable trend in the link duration, wavelength volatility, and node connectivity volatility.

Keywords: Wavelength assignment · Regular ISLs · Wavelength routing · WDM

1 Introduction

Nowadays, the inter-satellite microwave transmission has been difficult to fulfil the communication capacity demand. And space all-optical communication technology has the benefits of high communication rate, robust anti-interference capability, powerful security and confidentiality [1–4]. The European Data Relay System (EDRS) [5], the Japanese laser relay satellite system [6], and the Quantum Experiments at Space Scale (QUESS) launched in China in 2016 [7] all accomplished higher-rate optical communication. With the mature development of WDM technology and related optical

© ICST Institute for Computer Sciences, Social Informatics and Telecommunications Engineering 2019
Published by Springer Nature Switzerland AG 2019. All Rights Reserved
M. Jia et al. (Eds.): WiSATS 2019, LNICST 280, pp. 612–629, 2019.
https://doi.org/10.1007/978-3-030-19153-5_61

equipment, optical wavelength switching has been widely introduced commercially. Thus, using the wavelength routing technology based on WDM on satellite networks is a fairly advanced and practical solution for building future space-wide networks [8].

The RWA problem of optical networks has been studied currently in ground fiber optic networks. However, there exist relative motions of two satellites of distinct orbital planes, and the inter-satellite distance typically changes with period. And the position of satellites in the non-synchronous orbit constellation is continuously time-varying relative to the earth. So, this key issue of satellite optical networks is more complex than the ground. Therefore, this paper chose the regular ISLs topology, which has lower algorithm complexity and better stability than the link-arbitrary topology.

The LEO constellation has become a preferred option for countries to construct space-based networks because of its low transmission delay and expense. The LEO constellation system's design is commonly divided into the polar orbit constellation and the Delta constellation. Consequently, this paper chooses the representative 2π constellation NeLS [9] and the π constellation Iridium [10], and analyzes the RWA topic of these two constellations in detail.

In the past domestic and foreign research, some academics have proposed a number of algorithms for satellite network traffic, blocking rate and wavelength utilization analysis and improvement [11–14], but they lacked the analysis of wavelength demand and node connectivity. Sun et al. proposed that the deployment of LEO π-type polar orbit constellation is in line with the development trend of China's future integrated satellite network [15], and Tan et al. proposed a wavelength routing model based on 2π-type NeLS constellation, lacking the comparison with the π-type constellation [16].

In this paper, the model of regular potential ISLs is established, and the ISLs topology is generated under the condition of time-varying ISL nodes, which supplies link support for the RWA procedure. This paper also improves the Dijkstra routing algorithm strategy, simulates the number of wavelength resource required in the optical satellite network, and compares it with the arbitrary ISL topology [19].

2 Optical ISLs Model

2.1 Introduction to NeLS and Iridium

The Iridium constellation is the only near-polar orbit constellation at present that can achieve global seamless coverage even including Antarctic and Arctic. NeLS is the first global satellite network that prepares to take advantage of WDM ISL technology, which belongs to the typical Delta type [17]. The 3D orbits map of NeLS and Iridium can be obtained by STK simulation software (see Fig. 1).

At the same time, using STK satellite simulation software to analyze the 2D planar columnar expansion of the two constellations, we can see the difference between the two constellations and their respective advantages more intuitively (see Fig. 2). The coverage of the NeLS constellation on the ground is better and evenly distributed, especially in densely populated areas. While the Iridium constellation takes care of the polar regions and achieves global seamless coverage.

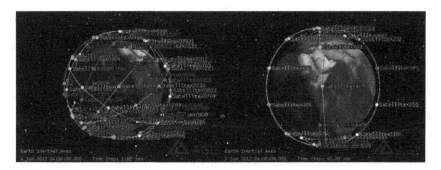

Fig. 1. 3D orbits map of NeLS (left) and Iridium (right) constellation.

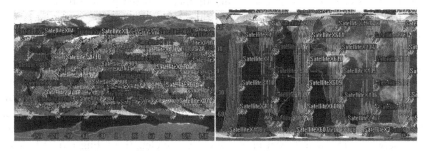

Fig. 2. 2D planar expansion map of the NeLS constellation (left) and Iridium constellation (right).

2.2 Mathematical Modeling of Satellites of the Constellations

According to the Walker representation [16, 18], the distribution of satellites in the constellation is expressed as N/P/F, where N stands for the total number of satellites in the constellation, P denotes the total number of orbits contained in the constellation, F means the phase factor of the constellation, and S represents the number of satellites in each orbit. According to the spatial geometric relationship, the following relationship can be obtained between the location of the k-th satellite in the i-th orbit of the constellation and the constellation parameters:

$$
x_{ik}(t) = - R\cos\theta \, \sin\left(\frac{2\pi i}{P}\right) \sin\left[\omega t + 2\pi\left(\frac{k}{S} + \frac{iF}{PS}\right)\right] + R\cos\left(\frac{2\pi i}{P}\right)\cos\left[\omega t + 2\pi\left(\frac{k}{S} + \frac{iF}{PS}\right)\right]
\tag{1}
$$

$$
y_{ik}(t) = R\cos\theta \, \cos\left(\frac{2\pi i}{P}\right) \sin\left[\omega t + 2\pi\left(\frac{k}{S} + \frac{iF}{PS}\right)\right] + R\sin\left(\frac{2\pi i}{P}\right)\cos\left[\omega t + 2\pi\left(\frac{k}{S} + \frac{iF}{PS}\right)\right]
\tag{2}
$$

$$z_{ik}(t) = Rsin\theta \, \sin\left[\omega t + 2\pi\left(\frac{k}{S} + \frac{iF}{PS}\right)\right] \tag{3}$$

Where:

$0 \leq i \leq P - 1, 0 \leq k \leq S - 1.$

Where:

R - Distance between the satellite and the earth's center;
ω - Orbital angular velocity of the satellite;
θ - Orbital inclination of the satellite.

Supposing that the k-th satellite in the i-th orbit of the constellation requires to build an ISL with the l-th satellite in the j-th orbit, we can obtain the link distance $D(t)$ between the two satellites:

$$D(t) = \sqrt{\begin{array}{c} \left[x_{ik}(t) - x_{jl}(t)\right]^2 + \left[y_{ik}(t) - y_{jl}(t)\right]^2 \\ + \left[z_{ik}(t) - z_{jl}(t)\right]^2 \end{array}} \tag{4}$$

2.3 Regular ISL Network Topology and Arbitrary ISL Network Topology

In the planar structure of the regular ISL network topology, each node establishes ISL with 2–4 satellites adjacent to the same orbit and 2–4 satellites in the front and behind adjacent orbits, and the topological shape is regular and stable. In the arbitrary ISL network topology, under the limitation of the number of satellite optical terminals, the ISLs can be established between all the potential link satellites within the allowable laser terminal link distance, while its topology shape is complicated and the link duration is unstable (see Fig. 3).

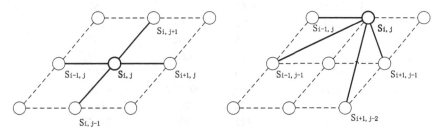

Fig. 3. Regular ISL network topology (left) and arbitrary ISL network topology (right) in some moment.

2.4 Regular ISL Network Topology and Its Time Stability

On the basis of the mathematical model obtained in part 2.3, we analyzed the link topology characteristics of a single satellite in the constellation, and select the regular link topology that can be used as a permanent link for simulation analysis. The simulation orbit parameters are based on the NeLS constellation and the Iridium constellation (see Table 1). We presented a two-dimensional model of the regular ISL topology at a certain time, verified and analyzed the stability characteristics of the potential communication links of a single satellite in one cycle in the system.

Link Topology Characteristics of a Single Satellite

Since each satellite of the constellation system is equivalent in the network, the motion characteristics of a single node are representative and universal, so we only analyze the link topology characteristics of one satellite. The link distance of the optical terminals on the satellite determines the communication coverage of the satellite, so we analyzed all satellites that can enter the satellite communication range and establish an ISL.

Table 1. Chief parameters of the NeLS constellation and Iridium constellation.

Parameters	NeLS	Iridium
Orbit inclination	55°	86.4°
Orital altitude	1200 km	780 km
Orbit period	6565 s	6660 s
Number of orbits	10	6
Number of satellites per orbit	12	11
Number of ISL terminals per satellite	4	4
Intraorbit ISL distance	3922 km	4029 km
Interorbit ISL distance	≤ 4909 km	≤ 4909 km
Inter plane spacing	3°	3°

Table 2. NeLS constellation potential link and its link duration.

	Satellite number	Duration(s)	Satellite number	Duration(s)
Intraorbit	0001	6566	0011	6565
Interorbit	0100	6566	0506	1653
	0110	2207	0507	1235
	0111	6566	0602	1247
	0209	1263	0603	1747
	0210	3006	0604	1714
	0211	2605	0605	1120
	0308	1526	0701	1814
	0309	2127	0702	2127
	0310	1814	0703	1526
	0406	1120	0800	2605
	0407	1714	0801	3006
	0408	1747	0802	1263
	0409	1247	0900	6566
	0504	1235	0901	2207
	0505	1653	0911	6566

Table 3. Iridium constellation potential link and its link duration.

	Satellite number	Duration(s)	Satellite number	Duration(s)
Intraorbit	0101	6600	0110	6600
Interorbit	0000	3126	0403	1480
	0001	2694	0404	1426
	0010	1216	0405	1430
	0200	3126	0406	1459
	0201	1214	0407	1480
	0210	2692	0408	1474
	0300	1650	0409	1466
	0301	1240	0410	1464
	0308	770	0500	1718
	0309	1460	0501	1460
	0310	1718	0502	770
	0400	1464	0509	1238
	0401	1466	0510	1650
	0402	1474		

Tables 2 and 3 show the satellite numbers of NeLS and Iridium in all communication ranges of satellite s0000 during the constellation period and the total duration of the corresponding links in detail. The satellite s0000 can establish an ISL with the two satellites before and after the same orbit in the whole period, and can also establish a permanent interorbit link with the remaining four satellites of different tracks (see Table 2). Therefore, in the simulation work of this paper, the satellite s0000 is selected to establish a regular link topology with four satellites, which are s0001, s0011 in the same orbit and s0100, s0900 in the different orbits. The satellite s0100 can establish an ISL with the two satellites in front and rear of the same orbit at any time during the entire period, and can also establish a half-cycle ISL with two satellites of different orbits (see Table 3). Therefore, in the simulation work of this paper, the satellite s0100 is selected to establish a regular link topology with four satellites, which are s0101, s0110 in the same orbit and s0000 and s0200 in the different orbits.

This type of regular topology conforms to the setting of the maximum degree of freedom of a single satellite node of 4, and the requirements of the optical terminals carried on the satellite are lower (see Fig. 4).

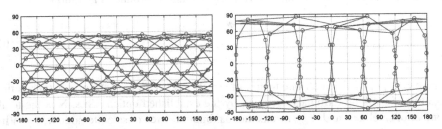

Fig. 4. 2D simulation of the potential link of the satellite network at a certain moment in the NeLS constellation (left) and the Iridium constellation (right).

Time Characteristics of Regular ISL Topology

For a single satellite, the quantity of potential links for NeLS is stable at four, and it lasts for the entire 6565 s period; the quantity of potential links for Iridium changes from 2 or 4 within a period, and the time of the number of links is 2 or 4 basically reached the entire 6660 s period (see Fig. 5).

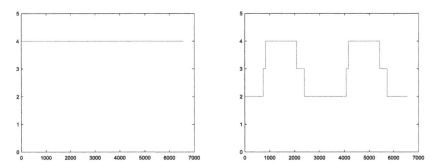

Fig. 5. The stability variation of the number of satellites in the potential link set of the NeLS constellation and the Iridium constellation within a period.

3   Optical ISLs Topology and RWA Algorithm

This paper defines the Satellite Connection Matrix (SCM):

$$C = \begin{pmatrix} c_{1,1} & c_{1,2} & \cdots & c_{1,N} \\ c_{2,1} & c_{2,2} & \cdots & c_{2,N} \\ \vdots & \vdots & \ddots & \vdots \\ c_{N,1} & c_{N,2} & \cdots & c_{N,N} \end{pmatrix} \tag{5}$$

Where $C \in \{0,1\}^{N \times N}$, $c_{m,n} = 0$ means the satellite m to satellite n does not have an ISL, and $c_{m,n} = 1$ means the satellite m has an ISL with satellite n. N represents the total quantity of satellites.

In this paper, we consider bidirectional connections, so $c_{m,n} = c_{n,m}$, i.e. C is a symmetric matrix. We proposed α to measure the proportion of active terminals in a satellite optical network link topology. The calculation formula is as follows:

$$\alpha = \frac{1}{N} \sum_{i=1}^{N} \sum_{j=1}^{N} \frac{c_{i,j}}{\phi_{max}} = \frac{\|CE\|_1}{N \cdot \phi_{max}} \tag{6}$$

Where $E \in \{1\}^{1 \times N}$ is an all-one matrix of size $1 \times N$. $\|CE_1\|$ is a 1-norm, which is the quantity of working terminals occupied by the established optical ISLs. N is the total number of satellites, and ϕ_{max} means the maximum degree of satellite node freedom(in this paper, $\phi_{max} = 4$). So $N \cdot \phi_{max}$ means the total of terminals in the optical ISL network.

3.1 Establish ISLs Topology of the Satellite Optical Network

When all satellites have established their sets of potential ISLs during the constellation period, our work will focus on the choice from sets to determine the topology of the satellite optical network. Our algorithm is based on the following rules:

- An ISL is randomly chosen from all potential links as an established ISL. The entire topology generation rules should follow: (1) Every potential link can only be chosen once; (2) The node degrees of freedom of the two satellites must be within the interval defined by the minimum and maximum values; (3) Confirm whether the connectivity of the satellite network topology satisfies the full link and whether α satisfies the demands.
- Repeat the above steps until the full topology is established.

In reality, there are always some pairs of satellite nodes that are not connectable because they may need to establish many ISLs to access each other. This situation will undoubtedly have a negative impact on network performance. Therefore, under the premise of complying with the wavelength continuity limit rule, the ISL hop count of the satellite optical network should not exceed an upper limit, that is, the maximum allowable link hop count of a single satellite, which we define as $N_{maxhops}$. After defining the hop limit between satellite nodes, the topology connectivity of the satellite optical network will be affected accordingly. For a more intuitive description, we define β as the normalized number of interconnectable node pairs relative to all the node pairs in the optical network.

$$\beta = \frac{2\mathcal{L}}{N(N-1)} \tag{7}$$

Where $\mathcal{L}$ represents the quantity of satellite node pairs that have interconnected and N denotes the total number of all satellites in the constellation.

3.2 The RWA Algorithm

To solve the RWA issue, the continuity and dissimilarity constraints of wavelength routing must be considered. Under the premise of satisfying the above two constraints, the idle communication wavelength can be allocated when the optical connection request arrives. In the RWA algorithm for satellite optical networks, different routing schemes mean the performance of the network because it is directly affected by the allocation of wavelength resources between satellites. Finding the optical path with the least link cost is the core issue of the routing algorithm. Based on the research of reference [4], this paper comprehensively considers the influence of on-board processing time and ISL distance on link cost, and establishes the optical path set of source-target satellites optical connection request based on Dijkstra algorithm. In order to make the simulation results more accurate, we consider the time-varying characteristics of the satellite constellation, and perform a random network topology simulation over thousands of times at each moment in the constellation cycle, and finally obtain the best optical path set of all source-target satellites and the result of wavelength assignment.

The total cost of the optical routing link has two major factors, one is the link cost of a single ISL, and the other is the on-board processing cost of the satellite node, which is calculated as follows.

$$W_{total}(t_i) = \sum_{j=1}^{N_{hops}} \left[\frac{d_j(t_i)}{c} + t_{j,p} \right] \tag{8}$$

Where N_{hops} is the jump numbers of the ISLs included in the optical path, $d_j(t_i)$ represents the j-th ISL distance of the path, c represents the speed of light, and $t_{j,p}$ is the processing cost of the terminals on the satellite node of the j-th ISL.

The detailed process is as follows:

- Establish the lowest cost optical path set and second lowest cost set;
- We sort the links in the optical path from high to low total cost and randomly select one of the costliest links in the optimal optical path set (because there may be several links have the same cost). The selected optical path is then assigned a dedicated wavelength that satisfies the wavelength dissimilarity constraint, in which case it is necessary to check whether the wavelength is free and has the smallest wavelength number in all ISLs through which the optical path passes;
- If the maximum number of channels in an ISL in the lowest cost optical path is greater than the second lowest cost optical path, in this situation, the lowest cost optical path currently requested will be replaced with the second lowest cost light path;
- According to the above steps, until all the link wavelength assignments are accomplished, the last calculated maximum wavelength number is the wavelength demand of the satellite optical network.

4 Simulation and Analysis of Results

Taking NeLS constellation and Iridium constellation as examples, this section analyzes and compares the wavelength resource demand and the node pairs connectivity β in a constellation cycle in the regular inter-satellite topology. In all simulation experiments we set $t_{j,p}$ 10 ms and $N_{maxhops}$ is [1, 6].

4.1 The Performance of Node Connectivity with $N_{maxhops}$

The dotted line in the figure indicates the change in the mean value of β, and the vertical line indicates the range of variation of β at the hop count (see Figs. 6 and 7). This is because for the same α, we generated 2600 different network topologies for the NeLS constellation and 4000 different kinds of network topology for the Iridium constellation, which is very convincing and representative. It can be concluded that when $N_{maxhops}$ increases, the average value of β and the overall trend will show an upward trend. For a fixed $N_{maxhops}$ value, it is desirable to increase the node connectivity β by increasing the α. In the same network case (with the same α and $N_{maxhops}$), the Iridium constellation displays a better β than the NeLS constellation.

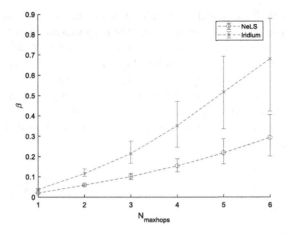

Fig. 6. The performance of β with $N_{maxhops}$ (α =0.6).

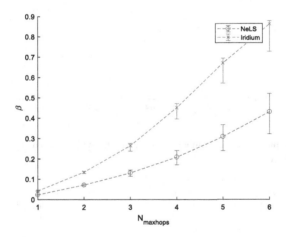

Fig. 7. The performance of β with $N_{maxhops}$ (α = 0.7).

4.2   The Performance of Requirement of Wavelengths with β and α

The dotted line indicates the trend of the average value of the number of wavelengths, the vertical line indicates its range of variation, and the horizontal line indicates the range of variation of the node connectivity (see Figs. 8 and 9). As can be concluded from the picture, when the node connectivity β is higher, the wavelength demand increases. For the same β, increasing α can effectively save wavelength resources. In the same network case (with the same α and β), the Iridium constellation requires fewer wavelength resources, apparently related to its smaller constellation system. As α increases, the rate of change in β and wavelength demand is smaller.

Comparing with Figs. 8 and 9, it can be seen that for the same $\alpha = 0.7$, the arbitrary topology of the NeLS constellation requires a maximum of 550 wavelengths, while the regular topology requires only a maximum of nearly 300 wavelengths, saving nearly half of the wavelength resources (see Figs. 10 and 11). The connectivity of the Iridium constellation in regular topology can reach a maximum of nearly 0.9, while in arbitrary link topology can only reach nearly 0.7, which improves the connectivity of 0.2 while reducing the wavelength requirement by nearly 100. It can be seen that the regular topology has a great improvement in wavelength demand and connectivity, especially for Iridium constellation.

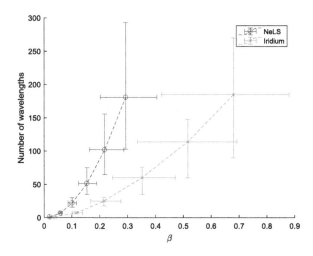

Fig. 8. The performance of the number of wavelengths with β when $\alpha = 0.6$ in the rule of regular ISLs topology.

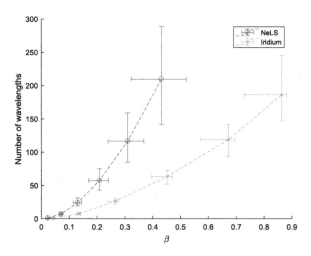

Fig. 9. The performance of the number of wavelengths with β when $\alpha = 0.7$ in the rule of regular ISLs topology.

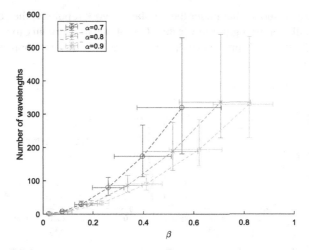

Fig. 10. The performance of the number of wavelengths with β in the rule of arbitrary ISLs topology (NeLS constellation).

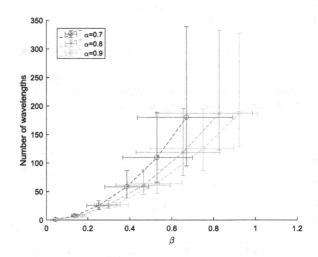

Fig. 11. The performance of the number of wavelengths with β in the rule of arbitrary ISLs topology (Iridium constellation).

4.3   The Performance of Wavelength Requirements and β with Different $N_{maxhops}$ in a Constellation Period (α= 0.7)

It can be seen from the comparison that the regular topology has a large reduction of wavelength requirement for the NeLS constellation than the arbitrary topology, and the wavelength requirements of these two constellations fluctuate less (see Figs. 12, 13, 14 and 15).

The comparison shows that under the regular network topology, the connectivity of the NeLS constellation is slightly lower than that of the arbitrary link topology, and the connectivity of the Iridium constellation has a significant improvement when $N_{maxhops} > 4$ (see Figs. 16, 17, 18 and 19).

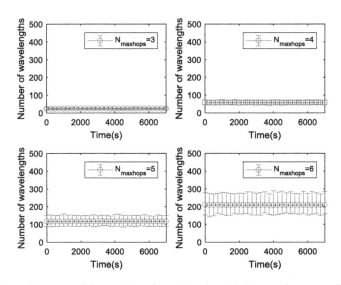

Fig. 12. The performance of the number of wavelengths with $N_{maxhops}$ in a constellation period in the rule of regular ISL topology (NeLS constellation).

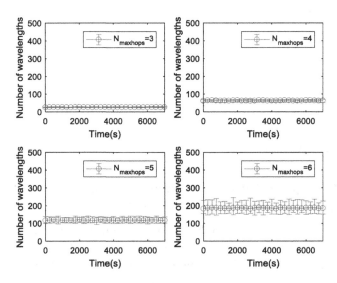

Fig. 13. The performance of the number of wavelengths with $N_{maxhops}$ in a constellation period in the rule of regular ISL topology (Iridium constellation).

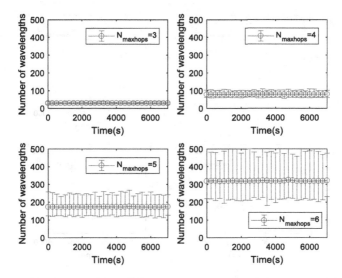

Fig. 14. The performance of the number of wavelengths with $N_{maxhops}$ in a constellation period in the rule of arbitrary ISL topology (NeLS constellation).

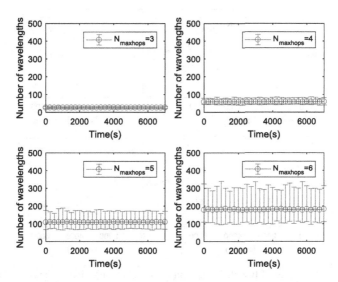

Fig. 15. The performance of the number of wavelengths with $N_{maxhops}$ in a constellation period in the rule of arbitrary ISL topology (Iridium constellation).

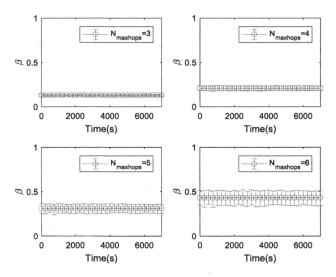

Fig. 16. The performance of β with $N_{maxhops}$ in a constellation period in the rule of regular ISL topology (NeLS constellation).

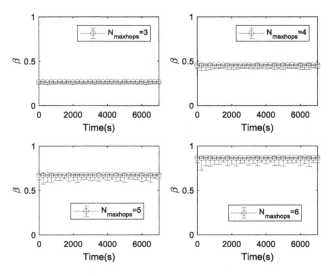

Fig. 17. The performance of β with $N_{maxhops}$ in a constellation period in the rule of regular ISL topology (Iridium constellation).

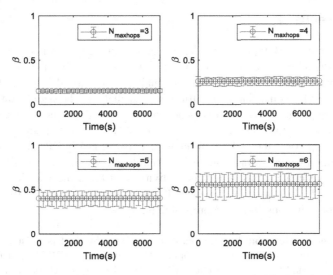

Fig. 18. The performance of β with $N_{maxhops}$ in a constellation period in the rule of arbitrary ISL topology (NeLS constellation).

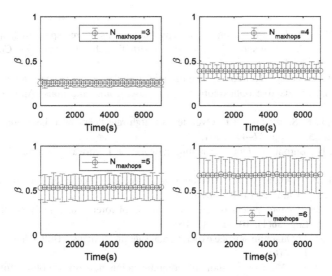

Fig. 19. The performance of β with $N_{maxhops}$ in a constellation period in the rule of arbitrary ISL topology (Iridium constellation).

5 Conclusions

In this paper, a network topology model for satellite optical networks with π-type and 2π-type constellations is established, which has a wide application space. And the RWA algorithm and wavelength demand analysis are carried out for the specific parameters of NeLS constellation and Iridium constellation. The correlation model and algorithm simulations given in this paper demonstrate that when we compare the regular network topology similar to the grid-like streets of Manhattan Island with the arbitrary link topology, the NeLS constellation can save nearly half of the wavelength resource requirement under the condition of slightly sacrificing node connectivity. And the Iridium constellation has better connectivity with the same wavelength resource requirements. The link duration, wavelength volatility and node connectivity volatility of the two constellations show a more stable trend.

Acknowledgments. This work has been partially supported by the Open Fund of State Key Laboratory of information Photonics and Optical Communications (BUPT) and the National Natural Science Foundation of China (No. 61701484) and the Research Fund of the manned space engineering (No. 18128060401).

References

1. Berman, G.P., et al.: Suppression of intensity fluctuations in free space high-speed optical communication based on spectral encoding of a partially coherent beam. Opt. Commun. **280**(2), 264–270 (2007)
2. Levine, B.M., et al.: Horizontal line-of-sight turbulence over near-ground paths and implications for adaptive optics corrections in laser communications. Appl. Opt. **37**(21), 4553 (1998)
3. Boroson, D.M., Scozzafava, J.J.: Overview of high-rate deep-space laser communications options, vol. 5338, pp. 37–49 (2004)
4. Karafolas, N., Baroni, S.: Optical satellite networks. J. Lightwave Technol. **18**(12), 1792–1806 (2000)
5. Jia, P., Li, H.: Looking at the development of foreign space laser communication from EDRS. Aerosp. China **3**, 14–17 (2016)
6. Yang, H.: Latest development progress and trends of foreign data realy satellite systems. Telecommun. Eng. **56**(1), 109–116 (2016)
7. Peng, C., Pan, J.: Quantum science experimental satellite "Micius". Bull. Chin. Acad. Sci. **31**(9), 1096–1104 (2016)
8. Dang, Z., Zhang, Y.: Optimization of communication network topology for navigation sharing among distributed satellites. Adv. Space Res. **51**(1), 143–152 (2013)
9. Koyama, Y., et al.: Components development for NeLS optical terminal. In: Free-Space Laser Communication Technologies XVII International Society for Optics and Photonics, pp. 217–224 (2005)
10. Wu, J., et al.: The iridium next system and its application. Satell. Appl. **6**, 25–29 (2010)
11. Dong, Y., Zhao, S., dan Ran, H., Li, Y., Zhu, Z.: Routing and wavelength assignment in a satellite optical network based on ant colony optimization with the small window strategy. J. Opt. Commun. Netw. **7**, 995–1000 (2015)

12. Liu, Z., et al.: Perfect match model based link assignment for optical satellite network. In: 2014 IEEE International Conference on Communications (ICC), Sydney, NSW, pp. 4149–4153 (2014)
13. Yang, Y., Xu, M., Wang, D., Wang, Y.: Towards energy-efficient routing in satellite networks. IEEE J. Sel. Areas Commun. **34**(12), 3869–3886 (2016)
14. Liu, Q., Yao, J., Liu, Z.: Research on wavelength routing algorithm based on multi-service in satellite optical networks. J. Syst. Simul. **29**(8), 1780–1787 (2017)
15. Sun, C., et al.: Development conception of space-ground inteyrated information network LEO mobile and broadband internet constellation. Telecommun. Sci. **12**, 43–52 (2017)
16. Tan, L., Yang, Q., Ma, J., Jiang, S.: Wavelength dimensioning of optical transport networks over nongeosychronous satellite constellations. J. Opt. Commun. Netw. **2**, 166–174 (2010)
17. Li, Y., Zhao, S., Wu, J.: A general evaluation criterion for coverage performance of LEO constellations. J. Astronaut. **35**(4), 410–417 (2014)
18. Zhu, L., Wu, T., Zhuo, Y.: Introduction to Satellite Communications, 4th edn. Publishing House of Electronics Industry, Beijing (2015)
19. Sun, X., Cao, S.: Wavelength routing assignment of optical networks on two typical LEO satellite constellations. In: 2018 Asia Communications and Photonics Conference (ACP), Hangzhou, pp. 1–3. IEEE (2018)

DOA Estimation Based on Bayesian Compressive Sensing

Suhang Li$^{(\boxtimes)}$, Yongkui Ma, Yulong Gao, and Jingxin Li

Changchun, China
suhang_li@163.com

Abstract. In this paper, Bayesian Compressive Sensing algorithm is studied. To deal with signals with multiple snapshots, we extend traditional Bayesian algorithm under the condition of single snapshot to multi-snapshot Bayesian Compressed Sensing (MBCS) algorithm and apply MBCS algorithm to direction of arrival (DOA) estimation of narrowband signals and wideband signals. Simulation shows that the application of BCS to DOA has certain advantages in algorithm performance.

Keywords: Bayesian Compressed Sensing · DOA · Wideband signal

1 Introduction

Direction of Arrival (DOA) estimation is one of the important branches of array signal processing [1]. Since the Second World War, it has developed rapidly and has been widely used in military and civilian fields. The classic DOA estimation algorithm is divided into subspace division and subspace fitting two categories [2]. The typical algorithm of the former is the multiple signal classification (MUSIC) algorithm. Until now, a number of derivative algorithms have been proposed. The basic idea of the MUSIC algorithm is to decompose the received data into signal subspaces and noise subspaces that are orthogonal to each other and perform spectral peak searching based on the orthogonality to estimate DOA [3]. The representative algorithm of subspace fitting category is maximum likelihood (ML) algorithm. Compared with the subspace decomposition algorithm, the subspace fitting algorithm has better estimation accuracy under the condition of low signal to noise ratio. But because of the high complexity, subspace fitting algorithm is limited in engineering applications. In 1989, Roy and Kailayh proposed the rotation-invariant subspace (ESPRIT) algorithm which eliminates the spectral peak searching compared with MUSIC algorithm and increases the operation speed [4]. For the DOA estimation of wideband signals, the basic idea of most algorithms is to decompose wideband signal into multiple narrow band parts and deal with them separately. Incoherent signal subspace algorithm (ISSM) is the easiest way to estimate DOA of wideband signals. It divides the wideband signal into several narrowband signals, and then applies the MUSIC method to each narrowband signal directly. The coherent signal subspace algorithm (CSSM) proposed by Wang and Kaveh [5] presents the concept of focusing matrix and focusing frequency. By constructing the focusing matrix, the data of each frequency point is transferred to the

M. Jia et al. (Eds.): WiSATS 2019, LNICST 280, pp. 630–639, 2019.
https://doi.org/10.1007/978-3-030-19153-5_62

focusing frequency and each realize the estimation of the coherent signal DOA. Compressive Sensing (CS) was proposed by Donoho and Tao in 2006 and it has attracted extensive attention from the industry and research. Traditional DOA estimation algorithms have some common shortcomings and it is due to the characteristic of signal subspace theory. The rapid development of CS theory provides a new idea for DOA estimation. Combining CS with DOA estimation can effectively utilize the sparse spatial characteristics of the incoming wave direction and it can overcome the disadvantage of traditional methods to a certain extent. Tropp proposed orthogonal matching pursuit (OMP) algorithm which selects the most matching atomic in the measurement matrix and computes the residual. It can solve the disadvantage that the matching pursuit (MP) algorithm cannot guarantee orthogonality and cannot obtain the optimal solution. [6] introduces the spatial coupling in coding theory and proposes the compressed sensing algorithm in coding theory. In [7], A compressed sensing algorithm based on projection matrix optimization is proposed. [8] applies compressed sensing to DOA estimation under the assumption that the dimension of received data is less than the number of array elements; the literature [9] proposed a new measurement matrix model applied to DOA estimation, and it is proved that the new model performs better when the RIP property is satisfied. The literature [10] proposes DOA estimation algorithm for multi-band signal based on compressed sensing and the detection accuracy is improved. Bayesian Compressed Sensing (BCS) is one of the latest achievements in compressed sensing theory, which was proposed by Ji and Xue in 2008. The idea is to use Bayesian statistics to make a priori assumptions about the received signal and noise, and then calculate its maximum posterior probability. Babacan introduced the Laplace Prior based on the BCS framework and proposed the LP-BCS algorithm [11]; Wu proposed multi-task Bayesian Compressive Sensing Algorithm (CMT-BCS) for the complex signal. In this paper, we research the DOA estimation based on Bayesian Compressed Sensing.

In the following section, DOA estimation based on Bayesian Compressed Sensing is studied. Section 2 introduces the signal model. Section 3 describes different Bayesian Compressed Sensing algorithms. Section 4 is the simulation result of algorithm. Finally, Sect. 5 shows the conclusion.

2 Signal Model

In the problem for estimating DOA, the array data model is the basis of all algorithms. For different array models, the algorithm should be adjusted accordingly. In this paper, we assume the antenna array is a uniform line array, that is, all the antennas are arranged in a straight line and the space of each antenna is same. The number of array elements is M and the distance between the antenna elements is d. Treating the first array element as the reference point, we can obtain that the position of kth array element can be expressed as follows.

$$r_k = (k - 1) \cdot d \tag{1}$$

The array signal model is shown in Fig. 1.

Fig. 1. Array signal model

2.1 Narrowband Signal Model

At present, there are several ways as follows to define narrowband signals.

(1) $B \ll f_0 \cdot B$ is the bandwidth of incoming signal and f_0 represents center frequency.
(2) $2v/c < < 1/(TB) \cdot v$ is the speed of source relative to the array and c is the velocity of light.
(3) $(M-1)d/c < < 1/B \cdot M$ represents the number of array elements, and d is the distance between elements.

In this paper, we adopt the first definition.

The incoming wave is far-field narrowband signal. For the ith signal, the received data can be expressed as (2)

$$s_i(t - \tau) = u_i(t - \tau)e^{j(\omega_0(t-\tau) + \varphi_i(t-\tau))} \tag{2}$$

u represents the amplitude of received signal, and ω_0 is the frequency of signal. Signal phase is marked by φ and time delay is denoted by τ.

For different elements of array, there exists a delay between elements. With the first antenna as the reference point, the delay of the kth antenna can be written as (3)

$$\tau_{ki} = (k-1) \cdot d \cdot \sin \theta_i / c \tag{3}$$

It is known that the amplitude and phase of narrowband signal are changing slowly and Eq. (4) can be obtained

$$\begin{aligned} u_i(t - \tau) &\approx u_i(t) \\ \varphi_i(t - \tau) &\approx \varphi_i(t) \end{aligned} \tag{4}$$

Then the received data of kth antenna from i^{th} incoming wave can be written as (5)

$$s_i(t - \tau_{ki}) = u_i(t)e^{j(\omega_0(t-\tau) + \varphi_i(t))} = s_i(t)e^{-j\omega_0\tau_{ki}} = s_i(t)e^{-j\omega_0\frac{(k-1)\cdot d\cdot\sin\theta_i}{c}} \tag{5}$$

When the number of incoming wave is N, the received signal of the kth antenna can be expressed as (6)

$$x_k(t) = \sum_{i=1}^{N} s_i(t - \tau_{ki}) + n_k(t) = \sum_{i=1}^{N} s_i(t)e^{-j\omega_0 \frac{(k-1)\cdot d\cdot \sin\theta_i}{c}} + n_k(t) \tag{6}$$

Then the received signal of array has the following form.

$$\begin{bmatrix} x_1(t) \\ \cdots \\ x_M(t) \end{bmatrix} = \begin{bmatrix} e^{-j\omega_0\tau_{11}} & \cdots & e^{-j\omega_0\tau_{1N}} \\ \cdots & \cdots & \cdots \\ e^{-j\omega_0\tau_{M1}} & \cdots & e^{-j\omega_0\tau_{MN}} \end{bmatrix} \begin{bmatrix} s_1(t) \\ \cdots \\ s_N(t) \end{bmatrix} + \begin{bmatrix} n_1(t) \\ \cdots \\ n_M(t) \end{bmatrix} \tag{7}$$

Equation (7) can be written in vector form as (8).

$$\mathbf{X} = \mathbf{AS} + \mathbf{N} \tag{8}$$

A represents array steering matrix whose size is $M \times N$. **S** is the signal to be estimated and **N** is Gaussian noise. The above is the narrowband signal model.

2.2   Wideband Signal Model

At present, there is no clear definition of the wideband signal. It is generally believed that signals which do not satisfy the definition of narrowband signals are wideband signals. For narrowband signals, the phase difference of the received signals of different array elements in the array is only related to the position of the array elements and the angle of the source. However, for the wideband signal, the phase difference of the received signals is not only related to the above two factors, but also related to the signal frequency and bandwidth. Therefore, the narrowband signal model cannot be applied to the wideband signal. It is usual to transform time domain form of signal into frequency domain form when we analyze wideband signals to use frequency and bandwidth information conveniently.

By performing DFT on the received signals, the received data of the kth array can be expressed as (9)

$$X_k(f) = \sum_{i=1}^{N} S_i(f)e^{-jf\frac{(k-1)\times d\times \sin q_i}{c}} + N_k(f) \tag{9}$$

Assuming that the lower frequency of incoming wave is f_L and the upper frequency is f_H, we can know that the signal of each sub-band can be expressed as (10) when the wideband signal is divided into J sub-band.

$$\mathbf{X}(f_j) = \mathbf{A}(f_j, \theta)\mathbf{S}(f_j) + \mathbf{N}(f_j), \ j = 0, 1, \ldots, J - 1 \tag{10}$$

$\mathbf{A}(f_j, \theta)$ is the frequency domain form of array steering matrix at f_j and it can be expressed as (11).

$$\mathbf{A}(f_j, \theta) = [\mathbf{a}(f_j, \theta_1), \mathbf{a}(f_j, \theta_2), \ldots, \mathbf{a}(f_j, \theta_N)], \, j = 0, 1, \ldots, J - 1 \quad (11)$$

$\mathbf{a}(f_j, \theta)$ is a column vector and has the following form.

$$\mathbf{a}(f_j, \theta_i) = \left[1, e^{-j \cdot f_j \frac{d \cdot \sin \theta_i}{c}}, \ldots, e^{-j \cdot f_j \frac{(M-1) \cdot d \cdot \sin \theta_i}{c}}\right]^T, \, i = 1, 2, \ldots, N, j = 0, 1, \ldots, J - 1 \quad (12)$$

The above is the array model for wideband signals.

3   Algorithm Description

3.1   MBCS Algorithm

DOA estimation must be performed under multiple snapshot conditions, this section presents a Bayesian Compression Sensing algorithm with multiple snapshots (MBCS) and apply it to narrowband and wideband DOA estimates.

Firstly, assuming that the noise is zero mean Gaussian white noise and the variance is σ^2, for each column of signal matrix $\mathbf{T}$ and sparse weight coefficient matrix $\mathbf{W}$, we have

$$p(\mathbf{t}_j | \mathbf{\omega}_j) = (2\pi\sigma^2)^{-N/2} \exp\left(-\frac{1}{2\sigma^2} \|\mathbf{t}_j - \mathbf{\Phi}\mathbf{\omega}_j\|^2\right) \quad (13)$$

Assume that each row element in the sparse weight coefficient matrix obeys Gaussian distribution whose mean is zero and variance is α_i. Then the distribution of $\mathbf{W}$ can be expressed as (14)

$$p(\mathbf{W}; \mathbf{\alpha}) = \prod_{i=1}^{M} p(\mathbf{\omega}_i; \alpha_i) \quad (14)$$

The posterior distribution of the signal can be obtained as (15) based on likelihood estimation and prior estimation.

$$p(\mathbf{\omega}_j | \mathbf{t}_j; \mathbf{\alpha}) = \frac{p(\mathbf{\omega}_j, \mathbf{t}_j; \mathbf{\alpha})}{\int p(\mathbf{\omega}_j, \mathbf{t}_j; \mathbf{\alpha}) d\mathbf{\omega}_j} = N(\mu_j, \mathbf{\Sigma}) \quad (15)$$

μ and Σ are the mean and variance, and can be expressed as follows.

$$\begin{aligned}
\mu &= [\mu_1, \mu_2, \ldots, \mu_L] = E[\mathbf{W} | \mathbf{T}; \mathbf{\alpha}] = \mathbf{\Lambda}\mathbf{\Phi}^T\mathbf{C}^{-1}\mathbf{T} \\
\Sigma &= \text{Cov}[\mathbf{\omega}_j | \mathbf{t}_j; \mathbf{\alpha}] = \mathbf{\Lambda} - \mathbf{\Lambda}\mathbf{\Phi}^T\mathbf{C}^{-1}\mathbf{\Phi}\mathbf{\Lambda}, \, j = 1, 2, \ldots, K
\end{aligned} \quad (16)$$

$\mathbf{\Lambda} = \text{diag}(\mathbf{\alpha})$, $\mathbf{C} = \sigma^2\mathbf{I} + \mathbf{\Phi}\mathbf{\Lambda}\mathbf{\Phi}^T$, and μ is the parameter to be estimated.

By marginalizing likelihood function, the log-likelihood function of $\mathbf{\alpha}$ can be obtained as follows.

$$L(\alpha) = -2\log_{10}\int p(\mathbf{T}|\mathbf{W})p(\mathbf{W};\alpha)d\mathbf{W}$$

$$= -2\log_{10}p(\mathbf{T};\alpha) = K\log_{10}|\mathbf{C}| + \sum_{j=1}^{K}\omega_{\cdot j}^{T}\mathbf{C}^{-1}\omega_{\cdot j} \tag{17}$$

Solve the derivative of $L(\alpha)$ and make derivative equal to zero. The extreme point of $L(\alpha)$ is

$$\alpha_{i}^{new} = \frac{\frac{1}{K}\|\mu_i\|^2}{1 - \alpha_i^{-1}\Sigma_{ii}} \tag{18}$$

Similarly, the estimated parameter σ^2 can be solved

$$\left(\sigma^2\right)^{new} = \frac{\frac{1}{K}\|\mathbf{T} - \Phi\mu\|_F^2}{N - M + \sum_{i=1}^{M}\frac{\Sigma_{ii}}{\gamma_i}} \tag{19}$$

3.2 DOA Estimation Based on MBCS Algorithm

Bayesian theory is only applicable to real-valued data. In order to apply it to DOA estimation, the signal model described in Sect. 2 cannot be directly used, and the signal model needs to be improved.

The complex signal data received by the array antenna is

$$\mathbf{y}_m = \mathbf{A}\mathbf{s}_m + \varepsilon_m, \; m = 1, 2, \ldots, M \tag{20}$$

Convert the complex signal into the form shown in Eq. (21)

$$\mathbf{T}_m = \Phi\mathbf{W} + \mathbf{N}_m, \; m = 1, 2, \ldots, M \tag{21}$$

$\mathbf{T}_m = [\mathrm{Re}\{\mathbf{y}_m\}, \mathrm{Im}\{\mathbf{y}_m\}]^T$ is the real matrix. $\mathbf{N}_m = [\mathrm{Re}\{\varepsilon_m\}, \mathrm{Im}\{\varepsilon_m\}]^T$ is the transformation of noise matrix, $\mathbf{W} = [\mathrm{Re}\{\mathbf{s}_m\}, \mathrm{Im}\{\mathbf{s}_m\}]^T$ is the transformation of signal matrix. The transformation of Φ is the corresponding real steering matrix and can be written as

$$\Phi = \begin{bmatrix} \mathrm{Re}\{\mathbf{A}\} & -\mathrm{Im}\{\mathbf{A}\} \\ \mathrm{Im}\{\mathbf{A}\} & \mathrm{Re}\{\mathbf{A}\} \end{bmatrix} \tag{22}$$

The algorithm steps applying LP-BCS to DOA estimation are as follows.

(1) Divide the angular space into equal spacing, and determine the real steering matrix Φ according to (22)
(2) Transform the received data according to (21)

(3) Solve the sparse coefficient vector with the algorithm, the DOA information can be obtained

Figure 2 is the simulation result. The simulation condition is: incident angle are 10°, 50°; snapshot number is 10; signal to noise ratio is 0 dB; array element number 10; grid division 181 copies.

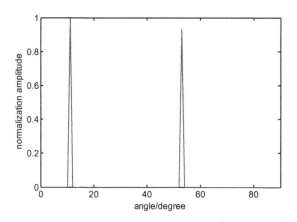

Fig. 2. Simulation result of MBCS

The steps for applying MBCS algorithm to wideband signal DOA estimation (MBCS-WDOA) are as follows:

(1) Sample the received signal with $L \times J$ points and divide signal into L groups.
(2) Transform the wideband signal into J narrowband signals by using discrete Fourier transform (DFT) to each group data.
(3) Construct measurement matrix of corresponding frequency point for each narrowband data.
(4) Apply MBCS algorithm to data for each frequency point and compute the result of each frequency point.
(5) Compute the average of the estimated values of each frequency point and solve the final result.

Figure 3 is the MBCS-WDOA simulation result. The simulation condition is: Incident angle is 40°; snapshot number is 6×128; signal to noise ratio is 0 dB; the number of array elements is 10; incident signal center frequency is 300 kHz; the bandwidth is 200 kHz.

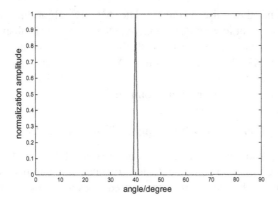

Fig. 3. Simulation result of MBCS-WDOA

4   Simulation Verification and Analysis

4.1   DOA Estimation for Narrowband Signal Based on MBCS

Figure 4 shows the estimation performance of MBCS, MUSIC and MMV-OMP. The simulation condition is: incidence angle is 10°; snapshot number is 10; array element number is 10.

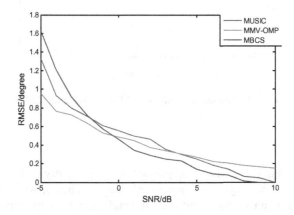

Fig. 4. Performance of MUSIC, MMV-OMP and MBCS

As can be seen from Fig. 4, at higher SNR, the performance of the MBCS is better than the MUSIC algorithm and MMV-OMP algorithm. This can be explained theoretically. The MBCS algorithm is essentially a process of learning the prior knowledge of signals and noise, that is, the estimation results of each time are related to the results of the previous calculation. When the signal-to-noise ratio is low, since the noise is random, and the MBCS algorithm has a simple a priori assumption on the signal, and the estimated hyper-parameter is less, the MBCS has a poor learning effect on the signal variance and the noise variance. The MUSIC algorithm utilizes subspace decomposition. Even if at low SNR, the eigenvalue of the signal subspace is still higher than that of noise subspace. However, with the increase of signal-to-noise ratio, the learning ability of MBCS is getting better. At this time, the advantage of MBCS multiple iteration learning to calculate the posterior probability is revealed, which can make full use of the better external environment.

4.2   DOA Estimation for Wideband Signal Based on MBCS

Figure 5 shows the estimation performance of MBCS, MUSIC and MMV-OMP. The simulation condition is: incidence angle is $10°$; snapshot number is 6×128; array element number is 10; Incident signal center frequency is 300 kHz, and bandwidth is 200 kHz.

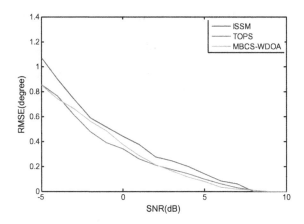

Fig. 5. Performance of MUSIC, MMV-OMP and MBCS

5   Conclusion

In this paper, we study Bayesian Compressed Sensing Theory and its application in DOA estimation. In the Bayesian Compressed Sensing Theory, we extend traditional Bayesian algorithm under the condition of single snapshot to multiple snapshots condition. Then MBCS algorithm is studied. Correspondingly, the likelihood function and parameter update formula of MBCS are given. In terms of DOA estimation, MBCS is applied in narrowband signal DOA estimation. At a higher signal-to-noise ratio, the performance is better than the other two compression sensing methods MMV-OMP and L1-SVD. The implementation scheme of MBCS-WDOA is given. Through simulation analysis, it is proved that its performance is better than ISSM, which is basically the same as the TOPS algorithm.

Acknowledgement. This work was supported by the Nation Science Foundation of China (Under Grant: 61671176).

References

1. Candès, E.J., Wakin, M.B.: An introduction to compressive sampling. IEEE Signal Process. Mag. **25**(2), 21–30 (2008)
2. Candès, E.J., Romberg, J., Tao, T.: Robust uncertainty principles: exact signal reconstruction from highly incomplete frequency information. IEEE Trans. Inf. Theory **52**(2), 489–509 (2006)
3. Vallet, P., Mestre, X., Loubaton, P.: Performance analysis of an improved MUSIC DoA estimator. IEEE Trans. Signal Process. **63**(23), 6407–6422 (2015)
4. Amiri, P.M., Ghofrani, S.: MUSIC algorithm for DOA estimation of coherent sources. IET Signal Process. **11**(4), 429–436 (2017)
5. Ghofrani, S., Amin, M.G., Zhang, Y.D.: High-resolution direction finding of non-stationary signals using matching pursuit. Signal Process. **93**(12), 3466–3478 (2013)
6. Parian, M.A., Ghofrani, S.: Using $\ell 1, 2$ mixed-norm MUSIC based on compressive sampling for direction of arrival estimation. In: IEEE International Symposium on Signal Processing and Information Technology, pp. 258–263 (2015)
7. Steinwandt, J., Roemer, F., Haardt, M., et al.: R-dimensional esprit-type algorithms for strictly second-order non-circular sources and their performance analysis. IEEE Trans. Signal Process. **62**(18), 4824–4838 (2014)
8. Donoho, D.L., Javanmard, A., Montanari, A.: Information-theoretically optimal compressed sensing via spatial coupling and approximate message passing. IEEE Trans. Inf. Theory **59** (11), 7434–7464 (2013)
9. Stanković, L., Orović, I., Stanković, S., et al.: Compressive sensing based separation of nonstationary and stationary signals overlapping in time-frequency. IEEE Trans. Signal Process. **61**(18), 4562–4572 (2013)
10. Li, G., Zhu, Z., Yang, D., et al.: On projection matrix optimization for compressive sensing systems. IEEE Trans. Signal Process. **61**(11), 2887–2898 (2013)
11. Ibrahim, M., Roemer, F., Del, G.G.: On the design of the measurement matrix for compressed sensing based DOA estimation. In: IEEE International Conference on Acoustics, Speech and Signal Processing, pp. 3631–3635 (2015)

A New Algorithm (ESA-DE)
for Designing FIR Digital Filters

LiBao Deng[(✉)], Haili Sun, and Lili Zhang

Harbin Institute of Technology, Weihai, Shandong, China
denglibao_paper@163.com

Abstract. This paper proposes a new algorithm called (ESA-DE) for software-designed realization of finite impulse response (FIR) filters. The determination of the optimal order of the filter is always a confusing problem. In this paper, we will confirm the optimal order of the filter. Differential evolution has obtained widely concern as one of the most promising intelligent optimization algorithms in the field of artificial intelligence. The new algorithm (ESA-DE) uses a new mechanism called elite guide with weight and two new self-adaptive parameter distribution techniques to enhance algorithm's diversity and convergence. Experiments prove that the new algorithm is at least superior to the basic DE and its variants jDE and ODE. The proposed algorithm is applied to solve practical problem that it is to design FIR digital filters, which overcomes the shortcomings of the traditional designing method. In addition, the practical problem about design for digital filter demonstrates that the ESA-DE has a better performance compared with the other three algorithms.

Keywords: FIR digital filters · Artificial intelligence · Differential evolution (DE)

1 Introduction

FIR is a kind of the digital filter [1] which is widely used for stability, amplitude's randomicity and limited sampling value. The window function method [2,3], optimal least-squares method (LSM) [4,5]and other traditional methods have problems on determining the boundary frequency of passband and stopband. The traditional optimization algorithms only pay attention to local information which can't meet the requirement of high precision of practical engineering problems because it is difficult to jump out of local optimum. Intelligent optimization methods with global optimization ability gradually emerge, including

This work was supported in part by National Natural Science Foundation of China (61401121).

genetic algorithm (GA) [6], particle swarm algorithm (PSO) [7] and differential evolutionary algorithm (DE) [8], etc. These algorithms simulate the evolutionary process of natural organisms or the behavior of social groups of organisms to form a scientific calculation method called artificial life computation. Scholars continuously devote to the artificial life and design research of digital filter with artificial life calculation.They put forward a new optimization algorithm [9,10] and various technologies [5,11–13] to design digital filter and achieve good optimization results.

The layout of the rest of the paper is as follows: Sect. 2 gives a brief introduction about principle of FIR digital filter and model establishment. Section 3 reviews the related works on the traditional DE. Section 4 elaborates the new algorithm with various strategies and comparative experiments results of several algorithms. Section 5 demonstrates design process of low-pass FIR digital filter. Finally, a conclusion is made in Sect. 6.

2   FIR Digital Filter Principle

In this section, principle and model of FIR digital filter is introduced.

2.1   Principle of FIR Digital Filter

The optimal design of digital filter is an important part of signal processing. It can be realized by hardware [14] and software while software implementation has become a trend of filter design. Both can process the digital discrete signal and change the frequency response or waveform of the input signal. They can prevent the interference signal from outputting and then output the required signal. FIR digital filter has a wide range of applications including speech recognition, image processing, communication , military target navigation [15,16], the trend of the economic market forecast, energy distribution of power system [17], and intelligent robot system automatically detecting [18] etc.

2.2   Establishment of FIR Digital Filter Model

We designed a linear phase FIR digital filter [18] and selected finite impact response $h(n)(1 \leqslant n \leqslant N-1$, N represents the filter order). The system function $H(z)$ is as follows:

$$H(z) = \sum_{n=0}^{N-1} h(n)z^{-n} \tag{1}$$

The frequency response function corresponding to the filter is as follows:

$$H(e^{jw}) = \sum_{n=0}^{N-1} h(n)e^{-jwn} \tag{2}$$

The filter has a linear phase and obtains four different amplitude responses in the frequency domain. One odd number is listed here ($\theta(w)$ is the phase frequency response) (Table 1).

Table 1. Parameter correspondence of amplitude responses

N = odd	$H(w)$ and $\theta(w)$	Relation of $H(w)$ and $h(n)$	The filter type
$h(n)$ = even symmetry	$\sum_{n=0}^{\frac{N-1}{2}} h_1(n)cos(wn)$ $-w\frac{N-1}{2}$	$h_1(0) = h(\frac{N-1}{2})$ $h_1(n) = 2h(\frac{N-1}{2} + n)$ $n = 1, 2, ..., \frac{N-1}{2}$	(1) Low pass (2) High pass (3) Band pass (4) Stop band

3   Classical DE

DE is a stochastic optimization algorithm based on the number of population NP, which searchs the optimal solution in the D dimensional space. We use $X_{i,G} = [x_{i,1,G}, x_{i,2,G}, ..., x_{i,D,G}]$ to represent the ith candidate solution in generation G, where $i = 1, 2, ..., NP$. For the classical DE [19], there are four following operations:initialization, mutation, crossover, and selection.

3.1   Initialization

We initialize the candidate solution between lower limit $X_{i,G} = [x_{1,min}, x_{2,min}, ..., x_{D,min}]$ and high limit $X_{i,G} = [x_{1,max}, x_{2,max}, ..., x_{D,max}]$. The following equation is used to initialize individuals in the initial population :

$$x_{i,j} = x_{j,min} + rand_{i,j}(0, 1) \cdot (x_{j,max} - x_{j,min}) \tag{3}$$

where $x_{j,min}$ and $x_{j,max}$ denote the lower and upper bound, It's a constant between $[0, 1]$.

3.2   Mutation

Mutation operation is the part of DE algorithm. Each target vector $X_{i,G}$ is viewed as the base vector once. And then, two target vectors $X_{i2,G}$ and $X_{i3,G}$ are selected from the population. The difference vector is generated. The difference vector is weighted and added to the basis vector. The mutation vector $V_{i,G} = [v_{i,1,G}, v_{i,2,G}, ..., v_{i,D,G}]$ is obtained. The basic variation strategy:

$$V_{i,G} = X_{i1,G} + F \cdot (X_{i2,G} - X_{i3,G}) \tag{4}$$

where $i = 1, 2, ..., NP$. index $i1, i2, i3 \in [1, NP]$, which is different from each other.

3.3   Crossover

The crossover operation is to mix the components of the target vector $X_{i,G}$ and the mutation vector $V_{i,G}$ and get the trial vector $U_{i,G} = [u_{i,1,G}, u_{i,2,G}, ..., u_{i,D,G}]$ which can be generated by the following formula:

$$u_{i,j,G} = \begin{cases} v_{i,j,G} & \text{if } rand_{i,j}(0,1) \leqslant CR \text{ or } j = j_{rand} \\ x_{i,j,G} & \text{otherwise} \end{cases} \tag{5}$$

where $i = 1, 2, ..., NP$. $rand_j(0,1)$ is randomly chosen from 0 to 1 for each j and each i according to a uniform distribution. the crossover factor CR is a constant between $[0, 1]$, which determines how many components of the trial vector from the mutation vector and affects the evolutionary speed of the algorithm. j_{rand} that is a integer keeps that one different parameter exists between the target vector $X_{i,G}$ and its trial vector $U_{i,G}$ at least.

3.4 Selection

The selection operation forms a new population by selecting the trial vector and corresponding target vector. According to their fitness values $f(\cdot)$, The vector with having the best fitness value is preserved. The implementation is as follows:

$$X_{i,G+1} = \begin{cases} U_{i,G} & \text{if } f(U_{i,G}) \leqslant f(X_{i,G}) \\ X_{i,G} & \text{otherwise} \end{cases} \tag{6}$$

where $f(\cdot)$ represents the fitness value of the function. In general, we optimize the minimum value of the problem.

3.5 Condition of Algorithm Termination

There are two kinds of circumstances to make algorithm to end. On the one hand, the number of iteration has reached maximum number of iteration, on the other hand, the error $f_{actual}(\cdot) - f(\cdot)$ between the ideal function value $f(\cdot)$ and actual output function value $f_{actual}(\cdot)$ is not more than 10^{-8}.

4 ESA-DE

The convergence speed of the algorithm is accelerated by using strategy of elite guidance with weight. We use adaptive F and CR to balance the exploration and exploitation. The description is as follows.

4.1 Strategy of Elite Guide with Weight

Variation strategy [23,24] has a direct impact on the performance of the algorithm. We aim to better find the global optimal solution, in the first place, population diversity should be maintained to avoid the algorithm falling into the local optimum. In the second place, the convergence speed should be guaranteed. Direction of the improvement which based on the above content that is strategy of elite guide with weight is put forward in this paper. It will retain the original difference vector of DE algorithm to ensure the population diversity. What's more, it will join a new difference vector and let the elite guide the worst evolve together to speed up the algorithm convergence through diagram Figs. 1a and 1b. In addition, the weight w is added to control the participation degree of two difference vectors to ensure the accuracy of the solution. The strategy equation is as follows:

$$X_1 = X_{r1} - X_{r2} \tag{7}$$

$$X_2 = X_{best} - X_{worst} \tag{8}$$

$$V = X_i + w \cdot F \cdot X_1 + (1 - w) \cdot F \cdot X_2 \tag{9}$$

where X_1 and X_2 represent two difference vectors, X_i, X_{r1} and X_{r2} are chosen at random from a population, $i \neq r1 \neq r2$; X_{best} is the best individual in the population, X_{worst} is the worst individual in the population; $w = 0.9$; F is the scale factor, which controls the magnitude of the difference vector between [0,1].

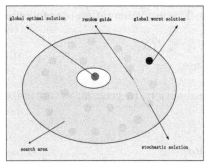 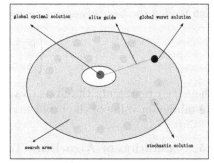

(a) *random-guide strategy*   (b) *elite-guide strategy*

Fig. 1. Mapping of logistic and sinusoidal

4.2   Parameter Adaptation

Parameter setting [25–28] is another important factor to affect the performance of the algorithm. The two main parameters of the DE algorithm are F and CR. Changeable parameters can improve the performance of the algorithm so we let the parameters change in each generation to adapt to the evolution of the algorithm. In order to improve the convergence speed of the algorithm and carry out local accurate search. We let F keep large to ensure the diversity of the population at an early stage. In the later stage of the algorithm evolution, F decreases gradually. Similarly, CR was large to ensure the convergence speed in the early stage. In the later stage of evolution, CR was small to ensure the diversity of population. Based on the above ideas, the distribution of F and CR is as follows:

$$F = F_{max} - \frac{F_{max} - F_{min}}{G_{max}} \cdot G \tag{10}$$

$$CR = \frac{CR_{min}}{1 + (\frac{CR_{min}}{CR_{max}} - 1) \cdot e^{-G}} \tag{11}$$

where G_{max} is maximum number of iteration, G is current iteration number, F_{max} and F_{min} are maximum and minimum value of variation factors, they are set to 0.9 and 0.3, CR_{max} and CR_{min} are maximum and minimum value of crossover factors, they are set to 0.8 and 0.5, algorithm flow is displayed algorithm 1.

Algorithm 1. Pseudocode of OTWDE algorithm

Begin
      $G\_max = 1000$; $NP = 100$;$w = 0.9$;
      $F\_min = 0.9$; $F\_max = 0.3$;$CR\_min = 0.8$; $CR\_max = 0.5$;
  Inilization
  Generate a random initial population $P_0 = [X_1, X_2, ..., X_{NP}]$
  while $G < G\_max$ **do**
    for $i = 1 : NP$ **do**
  According to 10 and 11 to update F and CR
  According to 9 to generate $V_{i,G}$
  According to 5 to generate $U_{i,G}$
  According to 6 to select the next generation $X_{i,G+1}$
      if $f(U_{i,j,g}) \leq f(X_{i,j,g})$ **then**
        $X_{i,j,G+1} = U_{i,j,G}$;
      else
        $X_{i,j,G+1} = X_{i,j,G}$
      end if
    end for
  end while

4.3 Test Function

For the evaluation of algorithm performance, there is no unified evaluation criterion in academia while the performance comparison of optimization algorithm is usually based on some typical problems called Benchmark [29,30]. In this paper, 6 classic universal test functions are selected, High Conditioned Elliptic Function f(1), Rastrigin Function f(2), Rosenbrock Function f(3), Cigar Function f(4), Griewank Function f(5), Schaffer Function f(6), respectively. The specific description is given Table 2 (Fig. 2).

4.4 Simulation Result

The performance of DE, jDE, ODE and ESA-DE algorithm is evaluated by the above 6 common test functions. The four algorithms run 50 times independently. F and CR are 0.5 and 0.3 for standard DE algorithm, respectively; The parameter setting of jDE and ODE is consistent with the original algorithm; For ESA-DE algorithm, $F_{max} = 0.9$, $F_{min} = 0.3$, $CR_{max} = 0.8$,$CR_{min} = 0.5$. The maximum number of iteration of the four algorithms is $G_{max} = 1000$. The population size is set $NP = 100$. We obtained the performance evaluation criterion of

Table 2. Specific description of test functions

Function name	Seach range	Optimum	Dimension
f_1	$[-30, 30]^D$	0	50
f_2	$[-5.12, 5.12]^D$	0	20
f_3	$[-30, 30]^D$	0	20
f_4	$[-30, 30]^D$	0	50
f_5	$[-500, 500]^D$	0	20
f_6	$[-100, 100]^D$	0	20

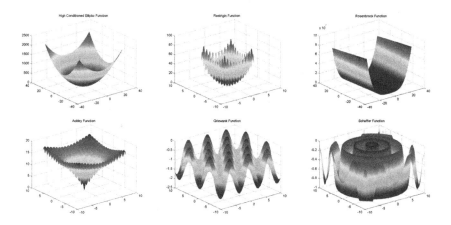

Fig. 2. 3-dimensional images of 2-dimensional functions of 6 test functions

test function: average error value of fitness (mean), standard deviation (std) and the success rate of the solution (SR) ($SR = SN/S$,SN is amounts that we find the optimal value among 50 times, S is the total number of 50 runs). Table 3 represents the data simulation results. Figure 3 is convergence figures of test functions. We see Table 3, ESA-DE is less than mean and standard error value of other algorithms for the mean and standard error value. The success rate of solution is also higher than other algorithms. It can illustrate that ESA-DE has higher robustness and precision about solution. We can conclude that ESA-DE converges earlier than other algorithms in earlier generation which means that ESA-DE converges faster From the convergence simulation diagram of Fig. 3. In conclusion, the improved algorithm is superior to the standard DE algorithm, jDE and ODE.

Table 3. Mean, standard deviation value and SR of ESA-DE, DE, jDE and ODE over 50 independent runs

Function	Algorithm	Mean	Std	SR
$f_1(50)$	ESA-DE	1.19E−14	8.46E−15	100%
	DE	1.57E−09	1.15E−09	100%
	jDE	6.94E−11	9.30E−11	100%
	ODE	1.55E−12	6.01E−13	100%
$f_2(30)$	ESA-DE	5.00E−10	3.50E−10	100%
	DE	9.05E+01	7.10E+00	0%
	jDE	5.70E+02	2.61E+01	0%
	ODE	2.38E+01	4.48E+00	13%
$f_3(30)$	ESA-DE	1.44E−02	1.22E−02	15%
	DE	3.67E+01	1.55E+01	0%
	jDE	3.28E+02	1.81E+02	0%
	ODE	1.23E−05	1.70E−05	40%
$f_4(50)$	ESA-DE	1.64E−16	1.00E−16	100%
	DE	1.49E−04	6.97E−05	0%
	jDE	4.92E−09	3.44E−09	90%
	ODE	5.73E−09	4.05E−08	87%
$f_5(30)$	ESA-DE	2.32E−13	2.18E−13	100%
	DE	2.28E+00	7.39E+00	0%
	jDE	3.78E−07	4.54E−06	40%
	ODE	5.69E−08	7.24E−09	93%
$f_6(30)$	ESA-DE	2.47E−08	1.10E−08	93%
	DE	8.93E+01	3.30E−01	0%
	jDE	1.44E−05	1.40E−06	30%
	ODE	1.85E−03	3.82E−04	0%

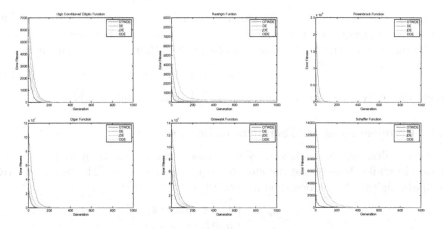

Fig. 3. Convergence figures of 6 test functions

5   Design of Low Pass FIR Digital Filter

The software-designed filter is a popular topic for digital signal processing of artificial intelligence in recent years. DE algorithm is booming in recent years. It has found application in various fields and achieved good results. Besides relying on theory, The test of algorithm design needs validation of test problems so we use DE to design filter.

5.1   Establish the Fitness Function Model

The difference evolution is used to evaluate individual's advantages and disadvantages through fitness value so you must choose the corresponding fitness function E according to the actual problem. The minimum square error optimization design of the FIR digital filter is required at the discrete frequency point w_i, and $i = 1, ..., M$. FIR digital filter and the ideal FIR digital filter are $|H(e^{jw_i})|$ and $|H_d(e^{jw_i})|$ respectively, The fitness function of the algorithm is shown as follows:

$$E = \sum_{i=1}^{M}[|H(e^{jw_i})| - |H_d(e^{jw_i})|]^2 = \sum_{i=1}^{M}[|\sum_{n=0}^{N-1} h(n)(e^{-jw_i})| - |H(e^{jw_i})|]^2 \quad (12)$$

where the smaller E, it shows that optimized parameters are better and the filter has a better performance.

5.2   Parameter Coding

We designed a FIR low-pass digital filter that N is odd which is based on the corresponding process of coefficient $h(n)$ and $h_1(n)$. We use the symmetry of $h_1(n)$ to get all coefficients of filter. $h_1(n)$ is encoded by matrix as follows:

$$\begin{bmatrix} H(w_1) \\ \cdots \\ H(w_M) \end{bmatrix} = \begin{bmatrix} 1 & cos(w_1) & \cdots & cos(\frac{N-1}{2}w_1) \\ \cdots & \cdots & \ddots & \cdots \\ 1 & cos(w_1) & \cdots & cos(\frac{N-1}{2}w_M) \end{bmatrix} \begin{bmatrix} h_1(0) \\ \cdots \\ h_1(\frac{N-1}{2}) \end{bmatrix} \quad (13)$$

where the matrix equation is written as $H = A \cdot h$. H represents sampling value vector of the frequency domain. A coefficient matrix. h represents the filter coefficient vector. The fitness function of the algorithm can be rewritten as:

$$E = (|A \cdot h_1 - H_d|)^{'}(|A \cdot h_1 - H_d|) \quad (14)$$

where the individual that we encode is a $\frac{N-1}{2}$ dimensional variable.

5.3   Requirements for Technical Indicators

Low-pass filter means that some signals below the cut-off frequency can pass smoothly while those above the cut-off frequency can't pass. The designed FIR low-pass digital filter is designed as follows:

$$H_d(e^{jw}) = \begin{cases} 1 & 0 \leqslant w < 0.4\pi \\ 0 & 0.5\pi \leqslant w < \pi \end{cases} \quad (15)$$

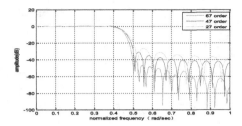

Fig. 4. Situation of order increasing

where the optimized filter parameter values are reserved with 5 decimal places.

5.4   Design Flow

The main steps of designing a linear phase digital filter using ESA-DE algorithm are as follows: (1) give the technical index of designed linear phase digital filter; (2) the parameters of ESA-DE algorithm are set according to the design requirement of FIR digital filter; (3) the population was randomly initialized within the parameter range and the fitness value was calculated; (4) carry out mutation, crossover and selection for each target individual; (5) repeat (4) until the end condition of the algorithm is satisfied and finally output FIR digital filter parameters.

5.5   Result Analysis

We first determine the optimal order of the digital low pass filter. We use four algorithms to design the filter according to the optimal order. Finally we prove the superiority of ESA-DE algorithm from the practical problems.

Determination of the Optimal Order. The order N will affect the approximation of the designed filter to the ideal filter. The distortion degree of sampling will be smaller for the greater N. The problem with great N is that complexity increases gradually. Even if the narrow pulse is wide, filtering effect will decline. This paper determines the optimal order size. We first applied ESA-DE to design FIR low pass digital filter. Cut-off frequecy of passband is set to 0.4π. Cut-off frequency of stopband is set to 0.5π. We select 64 sampling points. The simulation results are shown in Figs. 4 and 5.

Filter Design of Four Algorithms. Four algorithms are used to design FIR low-pass digital filters. The parameters encoding, requirements for technical indicators and design flow are the same as the above design method. It proves that the improved algorithm is better than standard DE algorithm, jDE and ODE through examples of practical problem. According to the above simulation results, the order of the filter is set to 67. The simulation results are shown in Fig. 6.

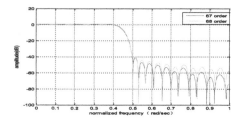

Fig. 5. Situation of order determination

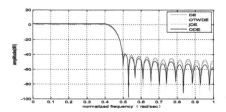

Fig. 6. Design situation of four algorithms

Filter Design of Four Algorithms. As can be seen from the simulation results, there is no significant difference in the optimization effect of several algorithms in the passband and transition zone. The passband ripple is basically 0, indicating that the robustness of the DE algorithm is very good. On the side of stopband attenuation, the designed filter attenuation amplitude for ESA-DE is greater than 30 dB. Attenuation amplitude of the designed filter for DE algorithm and jDE are all greater than 10 dB. The designed filter attenuation amplitude for the ODE is greater than 20 dB. It can also explain that ESA-DE is superior to the above three kinds of algorithms.

6   Conclusion

In this paper, the basic DE algorithm is improved. The improvements including two aspects: (1) Elite guiding strategy is used to make the best individual guide the worst individual (2) adaptive parameter mechanism is utilized in the different stages of evolution algorithm. Importantly, The optimal order of filter is determined. Posteriorly, basic DE algorithm, jDE and ODE are also used to design filters. The comparison experiments show that the proposed algorithm performs better than the above three algorithms in solving the practical problem from the opposite side. In the future, we will use the improved algorithm to try to solve magnitude-error and phase-error constrained optimal designs of finite impulse response (FIR) filter problem.

References

1. Haridas, N., Elias, E.: Low-complexity technique to get arbitrary variation in the bandwidth of a digital FIR filter. IET Sign. Process. **11**(4), 372–377 (2017)
2. Kumar, S., Mehra, R., Chandni.: Implementation and designing of FIR filters using Kaiser window for de-noising of electrocardiogram signals on FPGA. In: IEEE Power India International Conference, pp. 1–6. IEEE (2016)
3. Das, P., Naskar, S.K., Patra, S.N.: An approach to enhance performance of Kaiser window based filter. In: International Conference on Research in Computational Intelligence & Communication Networks, pp. 256–261. IEEE (2017)
4. Eghbali, A., et al.: Optimal least-squares FIR digital filters for compensation of chromatic dispersion in digital coherent optical receivers. J. Lightwave Technol. **32**(8), 1449–1456 (2014)
5. Yi, H., et al.: A new constraint model for optimal design of constrained FIR digital filters. In: Chinese Control Conference, pp. 5566–5571. IEEE (2017)
6. Nyathi, T., Pillay, N.: Comparison of a genetic algorithm to grammatical evolution for automated design of genetic programming classification algorithms. Expert Syst. Appl. **104**, 213–234 (2018)
7. Nobile, M.S., et al.: Fuzzy self-tuning PSO: a settings-free algorithm for global optimization. Swarm Evol. Comput. **39**, 70–85 (2017)
8. Price, K., Price, K.: Differential Evolution a Simple and Efficient Heuristic for Global Optimization over Continuous Spaces. Kluwer Academic Publishers, Dordrecht (1997)
9. Jiang, A., Kwan, H.K.: WLS design of sparse FIR digital filters. IEEE Trans. Circuits Syst. I Regul. Pap. **60**(1), 125–135 (2013)
10. Das, P., Naskar, S.K., Patra, S.N.: Adaptive global best steered Cuckoo search algorithm for FIR filter design. In: International Conference on Research in Computational Intelligence & Communication Networks, pp. 15–20 (2017)
11. Shiung, D., Yang, Y.Y., Yang, C.S.: Improving FIR filters by using cascade techniques tips & tricks. IEEE Sign. Process. Mag. **33**(3), 108–114 (2016)
12. Mason, J.S., Chit, N.N.: New approach to the design of FIR digital filters. In: IEE Proceedings G - Electronic Circuits and Systems, vol. 134, no. 4, pp. 167–180 (1987)
13. Bose, A., Chandra, A.: Conditional differential coefficients method for the realization of powers-of-two FIR filter. IEEE Trans. Comput.-Aided Des. Integr. Circ. Syst. **PP**(99), 1 (2018)
14. Chandra, A., Chattopadhyay, S.: Design of hardware efficient FIR filter: a review of the state-of-the-art approaches. Eng. Sci. Technol. Int. J. **19**(1), 212–226 (2016)
15. Tajima, S., Sencer, B., Shamoto, E.: Accurate interpolation of machining tool-paths based on FIR filtering. Precis. Eng. **52**, 332–344 (2018)
16. Eren, L., Akar, M., Devaney, M.J.: Motor current signature analysis via four-channel FIR filter banks. Measurement **89**, 322–327 (2016)
17. Xiong, H., Li, D.: Nuclear reactor doubling time calculation using FIR filter. Energy Procedia **39**, 3–11 (2013)
18. Pak, J.M., et al.: Maximum likelihood FIR filter for visual object tracking. Neurocomputing **216**(C), 543–553 (2016)
19. Ozer, A.B.: CIDE: chaotically initialized differential evolution. Expert Syst. Appl. **37**(6), 4632–4641 (2010)
20. May, R.M.: Simple mathematical models with very complicated dynamics. Nature **261**(5560), 459–467 (1976)

21. Peitgen, H.O.: Chaos and fractals: new frontiers of science. Math. Gaz. **79**(484), 241–255 (2004)
22. He, Y., et al.: Differential evolution algorithm combined with chaotic pattern search. Kybernetika-Praha **46**(4), 684–696 (2010)
23. Brest, J., Maučec, M.S.: Population size reduction for the differential evolution algorithm. Appl. Intell. **29**(3), 228–247 (2008)
24. Yang, Q., et al.: Multimodal estimation of distribution algorithms. IEEE Trans. Cybern. **47**(3), 636–650 (2017)
25. Ali, M.M.: Differential evolution with generalized differentials. J. Comput. Appl. Math. **235**(8), 2205–2216 (2011)
26. Weber, M., Neri, F., Tirronen, V.: A study on scale factor in distributed differential evolution. Inf. Sci. **181**(12), 2488–2511 (2011)
27. Zou, D., et al.: An improved differential evolution algorithm for the task assignment problem. Eng. Appl. Artif. Intell. **24**(4), 616–624 (2011)
28. Fu, H., Xu, J., Xu, J.: A Self-adaptive Differential Evolution Algorithm for Binary CSPs. Pergamon Press, Inc., Oxford (2011)
29. Zamuda, A., Brest, J., Mezura-Montes, E.: Structured population size reduction differential evolution with multiple mutation strategies on CEC 2013 real parameter optimization. In: 2013 IEEE Congress on Evolutionary Computation, Cancun, 2013, pp. 1925–1931 (2013). https://doi.org/10.1109/CEC.2013.6557794
30. Liang, J.J., Qu, B.Y., Suganthan, P.N.: Problem definitions and evaluation criteria for the CEC 2014 special session and competition on single objective real-parameter numerical optimization (2013)

Collaborative Visual SLAM Framework for a Multi-UAVs System Based on Mutually Loop Closing

Haifeng Yu[1], Hao Li[1], and Zhihua Yang[1,2(✉)]

[1] Communication Engineering Research Center, Harbin Institute of Technology (Shenzhen), Shenzhen, Guangdong, China
mryuhaifeng@163.com, lihao_hitsz@163.com, yangzhihua@hit.edu.cn
[2] Pengcheng Laboratory, Shenzhen, Guangdong, China

Abstract. In a typical visual Simultaneous Localization and Mapping (SLAM) algorithm integrated within a single unmanned aerial vehicle (UAV), the positioning drift will increase cumulatively due to the motion and dynamic of UAV platform, which could be efficiently alleviated by the introduction of loop detection. However, a large number of loop movements by a single UAV will result in too many turns of the drone with significant reduction of coverage area per unit time. Therefore, in this paper, we propose a collaborative framework of visual SLAM algorithm with a multiple UAVs system. In the proposed framework, a series of mutually closed loop will be detected and executed by multiple UAVs within the position map. By this coordination method, the position accuracy of the system could be obviously improved, through the experimental results compared with a single UAV SLAM system.

Keywords: Visual SLAM · Multi-UAVS · Loop closing · Mapping merge

1 Introduction

Simultaneous localization and mapping (SLAM) is an effective method to solve the problem of synchronous localization and map reconstruction in unknown environments. In recent years, the SLAM algorithm is attractively applied into the system of unmanned aerial vehicle (UAV), in order to locate the position of the UAV while generating the map especially in an unknown environment. One broad category of SLAM algorithms attempts to build and maintain a pose (position and orientation) graph, which consists of a group of UAV states (represented as nodes), and pose transformations (as edges, i.e., constraints). For each state, related poses and sensor data, e.g., camera images or laser scans, are contained. Generally, the drifting error from odometry can be reduced by detecting re-visited places and introducing loop closure constraints, with a global

© ICST Institute for Computer Sciences, Social Informatics and Telecommunications Engineering 2019
Published by Springer Nature Switzerland AG 2019. All Rights Reserved
M. Jia et al. (Eds.): WiSATS 2019, LNICST 280, pp. 653–664, 2019.
https://doi.org/10.1007/978-3-030-19153-5_64

graph optimization. In particular, the goal of graph optimization in this context is to find a configuration that minimizes the errors of the constrained pose estimations [1]. As a result, the expected map can be reconstructed at any time from the graph by superimposing the associated sensor data with a consistent configuration.

Typically, compared with the terrestrial robot system integrated with a SLAM, a drone platform has a faster and more flexible flight as making an exploration mission in a wide-range environment, leading to an easily loss of the feature information of objects and thus a sparse density of the resulted point cloud map. In recent days, a collaborative method by using multiple UAVs is elaborately employed for the SLAM, which can improve the robustness of positioning and the accuracy of the map with a less time. In particular, in a large-scale environment, a collective use of multiple UAVs can not only speed up the reconstruction of the map, but also improve the accuracy through multi-machine map fusion. In specific, during the mission, the UAVs team can branch off the cruise path and meet again at some place where they share their maps. Another advantage of multi-UAV collaboration is the detection capability on the overlap area. For example, a required redundancy of the data can be provided by other UAVs in the event of a loss of positioning of one certain UAV, which could help locating its own exact location. Therefore, in this paper, we propose a collaborative visual SLAM algorithmic framework for a multi-UAVs system based on mutually loop closing. In the proposed algorithm, a dense point cloud map is constructed by fusing multiple pose maps from different drones with detection on a series of key frames (site or scene identification) from different drone shooting scenes. The proposed algorithm is designed on the basis of a well-tailored ORB-SLAM2 framework and verified by a group of experiments in real scenes.

The remainder of this paper is structured as follows. Section 2 lists related research. Section 3 particularizes the posed problem and explains the proposed methods in details. In Sect. 4, we present experiment results and discussion. Finally, we summarize our work in Sect. 5.

2   Related Work

In the early SLAM, laser scanners were used as the main sensors of SLAM for estimating poses. In [2], an extended Kalman filter (EKF) method is exploited for relative observation between multiple robots. With the developments of camera technology, a variety of sensors have gradually replaced inexpensive lasers with inexpensive costs. In [3], the monocular cameras and the IMU are cooperatively employed to form a flexible three-dimensional platform of UAVs team, which is used to estimate the relative poses of UAVs on a simple experimental setup. In [4], Piasco et al. use a distributed stereo-vision system of multiple UAVs for collaborative localization with an EKF filtering algorithm. In [5], a UAV equipped with multiple cameras is used to estimate the trajectory of moving objects in the scene, while creating a 3-D map of a static object.

In order to improve the running speed, at present, non-linear optimization methods are gradually exploited in the SLAM to replace traditional filtering methods. In [6], a fully distributed system is proposed to realize collaborative SLAMs and evaluate them in a simulated environment. The main challenge for decentralized systems is more difficult to ensure data consistency and avoid duplicate calculations, compared with a centralized client-server architecture. In addition, in a central server-assisted system, computationally expensive algorithms can be handled on the server side, which does not necessarily limit real-time operations such as bundling adjustment and location identification. As a result, this allows a flying agent to use its only potentially limited resources for performing the most critical task, such as real-time visual ranging. In several cases, a centralized SLAM would utilize a cloud server instead of a central server to exchange data. In [7], the ground agent will update the related information of key-frames in the local map to the cloud system without checking the global map stored in the cloud. A centralized framework is proposed for a group of UAVs equipped with monocular cameras, in which each UAV performs visual odometry on its on-board processor.

3 Methodology

3.1 Algorithmic Framework

The method is applicable to a quadrotor UAV. The camera pose is consistent with the position of the rotor unmanned aerial vehicle. The environment map is constructed indoors by three or more drones. The maximum speed of the drone flight is $1\,\text{m/s}$, the turning angle is less than $30°$.

In this section, we devise a loop-closing enabled algorithmic framework of multi-UAVs SLAM system, as shown in Fig. 1. In specific, the proposed algorithm consists of two parts, which are separately executed at multi-UAVs system and central server. The proposed algorithm system use ORB-SLAM2 for locating and mapping at each UAV, meanwhile construct a complete map at central server by merging those sectional maps from different agent. Without loss of generality, in this paper, we assume that a reliable and real-time data transmission is ensured between UAVs and central server. In each UAV, a RGB Depth cameras and

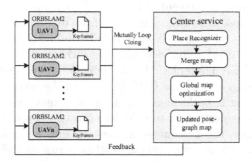

Fig. 1. Collaborative visual SLAM framework based on loop closing.

on-board processors are equipped for visual mileage calculations, which provides an estimate of the UAV platform attitude, with a 3D map of the environment in the local coordinate system.

Algorithm 1. Algorithm in Service

Begin
  $msgFlag \longleftarrow False$;
// receive the key frame from different UAVs
while $msgFlag \longleftarrow if\_connUAV()$ **do**;
  $[uavLabel, keyFrame] \longleftarrow recv\_keyFrame()$;
end while
// merge the maps
  $subMap \longleftarrow find\_olpregion(keyFrame, uavLabel)$;
  $mergeMap \longleftarrow merge\_submaps(submaps)$;
  $optMap \longleftarrow optimal\_Map(mergeMap)$;
  $optMap \longleftarrow update\_Map(optMap)$;
  $msgFlag \longleftarrow False$;
// feedback the optiaml maps to the different UAVs
while $msgFlag \longleftarrow if\_connUAV()$ **do**;
  $send\_map(uavLabel, optMap)$
end while
End

Algorithm 2. Algorithm in UAVs

Input: task
  $keyframe \longleftarrow run\_orbslam()$;
  $send\_keyFrame(keyFrame, centerService)$;
Output:

In the proposed algorithm, each UAV transmits a series of key frames (posture and shooting picture information in the local coordinates system) to the central server. Meanwhile, the central server will continuously monitor all observations and detect those same shooting scenes from different UAVs. In particular, we use the technology of Bag of Word (BOW) to quickly compare their image features and perform overlapping detection algorithms on the appearance. Once overlapping scenes from different UAVs are detected, a well-designed map fusion algorithm is started to extract the ORB features of the related two images, and then feature matching is performed to remove false matches. An iterative closest point algorithm is performed to calculate the two key frames for similarity transformation. Then, the two maps are merged into a single global map. At the same time, a bundle optimization algorithm is run on the global map. The updated pose of the keyframe image is fed back to each UAV to improve its local estimation and local map in turn.

3.2 Improved ORB-SLAM2

In this paper, we built a feature-based ORB-SLAM2 framework integrated with a stereo and RGB-D cameras based on the typical version of ORB-SLAM2 [8]. For reader convenience, the main components are summarized here, which includes three main parallel threads, as shown in Fig. 2.

(1) Tracking thread. It will localize the camera with every frame by finding those features matching the local map, and minimizing the re-projection error with motion-only Bundle Adjustment (BA).
(2) Local mapping thread. This thread will optimally manage the local map with local BA.
(3) Loop closing thread. It attempts to detect large loops and correct the accumulated drift by performing a pose-graph optimization.

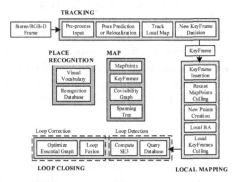

Fig. 2. The frame of ORBSLAM2

Compared with typical version of ORB-SLAM2, a dense point cloud map is constructed by utilizing a sparse point cloud with a RGD image to remap the point cloud map, and added into the proposed framework in this paper, which has a large amount of information for restoration on the environments more sparse point clouds in typical ORB-SLAM2. In particular, here, we use an incremental method to generate a dense surface model from a semi-dense point cloud. The proposed method first generates a dense surface mesh for every single scan, and creates corresponding image by doing edge-aware resampling and triangulating the surface points.

3.3 Place Recognizer

In the proposed framework, loop closing is performed in two steps. Firstly, a loop has to be detected and validated, which is called place recognizer. Secondly, the loop is corrected by optimizing the fused attitude map of pose-graph. In this framework, we incorporated a full bundle adjustment (BA) optimization after the maps are fused. Considering that this optimization might be very costly, we perform it in a separate thread, allowing the system to continue creating maps and detecting loops. However, this brings the challenge of merging the BA output with the current state of the map. If a new loop is detected while the optimization is running, the algorithm aborts the current optimization and proceeds to close the new loop, which will launch the full BA optimization again. Once the full BA finishes, the algorithm will merge the updated subset of keyframes and points, with the non-updated keyframes and points inserted while the optimization was running. This is done by propagating the correction of updated keyframes (i.e. the transformation from the non-optimized to the optimized pose) to non-updated keyframes through the spanning tree. Then, non-updated points are transformed according to the above correction. In this collaborative framework, the identification of the location and the fusion of those separated maps are handled in a central server, in which local maps in different coordinate systems are merged into a global map by finding similar scenes from different UAVs. In this framework, we extract ORB features from all keyframe images and use Bag of Words (BOW) to represent keyframe features as descriptors. We use the DBOW3 open source software package to create the dictionary and finally generate a descriptor that facilitates location detection. In specific, DBOW3 uses the k-means++ method to create visual dictionaries. Each frames picture is described by dictionary information. Finally, the same place is detected by comparing the degree of similarity of descriptors of each frame.

3.4   Map Merge

In order to achieve map merge, we use a iterative closest point (ICP) algorithm in [9], which tries to find a transformation that minimizes the distance between a set of corresponding points in two clouds. In this section, we tailored an augmented version of ICP which also includes surface normal and tangent information to improve the estimate results. Note that both the Sim3 [10] tracker and the ICP procedure use a gradient approach to find the solution. In theory, both methods could be used in any order. However, the ICP procedure was found to be most accurate if starting from a better estimation of the scale factor.

When used to register and align two sets of two-dimensional or three-dimensional points with relative motion, the ICP can continuously solve the optimal value by iterations. This issue could be modeled by finding the optimal solution of the least-squares problem as shown in (1).

$$\min E = \sum_{i=1}^{n} (q_i - (Rp_i + t))^2 \tag{1}$$

in which $P = \{p_i | i = 1, \ldots, n\}$ and $Q = \{q_i | i = 1, \ldots, n\}$ are respectively 3D feature point sets from different UAVs with the 3D coordinates of $(x, y, z)_i^T$. By continuously iterating the rotation matrix $\boldsymbol{R}$ and the translation matrix $\boldsymbol{t}$, we get a motion transformation matrix $\boldsymbol{T} = [\boldsymbol{R}, \boldsymbol{t}]$. Trough the motion transformation matrix $\boldsymbol{T}$, we can get the merge map form the source point set Q to the target point set P.

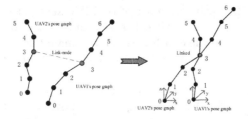

Fig. 3. Merged diagram of multi-UAVs pose graph.

The merged process of pose graph of multiple UAVs is shown in Fig. 3. In the figure, two third nodes are the separated pose nodes from two individual UAV paths for the same environment identified by the BOW algorithm. By the ICP, a transformation matrix T could be calculated and utilized for merging into a global pose graph in a unified coordinate system with the two different pose diagrams.

3.5   Global Map Optimization

Once the transformation is computed, new similarity constraints are added between the matched keyframes. The corresponding local maps are transformed into the global coordinate system by considering one of the two as reference (if it is the first map to be merged) or using the existing reference otherwise. After the new constraints have been added, a BA step is performed over the merged graph.

After the ICP procedure, we establish the relationships between different UAVs maps. Then, we use these images to triangulate some feature points with geometry. The constructed triangle could determine the position of the three-dimensional point. Finally, the coordinates of the three-dimensional point are calculated to re-project the camera matrix. This issue could be shown in (2).

$$\{R, t\} = \underset{R,t}{\arg\min} \sum_{i \in \chi} \rho(\|x^i_{(.)} - \pi_{(.)}(RX^i + t)\|^2_\Sigma) \tag{2}$$

In which $\boldsymbol{R} \in SO(3)$ is the camera orientation of BA optimizes and $\boldsymbol{t} \in \mathbb{R}^3$ is position. $\boldsymbol{X}^i \in \mathbb{R}^3$ and $\boldsymbol{x}^i_{(.)}$ expresses respectively the minimizing reprojection error between matched 3D points in world coordinates and keypoints. Either monocular $\boldsymbol{x}^i_m \in \mathbb{R}^2$ or stereo $\boldsymbol{x}^i_s \in \mathbb{R}^3$, with $i \in \chi$ the set of all matches.

We use general graph optimization (g2o) to solve the bundle adjustment. g2o is an open source framework that is mainly used to solve the problem based on graph optimization. The optimization problem is described the following formulation:

$$\{X^i, R_l, t_l \mid i \in p_L, l \in \kappa_L\} = \underset{X^i, R_L, t_l}{\arg\min} \sum_{k \in \kappa_L \cup \kappa_F} \sum_{j \in \chi_k} \rho(E_{k,j}) \tag{3}$$

where

$$E_{kj} = \|x^j_{(.)} - \pi_{(.)}(R_k X^i + t_k)\|^2_\sigma \tag{4}$$

In which, local BA optimizes a set of covisible keyframes κ_L and all points seen in those keyframe is p_L. All other keyframes κ_F, not in κ_L, observing points in p_L contribute to the cost function but remain fixed in the optimization. Defining χ_k as the set of matches between points in p_L and keypoints in a keyframe k.

The conversion relationship between the dense point cloud maps is same with the pose graph. Finally, according to the above algorithm, the two point cloud maps are merged. Finally, the overall map, consisted of keyframe poses as vertices and BA constraints as edges, is continuously optimized in parallel by using a general graph optimization framework in [10] for reducing the drifts both in scale and pose estimates.

3.6 Updated Pose Graph

When different UAVs visit the same place in the environment, new constraints are created in the global graph. If they cross each other path by multiple times, these resulted loop closure constraints will help in reducing the overall drifts.

Finally, the central server communicates the updated pose graph to individual UAVs, which can then use this information to update their localization estimate and the local maps. This overall feedback mechanism facilitates the extension of sensing capability of an individual UAV beyond the direct reach of their respective on-board sensors.

4 Experimental Results

In this experiment, the multi-UAV map fusion algorithm based on loopback detection is applied to three separate quantity acquisition and processing modules, and the generated keyframe information is merged to finally realize the fusion of 3D point cloud maps. The camera is ASUS's Xtion2. The stand-alone platform is a great deal for Dajiang, and the central processor is Lenovo's notebook. Finally, it analyzes the number of keyframes, algorithm implementation complexity, and compositional integrity. Verify the feasibility and advantages of the algorithm.

On each stand-alone platform, we use the ORB-SLAM2 algorithm to achieve stand-alone SLAM positioning and composition, as shown in Fig. 4, which is the RGB picture in left and ORB-SLAM2's feature tracking process in right. The blue and green colors in the picture indicate the extracted feature points and the matched feature points respectively.

A single agent runs ORB-SLAM2 to estimate is own pose, and builds a 3-dimensional point cloud map of the environment. Figure 5 shows the path maps and point cloud maps of the three agents. As can be seen from the figure, the dense point cloud map constructed by a single machine is relatively vague and has a relatively small amount of information. It can be seen from the path in the sparse map that no large loopback detection occurs.

Fig. 4. The features of ORB. (The bule points is all the ORB features and the green points is matched features). (Color figure online)

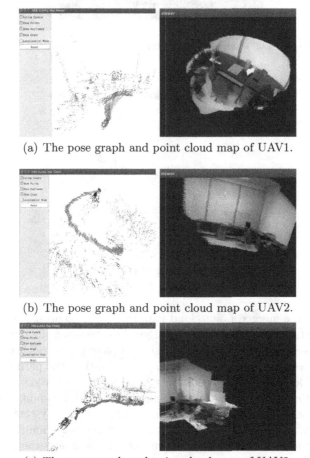

(a) The pose graph and point cloud map of UAV1.

(b) The pose graph and point cloud map of UAV2.

(c) The pose graph and point cloud map of UAV3.

Fig. 5. The pose graph and point cloud map.

According to the 3.2 map fusion algorithm, the keyframe data of the two platforms, based on the mutual loop detection, the fusion results of the map are shown in Fig. 6, and it can be clearly seen that the map obtained by the multi-machine fusion is better than the stand-alone, and the map can be used. Observed environmental information.

Fig. 6. The merged point cloud map of UAV1 and UAV2.

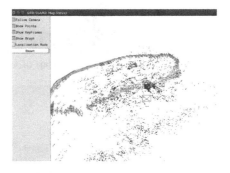

Fig. 7. The merged pose gragh.

It is shown the merged point cloud map in Fig. 6. According to the Collaborative Visual SLAM Framework merge Algorithm the point cloud maps from different agencies are merged into a relatively complete global point cloud map. In Fig. 7, we can see that through the fusion of information, the path map increases the number of loops, and the positioning accuracy is improved.

In Fig. 8, It describes the number of map points and the number of generated key frames in a stand-alone system and a multi-machine system, respectively. In the same environment, the number of map points of a multi-UAVs system is more than that of a stand-alone system. On the contrary, the number of key frames is less than that of a stand-alone system. It can be concluded that the multi-machine system can reduce the number of extracted keyframes and the complexity of the algorithm. However, the multi-machine system has the more map points, the more fusion map information, and the higher map accuracy.

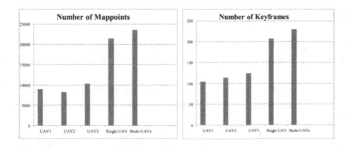

Fig. 8. The number of mappoints and keyframes.

Table 1. The number of looping closing

	Single UAV	MultI-UAV
Number of LC	6	13
Number of mutually LC	–	7

Table 1 describes the number of loop closing, in which, the number of reciprocating loops can be increased by multi-machine information fusion in a multi-machine system, thereby improving the positioning accuracy and robustness of the entire system.

5   Conclusions

We propose a collaborative framework of visual SLAM algorithm with a multiple UAVs system. While the small UAVs run real-time visual odometry onboard independently, the computationally more powerful central server aggregates their experiences, searches for loop closing and merges maps. Communicating merged and optimized information back to the agents, the agents are able to operate on updated information, enabling better and more consistent estimates.

In the proposed framework, a series of mutually closed loop will be detected and executed by multiple UAVs within the position map. Compared with some existing frameworks, the final feedback can improve the positioning accuracy of each agent. At the same time, there are also problems. The processing capability of the central server directly affects the real-time nature of map fusion and feedback. In practical applications, communication is used. The real-time nature of the entire framework is also an important part of it. A good communication environment, the availability and reliability of transmission are also important factors that determine the quality of the final map fusion.

Acknowledgments. The authors would like to express their high appreciations to the supports from the National Natural Science Foundation of China (61871426) and Basic Research Project of Shenzhen (JCYJ20170413110004682).

References

1. Deutsch, I., Liu, M., Siegwart, R.: A framework for multi-robot pose graph SLAM. In: IEEE International Conference on Real-Time Computing and Robotics, pp. 567–572 (2016)
2. Martinelli, A., Pont, F., Siegwart, R.: Multi-robot localization using relative observations. In: IEEE International Conference on Robotics and Automation, pp. 2797–2802 (2006)
3. Achtelik, M.W., Weiss, S., Chli, M., Dellaert, F.: Collaborative stereo. In: IEEE/RSJ International Conference on Intelligent Robots and Systems, pp. 2242–2248 (2011)
4. Piasco, N., Marzat, J., Sanfourche, M.: Collaborative localization and formation flying using distributed stereo-vision. In: IEEE International Conference on Robotics and Automation, pp. 1202–1207 (2016)
5. Mohanarajah, G., Usenko, V., Singh, M., D'Andrea, R., Waibel, M.: Cloud-based collaborative 3D mapping in real-time with low-cost robots. IEEE Trans. Autom. Sci. Eng. **12**(2), 423–431 (2015)
6. Kaess, M., Dellaert, F.: Probabilistic structure matching for visual slam with a multi-camera rig. Comput. Vis. Image Underst. **114**(2), 286–296 (2010)
7. Riazuelo, L., Civera, J., Montiel, J.M.M.: C2TAM: a cloud framework for cooperative tracking and mapping. Robot. Autonom. Syst. **62**(4), 401–413 (2014)
8. Mur-Artal, R., Montiel, J.M.M., Tards, J.D.: ORB-SLAM: a versatile and accurate monocular slam system. IEEE Trans. Robot. **31**(5), 1147–1163 (2017)
9. Holz, D., Behnke, S.: Sancta simplicitas - on the efficiency and achievable results of SLAM using ICP-based incremental registration. In: IEEE International Conference on Robotics and Automation, pp. 1380–1387 (2010)
10. Kim, A., Eustice, R.M.: Active visual SLAM for robotic area coverage: theory and experiment. Int. J. Robot. Res. **34**(4–5), 457–475 (2015)

Feature Extraction and Identification of Pipeline Intrusion Based on Phase-Sensitive Optical Time Domain Reflectometer

Zhanfeng Zhao, Duo Liu$^{(\boxtimes)}$, Longwei Wang, and Shujun Liu

Harbin Institute of Technology (Weihai), Weihai, China
1398108921@qq.com

Abstract. Since fiber distributed vibration sensing (DVS) system based on phase-sensitive optical time domain reflectometer (Φ-OTDR) has the characteristics of identifying intrusion signals, wide monitoring range and high system sensitivity, correct identification of intrusion types by the system is an important issue to promote the engineering of this technology. In this paper, based on the intrusion signal of Φ-OTDR system, a multi-dimensional feature extraction and selection method is proposed. The polynomial least squares method is used to remove the trend term from the vibration signal, and the wavelet threshold denoising method is used to reduce the noise interference. The short-time analysis in the time domain and the wavelet analysis in the wavelet domain are combined to extract the multi-dimensional characteristics of the signal. The feature selection is based on the QUICKREDUCT algorithm. The experimental results show that the feature vector obtained by this method is relatively complete, and it is less affected by the environment, and the recognition rate is higher, reaching over 92%.

Keywords: Φ-OTDR · Short-term analysis · Wavelet analysis · Feature extraction · Identification

1 Introduction

As fiber distributed vibration sensing (DVS) system based on phase-sensitive optical time domain reflectometer (Φ-OTDR) has the advantages of low cost, long service life, corrosion resistance, good electrical insulation and strong concealment, it can be applied to long-distance perimeter security, pipeline pre-warning, and quantitative vibration measurement. In the fiber pre-warning system, the classification and identification of external intrusion signals is very important. If a false alarm occurs, it will not only cause waste of manpower and material resources, but also may delay the processing time and even endanger the safety of life and property. Therefore, how to accurately identify the types of intrusion events has always been the key issue in the research of optical fiber pre-warning systems, and has received extensive attention from researchers [1].

In previous studies, Mahmud et al. generated a dynamic threshold based on the measured signal. The number of times a signal of a certain duration passes through the threshold and the length of time exceeding the threshold are used as signal

© ICST Institute for Computer Sciences, Social Informatics and Telecommunications Engineering 2019
Published by Springer Nature Switzerland AG 2019. All Rights Reserved
M. Jia et al. (Eds.): WiSATS 2019, LNICST 280, pp. 665–675, 2019.
https://doi.org/10.1007/978-3-030-19153-5_65

characteristics [2]. However, this method only extracts the time domain features of the signal and cannot fully represent the signal characteristics [3]. Xu used convolutional neural networks to identify and classify time-frequency analysis patterns of different intrusion methods, but the number of training samples required by convolutional neural networks is large, and the time-frequency analysis map is susceptible to noise in fiber-optic signals [4].

In addition, Qu used the classical modal algorithm to decompose the vibration signal into multiple frequency band signals, and extracted the kurtosis of each frequency band as a feature for identification. However, the signal time domain of the same intrusion type may also have multiple vibration forms, which resulted in the number of frequency bands in which the algorithm decomposed the signal cannot be determined [5]. Sun proposed a method based on image morphology to extract temporal and spatial two-dimensional signal features, and the recognition rate is high, but the fiber pre-warning system needs to be in an ideal working environment. The environmental noise and interference have great influence on the recognition result [5].

To solve these problems, this paper innovatively introduces the combination of short-term analysis in time domain and wavelet analysis in wavelet domain. Based on the measured data, a multi-dimensional feature extraction and feature selection method which can fully characterize the vibration signal feature is proposed. Secondly, this paper innovatively preprocesses the signal using polynomial least squares method and wavelet threshold denoising method, which removes the trend term caused by the system, and reduces the influence of environmental noise. Then, based on QUICK-REDUCT algorithm to select features, remove redundant information, and extract the optimal feature vector combination under different dimensions. Finally, using the probabilistic neural network (PNN) for training and testing, and the recognition rate is as high as 92%.

2 Principle and Preprocessing

2.1 Eliminate Trend Terms Using Least Squares

The vibration signal data collected in the vibration test often deviates from the baseline, and even deviates from the baseline changing with time due to the zero drift of the amplifier with temperature changes, the instability of the low frequency performance outside the sensor frequency range, and the environmental interference around the sensor. The entire process of deviating from the baseline over time is referred to as the trend term of the signal. It can be seen from Fig. 1.

Set the time domain signal of a certain position of the fiber to $\{x_k\}$, $k = 1, 2, 3, \cdots, n$, where n is the number of sampling points. Since the sampling is equally spaced, the sampling interval can be set to 1. Use a polynomial function to represent the trend item of the signal:

$$\hat{x}_k = a_0 + a_1 k + a_2 k^2 + \ldots + a_m k^m = \sum_{j=0}^{m} a_j k_j, k = 1, 2, \ldots, n \tag{1}$$

Theoretical derivation shows that the trend term obtained when m = 0 is a linear trend term, eliminating the linear trend term and obtaining:

$$y_k = x_k - \hat{x}_k = x_k - (a_0 + a_1 k), k = 1, 2, \ldots, n \tag{2}$$

The curve trend term is obtained when $m \geq 2$. In actual speech signal processing, $m = 1 \sim 3$ is usually taken. In this paper, $m = 3$ is obtained to obtain the curve trend term, and then the trend term is eliminated by using polynomial least squares method for the fiber sensing signal.

Taking the artificial tapping signal of the field experiment as an example, the sampling frequency of the signal is 2 kHz, the signal length is 10 s, and the trend term is eliminated by using the least squares method. The signal waveforms before and after the trend item are shown in Figs. 1 and 2.

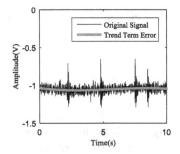   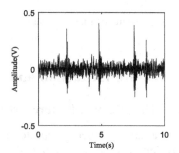

Fig. 1. Original signal curve   **Fig. 2.** Detrended term signal curve

2.2 Wavelet Threshold Method for Noise Reduction

Since the fiber sensing signal is susceptible to the background environment noise, how to retain the useful vibration signal to the utmost is a key problem in fiber optic vibration signal preprocessing. According to the characteristics that the vibration intrusion signal is a sudden signal, the conventional Fourier filter noise reduction method will simultaneously attenuate the vibration signal and the noise. However, wavelet analysis has a frequency zoom function, which can eliminate the sharp part of the signal and some weak small signals while eliminating noise. Therefore, the wavelet denoising algorithm is used to denoise the fiber vibration signal.

This section firstly uses a polynomial least squares method for a manual tapping signal with a length of 10 s to eliminate the trend error caused by the system to the fiber signal, Then, the wavelet threshold denoising is processed on the noisy fiber vibration intrusion signal after eliminating the trend term. The wavelet basis function used is db6 wavelet, and the number of decomposition layers is 7 layers. The waveform diagram before and after the vibration signal is denoised is shown in the figures below. Figure 3 is the waveform of the artificial tapping signal with no noise after eliminating the trend term. Figure 4 is the waveform of the artificial tap signal after noise reduction. Comparing the waveforms before and after noise reduction of the vibration signal, after the noise reduction by the wavelet threshold method, the high-frequency noise signal is obviously suppressed, and the sharp-changing part of the signal is better preserved, and the signal-to-noise ratio of the vibration intrusion signal is improved.

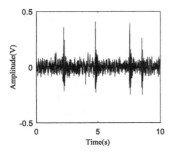
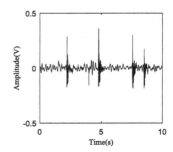

Fig. 3. Detrended term signal curve   **Fig. 4.** Heuristic threshold denoising result

3   Feature Extraction and Identification

3.1   Time Domain Feature Extraction

After a large number of repeated tests, the fiber-sensing signals of different vibration intrusion types can be found that their time-domain characteristic parameters will satisfy certain statistical characteristics, and if the number of repeated tests tends to infinity, the feature distribution of the same type of signal is the same. Based on the differences in the distribution of statistical characteristics of different types of vibration signals, the time domain characteristic parameters of the signals can be used to identify the type of vibration intrusion.

Variance and Maximum Energy Segment. The variance reflects the fluctuation and dispersion of the one-dimensional signal. Vibration intrusion can cause fluctuations in the fiber's time domain signal, so the variance can be used to indicate the degree of fluctuation of the fiber's vibration signal. The greater the fluctuation of the time domain signal, the greater the variance of the signal; and vice versa. Variance can be expressed as

$$D(X) = Var(X) = E\{[X - EX]^2\} = \frac{1}{n}\sum_{i=1}^{n}(x_i - EX)^2 \tag{3}$$

Theoretically, the fluctuations of non-invasive signals, artificial tapping signals, vehicle passing signals, and mechanical excavation signals depend on the time of action of the vibration intrusion on the fiber. However, in practical applications, as is shown in Figs. 5, 6, 7 and 8, the fiber sensing signal is susceptible to the influence of the surrounding environment, so the signal collected by the system is mixed with a lot of high frequency noise.

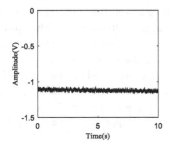

Fig. 5. No vibration intrusion signal

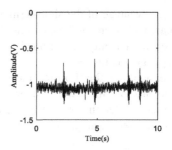

Fig. 6. Artificial tapping signal

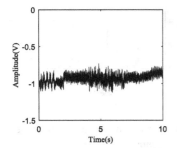

Fig. 7. Vehicle passing signal

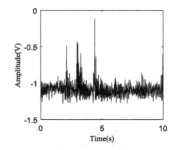

Fig. 8. Mechanical excavation signal

Based on a number of field experimental sample data with a time length of 10 s, the total energy of these four fiber signals is analyzed by observing the time domain waveforms of non-invasive signals, artificial tapping signals, vehicle passing signals and mechanical excavation signals. The duration of the vibration intrusion is different, and the duration of the vibration caused by the artificial tapping signal to the time domain signal is much less than 1 s; the vibration intrusion of the vehicle through the signal and the mechanical excavation signal takes a long time, which is reflected in the time domain signal. The vibration of several seconds continues to fluctuate, and there is a process of ascending, continuing, and descending. In order to minimize the influence of system noise, this section divides the sample data of 10 s into ten parts, each part is data with a time length of 1 s, and calculates the energy of ten time domain signals with a time length of 1 s, respectively. The larger of the ten energy values is the maximum energy segment characteristic of the time domain.

Short-term Average Amplitude. Fiber optic signals are unsteady, time-varying signals, but can be considered to be steady-state, time-invariant in "short-term" and "short-term" in milliseconds. According to this characteristic, the signal can be divided into several segments to analyze its characteristics, which is called short-term analysis technique of the signal, and each segment of the signal is called a frame signal.

The advantage of the short-term average amplitude is that it does not need to take the quadratic square, and the amplitude of the fiber signal is relatively small. Therefore, the short-term average amplitude is used to observe the signal. Firstly, the 10-s artificial tapping signal is processed by polynomial least squares method and wavelet threshold method, and then the short-term average amplitude method proposed in this section is used to analyze the short-term signal energy fluctuation. The frame processing is performed by Hanning window. The frame length is 30 ms, and the waveforms of the short-term average amplitudes of the four intrusion types are shown in Figs. 9, 10, 11 and 12.

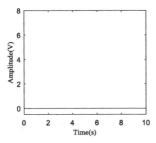

Fig. 9. Short-term average amplitude of vibration-free intrusion signal

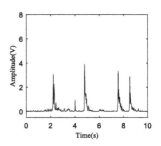

Fig. 10. Short-term average amplitude of artificial tapping signal

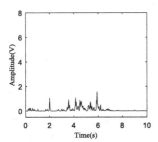

Fig. 11. Short-term average range of vehicles passing signal

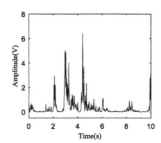

Fig. 12. Short-term average amplitude of mechanical excavation signal

It can be seen from the above figure that the high frequency noise of the original signal of the optical fiber is suppressed after calculating the short-term average amplitude, and the amplitude of the short-term average amplitude map of the non-invasive signal is almost constant to zero and does not change with time. In comparison, the short-term signal amplitude can express the amplitude characteristics of the fiber signal in the time domain.

The maximum segment of short-term average amplitude vibration is defined as the sum of the amplitudes of each vibration segment exceeding the threshold after the short-term amplitude analysis of the signal, and the maximum value is taken as the maximum segment of the vibration energy in all the vibration segments. The sum of short-term average amplitude vibrations is defined as the short-range amplitude analysis of the signal, and all the vibration segments exceeding the threshold are counted, and the sum of the amplitudes of all the vibration segments is obtained as the sum of the vibration energies.

3.2 Wavelet Domain Feature Extraction

In the foregoing, the characteristic parameters of the signal are analyzed from the perspective of time domain. The time domain features are mainly extracted by the amplitude variation. However, the characteristic parameters in a single domain cannot fully reflect the complex distribution of the intrusion signal. Therefore, this section from the wavelet domain The angle of the signal is analyzed. In this paper, discrete wavelet transform is used to analyze the signal in multiple resolutions, and the fraction of wavelet energy at each scale is extracted as the characteristic parameter of wavelet domain.

Considering that the Db wavelet has the characteristics of describing the non-stationary signal as a whole, combined with the results of multiple experiments [7], this paper selects the db6 wavelet and performs 7-layer wavelet decomposition on all the measured samples. The wavelet energy of each scale is then calculated and normalized to eliminate the effect of amplitude. After wavelet decomposition of the four types of samples, the statistical average results of the obtained wavelet energy ratio are shown in Figs. 13, 14, 15 and 16. The comparison shows that the energy ratios of different

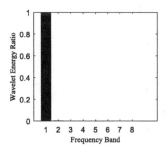

Fig. 13. Wavelet energy ratio of vibration-free intrusion signal

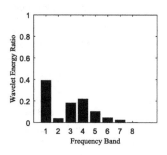

Fig. 14. Wavelet energy ratio of artificial tapping signal

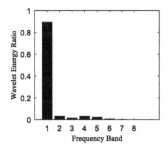

Fig. 15. Wavelet energy ratio of vehicle passing signal

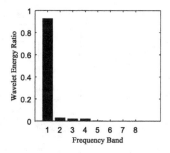

Fig. 16. Wavelet energy ratio of mechanical excavation signal

frequency bands without intrusion and manual tapping are significantly different. The distribution of vehicle passing and mechanical excavation is similar, but the difference between the characteristics of the first two intrusion signals is obvious.

4   Feature Evaluation and Identification

4.1   Feature Evaluation

In this paper, 12 eigenvalues are obtained after extracting the time domain and wavelet domain features of the four types of intrusion events, which are the maximum energy segment, the variance, the short-term average amplitude vibration maximum segment, the short-term average amplitude vibration sum, and the wavelet decomposition from the low frequency band to the high frequency band.

Jensen proposed the QUICKREDUCT algorithm for attribute reduction of rough sets [8]: the attribute set is initialized to an empty set, and attributes are added to it at a time. If this attribute is added, the attribute is retained and the attribute is retained. Otherwise, it is discarded. According to this idea, the design is as follows (Fig. 17):

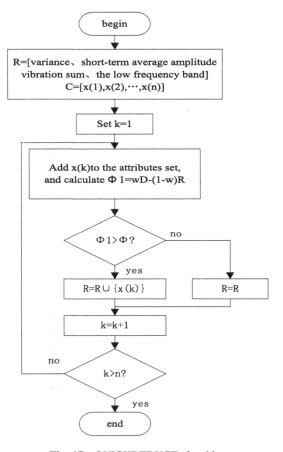

Fig. 17. QUICKREDUCT algorithm

Among them, x(k) is a variety of features, D is the correlation between the selected feature subset and the state category, and R is the redundancy between the various features.

Using the QUICKREDUCT algorithm, the optimal eigenvectors of different feature dimensions are shown in Table 1.

Table 1. Optimal eigenvectors of different dimensions

Dimension	Optimal feature vector combination
4	2 4 5 12
5	2 4 5 11 12
6	2 4 5 10 11 12
7	2 4 5 9 10 11 12
8	2 4 5 8 9 10 11 12
9	2 4 5 6 8 9 10 11 12
10	2 4 5 6 7 8 9 10 11 12
11	1 2 4 5 6 7 8 9 10 11 12
12	1 2 3 4 5 6 7 8 9 10 11 12

Through the above algorithm, the optimal feature vector corresponding to different feature vector dimensions is obtained. Compared with the exhaustive method, all the eigenvectors are calculated by the classifier. The method of this paper is to calculate the optimal eigenvectors corresponding to different dimensions, which can reduce the computational complexity.

4.2 Identification Based on PNN

Probabilistic neural network (PNN) consists of input layer, hidden layer, summation layer and output layer, and its structure is shown in the Fig. 18.

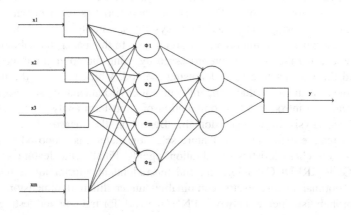

Fig. 18. Probabilistic neural network

Compared with the commonly used BP and radial basis neural networks, PNN has the advantages of simple network learning process, good expansion performance, few parameters and short training time. These advantages not only meet the real-time requirements of the system, but also reduce the impact of parameter settings on classification recognition [9]. Therefore, this paper chooses PNN neural network as the classifier of fiber-optic early warning system, and estimates the correct rate of classifier identification by double cross-validation method.

In general, the width parameter of the PNN, that is, the standard deviation is usually taken as 0.1. This paper uses 640 measured data samples to train tests. Among them, there are 196 groups of non-invasive sample data, 178 sets of manual tapping sample data, 126 sets of data after vehicle passing, and 140 sets of data for mechanical mining. Combined with the 5-fold cross-validation method, the average recognition accuracy of the optimal eigenvectors of different dimensions is obtained, as shown in Table 2.

Table 2. Average accuracy of identification of different eigenvalues

Feature vector dimension	Average recognition accuracy
4	92.8670%
5	93.7494%
6	92.8755%
7	93.7238%
8	92.9889%
9	93.2788%
10	92.8824%
11	92.6991%
12	93.7451%

5   Conclusion

Since fiber distributed vibration sensing (DVS) system based on phase-sensitive optical time domain reflectometer (Φ-OTDR) has the characteristics of identifying intrusion signals, wide monitoring range and high system sensitivity. The identification of vibration signal types is an important research topic. In this paper, the vibration signal is preprocessed, and the signal is preprocessed by using the polynomial least squares method and the wavelet threshold denoising method, which removes the trend term caused by the system, and reduces the influence of environmental noise. Secondly, this paper innovatively introduces the combination of short-term analysis in time domain and wavelet analysis in wavelet domain. Based on the measured data, a multi-dimensional feature extraction and feature selection method is proposed, which fully characterizes the characteristics of vibration signals. Finally, the feature selection is based on QUICKREDUCT algorithm, and the redundant information is removed to extract the optimal feature vector combination under different dimensions. Finally, using the probabilistic neural network (PNN) network for training and testing, and the recognition rate is over 92%.

Acknowledgement. Thanks to the support of Harbin Institute of Technology and Weihai Fund.

References

1. Ye, Q., Pan, Z., Wang, Z.: Progress of research and applications of phase-sensitive optical time domain reflectometry. Chin. J. Lasers **44**(06), 7–20 (2017)
2. Mahmoud, S., Visagathilagar, Y., Katsifolis, J.: Real-time distributed fiber optic sensor for security systems: performance, event classification and nuisance mitigation. Photonic Sens. **2**(3), 225–236 (2012)
3. Mahmoud, S., Katsifolis, J.: Robust event classification for a fiber optic perimeter intrusion detection system using level crossing features and artificial neural networks. In: SPIE Defense, Security, and Sensing. International Society for Optics and Photonics (2010)
4. Xu, C., Guan, J., Bao, M., et al.: Pattern recognition based on time-frequency analysis and convolutional neural networks for vibrational events in Φ-OTDR. Opt. Eng. **57**(1), 1 (2018)
5. Qu, Z., Li, J., Qi, S.: Signal analysis method for safe distributed optical fiber early warning system based on EMD. J. Tianjin Univ.: Nat. Sci. Eng. Technol. **40**(1), 73–77 (2007)
6. Sun, Q., Feng, W., Zeng, W.: Pattern recognition of optical fiber early warning system based on image processing. Opt. Precis. Eng. **23**(2), 334–341 (2015)
7. Sun, Q.: Research on pattern recognition method of Φ-OTDR optical fiber early warning system. Tianjin University (2015)
8. Jensen, R., Shen, Q.: Fuzzy-rough sets for descriptive dimensionality reduction. In: IEEE International Conference on Fuzzy Systems, vol. 1, pp. 29–34 (2002)
9. Hu, H., Hu, X., Guan, X.: Forecasting method of crude oil output based on optimization of LSSVM by particle swarm algorithm. In: International Conference on Information Science and Control Engineering. IEEE Computer Society, pp. 334–338 (2017)

Detection of Print Head Defect Based on Image Processing Technology

Zhanfeng Zhao, Duo Liu$^{(\boxtimes)}$, and Longwei Wang

Harbin Institute of Technology (Weihai), Weihai, China
1398108921@qq.com

Abstract. In the detection of dead pixels in the print head, this paper innovatively proposes a dead pixel detection algorithm based on image processing technology for the low efficiency of manual detection and high labor cost. Firstly, the ROI is extracted based on the maximum connected region. Secondly, the binarized image is preprocessed by morphological processing, and then the texture is extracted based on the periodic structural features of the image. The specific steps of texture extraction are as follows: Firstly, this paper locates the largest connected area and gains the row and column of the connected area according to the polynomial fit. Secondly, according to the up and down translation, a column of texture regions is obtained, and then other texture regions are obtained according to the left and right translation. In addition, the Canny operator is used to detect the edge of the image, getting an image with texture edges and dead pixels. Perform a close operation on the image to remove dead pixels, and then subtracted from the original image, the dead pixels in the print head can be detected. The experimental results show that the algorithm not only can accurately detect the dead pixels in the print head image, but also has low complexity and short processing time, which is good for engineering practicability.

Keywords: Dead pixel detection · Image processing technology ·
Texture extraction · Canny operator

1 Introduction

In the process of human-computer interaction, the printer is an important device for information data output, and the quality of the print head will directly influence the user's reading and judgment of the output information [1]. In the production process, there are many uncertainties, such as the material itself and the fabrication process, which may lead to the surface of the printing head which is not smooth and produces micron-sized bulges that are difficult to be distinguished by the naked eye, which directly leads to the unqualified products [2]. Therefore, strict inspection must be carried out before the production.

The traditional detection is carried out by visual inspection by the employee under the microscope. However, the method is susceptible to environment, attention and other human factors, and has a certain randomness, which is relatively easy to cause large human error. In addition, employees for a long time continuous work will cause

M. Jia et al. (Eds.): WiSATS 2019, LNICST 280, pp. 676–686, 2019.
https://doi.org/10.1007/978-3-030-19153-5_66

visual fatigue. The existence of many factors will result in low detection efficiency, which will adversely affect the efficiency of the company [3].

With the development of domestic industrialization, image processing technology and machine vision are flourishing in China. The technology of detecting surface defects by machine vision has been applied in many industrial fields [4]. In the detection of flaws for small spots, the image reconstruction method using singular value decomposition proposed by Tsai can accurately detect minute defects, but since most of the tiny singular points of the print head image are not defects, the method is not suitable for processing the data in this paper [5]. He proposed a method based on partial image template matching to achieve micron-level defect detection, but the algorithm is complex and takes a long time, which is not conducive to the realization of engineering automation [6].

Aiming at the above problems, this paper based on the periodic texture features of the print head image, the polynomial fitting and Canny edge detection operator are introduced into the dead pixel detection of the print head image, and the corresponding dead-point detection algorithm is proposed. The test results show that the algorithm can accurately and effectively detect the dead pixels in the print head image, and provides a feasible algorithm for the detection of dead pixels in the print head image.

2 Principle and Preprocessing

In the production process, due to many uncertain factors such as the manufacturing process and the material itself, the surface of the print head is often not smooth, resulting in micro-scale fine protrusions. In order to detect these tiny protrusions by computer vision, this paper uses the blue light strip diffusion mode of the optical microscope camera for image acquisition, and the acquisition work is done on the experimental bench.

2.1 Print Head Area Segmentation

Since the acquired image contains other areas than the print head image, the ROI (region of interest) is extracted firstly, that is, the print head image area is segmented, and then the print head image is subjected to dead pixel detection. According to the structural characteristics of the acquired image, the maximum connected component is used to obtain the rectangular area of the print head to achieve accurate segmentation of the print head.

Image graying is a method of processing color images. It is a single-channel image that not only makes analysis easier, but also preserves the distribution of chrominance and brightness of the original color image, so this paper convert color images into grayscale images. There are many different types of color images. In this paper, RGB images are obtained. There are usually three methods for converting RGB images into grayscale images: maximum value method, average value method, and weighted average method. This paper uses an algorithm for weighted averaging of RGB components:

$$gray = 0.2989R + 0.5870G + 0.1140B \qquad (1)$$

Among them, gray is the converted gray value. R, G, and B are the values of the three channels corresponding to the RGB color image. The resulting grayscale image is shown in Fig. 1:

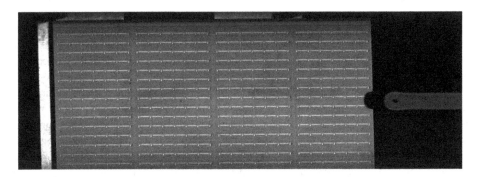

Fig. 1. Grayscale image

After obtaining the gray image, the gray image is segmented by threshold value, and the apparent foreground and the background are segmented. The so-called threshold segmentation is to set an appropriate threshold, and the pixel point higher than the threshold is determined as the target point of interest. The pixel points below the threshold are judged as background target points. There are many methods for threshold selection: histogram method, bimodal method, iterative method, Otsu method, gray scale stretching method, etc. Based on the characteristics of image data obtained, this paper uses the Otsu method for threshold selection, which is a global threshold acquisition method based on the maximum inter-class variance. Suppose that the segmentation threshold of the foreground and the background is T, and the ratio of foreground points to image is ω_0, and the average gray value is u_0. The ratio of background points to image is ω_1, the average gray value u_1. The total average gray value of the image is u, and the variance of the foreground and background images is g. Then there is

$$u = \omega_0 \times u_0 + \omega_1 \times u_1 \qquad (2)$$

$$g = \omega_0 \times (u_0 - u)^2 + \omega_1 \times (u_1 - u)^2 \qquad (3)$$

Equation (4) can be obtained from Eqs. (2) and (3):

$$g = \omega_0 \times \omega_1 \times (u_0 - u_1)^2 \qquad (4)$$

Or

$$g = \frac{\omega_0}{1 - \omega_0} \times (u_0 - u)^2 \tag{5}$$

When the variance is maximum, it can be considered that the differences between the foreground and background are the largest at this time, and the gray value T at this time is the optimal threshold.

Suppose that the gray value of the grayscale image at coordinates (x, y) is f(x, y), and the result after the threshold processing is g(x, y), and the threshold is T, then

$$g(i,j) = \begin{cases} 1 & f(i,j) \geq T \\ 0 & f(i,j) < T \end{cases} \tag{6}$$

Where 1 is the print head pixel and 0 is the background pixel. Threshold segmentation results are shown in Fig. 2:

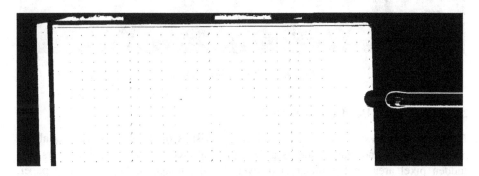

Fig. 2. Image after the first binarization

It can be seen that there are many small singular points from Fig. 2. In order to prevent these singular points from affecting the extraction of the maximum connected components, the morphological closing operation is used to remove them, and the structural elements are disc-shaped. The results are shown in Fig. 3:

Fig. 3. Image after the first closing operation

As can be seen from the Fig. 3, after the morphological processing, the small singular points are eliminated, and the maximum white connected area is the rectangular area of the print head to be extracted. This paper obtains the starting point coordinates and the length and width data of the rectangular area and then correspond to the original image, and achieve accurate segmentation of the print head image, as shown in the Fig. 4:

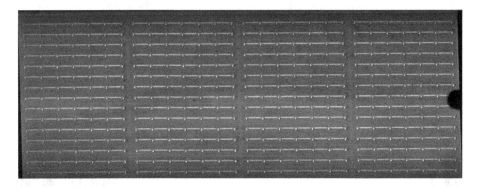

Fig. 4. Split print head image

2.2 Print Head Dead Pixels Detection

Through the analysis of the dead pixel characteristics of the previously unqualified products, it is found that if there is a dead pixel at a certain position, it appears as a sudden pixel area on the image. However, for the images collected in this paper, because the periodic texture contains some pixel mutation points, even if there are no dead pixels, the conventional detection method will detect the sudden change point. Therefore, how to eliminate pixel mutation points in periodic texture while detecting really bad points is the key point of this algorithm. This article considers that in actual engineering applications someone do not care whether the region where the periodic texture is located contains dead pixels. Therefore, the core idea of the algorithm is firstly to extract the region where the periodic texture is located and change all the regions into bright color. Secondly, use the Canny operator for edge detection on the newly obtained image, and then combined with the corresponding morphological processing, the dead pixels are detected by the difference. The specific steps are as follows:

Texture Area Extraction. It can be seen from Fig. 4 that the texture in the image has a certain arrangement regular, and this particular arrangement regular has great significance for the acquisition of the texture region. In this paper, the method of obtaining the texture region is as follows: Firstly, the binarization of Fig. 4 is performed. Secondly, the maximum connected component is extracted. Suppose that the coordinate of the starting point of the largest connected component is (x_1, y_1), and the length is h_1 and the width is w1. According to Eqs. (7) and (8) we can obtain a series of horizontal and vertical points respectively, where the horizontal and vertical points are not strictly horizontal and vertical, but have a certain angle of inclination.

$$abs(x - x_1 \leq 20)\&\&abs(w \times h - w_1 \times h_1) < (w_1 - 5) \times (h_1 - 5) \qquad (7)$$

$$abs(y - y_1 \leq 6)\&\&abs(w \times h - w_1 \times h_1) < (w_1 - 5) \times (h_1 - 5) \qquad (8)$$

In the formula, the new starting point is (x, y), and the length and width of the connected component with the starting point (x, y) are h, w respectively.

Then this article uses the obtained series of horizontal and vertical points to perform polynomial fitting to obtain two intersecting straight lines. The polynomial fitting selects a first-order polynomial, which is consistent with the structural features of the image. And take (x_1, y_1) as the starting point and take the two lines as the axis. Then make the left and right and up and down translation. The step length of the translation can be determined by the shortest distance between the horizontal point and the vertical point to the starting point.

Dead Pixels Detection. After extracting the texture region and turning it into a bright color, this paper uses the Canny operator for edge detection. Canny edge detection has four parts: Firstly, smoothing the image with Gaussian filter. Secondly, calculating the gradient amplitude and direction with first-order partial derivative finite difference. Thirdly, non-maximum suppression of gradient magnitude. Finally, detection and joining of edges using a dual threshold algorithm. This paper directly calls the edge function with the Canny operator, and the upper bound of the threshold was calculated as 0.08.

After the edge detection, both the edge and the dead pixels are detected. Since the dead point is roughly circular and is very different from the background edge, this article use the circular structure element to perform the morphological closing operation on the image after edge detection, which get the background edge that gets rid of the dead pixels. The background edge is then subtracted from the original image, and the dead pixels in the print head image are detected.

The advantages of this algorithm are that it can not only avoid complex illumination compensation of the image before binarization, but also accurately detect the dead pixels in the print head image. In addition, the algorithm has low complexity and short running time.

3   Experiment and Result Analysis

This paper uses the blue-ray diffuse mode of the optical microscope camera for image acquisition, and the acquisition work is done on the experimental bench. After the image segmentation of the collected print head image is performed according to the maximum connected component method proposed in this paper, the algorithm proposed in this paper is used to detect the dead pixels. First, the segmented image is binarized, as shown in Fig. 5.

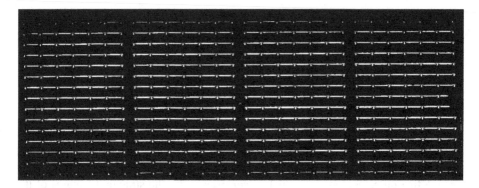

Fig. 5. Image after the second binarization

It can be seen from the above figure that the binarization result of the edge region is not ideal due to uneven illumination, which further affects the extraction of the texture region. However, the traditional illumination compensation method is not suitable for processing the image. Therefore, the polynomial fitting method mentioned above is used to extract the texture region. The results of the polynomial fitting are shown in Fig. 6.

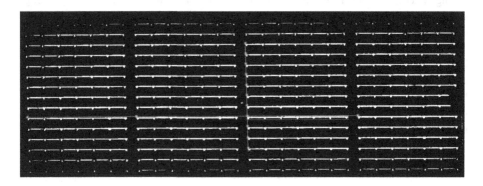

Fig. 6. Polynomial fitting result

According to Fig. 6, this paper uses the straight line shown in the figure as the axis, respectively, up and down and left and right to obtain the texture area, as shown in Fig. 7:

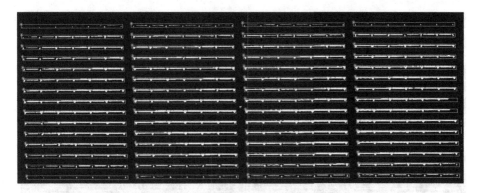

Fig. 7. Texture area positioning result

Turn it into a bright color, that is, set the gray value of the texture area to 255, and the resulting image is shown in Fig. 8:

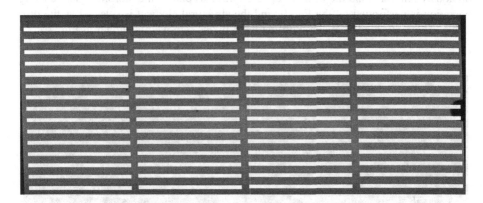

Fig. 8. Remove texture area results

Next, the Canny operator is used for edge detection. This paper directly calls the edge function and selects the Canny operator. The threshold is calculated as 0.08. The processing results are shown in Fig. 9.

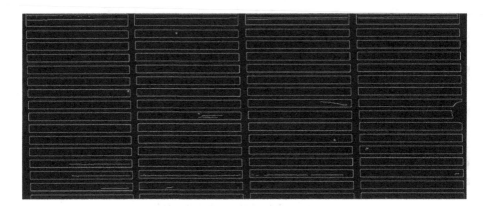

Fig. 9. Edge detection result using canny operator

It can be seen from Fig. 9 that both the texture edge and the dead pixels are detected at the same time. However, since the shape of texture edge and dead pixels are obviously different, and the dead pixels occupies less pixels, the morphological closing operation is performed on the Fig. 9, and the structural element is selected as the disc shape. The texture edge image with the dead pixels removed is shown in Fig. 10.

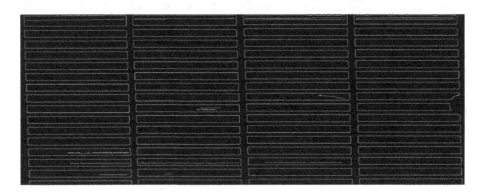

Fig. 10. Image after the second closing operation

By subtracting the Fig. 9 from the Fig. 10, the dead pixels can be detected, as shown in Fig. 11.

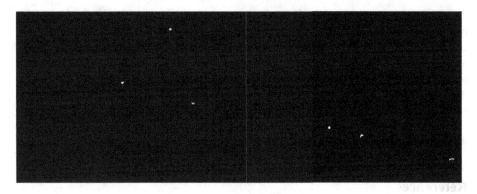

Fig. 11. Dead pixels detection result

Corresponding to the original image of the location of the dead pixels, as shown in Fig. 12. By comparing with Fig. 1, it can be seen that the locations of the dead pixels are all located.

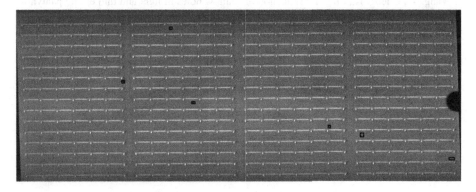

Fig. 12. Dead pixels positioning result

At this point, this paper accurately detected all the dead pixels in the print head image.

4   Conclusion

This paper combines the principle of computer vision and the corresponding software platform to propose a specific algorithm and processing flow for the detection of dead pixels in the print head. The experimental results show that the proposed maximum connected component algorithm can accurately segment the print head region. The polynomial fitting method can not only accurately acquire the texture region, but also remove the influence of illumination unevenness. Canny operator is used for edge detection and then morphological closing operation is performed. Then the dead pixels can be detected quickly and accurately by subtracting from the previous image, so we can make a judgment on whether the print head product is qualified. And the proposed algorithm has low complexity and short running time, which meets the requirements of real-time system. With the mass production of the print head, the print head dead pixels detection idea and detection method proposed in this paper have great theoretical reference and practical value for the print head production enterprise.

Acknowledgement. Thanks to the support of Harbin Institute of Technology and Weihai Fund.

References

1. Cai, X.: Analysis of dead pixels in liquid crystal screen using machine vision. Electron. Test (09), 47–48 (2017)
2. Li, W., Cheng, L.: New progress in fabric defect detection based on machine vision and image processing. J. Text. Res. **35**(03), 158–164 (2014)
3. Dou, Z., Zhang, Q., Zhou, Y., Liu, J.: Detection of dead pixels in liquid crystal screen based on machine vision. J. Beijing Univ. Inf. Sci. Technol. (Nat. Sci.) **30**(05), 87–92 (2015)
4. Wang, Y., Cheng, K., Sun, Y.: Detection of shallow holes in light and thin elastic pantyhose based on machine vision. Wool Spinn. Technol. **45**(08), 80–84 (2017)
5. Lu, C.J., Tsai, D.M.: Automatic defect inspection for LCDs using singular value decomposition. Int. J. Adv. Manuf. Technol. **25**(1), 53–61 (2005)
6. He, Z.: Research on TFT-LCD micro-scale defect detection method based on image processing technology. Harbin Institute of Technology (2007)

Half-Duplex Two-Way AF Relaying Network with Energy Harvesting

Weilin Zhao[1(⊠)], Weidang Lu[1], Yu Zhang[1], Bo Li[2], Xin Liu[3], and Zhenyu Na[4]

[1] College of Information Engineering, Zhejiang University of Technology,
Hangzhou 310023, China
1019653554@qq.com
[2] School of Information and Electrical Engineering,
Harbin Institute of Technology, Weihai 264209, China
[3] School of Electronic Information and Electrical Engineering,
Dalian University of Technology, Dalian 116024, Liaoning, China
[4] School of Information Science and Technology, Dalian Maritime University,
Dalian 116026, China

Abstract. In this paper, we consider a three-node, half-duplex two-way relaying wireless network where an amplify-and-forward relay harvests energy from radio frequency wave transmitted by the two source nodes. Different from time switching (TS) and power splitting (PS), we group subcarriers to realize the information decoding (ID) and energy harvesting (EH) separately. This two-way relaying transmission is consisted of two phases, which is more efficiency and complicated than one-way relaying. System is orthogonal frequency division multiplexing modulated, and subcarrier grouping scheme is the same for the two source nodes. Subcarrier power of source nodes is average allocated, while that of relay is optimized. In this amplify-and-forward relaying network, subcarrier pairing is also under consideration. With the aim of sum rate maximized, we purpose a joint subcarrier grouping, relay subcarrier pairing and power allocation scheme. We use dual decomposition method to solve this problem, after transforming it into an equivalent convex optimization problem. Simulation results also show the impact of the relay location on subcarrier grouping and on sum rate.

Keywords: TWR network · Energy harvesting · Subcarrier grouping

1 Introduction

Nowadays, simultaneous wireless information and power transfer (SWIPT) has attracted significant research interests, which could harvest energy from radio frequency (RF) signals, since RF signals could also be considered as a kind of energy. Compared with other nature resources, RF signals are more stable and reliable, providing a potential method to prolong lifetime of wireless devices and having high potential especially in wireless communication area [1, 2].

In general, there are two practical schemes in SWIPT, one is time switching (TS) and the other is power splitting (PS) [3, 4]. In the TS scheme, the receiver

M. Jia et al. (Eds.): WiSATS 2019, LNICST 280, pp. 687–695, 2019.
https://doi.org/10.1007/978-3-030-19153-5_67

switches between information decoding (ID) and energy harvesting (EH). As for PS scheme, the receiver splits the received signal into two signal streams by a power splitter, then processes ID and EH respectively. Combine relaying protocols with SWIPT, many works have done on various forms relaying networks, in Amplify-and-Forward (AF) or Decode-and-Forward (DF) relay, in one-way relay (OWR) [5–7] or two-way relay (TWR) [3, 8, 9] protocols. [5] proposed TS based SWIPT in AF and DF relaying one-way cooperative communications, analyzed achievable throughput. In [7] PS and TS transmission protocols are compared in one-way AF relaying networks, the TSR (time switching relaying) protocol outperforms the PSR (power splitting relaying) protocol in terms of throughput at low signal-to-noise-ratios and high transmission rates. [4] introduced optimal PS in two-way DF relay networks. Optimal power allocated is derived to achieve the maximum achievable sum rate, and performance is compared with that of AF relay protocols.

In this paper, we address OFDM based half-duplex two-way AF relaying network with energy harvesting. Instead of PS and TS scheme, we adopt OFDM modulation method, where subcarriers are divided into two groups to achieve information decoding and energy harvesting separately. We assume that source nodes are stable power supplied, while relay node is powered by the energy harvested from the RF signal of the source nodes.

2 System Model

Our model is consisted of two source nodes S1, S2, and one AF relay node R. A completed transmission is composed of two equal length phases. During the first phase, source nodes S1 and S2, transmit its signal $x_{1,k}$, $x_{2,k}$ to relay over subcarrier k. $h_{1,k}$ and $h_{2,k}$ denote the channel coefficient of the S1 $\rightarrow$ R link and S2 $\rightarrow$ R link over subcarrier k. Direct link is not taken into consideration here due to the bad channel state. We assumed that noise at each node is complex Gaussian random variables, subject to $CN(0, \sigma_k^2)$. The received signal at relay can be given as

$$y_{R,k} = h_{1,k}\sqrt{p_{s1,k}^I}x_{1,k} + h_{2,k}\sqrt{p_{s2,k}^I}x_{2,k} + n_{R,k} \tag{1}$$

According to the subcarrier ordinal, signals are divided into 2 groups, G_1 and G_2. Where $G_1 + G_2 = K$. Specifically, signals with subcarrier numbers belonging to G_1 are used for information decoding, and with that belonging to G_2 are used for energy harvesting. Therefore, energy harvested at relay can be given as

$$Q = \sum_{k \in G_2} \zeta(p_{s1,k}^E|h_{1,k}|^2 + p_{s2,k}^E|h_{2,k}|^2 + \sigma_k^2) \tag{2}$$

ζ represents the conversion efficiency of energy harvesting.

In the second phase, the relay amplifies and forwards the information using the energy Q after pairing the subcarriers in G_1. $\rho_{k,k'}$ represents the indicator of subcarrier pairing. $\rho_{k,k'} = 1$ represents that subcarrier ordinal k in the first phase is paired with subcarrier ordinal k' in the second phase. It should be noted that one subcarrier could only be paired with one subcarrier in the second phase, that is $\sum_{k'=1}^{K} \rho_{k,k'} = 1, \forall k$. $h_{3,k'}$ and $h_{4,k'}$ denote the channel coefficient of the R $\rightarrow$ S1 link and R $\rightarrow$ S2 link over subcarrier k' in the second phase. And $\beta_{k,k'}$ is the amplification factor, satisfying:

$$\beta_{k,k'}^2 = \frac{p_{r,k'}}{p_{s1,k}^I |h_{1,k}|^2 + p_{s2,k}^I |h_{2,k}|^2 + \sigma_k^2} \tag{3}$$

The signal-to-noise ratio at node S_i is expressed as $SNR_{k,k'}^i$, devoted as

$$\text{SNR}_{k,k'}^1 = \frac{\beta_{k,k'}^2 |h_{3,k'}|^2 |h_{2,k}|^2 p_{s2,k}^I}{\left(\beta_{k,k'}^2 |h_{3,k'}|^2 + 1\right)\sigma_k^2} \tag{4}$$

$$\text{SNR}_{k,k'}^2 = \frac{\beta_{k,k'}^2 |h_{4,k'}|^2 |h_{1,k}|^2 p_{s1,k}^I}{\left(\beta_{k,k'}^2 |h_{4,k'}|^2 + 1\right)\sigma_k^2} \tag{5}$$

Thus, information rate of the two opposite links can be described as

$$R_{s1} = \sum_{k\in G_1} \sum_{k'=1}^{K} \rho_{k,k'} \frac{1}{2}\ln(1 + \text{SNR}_{k,k'}^1) \tag{6}$$

$$R_{s2} = \sum_{k\in G_1} \sum_{k'=1}^{K} \rho_{k,k'} \frac{1}{2}\ln(1 + \text{SNR}_{k,k'}^2) \tag{7}$$

Total transmission rate R_s can be given as

$$R_s = R_{s1} + R_{s2} \tag{8}$$

3   Problem Formulation and Optimal Solution

Our target is to maximize the total transmission rate by jointly determining the subcarrier grouping $\mathcal{G} = \{G_1, G_2\}$, relay subcarrier power $p = \{p_{r,k'}\}$ and subcarrier pairing $\rho = \{\rho_{k,k'}\}$ with energy constraints. Subcarriers' power of source node here is average allocated. The problem can be formulated as

$$\max_{\{\mathcal{G},\mathcal{P},\rho\}} R_s \tag{9}$$

subject to

$$
\begin{cases}
\sum\limits_{k\varepsilon G_1} \sum\limits_{k'=1}^{K} \rho_{k,k'} p_{r,k'} \leq Q \\
\rho_{k,k'} \varepsilon \{0, 1\} \\
\sum\limits_{k'=1}^{K} \rho_{k,k'} = 1, \forall k
\end{cases}
$$

The optimization problem in (9) is a mixed integer non-convex problem. If the "time-sharing" condition [10] is satisfied, which will be always satisfied when the number of subcarriers is larger, the duality gap of the nonconvex optimization problem is zero.

By constructing a Lagrangian function

$$g(\alpha) = \max_{\{\mathcal{G},\mathcal{P},\rho\}} L(\mathcal{G}, \mathcal{P}, \rho) \tag{10}$$

where

$$L(\mathcal{G}, \mathcal{P}, \rho) = R_s + \alpha(Q - \sum_{k\in G_1} \sum_{k'=1}^{K} \rho_{k,k'} p_{r,k'}) \tag{11}$$

And α denotes non-negative Lagrange multiplier subject to power constraints. The dual optimization problem can be expressed as

$$\min_{\alpha} g(\alpha) \tag{12}$$

The minimization problem can be solved by using the sub-gradient based methods. The sub-gradient can be given as

$$\alpha = (Q - \sum_{k\in G_1} \sum_{k'=1}^{K} \rho_{k,k'} p_{r,k'}) \tag{13}$$

α is updated by $\alpha^{t+1} = \alpha^t - \xi^t \alpha$, ξ^t is the step size. And the optimal variables can be obtained with the following two steps.

Step 1: assume we had already know $\mathcal{G}$, ρ, deriving the optimal $\mathcal{P}$.
The partial derivatives of the Lagrangian in (11) with respective to the optimization variables $p_{r,k'}$ is show as

$$\frac{\partial L}{\partial p_{r,k'}} = -\alpha + \frac{1}{2} \frac{p_{s2,k}^I \gamma_{2,k} \gamma_{3,k'} (p_{s1,k}^I \gamma_{1,k} + p_{s2,k}^I \gamma_{2,k} + 1)}{(p_{s1,k}^I \gamma_{1,k} + p_{s2,k}^I \gamma_{2,k} + p_{r,k'} \gamma_{3,k'} + 1)(p_{s1,k}^I \gamma_{1,k} + p_{s2,k}^I \gamma_{2,k} + p_{r,k'} \gamma_{3,k'} + p_{s2,k}^I \gamma_{2,k} p_{r,k'} \gamma_{3,k'} + 1)}$$

$$+ \frac{1}{2} \frac{p_{s1,k}^I \gamma_{1,k} \gamma_{4,k'} (p_{s1,k}^I \gamma_{1,k} + p_{s2,k}^I \gamma_{2,k} + 1)}{(p_{s1,k}^I \gamma_{1,k} + p_{s2,k}^I \gamma_{2,k} + p_{r,k'} \gamma_{4,k'} + 1)(p_{s1,k}^I \gamma_{1,k} + p_{s2,k}^I \gamma_{2,k} + p_{r,k'} \gamma_{4,k'} + p_{s1,k}^I \gamma_{1,k} p_{r,k'} \gamma_{4,k'} + 1)}$$

$$(14)$$

where $\gamma_{1,k} = \frac{|h_{1,k}|^2}{\sigma_k^2}, \gamma_{2,k} = \frac{|h_{2,k}|^2}{\sigma_k^2}, \gamma_{3,k'} = \frac{|h_{3,k'}|^2}{\sigma_k^2}, \gamma_{4,k'} = \frac{|h_{4,k'}|^2}{\sigma_k^2}$. Due to KKT condition, the partial derivative of the Lagrange function is equal to zero at the optimal solution, $\mathcal{P}^* = \{p_{r,k'}^*\}$ is the positive solution of quartic Eq. (15)

$$a_4 p_{r,k'}^4 + a_3 p_{r,k'}^3 + a_2 p_{r,k'}^2 + a_1 p_{r,k'} + a_0 = 0 \qquad (15)$$

Where

$$a_4 = \frac{2\alpha}{X(k)} \left(1 + p_{s1,k}^I \gamma_{1,k}\right) \left(1 + p_{s2,k}^I \gamma_{2,k}\right) \gamma_{3,k'}^2 \gamma_{4,k'}^2$$

$$a_3 = 2\alpha \gamma_{3,k'} \gamma_{4,k'} \left(\left(1 + p_{s1,k}^I \gamma_{1,k}\right)\left(2 + p_{s2,k}^I \gamma_{2,k}\right) \gamma_{4,k'} + (2 + p_{s1,k}^I \gamma_{1,k})(1 + p_{s2,k}^I \gamma_{2,k}) \gamma_{3,k'}\right)$$

$$a_2 = \left(2\alpha X(k) - p_{s2,k}^I \gamma_{2,k} \gamma_{3,k'}\right) \left(1 + p_{s1,k}^I \gamma_{1,k}\right) \gamma_{4,k'}^2$$
$$+ (2\alpha X(k) - p_{s1,k}^I \gamma_{1,k} \gamma_{4,k'})(1 + p_{s2,k}^I \gamma_{2,k}) \gamma_{3,k'}^2$$
$$+ 2\alpha \left(4 + p_{s1,k}^I \gamma_{1,k} p_{s2,k}^I \gamma_{2,k} + 2 p_{s1,k}^I \gamma_{1,k} + 2 p_{s2,k}^I \gamma_{2,k}\right) X(k) \gamma_{3,k'} \gamma_{4,k'}$$

$$a_1 = \left(2\alpha X(k) - p_{s2,k}^I \gamma_{2,k} \gamma_{3,k'}\right) \left(2 + p_{s1,k}^I \gamma_{1,k}\right) X(k) \gamma_{4,k'}$$
$$+ \left(2\alpha X(k) - p_{s1,k}^I \gamma_{1,k} \gamma_{4,k'}\right)(2 + p_{s2,k}^I \gamma_{2,k}) X(k) \gamma_{3,k'}$$

$$a_0 = X(k)^2 \left(2\alpha X(k) - p_{s2,k}^I \gamma_{2,k} \gamma_{3,k'} - p_{s1,k}^I \gamma_{1,k} \gamma_{4,k'}\right)$$

$$X(k) = 1 + p_{s1,k}^I \gamma_{1,k} + p_{s2,k}^I \gamma_{2,k}$$

Step 2: deriving the optimal ρ, $\mathcal{G}$ with $\mathcal{P}^*$.

Substituting the optimal $\mathcal{P}^*$ into (11), and taking some mathematical operation, formula can be rewritten as (16)

$$L = \sum_{k \in K} \alpha \zeta (p_{s1,k}^E |h_{1,k}|^2 + p_{s2,k}^E |h_{2,k}|^2 + \sigma_k^2)$$

$$+ \sum_{k \in G_1} \{ \sum_{k'=1}^{K} \rho_{k,k'} E_{k,k'} - \alpha \zeta (p_{s1,k}^E |h_{1,k}|^2 + p_{s2,k}^E |h_{2,k}|^2 + \sigma_k^2) \qquad (16)$$

where

$$E_{k,k'} = \frac{1}{2}\ln\left(1 + \text{SNR}_{k,k'}^1\right) + \frac{1}{2}\ln\left(1 + \text{SNR}_{k,k'}^2\right) - \alpha p_{r,k'} \qquad (17)$$

We can see only $E_{k,k'}$ is related to ρ, therefore, the optimal subcarrier pairing can be obtained by finding the maximum $E_{k,k'}$ in order. After obtaining ρ^*, we denote

$$F_k = \sum_{k'=1}^{K} \rho_{k,k'} E_{k,k'} - \alpha\zeta(p_{s1,k}^E |h_{1,k}|^2 + p_{s2,k}^E |h_{2,k}|^2 + \sigma_k^2) \qquad (18)$$

Then, we can rewrite (16) as

$$L = \sum_{k\in K} \alpha\zeta(p_{s1,k}^E |h_{1,k}|^2 + p_{s2,k}^E |h_{2,k}|^2 + \sigma_k^2) + \sum_{k\in G_1} F_k \qquad (19)$$

Similarly, only F_k is related to G_1, we only need to find all the $k's$ that make F_k positive. Then, all these $k's$ form G_1.

$$G_1^* = \arg\ \max_{G_1}\ \sum_{k\in G_1} F_k \qquad (20)$$

Finally, the optimal G_2 can be given as $G_2^* = K - G_1^*$. So far, with given dual variable, we have got all the optimal variables. By updating the dual variable, the joint optimization problem can be finally solved.

4 Simulation Results

In this section, we provide simulation results of our algorithm. We set the distance between S1 and S2 to be 5 m and the relay is located on the line connecting the two source nodes. Channel coefficient $h_{i,k} \sim CN(0, d_i^{-v})$, where d_i representing the distance between S_i, $i \in (1, 2)$ and relay, and path-loss index v is set to be 3. For simplicity, we use d_1, the distance between S1 and relay to represent the position of relay in the following figures. The number of subcarriers K is set to be 32. Energy harvesting conversion efficiency is set to be 1. No otherwise explanation, sum transmission power of each source node is devoted as Ps, which is set to be 1mW, d_1 is 2 m, and variance of noise is set to be -30 dBm.

Figure 1 shows the subcarrier grouping of source node, which is the same for two source nodes in our algorithm. Figure 2 shows the power allocation of relay after subcarrier pairing. Although there is no information about the one-to-one pairing of subcarriers, it can be seen that the pairing of subcarriers is completed. The number of subcarriers used for information, that is, the number of red stripes in the graph is 16, is the same as the number of subcarriers in the relay node.

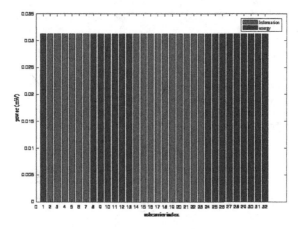

Fig. 1. Power allocation of source nodes (Color figure online)

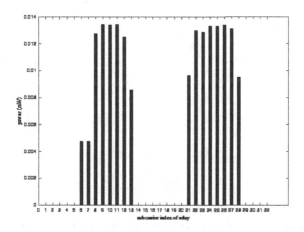

Fig. 2. Power allocation of relay

Figure 3 shows the sum rate versus relay location, when Ps is set to be 1 mW, 1.5 mW and 2 mW, respectively. All the curves descend first and then rise, reach the lowest value when relay is exactly at the middle of S1 and S2. curves are symmetric about $d_1 = 2.5$ m.

Figure 4 shows the harvested energy and the ratio of subcarriers number in G_2 change with d_1. When relay approaches the central position, more subcarriers can be seen for energy transmission (the orange circle), but the energy collected is still declining, because overall channel condition is not good. It is also consistent with the conclusion in Fig. 3, sum rate reaches the lowest value when d_1 is 2.5 m.

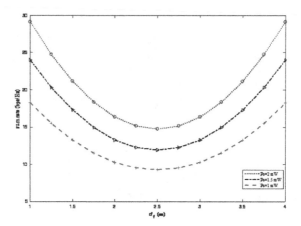

Fig. 3. Sum rate versus d_1

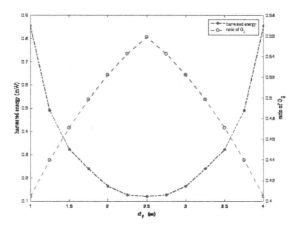

Fig. 4. Harvested energy and the number of subcarriers in G_2 versus d_1 (Color figure online)

5   Conclusion

In this paper, we investigated SWIPT in a two-way AF relaying network, which adopts OFDM technology. Different from TS and PS, the received OFDM subcarriers are partitioned into two groups for information decoding and energy harvesting separately. With the aim of sum rate maximized, we purpose a joint subcarrier grouping, subcarrier pairing and power allocation scheme. Our results also demonstrate the impact of relay location on subcarrier grouping and on sum rate.

Acknowledgement. This work was supported in part by the National Natural Science Foundation of China under Grants 61871348 and 61601221, by the Project funded by China Postdoctoral Science Foundation under Grant 2017M612027.

References

1. Lu, X., Wang, P., Niyato, D., et al.: Wireless networks with RF energy harvesting: a contemporary survey. IEEE Commun. Surv. Tutor. **17**(2), 757–789 (2015)
2. Ozel, O., Tutuncuoglu, K., Ulukus, S., et al.: Fundamental limits of energy harvesting communications. IEEE Commun. Mag. **53**(4), 126–132 (2015)
3. Do, T.P., Song, I., Kim, Y.H.: Simultaneous wireless transfer of power and information in a decode-and-forward two-way relaying network. IEEE Trans. Wireless Commun. **16**(3), 1579–1592 (2017)
4. Peng, C., Li, F., Liu, H.: Optimal power splitting in two-way decode-and-forward relay networks. IEEE Commun. Lett. **21**(9), 2009–2012 (2017)
5. Nasir, A.A., Zhou, X., Durrani, S., et al.: Wireless-powered relays in cooperative communications: time-switching relaying protocols and throughput analysis. IEEE Trans. Commun. **63**(5), 1607–1622 (2015)
6. Zhu, G., Zhong, C., Suraweera, H.A., et al.: Wireless information and power transfer in relay systems with multiple antennas and interference. IEEE Trans. Commun. **63**(4), 1400–1418 (2015)
7. Nasir, A.A., Zhou, X., Durrani, S., et al.: Relaying protocols for wireless energy harvesting and information processing. IEEE Trans. Wireless Commun. **12**(7), 3622–3636 (2013)
8. Zhou, X., Li, Q.: Energy efficiency optimisation for SWIPT AF two-way relay networks. Electron. Lett. **53**(6), 436–438 (2017)
9. Wang, L., Hu, F., et al.: Wireless information and power transfer to maximize information throughput in WBAN. IEEE Internet Things J. **4**(5), 1663–1670 (2017)
10. Wei, Y., Lui, R.: Dual methods for nonconvex spectrum optimization of multicarrier systems. IEEE Trans. Commun. **54**(7), 1310–1322 (2006)

Optimized Power Allocation for Weighted Complementary Coded-CDMA Systems

Zaiyang Jiang[1,2,3(✉)], Siyue Sun[2], Guang Liang[2], and Huawang Li[2]

[1] Shanghai Institute of Micro-system and Information Technology,
Chinese Academy of Science, Shanghai 200050, China
arthur91@mail.ustc.edu.cn
[2] Shanghai Engineering Center for Micro-satellites, Shanghai 201210, China
[3] University of Chinese Academy of Sciences, Beijing 100049, China

Abstract. Complementary codes (CCs) have opened up a whole new frontier in Code Division Multiple Access (CDMA) techniques due to the ideal correlation properties. However, the equal gain combination must be satisfied in such CDMA system, which constrains the system performance over frequency selective fading channels. This paper aims to propose a set of weighted complementary codes (WCCs) to enable variable combination parameters while maintaining ideal correlation properties. Such new WCCs can provide power allocation with more freedom, and more importantly, an optimized power allocation can improve the bit error probability performance of CDMA systems as proved at the end of this paper.

Keywords: Weighted complementary codes · WCC-CDMA system ·
Multiple access interference · Multi-path interference · Power allocation

1 Introduction

CDMA systems have been considered as interference-limited systems in the past decade, due to the fact that ideal correlation properties cannot be achieved with one-dimensional spreading codes. As a consequence, these codes could lead to multi-path interference (MPI) and multiple access interference (MAI), as they only considered periodic auto-correlation functions (ACFs) and periodic cross-correlation functions (CCFs) while aperiodic ACFs and/or CCFs were neglected [1]. A possible solution was to design a spreading code based on CCs [2–4], which have taken account of periodic and aperiodic ACFs and/or CCFs. The systems

This work was partly supported by National Nature Science Foundation Program of China (No. 61601295), Shanghai Sailing Program (16YF1411000) and CAS Innovation Fund (No. CXJJ-16S033).

© ICST Institute for Computer Sciences, Social Informatics and Telecommunications Engineering 2019
Published by Springer Nature Switzerland AG 2019. All Rights Reserved
M. Jia et al. (Eds.): WiSATS 2019, LNICST 280, pp. 696–706, 2019.
https://doi.org/10.1007/978-3-030-19153-5_68

employing such spreading codes are named Complementary Coded-CDMA (CC-CDMA) systems, which are interference-free [5]. However, orthogonality cannot be recovered in frequency selective channels, which again introduces the interference problems. The previous constructions of CCs were so inflexible that the gains of subcodes of each channel had to be equal [6,7], which means that the channels can only result in an equal gain regardless of how they perform. Therefore, CC-CDMA systems needed to satisfy an equal gain of correlation coefficients. The previous academic literature only attempted to resolve this problem through the design optimization of traditional CC-CDMA systems, where the designs were highly complicated and the use of diversity gain was insufficient. In this sense, it is vital to develop much smarter codes while keeping the properties of periodic and aperiodic ACFs and/or CCFs at the same time.

This paper aims to solve the problem by proposing a new construction of WCCs to enable the allocation of more power to better channels and thereby reduce the BER. WCC-CDMA systems no longer require equal transmitter powers and equal combination gains of channels, because of the ideal correlation properties of subcodes. According to the water filling algorithm, the allocation of more power to better channels can result in the improvement of capacity, so that there will be a declined bit error rate (BER). Systems employing a set of WCCs are weighted complementary coded-CDMA (WCC-CDMA) systems.

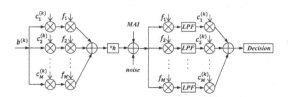

Fig. 1. The architecture of an FDM CC-CDMA system with k users taking transceiver

2   System Model

This paper considers the same CC-CDMA architecture as that in [8]. Figure 1 shows a classic frequency division multiplex (FDM) CC-CDMA system architecture. The signature codes are a set of CCs $\mathbb{C}(M, N, K)$, where M is the flock size, which is the number of element sequences; N is the code length, which is the same length of each element sequence; and K is the set size, which is the maximum number of users. MN is the "congregated length" of a CC, and it determines the processing gain of the corresponding CC-CDMA system [9]. The CC assigned to user k is represented by $C^{(k)} = \left\{ c_m^{(k)} \right\}_{m=1}^{M}$, $k \in \{1, 2, \cdots, K\}$, the mth sequence is $c_m^{(k)} = [c_{m,1}^{(k)}, c_{m,2}^{(k)}, \cdots, c_{m,N}^{(k)}]$, where $c_{m,n}^{(k)} \in \{-1, 1\}$, $m \in \{1, \cdots, M\}$, and $n \in \{1, \cdots, N\}$.

The correlation properties of CCs are expressed as

$$\rho(C^{(k_1)}, C^{(k_2)}; \tau) = \sum_{m=1}^{M} \phi(c_m^{(k_1)}, c_m^{(k_2)}; \tau) \tag{1}$$

where $C^{(k_1)}, C^{(k_2)} \in C(M, N, K)$, $k_1, k_2 \in \{1, 2, \cdots, K\}$, τ is the delay of element sequences, and $\phi(c_m^{(k_1)}, c_m^{(k_2)}; \tau)$ is the aperiodic correlation function of $c_m^{(k_1)}$ and $c_m^{(k_2)}$. When $k_1 = k_2$, (1) is the aperiodic auto-correlation function (ACF); otherwise, it is the aperiodic cross-correlation function (CCF).

The ACF of a CC is ideal if it is a delta function. The CCF of a set of CC is ideal if and only if it is a zero function. The ideal correlation properties can be expressed as

$$\rho(C^{(k_1)}, C^{(k_2)}; \tau) = \begin{cases} MN, & k_1 = k_2 \ and \ \tau = 0, \\ 0, & otherwise. \end{cases} \tag{2}$$

where $-N < \tau < N$, and $\forall k_1, k_2 \in \{1, \ldots, K\}$.

Let $b^{(k)}(i)$ be the source data for user k, where $b^{(k)}(i) \in \{-1, 1\}$, $i \in \{0, 1, \cdots, B-1\}$, and B is data block length. The source data is spread by $C^{(k)}$, as

$$s_m^{(k)}(t) = \sqrt{p} \sum_{i=0}^{B-1} b^{(k)}(i) C_m^{(k)}(t - iT_b) \tag{3}$$

where p is the transmitter power, T_b is bit interval. $C_m^{(k)}(t)$ is chip waveform of the mth element sequence, as

$$C_m^{(k)}(t) = \sum_{n=1}^{N} c_{m,n}^{(k)} q(t - nT_c + T_c) \tag{4}$$

where $q(t)$ is the impulse of chip waveform-shaping filter, as

$$q(t) = \begin{cases} \frac{1}{\sqrt{T_C}}, & 0 \le t \le T_C, \\ 0, & otherwise. \end{cases} \tag{5}$$

At the receiver of user k, the signal received can be written as

$$r_m^{(k)}(t) = h_m \sum_{k=1}^{K} s_m^{(k)}(t) + n_m(t) \tag{6}$$

where $h_m = |h_m| e^{j\varphi_m}$ is the channel coefficient from base stations to the receiver of user k, $n_m(t)$ is white Gaussian noise with zero mean and variance $\sigma_n^2 = N_0/T_c$, where N_0 is the power spectrum density of the complex additive white Gaussian noise (AWGN), assuming that M noises samples are uncorrelated.

3   Scalable Complementary Sets of Sequence

This section starts with the introduction of special CCs namely, WCCs, and prove that the correlation properties of WCCs is perfect with a delay τ, where $\tau = 0, 2, 4, \cdots$.

It has been known that a Hadamard Matrix H_N is an N-order matrix, satisfying

$$H_N H_N^T = H_N^T H_N = N I_N \tag{7}$$

where $H_N \in \{-1, 1\}$, H_N^T is the transpose of H_N and I_N is the identity matrix of order N. (7) implies the orthogonality of any two sequences given by rows of H_N. The Sylvester-type Hadamard matrices with $N = 2^n (n \geq 0)$ can be generated as

$$H_{2N} = \begin{bmatrix} H_N & H_N \\ H_N & -H_N \end{bmatrix} \tag{8}$$

Inspired by (8), the construction of Hadamard matrices of order $N = 2^n (n \geq 0)$ can be formulated by a new recursive procedure as

$$H_{2N} = \begin{bmatrix} H_N & \tilde{H}_N \\ H_N & -\tilde{H}_N \end{bmatrix} \tag{9}$$

where $\tilde{H}_N = P_N H_N Q_N$, P_N and Q_N are orthogonal matrices as

$$P_N P_N^T = P_N^T P_N = Q_N Q_N^T = Q_N^T Q_N = I_N \tag{10}$$

assuming that

$$P_N = \begin{bmatrix} 0 & I_{\frac{N}{2}} \\ I_{\frac{N}{2}} & 0 \end{bmatrix} \tag{11}$$

and

$$Q_N = I_N \tag{12}$$

(11) and (12) represent that $\tilde{H}_N$ results from the exchange of the upper and lower half part of H_N. Therefore, if H_N is a CC of N-order, then $\tilde{H}_N$ is a CC of N-order. Let $H_2^{(0)} = \begin{bmatrix} +1 & +1 \\ +1 & -1 \end{bmatrix}$ and $H_2^{(1)} = \tilde{H}_2^{(0)} = \begin{bmatrix} +1 & -1 \\ +1 & +1 \end{bmatrix}$, a CC set of 2-order can be formed. Through (9), we obtain a CC set of N-order from the set of N-1-order, recursively. The CC set of N-order can be expressed

$$c_{m,n}^{(k)} = (-1)^{\sum_{r=0}^{L-2} (n_{r+1} \oplus m_r \oplus k_r) n_r + (m_{L-1} \oplus k_{L-1}) n_{L-1}} \tag{13}$$

where $m \in \{1, 2, \cdots, M\}$, $n \in \{1, 2, \cdots, N\}$, $k \in \{1, 2, \cdots, K\}$, $K = M = N = 2^L (L \geq 1)$, and m in the radix-2 form is expressed as [10]. Therefore

$$m \equiv (m_{L-1} m_{L-2} \cdots m_0) = \sum_{r=0}^{L-1} 2^r m_r \tag{14}$$

Now, we add a coefficient to (1) and (2), and get

$$\rho(C^{(k_1)}, C^{(k_2)}; \tau; W) = \sum_{m=1}^{M} w_m \phi(c_m^{(k_1)}, c_m^{(k_2)}; \tau) \tag{15}$$

$$\rho(C^{(k_1)}, C^{(k_2)}; \tau; W) = \begin{cases} MN, & k_1 = k_2 \ and \ \tau = 0, \\ 0, & otherwise. \end{cases} \tag{16}$$

Let $L = 2$, we get a set of C_4. Substituting C_4 into (16), we can obtain $W = \{w_1, \cdots, w_4\}$ satisfying

$$w_1 + w_2 = w_3 + w_4 \tag{17}$$

when τ is an even number ($\tau = 0, 2, 4, \cdots$).

In order to prove $\rho(H_N^{(k_1)}, H_N^{(k_2)}; \tau; w) = 0$, we need to prove that the open statement $s(n)$ is true, where $s(n)$ denotes a mathematical statement of $\rho(H_{2^n}^{(k_1)}, H_{2^n}^{(k_2)}; \tau; w) = 0$, $N = 2^n$, $n = 1, 2, \cdots$, $\tau = 2 - N, \cdots, 0, 2, \cdots, N - 2$, $k_1 \neq k_2$ and $W = (w_1, \cdots, w_N)$ satisfying

$$w_1 + w_2 = w_3 + w_4 = \cdots = w_{N-1} + w_N \tag{18}$$

For $n = 1$

$$s(1) : \rho(H_2^{(k_1)}, H_2^{(k_2)}; \tau; w) = 0 \tag{19}$$

So, $s(1)$ is true. Assuming s(n) is true for $n = N$,

$$s(N) : \rho(H_{2^N}^{(k_1)}, H_{2^N}^{(k_2)}; \tau; w) = 0 \tag{20}$$

To establish the truth of $s(N + 1)$, we need to show that

if $1 \leq k < 2^N$

$$H_{2^{N+1}}^{(k)} = \begin{bmatrix} H_{2^N}^{(k')} & H_{2^N}^{(g)} \\ H_{2^N}^{(k')} & -H_{2^N}^{(g)} \end{bmatrix} \tag{21}$$

if $2^N \leq k < 2^{N+1}$

$$H_{2^{N+1}}^{(k)} = \begin{bmatrix} H_{2^N}^{(k')} & -H_{2^N}^{(g)} \\ H_{2^N}^{(k')} & H_{2^N}^{(g)} \end{bmatrix} \tag{22}$$

where $k' \equiv k (mod 2^N)$ and $g = |2^N - k'|$.

$$s(N + 1) : \rho(H_{2^{N+1}}^{(k_1)}, H_{2^{N+1}}^{(k_2)}; \tau; w) = 0 \tag{23}$$

Consequently, $s(N)$ is true for all $n \in Z^+$ based on the Principle of Finite Induction.

4   QPSK in CC-CDMA System

In the section above, we have proved the ideal correlation properties of WCCs, while chip delay τ is an even number. In this section, we will prove that the chip delay τ is an even number by QPSK modulation. Figure 2 shows the chip delay by BPSK and QPSK. It is obvious that the chip delay τ is even by QPSK. In addition, the chip delay is even in some other higher order modulation schemes, for example 16QAM.

The signal after QPSK is

$$
\begin{aligned}
s_m^{(g)}(t) &= I_m^{(g)}(t) + jQ_m^{(g)}(t) \\
&= \sum_{i=1}^{B} b_k(i) C_{I,m}^{(g)}(t - iT_s + T_s) \\
&\quad + j \sum_{i=1}^{B} b_k(i) C_{Q,m}^{(g)}(t - iT_s + T_s)
\end{aligned}
\tag{24}
$$

where T_s is the symbol interval and the source data is spread by $C_{I,m}^{(g)}(t)$ and $C_{Q,m}^{(g)}(t)$.

$$
C_{I,m}^{(g)}(t) = \sum_{i=1}^{N/2} c_{m,2i-1}^{(g)} q(t - iT_c + T_c)
\tag{25}
$$

$$
C_{Q,m}^{(g)}(t) = \sum_{i=1}^{N/2} c_{m,2i}^{(g)} q(t - iT_c + T_c)
\tag{26}
$$

At the receiver of user g, the signal received can be written as

$$
\widehat{I}_m^{(g)}(t) = \sum_{l=1}^{L} \sum_{k=1}^{K} h_l^{(k)} I_m^{(k)}(t - \tau_{k,l}) + n_{I,m}(t)
\tag{27}
$$

$$
\widehat{Q}_m^{(g)}(t) = \sum_{l=1}^{L} \sum_{k=1}^{K} h_l^{(k)} Q_m^{(k)}(t - \tau_{k,l}) + n_{Q,m}(t)
\tag{28}
$$

where $n_{I,m}(t)$ and $n_{Q,m}(t)$ are noise after demodulation through channels I and Q, respectively. $h_l^{(k)}$ is the fading coefficient of the lth path of the channel for signal sent by user k. $\tau_{k,l}$ is the delay on the lth path of user k. In this paper, only the effect of asynchronous fading channels on baseband signals is considered. Therefore, for user p and the mth sequence, the first paths of channels I and Q are despread as

$$
\Im_{m,1}^{(p)} = \frac{1}{MN} \sum_{k=1}^{K} \sum_{l=1}^{L} h_l^k b_k \sum_{i=1}^{N/2-\delta} g_{m,2i-1}^{(k)} g_{m,2i+2\delta-1}^{(p)} + \omega_{I,m}
\tag{29}
$$

$$\mathfrak{Q}_{m,1}^{(p)} = \frac{1}{MN} \sum_{k=1}^{K} \sum_{l=1}^{L} h_l^k b_k \sum_{i=1}^{N/2-\delta} g_{m,2i}^{(k)} g_{m,2i+2\delta}^{(p)} + \omega_{Q,m} \tag{30}$$

where $\delta = (\tau_{p,1} - \tau_{k,l})/T_c$, $\delta \in \left\{0, 1, \cdots, \frac{N}{2} - 1\right\}$

$$\widehat{b}_{p,1} = \sum_{m=1}^{M} (\mathfrak{I}_{m,1}^{(p)} + \mathfrak{Q}_{m,1}^{(p)})$$

$$= \frac{1}{MN} \sum_{k=1}^{K} \sum_{l=1}^{L} h_l^k b_k \sum_{m=1}^{M} \sum_{n=1}^{N/2-\delta} \underbrace{g_{m,n}^{(k)} g_{m,n+2\delta}^{(p)}}_{\rho(G^{(k)}, G^{(p)}; 2\delta)} + \omega \tag{31}$$

It is obvious that two neighboring chips are modulated to the same symbol by QPSK. Moreover the delay caused by asynchronous communication or multipath transmission is an even number at the receiver.

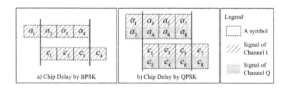

Fig. 2. Chip delay by BPSK and QPSK modulation

5   Power Allocation in WCC-CDMA System

Based on the discussions in the above two sections, WCCs modulated by QPSK can achieve ideal correlation properties of subcodes, which equal transmitter powers and equal combination gains of channels are no longer required.

This section starts with two combining algorithms at the receiver. Maximum ratio combining (MRC) in a CC-CDMA system is employed to get a maximum frequency diversity gain. M filtered signal can be combined with MRC as

$$\widehat{b}_{mrc}^{(g)}(j) = \sum_{m=1}^{M} [h_m^{(g)}] \cdot y_m^{(g)}(j)$$

$$= N\sqrt{\overline{p_r}^{(g)}} \sum_{m=1}^{M} |h_m^{(g)}| b^{(g)}(j) + I_{mrc}^{(g)} + \omega_{mrc} \tag{32}$$

where '*' denotes complex conjugate operation, $I_{mrc}^{(g)}$ is the multi-user interference (MUI) under MRC, ω_{mrc} is the noise, and $\overline{p_r}^{(g)} = \frac{E_b}{MNT_c}$.

Equal gain combining (EGC) in a CC-CDMA system is employed to equalize frequency diversity gain. M filtered signal can be combined with EGC as

$$\widehat{b}_{egc}^{(g)}(j) = \sum_{m=1}^{M} [h_m^{(g)}] * y_m^{(g)}(j)/|h_m^{(g)}|$$
$$= N\sqrt{\overline{p_r}^{(g)}} \sum_{m=1}^{M} b^{(g)}(j)|h_m^{(g)}| + I_{egc}^{(g)} + \omega_{egc} \tag{33}$$

From the above analysis, it can be suggested that the MUI problem still exists despite the fact that CCs correlation properties are perfect. The problem is that the ideal correlation of CCs cannot be regained by combining algorithm at a receiver, because channel gains vary with different sub-carriers of users. In order to solve this problem, this paper will propose a technology of power allocation.

As defined in (18), we can obtain one constraint equation as

$$\sqrt{P_1} + \sqrt{P_2} = \cdots = \sqrt{P_{M-1}} + \sqrt{P_M} \tag{34}$$

where P_m is the transmitter power for the mth channel. Assuming that

$$\sum_{m=1}^{M} P_m = M \tag{35}$$

As proposed by R. G. Gallager

$$C = \frac{B}{N} \sum_{m=1}^{M} \log_2(1 + H_m P_m) \tag{36}$$

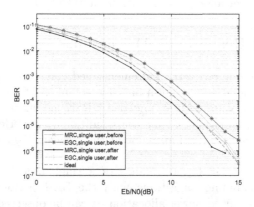

Fig. 3. BER performance of power allocation of weighted-combined uplink CC-CDMA systems for a single user in an asynchronous scenario

where C is the total channel capacity of CC-CDMA system and B is the bandwidth of the system. Under the constraint condition that the total power is constant, the maximum of C can be described as

$$C^* = \max \frac{B}{N} \sum_{m=1}^{M} \log_2(1 + H_m P_m) \tag{37}$$

Construct a function L as

$$L = \sum_{m=1}^{M} \log_2(1 + H_m P_m) - \lambda(\sum_{m=1}^{M} P_m - P_{total}) \tag{38}$$

where $P_{total} = M$. Let $\frac{\partial L}{\partial P_m} = 0$, we get

$$P_m + \frac{1}{H_m} = P_n + \frac{1}{H_n} \tag{39}$$

Considering (34), we make a trade-off between the maximum total channel capacity and the amount of calculation, as follows

$$\begin{cases} P`_{2k-1} = [\frac{s}{2} + \frac{1}{s}(\frac{1}{H_{2k}} - \frac{1}{H_{2k-1}})]^2 \\ P`_{2k} = [\frac{s}{2} + \frac{1}{s}(\frac{1}{H_{2k-1}} - \frac{1}{H_{2k}})]^2 \end{cases} \tag{40}$$

where we assume $s = \sqrt{P`_{2k-1}} + \sqrt{P`_{2k}}$ is a constant and $k = (1, \cdots, \frac{M}{2})$. Substituting (40) into (35)

$$P_m = \frac{M P`_m}{\sum\limits_{m=1}^{M} P`_m} \tag{41}$$

where P_m is the power allocation algorithm for WCC-CDMA systems.

6   Numerical Results and Discussions

In this section, we will verify the aforementioned correctness of the analytical results through simulation. In addition to a set of WCCs $\mathbb{C}(M, N, K)$ (13), the uplink communication with an uncoded QPSK modulation also need to be considered in the simulation. Under the condition that perfect channel state information (CSI) is considered available at the receiver, Figs. 3 and 4 illustrate the simulation results.

Figure 3 compares BER performance of a single-user CC-CDMA system under different combining algorithms with the BER performance of WCC-CDMA through optimized power allocation. It can be observed that both EGC and MRC for a single user can be improved after power allocation. In particular, it should be noted that MRC is even better than the ideal curve of BER (i.e. the best performance of BER without power allocation).

Figure 4 compares BER performance of a CC-CDMA system for multiple users under different detecting algorithms with the BER performance of WCC-CDMA through power allocation. The simulation result shows that, after power allocation, BER of MRC for multiple users is nearly the same when EbN0 is low, and slightly worse when EbN0 is high; however, BER of EGC for multiple users is improved regardless of EbN0.

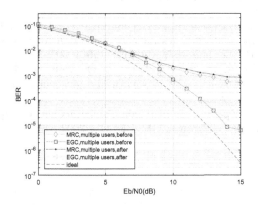

Fig. 4. BER performance of power allocation of weighted-combined uplink CC-CDMA systems for 8 users in an asynchronous scenario

7 Conclusion

This paper proposed a type of weighted complementary codes (WCCs), which enables the variation of combination parameters while remaining under the constraint of ideal correlation properties. It has been proven that the constructed WCCs can bring more freedom on the variation of power allocation, which can therefore improve the BER performance of a CC-CDMA system. Given consideration to the unicity of WCCs constructed in this paper, the construction of generalized WCCs is recommended for a possible direction of future work.

References

1. Chen, H.-H., Chiu, H.-W., Guizani, M.: Orthogonal complementary codes for interference-free CDMA technologies. IEEE Wirel. Commun. **13**(1), 68–79 (2006)
2. Golay, M.: Complementary series. IRE Trans. Inf. Theory **7**(2), 82–87 (1961)
3. Tseng, C.-C., Liu, C.: Complementary sets of sequences. IEEE Trans. Inf. Theory **18**(5), 644–652 (1972)
4. Suehiro, N., Hatori, M.: N-shift cross-orthogonal sequences. IEEE Trans. Inf. Theory **34**(1), 143–146 (1988)

5. Sun, S.-Y., Chen, H.-H., Meng, W.-X.: A survey on complementary-coded MIMO CDMA wireless communications. IEEE Commun. Surv. Tutorials **17**(1), 52–69 (2015)
6. Chen, H.-H., Chiu, H.-W.: Design of perfect complementary codes to implement interference-free CDMA systems. In: Global Telecommunications Conference, GLOBECOM 2004, vol. 2, pp. 1096–1100. IEEE (2004)
7. Sun, S.: Research on complementary coded multi-user wireless communication techniques and code design. Ph.D. dissertation, Harbin Institute of Technology (2014)
8. Chen, H.-H., Yeh, J.-F., Suehiro, N.: A multicarrier CDMA architecture based on orthogonal complementary codes for new generations of wideband wireless communications. IEEE Commun. Mag. **39**(10), 126–135 (2001)
9. Meng, W.-X., Sun, S.-Y., Chen, H.-H., Li, J.-Q.: Multi-user interference cancellation in complementary coded CDMA with diversity gain. IEEE Wirel. Commun. Lett. **2**(3), 303–306 (2013)
10. Huang, X., Li, Y.: Scalable complete complementary sets of sequences. In: Global Telecommunications Conference, GLOBECOM 2002, vol. 2, pp. 1056–1060. IEEE (2002)

Low Complexity Sensing Algorithm
of Periodic Impulsive Interference

Yingtao Niu[1(✉)], Yutao Wang[2], and Cheng Li[1]

[1] National University of Defense Technology, Nanjing, China
niuyingtao78@hotmail.com, lchnudt@gmail.com
[2] Army Engineering University of PLA, Nanjing, China
wang_yutao@plaaeu.cn

Abstract. In this paper, a low complexity sensing algorithm based on power spectrum density (PSD) for periodic impulsive interference is proposed. First, the PSD is computed by modified periodogram. Then the time occupancy of spectrum by interference and time interval of interference is computed in multiple detections to determine the presence of impulsive interference. Finally, main parameters of impulsive interference, such as period, duty cycle, bandwidth, and the peak power, are estimated. The computation afford of the proposed algorithm is quite low. The simulation results show that the sensing performance can satisfy the requirement of spectrum sensing.

Keywords: Impulsive interference · Sensing · Low complexity

1 Introduction

Nowadays, numerous wireless communication systems are deployed for variety of different fields of applications. Without doubt, wireless communication may be exposed to various interference, and noise, due to the open nature of wireless channel [1]. Periodic impulsive interference is a kind of typical interference which can significantly impact the performance of wireless communication systems. For example, impulsive interference generated by high-voltage equipment such as transformers, power lines, and switch-gear within substations has a significant influence for wireless communication in a smart grid context [2]. Wireless DVB-T signals may be impaired by impulsive interference, which is caused by house appliances [3]. In aeronautical communications, L-band digital aeronautical communications system will be exposed to impulsive interference from distance measuring equipment (DME) [4]. In military applications, pulsed jamming can disrupt reliable data transmission or reception of military communication system [5]. Whether it is generated unintentionally or by an opponent, impulsive interference or pulsed jamming can cause a substantial increase in the bit error rate of a communication system relative to the rate caused by continuous interference with the same average power. Therefore, we focus on the detection and parameters estimation of impulsive interference as base of anti-impulsive-interference technology.

Recently, there has been a lot of research on the mitigation of impulsive interference. The popular method to compensate for the performance loss is concatenated

M. Jia et al. (Eds.): WiSATS 2019, LNICST 280, pp. 707–716, 2019.
https://doi.org/10.1007/978-3-030-19153-5_69

forward error correction coding combined with frequency-domain block interleaving [6, 7]. Optimal power allocation with respect to sum capacity affected by additive independent Class A impulse noise is proposed [8]. The performance of frame synchronizer in Consultative Committee for Space Data Systems (CCSDS) under pulsed jamming conditions is researched [9]. An efficient statistical processing of impulsive interference of distance measuring equipment (DME) is proposed [4]. In [3], blanking nonlinearity for mitigating impulsive interference in OFDM systems is investigated. However, none of the existed references have researched the sensing algorithm of impulsive interference.

In this paper, we present a low complexity sensing algorithm based on power spectrum density (PSD) for periodic impulsive interference. Based on the sensing results, one can know the presence and main parameters of impulsive interference and exploit the spectrum hole in impulsive interference environment. The outline of this paper is as follows. Section 2 describes the system model under investigation. Section 3 present the impulsive interference sensing algorithm based on PSD in detail. Section 4 presents computer simulation results. Finally, in Sect. 5, some concluding remarks are provided.

2 System Model

Impulsive interference is interference that occurs periodically or sporadically for brief durations. Its characteristics are time-varying power with large peak power and low average power. In this paper, the sensing problem of periodic impulsive interference is researched. Some of the important design issues associated with the sensing algorithm for impulsive interference are as follows:

(1) Low complexity, in order to lower the calculation delay required to sense the impulsive interference.
(2) Not requiring prior knowledge, in order to account for the difficulty of acquiring prior knowledge of impulsive interference signals in wireless communication systems.
(3) Strong adaptability. The sensing algorithm should take wide range of period, duty cycle and bandwidth of impulsive interference into consideration.

Therefore, the sensing algorithm for impulsive interference based on PSD is investigated. The following assumptions are given in the paper.

(1) Sensing duration of one time is equal to PSD estimation interval T_d.
(2) The starting time of PSD estimation is assumed to be the starting time of impulsive interference.
(3) The interference time and interference-free time of impulsive interference is all the integral multiple of T_d.

The block diagram of sensing system of impulsive interference is shown as Fig. 1.

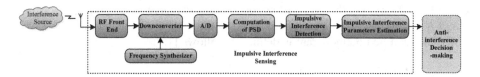

Fig. 1. Block diagram of impulsive sensing system

In the sensing system, a broadband radio frequency (RF) front end with a bandwidth W that covers target spectrum should be equipped. The automatic gain control (AGC) is not exploited in the RF front end to detect the actual signal power. By designing the appropriate gain of RF front end, strong impulsive interference will fall on the linear range of RF front end. After the received signal is processed by the RF front end, downconverter, and ADC, impulsive interference is sensed at an intermediate frequency. Therefore, the discrete time received signal after processing by ADC is given by

$$r(n) = I_{pul}(n) + w(n) \tag{1}$$

where $w(n)$ is AWGN with zero mean and unknown variance σ_w^2, $I_{pul}(n)$ is impulsive interference denoted as

$$
\begin{aligned}
I_{pul}(n) &= AI(n) \sum_{i=0}^{\infty} D_\tau(n - iT) \\
&= AI(n) \sum_{i=0}^{\infty} [U(n - n_1 - iT) - U(n - n_2 - iT)]
\end{aligned}
\tag{2}
$$

where A is amplitude of impulsive interference, $I(n)$ is continuous interference waveform with zero mean and unknown variance σ_I^2, $D_\tau(n)$ is rectangular pulse with the duration $\tau = n_2 - n_1$, T is the period of impulsive interference, $U(n)$ is the unit step function. $U(n) = 1$, $n \geq 0$, and $U(n) = 0$, $n < 0$.

3 Detection and Parameters Estimation of Periodic Impulsive Interference

In this section, the presence of periodic impulsive interference is determined by detection algorithm firstly. Then the parameters of periodic impulsive interference are estimated.

3.1 Detection of Periodic Impulsive Interference

The most popular PSD estimation algorithm is periodogram, which has very low complexity. Therefore, the modified periodogram is explored in the proposed scheme. Every N received samples which correspond to the sensing duration T_d are computed PSD. The modified periodogram is defined as follows [10]:

$$S(f_i) = \frac{\frac{1}{F_sN}\left|\sum\limits_{n=1}^{N} win_n r(n)e^{-j2\pi f_i n}\right|^2}{\frac{1}{N}\sum\limits_{n=1}^{N}|win_n|^2}, i = 1, 2, \ldots, N \tag{3}$$

where win_n is a window, F_s is the sample frequency. In the proposed sensing scheme, PSD is calculated every T_d. To smoothen the PSD with large fluctuation generated by the periodogram, a moving average filter is exploited, which has very low complexity and processing delay. The filter can be written as follows:

$$S_{sm}(f_i) = \frac{1}{2M+1}\sum\limits_{j=-M}^{M} S(f_{i-j}) \tag{4}$$

where $S_{sm}(f_i)$ is the smoothened PSD in f_i. In this paper, $M = 2$ is used, which can reconcile good smoothening effect and low errors of PSD. The PSD vector after smoothening at kth PSD estimation interval is written as

$$\mathbf{S}_{smooth}(\mathbf{f}, k) = [S_{sm}(f_1, k), S_{sm}(f_2, k), \ldots, S_{sm}(f_N, k)] \tag{5}$$

The spectral resolution of every PSD point is

$$\Delta f = \frac{W}{N} \tag{6}$$

where W is the bandwidth of RF front end.

To determine the presence of impulsive interference, the detection threshold α_{th} should be chosen. The PSD with a magnitude exceeding threshold are considered interference. However, the determination of the threshold is a sensitive task because of unknown σ_w^2. Therefore, we determine α_{th} by method in [11]. $\mathbf{S}_{smooth}(f, n)$ is sorted in descending order firstly. Then a mean value α_{mean} is computed by 20% largest values of PSD. Finally, the initial threshold α_{th} is set to be proportional to α_{mean}. In general, $\alpha_{th} = 0.7\alpha_{mean}$ is obtained.

After K detections, the PSD matrix $\mathbf{S}$ can be denoted as

$$\mathbf{S} = [\mathbf{S}_{smooth}(\mathbf{f}, 1), \mathbf{S}_{smooth}(\mathbf{f}, 2), \ldots, \mathbf{S}_{smooth}(\mathbf{f}, K)]^T \tag{7}$$

where the superscript T denote transpose. $\mathbf{S}$ is also denoted as

$$\mathbf{S} = \left[\mathbf{S}_f(f_1, \mathbf{K}),\, \mathbf{S}_f(f_2, \mathbf{K}), \ldots, \mathbf{S}_f(f_N, \mathbf{K}) \right] \qquad (8)$$

where $\mathbf{S}_f(f_n, \mathbf{K}) = [S_{sm}(f_n, 1), S_{sm}(f_n, 2), \ldots, S_{sm}(f_n, K)]$. $\mathbf{S}$ is processed as a dual value according to α_{th}, i.e.,

$$S_2(f_n, k) = \begin{cases} 1, S_{sm}(f_n, k) \geq \alpha_{th} \\ 0, S_{sm}(f_n, k) < \alpha_{th} \end{cases}, \; n = 1, 2, 3, \ldots, N, k = 1, 2, 3, \ldots, K \qquad (9)$$

Then we compute the occupancy of spectrum by interference in K detections.

$$\rho(f_n) = \frac{\sum\limits_{k=1}^{K} S_2(f_n, k)}{K} \qquad (10)$$

According to experience, we can set the upper and lower threshold of the occupancy of spectrum by interference as ρ_1 and ρ_2. Impulsive interference is considered as presence in the spectrum with occupancy between ρ_1 and ρ_2. The spectrum with occupancy below ρ_1 is considered as that only AWGN exist. That is

$$\begin{cases} \rho(f_n) < \rho_1, \text{ only AWGN exist} \\ \rho_1 \leq \rho(f_n) \leq \rho_2, \text{ impulsive interference and AWGN may exist} \\ \rho(f_n) > \rho_2, \text{ constant interference and AWGN exist} \end{cases} \qquad (11)$$

Then the time slot and frequency range of impulsive interference can be determined initially. The f_n with $\rho_1 \leq \rho(f_n) \leq \rho_2$ is the candidate frequency of periodic impulsive interference. $\mathbf{S}_2(f_n, \mathbf{K}) = [S_2(f_n, 1), S_2(f_n, 2), \ldots, S_2(f_n, K)]$ is dual-value PSD of f_n. If the index of element in $\mathbf{S}_2(f_n, \mathbf{K})$ begin from 1, the index of element "1" in $\mathbf{S}_2(f_n, \mathbf{K})$ can compose vector of interference index

$$\mathbf{IND1} = [index_1, index_2, \ldots, index_{M_1}] \qquad (12)$$

M_1 elements are assumed to compose $\mathbf{IND1}$. Then the elements in $\mathbf{IND1}$ is performed self-difference operation:

$$\mathbf{IND2} = [(index_2 - index_1 - 1), (index_3 - index_2 - 1), \ldots, (index_{M_1} - index_{M_1-1} - 1)] \qquad (13)$$

The non-zero elements in $\mathbf{IND2}$ compose vector $\mathbf{IND3}$. We assume $\mathbf{IND3}$ is composed of M_2 elements, i.e. $\mathbf{IND3} = [ind_1, ind_2, \ldots, ind_{M_2}]$. The mean of all elements in $\mathbf{IND3}$ is

$$Mean = \frac{\sum_{m=1}^{M_2} ind_m}{M_2} \tag{14}$$

The upper and lower threshold are set as β_1 and β_2.

$$\beta_1 = \text{Ceil}(Mean) + 1 \tag{15}$$

$$\beta_2 = \text{floor}(Mean) - 1 \tag{16}$$

where $\text{Ceil}(\bullet)$ and $\text{Floor}(\bullet)$ denote round toward positive infinity and negative infinity respectively. If

$$\beta_1 \leq 80\% \text{ elements of } \mathbf{IND3} \leq \beta_2 \tag{17}$$

f_n is determined as the frequency with periodic impulsive interference, and is kept a record. All the f_n satisfied with (17) can compose the frequency vector of impulsive interference

$$\mathbf{f}_{im} = [f_{im1}, f_{im2}, \ldots, f_{imN_1}] \tag{18}$$

3.2   Parameters Estimation of Periodic Impulsive Interference

The parameters of periodic impulsive interference include period, duty cycle, the mean power, the peak power, etc. The interference-free time in a period is approximated as

$$T_{fr} = Mean \bullet T_d \tag{19}$$

During the total sensing time KT_d, the number of period is

$$M_3 = M_2 + 1 \tag{20}$$

Interference time in a period is approximated as

$$T_{in} = \frac{M_1}{M_3} T_d \tag{21}$$

A period of impulsive interference is approximated as

$$T_p = \frac{K}{M_3} T_d \tag{22}$$

The duty cycle of periodic impulsive interference is

$$DR = \frac{T_{in}}{T_p} = \frac{M_1}{K} \tag{23}$$

The average power of periodic impulsive interference can be calculated by the PSD $S_{sm}(f_n, k)$ corresponding to the interference index vector **IND1**.

$$P_{aver}(f_n) = \frac{\Delta f \sum\limits_{k \in \mathbf{IND1}} S_{sm}(f_n, K)}{K T_d} \tag{24}$$

The peak power of impulsive interference can be estimated as

$$P_{peak}(f_n) = \frac{P_{aver}(f_n)}{DR} \tag{25}$$

The bandwidth of impulsive interference can be estimated as

$$B_{im} = f_{imN_1} - f_{im1} \tag{26}$$

4 Simulation Results

The simulation is performed in intermediate frequency. Sampling frequency, PSD detection duration, and PSD detection period are 20 MHz, 100 µs and 100 µs, respectively. The impulsive interference's central frequency and bandwidth is 5 MHz and 0.4 MHz. The impulsive interference period is 10 ms. AWGN exist in the wireless environment. The duty cycle is 0.1, 0.2 0.3 0.4, respectively. The 10000 trials are performed in simulation. NMSE (Normalized Mean Square Error) of parameters estimation is computed.

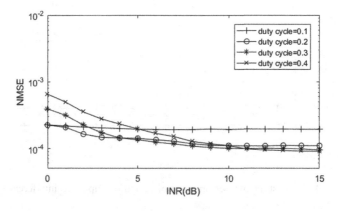

Fig. 2. The estimation performance of peak power of impulsive interference

Figure 2 shows the estimation performance of peak power of impulsive interference as a function of INR (Interference-to-Noise Ratio). From the figure, we can find that the NMSE of estimation value of peak power with duty cycle = 0.1 keeps steady. However, the NMSE deteriorates with the INR decrease when duty cycle = 0.2, 0.3 and 0.4. The small duty cycle is, the larger peak power is. Therefore, the noise has little effect on the estimation performance of peak power when the duty cycle is small.

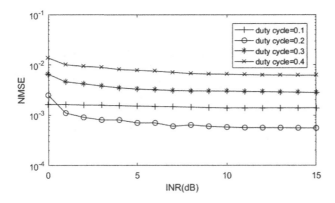

Fig. 3. The estimation performance of bandwidth of impulsive interference

Figure 3 shows the estimation performance of bandwidth of impulsive interference as a function of INR. Similar to Fig. 3, the NMSE of estimation value of bandwidth with duty cycle = 0.1 keeps steady. However, the NMSE deteriorates with the INR decrease when duty cycle = 0.2, 0.3 and 0.4. The larger duty cycle lead to the lower peak power, which is affected largely by noise when INR is low.

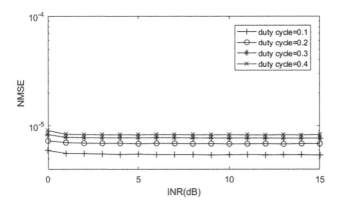

Fig. 4. The estimation performance of period of impulsive interference

Figure 4 shows the estimation performance of period of impulsive interference as a function of INR. Difference with Figs. 2 and 3, the NMSE of period is quite steady with INR. But with the increase of duty cycle, the NMSE deteriorates slightly.

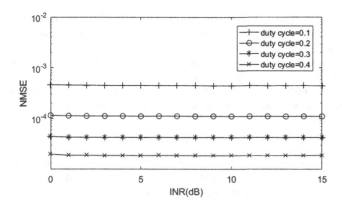

Fig. 5. The estimation performance of duty cycle of impulsive interference

Figure 5 shows the estimation performance of duty cycle of impulsive interference as a function of INR. Difference with all above simulation results, the larger duty cycle implies the better NMSE performance. The reason lies in the detection period is fixed. The large duty cycle includes more detection periods, which improve the estimation performance.

In summary, the NMSE of parameters estimation can satisfy the sensing requirement of interference.

5   Conclusion

In this paper, a low complexity sensing algorithm based on power spectrum density (PSD) for periodic impulsive interference is proposed. First, the modified periodogram is computed. Then the time occupancy of spectrum by interference and time interval of interference is computed in multiple detections to determine the presence of impulsive interference. Finally, main parameters of impulsive interference, such as period, duty cycle, bandwidth, and the peak power, are estimated. The computation afford of the proposed algorithm is quite low. The simulation results show that the sensing performance can satisfy the requirement of spectrum sensing.

References

1. Fragkiadakis, A.G., Tragos, E.Z., Askoxylakis, I.G.: A survey on security threats and detection techniques in cognitive radio networks. IEEE Commun. Surv. Tutor. **15**, 428–444 (2013)
2. Lin, J., Pande, T., Kim, I.H., Batra, A., Evans, B.L.: Time-frequency modulation diversity to combat periodic impulsive noise in narrowband powerline communications. IEEE Trans. Commun. **63**, 1837–1849 (2015)
3. Epple, U., Schnell, M.: Advanced blanking nonlinearity for mitigating impulsive interference in OFDM systems. IEEE Trans. Veh. Technol. **66**, 146–158 (2017)
4. Saaifan, K.A., Elshahed, A., Henkel, W.: Cancellation of distance measuring equipment interference for aeronautical communications. IEEE Trans. Aerosp. Electron. Syst. **53**, 3104–3114 (2017)
5. Poisel, R.A.: Modern Communication Jamming Principles and Techniques, 2nd edn. Artech House, Norwood (2011)
6. IEEE: IEEE Standard for Low-Frequency (Less Than 500 kHz) Narrowband Power Line Communications for Smart Grid Applications, in 1901.2-2013 (2013)
7. ITU: Narrowband orthogonal frequency division multiplexing power line communication transceivers for G3-PLC networks, in G.9903 Geneva, Switzerland (2014)
8. Axell, E., Eliardsson, P., Tengstrand, S.Ö., Wiklundh, K.: Power control in interference channels with class a impulse noise. IEEE Wirel. Commun. Lett. **6**, 102–105 (2017)
9. Noels, N., Moeneclaey, M.: Performance of advanced telecommand frame synchronizer under pulsed jamming conditions. In: IEEE ICC 2017 (2017)
10. Zhang, X.: Modern Signal Processing. Tsinghua University Press, Beijing (2002)
11. Niu, Y., Yao, F., Wang, M., Chen, J.: Anti-chirp-jamming communication based on the cognitive cycle. Int. J. Electron. Commun. **66**, 547–560 (2012)

Blind Source Separation for Satellite Communication Anti-jamming

Hua Yang[1], Hang Zhang[1(✉)], Jiang Zhang[2], Liu Yang[1],
and Pengfei Wang[1]

[1] College of Communication and Engineering,
Army Engineering University of PLA, Nanjing 210007, Jiangsu, China
zhanghangnj@126.com
[2] 63rd Research Institute, National University of Defense Technology,
Nanjing 210007, Jiangsu, China

Abstract. In this paper, the feasibility of applying blind source separation (BSS) to satellite communication (SatCom) anti-jamming is studied. And an EASI-based BSS method is introduced for anti-jamming processing for SatCom system. This method achieves the elimination of jamming signal by separation. Meanwhile, the anti-jamming ability of this method is completely dissected herein. Experimental simulations are conducted to demonstrate the availability of the EASI-based anti-jamming processing method. Simulation results show that the EASI-based method can effectively separate the jamming signal. And, after EASI-based anti-jamming processing, the signal-to-jamming-plus-noise ratio nearly approximates the signal-to-noise ratio and the available transmission rate of SatCom system approaches the theory rate.

Keywords: Satellite communication anti-jamming ·
Blind source separation · EASI · Transmission rate

1 Introduction

Contrasted to conventional ground communication, satellite communication (SatCom) [1–3] can cover larger area and connect longer distance due to its inherent height advantage. Especially, in some rough terrains (e.g., high mountain, canyon and ocean, etc.) that can't build the base station for ground communication, the function of SatCom is irreplaceable. Therefore, not surprisingly, SatCom plays a very important role in both of civilian and military communication fields. For modern warfare, military SatCom even serves as a multiplier role for the winning of warfare, as it can significantly enhance the capacity of cross-regional command, control and cooperation, e.g., in the C^4ISR systems [4,5].

However, as communication satellite exposes in the space and its orbit is relatively stationary (e.g., the geostationary orbit), it is easy to be jammed by

Supported by National Natural Science Foundation of China under Grant 61671475.

M. Jia et al. (Eds.): WiSATS 2019, LNICST 280, pp. 717–726, 2019.
https://doi.org/10.1007/978-3-030-19153-5_70

hostile jammer no matter in uplink or downlink. There are many jamming styles, including single or multi-tone jamming, barrage or full band jamming [6], etc. When communication satellite is jammed, the quality of communication signal will be badly deteriorated that leads to the degradation of communication quality even communication outage. It would be fatal for the communication parties in the warfare, if without effective anti-jamming countermeasures. To cope with jamming signal, many methods can be employed, e.g., spread spectrum, adaptive antenna, and post anti-jamming signal processing [7], etc. Among these, post anti-jamming signal processing method is preferred, as it has lower complexity and higher transferability. It can be flexibly implemented in uplink or downlink.

Blind source separation (BSS) [8,9] is viewed as a powerful anti-jamming or interference cancellation method, due to its capacity of separating mixture of signals that are non-Gaussian and mutually statistically independent. Because the preconditions are easy to be satisfied, BSS can cope with various jamming or interference patterns. As in [10], a BSS-based radar anti-jamming approach is proposed to improve the tracking ability of radar systems. In [11], BSS is employed to cancel the jamming signal in frequency hopping communication system. In [12] and [13], BSS is used to deal with the self-interference problem for full-duplex communication systems. For BSS-based SatCom anti-jamming, there are also many literatures. As in [7], BSS is applied to eliminate the jamming signal encountering in the uplink of satellite communication systems. In [14], an adjacent satellite interference cancellation method based on BSS is introduced. A satellite communication system that removes unwanted in-band interference by BSS technology is investigated in [15]. Although, many literatures have studied the application of BSS to SatCom anti-jamming. However, they only concentrate on the separation of communication signal and jamming signal and lack comprehensive analysis of the anti-jamming ability of BSS-based method.

In this paper, we will fully analyze the anti-jamming ability of BSS-based method, and an EASI-based anti-jamming processing method is correspondingly introduced. In addition, experimental simulations are conducted to verify the analysis, including the anti-jamming ability and available transmission rate of the EASI-based method are evaluated.

2   System Model

Assume that there are deployed with two receiving antennas in the communication satellite or ground receiver, then the baseband received signal model under jammed environment at a sampling time can be formulated as

$$\mathbf{x} = \mathbf{H}\mathbf{s} + \mathbf{n} \tag{1}$$

where $\mathbf{x} = [x_1, x_2]^T$ denotes the received signal vector, $\mathbf{s} = [s_1, s_2]^T$ represents the transmitted signal vector with s_1 being the communication signal and s_2 being the jamming signal, $\mathbf{H} \in \mathbb{C}^{2 \times 2}$ is the channel coefficient matrix and is assumed to be flat fading, and $\mathbf{n} \in \mathbb{C}^{2 \times 1}$ is the additive white Gaussian noise vector with zero mean and σ_n^2 variance.

The jamming signal s_2 badly deteriorates the quality of communication signal s_1. And signal-to-jamming-plus-noise ratio (SJNR) is used to measure the quality of communication signal, that is

$$SJNR_i = \frac{|h_{i1}s_1|^2}{|h_{i2}s_2|^2 + \sigma_n^2}, \ i = 1, 2 \tag{2}$$

where h_{ij} is the (i, j) th element of $\mathbf{H}$. Without effective jamming elimination or suppression, the SJNR condition would be very low as jamming signal usually has stronger power level than communication signal, which leads to the degradation of communication quality (i.e., symbol error ratio (SER) increasing) even communication outage when SER increasing to an intolerable level. For military communication, it would be fatal. Therefore, it is vital to resort to corresponding anti-jamming processing method to deal with possible encountered jamming signal.

3 BSS for Anti-jamming

As communication signal and jamming signal come from different transmitters, naturally, they can be treated as mutually statistically independent source signals. Meanwhile, they are also non-Gaussian. These make it feasible to utilize BSS [8,9] to separate the mixture of communication signal and jamming signal.

BSS can estimate a separating matrix $\mathbf{W} \in \mathbb{C}^{2 \times 2}$ to separate the received signal vector $\mathbf{x}$ (i.e., the mixture of communication signal and jamming signal) and then make the elements among the separated signal vector $\mathbf{y}$ (defined as $\mathbf{y} = \mathbf{W}\mathbf{x}$) be mutually statistically independent signals. In fact, BSS procedure renders the product of separating matrix $\mathbf{W}$ and channel matrix $\mathbf{H}$ be equivalent to a generalized permutation matrix (i.e., there is only one non-zero element in each row and column). In that case, the separated signal vector $\mathbf{y}$ is a valid estimation of the transmitted signal vector $\mathbf{s}$. There are up to an ambiguity of order and scaling (amplitude and phase), and some noise disturbance between the two signal vectors. That is

$$\mathbf{y} = \mathbf{W}\mathbf{x} = \mathbf{W}\mathbf{H}\mathbf{s} + \mathbf{W}\mathbf{n} = \mathbf{G}\mathbf{s} + \tilde{\mathbf{n}} \tag{3}$$

where $\mathbf{G}$ denotes the generalized permutation matrix, and $\tilde{\mathbf{n}} = \mathbf{W}\mathbf{n}$ is the noise disturbance. In other words, communication signal and jamming signal are no longer mixed together in the separated signal vector $\mathbf{y}$. The negative effect of jamming signal on communication signal is eliminated, and then the anti-jamming purpose is achieved.

3.1 EASI-Based Anti-jamming Processing Method

Many effective BSS algorithms can be employed to implement the separation of communication signal and jamming signal for the target of SatCom antijamming, including EASI [16], JADE [17] and FastICA [18]. In this paper, we will primarily introduce an EASI-based anti-jamming processing method.

The iterative equation of separating matrix $\mathbf{W}$ of EASI algorithm is formulated as

$$\mathbf{W}[k+1] = \mathbf{W}[k] - \mu \left(\mathbf{y}[k]\mathbf{y}^H[k] - \mathbf{I} + \boldsymbol{\varphi}\left(\mathbf{y}[k]\right)\mathbf{y}^H[k] - \mathbf{y}[k]\boldsymbol{\varphi}^H\left(\mathbf{y}[k]\right) \right)\mathbf{W}[k] \tag{4}$$

where k denotes the sampling time index, $\mu \in (0, 1]$ represents the step size, $\boldsymbol{\varphi}(\mathbf{y}) = [\varphi_y(y_1), \varphi_y(y_2), \ldots, \varphi_y(y_N)]^T$ with $\varphi_y(y_i)$ being the nonlinear kernel function (NKF) of the ith element y_i of $\mathbf{y}$ and N being the number of source signals, superscript ^{H} is the conjugate transpose operator, and $\mathbf{I} \in \mathbb{R}^{N \times N}$ is the identity matrix.

For the stability of algorithm, there is a normalized version, that is

$$\mathbf{W}[k+1] = \mathbf{W}[k] - \mu \left(\frac{\mathbf{y}[k]\mathbf{y}^H[k] - \mathbf{I}}{1 + \mu\mathbf{y}^H[k]\mathbf{y}[k]} + \frac{\boldsymbol{\varphi}\left(\mathbf{y}[k]\right)\mathbf{y}^H[k] - \mathbf{y}[k]\boldsymbol{\varphi}^H\left(\mathbf{y}[k]\right)}{1 + \mu\left|\mathbf{y}^H[k]\boldsymbol{\varphi}\left(\mathbf{y}[k]\right)\right|} \right)\mathbf{W}[k] \tag{5}$$

After separating matrix $\mathbf{W}$ is well estimated, the anti-jamming processing can be implemented as in (3). Certainly, subsequent extraction and phase recovery for the communication signal are necessary, however, we don't intend to elaborate as these are out the scope of this paper.

And the SJNR after EASI-based anti-jamming processing can be expressed as

$$SJNR_{\text{EASI}} = \frac{\max\limits_{i}\left\{\left|g_{i1}s_1\right|^2\right\}}{\left|g_{i2}s_2\right|^2 + \sigma_n^2\|\mathbf{w}_i\|^2} \tag{6}$$

where g_{ij} denotes the (i, j)th entry of $\mathbf{G}$, and $\mathbf{w}_i$ is the ith row of $\mathbf{W}$. As $\mathbf{G}$ is equivalent to a generalized permutation matrix, $g_{i2} \approx 0$, the jamming item $\left|g_{i2}s_2\right|^2$ approaches zero. In addition, the noise power may be enhanced, however, its effect is little or negligible. Then, the SJNR is improved.

3.2 Anti-jamming Ability Analysis

As only requiring source signals to be mutually statistically independent, EASI algorithm can adapt to various jamming patterns, including single or multi tone jamming, barrage or full band jamming, etc. And, not constrained in SatCom anti-jamming, EASI algorithm can also be applied to unintentional interference cancellation, e.g., co-channel interference cancellation in MIMO system, and self-interference cancellation in full-duplex communication system [12,13].

In addition, EASI algorithm is capable of countering strong jamming signal. Essentially, when the iteration of separating matrix $\mathbf{W}$ arrives a stationary point, the update term in (4) would be zero, that is

$$\mathrm{E}\left\{\mathbf{y}\mathbf{y}^H - \mathbf{I} + \boldsymbol{\varphi}(\mathbf{y})\mathbf{y}^H - \mathbf{y}\boldsymbol{\varphi}^H(\mathbf{y})\right\} = \mathbf{0} \tag{7}$$

where $\mathrm{E}\{\cdot\}$ denotes the expectation operator, and $\mathbf{0}$ represents the zero matrix. And Eq. (7) can be decomposed into symmetric and skew-symmetric parts, namely

$$\mathrm{E}\left\{\mathbf{y}\mathbf{y}^H - \mathbf{I}\right\} = \mathbf{0} \tag{8}$$

$$\mathrm{E}\left\{\varphi(\mathbf{y})\mathbf{y}^H - \mathbf{y}\varphi^H(\mathbf{y})\right\} = \mathbf{0} \tag{9}$$

Equation (8) ensures the separated signal vector $\mathbf{y}$ being spatially white, and (9) guarantees the components among the separated signal vector $\mathbf{y}$ being mutually statistically independent. Seemingly, there are nothing special. However, in the anti-jamming context, these characteristics make a big difference. The mutually statistically independent condition makes the communication signal and jamming signal no longer be mixed together, then the negative effect of jamming signal on communication signal is eliminated. And the spatially white condition makes the separated communication signal and jamming signal be unit variance. What it means? The separated jamming signal would be suppressed to the same power level as communication signal no matter how strong the emitted jamming signal is, which makes EASI algorithm be capable of countering strong jamming signal. Therefore, we can conclude that EASI algorithm is a powerful anti-jamming processing method.

4   Experimental Simulations

In this section, EASI algorithm is experimentally employed to perform the anti-jamming processing for SatCom system in the downlink. In the simulations, we assume that quadrature amplitude modulation (QAM) is adopted as the modulation scheme for communication signal, and the jamming pattern is single tone jamming. The channel is assumed to be block flat, its coefficients are randomly generated complex variables with absolute value belonging to $(0, 1)$, and the length of symbol block is set to 1000. In addition, the symbol rate is set to 2.4 kHz, the roll-off factor of shaping filter is set to 0.35, the jamming frequency point in baseband is set to $800\,\mathrm{Hz}$, and the baseband signal sampling frequency Fs is set to 19.2 kHz. For EASI algorithm, the step size μ is set to 0.002, and the NKF is set to $\varphi_y(y_i) = y_i|y_i|^2$.

4.1   Anti-jamming Ability

First, we evaluate the anti-jamming ability of EASI algorithm. The waveform (only the real part) and spectrum of the communication signal (4QAM), jamming signal, and received signal are illustrated in Fig. 1. The signal-to-noise ratio (SNR) is 20 dB, and the jamming-to-signal ratio (JSR) equals 50 dB. And in Fig. 2, the waveform and spectrum of the separated communication signal and jamming signal are plotted. Although the jamming signal is overwhelming to the communication signal in the received signal as shown in Fig. 1, we can note that the communication signal and jamming signal are effectively separated both in waveform and spectrum from Fig. 2. And, the separated jamming signal nearly has the same power level as the separated communication signal. These prove the separation and suppression abilities of EASI algorithm to strong jamming signal.

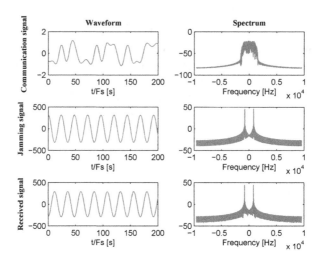

Fig. 1. Waveform and spectrum of the communication signal, jamming signal, and received signal. SNR = 20 dB, and JSR = 50 dB.

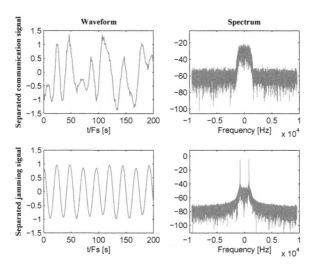

Fig. 2. Waveform and spectrum of the separated communication signal and jamming signal.

In Fig. 3, the constellations of the received signals, separated communication signal and separated jamming signal are shown. We can observe that the communication signal is submerged by the strong jamming signal in the received signals. However, after BSS-based anti-jamming processing, the constellation of communication signal is effectively recovered. And there is a phase offset due to the inherent ambiguity of BSS procedure.

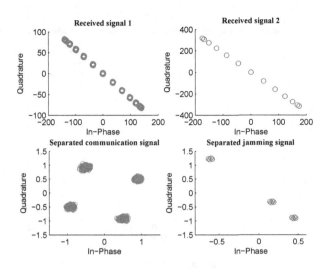

Fig. 3. Constellations of the received signals, separated communication signal and separated jamming signal.

In Fig. 4, the symbol SJNR curves in different JSR conditions are shown. The SJNR_NJC means the no jamming cancellation case (NJC), and the SJNR_EASI means the EASI-based anti-jamming processing case. We can note that the symbol SJNR curve with EASI-based anti-jamming processing almost approximates the SNR condition and is unaffected by the JSR condition. It also demonstrates the strong anti-jamming ability of EASI algorithm.

4.2 Available Transmission Rate

Secondly, we theoretically assess the available transmission rate for the SatCom system with EASI-based anti-jamming processing. And the transmission rate is calculated as [19]

$$R = \log_2(M) * (1 - SER(M, SJNR)) \, [\text{bps/Hz}] \tag{10}$$

with

$$SER(M, SJNR) = 1 - \left[1 - \left(1 - \frac{1}{\sqrt{M}} \right) * \text{erfc} \left(\sqrt{\frac{1.5 * SJNR}{M - 1}} \right) \right]^2 \tag{11}$$

where M denotes the modulation order, $SER(\cdot)$ is the symbol error ratio function, and erfc$(\cdot)$ is the complementary error function.

From Fig. 5, we can know that the available transmission rates with EASI-based anti-jamming processing approximate the theory value in different modulation order, and the NJC cases drop fast when JSR increasing. It indicates that the quality of communication can be effectively ensured with EASI-based anti-jamming processing.

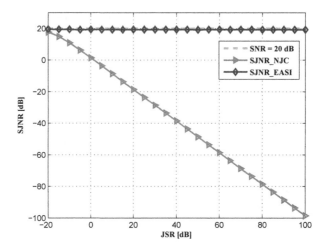

Fig. 4. Symbol SJNR versus JSR.

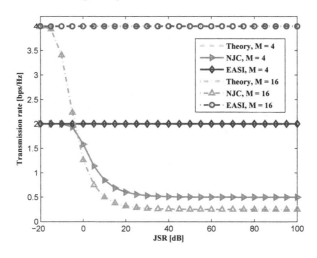

Fig. 5. Transmission rate versus JSR.

5   Conclusions

In this paper, the issue that employing BSS to SatCom anti-jamming is investigated, and an EASI-based anti-jamming processing method is introduced. By separating the received signal basing on the independence between communication signal and jamming signal, this method is capable of eliminating the negative effect of jamming signal on communication signal. Meanwhile, from the perspective of algorithm, the anti-jamming ability of this method is fully analyzed herein. Experimental simulations are carried out to prove the availability of the EASI-based anti-jamming processing method. The simulation results show that the EASI-based method can effectively separate the mixture of communication signal and jamming signal. And, with EASI-based anti-jamming processing, the SJNR nearly approximates the SNR condition and the available transmission rate approaches the theory rate.

References

1. Matin, M.A.: Satellite communication systems. In: Communication Systems for Electrical Engineers. SECE, pp. 107–124. Springer, Cham (2018). https://doi.org/10.1007/978-3-319-70129-5_7
2. Elbert, B.R.: The Satellite Communication Applications Handbook. (Artech House Space Applications Series). Artech House Inc., Norwood (2003)
3. Fritz, D.A., Doshi, B.T., Oak, A.C., et al.: Military satellite communications: Space-based communications for the global information grid. Johns Hopkins APL Tech. Dig. **27**(1), 32–40 (2006)
4. Jinfeng, Z., Chen, Z., Songhua, H., et al.: An effects analysis method for C4ISR system structure based on information flow. In: 2017 36th Chinese Control Conference (CCC), pp. 10149–10154. IEEE (2017)
5. Zhou, F., Ding, R., Yi, K.: The research of C4ISR system design and modeling method based on model. In: Proceedings of the 2017 The 7th International Conference on Computer Engineering and Networks, CENet2017, 22–23 July 2017 Shanghai, China (2017)
6. Rao, G.K., Rao, R.S.H.: Status study on sustainability of satellite communication systems under hostile jamming environment. In: 2011 Annual IEEE India Conference on (INDICON), pp. 1–7. IEEE (2011)
7. Lin, B., Zhang, B.N., Guo, D.S.: Blind source separation in noisy environment and applications in satellite communication anti-jamming. In: Asia-Pacific Conference on Computational Intelligence and Industrial Applications, PACIIA 2009, pp. 96-99. IEEE (2009)
8. Naik, G.R., Wang, W.: Blind Source Separation. Springer, Heidelberg (2014). https://doi.org/10.1007/978-3-642-55016-4
9. Comon, P., Jutten, C.: Handbook of Blind Source Separation: Independent Component Analysis and Applications. Academic Press, Cambridge (2010)
10. Huang, G.M., Yang, L.X., Su, G.Q., Blind source separation used for radar anti-jamming. In Proceedings of 2003 International Conference on Neural Networks and Signals Processing (2003)
11. Zhu, X., Liu, Y., Zhang, X.: A blind source separation-based anti-jamming method by space pre-whitening. In: 2016 7th IEEE International Conference on Software Engineering and Service Science (ICSESS), pp. 454–457. IEEE (2016)
12. Li, J., Zhang, H., Fan, M.: Digital self-interference cancellation based on independent component analysis for co-time co-frequency full-duplex communication systems. IEEE Access **PP**(99), 1 (2017)
13. Yang, H., Zhang, H., Zhang, J., et al.: Digital self-interference cancellation based on blind source separation and spectral efficiency analysis for the full-duplex communication systems. IEEE Access **6**, 43946–43955 (2018)
14. Li, C., Zhu, L., Zhang, Z.: Underdetermined blind separation of adjacent satellite interference in modern satellite communication systems (2017)
15. Downey, M.L., Chu, J.C.: System for and method of removing unwanted inband signals from a received communication signal: U.S. Patent 9,537,521, 3 January 2017

16. Cardoso, J.F., Laheld, B.H.: Equivariant adaptive source separation. IEEE Trans. Sig. Process. **44**(12), 3017–3030 (1996)
17. Nordhausen, K., Cardoso, J.F., Miettinen, J., et al.: JADE: Blind source separation methods based on joint diagonalization and some BSS performance criteria. J. Stat. Softw. **76**, 1–31 (2017)
18. Hyvärinen, A., Oja, E.: A fast fixed-point algorithm for independent component analysis. Neural Comput. **9**, 1483–1492 (1997)
19. Catreux, S., Driessen, P.F., Greenstein, L.J.: Data throughputs using multiple-input multiple-output (MIMO) techniques in a noise-limited cellular environment. IEEE Trans. Wirel. Commun. **1**(2), 226–235 (2002)

Low Complexity Decoding Scheme for LDPC Codes Based on Belief Propagation Algorithm

Wenshuo Zhang, Liming Zheng, Yue Wu$^{(\boxtimes)}$, Gang Wang, and Aijun Liu

Communication Research Center, Harbin Institute of Technology, Harbin, China
17S005039@stu.hit.edu.cn, {zheng,wuy,gwang51}@hit.edu.cn,
hitlaj@163.com

Abstract. The low-density parity check codes (LDPC codes) are block codes whose performances are close to the Shannon limit. LDPC codes have the strong ability for error correction. The decoding algorithm of LDPC codes has a great influence on their performances. The belief propagation (BP) algorithm is a commonly used soft decision decoding algorithm. The algorithm decodes by information iterations, and its complexity does not increase rapidly with the increase of code length. This paper mainly analyze the probabilistic domain BP decoding algorithm, log-domain BP decoding algorithm and minimum sum decoding algorithm, the bit error performance of LDPC codes under BP algorithm is studied, and the influence of the number of iterations on the BP decoding algorithm is also shown by simulation results.

Keywords: LDPC codes · Soft decision decoding algorithm ·
BP algorithm

1 Introduction

Robert Gallager discussed error correction codes based on low-density parity check codes (LDPC codes) in 1962 [1]. In 1990's, LDPC codes were rediscovered by MacKay and Neal [2]. LDPC codes are linear block codes whose performances are close to the Shannon limit [3]. The LDPC codes are low-density parity check codes, and they are constructed according to a low-density sparse check matrix or a tanner graph. A low-density check code of length n corresponds to the sparse check matrix $\mathbf{H}$ and represented by $\mathbf{H}$(n,p,q). There are q non-zero elements in each row of $\mathbf{H}$ and p non-zero elements in each column. Both p and q are very small compared to m and n, which makes the number of non-zero elements in the check matrix is much smaller than the number of zero elements.

The low-density sparse check matrix can be constructed by Gallager construction method [1] and progressive edge-growth (PEG) method [4], The PEG construction method establishes an edge link between a information node and

© ICST Institute for Computer Sciences, Social Informatics and Telecommunications Engineering 2019
Published by Springer Nature Switzerland AG 2019. All Rights Reserved
M. Jia et al. (Eds.): WiSATS 2019, LNICST 280, pp. 727–737, 2019.
https://doi.org/10.1007/978-3-030-19153-5_71

a check node according to the edge-by-edge method [5]. MacKay and Neal have showed LDPC codes can have very good performances when decoded with the belief-propagation (BP) algorithm [2]. Linear functions make the implementation of the BP algorithm difficult, so the BP algorithm is simplified in BP-based algorithm [6], it can reduce the complexity but it makes decoding performance decline. Among all the BP-based algorithms, LLR BP decoding algorithm [7] improve LDPC codes performance greatly. The UMP_BP_based (minimum and) algorithm reduce the computational complexity to a great extent.

This paper is organized as follows. Section 2 corresponds to general construction methods of the low-density sparse check matrix. Section 3 describes the BP-Based algorithm and its different variants. Simulation results are proposed in Sect. 4. Finally, the conclusion and perspectives of this paper are given in Sect. 5.

2   Construction Methods of Low-Density Sparse Check Matrix

Gallager Construction Method. The Gallager construction method is a construction method given by Gallager when the LDPC codes are proposed [1]. The basic idea is to give the row weight d_v and column weight d_c of the $\mathbf{H}$ matrix and make it satisfy the constraint $d_c \geq 3$. The $\mathbf{H}$ matrix is divided into sub-matrices by row, and the sub-matrices have only one non-zero element per column. In the first sub-matrix, non-zero elements in row i start from column $(i-1)d_v + 1$ to column id_v and the rest elements are zero elements. Except for the first sub-matrix, the remaining sub-matrices are obtained by column transformation of the first matrix.

The following matrix (1) is a typical Gallager check matrix $\mathbf{H}(20, 3, 4)$. It can be seen that in the first five rows, that is, In the first sub-matrix, the elements in row i are non-zero elements form column $(i-1)d_v + 1$ to column id_v and the rest elements are zero elements. The remaining two sub-matrices are all obtained from the first sub-matrix by switching the column randomly.

$$
\mathbf{H} =
\begin{bmatrix}
1\,1\,1\,1\,0\,0\,0\,0\,0\,0\,0\,0\,0\,0\,0\,0\,0\,0\,0\,0 \\
0\,0\,0\,0\,1\,1\,1\,1\,0\,0\,0\,0\,0\,0\,0\,0\,0\,0\,0\,0 \\
0\,0\,0\,0\,0\,0\,0\,0\,1\,1\,1\,1\,0\,0\,0\,0\,0\,0\,0\,0 \\
0\,0\,0\,0\,0\,0\,0\,0\,0\,0\,0\,0\,1\,1\,1\,1\,0\,0\,0\,0 \\
0\,0\,0\,0\,0\,0\,0\,0\,0\,0\,0\,0\,0\,0\,0\,0\,1\,1\,1\,1 \\
1\,0\,0\,0\,1\,0\,0\,0\,1\,0\,0\,0\,1\,0\,0\,0\,0\,0\,0\,0 \\
0\,1\,0\,0\,0\,1\,0\,0\,0\,1\,0\,0\,0\,0\,0\,0\,1\,0\,0\,0 \\
0\,0\,1\,0\,0\,0\,1\,0\,0\,0\,0\,0\,1\,0\,0\,0\,1\,0\,0 \\
0\,0\,0\,1\,0\,0\,0\,0\,0\,1\,0\,0\,0\,1\,0\,0\,0\,0\,1\,0 \\
0\,0\,0\,0\,0\,0\,0\,1\,0\,0\,0\,1\,0\,0\,0\,1\,0\,0\,0\,1 \\
1\,0\,0\,0\,0\,1\,0\,0\,0\,0\,1\,0\,0\,0\,0\,0\,1\,0\,0 \\
0\,1\,0\,0\,0\,0\,1\,0\,0\,1\,0\,0\,0\,1\,0\,0\,0\,0 \\
0\,0\,1\,0\,0\,0\,0\,1\,0\,0\,0\,0\,1\,0\,0\,0\,0\,0\,1\,0 \\
0\,0\,0\,1\,0\,0\,0\,0\,1\,0\,0\,0\,0\,1\,0\,0\,1\,0\,0\,0 \\
0\,0\,0\,0\,1\,0\,0\,0\,0\,1\,0\,0\,0\,0\,1\,0\,0\,0\,0\,1 \\
\end{bmatrix}
\tag{1}
$$

PEG Construction Method. The following matrix (2) is a **H** matrix in binary domain. And its corresponding tenner graph is shown in Fig. 1.

$$\mathbf{H} = \begin{bmatrix} 1 & 1 & 1 & 0 & 0 & 1 & 1 & 0 & 0 & 0 & 1 & 0 \\ 1 & 1 & 1 & 1 & 1 & 0 & 0 & 0 & 0 & 0 & 0 & 1 \\ 0 & 0 & 0 & 0 & 0 & 1 & 1 & 1 & 0 & 1 & 1 & 1 \\ 1 & 0 & 0 & 1 & 0 & 0 & 0 & 1 & 1 & 1 & 0 & 1 \\ 0 & 1 & 0 & 1 & 1 & 0 & 1 & 1 & 1 & 0 & 0 & 0 \\ 0 & 0 & 1 & 0 & 1 & 1 & 0 & 0 & 1 & 1 & 1 & 0 \end{bmatrix} \tag{2}$$

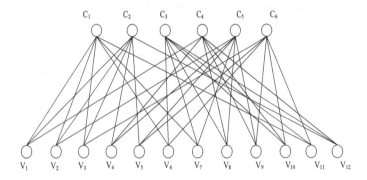

Fig. 1. The tanner graph corresponding to check matrix in (2).

The PEG construction method establishes an edge link between an information node and a check node according to the edge-by-edge method. When a new edge is added, it maximum the girth of the graph. The degree sequence of the information nodes is defined by the following Eq. (3).

$$D_b = (d_{b0}, d_{b1}, \cdots d_{bn-1}) \tag{3}$$

Where d_{bi} is the degree of the ith information node, it satisfies the non-decreasing order $d_{b0} \leq d_{b1} \leq \cdots \leq d_{bm-1}$. From the point of view, the information node set is V_b, the set of edges is $E = E_{b0} \cup E_{b1} \cup \cdots \cup E_{bn-1}$, E_{bi} corresponding to the information nodes b_i $(0 \leq i \leq n - 1)$. The kth edge connected to the information nodes b_i is defined as $E_{b_i}^k$ $(0 \leq k \leq db_i - 1)$. If nodes x and y are connected, then (x, y) is an edge, and the set of nodes connected to node x is called the neighbors of x. According to the tanner graph, for a given information node b_i, a tree graph with a depth of l is expanded along the information node b_i. The set of all the check nodes included at this time is called the neighbor of the information nodes b_i with l depth, and is represented as $N_{b_i}^l$. It means that we start from node b_i then go through all the edges connected to the check nodes, removing the edges that we have passed until we get the desired depth. There may be some nodes and edges appearing multiple times in this process.

The process of setting the edge should satisfy the requirement that the newly introduced edge has the smallest effect on the girth of the graph. Therefore, the key is to find the check node that is the farthest from this information node and then set a new edge between them. The PEG algorithm is summarized as follows.

Algorithm for PEG

For i=0 to n-1

For k=0 to n-1

If k=0

Then the edge $(b_i, c_j) \rightarrow E^0_{b_i}$, where $E^0_{b_i}$ is the first incident edge of the information nodes b_i, c_j is the check node with the lowest degree in the current graph set $E_{b_0} \cup E_{b_1} \cup ... \cup E_{b_{i-1}}$.

Else

Based on the current set of graphs, expand the information nodes b_i to a sub map of depth l until the number of elements in the collection $N^l_{b_i}$ reaches m, or $\overline{N}^l_{b_i} \neq \varphi$ but $\overline{N}^{l+1}_{b_i} = \varphi$. Then, there exists $(b_i, c_j) \rightarrow E^0_{b_k}$, where $E^0_{b_k}$ is the kth incident edge of the information nodes b_i, which c_j is the check node with the lowest degree in the set $\overline{N}^l_{b_i}$.

End If

End

End

According to the algorithm above, The first layer of the sub-graph whose depth is l of Fig. 1 is shown in Fig. 2.

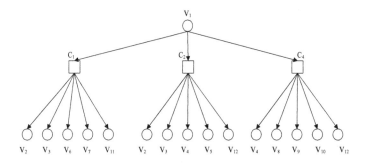

Fig. 2. The first layer of Fig. 1.

3   Decoding Methods of LDPC Codes

There are mainly two types of decoding algorithms for LDPC codes, mainly based on hard decision decoding and soft decision decoding. The advantage of decoding based on hard decision is mainly that the amount of computation is small [8]. The soft decision uses posterior probability decoding, which can achieve good performance. The decoding algorithm based on BP is the most popular decoding scheme, mainly including probability BP and LLR BP. The basic idea is to process the check nodes and information nodes for each iteration. Figure 3 shows various decoding algorithms based on BP.

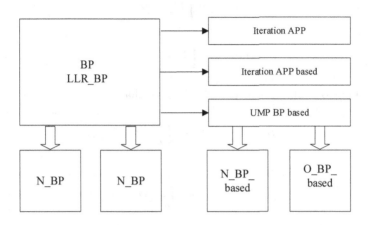

Fig. 3. Decoding algorithms based on BP.

Probabilistic BP Algorithm. Each modulated codeword $C = (c_1, c_2, ..., c_n)$ is mapped to a transmission sequence $X = (x_1, x_2, ..., x_n)$, and the received sequence is $Y = (y_1, y_2, ..., y_n)$.

The external probability that check node j passes to information node i, under the condition of given information bits and other information bits with independent probability distribution, is the probability that check equation j is met. It is represented as $r_{ji}(b)(b = 0, 1)$. The external probability information passed from information node i to check node j, that is, after obtaining the external information of channels and all the check nodes except j, the probability of the information nodes that is judged as $c_i = b$ and is represented as $q_{ij}(b)$. The set of the check nodes connected to the information nodes i is represented as $C(i)$. A collection of connected information nodes by the check node j is represented by $R(j)$. A set of check nodes connected to the information nodes i except j is represented as $C(i)\backslash j$. A set of information nodes connected to the check node j except i is represented as $R(j)\backslash i$. c_{kj} is the kth bit in the included jth check equation. y_{kj} is the corresponding received value to the c_{kj}, the bit in $\hat{c}$ satisfies the d_c check equation which include c_i is represented as S_i. The posterior probability of the transmitted bit (or information node) which is determined as $c_i = 1$ after receiving y_i is P_i. The posterior probability to judge the kth bit that is included in the jth check equation which contains c_i as $c_{kj} = 1$ after receiving y_{kj} is P_{kj}.

$$P_i = \Pr(c_i = 1|y_i) \tag{4}$$

$$P_{kj} = \Pr(c_{kj} = 1|y_{kj}) \tag{5}$$

For a binary sequence $\alpha = (a_1, a_2, ..., a_m)$, where $p(a_k = 1) = p_k$, the probability that α has an even number of 1 and an odd number of 1 are as follows (6) and (7) respectively [8].

$$1/2 + 1/2 \prod_{k=1}^{m} (1 - 2p_k) \tag{6}$$

$$1/2 - 1/2 \prod_{k=1}^{m} (1 - 2p_k) \tag{7}$$

According to Gallager's theory [1] we know that,

$$r_{ji}(0) = 1/2 + 1/2 \prod_{i' \in R_j \backslash i}^{m} (1 - 2p_{i'j}) \tag{8}$$

$$r_{ji}(1) = 1/2 - 1/2 \prod_{i' \in R_j \backslash i}^{m} (1 - 2p_{i'j}) \tag{9}$$

Gallager's theory gives the calculation method of posterior probability when the bit rates are independent to each other. The Gallager's theory can be rewritten as,

$$\frac{P(c_i = 0|\bar{y}, S_i)}{P(c_i = 1|\bar{y}, S_i)} = \frac{1 - P_i}{P_i} \frac{\prod\limits_{j \in C_i} r_{ji}(0)}{\prod\limits_{j \in C_i} r_{ji}(1)} \tag{10}$$

$$q_{ij}(0) = (1 - P) \prod_{j' \in C_i \backslash j} r_{j'i}(0) \quad q_{ij}(1) = P_i \prod_{j' \in C_i \backslash j} r_{j'i}(1) \tag{11}$$

Therefore, the BP decoding step is summarized as follows,

Initialization. Calculate the initial probability $P_i(1)$, $P_i(0) = 1 - P_i(1)(i = 1, 2, 3, ..., n)$ that the channel passes to the information nodes. Then, for each information node i and the adjacent check node $j \in C(i)$, an initial message from the information nodes to the check node is set as,

$$q_{ij}^{(0)}(0) = P_i(0) \tag{12}$$

$$q_{ij}^{(0)}(1) = P_i(1) \tag{13}$$

Iterative Processing. Step 1: Information processing of check nodes

For check node j and its adjacent information nodes $i \in R(j)$, in the first iteration, the message that the information nodes passes to the check nodes is calculated.

$$\begin{cases} r^l_{ji}(0) = 1/2 + 1/2 \prod_{i' \in R_j \setminus i} (1 - 2q^{(l-1)}_{i'j}(1)) \\ r^l_{ji}(1) = 1/2 - 1/2 \prod_{i' \in R_j \setminus i} (1 - 2q^{(l-1)}_{i'j}(1)) \end{cases} \tag{14}$$

Step 2: Information processing of information nodes

For information nodes i and its neighboring check nodes $j \in C(i)$, the message that the check nodes passes to the information nodes is calculated.

$$\begin{cases} q^l_{ij}(0) = k_{ij} P_i(0) \prod_{j' \in C_j \setminus j} r^{(l)}_{j'i}(0) \\ q^l_{ij}(1) = k_{ij} P_i(1) \prod_{j' \in C_j \setminus j} r^{(l)}_{j'i}(1) \end{cases} \tag{15}$$

k_{ij} is the correction factor that makes $q^{(l)}_{ij}(0) + q^{(l)}_{ij}(1) = 1$.

Step 3: Decoding decision

Hard decision messages are computed for all information nodes.

$$\begin{cases} q^l_i(0) = k_i P_i(0) \prod_{j \in C_j} r^{(l)}_{ji}(0) \\ q^l_i(1) = k_i P_i(1) \prod_{j \in C_j} r^{(l)}_{ji}(1) \end{cases} \tag{16}$$

Where k_i is the correction factor, so that $q^{(l)}_i(0) + q^{(l)}_i(1) = 1$. If $q^{(l)}_i(1) > q^{(l)}_i(0)$, then, $\hat{c}_i = 1$, otherwise $\hat{c}_i = 0$.

Stop. If the maximum number of iterations is reached or $\mathbf{H}\hat{c}^T = 0$, the operation ends, otherwise the iteration is continued from step 1.

LLR BP Algorithm. When the probability BP algorithm is represented by a likelihood ratio the LLR BP [4] algorithm is obtained, and the multiplication operation is converted into an additional operation to reduce the operation time. The likelihood is defined as follows. The channel initial message is defined by the following Eq. (17).

$$L(P_i) = \ln \frac{P_i(0)}{P_i(1)} = \ln \frac{P_r\{x_i = 1|y_i\}}{P_r\{x_i = -1|y_i\}} \tag{17}$$

The message that the check node passes to the information node is defined as the following Eq. (18).

$$Lr_{ji} = \ln \frac{r_{ji}(0)}{r_{ji}(1)} \tag{18}$$

The information that the information node passes to the check node is calculated in (19).

$$Lq_{ij} = \ln \frac{q_{ij}(0)}{q_{ij}(1)} \tag{19}$$

All messages collected by the information nodes by (20).

$$Lq_i = \ln \frac{q_i(0)}{q_i(1)} \tag{20}$$

Then check nodes message processing can be written as formula (21).

$$1 - 2r_{ij}(1) = 1 + \prod_{i' \varepsilon R_j \backslash i} (1 - 2q_{i'j}(1)) \tag{21}$$

Information nodes message processing can be written as formula (22).

$$L(q_{ij}) = L(P_i) + \prod_{j' \in C_i \backslash j} L(r_{j'i}) \tag{22}$$

Therefore, the LLR BP algorithm is summarized as follows,

Initialization. Calculate the initial probability likelihood ratio $L(P_i)$ passed from the channel to the information nodes. Then, for each information node i and the adjacent check node $j \in C(i)$, the initial message that the information node passes to the check node is (23).

$$L^{(0)}(q_{ij}) = L(P_i) \tag{23}$$

Iterative Processing. Step 1: Information processing of Check nodes

For check node j and its adjacent information nodes $i \in R(j)$, in the first iteration, the message that the information nodes passes to the check node is calculated.

$$L^{(l)}(r_{ji}) = 2\tanh^{-1}(\prod_{i' \in R_j \backslash i} \tanh(1/2L^{(l-1)}(q_{i'j}))) \tag{24}$$

Step 2: Information processing of information nodes

For information node i and its neighboring check node $j \in C(i)$, a message is sent from the check node to the information note.

$$L^{(l)}(q_{ij}) = l(P_i) + \prod_{j' \in C_i \backslash j} L^{(l)}(r_{j'i}) \tag{25}$$

Step 3: Decoding decision

Hard decision messages are computed for all information nodes.

$$L^{(l)}(q_i) = l(P_i) + \prod_{j' \in C_i} L^{(l)}(r_{ji}) \tag{26}$$

If $L^{(l)}(q_i) > 0$, then $\hat{c}_i = 0$, otherwise $\hat{c}_i = 1$.

Stop. If the maximum number of iterations is reached or $\mathbf{H}\hat{\mathbf{c}}^T = 0$, the operation ends, otherwise the iteration is continued from step 1.

If the nature of the utilization $\tanh x, \tanh^{-1} x$ is used, the formula of the check node processing in the LLR BP algorithm is processed, and the Eq. (27) can be obtained.

$$L(r_{ji}) = \prod_{i' \in R_j \backslash i} \mathrm{sgn}(L(q_{ij})) \cdot \min(|L(q_{i'j})|) \qquad (27)$$

If it is processed by the above formula, it is called the minimum sum or maximum product algorithm. This processing can make the iteration of the check nodes much more simple.

4   LDPC Codes Simulation Results and Performance Analysis

When a low-density parity check matrix $\mathbf{H}$ is choosen, we decode the (2048,1024) LDPC codes recommended by CCSDS standard with minimum sum decoding algorithm the simulation result shows the bit error rate performance in Figs. 4 and 5.

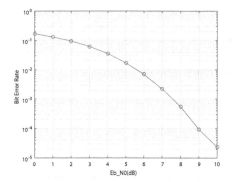 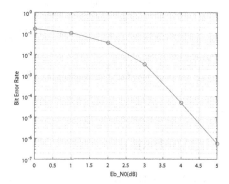

Fig. 4. BER performance with minimum sum decoding algorithm (iteration number = 1)

Fig. 5. BER performance with minimum sum decoding algorithm (iteration number = 5)

Under the condition that the code length is fixed, as the signal-to-noise ratio increases, the bit error rate decreases. In the case of iteration number is 1, the LDPC codes performance can reach about 10^{-5} at 10 dB. In the case of iteration number is 5, the LDPC codes performance can reach about 10^{-6} at 5 dB. It seems the iteration number has significant impact on bit error rate performance of LDPC codes. So the influence of number of iterations is studied in Fig. 6. Simulation result in Fig. 6 shows that the BP decoding algorithm can receive better performance with the increasing number of iterations. Under the same signal-to-noise ratio condition, the bit error rate decreases with the increase of the number of iterations. When the number of iterations is 1, 5, 10, 15, the bit error rate increases with the number of iterations. The degradation is very fast, and the decoding performance is greatly improved. However, when the number of iterations is further increased, the bit error rate decreases at a slower speed, and the increase in the number of iterations leads to an increase in the demand for hardware resources.

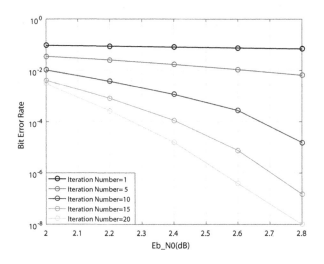

Fig. 6. BER performance with different iteration numbers.

5   Conclusion

According to the LDPC codes decoding methods applied in this paper, the increase of iteration numbers have a significant influence on bit error performance under the same code length and signal-to-noise ratio. With the increase of iteration numbers the bit error rate drop dramatically. This paper has analyzed BP based decoding algorithms and the simulation results suggest that the LDPC codes have a strong capability to correct error bits during the transmission of information.

Acknowledgments. This work was supported by National Natural Science Foundation of China (NSFC) (61671184).

References

1. Gallager, R.G.: Low-density parity-check codes. IRE Trans. Inf. Theory, **IT-18**, 21–28 (1962)
2. MacKay, D.J.C., Neal, R.M.: Near Shannon limit performance of low density parity check codes. Electron. Lett. **32**(18), 1645–1646 (1996)
3. Richardson, T.J., Shokrollahi, M.A., Urbanke, R.: Design of capacity-approaching irregular low-densityparity-check codes. IEEE Trans. Inf. Theory **47**, 619–637 (2001)
4. Hu, X.-Y., Eleftheriou, E., Arnold, D.-M.: Regular and irregular progressive edge-growth tanner graphs. IEEE Trans. Inform. Theory **51**, 386–98 (2005)
5. Prompakdee, P., Phakphisut, W., Supnithi, P.: Quasi cyclic-LDPC codes based on PEG algorithm with maximized girth property. In: IEEE International Symposium on Intelligent Signal Processing and Communications Systems, pp. 1–4 (2012)
6. Fossorier, M.P.C., Mihaljevic, M., Imai, I.: Reduced complexity iterative decoding of low density parity check codes based on belief propagation. IEEE Trans. Commun. **47**, 673–680 (1999)
7. Ning, H., Hua, Q.: Research of LDPC decoding based on modified LLR BP algorithm. J. Southwest Univ. (Nat. Sci. Ed.) 119–124 (2009)
8. Jia, H.: Principle and Application of LDPC, 1st edn. People's Posts and Telecommunications Press, Beijing (2009)

Joint Uplink and Downlink Optimization for Wireless Powered NOMA OFDM Communication Systems

Mengshu Zhang[1], Zhenyu Na[1], Mei Yang[1(✉)], Weidang Lu[2], and Xin Liu[3]

[1] Dalian Maritime University, Dalian 116026, China
yangmei@dlmu.edu.cn
[2] Zhejiang University of Technology, Hangzhou 310023, China
[3] Dalian University of Technology, Dalian 116024, China

Abstract. In this paper, an Orthogonal Frequency Division Multiplexing (OFDM) wireless communication system is investigated. For downlink, users perform Information Decoding (ID) and Energy Harvesting (EH) simultaneously. For uplink, users transmit information to Base Station (BS), while BS performs the Non-Orthogonal Multiple Access (NOMA) to decode information from users. In order to maximize the total uplink ID rate in the condition that the total downlink ID rate is ensured, a joint uplink and downlink optimization method based on power and subcarrier allocation is proposed. As shown in simulation results, compared with the existing method, the proposed method can implement the maximum harvested energy for users in the downlink and achieve higher total uplink ID rate.

Keywords: OFDM · Energy harvesting · Information decoding · NOMA

1 Introduction

Driven by the rapid evolvement of mobile networks and the growing demands for the Internet of Things (IoT) services, higher capacity, higher transmission rate, denser network deployment and lower time delay become necessary for the 5th Generation (5G) communication [1]. In that case, it will inevitably lead to the scarcity of resource, which may cause serious economic and environmental problems in use of traditional schemes. Thus, new schemes for increasing resource utilization becomes the precondition for implementing these technical requirements.

On the one hand, the Wireless Powered Communication (WPC) attracts broad attention, in which the energy can be harvested from environmental Radio Frequency (RF) signals [2]. So far, plenty of optimization methods are designed for WPC-based systems, such as [3] and [4]. However, most of the designed schemes for WPC only keep eyes on uplink or downlink without taking joint uplink and downlink optimization into account.

On the other hand, as an effective method for improving spectrum efficiency, Non-Orthogonal Multiple Access (NOMA) has received much attention recently. The core

M. Jia et al. (Eds.): WiSATS 2019, LNICST 280, pp. 738–746, 2019.
https://doi.org/10.1007/978-3-030-19153-5_72

idea of NOMA is that different proportion of transmit power multiple are allocated to users to achieve the simultaneously access [5]. Many researches focus on the combination of NOMA and other techniques, such as Sparse Code Multiple Access (SCMA), Pattern Division Multiple Access (PDMA) [6] and Mobile Edge Computing (MEC) [7]. But there are few works for WPC NOMA.

In this paper, an OFDM wireless system based on WPC NOMA is studied to optimize the total uplink Information Decoding (ID) rate. Unlike conventional methods, the proposed method can obtain the maximum energy in the downlink and higher total uplink ID rate.

2   System Model and Problem Formulation

2.1   System Model

An OFDM-based wireless communication system with one BS and N users is studied and shown in Fig. 1. In the downlink, ID and Energy Harvesting (EH) are simultaneously performed by users. In the uplink, ID is performed by BS based on NOMA. The user set is represented by $\mathbf{N} = \{1, 2, \ldots, N\}$. The total bandwidth is equally split into K subchannels for K subcarriers. The subcarrier set is represented by $\mathbf{K} = \{1, 2, \ldots, K\}$. For subcarrier k assigned to user n, the channel gain coefficient is represented by $h_{k,n}$. The factor for subcarrier allocation is represented by $a_{k,n}$. It is set that $a_{k,n} = 1$ if subcarrier k is assigned to user n, otherwise, $a_{k,n} = 0$. The total transmit power is represented by P. The power assigned to subcarrier k for user n is represented by $p_{k,n}$.

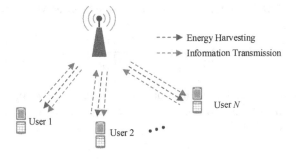

Fig. 1. System model.

2.2   Problem Formulation

In the downlink, subcarriers for ID is allocated to group $\mathbf{K^I}$ and others for EH is allocated to group $\mathbf{K^E}$, where $\mathbf{K^I}, \mathbf{K^E} \subseteq \mathbf{K}$ and $\mathbf{K^I} + \mathbf{K^E} = \mathbf{K}$. $\mathbf{K^I}$ is used for ID while $\mathbf{K^E}$ is used for EH. Each subcarrier is only utilized for ID or EH.

The downlink ID rate on subcarrier k is formulated by

$$R_k = \sum_{n=1}^{N} a_{k,n} \ln(1 + \frac{h_{k,n}^2 p_{k,n}}{\sigma_{k,n}^2}), k \in \mathbf{K_I}, n \in \mathbf{N} \tag{1}$$

Where $\sigma_{k,n}^2$ represents the noise on subcarrier k to user n. The EH on subcarrier k is given by

$$E_k = \eta \sum_{n=1}^{N} a_{k,n} \left(h_{k,n}^2 p_{k,n} + \sigma_{k,n}^2 \right), k \in \mathbf{K_E}, n \in \mathbf{N} \tag{2}$$

Where $\eta \in (0, 1)$ represents the receiver's energy conversion efficiency.

After EH is performed in the downlink, energy obtained by users is available to perform information transmission to BS in the uplink. Then, BS can perform ID based on NOMA. For simplicity, subcarriers in $\mathbf{K^E}$ can be sorted as a fixed decoding order, which is assumed to be the ascending order of $h_{k,n}$, and renumbered from 1 to M. In use of SIC, when the signal from one subcarrier is decoded, signals from who have higher decoding order than the decoded one are treated as noise. The transmit power on subcarrier m for user n is represented by $p_{m,n} = E_{m,n}$. Thus, the ID rate on subcarrier m can be given by

$$R_m = \sum_{n=1}^{N} a_{m,n} \ln(1 + \frac{h_{m,n}^2 p_{m,n}}{\sum_{j=m+1}^{M} h_{j,n}^2 p_{j,n} + \sigma_{m,n}^2}), n \in \mathbf{N} \tag{3}$$

After the ID of M-1 subcarriers, the ID rate on subcarrier M can be given by

$$R_M = \sum_{n=1}^{N} a_{M,n} \ln(1 + \frac{h_{M,n}^2 p_{M,n}}{\sigma_{M,n}^2}), n \in \mathbf{N} \tag{4}$$

The optimization objective of this paper is to maximize the total uplink ID rate while the threshold of total downlink ID rate can be ensured. Thus, the optimization objective can be formulated as

$$\max_{R_m} \sum_{m=1}^{M} R_m \tag{5}$$

Subject to

$$\sum_{n=1}^{N} \sum_{k \in \mathbf{K^I}} a_{k,n} \ln(1 + \frac{h_{k,n}^2 p_{k,n}}{\sigma_{k,n}^2}) \geq R_T \tag{6}$$

Where R_T represents the threshold of total downlink ID rate, so that the total ID rate must be more than or equal to R_T. As known that one subcarrier is only used for ID or

EH, so that $\sum_{n=1}^{N} a_{k,n} = 1$. It is noted that, in (3) and (4), the ID rate on subcarrier m in the uplink is only determined by $p_{m,n}$. Thus, the original optimization objective can be regarded as a maximization of EH in the downlink. The optimization objective can be arranged as

$$\max_{\varphi_{k,n}, p_{k,n}} \eta \sum_{n=1}^{N} \sum_{k \in \mathbf{K}^{\mathbf{E}}} a_{k,n} (h_{k,n}^2 p_{k,n} + \sigma_{k,n}^2)$$

$$\text{s.t.} \sum_{n=1}^{N} \sum_{k \in \mathbf{K}^{\mathbf{I}}} a_{k,n} \ln(1 + \frac{h_{k,n}^2 p_{k,n}}{\sigma_{k,n}^2}) \geq R_T$$

$$\sum_{n=1}^{N} a_{k,n} = 1, \ a_{k,n} = 0, 1 \quad (7)$$

$$\sum_{n}^{N} \sum_{k=1}^{K} a_{k,n} p_{k,n} \leq P$$

$$\mathbf{K}^{\mathbf{I}} + \mathbf{K}^{\mathbf{E}} = \mathbf{K}$$

3 Optimal Solution

An iteration method based on Lagrange Multiplier is designed to achieve the optimization objective proposed in Sect. 2. Obviously, the optimization problem in (7) is nonconvex that requires to be broken down into parts to solve. It is set that $p_{k,n}$, $\mathbf{K}^{\mathbf{I}}$ and $\mathbf{K}^{\mathbf{E}}$ are given first. Taking no account of fairness, subcarrier k is allocated to user n by finding the maximum $h_{k,n}$ for it, so that $a_{k,n} = 1$. Thus, (7) is arranged as

$$\max_{p_{k,n}} \eta \sum_{n=1}^{N} \sum_{k \in \mathbf{K}^{\mathbf{E}}} a_{k,n} (h_{k,n}^2 p_{k,n} + \sigma_{k,n}^2)$$

$$\text{s.t.} \sum_{n=1}^{N} \sum_{k \in \mathbf{K}^{\mathbf{I}}} a_{k,n} \ln(1 + \frac{h_{k,n}^2 p_{k,n}}{\sigma_{k,n}^2}) \geq R_T \quad (8)$$

$$\sum_{n=1}^{N} \sum_{k=1}^{K} a_{k,n} p_{k,n} \leq P$$

The optimization problem in (8) is convex so that it can be settled based on the Lagrange Multiplier. Then, the Lagrange dual function of (8) can be formulated as

$$g(\mathbf{\Lambda}) = \max_{\mathbf{P}, \mathbf{K}} \mathcal{L}(\mathbf{P}, \mathbf{K}) \quad (9)$$

Where $\mathbf{P} = \{p_{1,n}, p_{2,n}, ..., p_{k,n}\}$ is the allocated power set and $\mathbf{K} = \{\mathbf{K}^{\mathbf{I}}, \mathbf{K}^{\mathbf{E}}\}$ is the subcarrier set. The expression of $\mathcal{L}(\mathbf{P}, \mathbf{K})$ is given by

$$\mathcal{L}(\mathbf{P}, \mathbf{K}) = \eta \sum_{n=1}^{N} \sum_{k \in \mathbf{K}^{\mathbf{E}}} a_{k,n}(h_{k,n}^2 p_{k,n} + \sigma_{k,n}^2) + \lambda_1 \left(\sum_{n=1}^{N} \sum_{k \in \mathbf{K}^{\mathbf{I}}} a_{k,n} \ln(1 + \frac{h_{k,n}^2 p_{k,n}}{\sigma_{k,n}^2}) - R_T \right)$$
$$+ \lambda_2 (P - \sum_{n=1}^{N} \sum_{k=1}^{K} a_{k,n} p_{k,n})$$

$$(10)$$

Where $\Lambda = (\lambda_1, \lambda_2)$ is the non-negative dual variable depending on P and total ID rate. Then, the dual optimization problem is able to be transformed to

$$\min_{\Lambda} g(\Lambda) \qquad (11)$$

Based on the subgradient method, (11) can be obtained owing to the differentiability of $g(\Lambda)$. The subgradients can be expressed as

$$\Delta \lambda_1 = \sum_{n=1}^{N} \sum_{k \in \mathbf{K}^{\mathbf{I}}} a_{k,n} \ln(1 + \frac{h_{k,n}^2 p_{k,n}}{\sigma_{k,n}^2}) - R_T \qquad (12)$$

$$\Delta \lambda_2 = P - \sum_{n=1}^{N} \sum_{k=1}^{K} a_{k,n} p_{k,n} \qquad (13)$$

Λ can be update by iteration in use of $\Lambda(t + 1) = \Lambda(t) + v(t) \cdot \Delta \Lambda$, where $\Delta \Lambda = (\Delta \lambda_1, \Delta \lambda_2)$, t represents iterations and v represents negative step size. With the increase of t, $\mathbf{P}$ and $\mathbf{K}$ can be optimized by iteration until Λ converges. In this case, the objective of (11) can be achieved.

The optimization of $\mathbf{P}$ and $\mathbf{K}$ can be performed based on the variable control method. $\mathbf{P}$ can be maximized first with a fixed $\mathbf{K}$ so that $p_{k,n}$ can be obtained by partial derivatives of (10), which are expressed as

$$\frac{\partial \mathcal{L}(\mathbf{P}, \mathbf{K})}{\partial p_{k,n}} = \frac{\sum_{n=1}^{N} \lambda_1 a_{k,n} h_{k,n}^2}{\sigma_{k,n}^2 + h_{k,n}^2 p_{k,n}} - \lambda_2, k \in \mathbf{K}^{\mathbf{I}} \qquad (14)$$

$$\frac{\partial \mathcal{L}(\mathbf{P}, \mathbf{K})}{\partial p_{k,n}} = \sum_{n=1}^{N} a_{k,n} h_{k,n}^2 \eta - \lambda_2, k \in \mathbf{K}^{\mathbf{E}} \qquad (15)$$

According to the Karush-Kuhn-Tucker condition, the desired $p_{k,n}$ can be obtained when (14) and (15) equal to 0. Therefore, when $k \in \mathbf{K}^{\mathbf{I}}$, the desired $p_{k,n}$ can be formulated by

$$p_{k,n} = \frac{\lambda_1}{\lambda_2} - \frac{\sum\limits_{n=1}^{N} a_{k,n}\sigma_{k,n}^2}{h_{k,n}^2} \tag{16}$$

Obviously, (15) can not be set to zero unless $h_{k,n}\eta = \lambda_2$. For the sake of improving power utilization and obtaining more energy, the linear water-filling method can be utilized to reassign the power not be used for ID. For simplicity, $a_{k,n}$ is not participated in following derivation. Thus, the Lagrange function is expressed as

$$\mathcal{L}(\lambda_2, p_i) = \ln(1 + \frac{h_i^2 p_i}{\sigma_i^2}) + \lambda_2(P_E - \sum_{i \in \mathbf{K}^E} p_i) \tag{17}$$

Where subcarrier i belongs to $\mathbf{K}^E$. P_E represents the power unutilized for ID. Thus, the following derivation based on the partial derivative of (17) is expressed by

$$p_i = (\frac{1}{\lambda_2} - \frac{\sigma_i^2}{h_i^2})^+ \Rightarrow \frac{\sigma_i^2}{h_i^2} + p_i = \frac{\sigma_k^2}{h_k^2} + p_k \Rightarrow p_i = p_k + \frac{\sigma_k^2}{h_k^2} - \frac{\sigma_i^2}{h_i^2}$$
$$\Rightarrow N_E(p_k + \frac{\sigma_k^2}{h_k^2}) - \sum_{i \in \mathbf{K}^E} \frac{\sigma_i^2}{h_i^2} = P_E \tag{18}$$

Where subcarrier k is another one of $\mathbf{K}^E$ except subcarrier i. N_E represents the number of subcarriers in $\mathbf{K}^E$. The desired p_k for subcarrier k in $\mathbf{K}^E$ can be obtained as

$$p_k = \frac{1}{N_E}(P_E - \frac{N_E\sigma_k^2}{h_k^2} + \sum_{i \in \mathbf{K}^E} \frac{\sigma_i^2}{h_i^2}) \tag{19}$$

Afterwards, the optimized $\mathbf{K}^I$ and $\mathbf{K}^E$ can be obtained by substituting (16) and (19) into (10). The simplification process is given by

$$\mathcal{L} = \eta \sum_{n=1}^{N} \sum_{k \in \mathbf{K}^E} a_{k,n}(h_{k,n}^2 p_{k,n} + \sigma_{k,n}^2) + \lambda_1[\sum_{n=1}^{N} \sum_{k \in \mathbf{K}^I} a_{k,n} \ln(1 + \frac{h_{k,n}^2 p_{k,n}}{\sigma_{k,n}^2}) - R_T] + \lambda_2(P - \sum_{n=1}^{N} \sum_{k=1}^{K} a_{k,n} p_{k,n})$$
$$= \sum_{k \in \mathbf{K}^I} Y_k + \sum_{n=1}^{N} \sum_{k=1}^{K} a_{k,n}[\eta(h_{k,n}^2 p_{k,n} + \sigma_{k,n}^2) - \lambda_2 p_{k,n}] - \lambda_1 R_T + \lambda_2 P \tag{20}$$

Where

$$Y_k = \sum_{n=1}^{N} a_{k,n}[\lambda_1 \ln(1 + \frac{h_{k,n}^2 p_{k,n}}{\sigma_{k,n}^2}) - \eta(h_{k,n}^2 p_{k,n} + \sigma_{k,n}^2)] \tag{21}$$

Obviously, Y_k is the only part relative to $\mathbf{K}^I$. By finding subcarriers making Y_k positive, the optimized $\mathbf{K}^I$ can be obtained. Other subcarriers are allocated to $\mathbf{K}^E$.

Afterwards, the update of $\Delta\Lambda$ for the next iteration can be achieved by substituting the optimized $\mathbf{P}$ and $\mathbf{K}$ into (12) and (13). Based on iteration, the maximum EH can be achieved until Λ converges.

Afterwards, the desired transmit power $p_{m,n}$ in the uplink can be obtained based on the optimal harvested energy discussed above. For simplicity, $a_{k,n}$ is not considered in the following discussion. It is assumed that σ_m^2 is set to 1. The maximum sum ID rate in the uplink can be given by

$$R_u = \sum_{m=1}^{M-1} \ln\left(1 + \frac{h_m^2 p_m}{\sum\limits_{j=m+1}^{M} h_k^2 p_k + \sigma_m^2}\right) + \ln\left(1 + \frac{h_M^2 p_M}{\sigma_M^2}\right) = \ln\left(2 + \sum_{m=1}^{M} h_m^2 p_m\right) \quad (22)$$

4 Simulation

The performance of the proposed method is investigated based on simulation results. It is set that $N = 4$, $K = 16$, $\sigma_{k,n}^2 = 1$, $\eta = 0.8$, and $h_{k,n}$ are known at all receivers. The total bandwidth is set to 1 MHz. The signals are assumed to be perfectly synchronized. For iteration, it is set that $\lambda_1 = 2.2$ and $\lambda_2 = 0.6$. The step sizes are set to 0.02 and 0.002, respectively. The threshold of total downlink ID rate R_T is set to 6Mbps.

The method proposed is considered as Method 1. The other method defined as Method 2 is considered in which P is equally allocated to subcarriers. When two methods are performed in the downlink, the results of total uplink ID rate are shown in Fig. 2. With the increase of P, the total ID rate based on Method 1 is higher than that based on Method 2.

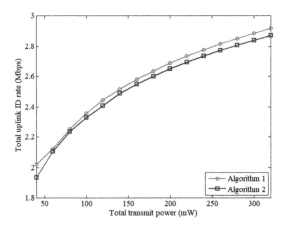

Fig. 2. Total uplink ID rate based on Method 1 and Method 2.

For uplink, the performance based on NOMA is contrasted with that based on Time Division Multiple Access (TDMA) which is a common type of orthogonal multiple access (OMA). While EH is constantly performed for downlink, the results of total uplink ID rate based on NOMA and TDMA are shown in Fig. 3 Obviously, the performance of total ID rate based on NOMA is much better than that based on TDMA.

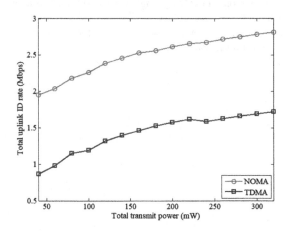

Fig. 3. Total uplink ID rate based on NOMA and TDMA

5   Conclusion

In this paper, a joint uplink and downlink optimization method for wireless powered NOMA OFDM communication system is proposed. Owing to that the total uplink ID rate is only influenced by downlink EH, for achieving the objective, an iteration algorithm based on Lagrange Multiplier is designed. In the downlink, the energy obtained by users can be optimized based on the joint power and subcarrier allocation optimization by iteration. Afterwards, NOMA and SIC are used for uplink at BS to perform ID and improve the total uplink ID rate. As shown in simulation results, in the same condition, the proposed method can increase the energy harvested for uplink and obtain a higher uplink ID rate than traditional methods.

References

1. Rizvi, S., Aziz, A., Jilani, M.T., Armi, N., Muhammad, G., Butt, S.H.: An investigation of energy efficiency in 5G wireless networks. In: 2017 International Conference on Circuits, System and Simulation (ICCSS), London, pp. 142–145 (2017)
2. Zhang, R., Ho, C.K.: MIMO broadcasting for simultaneous wireless information and power transfer. IEEE Trans. Wirel. Commun. **12**(5), 1989–2001 (2013)
3. Lu, W., Gong, Y., Wu, J., Peng, H., Hua, J.: Simultaneous wireless information and power transfer based on joint subcarrier and power allocation in OFDM systems. IEEE Access **5**, 2763–2770 (2017)

4. Na, Z., Li, X., Liu, X., Deng, Z.: Subcarrier allocation based simultaneous wireless information and power transfer for multiuser OFDM systems. EURASIP J. Wirel. Commun. Netw. **2017**(1), 148 (2017)
5. Ding, Z., Lei, X., Karagiannidis, G.K., Schober, R., Yuan, J., Bhargava, V.K.: A survey on non-orthogonal multiple access for 5G networks: research challenges and future trends. IEEE J. Sel. Areas Commun. **35**(10), 2181–2195 (2017)
6. Zeng, J., et al.: Investigation on evolving single-carrier NOMA into multi-carrier NOMA in 5G. IEEE Access **6**, 48268–48288 (2018)
7. Kiani, A., Ansari, N.: Edge computing aware NOMA for 5G networks. IEEE Internet of Things J. **5**(2), 1299–1306 (2018)

Research on Detection Algorithm of DSSS Signals Under Alpha Stable Distribution Noise

Weichao Yang$^{(\boxtimes)}$ and Yu Du

China Academy of Space Technology (Xi'an), Xi'an 710100, China
yangweichao2008@163.com

Abstract. The detection algorithm of direct sequence spread spectrum (DSSS) signals based on power spectrum reprocessing will significantly degrade in Alpha stable distribution noise environment, in order to solve this problem, the concept of generalized power spectrum reprocessing was proposed. On the basis of studying the generalized power spectrum reprocessing feature of the DSSS signals, the pulse spectrum was extracted as the detection feature to achieve effective detection. Simulation results show that the performance of this method have good performance both in the Alpha stable distribution noise.

Keywords: Signal detection · DSSS signals · Alpha stable distribution noise · Generalized power spectrum reprocessing

1 Introduction

DSSS is a channel transmission technology widely used in modern communication, it has very high processing gain. The source signal is often hidden in the noise after direct expansion processing, the special character determines its hard to detect. At present, the commonly used detection methods include auto-correlation accumulation [1], cyclostationarity spectral correlation [2], higher-order cumulants [3], cepstrum [4], power spectrum reprocessing [5, 6], etc. Power spectrum reprocessing can be seen as an improved version of cepstrum, its computational complexity is slightly lower than the cepstrum. Cepstrum and the power spectrum reprocessing is used to detect DSSS signals, is the use of periodicity of pseudo-code components in the frequency domain and time domain, through power spectrum reprocessing, the pseudo-time domain or the inverted frequency domain will show up this periodicity, it becomes a useful characteristics of signal detection. Thus, the advantages of cepstrum and power spectrum reprocessing are that it can not only detect the presence of DSSS signals in the noise, and can effectively identify the DSSS signal and normal signal.

Most of previous researches on the detection of DSSS signals employed Gaussian distribution as the model of background noise. With the increasing complexity of channel environment, the Gaussian distribution has been unable to effectively describe some noise, especially some significant short-time impulse noise with large amplitude, such as electromagnetic pulse noise, low-frequency atmospheric noise, multi-user interference, etc. More and more researchers confirmed that the Alpha stable distribution is a more effective noise model, and have done a lot of researches on signal

© ICST Institute for Computer Sciences, Social Informatics and Telecommunications Engineering 2019
Published by Springer Nature Switzerland AG 2019. All Rights Reserved
M. Jia et al. (Eds.): WiSATS 2019, LNICST 280, pp. 747–754, 2019.
https://doi.org/10.1007/978-3-030-19153-5_73

processing in Alpha stable distribution noise [7–11], therefore, this article studies the detection method of DSSS signals under Alpha stable distribution noise. Alpha stable distribution sequence does not have a second-order statistics and above, this nature determines the above mentioned detection methods of DSSS signals will fail. It can be seen from the Figs. 1 and 2 that the Alpha stable distribution noise destroys the spectral characteristics of the power spectrum reprocessing, and the corresponding DSSS signal detection algorithm will also fail. Aiming at this problem, based on the idea of reference [12], power spectrum reprocessing is extended, and the concept of generalized power spectrum reprocessing is proposed. It is applied to the detection of DSSS signal under Alpha stable distribution noise and achieves good results.

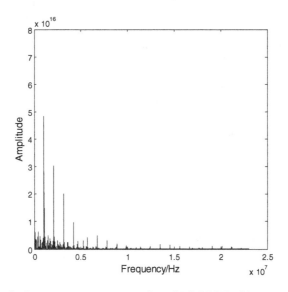

Fig. 1. Power spectrum reprocessing of DS-BPSK with non-noise

2 Algorithm Principle

The generalized auto-correlation function of the signal $x(t)$ is defined as:

$$GR_x(\tau) = E[f\{x(t+\tau)\}f^*\{x(t)\}] \tag{1}$$

In the above formula, $f(x) = \dfrac{\arctan(|x+jH(x)|)}{|x+jH(x)|}x$, $H(\cdot)$ represents the Hilbert transform.

The generalized power spectrum is the Fourier transform of generalized auto-correlation function:

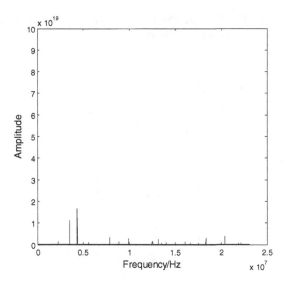

Fig. 2. Power spectrum reprocessing of DS-BPSK with Alpha stable distribution noise

$$GP_x(f) = \int_{-\infty}^{\infty} GR_x(\tau)e^{-j2\pi f\tau}d\tau \tag{2}$$

Similarly, assuming that the auto-correlation function of the generalized power spectrum $GP_x(f)$ is $G^2R_x(\tau)$, its generalized power spectrum reprocessing is defined as:

$$G^2P_x(f) = \int_{-\infty}^{\infty} G^2R_x(\tau)e^{-j2\pi f\tau}d\tau \tag{3}$$

In practical applications, the generalized power spectrum reprocessing can be approximated by the following formula:

$$G^2P_x = \left| FFT\left| FFT(f(x))\right|^2 \right|^2 \tag{4}$$

It is mentioned in the reference [11] that the generalized transform does not change the period characteristics of the spread code of DSSS signal. The generalized power spectrum reprocessing must have similar spectral characteristics to the traditional power spectrum reprocessing.

The noisy DSSS signal received by the receiver can be expressed as:

$$x(t) = s(t) + n(t) = Ad(t)p(t)\cos(\omega_c t + \varphi_0) + n(t) \tag{5}$$

In the above formula, A represents the amplitude of the DSSS signal, $d(t)$ represents the information code sequence, $p(t)$ represents the spread code sequence, ω_c represents the carrier frequency, φ_0 represents the initial phase, and $n(t)$ represents the Alpha stable distribution noise.

Combined with the Eqs. (4) and (5), the generalized power spectrum reprocessing of DSSS signal can be obtained as follows:

$$G^2 P_s(f') = \left| \text{FFT} \left[\frac{(N+1)\left(\arctan^2 A\right)}{4\pi N^2} \text{Sa}^2\left((f-f_c)\pi T_p\right) \sum_{\substack{k=-\infty \\ k\neq 0}}^{k=\infty} \delta\left(f-f_c-\frac{k}{T_0}\right) \right] \right|^2$$

$$= \begin{cases} \left| \left| \frac{(N+1)\left(\arctan^2 A\right)}{4\pi N^2} e^{-j2\pi d f_c} \left\{ \frac{1}{2\pi^2 T_p}\left(1-\frac{|f'|}{T_p}\right) * \right. \right. \\ \left. \left. 4\pi^2 T_0 \sum_{\substack{k=-\infty \\ k\neq 0}}^{k=\infty} \delta(f'-kT_0) \right\} \right|^2 \right|, & |f'| \leq T_p \\[6mm] 0, & |f'| > T_p \end{cases}$$

$$= \begin{cases} \left| \frac{(N+1)\left(\arctan^2 A\right)}{2\pi N} \sum_{\substack{k=-\infty \\ k\neq 0}}^{k=\infty} \left(1-\frac{|f'-kT_0|}{T_p}\right) \times \right. \\ \left. e^{-j2\pi d f_c} \right|^2, & |f'-kT_0| \leq T_p \\[6mm] 0, & |f'-kT_0| > T_p \end{cases} \tag{6}$$

It can be seen from the above equation that in the generalized power spectrum reprocessing, the signal energy is concentrated at some sharp triangular pulse sequences. Figure 3 shows a generalized power spectrum reprocessing graph with the same noise as in Fig. 2. It can be seen from the figure that the spectral characteristics have been greatly improved. Therefore, the generalized power spectrum reprocessing can be used as a detection feature of DSSS signal under Alpha stable distribution noise.

For the generalized power spectrum reprocessing of DSSS signal, after a large number of simulation analysis, the ratio of the maximum value to the mean value in the spectral domain is used to describe the sharp pulse characteristics, and the ratio is used as the detection feature.

$$th = \frac{\max\left(G^2 P_s\right)}{\text{mean}\left(G^2 P_s\right)} \tag{7}$$

According to the simulation experience value, when the decision threshold is 25, the effective detection of the DSSS signal under a certain mixed SNR can be realized.

3 Algorithm Step

The detection algorithm steps are as follows:

(1) Calculate the generalized power spectrum reprocessing of the received signal;
(2) The detected feature value is calculated according to Eq. (7) (In order to avoid the influence of the DC term, the calculation here does not include the zero frequency);
(3) Decision: if $th \geq 25$, there is a DSSS signal; otherwise there is only noise.

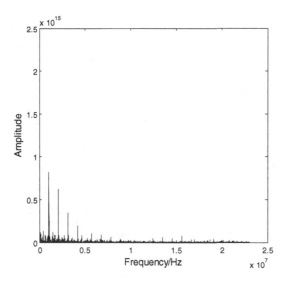

Fig. 3. Generalized power spectrum reprocessing of DS-BPSK

4 Simulation Analysis

(1) Verify detection algorithm performance based on power spectrum reprocessing. The parameters of DSSS signal are as follows: the modulation type is DS-BPSK, the spread code is Gold, the symbol rate of spread code is 3.84 M bit/s, the spread spectrum gain is 23 dB, the sampling frequency is 46.08 MHz, the carrier frequency is 5 MHz, the number of point is 16384. The detection results are shown in the Figs. 4 and 5.

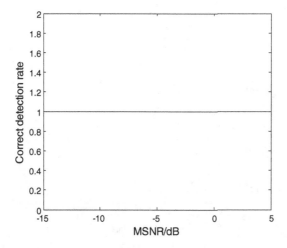

Fig. 4. Correct detection rate

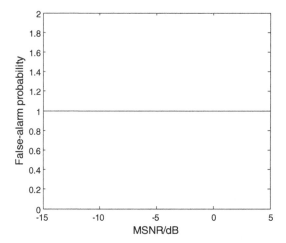

Fig. 5. False-alarm probability

It can be seen from the above figure that under the framework of the proposed algorithm, in the whole mixed SNR range, the correct detection rate and false alarm probability of the algorithm based on the power spectrum reprocessing are both 100%. As can be seen from Fig. 2, regardless of whether there is a target signal, there is an irregular impact line in the power spectrum reprocessing of the received signal, which will cause misjudgment. In other words, the influence of noise dominates the decision process. This shows that the algorithm based on the power spectrum reprocessing has failed.

(2) Verify detection algorithm performance based on generalized power spectrum reprocessing. The signal parameters are the same as simulation 1. The detection results are shown in the Figs. 6 and 7.

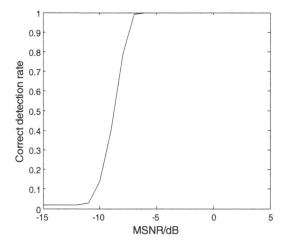

Fig. 6. Correct detection rate

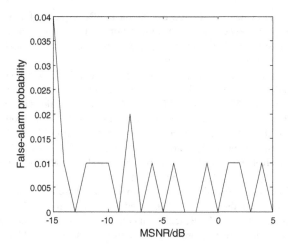

Fig. 7. False-alarm probability

It can be seen from Fig. 6 that when, the correct detection rate is greater than 90%, and the false-alarm probability is not more than 1%, indicating that the proposed algorithm can achieve effective detection of DSSS signal under a certain mixed SNR.

5 Conclusion

In this paper, the concept of generalized power spectrum reprocessing is proposed, which solves the problem of power spectrum reprocessing failure under Alpha stable distribution noise. On this basis, a new detection method of DSSS signal is proposed, which extends the application range of power spectrum reprocessing from Gaussian noise background to the Alpha stable distribution noise.

References

1. Huang, X.L., Shao, H.Z., Huang, W.: A new detection method for DSSS signal in multipath channel. Sig. Process. **27**(12), 1925–1930 (2011)
2. Liu, W.X., Peng, H., Yang, X.: A modified algorithm for bind detection of the burst DSSS signal. Sig. Process. **29**(7), 857–864 (2013)
3. Zhao, Z.J., Wu, J., Xu, C.Y.: The study on the detection methods of DSSS/QPSK signal based on the fourth-order cumulants. Acta Electronica Sinica **35**(6), 1046–1049 (2007)
4. Zhang, G.Q., Dong, Y.Z., Liu, P.X.: Detection of underwater acoustic DSSS signals using the cepstrum method based on a power spectral density average. J. Harbin Eng. Univ. **31**(7), 863–867 (2010)
5. Zhang, T.Q., Miao, P., Ma, G.N.: Period estimation of the PN sequence for direct sequence spread spectrum in multipath environment. Chin. J. Radio Sci. **24**(5), 973–978 (2009)

6. Zhang, Y., Wu, H., Chen, Y.: Period estimation of PN sequence for weak DSSS signals based on improved power spectrum reprocessing in non-cooperative communication systems. In: International Conference on Control Engineering and Communication Technology, Shenyang, China, pp. 924–927 (2012)

7. Chavali, V.G., Da, S., Claudio, R.: Detection of digital amplitude-phase modulated signals in symmetric alpha-stable noise. IEEE Trans. Commun. **60**(11), 3365–3375 (2012)

8. Mahmood, A., Chitre, M., Armand, M.A.: PSK communication with pass-band additive symmetric alpha-stable noise. IEEE Trans. Commun. **60**(10), 2990–3000 (2012)

9. Zhang, J.F., Qiu, T.S., Aimin, S.: A novel correntropy based DOA estimation algorithm in impulsive noise environments. Sig. Process. **104**(11), 346–357 (2014)

10. Jin, Y., Ji, H.B.: Robust symbol rate estimation of PSK signals under the cyclostationary framework. Circ. Syst. Sig. Process. **33**(2), 599–612 (2014)

11. Zhu, X.M., Zhu, W.P., Benoit, C.: Spectrum sensing based on fractional lower order moments for cognitive radios α-stable distributed noise. Sig. Process. **111**(6), 94–105 (2015)

12. Zhao, C.H., Yang, W.C., Ma, S.: Research on communication signal modulation recognition based on the generalized second-order cyclic statistics. J. Commun. **32**(1), 144–150 (2011)

Radar Detection Based on Pilot Signals of LTE Base Stations

Yun Zhang, Jinze Li$^{(\boxtimes)}$, Yang Li, and Nan Qiao

Harbin Institute of Technology, Harbin 150001, China
buwai12877@163.com

Abstract. This paper presented a new signal design method for target detection. As the development of communication equipment, wireless communication has gradually developed to high frequency band and large bandwidth, which makes communication and radar systems gradually have common characteristics in frequency occupancy, system architecture and antenna composition technology. In the context of the LTE base station signal, the pilot signal is inserted into the frame format of the OFDM signal to enhance the target detection performance of the base station. The signal is affected by Doppler shift and the velocity resolution is degraded. This paper presents a new method to improve the speed resolution of the target. Simulation and experiment proved the method has good effect.

Keywords: OFDM · LTE base station · Target detection · Signal sharing

1 Introduction

1.1 A Subsection Sample

In recent years, research on communication radar integration has been ongoing. With the evolution of 4G and 5G, OFDM technology has become one of the most critical technologies of LTE [1]. At the end of the twentieth century, OFDM technology first appeared in radar systems. Jankiraman found that OFDM radar has good velocity range resolution, low autocorrelation side lobes and high probability of interception [2]. The characteristics of OFDM that exhibits anti-clutter interference and suppression of multipath fading in communication systems are also used in radar systems. Martin Braun and Yves Koch proposed a radar and communication system using 24 GHz OFDM signals [3]. However, the convergence of radar and communication poses some problems. If the OFDM waveform is only used for radar transmission, the detection performance will deteriorate. Therefore, some processing of the OFDM signal is required to ensure the performance of the communication while improving the performance of the radar system. Therefore, the coding of OFDM and the frame structure of OFDM require a reliable design. Ruggiano studies OFDM radar signals from the perspective of waveform design and optimization [4], and analyzes the wide-band ambiguity function (WAF) in radar integrated systems to compare the performance of narrow-band ambiguity functions (NAF). The system combines the possibility of an integrated system, and the radar-communication integrated system combines the characteristics of high resolution and large data rate. Extending the radar-communication concept into a multi-path, multi-user environment, faced with the challenge of real multipath scene settings near the radar. Interference signals severely damage the dynamic range of the radar. Some researchers have implemented inter-ference cancellation schemes using the received availability of radar communication signals [5]. The interference cancellation scheme utilizes information extracted from regularly spaced pilot symbols within an OFDM frame. The frequency offset infor-mation is extracted from the channel estimation matrix by a frequency offset estimator.

The focus of this paper is to share the target detection using the pilot signal of OFDM, and obtain the distance and speed for the moving target in the cell range. The pilot signal is inserted in the frame format of the OFDM signal for better resolution.

2   Theory Basis and Simulation Configuration

2.1   Shared Signal Form and Transceiver Mode

The OFDM waveform transmitted by the base station is radiated in the cell and reflected by objects in the cell, such as a vehicle, which can be received by the passive detection radar. The detection radar needs to determine which of the received signals is the waveform reflected by the vehicle at that time. A signal having a special form, such as a pilot signal, can be inserted in the frame format of the transmitted signal. Pilot signals have a synchronous effect.

The radar part of the communication radar integrated system is the bistatic radar [6]. The definition of bistatic radar is to use transmitters and receivers separated by a certain distance. The receiver is passive detection, and the transmitter is a civilian base station as a radiation source, as shown in Fig. 1.

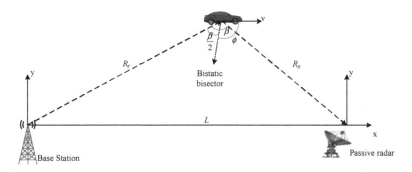

Fig. 1. Shared signal based on bistatic receiving model

In this mode of operation, there is no need to switch the mode of communication or radar, only need to change the format of the transmitted waveform slightly, which can be used for passive detection. The operation not only can synchronize signals, but also improve the performance of target detection. Frame format of the transmitted signal is shown in Fig. 2. The physical layer protocol data unit (PPDU) frame structure is defined in the 802.11a standard, that is, the data structure generated by the baseband transmission processor.

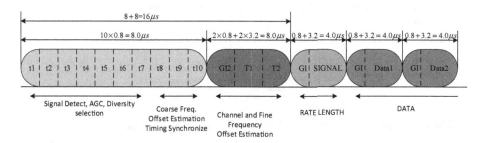

Fig. 2. PPDU frame format

2.2 Signal Model and the Ambiguity Function

An OFDM multi-carrier signal [7] can be considered as a parallel stream carrier waveform with orthogonal multiple carrier signals, each modulated with different transmission information, and the signal can be expressed as

$$x(t) = \sum_{\mu=0}^{N_{sym}-1} \sum_{n=0}^{N_c} a(\mu N_c + n) \exp(j2\pi f_n t) rect(\frac{t - \mu T_{OFDM}}{T_{OFDM}}) \qquad (1)$$

with μ representing the sequence number of each OFDM symbol within the total amount of N_{sym}, n being serial number of a single subcarrier within the total amount of N_c subcarriers, a denoting the complex modulation symbols, f_n representing the individual subcarrier frequency, $T_{OFDM} = T + T_G$ being the total duration of an OFDM symbol, consisting of the OFDM symbol duration T and the cyclic prefix time T_G, $rect(t/T_{OFDM})$ denoting a rectangular window time for a duration T_{OFDM}. Time and frequency domain structure of OFDM waveform is shown as Fig. 3 [6].

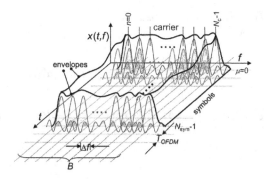

Fig. 3. Time and frequency domain structure of OFDM

During an OFDM symbol time, its frequency domain contains a large number of subcarriers, and the necessary modulation information is carried on these subcarriers, which can achieve a high data transmission rate. The OFDM waveform in the time domain looks like noise which has good transmission performance.

As one of the important indicators of radar signal design, the ambiguity function can analyze whether the OFDM signal can show good detection performance in the radar system.

Taking a single OFDM signal as followed

$$s(t) = \sum_{n=0}^{N-1} a(n) \exp(j2\pi n \Delta f t) \tag{2}$$

The echo signal of a single OFDM signal reflected by a target

$$r(t) = s(t - \tau)e^{j2\pi f_d t} + n(t) \tag{3}$$

with Δf denoting subcarrier spacing, τ being echo delay time, f_d being doppler shift, $n(t)$ representing gaussian white noise.

The ambiguity function of a single OFDM signal can be expressed as

$$\chi(\tau, f_d) = \int_{-\infty}^{\infty} r^*(t)s(t)dt$$

$$= \sum_{l=0}^{M-1} \sum_{k=0}^{N-1} \exp(j2\pi l \Delta f \tau)a(k)a^*(l) \int_{-\infty}^{\infty} \exp\{j2\pi(k\Delta f - l\Delta f - f_d)\}dt \tag{4}$$

Extract some integral items

$$\int_{T_{\min}}^{T_{\max}} \exp(-j2\pi f t)dt = T_d \sin c(\pi f T_d) \exp(-j2\pi f T_a) \tag{5}$$

with $T_d = T_{\max} - T_{\min}$, $T_a = (T_{\max} - T_{\min})/2$.
$\chi(\tau, f_d)$ can be expressed as

$$\chi(\tau, f_d) = \sum_{l=0}^{M-1} \sum_{k=0}^{N-1} \exp(j2\pi l \Delta f \tau)a(k)a^*(l)$$

$$\cdot \sin c\{\pi(l\Delta f + f_d - k\Delta f)T_d\} \exp\{j2\pi(k\Delta f - l\Delta f - f_d)T_a\} \tag{6}$$

According to the basic definition of OFDM, the subcarriers in the frequency domain have orthogonality, so only when $k = l$, the value of $\chi(\tau, f_d)$ is the largest, that is, the larger energy is displayed on the ambiguity function. The expression in this case is

$$\chi(\tau, f_d) = \sum_{l=0}^{M-1} \sum_{k=0}^{N-1} \exp(j2\pi l\Delta f \tau) a(k) a^*(l)$$

$$\cdot \sin c\{\pi(f_d - k\Delta f)T_d\} \exp\{j\pi(f_d - k\Delta f)T_a\} \tag{7}$$

When $\tau = 0, f_d \neq 0$, the two-dimensional ambiguity function is transformed into a velocity ambiguity function.

$$\chi(0, f_d) = \sum_{k=0}^{N-1} a(k) a^*(k) \sin c\left\{\pi\left(\frac{f_d}{\Delta f} - k\right)\right\} \exp\{-j\pi(f_d - k\Delta f)T\} \tag{8}$$

with T representing the duration of this OFDM signal, and its speed resolution is determined by the $\sin c$ function with a speed resolution of $1/T$.

When $\tau \neq 0, f_d = 0$ the two-dimensional ambiguity function is transformed into a distance ambiguity function.

$$\chi(\tau, 0) = \sum_{k=0}^{N-1} a(k) a^*(k) \exp\left(j2\pi \frac{k}{N} B\tau\right) \tag{9}$$

with B represents the subcarrier bandwidth. When $\tau = 1/B$, $\chi(\tau, 0) = 0$. In other words, the distance resolution is $c/2B$.

2.3   Pilot Signal

The pilot is a channel estimation method based on auxiliary information. If the pilot is periodically allocated to the OFDM block in the time domain, the pilot is suitable for the slow fading wireless channel [8]. The shape structure of the pilot determines the applicable range of the pilot channel estimate. In the mobile communication system, the coherent monitoring and decoding of data requires prior knowledge of the channel information between the transmitting and receiving antennas. In order to obtain the frequency response of the mobile channel, a common method is the pilot assisted channel estimation algorithm, that is, using the pilot signal to the channel. The channel estimation is performed by sampling at different points in the time domain space and then using interpolation filtering to obtain the frequency response value of the entire channel. Three common pilot structures are shown in Fig. 4.

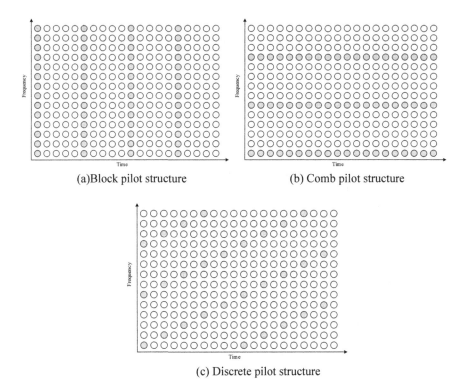

(a)Block pilot structure   (b) Comb pilot structure

(c) Discrete pilot structure

Fig. 4. Three common pilot structures

For the signal transmitted by the base station, this paper proposes a new type of discrete pilot structure which is shown as Fig. 5.

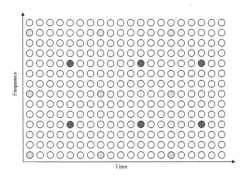

Fig. 5. Pilot structure based on cell-specific reference signal

This kind of structure optimizes moving objects in a cell. The LTE system can operate under high-speed mobile conditions, so the required time interval between reference symbols can be 500 km/h from the maximum Doppler LTE system it supports. The Doppler shift is $f_d = f_c v/c$, with f_c being carrier frequency, v being speed of users, c being Speed of light. Assuming $f_c = 2\,\text{GHz}$, $v = 500\,\text{km/h}$ then the Doppler shift is $f_d \approx 950\,\text{Hz}$. According to the Nyquist sampling theorem, the minimum sampling frequency that can recover the channel is $T_d = 1/(2f_d) \approx 0.5\,\text{ms}$. In other words, two reference symbols are needed for each time slot in the time domain in order to correctly estimate the channel. In the frequency domain, on each OFDM symbol containing reference symbols, there is one reference symbol between every 6 subcarriers. However, reference symbols are staggered, so in each resource block, there is one reference symbol between every three subcarriers.

Table 1. The parameters of the bistatic system

Symbol	Parameter	Value
B	Signal bandwidth	20 MHz
f_c	Carrier frequency	2.6 GHz
N_c	Number of subcarriers	1200
N_{sym}	Number of symbols	120
Δf	Subcarrier spacing	15 kHz
T	OFDM symbol duration	10 ms
F_n	Noise bandwidth	2 dB
$(S/N)_{\min}$	Minimum signal to noise ratio	20 dB
P_T	Transmitter power	20 W
G_T	Transmitter antenna power gain	30
G_R	Receiver antenna power gain	30
σ_B	Cross-sectional area	3–20 m²

2.4 Detection Performance Analysis

Figure 1 shows the geometric relationship of the bistatic radar. According to this structure, the bistatic radar equation can be obtained.

$$(R_T R_R)_{\max} = \left[\frac{P_T G_T G_R \lambda^2 \sigma_B}{(4\pi)^3 P_{R\min}} \right]^{\frac{1}{2}} \qquad (10)$$

with P_T being the transmitter power, G_T being the transmitter antenna power gain, G_R being the receiver antenna power gain, λ being the wavelength of the transmitted signal, σ_B being the cross-sectional area of the target, and $R_T R_R$ being the distance product.

The minimum detection power of the receiver is

$$P_{R\min} = kF_nT_sB_n \left(\frac{S}{N}\right)_{\min} \tag{11}$$

with k being the Boltzmann constant ($k = 1.38 \times 10^{-23}$ J/K), F_n being receiver detector front noise bandwidth, T_s being the receiver noise temperature, the standard reference temperature being 290 K, B_n being the noise bandwidth before the receiver detector, $(S/N)_{\min}$ being the minimum signal to noise ratio received.

The parameters of the bistatic system are shown in Table 1. From the table can calculate the distance resolution which is

$$\Delta R = \frac{c_0}{2B\cos\left(\frac{\beta}{2}\right)} \tag{12}$$

Speed resolution is expressed as

$$\Delta V = \frac{\lambda}{2T\cos\left(\frac{\beta}{2}\right)} \tag{13}$$

3 Simulation and Results

The regular pilot leads to the appearance of a blur function secondary peak of the OFDM signal, which is a bad influence for target detection. The pilot does not necessarily fill the entire symbol area, but rather exists in a certain interval. Pilot signals have some important characteristics which are shown in the Table 2.

Table 2. The parameters of the pilot signal

Characteristic parameter	Symbol	Comment
Data amplitude	σ_d	Average amplitude of data within the data frame
Pilot amplitude	σ_P	Average amplitude of data within the data frame
Translation distance	m	Translation distance between symbols in a data frame, an integer
Translation distance	p	Translation distance of adjacent symbol pilots in a data frame, integer
Pilot region ratio	α	Proportion of subcarriers containing pilot regions,
Pilot density	k	Proportion of the number of pilots in a data frame, $k \approx \alpha/m$

Assuming $R_T = 2$ km, according to the parameters discussed, the minimum detection power of the receiver can be obtained as $P_{Rmin} = -84.95$ dbmW. The echo power of the target located in the radiation range of the base station base station is shown in Fig. 6.

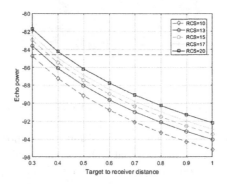

Fig. 6. Echo power for target distance diagram

In the case of a 20M bandwidth communication signal and dual base station target detection, for a target within a cell communication range of the base station (2 km) and its cross-sectional area is relatively large, theoretically the distance from the target antenna to the receiving antenna is 0.45 km. The echo power is greater than the minimum detectable power of the receiver, that is, the target within 0.45 km can be detected. In order to obtain a better detection range, the signal bandwidth can be increased or the transmission power can be increased, and the waveform can be optimized as necessary. With $\beta = 15°$, the distance resolution of bistatic radar is $\Delta R = 7.57$ m, while the speed resolution is 0.58 m/s.

Change the waveform of the transmitted wave under the model of the dual base station. Figures 7 and 8 shows the ambiguity function of block pilot and comb pilot.

The ambiguity function of the new discrete pilot structure designed in this paper is shown in the Fig. 9. The parameters of the pilot structure are $\sigma_P = 1$, $m = 3$, $P = 6$, $\alpha \approx 0.143$, $k \approx 0.048$.

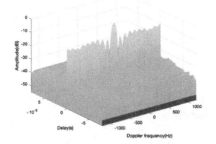

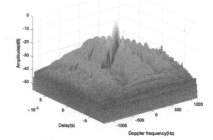

Fig. 7. The ambiguity function of block pilot

Fig. 8. The ambiguity function of comb pilot

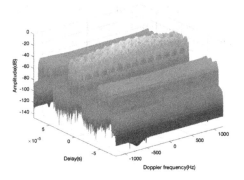

Fig. 9. The ambiguity function of the new pilot discrete

The regular pilot does not contribute to the distance resolution and speed resolution of the downlink OFDM signal. In the actual LTE system, the regular pilot is applied in the uplink, and the scattered pilot is applied in the downlink, the pilot not only enables synchronization and channel estimation, but also improves the speed resolution without affecting the distance resolution. The effect of the scattered pilot on the range resolution is unfavorable, and a higher amplitude side lobe are generated around the main lobe of the origin.

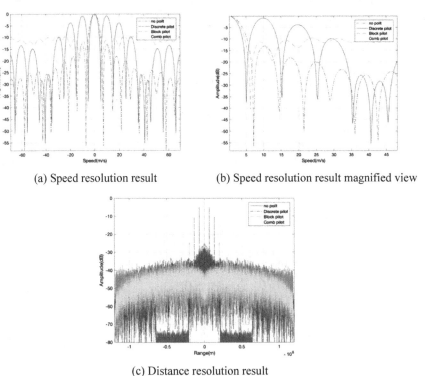

(a) Speed resolution result   (b) Speed resolution result magnified view

(c) Distance resolution result

Fig. 10. Different pilot structure resolution comparison results

Specifically observe the impact of various pilot structures on resolution which is shown as Fig. 10.

From the comparison of the velocity ambiguity function, the main lobes of the velocity ambiguity function inserted into the discrete pilot and the inserted block pilot are narrower than the main lobes without the pilot signal inserted, indicating that the velocity resolution is better, and the insertion is better. The speed resolution of the comb pilot is almost unchanged from that of the unplugged pilot. From the distance ambiguity function, it can be seen that the autocorrelation is reflected in the frequency domain position of the inserted pilot, but around the very narrow main lobe. A narrow side lobe closer to the main lobe are generated, but because the peak ratio of the main lobe and the side lobe main lobe are within an acceptable range, the detection performance of the pilot signal is better to traditional method.

4 Conclusion

This paper proposes a radar communication shared signal waveform, which can achieve higher resolution while using OFDM signals for target detection. Firstly, the ambiguity function of OFDM signal is derived, and then the ambiguity function of OFDM signal in various pilot forms is analyzed. The simulation results show that the proposed discrete pilot form has higher speed resolution than other forms. Therefore, the proposed method can effectively solve the Doppler ambiguity problem and improve the target detection ability.

Acknowledgement. Thanks for the National Natural Science Foundation of China (61201308 and 61201304). And it was supported by Key Laboratory of Marine Environmental Monitoring and Information Processing, Ministry of Industry and Information Technology.

References

1. Parkvall, S., Furuskar, A., Dahlman, E.: Evolution of LTE toward IMT-advanced. IEEE Commun. Mag. **49**(2), 84–91 (2011)
2. Jankiraman, M., Prasad, R.: A novel algorithmic synchronization technique for OFDM based wireless multimedia communications. In: IEEE International Conference on Communications, vol. 1, pp. 528–588. IEEE (1999)
3. Braun, M., Koch, Y., Sturm, C.: Signal design and coding for high-bandwidth OFDM in car-to-car communications. In: Vehicular Technology Conference Fall, pp. 1–5. IEEE (2010)
4. Ruggiano, M., Genderen, P.V.: Wideband ambiguity function and optimized coded radar signals. In: European Radar Conference, EuRAD 2007, pp. 142–145. IEEE (2007)
5. Colone, F., Woodbridge, K., Guo, H.: Ambiguity function analysis of wireless LAN transmissions for passive radar. IEEE Trans. Aerosp. Electron. Syst. **47**(1), 240–264 (2011)
6. Abdullah, R.S.A.R., Salah, A.A., Ismail, A., et al.: LTE-based passive bistatic radar system for detection of ground-moving targets. Etri J. **38**(2), 302–313 (2016)
7. Sturm, C., Wiesbeck, W.: Waveform design and signal processing aspects for fusion of wireless communications and radar sensing. Proc. IEEE **99**(7), 1236–1259 (2011)
8. Zhao, Y., Huang, A.: A novel channel estimation method for OFDM mobile communication systems based on pilot signals and transform-domain processing. In: IEEE 1997 Vehicular Technology Conference, pp. 2089–2093. IEEE Xplore (1997)

Design and Implementation of Stereo Vision System Based on FPGA

Qian Wang[⊠], Xin Gu, Hua Wang, and Guowei Yao

Research and Development Center,
China Academy of Launch Vehicle Technology, Beijing, China
aoranqian@126.com, nync396@126.com,
e_visawang@aliyun.com, 75312309@qq.com

Abstract. By comparing the different methods of vehicle ranging, the stereo vision system is selected for obstacle imaging and ranging. In response to low data transmission rate and low real-time performance and low resolution of the traditional ranging system design method, the stereo vision system is designed with integrated multi-core ARM and FPGA SOC. The system adopts image acquisition, distortion correction, target detection and tracking the image of the obstacle in front of the vehicle to compute the obstacle distance information. The delay and the power consumption of the system is measured by experiments, and it indicates that the system is suitable for vehicle-assisted driving and other image processing technologies field.

Keywords: Obstacle detection · Range finder · Stereo vision · Image match · System design

1 Introduction

With the rapid increase in car ownership, traffic safety has become an important issue for the public [1]. Therefore, the automobile active collision avoidance system based on the intelligent traffic system has become a research hotpot. The active collision avoidance system obtains the distance information of pedestrians and vehicles by sensor technology and transmits it to the drivers to realize the assisted driving of the vehicle. And the distance information also can assist the future car auto-driving collision avoidance system to make a decision.

This paper describes the design and implementation method of stereo vision system based on FPGA, the distance information can be generated by comparing binocular detection images, and the front obstacle distance image can also be output. At the same time, the paper provides the actual engineering indexes such as system delay and power consumption.

2 Obstacle Detection Method

At present, millimeter wave radar, laser ranging and depth vision imaging are normally used to detect obstacles. The following is a brief introduction.

© ICST Institute for Computer Sciences, Social Informatics and Telecommunications Engineering 2019
Published by Springer Nature Switzerland AG 2019. All Rights Reserved
M. Jia et al. (Eds.): WiSATS 2019, LNICST 280, pp. 766–774, 2019.
https://doi.org/10.1007/978-3-030-19153-5_75

2.1   Monocular Vision Measurement

Monocular vision measurement is a kind of passive ranging method, that needs to obtain the position information in the three-dimensional space from the two-dimensional image information. The characteristics of it is small size, low power consumption and good stability. This method usually detects the vehicle distance by mapping the width of the vehicle in the camera. If the road width has changed or no driveway, there may be a mistake or the distance can not be detected [2].

2.2   Millimeter Wave Radar Ranging

Millimeter-wave radar works in the millimeter-wave band. The 60 GHz, 120 GHz and 180 GHz bands are generally used on Car-borne radar. The ranging methods mainly include continuous wave radar ranging and pulsed radar ranging, which principle are the same. The distance is mainly calculated by measuring the time difference between transmission and reception [3]. The characteristic of this method is high resolution, frequency bandwidth, and can distinguish multiple small targets at the same time, with imaging capability, but in rain and fog weather, millimeter wave loss is serious, which is not conducive to imaging.

2.3   Laser Ranging

Laser distance measurement also belongs to radar distance measurement, which working principle is similar to the millimeter wave distance measurement but using light source to emit. Due to the narrow beam, short wavelength, and high resolution of the laser, a variety of information such as the emission characteristics, distance, and velocity of the target can be obtained [4]. However, weak global ability, low accuracy, and missed detection are weaknesses of this method.

2.4   Stereo Vision Ranging

Binocular stereo vision is based on the parallax principle and uses an imaging device to obtain two images of a measured object from different positions. According to calculating the positional deviation between the corresponding points of the image to obtain three-dimensional geometric information of an object. In actual application, the camera captures the image first, then uses a series of algorithms in the processor to find the same two-dimensional pixel points in two images at different viewing angles, and calculates three-dimensional information of the object according to the information such as the focal length and baseline distance of the camera [5].

This measurement method has the advantages of high efficiency, suitable precision, simple system structure, low cost. For the measurement of moving objects, the stereo vision method is a more effective measurement method because the image acquisition is completed instantaneously.

Comparing and analyzing the different ranging methods, and considering the factors such as the reliability and safety of the application in the automobile driving, this paper chooses to use FPGA to realize the Stereo Vision system.

The advantages and disadvantages of vehicle-mounted ranging methods are shown in Table 1 [5].

Table 1. Comparison of different ranging methods

	Stereo vision ranging	Monocular vision measurement	Laser ranging	Millimeter wave radar ranging
100 m ranging	O	×	◎	◎
View angle	◎	◎	△	△
Range accuracy	O	×	◎	◎
Depth accuracy	◎	O	△	△
Lane detection	◎	O	×	×
Rain, snow	O	O	O	◎
Fog	△	△	△	◎
Night	O	O	◎	◎
Target dependencies	O	O	△	△
Safety	◎	◎	△	O
Cost	△	◎	O	△

注: ◎Good ○Better △General ×Poor

3 System Design and Implementation

3.1 Hardware Components

Visual system includes binocular camera and data processing board binocular camera is used for taking image, data processing board is used for processing a series of algorithms.

(1) Binocular camera

The system uses the D5M binocular digital camera from You-Your company to obtain left and right visual images.

The output of this camera is 500M pixels. The system design around the camera spacing can be placed as 6 cm, 10 cm, 15 cm and 20 cm.

(2) Visual image

Traditional imaging processing systems are mostly implemented in the form of FPGA +DSP. However, due to the complexity of interface design for data interaction between chips and insufficient data transmission bandwidth, problems such as insufficient imaging resolution and poor real-time performance are caused. In response to these problems, the FPGA of the cyclone system which is produced by Altera Corporation is used in this system. It's a kind of medium scale logic processor and will not increase the R&D cost. It integrates multi-core Cortex-A9 processing Device, FPGA (referring to the internal logic part) communicates with ARM via AXI interface, communication clock is 400 MHz, bit width is 32 bit/64 bit/128 bit optional, FPGA can also read ARM external plug DDR directly at 500 MB rate, and FPGA integrates DDR, etc. Universal peripheral interface to meet application requirements (Fig. 1).

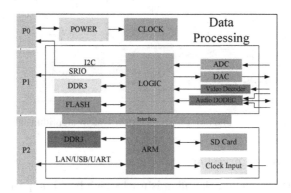

Fig. 1. The diagram of visual image processing board

The structure of the visual image processing board is shown in Fig. 2. The board is integrated into the VPX processing platform as a 3U board. Therefore, the external interface complies with the VPX standard. There are three groups of standard connectors: P0, P1, and P2. The board can be interpolated with other internal platforms. The board performs SRIO serial data transmission, which is beneficial for function expansion.

In the image processing board, DDR3 and FLASH are externally connected to the FPGA to receive frame data. At the same time, an analog interface is integrated to perform analog-to-digital conversion. The FPGA also has external audio and video interfaces and can directly process audio and video signals. The DDR3 which connects to ARM is used to storage the image and distance processing data, and the external SD CARD is used for program self-loading.

3.2   Image Processing Software

In the stereo vision system, the core is Cyclone V5 series SOC which includes two parts, FPGA and ARM. The FPGA in the SOC complete the image data acquisition and transmission, and performs image distortion correction, stereo visual imaging and target detection; ARM run Linux system and completes the target tracking, transfer the image data through Gigabit Ethernet to the host computer to display. The image processing software module is divided as shown below.

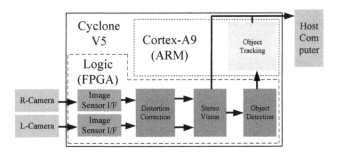

Fig. 2. The diagram of stereo vision system algorithm flow

(1) Image Distortion Correction

The fish-eye image correction algorithm is used which based on positioning retrieval. The standard coordinate system OXY is established according to the spherical coordinate model $(x − x0)2 + (y − y0)2 + (z − z0)2 = r2$ in this fish-eye imaging principle. Assume that the fish-eye lens is located at the coordinate origin O, and its shooting direction is along the OZ axis, the fish-eye image falls on the OXY plane after shooting.

Suppose the point q on the OXY plane is the imaging of an imaging point q′ in the imaging visual field region. When the distance (l) between the imaging point (q) and the coordinate origin (o) is less than or equal to the quarter of the spherical radius (r) of the spherical coordinate model in the imaging principle of the fish-eye lens, the distance between the fish-eye unfolded image point (q′) and the unfolded image center position (o′) is obtained from the following equation.

$$l' = \frac{l}{\sqrt{1 - \left(\frac{l}{r}\right)^2}} \tag{1}$$

If the distance (l) between the imaging point (q) and the coordinate origin (o) is greater than or equal to one fourth of the spherical radius (r) of the spherical coordinate model in the imaging principle of the fish-eye lens, the distance between fish-eye expansion image point (q′) and the expanded image Center position (o′) are obtained from Expression (2).

$$l' = \frac{l - m}{\sqrt{1 - \left(\frac{l-m}{r}\right)^2}} + n \tag{2}$$

l′ is the distance between the unfolded image point q′ and the unfolded image center position o′, and l is the distance between the projected imaging point q and the projection coordinate origin o, r is the spherical radius of the fish-eye imaging spherical coordinate model, m and n are correct-parameters. Finally, the position of the image point q′ in the unfolded image is calculated by Eq. 3 and the angle θ which is formed by the imaging point q in the OXY plane.

$$\left\{ \begin{array}{c} q'_x = l' \times ctg\theta \\ q'_v = l' \times tg\theta \end{array} \right\} \tag{3}$$

(2) Stereo Vision

In this paper, SAD (Sum of absolute difference) algorithm is used to perform block matching on the images captured by the left and right cameras (4×4 image blocks are used) to obtain the parallax of the two images. The SAD method is calculated as follows:

$$\min_{d=d_{min}}^{d_{max}} \sum_{i=-w}^{w} \sum_{j=-w}^{w} \left| I_{right}(x+i)(y+j) - I_{left}(x+i+d)(y+j) \right| \tag{4}$$

D_{max} and D_{min} are the maximum disparity and the minimum disparity value, d is the disparity value and w is the matching template size, I right and I left are the gray values of the points to be matched on the right and left two images.

- target tracking

Target tracking Using 3D-coordinate data and motion-vector data, the algorithm predicts the object's location in the next following frame, and then the object data in the first frame will be linked with the actual object data in the next frame. Vehicle A and vehicle B are moving in a frame at the same time, but vehicle C is tracking each of them separately by calculating their direction and speed.

(3) Object detection

- Object detection

It is a moving object detection method under a typical dynamic background.

- Retrieves the current frame image fcur(x, y) captured by the right camera and the previous frame image fpre(x, y) by Fourier transform to obtain Fcur(u, v) and Fpre (u, v) according to FFT;
- Estimate the global motion parameter;
- Perform inverse Fourier transform to calculate rotation angle θ_0 and scaling parameter σ;
- On the basis of the previous step, calculate the translation (x_0, y_0);

- Based on the estimated global motion variables σ, θ_0, and (x_0, y_0), fcur(x, y) is used as a benchmark to perform background matching on fpre(x, y) by bilinear interpolation.
- The difference between pre (x, y) and fcur (x, y) is calculated to get d(x, y), of two value image and the morphological image processing is used to extract the moving target
- Cycle through the steps above.

• Distance calculation

Two cameras of the same mode with a focal length of f and an optical center distance of b are used to calculate distance. The optical axes of the two cameras are parallel. Using the target detection to extract the target area, select the matching point pair (xl, yl), (xr, yr) with the best matching effect in the target area, and use the following formula to calculate the target distance:

$$R = \frac{bf}{(x_l - x_r)d_x} \tag{5}$$

xl − xr is called parallax, which means the position difference of the target on the left and right images captured by the camera. This value is obtained by matching the image feature points and finding the corresponding matching points on the left and right images; d_x represents the physical length of the unit pixel in the horizontal direction.

• target tracking

Target tracking Using 3D-coordinate data and motion-vector data, the algorithm predicts the object's location in the next following frame, and then the object data in the first frame will be linked with the actual object data in the next frame.

4   Experimental Result

The stereo vision system designed in this paper is used for target detection and tracking experiments. The camera's baseline are 10 cm and 20 cm and the camera's field of view was 42°, the pixel was 1280 * 720, and the frame rate was 30fps.

The video output of the vision system is shown in Fig. 3a–c, where the image output from Fig. A and Fig. B is the same static scene, Fig. A is the indoor image directly output by the camera without performing the stereo imaging algorithm, and the outline of the door frame and wall decoration can be recognized; Fig. B is the implementation of the algorithm, which marks target in the field of view by color. As the distance grows, the color becomes colder, and putting the mouse on the recognized target image, the distance of the target can be displayed.

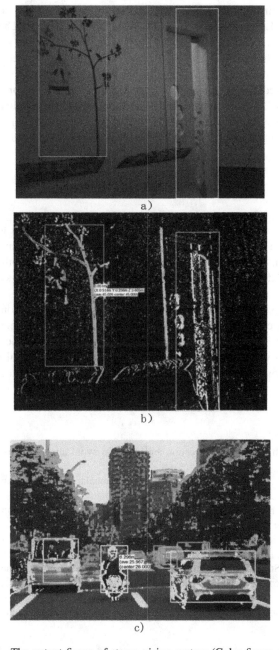

a)

b)

c)

Fig. 3. The output figure of stereo vision system (Color figure online)

Figures c shows the moving target output image. Due to the target position is changing, optical camera image is not given. From the figures, the system can identify people, vehicles, and buildings in front of the visual field and output the distance of specific target.

Through experiments, it can be seen that the processor FPGA consumes 23K of ALM, about 32K LE resources, and RAM usage is about 4 Mbit. The entire software code runs about 50 lines of delay, about 2–3 ms under 720p frame rate. The final test results show that when the baseline is 10 cm, the maximum perceived distance is about 160 m, the error is about 2.3%; with the baseline of the camera being 20 cm, the maximum perceived distance is about 330 m, and the distance error is about 1.1%.

Then using FPGA to achieve stereo vision system design, hardware development costs are low, the system output delay is small, the system's power consumption can also be controlled at about 1.5 W, does have the conditions for large-scale engineering applications.

5   Conclusion

Compared with monocular imaging, stereo vision system collects a lot of target contour, behavior and distance information, and with the development cost reduction, system power consumption reduction and frame processing capability, depth vision system is more and more widely used in the car's driver assistance system. However, the application of in-depth visual technology is not limited to this technology. The technology can also be applied to taxis to report real-time road conditions for road navigation. It can even be applied to aerospace assistance for spacecraft docking and parking. With the development of stereo visual technology, the application potential of this technology in various fields such as industrial inspection, virtual reality, etc. This technology will continue to emerge and drive the climax of technological change [6].

References

1. Lu, H.: Research on obstacle detection and obstacle avoid ancestrai. DongHua University, pp. 1–2 (2012)
2. Liu, Q., Pan, M., Li, Y.-w.: Design of vehicle monocular ranging system based on FPGA. Chin. J. Liq. Cryst. Displays **29**(3), 422–428 (2014)
3. Liao, S.-j., Liu, R., Cui, D.-Q.: Research on vehicle collision Prevention system based on Millimeter Wave Radar ranging, Technology and Market (2010)
4. Hua, Z.: Head detection and counting method based on stereo vision. Hunan University, pp. 16–17 (2015). 20150411
5. Saneyoshi, K.: Stereo vision system on automobile for collision avoidance. In: MVA 2011 IAPR Conference on Machine Vision Applications, Nara, Japan, 13–15 June 2011, p. 399 (2011)
6. Wang, X.-j., Zhou, C.-y., Zou, Z.-R.: Overview of stereoscopic vision. Comput. Knowl. Technol. (2005)

Author Index

Printed in the United States
By Bookmasters